To Carleton
with kind regards

Patt Sachs

Dec. 2007

GLOBAL JIHAD
The Future in the Face of Militant Islam

Patrick Sookhdeo Ph.D., D.D., F.Sy.I.

Global Jihad : The Future in the Face of Militant Islam

Published in the United States of America by Isaac Publishing
6729 Curran St
McLean
VA 22101

Copyright © 2007 Patrick Sookhdeo

Second Printing, November 2007

ISBN   09787141-2-1   978-0-9787141-2-3

Printed in the United States of America

The jihad is the Islamic *bellum justum* and may be regarded as the very basis of Islam's relationships with other nations.

Majid Khadduri[1]

Jihad is the signature tune of Islamic history.

M.J. Akbar[2]

God loves Muslims to be arrogant while fighting. It manifests that he is indifferent to the enemy and determined to vanquish him.

Abdullah Ghoshah[3]

The Prophet (peace be upon him) said: I am commanded to fight with men till they testify that there is no god but Allah, and that Muhammad is His servant and His Apostle, face our qiblah (direction of prayer), eat what we slaughter, and pray like us. When they do that, their life and property are unlawful for us except what is due to them. They will have the same rights as the Muslims have, and have the same responsibilities as the Muslims have. *Narrated by Anas ibn Malik, Sunan Abu Dawud, Book 14, Number 2635.*

Contents

Foreword. 4
Author's Note 8
Acknowledgements 11
Introduction. 12
  1 Some Causes Offered for Islamic Radicalism and Terrorism 24
  2 Sources and their Interpretation 46
  3 Qur'an, *Hadith* and *Shari'a* 60
  4 *Jihad* and the Sacralising of Territory 84
  5 The Theology of War and Empire-Building. 98
  6 *Jihad*, Eschatology and Messianism 128
  7 The Practicalities of *Jihad* 140
  8 The Islamic Concept of Peace 188
  9 *Taqiyya* 196
10 History: Muhammad and his Successors. 210
11 The Negative Impact of Islamic *Jihad* on Vanquished Populations 240
12 Violent Sects and Movements: Past and Present. 270
13 The Motivation of Terrorists and Suicide Bombers 322
14 The Making of an Islamic Terrorist 344
15 Contemporary Muslim Debate on *Jihad* .356
16 Muslims Against Violence—Progressive Reformers 374
17 Responses to Islamic Terrorism 396
18 Conclusion 422
Appendix 1 Traditional Divisions in Islam. 446
Appendix 2 Modern Trends in Islam 447
Appendix 3 Various Networks of Radical Islam. .448
Appendix 4 "Bin Laden" Audiotape. 450
Appendix 5 Editorial in *Al-Masaa* (2 February 2004) 456
Appendix 6 The Zarqawi Document 458
Appendix 7 Fighting Terrorism: Recommendations by Arab Reformists 466
Glossary 480
Bibliography 490
References and Notes. 540
Index of Qur'an references 642
Index of *Hadith* references 643
Index. 644

Qur'anic references are given as the surah (chapter) number followed by the number of the verse within the surah. All are from A. Yusuf Ali's *The Holy Qur'an: Text, Translation and Commentary* (Leicester: The Islamic Foundation, 1975) unless otherwise stated. Verse numbers vary slightly between different translations of the Qur'an so if using another version it may be necessary to search in the verses just preceding or just following the number given here to find the verse cited.

Foreword

I have long had misgivings about the phrase "global war on terror". Terror defines only some of the tactics used, not the conflict as a whole, and in any case has always been a subjective term. One man's terrorist is another's freedom-fighter, and my bomber-pilot may be your terror-flier. Moreover, it seems to me that the word struggle, with its notion of a long and obdurate (but sometimes low-key) conflict, fits the reality of the situation much better than war, too often seen as embodying a clash between armed forces. Call it what we will, though, I believe that Patrick Sookhdeo is absolutely right to see the struggle as being both global and long-term, and to identify the importance of militant Islam as its philosophical mainspring.

The real merit of his book is to make the ingredients of that militancy clear, particularly to members of a largely secularised society whose own toleration induces them to ignore or doubt the corrosive intensity of the beliefs of some others. The world-view and strategic objectives shaped by these beliefs are well set out in the pages that follow, and Dr Sookhdeo carefully explores the various meanings of *jihad* and warns of the way in which Islamist apocalyptic discourse is rife, especially on those internet sites which have such a great impact, particularly on the young.

One of the most serious problems confronting us is that our own strategic view is lamentably vague: we burble genially about things that we admire, like democratic values, free market economies or the rights of women, but find it hard to translate these general desiderata into practical policy. For instance, any meaningful policy in Afghanistan must address the issue of the poppy crop from its very inception, for it is an inescapable truth of counter-insurgency that armed force is never, by and of itself, more than part of the solution to a complex, multi-layered problem. This has been clear to theorists and successful practitioners for at least a century, and it is disturbing to find simple truths belatedly rediscovered. Where no genuine strategy exists, we compensate, as far as we can, with tactical or technical excellence, as if we imagine that by winning a series of battles we must inevitably win the war as well. In practice the reverse is often true, for too often we score short-term successes by doing things that are likely to make our ultimate defeat more likely. For instance, whatever advantages may have been gleaned from Guantanamo will, in the long term (and this is a conflict in which the long term really matters) be submerged by the fact that the place's very existence helps spawn a mass of radicalised young men eager to avenge injustices inflicted on their brothers. In the context of a conventional war against Saddam Hussein the entry of US tanks into Baghdad seemed the very icon of victory. Yet to thousands of Muslims, many of whom had neither affection for Saddam nor real quarrel with the West, it was a symbol of unspeakable humiliation. We are tactics-driven but somehow "strategy-lite".

In contrast, our opponents are far less good at winning battles and engagements. In Iraq, for example, the rise of the suicide bomber paralleled the bloody defeat of militias, who shot a lot but hit a little, in dozens of small actions. If coalition forces make a premature withdrawal from Iraq or Afghanistan, it will not be because they have lost a modern Dien Bien Phu, some decisive clash that breaks their armies. It will be because their civilian populations, not persuaded that these are life and death struggles in which the real national interest is engaged, will have their confidence fatally eroded by a constant trickle of casualties which units in the field will find painful (for it is never pleasant

5

to have valued comrades killed and wounded) but, in the context of the job they trained to do, tolerable. Failure will be strategic, not tactical. Had the Americans in Iraq displayed, three years ago, the acumen and cultural understanding they now exhibit, then things might be very different. However, I cannot imagine a would-be US president or British prime minister entering an election announcing that his (or, indeed, her) policy for Iraq is rather more of much the same.

In contrast, while our opponents have tactical weaknesses, they have enormous strategic strengths, and this book helps us understand why. Al Qa'eda's war aim is "complete victory over infidel powers and the establishment of the Islamic caliphate". The war will be prosecuted by a "one thousand wound" policy which will pit Muslim patience and endurance against Western demands for quick solutions and easy answers. While recruits to conventional armed forces are motivated by a variety of motives, pay and pensions amongst them, recruits to Islamic militant groups "enter a world where their rage is directed, channelled and given a sense of purpose and an outlet". Conventional armed forces are shackled by rules of engagement and the law of armed conflict. How can they not be, given the primacy of law in the societies which produce them, and the recognition that the effects of illegal action are often counter-productive? In contrast, one of Al-Qa'eda's training manuals justifies the torture or murder of hostages, using a version of Islamic teaching to justify itself.

Patrick Sookhdeo concludes that to gain ultimate victory over the Islamists will "require the exercise of the will and a right understanding of the situation." "Do those engaged in such a task have the necessary will to achieve the end required," he asks. "Do they properly understand what they are up against?" In most cases they do not. We believe that truths that seem so self-evident to us must be as appealing to others. Our cultural arrogance makes it hard for us to grasp the very real appeal of, say, a Sadrist militia in Iraq or the Taliban in Afghanistan. We confuse tactics with strategy: current fascination with "exit strategy" from

Iraq demonstrates all too clearly that we do not understand that strategy is not a short-term expedient. Lastly, we seem reluctant to explain to our own population, which lies in the very pit of our stomach for the fight, why the struggle matters to us. There is no such intellectual vacuum amongst our opponents.

This is not a struggle that will be won by counter-radicalism, by meeting crescent with cross. It will instead be won by clothing legitimate aspirations and values like tolerance and respect with real strategic shape, by emphasising that we have no quarrel with Muslims in general, but by straining every nerve – economic, diplomatic, psychological and military – to starve and isolate fundamentalist extremism, to guard against its baneful effects, and to deny it safe havens. Western nations with substantial Muslim minorities must be aware of the danger that, as another study has observed, "Valid criticism of Islam or Muslims is hindered by accusations of Islamophobia". Some may see this book in precisely that light.

Tactics without strategy, warned Sun Tzŭ, is the noise before defeat. Patrick Sookhdeo's book tells us much about our opponents' strategy. We would do well to understand it, to recognise its attraction and its force, and to meet it with a strategy of our own. We will have no excuse for saying that we were not warned.

Richard Holmes

Richard Holmes is Professor of Military and Security Studies at Cranfield University. He has presented several BBC documentary series, and writes widely on military topics: his most recent book was Dusty Warriors: Modern Soldiers at War (HarperCollins 2006).

Author's Note

Radical Islam has declared war on the West. It is the manifestation of a theology that is rooted in classical Islam. Traditional Islam which, developing under colonial pressure, saw a break from violence, from the totality of *shari'a* and from political activisim, is now gradually being subsumed into classical Islam. The challenge for the West is not to declare war on Islam the personal faith of the mainly peaceful majority of Muslim people, but rather to declare war on the Islamic theology, philosophy and ideology that motivate and sanction fanaticism, extremism, violence and terrorism.

Earlier this year I had a cup of tea with a Muslim Arab diplomat who was holidaying in London. He shared with me his feelings about Islam. He told me that he completely rejected the classical Islam embraced by modern Islamic extremists, particularly its violent aspects. He longed to see his faith transformed by reason, liberalised and endorsing a separation of religion and state. He wanted all Muslims to be able to function comfortably within a secular, plural society, indeed to embrace such a society. "Why don't Western leaders work with liberal Muslims?" he asked, "Why do they always focus on conservative Muslims?" He confided to me how anxious he was about his teenage son living in the UK, who was being drawn towards Islamic extremism, and told me of the hours he had spent on the phone from the Middle East to the lad, trying to persuade him towards a liberal interpretation of Islam. "British people are like ostriches with their heads in the sand, oblivious to what is going on around them," he said.

I was greatly struck by my conversation with this intelligent, warm and very worried man. Our discussion took place just as I was putting the final touches to this work, in which I seek to address the issue of violence – whether offensive or defensive – within the Islamic tradition. The mantra "Islam is peace" is heard so often in the West today, and yet this is true only in the sense of peace borne out of a religious war resulting in the submission of the enemy. To make the statement "Islam is peace" true in an objective sense, the majority of Muslims and their religious leaders must interpret their faith in the same liberal, rational and privatised way as does this diplomat.

At the moment this is a dangerous course for a Muslim to take. A 22-year-old Muslim called Abdelkareem Suleiman was given a four-year jail sentence in Egypt on February 22nd 2007 because of what he wrote in his blog about violence in Islam, both now and in the time of the Islamic prophet Muhammad.[4] Commenting on anti-Christian riots which took place in Alexandria in October 2005, Suleiman wrote,

> The Muslims have taken the mask off to show their true hateful face, and they have shown the world that they are at the top of their brutality, inhumanity and thievery.

> Some may think that the action of Muslims does not represent Islam and has no relationship with the teachings of Islam that was brought by Mohammed fourteen centuries ago, but the truth is that their action is not different from the Islamic teachings in its original form.

In a mirror image of the attitudes of the diplomat and his son, this young man's father has disowned him and called for his execution under Islamic law.

We live in depressing times, as leaders, both political and military, whether in the Islamic or the non-Islamic world, grapple with issues that seem to be insoluble. The apparent intractability of modern conflicts, in particular Iraq, can easily lead to despair. However, we can find hope not only in the Iraqi diplomat but also in countless other Muslims like him who seek the way of peace and reason. For this to be done, the Muslim world – its clerics, theologians, political leaders and *umma* – must rise up and engage in a radical reformation of Islam. This reformation will re-interpret the Qur'an so as to reject religious violence, will advocate a total separation of religion from state, and will argue for full equality of all citizens under a law based on international norms not on *shari'a*. This will include the reinterpretation of the Medinan Qur'anic passages on violence, the rejection of the *hadith* and *sunna* as authoritative sources, and the adaptation of *shari'a* from a public legal code to a personal code of conduct and morality.

The discussion on what term to use to describe the violence contained within the Islamic tradition is an ongoing one. Many people are at pains to distinguish "Islamist terrorism" from what they believe to be the unacceptable term "Islamic terrorism". However this is really a meaningless distinction, for, as this work will seek to show, Islamism is simply the essence of classical Islam, and violence and terror are found within both of them. To understand this fully is to understand the multi-dimensional nature of *jihad* (struggle), which is spiritual, moral, economic, political and military. Although such terrorism is inspired by the major sources of Islam, this of course does not mean that all Muslims are terrorists. Furthermore there are some movements which seek to reinterpret these sources in a more peaceable way, leading to the rejection of violence. In this work both terms are used.

The scope of this work is limited in that it focuses principally on theology. Whilst it is recognised that theology is often formed in contexts, both past and present, this work will do no more than touch on the geo-political, economic, historical and other issues which form the background to present conflicts relatng to Islam. It is my hope that this work will contribute to the multi-faceted efforts of people of good will and of many faiths or no faith, all around the world, who are seeking to make sense of what is happening and to work for a world in which peace, stability and freedom can co-exist.

Patrick Sookhdeo, September 2007

Acknowledgements

I would like to express my gratitude to the many colleagues and friends whose advice and assistance have been invaluable to me in preparing this book. Outstanding amongst these are Ivar Hellberg of Cranfield University, Reuven Paz of PRISM, and David Zeidan of the Institute for the Study of Islam and Christianity. Numerous others have also contributed comments, corrections and help of many kinds. Responsibility for any remaining errors is, of course, mine alone.

Introduction

The US defence establishment has recently rebranded its war on terrorism as a "long war", reflecting a shift in strategic thinking.[5] This is evident in the 2006 Quadrennial Defense Review (QDR) of the US Department of Defense where the term "long war" is repeatedly used:

> The United States is a nation engaged in what will be a long war… The Department of Defense conducted the 2006 Quadrennial Defense Review (QDR) in the fourth year of a long war, a war that is irregular in its nature… The long war against terrorist networks extends far beyond the borders of Iraq and Afghanistan and includes many operations characterized by irregular warfare – operations in which the enemy is not a regular military force of a nation-state.[6]

It is now clear that the war is not short-term and limited to specific battlefields like Afghanistan and Iraq, but is a long-term war being fought globally in many countries which will continue for many years to come.[7] This new thinking includes a shift from a strategy of large-scale military operations to a rapid deployment of highly mobile counter-terrorism forces. The new strategy recognises that the war cannot be confined to its military aspects, but has political and ideological connotations and that the battles must be won in the realm of ideas as well as of arms. This ideological aspect has been taken up in a 2005 study by a NATO think-tank has recognised the role that Islamism has to play in this war.[8]

But the war on Islamic terrorism is just one aspect of a "long war" which has lasted 1400 years already. This is the history of

Islamic expansion and pursuit of political dominance which are best expressed in the Islamic doctrine, institution and practice of *jihad*. Based on the models of Muhammad and the early Islamic state, *jihad* has determined the relations of Muslims to non-Muslims ever since, including the theory, ideology, rules and practicalities of waging war. The foreign policy of the Muslim state is linked to *jihad* which is the basis of the relationship between Muslims and non-Muslims.[9]

While modern Muslim apologetics tries to reinterpret *jihad* in purely defensive modes (in a moral sense as against evil in society and in a spiritual sense as the individual's fight against temptation and personal sin), there is no doubt that in Islamic history *jihad* has normally been viewed, both in traditional Islamic law (*shari'a*) and in Islamic practice, as the armed conflict against non-Muslims (and against heretical or apostate Muslims) permanently waged to ensure the victory of God's chosen community and religion, the *umma* (the whole body of Muslims worldwide), over all polytheistic powers, peoples and lands.

Only under severe constraints, when non-Islamic power was overwhelming, could the *jihad* imperative be suppressed for a while, as under colonial rule. This concession derived from *shari'a* principles of *darura* (necessity) and *maslaha* (public good) which permit the breaking of *shari'a* principles when Muslims are weak and Islam is in danger. Such suspension of *jihad* however, is always temporary and *jihad* can be reactivated at any time if Muslim strength is deemed capable of changing the balance of power and reasserting Islamic dominance.

The late Sheikh Abdel-Aziz Ibn Baz, then Grand Mufti of Saudi Arabia, at the request of the King, reluctantly issued a *fatwa* in 1990 related to the Gulf War of that year, declaring that it was legitimate for the Saudi ruler to invite non-Muslim troops to help defend the kingdom. It included the sentence:

> Even though the Americans are, in the conservative religious view, equivalent to nonbelievers, as they are not Muslims, they deserve support because they are here to defend Islam.[10]

Contemporary apologists for Islam, both Western and Muslim, tend to ignore the long history of the violent *jihadi* expansion of Islam, sanitising it by using language that implies a peaceful expansion happily accepted by non-Muslims. No mention is made of the military invasions, battles, looting, destruction, enslavement of civilians, or mass migration of Arab tribes to settle on the best parts of the conquered territories. Such scholars sometimes assert that early Muslims who took a more aggressive stance on war were merely heterodox sects like the Khariji,[11] who they argue were not part of mainstream Islam. Nevertheless the scholars' own efforts to counter and argue away the classical Islamic teaching on war do seem by implication to acknowledge how widely accepted this doctrine has been for many centuries. It is still the benchmark against which all other teaching on war is compared.

Most Western societies have long accepted the secular paradigm that relegates religion to the margins of society. They have come to terms with the privatisation of religion and its removal from the political centre of power and the public debate on morals and society. Muslims, by contrast, are in the process of regaining their lost confidence after several centuries of colonialism, and have embarked on a strategy aimed at reintegrating faith and politics in accord with the classical tenets of Islam. This process is taking place not only in Muslim states but also in countries of the non-Muslim developing world and in Western states with Muslim minorities.

Pakistani Brigadier S.K. Malik strikingly illustrates this difference in attitude in a military text book for the Pakistani army. Brigadier Malik quotes Edward Meade Earle as follows: "War is not an act of God. It grows out of what people, statesmen and nations do or fail to do." Malik then comments that "Meade's thesis is fully representative of the traditional thinking on the subject. The Quranic view on war is, however, altogether different. According to the Book, the initiation of war is for the Cause of God."[12] He also describes the place of military strategy within what he calls the total strategy of *jihad* according to the Qur'an.

> 'Jehad', the Quranic concept of total strategy, demands the preparation and application of total national power and military instrument is one of its elements. As a component of the total strategy, the military strategy aims at striking terror into the hearts

of the enemy from the preparatory stage of war while providing effective safeguards against being terror-stricken by the enemy.[13]

The foreword to Malik's book is by General M. Zia-ul-Haq, then Chief of the Army Staff and later president of Pakistan, who also affirms the pivotal place of the Qur'anic concept of *jihad* in the late twentieth century Pakistani army.[14]

Of course there are many variants of Islam. Most Muslims want simply to live a peaceful life enjoying democratic freedoms and opportunities as well as economic wellbeing, caring little for traditional Islamic concepts and teachings. Some Muslims are sincerely working for democratic values and human rights. Some want to focus on personal faith led by reason, rather than the public power aspects of Islam. Furthermore it must not be forgotten that there is a peaceable tradition within Islam, albeit the concept of peace has been understood in a variety of ways in different places and at different times, sometimes as coexistence on equal terms, sometimes more as submission to a *pax Islamica*, exceptionally even a kind of pacifism (usually more pragmatic than principled). Also, Islam was considerably different from the classical model when under Western colonial control it lost its political power; it became principally a faith without its traditional ideological dimensions.

However, despite these variations, it is true that the majority opinion in Muslim states is very much impacted by traditional and Islamist[15] concepts. Liberals in Muslim states are a minority, cowed by the vehement drive against them which includes physical violence and the threat of being legally labelled as apostates with all that entails. The limits of the possible in all contemporary Muslim countries are being determined by Islamist discourse, and most regimes submit to Islamist demands because of their fear of destabilisation and of delegitimisation. In the West, Muslim liberals have the freedom to express their views, but still face the ire of community leaderships heavily influenced by the power-centres in their countries of origin and by the resource-rich Wahhabi Saudis who fund much of their activity.

Much contemporary Muslim intellectual activity is aimed at masking the real intent of Islamist ideologues and movements behind a façade of fashionable Western leftist discourse. For many in the Western hard left, Westerners are reactionary oppressors while under-developed nations and minority groups in the West are oppressed victims. Western democracies are castigated as oppressive, racist and neo-colonial, while Islamists are praised as representing the revolt of the oppressed against their (Western) oppressors.

Radical Islamists, driven by a similar hatred of Western culture, especially its Judaeo-Christian basis and its liberal tradition, have forged a bizarre alliance with Western postmodern leftists and have appropriated their discourse as a way of gaining sympathy in the West and of camouflaging their real objectives.

Leftist intellectuals have functioned as the "Trojan horse" of Islamists in Europe and America - presenting a sanitised view of Islam; ignoring the excesses of its terrorist manifestations; concealing Islamism's totalitarian, fascist and hate-filled ideologies; while reinforcing the Western guilt syndrome over past colonialism and imperialism and "politically correct" attitudes to Muslim minorities in the West as well as to Islam in general. They tend to attribute all the world's problems to the West and ignore the deep fault lines in non-Western, including Islamic, societies and states. Their discourse encourages self-pity in non-Westerners and thus hinders progress in their societies, for conspiracy theories and scapegoating are used to justify their underdevelopment. This justification hampers any real effort at self-criticism and self-improvement.[16]

Many Western journalists, politicians and academics seem to have been intimidated by this discourse. Keen to support multiculturalism and fearful of being thought reactionary, illiberal, racist or Islamophobic, they repeat the view that stresses only Islam's peaceful and harmonious aspects and either denies the intolerant, violent episodes or attributes them to a few marginalised heretical groups that have nothing to do with "true Islam".[17]

Such a position is not held only by some leftist intellectuals and journalists, but is also used by politicians of many hues and by military strategists. In order to counter radical Islamist ideologies, they are arguing along the lines that *jihadis* "have hijacked Islam with their destructive interpretation of Islamic scripture".[18] Tony

Blair, when Prime Minister of the UK, expressed a similar view of radical Islamists not belonging to true Islam:

> The extremism is not the true voice of Islam. Neither is that voice necessarily to be found in those who are from one part only of Islamic thought, however assertively that voice makes itself heard. It is, as ever, to be found in the calm, but too often unheard beliefs of the many Muslims, millions of them the world over, including in Europe, who want what we all want: to be ourselves free and for others to be free also; who regard tolerance as a virtue and respect for the faith of others as part of our own faith. That is what this battle is about, within Islam and outside of it; it is a battle of values and progress; and therefore it is one we must win.[19]

Masked by the victim culture and discourse that seem to be merely seeking compensation for past wrongs and a respectable niche for Islam in the contemporary world, the real aim of Islamist movements is to emulate the early model of universal Muslim hegemony in politics and culture.

> We aim to establish Allah's religion in its entirety, in every soul and upon every inch of this earth, in every home, institution and society.[20]

Abul A'la Mawdudi (Indian sub-continent, 1903-79), one of the fathers of modern Islamism, stated that:

> The aim of Islam is to bring about a world revolution... the Muslim Party should not be content just with establishing the Islamic system of government in one territory, but should extend its sway as far as possible all around...if the Muslim Party commands enough resources, it will eliminate unislamic governments and establish the power of Islamic government in their place.[21]

This then is the ultimate goal of Islam: a worldwide Islamic government based on *shari'a*.

While it is true that Western colonialism dominated the majority of Muslims for various periods of time until the middle of the twentieth century, most Muslim states have now been independent for decades. So it is remarkable that a world community of over 1.2 billion, comprising some 52 independent Muslim-majority states (having significant large minorities in over 40 other states), controlling more than half the world's oil resources and constituting the largest voting bloc in the United Nations, continues to see itself as a victim of forces beyond its control.

Even the seemingly moderate former Prime Minister of economically successful Malaysia, Mahathir Mohamad, complained in his opening address at the 10th Summit of the Organisation of the Islamic Conference in Putrajaya, Malaysia (October 16th 2003) that:

> We are all Muslims. We are all oppressed. We are all being humiliated... We are now 1.3 billion strong. We have the biggest oil reserve in the world. We have great wealth. We are not as ignorant as the Jahilliah [non-Muslims of pre-Islamic Arabia] who embraced Islam. We are familiar with the workings of the world's economy and finances. We control 50 out of the 180 countries in the world. Our votes can make or break international organisations. Yet we seem more helpless than the small number of Jahilliah converts who accepted the Prophet as their leader. Why? Is it because of Allah's will or is it because we have interpreted our religion wrongly, or failed to abide by the correct teachings of our religion, or done the wrong things?... Today we, the whole Muslim ummah are treated with contempt and dishonour. Our religion is denigrated. Our holy places desecrated. Our countries are occupied. Our people starved and killed. None of our countries are truly independent. We are under pressure to conform to our oppressors' wishes about how we should behave, how we should govern our lands, how we should think even... There is a feeling of hopelessness among the Muslim countries and their people... The Muslims will forever be oppressed and dominated by the Europeans and the Jews. They will forever be poor, backward and weak... It cannot be that there is no other way. 1.3 billion Muslims cannot be defeated by a few million Jews... We are actually very strong. 1.3 billion people cannot be simply wiped out. The Europeans killed six million Jews out of 12 million.

But today the Jews rule this world by proxy. They get others to fight and die for them... We are up against a people who think. They survived 2000 years of pogroms not by hitting back, but by thinking. They invented and successfully promoted Socialism, Communism, human rights and democracy so that persecuting them would appear to be wrong, so they may enjoy equal rights with others. With these they have now gained control of the most powerful countries and they, this tiny community, have become a world power. We cannot fight them through brawn alone. We must use our brains also.[22]

Some scholars see this attitude as having been formed in the earliest years of Islam when the Muslim community under Muhammad in Mecca was a persecuted minority group facing hostility from pagans, Christians and Jews. This persecution was short-lived and was soon brought to an end – indeed reversed - after Muhammad's establishment of an Islamic state in Medina, the conquest of Mecca and the rapid Muslim expansion that followed, establishing a vast Muslim empire. Of course at first Muslims were a relatively small governing elite amongst larger indigenous Christian, Zoroastrian, Jewish (and later Hindu) populations, and may have feared the possibility of being overwhelmed by their non-Muslim subjects. The sense of insecurity seem to have been consecrated and preserved in perpetuity by being included in the holy canon of Islam (*Qur'an*, *hadith* and *sira*), which has such a formative effect on most Muslims. These feelings of victimhood have been redirected into feelings of rage against the West as the main cause of Muslim weakness and humiliation.[23]

In the modern era, Western imperialism and colonial control of most Muslim lands caused Muslim consternation as they sought to discover the roots of Muslim weakness. But Islamists also argue that another cause for the decline of Muslim power is what they consider the deviation of most Muslims from true original Islam. A result of this view is the labelling of all systems not based on Islam and *shari'a* as evil, corrupt or apostate, thus meriting destruction and replacement by a true Islamic state.

Modern Islamists have developed a many-pronged approach to achieve their goal of worldwide Islamic government. The spiritual revival of individual Muslims and the Islamising of all Muslim societies and states are two important elements. Another element is the weakening of all non-Muslim societies and states by infiltrating their structures and institutions with a view to their gradual islamisation.

Radical Islamists hold that a valid method for achieving their aims is by *jihad*, which they understand in the traditional sense of military warfare. Indeed, traditionally *jihad* goes beyond mere warfare and can be described as a comprehensive religious, military, political and economic system. For in *jihad* religious doctrine motivates military aggression and political expansion. The economic wealth generated by the looting of newly conquered regions provides for the maintenance and expansion of the system.

Fathi Yakan, a Lebanese Muslim Brotherhood leader and head of its affiliate in Lebanon, al-Jama'a al-Islamiyya, clearly states that the goal of contemporary *jihad*, which is not an intellectual debate but a real battle, is the establishment of the universal Islamic state implementing *shari'a*:

> The logic of confrontation in the present age, not to speak of the logic of Islam and the Shari'ah, dictate that the Islamic forces should be united in one struggle to strike at Jahiliyyah [ignorance, as in pre-Islamic times)] and establish a state which enforces the law of Allah and undertakes the role of guiding mankind... Moreover, the war between Islam and Jahiliyah is no more a merely intellectual debate but it has become a fierce, bloody struggle in the literal sense of these words.[24]

Jihad is at the heart of the Islamic system of dealing with non-Muslims, not only externally but also internally within the Islamic state. In the *dhimma* system, Jewish and Christian minorities living in Islamic states are protected from *jihad* but must in return accept the demeaning regulations imposed upon them, including the payment of the poll tax (jizya, conceived of as a payment for the privilege of being allowed to live in the Islamic state). Thus it could be said that *dhimmis* paid for their own humiliation and for the maintenance of the system that kept them in subservience. Any perceived failures by the *dhimmi* to obey the regulations were considered to release the Muslims from the constraints of the *dhimmi* pact i.e. to allow them to wage *jihad* against the *dhimmis*.

Yakan argues that the main duty of Islamic movements today is the breeding of *jihad* fighters who will join the various locations in the world where *jihad* is possible and promises success. The only consideration in this fight is the welfare of Islam, an argument that basically says that the end justifies the means:

> The Islamic movement should be barracks producing mujahidin and heroes more than it should be an ideological institution spreading mere Islamic culture and concepts among the people... In this respect the basis from which the movement should emanate should be the welfare of Islam above any consideration, and wherever the welfare of Islam can be realised there must be a drive forward whatever sacrifices it may call for.[25]

Likewise Sheikh Muhammad Taher of the Leeds Grand Mosque, UK, who makes clear elsewhere his belief that *jihad* includes actual fighting, urges that Muslim youngsters, both male and female, should be brought up as *jihad* warriors:

> One of the greatest lessons, dear brothers and sisters, is the Jihadi upbringing for the youth, and the role of the Mujahidat of the women, and the role of the virtues [sic] mother.[26]

These then are some of the religious motivations driving the modern revival of *jihadi* activities. It is such theological and ideological principles on which this book will primarily focus. It is recognised that there are many other causal factors which contribute to the long war, but, as this book will seek to show, the doctrinal underpinning is the real driving force.

It is instructive to compare Islam, and its basic ideological content, with Christianity, which has no such basis. When, at certain periods of history, Christianity became an ideology, power became central and with it violence. Most Christians in the West now rightly return back to the New Testament roots of their faith, and in making that return, as they have done at various times in history, they reject both power and violence in the cause of religion. The Reformation of the Western Church was an important factor in the growing move towards the separation of Church and state, but Islam has not (yet) undergone any such development.

1
Some Causes Offered for Islamic Radicalism and Terrorism

The world's second largest religion, with around 1.2 billion adherents, Islam is a complex faith consisting of a variety of often conflicting theological, sectarian, ethnic, linguistic, political and cultural elements. It is therefore difficult to generalise about the modern Islamic world. Any serious study of specific elements within Islam must include what a variety of Muslims say about these subjects as well as the observations of non-Muslim experts. Both Muslim and non-Muslim observers offer a variety of possible causes for the evident current radicalisation of many Muslims, and for the proliferation of militancy, radicalism, violence and terrorism within Muslim communities around the world.

Challenges facing the Muslim World

The contemporary Muslim world faces a series of challenges which can lead to feelings of resentment and victimisation. This is well described by Abu Sulayman, a Saudi scholar and founding member of the International Institute of Islamic Thought:

> Internally weak, relatively backward, frustrated, conflict-ridden, suffering from internal tensions, and often controlled and abused by foreign powers, the Muslim world is in a state of crisis. For Muslims, all of modern history is a tragedy.[27]

Out of the top 40 most at risk states in the Failed State Index of 2006, 20 were from Muslim majority countries.[28] This is a considerable number when it is remembered that there are in total 52 nations which have more than 50% Muslim populations. As

Muhammad Ahsan, an independent researcher on globalisation and under-development related to the Muslim world, notes:

> Whether it is an overall picture of human development, or these are its various components, e.g., education, human security, elimination of human deprivation and formation of human [capital], Muslim countries are much behind non-Muslim countries.[29]

1. Legacy of colonialism

The Western colonial period is still a source of bitterness for many Muslims and is often blamed for the troubles of contemporary Muslim societies. As Abu Sulayman states:

> In Muslim countries it is customary to blame external powers and imperialism for all manner of ills.[30]

Khurshid Ahmad, a main leader of the Jama'at-i Islami in Pakistan and a prominent politician and economist, argues that colonialism deprived Islam of its former glory and political power and hegemony:

> For the Middle-East the Western colonial powers had a horrible plan. Pan-Arab nationalism and lust for power were the destructive instruments applied to snatch political freedom from the Middle-Eastern Muslim rulers. About a dozen powerless states under the European command emerged on world map as a result of Sykes-Picot Agreement (1916) and Balfour Declaration (1917). As such, the plan was to divide Middle-East into pieces on one hand and on the other to create conditions facilitating creation of a Jewish state among Arabs. The machination ultimately bore fruit and Israel was established in the heart of Muslim ummah with due understanding among USA, UK and USSR with connivance of UN. This way, all those rulers, tribes and people who once enjoyed power, pelf [sic] and freedom were eliminated from world politics for ever. Muslims, who enjoyed world leadership status for more than 12 centuries, were thus deprived of this position for the first time in history. Except in a few semi-independent states (Afghanistan, Turkey, Yemen and Arab Peninsula), the Muslim might and political authority - the

symbols of Muslim ummah's dignity - was totally eliminated from around the globe.[31]

Modern Western intervention, particularly in Iraq, reminds many Muslims of the imperial age and generally produces a hostile reaction, as Abid Ullah Jan, a Pakistani writer explains:

> Any direct Western intervention in Muslim countries – even at the behest of the government in power – invariably creates a hostile reaction among the masses boosting the appeal of resistance movements.[32]

Some Muslims also interpret the colonial period as a time when Muslims were tempted to turn away from Islam through Western cultural, economic, political and Christian missionary influences. As Ayatollah Khomeini stated:

> Then more than three centuries ago, came the evil colonists who found in the Muslim world their long sought object. To achieve their ambitions they laboured to create the conditions which would lead to the annihilation of Islam. Missionaries, Orientalists, the information media – all are in the service of the colonialist countries and all are guilty of distorting Islam in a way that has caused many Muslims to steer away from it and not to find their way back to it.[33]

Continued dependence on the West is seen as aggressive neo-colonialism in which globalisation is but the latest of the tools used to perpetuate Western dominance and marginalise Islam. Tariq Ramadan, a leading popular European Islamic academic and thinker of Egyptian background, who promotes an independent European Islam, describes this mindset:

> The temptation is high, in the heart of this reality, to blame the collapse on the Other, the exploiter, the rich, the West and no bones are ever made about, throughout the Arab and Islamic world, eliciting all the arguments available to "explain" the situation this way. From old political colonisation to the modern forms of economic control, from the divisions maintained to the cultural imperialism imposed, from governments to multinationals who

dictate their will to dominate from their Western base, the causes are clear and the situation understood: Muslims are suffering from a multi-faceted form of oppression.[34]

2. Poverty

While a few Muslim oil states are fabulously rich, at a global level the Muslim world faces severe poverty. Most majority Muslim countries are in the developing world and few of them show signs of the rising prosperity of India and China. Many Muslim countries have significant social and economic stratification, which leaves them with poor under classes.

> Results of a survey of 15 Arab countries found that 32 million people suffer from malnutrition. This figure represents nearly 12% of the total population of the countries concerned. The same study found that even in some of the wealthiest Arab states, such as Kuwait and the United Arab Emirates, certain population groups are not adequately nourished.[35]

Some Muslims highlight poverty and inequality as the main causes of radicalism and terrorism. President Zine El-Abidine Ben Ali of Tunisia has said:

> Aware that religion-masked extremism feeds on poverty, deprivation and ignorance, we have endeavored to tackle its roots socially, economically, culturally and educationally, and to address the conditions conducive to its emergence and propagation.[36]

Others point out that these problems are not unique to Muslims. As Abdul Rahman Al-Rashed, general manager of Al-Arab television, argues that:

> The importance of improving living standards and increasing job opportunities are legitimate and valid requests that are completely independent of terrorism and such requests are not the dilemma of Arabs or Muslims alone.[37]

Timur Kuran, a lecturer on economics of Turkish background, King Faisal Professor of Islamic Thought and Culture at the University of Southern California, refutes the theory that poverty is the main cause for Islamic radicalism:

Does it follow that poverty is responsible for whatever clash we observe between Islam and the West? Will the current tensions subside if measures are taken to uplift the Islamic world's desperately poor sectors? While it would be comforting to believe that a quick-fix exists, it is doubtful that the problems will respond to economic incentives alone. After all, the hijackers of September 11 were not unemployable souls living at the margins of subsistence. Holding university degrees, some of them were perfectly capable of achieving prosperity through legitimate means. What motivated *them* was not material deprivation but an all-consuming ideology. They were not just Muslims but also Islamists pursuing goals they considered higher than life itself.[38]

It must be noted that many Muslim terrorists come from affluent and well educated middle class backgrounds and, therefore, the resentment and alienation they have felt cannot be explained by focussing upon their personal material deprivation.

Following the demise of communism, Islam emerged as the main force in the developing world strong enough to stand up to US-led capitalism and globalisation. Islamic political leaders express their protests in Islamic idiom that Muslim masses understand and respond to. Such movements are partly fuelled by the failure of all alternative ideologies and systems in the newly independent Muslim states to deliver development and prosperity. These failures nourish a culture of alienation and despair coupled with anti-Westernism in most Muslim states and societies. The Western far left has allied itself to the Islamist radicals, justifying their use of violence as a legitimate response to Western capitalist oppression.[39] As Professor Fred Halliday, a British academic expert on the Middle East and on international relations, has argued:

It is striking, however, that - beyond such often visceral reactions – there are signs of a far more developed and politically articulated accommodation in many parts of the   world between Islamism as a political force and many groups of the left. The latter show every indication of appearing to see some combination of al-Qaida, the Muslim Brotherhood, Hizbollah, Hamas, and (not least) Iranian president, Mahmoud Ahmadinejad as exemplifying a new form of international anti-imperialism that matches – even completes – their own historic project. This putative combined movement may be in the eyes of such leftist groups and intellectual trends hampered by "false consciousness", but this does not compromise the impulse to "objectively" support or at least indulge them. The trend is unmistakable. Thus the Venezuelan leader Hugo Chávez flies to Tehran to embrace the Iranian president. London's mayor Ken Livingstone, and the vocal Respect party member of the British parliament George Galloway, welcome the visit to the city of the Egyptian cleric (and Muslim Brotherhood figurehead) Yusuf al-Qaradawi. Many in the sectarian leftist factions (and beyond) who marched against the impending Iraq war showed no qualms about their alignment with radical Muslim organisations, one that has since spiralled from a tactical cooperation to something far more elaborated. It is fascinating to see in the publications of leftist groups and commentators, for example, how history is being rewritten and the language of political argument adjusted to (as it were) accommodate this new accommodation.[40]

3. Demographic Pressures

Growing populations lead to conflict as resources become scarce. Increases in population can lead to greater social and economic stratification. The CIA predicts that by 2015 "in much of the Middle East, populations will be significantly larger, poorer, more urban and disillusioned."[41]

As more than half the population is under 20 years of age in nearly all Middle Eastern countries this will create significant population pressures.[42] As Middle East expert Graham E. Fuller explains:

> The existence of a relatively large youth cohort within the population of Middle Eastern societies serves to exacerbate nearly all dimensions of its political, social and economic problems. It is youth that often translates broader social problems into an explosive and radicalizing mixture… The rapid population growth is such that youths under the age of 24 now make up 50%–65% of the population of the Middle East. This places immense strains

on the entire infrastructure of the state, especially on educational services that are already poor and declining in quality, and creates greater dissatisfaction among the most volatile elements of society. Social services need to be expanded as well to meet the growing population, but most states have been failing to meet the challenge. The slack is then usually taken up by Islamist organizations that are able to provide many of these services and gain increased support from the population. States likewise cannot employ the growing number of university graduates, heightening overall unemployment, also a volatile force.[43]

In Indonesia there will also be significant rises in population with the population of Jakarta predicted to rise from its current 9.5 million to 21.2 million by 2015.

4. Local political conflicts

There are hardly any Muslim-majority governments which are liberal democracies as understood in the Western sense. Non-democratic countries face problems accommodating marginal elements; excluded from politics, many turn to radicalism and violence. Authoritarian regimes leave large sections of the population discontented. Muslim violence against other Muslims is endemic across the Muslim world, as Salim Mansur, professor of political science at the University of Western Ontario, Canada, argues:

> The phenomenon of Muslim violence against Muslims demands attention, for it is primarily this inner conflict which periodically spills over beyond the borders of the Muslim world. More Muslims have been killed by Muslims, more Muslims continue to be victimized by Muslims, and more Muslims are in danger of dying at the hands of Muslims than non-Muslims. This is a subject that demands a wider examination and attention than has been given by Muslims and non-Muslims alike. Of Muslim violence against Muslims, we are concerned here primarily with the politically organized violence of those in power against those who are contesting that power, and the appeal to Islam is made in common by all parties in the conflict.[44]

In the Middle East and other parts of the Muslim world, society is characterised by clannism in all its forms (tribal, ethnic, religious) which demands loyalty in return for protection. This becomes a constraint on the development of the individual and ultimately on the development of society as a whole. Clannism is also a destabilising factor in politics, leading to factionalism which makes liberal-democracy difficult, perhaps impossible, to sustain in many Muslim majority countries. As the United Nations produced Arab Human Development Report 2004 explains for Arab states (but also true for most Muslim states):

> Freedoms in Arab countries are threatened by two kinds of power: that of undemocratic regimes oblivious to the welfare of their peoples, and that of tradition and tribalism, sometimes under the cover of religion. These twin forces have combined to curtail freedoms and fundamental rights and have weakened the good citizen's strength and ability to advance.[45]

5. Palestine (and similar causes)

A significant source of resentment throughout the Muslim world is caused by the perceived oppression of the Palestinians at the hands of non-Muslims. As Iqbal Sacranie, then Secretary General of the Muslim Council of Britain, declared:

> Despite their many differences and political persuasions, Muslims scholars are united and resolute about one issue. They agree that the question of Palestine and the status of Jerusalem is the foremost international concern on the agenda of Muslims... The Muslim Council of Britain, therefore, views the illegal occupation of Jerusalem as a Muslim issue and not as a Palestinian issue.[46]

The Islamisation of the Israeli-Palestinian conflict has made it a central unifying cause for the whole *umma*, linking it to the early Islamic past and to the future End-Time apocalypse. As Abid Ullah Jan, a Pakistani Islamist writer, states:

> It is not an Israeli Palestinian conflict... the ongoing conflict in the Middle East is a religious issue... Jerusalem is the key to understanding the historical process of the Middle East and

the world at large. The most important of all subjects dealt with in the Qur'an that must be taught in Islamic educational institutions today is the subject of 'Jerusalem in the Qur'an'... The Muslims also believe that Jerusalem has a destiny that will validate Islam's claim to Truth and invalidate the current Christian and Jewish claims.[47]

Jerusalem has been elevated to become the unifying symbol of a Muslim world plagued by internal rivalries. It was the reason for the creation of the Organisation of the Islamic Conference, which now links 56 governments of Muslim-majority states, and has remained its central concern:

> The problem of Al-Quds (Jerusalem) is the *raison d'etre* of the emergence of the OIC, and it has remained its single dominant obsession...Only the Al-Quds issue itself was sufficiently strong and grave to impel the Muslims to unite.[48]

The feeling that Muslims are everywhere under siege and being subjugated by aggressive non-Muslims is supported by the cases of Iraq, Afghanistan, Chechnya, Kashmir, the southern Philippines and southern Thailand among others.

6. Loss of identity – alienated and marginalised youth

Modern social and cultural changes originating from the West are seen to "threaten to dilute Islamic identity by a syncretistic mix with un-Islamic elements".[49] The positive aspects of modernisation are seen to have benefited only a few, while the majority have felt mainly its negative fallout – rural migration and rapid urbanisation, the breakdown of traditional family values, the population explosion, high unemployment, and the sharp inequalities in wealth distribution and a general climate of disillusionment and despair.[50] These economic, social and cultural changes, which are overwhelming in their rapidity, have resulted in an acute sense of dislocation, identity loss, alienation and purposelessness[51] that form the socio-psychological background to the Islamic resurgence.[52]

Muslim youth in the West frequently feel rootless - lost between their parents' traditional Islamic identity and secularism. As the British Muslim journalist Maruf Khwaja explains:

British Muslims are more likely than people of other creeds to have identity crises, and tend towards insularity and alienation from the mainstream. One source of these crises is the yet unresolved issue of whether religious or national identity should take precedence in the Muslim's acute sense of awareness.[53]

Middle-class youth in Muslim-majority countries struggle with similar feelings as the societies in which they live are exposed to modernity. In both cases many turn to Islamism as an alternative.

Globalisation and the attendant spread of electronic mass media are causing a shift from localised forms of Islam (perhaps focused on local Muslim saints) to more universal forms focusing on the source texts. Transnational pan-Islamic identities are encouraged by most Islamists and *jihadis* who reject the nation-state as a non-Islamic innovation and who yearn for the universal caliphate to be restored. Muslim youth, who are often better educated than their parents, are especially susceptible to this radicalising trend.

7. Honour and shame

Honour and shame are an important component of Islamic culture. According to Akbar S. Ahmed, former High Commissioner of Pakistan to the UK and distinguished anthropologist, writer and filmmaker, under the stress of modernity revenge becomes an ever greater component of the honour syndrome, which is always so prominent in Islamic culture:

> Today, notions of honor under attack remain an important discourse in political rhetoric and even behavior in much of the Muslim world. That is why The Satanic Verses controversy drew in Muslims from Bradford to Bombay. Muslims felt the Prophet of Islam and his wives had been dishonoured... A feeling of loss of honor is not new. What is new is the sense of apocalyptic disruption, which forces individuals to reconsider the intrepretation of honor and invariably emphasize revenge as its simplest expression.[54]

In most Muslim societies it is still true that only blood can really wipe out shame and humiliation: the greater the shame, the greater the bloodshed needed to wipe it out. Most Muslims feel humiliated and shamed by the West which they feel has dominated, manipulated and betrayed them. This is why the attack on the Twin Towers in 2001 was seen by many Muslims as a just retribution. The greatest humiliations Osama bin Laden mentioned to justify his actions are the abolition of the caliphate by Attaturk in 1924, the Jewish takeover of Palestine in 1948, the sanctions against Iraq (starting in 1990), and the stationing of American infidel troops in Saudi Arabia, the Holy Land of Islam in 1991. Osama bin Laden also declared:

> Without shedding blood no degradation and branding can be removed from the forehead… Death is better than humiliation! Some scandals and shame will never be otherwise eradicated".[55]

8. Western invasion of Afghanistan and Iraq, war on terror, foreign policy

The US-led invasions of Afghanistan and Iraq are seen by many Muslims as attacks on Islam itself. The US-proclaimed "war on terror" is also seen as a pretext to attack and occupy Muslim states and take control of their oil resources. The anti-war campaigns in the West have the support of most Muslims, who blame American and British foreign policy as the main cause of the radicalisation of Islamic youth and the proliferation of terrorism. As Ehsan Masood, a British Muslim journalist and project director of the Gateway Trust, said:

> At least until 7/7, too many Muslims glibly described British involvement in Afghanistan and Iraq as a simple war against Muslims.[56]

Or as Aftab Malik, a British Muslim journalist and author and a Visiting Fellow at the Centre for Ethnicity and Culture at the University of Birmingham, argues about the war on terror:

> The pain and anger inherent throughout the Muslim world has spilled over to Muslims in the west, who increasingly see the "war on terror" as a war on Islam.[57]

Parveen Akhtar, a British Muslim PhD research student, comments:

> My argument is essentially that after September 11 and the wars in Afghanistan and Iraq, radical Islamic groups are able to utilize this return to religion by uniting the various grievances of Muslims around the world. A very simple dichotomy is created between 'Muslims' and 'the West'.[58]

Muslim advisors to the British Home Office, part of the working parties set up by Home Secretary Charles Clarke in the aftermath of the July 2005 bombings in London, argued that:

> British foreign policy - especially in the Middle East - cannot be left unconsidered as a factor in the motivations of criminal extremists... We believe it is a key contributory factor.[59]

9. The corrupt secular West and its polluting impact

The Western concept of secularism, the separation of religion from politics, is totally foreign to most Muslims who view it as an imported Western ideology forced on Muslim states against their will. They hold that secularism is imposed in order to undermine Islam, and Western cultural influences are termed an "intellectual invasion" (*al-ghazw al-fikri*) more dangerous than the former political and military dominance.[60] Secularism is viewed as a rebellion against God and his law. Modern secular Western civilisation is considered to be essentially irreligious and materialistic even when it tolerates religion, for it ignores any absolute moral framework in favour of utilitarian pragmatism.[61] The ordinary European, claimed Sayyid Qutb, the main ideologue of the Muslim Brotherhood, the first modern Islamist movement,

> Whether democrat or fascist or Bolshevik, worker or intellectual, knows only one positive religion and that is the worship of material progress, that is, the belief that there is no other goal in life than to make this one life itself more and more comfortable... The temples of this religion are the large factories, the cinemas, the chemical laboratories, the dance halls and the electrical power plants, while its priests are the

bankers, the engineers, the movie stars, the leaders of industry and the heroes of aviation.[62]

Syed Abul Hasan Ali Nadwi, a renowned Islamic scholar, sees the dominance of Western culture over Muslims as a tragedy:

> We ape the West in manners and modes of living. What is worse we even depend for our moral and religious precepts on researches done by Western scholars: even the Islamic sciences are judged from the standpoint evolved by Western educational institutions... The insufferable weight upon every Islamic people of alien, crazy concepts, of values that have no grounding in, that even contradict, the principles of Islam and the demands of its own conscience – this insufferable weight is provoking everywhere a crisis of identity, a deep anxiety, a grave malaise – mental and spiritual.[63]

In Britain a YouGov poll in July 2005 found that nearly a third of British Muslims believe that "Western society is decadent and immoral and that Muslims should seek to bring it to an end".[64]

10. The *umma* as the core identity

The concept of the *umma*, the global Muslim community, is central to Muslim thought. For many Muslims, loyalty to the *umma* overrides loyalty to their nation-state. In this view, politics and war are simply the means of advancing the cause of the whole worldwide Muslim community. Abdel Beri Atwan, editor of the London-based *al-Quds al-Arabi*, notes this difference between Islam and other religions:

> Islam is very different from most of the celestial and non-celestial religions... The Islamic creed and the concept of the nation, surpass the concept of citizenship and nationality. A Muslim person is a Muslim first, then Pakistani or Indian or Egyptian or British. If this concept had retreated for many reasons, among which is the spread of secularism during the times of the leftist or communist tide, these campaigns that are looming in the West and are targeting Islam, have began to bring it back strongly in these last few years.[65]

Amir Taheri, an Iranian journalist, notes that a disturbing facet of prioritising loyalty to the *umma* is the ultimate denial of acccepted categories of good and evil. This attitude assumes that any Muslim cause or regime is inherently exempt from moral judgments and deserves the unquestioning support of all Muslims worldwide.[66]

11. Crisis of weak legitimacy of Muslim states and regimes

Most Muslim states are characterised by autocratic regimes and by a continuing segmentation of society along tribal, ethnic, and religious lines.[67] Radicals tend to blame the modern secular nation-state and its Westernised elites for all the ills of society.[68] Hrair Dekmejian, Professor of political science at the University of New York, explains that the political, social and economic failures of secular Muslim states are an important contributor to the rise of extremist Islamism demanding radical change.

> The most immediate consequence of identity crisis and alienation is the precipitous decline in the legitimacy of ruling elites and institutions... This legitimacy crisis had been reinforced by the failure of these leaders in the political, economic and social domains.[69]

Soumaya al-Ghannouchi, a Muslim researcher in the history of ideas at the School of Oriental and African Studies, University of London, deals with the growing illegitimacy of Arab regimes that results in the rise of autonomous Islamist movements bent on replacing the illegitimate regimes:

> Increasingly, the Arab public feels that the political system is unfit to respond to the question of destiny and provide the basics for preserving sovereignty. There is a striking dichotomy at the heart of the Arab state... Disillusionment with the official political order and growing cynicism about its ability to preserve a semblance of sovereignty, liberate occupied land, or safeguard national interests has brought new actors onto the stage of Arab politics. These non-state players, which include Hizbollah in Lebanon and several armed groups in Palestine, are increasingly occupying the centre of the public sphere in the Middle East, profiting

from the declining legitimacy of the political elite tied to the stakes of foreign dominance in the region and lacking popular support to speak of.[70]

12. Resentment towards the United States

Many Muslims see the US as heir to imperial European political power and as the recognised leader of the Western world. They accuse it of being intent on maintaining Western dominance through neo-colonial means such as dependency, economic superiority, globalisation and cultural influence. It is also accused of forcing governments of developing countries to implement International Monetary Fund and World Bank policies that worsen the lot of the poor, and of supporting repressive regimes in Muslim countries in order to secure vital oil supplies from the Middle East. Finally the United States is viewed as the main source of the modern immoral culture, including sexual permissiveness and pornography, which lies behind the breakdown of the family and the erosion of traditional values. This culture is exported to Muslim societies and is seen as corrupting young people, leading to drug abuse and fostering an explosion in crime all over the world. America has thus become the great enemy of the Muslim World or, as it is known in Iran, the Great Satan.

Ayatollah Khamenei, Supreme Guardian of the Islamic Republic of Iran, sees the history of the relations between the United States and Iran as a history of

> America delivering blows to us, betraying us, stabbing us in the back by plotting coups d'etat.[71]

In the Iran-Iraq war of the 1980s America supported Iraq against Iran. America has harmed Iran more than anyone else, says Khamenei, and it fully deserves the title

> "The Great Satan" because "it engages in evil, in treachery, in murder and because it is arrogant." America is also "the greatest supporter of the Zionist regime which has thrown out an Islamic nation from its homeland.[72]

Tariq Hilmi, an Egyptian Islamist, gives a long list of reasons why Muslims should hate America:

This is the America that declared war against Islam and the Muslims under the title of world terrorism. This is the America that gives unlimited and unconditional support for the Zionist entity. This is the America that wants the Muslims to surrender and submit to the forces of occupation, otherwise they are considered terrorists. This is the America that is using weapons that are internationally prohibited to crush the Muslims of Iraq and Afghanistan, and is using its planes and missiles to attack the Muslims in Palestine. This is the America that protects the agent governments in the Islamic world, which act against the will of the Muslim peoples... The history of America is full of evilness against humanity... This is the America that occupies the world with the culture of sex and deviation. This is the pagan civilization in Christian disguise... This is the American civilization whose object is the body and its means is materialism. The spirit has no place in the system of American values. They are dressed with Christian clothes on hearts that know nothing but stealing, robbing, and occupying the possessions of others. Has America left one place in our lives as Muslims without corrupting it?[73]

13. Climate change

Much of the Muslim population of the world live in areas which are likely to suffer the most from climate change:

1. Parts of the Middle East and North Africa will witness increased desertification. The CIA has predicted that there will be chronic water shortages in Egypt and Syria in coming years.[74]

2. Bangladesh is the country most vulnerable to rises in sea levels. Catastrophic floods in the past have previously caused widespread damage as far as 100 km inland.

As Muslim countries are among the poorest in the world they will be less able than others to deal with the potential effects of climate change. Where there is a lack of properly developed infrastructure and/or inefficient and corrupt government it will be particularly difficult to cope with serious environmental problems when they arise.

An excerpt from the synopsis of a recent seminar, "The Impacts of Climate Change on the Islamic World" held at the Oxford Centre for Islamic Studies reveals the extent of the problem:

> Professor Francis Robinson said that the Islamic world was particularly vulnerable to climate change. He drew attention to six main factors. First came the effects of rising sea levels, with their effects on coastal communities (one Muslim state - the Maldives - might be totally eliminated and Bangladesh could lose two thirds of its territory). As a result there would be destruction of livelihoods, loss of life in violent weather events, and large movements of people in search of somewhere to live. Secondly, there were the effects of the warming of the oceans. These included destruction of coral reefs and significant changes in fish populations. Hurricanes and cyclones would become more intense and severe. Thirdly, patterns of drought and rainfall would change, with enormous consequences for human populations. Fourthly, water supplies would be diminished from the melting of Himalayan and other glaciers. The supply of water might first increase but then diminish severely. Fifthly, there would be new patterns of disease with the proliferation of old and new micro-organisms. Lastly, change, which many in the past believed to be slow, might in fact be relatively fast. We were now trying to identify the tipping points of change.[75]

The hardship, suffering and accompanying natural disasters which will be caused by such climate change may be interpreted by Muslims as a punishment from God because of their failure either to be faithful to him or to implement *shari'a*. Furthermore those worst affected and least able to help themselves may then become radicalised by religious extremists. Increasingly Muslim writers view these catastrophes as part of an End-Time scenario when the final battle will be waged between the expected End-Time deliverer the *mahdi*, the Anti-Christ and Jesus ('Isa). The Turkish Islamic writer, Harun Yahya, in his book *The Signs of the Last Days*, has this to say on global warming:

In short, we are now living in that age of confusion and disorder in which yet another sign of the End Times is manifested. This sign is a stern warning that people should begin immediately to live their lives according to the moral teachings of the Qur'an... In the last ten years, disasters caused by climactic changes are a novel phenomenon. A dangerous and unwanted by-product of industry is global warming. Industry is gradually disturbing the balance in the world's atmosphere, giving rise to climactic changes. The year of 1998 was the hottest on earth since records have been kept... Therefore, all this destruction brought upon the great cities by these calamities is an important sign in each case.[76]

Climate change is thus likely to become a factor in Islamic radicalism and terrorism in future decades.

14. Muslim conspiracy theories

Conspiracy theories are popular at all levels of Muslim society around the world. Many Muslims believe that the Christian West, Jewish Zionism and secularism are combining to corrupt, divide and destroy Islam. According to such theories, governments in Muslim states are viewed as puppets of these three forces, betraying their countries into dependence and secularisation. Orientalists and Christian clergy are blamed for supporting all anti-Islamic activities in the world, conspiring against Islam, slandering its history, and degrading Muhammad and his Companions.[77] The US-led invasion of Iraq in 2003 is seen as part of the world-wide anti-Muslim conspiracy.

Ayatollah Ruhollah Khomeini, founder and Supreme Guide of the Islamic Republic of Iran, had this to say about the conspiracies of Jews and Christians against Islam:

Since its inception, Islam was afflicted with the Jews who distorted the reputation of Islam by assaulting and slandering it, and this has continued to our present day. The Crusades made the Christian West realise that Islam with its laws and beliefs was the biggest obstacle to their control and domination of the world. That is why they harboured resentment and treated it unjustly. Then more than three centuries ago, came the evil colonists who found in the

Muslim world their long sought object. To achieve their ambitions they laboured to create the conditions which would lead to the annihilation of Islam. Missionaries, Orientalists, the information media – all are in the service of the colonialist countries and all are guilty of distorting Islam in a way that has caused many Muslims to steer away from it and not find their way back to it. Whilst Islam is the religion of struggle for right, justice, freedom and independence, those enemies have portrayed it in a distorted manner, even in the academic world, aiming at extinguishing its flame and robbing it of its revolutionary character. They teach that Islam has no relevance to society and government and is only concerned with private rituals. These enemies have implanted their falsehoods in the minds of the Muslim people with the help of their agents, and have managed to eliminate Islam's judiciary and political laws from the sphere of application, replacing them by European laws. The colonialists and their lackeys claim there is a separation between state and religion, so they can isolate Islam from the affairs of society and keep the ulama' away from the people. When they have separated and isolated us they can take away our resources and rule us.[78]

According to Aftab Malik,

Young Muslims feel both powerless and guilty over their inability to help fellow-Muslims against the encroachments of "Zionist forces" and "crusader Americans". In face of an onslaught of conspiracy theories and *jihadist* videos, they are encouraged – even brainwashed – into complicity with the notion that Islam itself is under siege.[79]

Many Muslims do not believe that Muslims were behind the September 11th 2001 attacks on the twin towers in New York. They allege that it was the American CIA or the Israeli Mossad who masterminded these attacks. A recent survey studying Muslim and Western attitudes to each other reveals that:

In one of the survey's most striking findings, majorities in Indonesia, Turkey, Egypt, and Jordan say that they do *not* believe groups of Arabs carried out the Sept. 11, 2001 terrorist attacks. The percentage of Turks expressing disbelief that Arabs carried out the 9/11 attacks has increased from 43% in a 2002 Gallup survey to 59% currently. And this attitude is not limited to Muslims in predominantly Muslim countries – 56% of British Muslims say they do not believe Arabs carried out the terror attacks against the U.S., compared with just 17% who do.[80]

Conclusion

There can be no doubt that Muslims across the world face serious pressures and hardships. Muslim countries face enough real adversity and suffering for their populations to feel strong resentment and anger which can manifest itself in support for violence against perceived enemies.

However Muslims are not alone in facing such problems and the problems themselves should not be exaggerated, as they are typical of many nations in the developing world. Members of most religious and ethnic groups around the world face similar challenges. In fact, it can be argued that some areas, particularly sub-Saharan Africa, face greater problems than the Muslim world, and the violence in the Congo is partly due to similar causes. However, few religious communities in the present time engage in violence across the world to the same degree as Muslims. Certainly, in some contexts, members of most religions have been willing to resort to violence. Local grievances combined with a strong allegiance to a collective religious identity can lead to instability and conflict. The example of Sri Lanka shows that this includes even those religions with a reputation for "peacefulness" such as Buddhism and Hinduism.

Muslim states also include a few very wealthy oil states and several others with developing oil capacities. Much of this wealth is however invested in the West, used to promote radical forms of Islam (including violence and terrorism), and spent on procurement of expensive weapons systems. The potential for real development programmes in the poorer countries financed by the rich states is not being fulfilled.

Today almost every country which has either a majority Muslim population or a significant Muslim minority (including Western countries) has faced terrorist threats or actual terrorist violence perpetrated in the name of Islam. No other religious group in recent times have been shown to pose such a threat of violence and terrorism across the globe as consistently as Muslims do. Is there something distinctive about Islam as a religion that makes it more likely to justify violence than other religions? The British Muslim journalist, Rageh Omar, posed an important question when he said about the 7/7 bombers who attacked London in 2005:

> Why was it four Muslims who blew themselves up? Why have other marginalised communities not produced suicide bombers?[81]

The answer to this question lies in the legitimacy that the Muslim source texts, classical Islamic theology, and paradigmatic early Muslim history give to violence against non-Muslims and to the ways in which modern Islamists, drawing on these sources, have formed ideologies which justify violence in a modern context.

Currently Muslim minorities are causing problems in most of the majority of countries where they live. In Western countries this is shown in calls for the adoption of *shari'a* law, by Muslims being unwilling to integrate to the same degree as other religious minorities, and by both indirect and direct support for terrorism. Recently Libyan president Mu'ammar Qadhafi claimed that the rising numbers of Muslims in Europe could lead to Islam taking Europe over without violent force:

> We have fifty million Muslims in Europe. There are signs that Allah will grant Islam victory in Europe – without swords, without guns, without conquests. The fifty million Muslims of Europe will turn it into a Muslim continent within a few decades.[82]

Assimilation of immigrant populations is becoming harder in general in the age of globalisation as diasporas maintain much closer contact with their home nation through modern communications and cheap air flights. Indeed some are beginning to argue that because of these factors assimilation may now be impossible. Muslim populations are especially hard to assimilate because their religion permeates much further into social, political and legal spheres than other religions and because it encourages religious identity to be placed above national identity.

2
Sources and their Interpretation

Is the cup half full of water, or is it half empty? Human interpretation of basic data can be influenced by many different factors, exterior and interior, conscious and subconscious. This is particularly true in the religious arena, where basic sources are liable to be given a whole spectrum of interpretations, for ultimately there is no way of proving or disproving any particular believer's understanding of a religious text.

While there are small minorities of liberal and secular Muslims, the majority of the world's Muslims today continue to champion the traditional classical version of Islam as the only true God-given and unchangeable religion which must not be criticised, disparaged or tampered with. The Islamist version of Islam which has recently become dominant in most Muslim societies further strengthens and radicalises such traditional views. Islamism (revivalist Islam, political Islam, Islamic fundamentalism) is an integral part of Islam and its influence is growing rapidly across the Muslim world.

Most Muslims claim that God revealed their holy book, the Qur'an, to Muhammad, the founder of Islam (c.570–632), whom they see as the last and greatest prophet who was given God's final revelation to humanity. The Arabic word "Islam" means submission. Muslims are those who submit to God (Allah in Arabic) and his will and law as presented by Muhammad. For Muslims, Allah's will is expressed in the Qur'an and in the *hadith* (traditions) which record the *sunna* (Muhammad's life, deeds and sayings). Muslims hold that Islam was not a new religion, but a continuation and culmination of God's revelations through earlier prophets such as Abraham, Moses and Jesus.

For Muslims, Islam is not merely a personal faith, but a total way of life, an all-encompassing religious, social and political system, a world-view, civilisation and culture. Islam includes a legal system of detailed regulations (*shari'a*), based on the Muslim source texts, ruling every aspect of a Muslim's life. It covers family affairs, behavioural norms, criminal justice, politics and economics. Parts of *shari'a* are incorporated in the legal systems of a number of Islamic countries today, and even where it is not formally acknowledged in law or constitution, *shari'a* still exerts a powerful influence in Muslim societies.

Problems of Muslim source texts

The traditional "official" Muslim view of Islamic history is based exclusively on Muslim sources, the earliest of which were written some 150 years after the events they describe, and are uncorroborated by external evidence.[83] The most important source, the Qur'an, is viewed as divinely inspired, perfectly preserved and without error in all its assertions, including those on history. Muslims believe that the original is engraved in Arabic on a stone tablet in heaven and that its contents were revealed piecemeal to Muhammad during the last twenty-three years of his life (610-632). Various collections of the revelations were put together, differing slightly from each other, but between 650 and 656 efforts were made to suppress all but one of these

Second in importance and authority as a source text are the *hadith*, traditional accounts of what Muhammad said and did. They gain their authority from Muhammad's own command in his farewell sermon to hold on to two things he was leaving them that would prevent them going astray – the Qur'an and the *hadith*.[84] Further authority is given by a verse in the Qur'an which urges Muslims to follow Muhammad's example:

> Ye have indeed in the Apostle of God a beautiful pattern (of conduct). Q 33:21[85]

The stories are numerous, and different scholars have made their own collections, the largest ones dating from two or three centuries after Muhammad. Much scholarly effort has been put into ascertaining which of the many stories are the most reliable. Validity is traditionally judged by the chain of transmission i.e. the list of people by whom the story was passed down. The most dependable collections are recognisable by the word *sahih* (true) before the name of the compiler. Most Muslims believe that the methods of *hadith* collection and codification were reliable, recording only the correct information and filtering out the false narratives in a divinely controlled process. For most Muslims, *hadith* are seen as divinely inspired and second only to the Qur'an as a source of divine guidance. In practice they often take precedence over the literal Qur'anic statements, as they explain and interpret the Qur'an's meaning and are heavily used to establish legal rulings.

The source texts are thus considered to be divinely inspired, inerrant and perfect. The Muslim view implies that Islam broke into the world in the seventh century as a complete system. This traditional view does not allow for any processes of development in the nascent Muslim community except as found in its sacred sources.

While some Western scholars have largely accepted Muslim views on the origins and development of Islam and the reliability of Muslim sources, others have rejected the traditional Muslim account, claiming it was a later theological construct presented as history. The latter view is based on the paucity of non-Muslim corroborating materials and the alleged unreliability of the Muslim sources. According to this approach, the Muslim account of Islam's early history was developed as a later political rationalisation of history in order to defend the established order.[86]

In this view, *hadith* do not record the real words and deeds of Muhammad and his companions, but are the product of later disputes within the Muslim community in the first two centuries of Islam. A large number of *hadith* were created by various factions competing for political power or for doctrinal dominance during the Umayyad (661-750) and 'Abbasid (750-1258) periods. Muhammad's authority was invoked by every group to support its own ideas and causes. *Hadith* are thus a reflection of later Muslim communities, their aspirations and struggles, and mirror the development of Islam in the eighth to tenth centuries. *Hadith* assimilated foreign material including passages from the Old and New Testaments, Rabbinic sayings, apocryphal gospels, Greek philosophers and Persian and Indian wisdom.[87]

Some recent revisionist theories by Western academics reject the entire Muslim version of early Islamic history, regarding it as a later fabrication, and go beyond the scholarly views on the invention of *hadith* to a complete rewriting of the early history of Islam. Looking at external evidence from Jewish and Christian sources of the period, they argue that the Arabs were influenced by Jewish messianic ideas. According to these theories, both Muslim Arabs and Jews were hostile to Christianity and formed an alliance that lasted well beyond Muhammad's lifetime. Muslim Arab and Jewish tribes, they claim, migrated first in the direction of the Jewish Holy Land (Palestine) to claim it from Christian Byzantium as God's covenanted land to Abraham and his descendants, before expanding into other neighbouring lands (Syria, Egypt, Iraq). At some time following the conquest of Jerusalem a break occurred with the Jews and there was a softening of attitudes towards Christians, while many religious ideas were also borrowed from the Samaritan community.[88]

In this view, the religious development of Islam followed its political development and served to legitimate it. Qur'an and *hadith* developed gradually as the needs arose to legitimate political structures and power centres. Islam as we know it emerged as an independent religion only thorough a long process of struggle for identity among the disparate peoples in the conquered areas: Eastern Christians, Jews, Samaritans and Arabs. Islam thus evolved out of Jewish, Samaritan, Hellenistic, Roman-Byzantine, Eastern Christian and pre-Islamic Arabic practices and ideas as found in the various regions. The figure of Muhammad was later created as an Arab Prophet on the model of Moses, leading the Arabs in an exodus to receive a new revelation at an Arabian sacred mountain.[89]

Some Western scholars radically question the Muslim account of the assembling of the Qur'an, using methods adapted from biblical textual analysis. They argue that the Qur'an was not a product of Muhammad's lifetime, but was collected much later out of a fragmentary oral tradition which included some of Muhammad's sayings as well as a large quantity of exegetical and explanatory materials developed in the course of polemical disputes with Jews and Christians after the Arab conquests. Both Qur'an and *hadith* grew out of sectarian controversies over the first two centuries of Islam and were then projected back on to an invented Arabian origin. This revisionist theory suggests that Islam's religious institutions emerged at least two centuries after Muhammad's time, to ideologically consolidate the Arab conquest. The Arabs, anxious to forge an identity different from that of the more advanced religions and cultures of the peoples they conquered, developed a religion that would maintain their new identity, and attributed the materials used to a mythic figure of an Arab Prophet who had reaffirmed the ancient Mosaic code of law. This theory fits in with available palaeographic evidence which places the development of the Arabic script much later than the Muslim sources. It also provides explanations for certain archaeological problems, such as the *qiblas* of certain early mosques in Iraq facing Jerusalem rather than Mecca.[90]

Gerd R. Puin, a German scholar, has examined ancient Qur'anic manuscripts written in the early Hijazi Arabic script discovered in a mosque in Yemen in 1972. He discovered unconventional verse orders, textual variations and rare styles of orthography diverging from the accepted version. According to Puin, his discoveries indicate that the Qur'an is composed of a cocktail of texts, some preceding Islam, evolving over hundreds of years rather than a text fixed in the early years of Islam just after Muhammad's death.[91]

John Wansbrough, one of the leading Western scholars of early Islam, stressed the importance of Rabbinic Jewish influences on early Islam, arguing that Islamic doctrine, and even the figure of Muhammad, were modelled on rabbinic Jewish prototypes. He also claimed that the definitive text of the Qur'an was fixed after the ninth century.[92] According to Patricia Crone, Muhammad mobilised Jewish monotheism against dominant Christianity. The Byzantine persecution of the Jews played a crucial role in the launching

Muhammad's movement. Crone posits a Jewish-Arab symbiosis in north-west Arabia which was manipulated by Muhammad to achieve Arab supremacy.[93]

This revisionist version rejects the centrality of Mecca in early Islam, based on the lack of any mention of Mecca in non-Muslim sources and on the fact of the first *qibla* facing Jerusalem. The centre of the Arab-Jewish alliance is placed in north-west Arabia and the real *hijra* was not from Mecca to Medina, but from north-west Arabia to Palestine. These migrants were not called Muslims, a term first found only at the end of the seventh century, but *mahgraye* or *muhajirun*, from the Semitic root *hgr* which has connotations of migration in Hebrew and Aramaic.[94]

According to Crone and Cook, Islam only took on a specific identity in the late seventh century, while *shari'a* was only developed in the 'Abbasid era in Iraq by Shafi'i (768-820) and his contemporaries following the Babylonian Jewish Rabbinical model of sanctifying the oral law and relating it back to Moses. During the Umayyad period there had been no Islamic law at all – only customary law.[95]

Violent reaction by Muslim scholars to revisionist Western theories has had the effect of dampening some of the interest in these investigations. Islamist influence in Western academia has also worked to empower politically correct views that include the acceptance of the Muslim version of history. Academics who express doubts on these issues find themselves open to ridicule, isolation, harassment and even threats of violence.

In this book, which seeks to help the reader to understand what motivates Muslims to violence, war and terrorism, the history of early Islam follows the accepted scholarly view based mainly on Muslim sources, rather than the views of modern revisionist scholars. It represents more what *Muslims believe about their early history* as based on Muslim source texts rather than *historical evidence*.

Interpretations of *jihad*

There is plenty of scope for contrasting interpretations in many areas of life. America's "war on terror", following the tragic events of September 11th 2001, is considered a "war on Islam" by many Muslims despite repeated denials by western leaders.

The theme of this book is the doctrine of war in Islam, a subject which is surrounded by much confusion. What we can be sure of is that a discussion of war features overtly in Islamic theology and thought from its earliest days until now. We can also be sure that there are a multitude of different interpretations which are sincerely held and practised by different individual Muslims.

An example of difference in interpretation can be clearly seen in the varying understandings of the word "*jihad*" (literally "striving"). For some Muslims this means military war to spread Islam as a religious and political system – *jihad* of the sword. For others it is a spiritual struggle against temptation and sin to improve and purify oneself – *jihad* of the heart. Intermediate are two other possibilities – *jihad* of the tongue[96] and of the hands, aimed at correcting wrongs and supporting what is right.

It is worth noting here that the term "holy war", so often used as an English translation of "*jihad*", did not exist in classical Arabic usage. There is a word for war (*harb*) and a word for holy (*muqaddas*) which are sometimes put together in modern Arabic, but were never combined in classical Arabic. However, the use of the term "holy war" in the sense of "war ordained by God" can be supported by the fact that the word "*jihad*" in the Islamic source texts is commonly followed by the phrase "in the way [i.e. path] of God" and by the fact that the military meaning of *jihad* was predominant in the understanding of the classical Islamic theologians and jurists.[97]

Although Islamic terrorists – who are included in those who consider *jihad* to be military war – are relatively few in number, they should not necessarily be considered a marginalised fringe group rejected by the mainstream of Islamic society as "not real Muslims". Their guiding principles are not a modern aberration of some undeniably peaceful true Islam but have deep roots in Islamic history and theology. Such terrorists are simply following a particular interpretation of the sources of Islam. They have selected and prioritised certain aspects and texts of Islamic source material. Other interpretations take the same source material and come to a different conclusion. Those who deny the validity of the terrorists' interpretation are usually very liberal

Muslims, whose own interpretations of Islam are unacceptable to the majority. One such example is Bassam Tibi, Professor of International Relations at the University of Göttingen, Germany and formerly Bosch Fellow and Research Associate at Harvard University, who states categorically: "The terrorism of Islamic fundamentalists is not a *jihad* in the authentic tradition – even though they conceive of their actions as a *jihad*."[98] It should be noted that others may make similar public denials not through conviction but for tactical reasons.

Contemporary Islam has also produced a range of newer perspectives on war, making a discussion of the subject more complex than it would have been in an earlier age. In the past there was much more of a consensus (albeit always with some dissident variations) on what a Muslim should believe about war. This classical historic understanding has now been challenged by many alternative interpretations. This book seeks to examine the *classical* Islamic doctrine of war, for this is still the interpretation with which all other interpretations are compared and contrasted by their respective proponents. It is also the doctrine still followed closely by many modern Muslims as will be seen in the latter part of the book.

The development of the classical doctrine

The Islamic doctrine of war was developed over a period of time by the same processes which Islamic scholars used to develop other areas of Islamic doctrine and law.

Working from two sources, the Qur'an and *hadith*, Islamic jurists gradually evolved the detailed body of legislation known as *shari'a*. There are at least eight recognised versions of *shari'a*, the main ones being the four different Sunni schools of law and the Twelver Shi'a school – each being favoured in different parts of the world. The Sunni schools were founded by Hanifa, Malik, Shafi'i and Hanbal, the Shi'a school by Imam Ja'far al-Sadiq. Although differing on minor points, these five schools agree on basic issues. These enormously detailed sets of rules to regulate every aspect of devotional, family, social, economic, military and political life were derived from the Qur'an and *hadith* by a logical reasoning process known as *ijtihad*. It is worth taking some time to look at the main types of problems facing those engaged in *ijtihad*.

Firstly, despite the fact that the Qur'an and Muhammad's own words and actions were all held to be divinely inspired, there often appeared to be a conflict of opinion between these various sources. Even within the Qur'an itself there were many verses which seemed to contradict each other. Furthermore the Qur'anic text is often remarkably vague and ambiguous; many individual verses are open to a multitude of interpretations. (Some examples are given in chapter 15.) So although the Qur'an was more authoritative, the *hadith* were often easier to understand. Then there was the problem of how to legislate on issues not actually mentioned in either the Qur'an or the *hadith*.

Some rules and tools were devised to guide the scholars in their perplexity. Firstly there was the concept of *naskh*. This term is most often translated into English as "abrogation" and describes a simple rule of Qur'anic interpretation whereby in any case of self-contradiction within the Qur'an the later-dated verse (*nasikh*, that which abrogates) is assumed to take precedence over the earlier verse (*mansukh*, that which is abrogated). Some scholars emphasise that this does not mean the earlier verse is actually untrue and cancelled out, but that it has been subordinated to and modified by the later verse. The application of this simple rule is made complex in practice by the fact that the Qur'an is not arranged in chronological order so considerable scholarship is needed to know the relative dates of any two verses, and in some cases scholars differ. The huge impact of *naskh* on the classical Islamic doctrine of war is explained in chapter 3.

Other tools of *ijtihad* included *ijma'* (the consensus of Muslim scholars on any given subject) and *quays* (analogical reasoning, helpful when trying to derive laws on subjects not covered in the sources). Other factors taken into consideration, but carrying less weight, included the prevailing customs of pre-Islamic Arabia and various general principles such as the public good, a harm must not be removed by means of a greater harm, etc.[99]

The founders of the five schools of Islamic law lived in the eighth century and the first half of the ninth century. From the tenth century onwards, scholars of the various schools of law gradually reached a consensus that all essential questions of law had been comprehensively discussed and settled by the great founding scholars. Later scholars were not deemed to have the necessary qualifications for independent legal reasoning (*jihad*), and all future activity had to be confined to the explanation, application and interpretation of doctrines already laid down once and for all. This "closing of the gates of *jihad*" opened the way for the practice of *taqlid*, (imitating the example of the great scholars), which meant the unquestioning acceptance of the decisions of the established schools and authorities.[100] Deviation from the jurists' opinions of the past was disapproved and considered sinful. The *shari'a* was now seen as a set of static and unchanging norms. Since that time the *shari'a* has been viewed as a complete code from which there can be no variation.

This development created a great reluctance amongst the majority of Sunni Muslims to indulge in *ijtihad* even to this day. The belief that the door or gates of *ijtihad* have yet to be re-opened (if ever), is reinforced by a belief that *ijtihad* can only be practised by scholars of unusual personal piety as well as unusual learning.[101] Hence it is that the majority of today's Sunni Muslims see it as heresy to consider altering or updating the *shari'a*.[102]

Nevertheless, since the closing of the gates of *ijtihad*, there have been many individual Muslims who have departed from the standard teaching. Two of the best known in medieval times were al-Ghazali (d.1111) who promoted Sufism (Islamic mysticism) and Ibn Rushd (also known as Averroes, 1126-98) who took a rationalist approach.

Modern calls to return to the original sources and make a new *ijtihad* may seek to reform Islam in one or other of two directions. Some seek a modernisation and liberalisation to keep Islam in step with other contemporary civilisations; others seek to create a stricter and more puritanical faith completely unblemished by any outside influence.

Other sources

Non-Muslim scholars have identified some non-Islamic sources of the Islamic doctrine of war. The influence of these external sources would be denied by devout Muslims, who would not wish to acknowledge that uninspired human input had played any part in the development of their faith. But for the sake of completeness it may be helpful to outline the main factors.[103]

Pre-Islamic factors include:

1. Pre-Islamic traditions of northern Arabia

In this lawless tribal society, hostility to all other tribes was presumed, unless a specific agreement had been made with a particular tribe. The inter-tribal raid (*ghazwa* or razzia) was a frequent and normal part of life. In many ways the raids were more like sport than war. The result was generally a redistribution of wealth (e.g. livestock) or women from the losing tribe to the winning tribe, and loss of life was rare. There appear to have been at least some rules governing the conduct of *gnaws*, including a prohibition on attacking non-combatants with lethal intent. Harming women and children was probably considered dishonourable.

There was also another kind of tribal conflict called *manic*, which was rarer and more bloody. These were generally disputes over resources like grazing ground or wells and only arose in exceptional circumstances such as severe drought. *Manic* was effectively a battle for the survival of the tribe.

2. Byzantium

Byzantine culture had an ideology of imperial victory (derived from Roman ideas) and divine aid (derived from Judaism). Muslim rulers would most likely have felt the need to affirm the same two concepts in respect of the Islamic state. Byzantine culture can also be seen as having had an influence on the development of the Islamic concept of the unity of the Islamic state under a single ruler (caliph or imam). Only the state, under its head, can launch a *jihad*. The Byzantines viewed war as a great evil and had some notion of the possibility of a just war, for example, against external enemies in self-defence. Justice and mercy were supposed to characterise the emperor's dealings with his own people.

3. Sassanid Persians

The Sassanids had an ideology of imperial victory and divine support similar to that of the Byzantines. They appear to have held that only defensive war was justified, but that included defence of their religion (Zoroastrianism) as well as of their territory. Sometimes there seems to have been a requirement for the emperor to act justly, as in Byzantine culture, though there does not appear to have been a similar requirement for him to act mercifully, at least not in the context of keeping order within his empire. External enemies could be dealt with severely.

4. The ever-present reality of war

The daily reality of war must have shaped popular attitudes. For example, the Byzantine emperor was not, despite the ideology, always victorious in battle, which would surely have created some question marks in the minds of his subjects.

5. Apocalyptic traditions

Traditions concerning the imminent end of the world were very widespread. With Jewish, Christian or Hellenistic roots, these prophecies often foretold war - even defeat - as a precursor to the End Times and ultimate victory. Apocalyptic thought appears to have been particularly popular in the Christian kingdom of Axum (Ethiopia). It must also have brought comfort to the beleaguered Byzantines, who lost huge areas of territory to the Persians in the early seventh century and then again to the Muslims a few years later. Islam has a full and detailed eschatology in which war is a key portent. Possibly Muhammad and his followers saw themselves as instruments of God, cleansing the world by eliminating false belief in preparation for the Day of Judgement. (See also chapter 6.)

Later influences on the Islamic doctrine of war include:
1. The Crusades
While the Crusades had no effect on the theory or conduct of *jihad*[104] they are worth mentioning as they appear to have produced a heightened religious fervour because the Muslims were once more fighting Christians (albeit Europeans). This reminded them of the golden age of early Islam when their ancestors had swept to victory against the Byzantine Christians.

2. Eurasian steppe traditions
This influence came from the Turkish and Mongol tribes of central Asia who were introduced to the Islamic world as slaves, troops or migrants from the ninth century onwards. They eventually established a number of Muslim regimes in different parts of the world lasting from the eleventh to the twentieth centuries. The main departure from classical Islamic doctrine was the concept that a ruler had absolute authority to make "secular" state law, independent of any religious law. This created a tension between two parallel law systems, as was seen markedly in the Ottoman Empire.

3
Qur'an, *Hadith* and *Shari'a*

The word *jihad* has a long and complex history and set of meanings in Islam. While many twenty-first century Muslims would condemn the use of war or terrorism in the name of Islam, and while Muslim apologists in the West generally claim that *jihad* is merely a spiritual struggle against sin, there is no doubt that the accepted traditional and classical view of *jihad* was that of a holy war, an armed struggle, for establishing the dominion of Islam.[105] This should be no surprise given the fact that the source texts of Islam contain some passages which can without difficulty be interpreted to permit, command or even glorify violence of this kind. This violence is targeted primarily against polytheists, but also against Jews and Christians, and against erring Muslims.

Jihad is a concept taught by Muhammad and accepted as a central permanent religious duty. Indeed it is regarded by some Muslims as one of the most important acts of worship. Yusuf al-Qaradhawi, the popular Qatar-based cleric who plays a leading role in the Muslim Brotherhood, has made clear elsewhere that he interprets *jihad* as physical warfare and says:

> Islam regards *jihad* as the greatest act of worship… It is a sacred religious duty and an act of worship which brings Muslims closer to Allah.[106]

Jihad has always been a popular concept in Islam, evoking deep emotions of identification and sympathy. It has been invoked innumerable times in Muslim history to justify wars against various enemies, and is not merely defensive, as some apologists for Islam claim. S. Abdullah Schleifer, a convert to Islam who teaches TV journalism at the American University in Cairo, explains:

> Modern scholarship, in accord with traditional Islamic jurisprudence, has generally treated jihad in the context of military action as the one form of war which is permissible in principle in Islam; as the instrument of Islam's universal mission and, if need be, in the defence of Islam; and as an individual duty and collective obligation upon the community of Islam... jihad came to be used by the Muslims to generally signify the sacralization of combat; the holy war particularly as understood in the use of the expression: jihad fi sabil Allah fighting in the way of God, or for His sake, in the cause of Religion.[107]

Muslim attitudes to violence are grounded in classical Islamic theology as derived from the Qur'an, *hadith* and *shari'a*, as well as by the normative example of Muhammad and the experiences of violent conflicts in the early history of Islam. These factors provide the theoretical framework and paradigms within which violence, its causes and the means it may employ are discussed, legitimated and implemented.

Muhammad's Example

During his early years of prophethood in Mecca (610-622), Muhammad focused on prayer and meditation. His approach to Jews, Christians and other non-Muslims was peaceful, cooperative and non-violent. After opposition and persecution forced him to flee to Medina in 622, he became the spiritual, political and military leader of an Islamic state. While in Medina he believed that God gave him permission to fight those who were persecuting the Muslims.[108]

As Muhammad gained power, especially after his migration (*hijra*) from Mecca to Medina, he became much more aggressive in his pronouncements and actions[109] against his opponents, whether pagans, Jews, Christians or Muslim "hypocrites". He turned against his Jewish allies, massacring many, enslaving others and expelling them from their lands. He raided trade caravans to punish his Meccan enemies and to gain loot for himself and his supporters and developed the *ghazwa* into the *jihad*. He also instigated the assassination of individuals who had criticised him. It is recorded that Muhammad himself participated personally in at least 27 campaigns while organising 59 others led by commanders appointed by him.[110] As he is considered by Muslims to be the perfect example whom they should imitate in every detail, his belligerence and the methods he employed are considered a model for Muslims to emulate.

Muhammad declared that *jihad* was the special mark of his ministry and religion. As Schleifer explains this was interpreted by his early followers in a military sense:

> Yet it is in this very domain that the Prophet acknowledges his own combative mission: "Every prophet has his vocation and my vocation is jihad." The earliest biographies of the Prophet, written but one generation removed, were called kitab al-maghazi, Book of Military Expeditions, and the enduring term, from the 8th century, for the Prophet's biography - sira - was adopted by scholars and jurists in its plural form - siyar - as a technical heading for the early collections of hadiths or fikr bearing on warfare.[111]

For Muslims studying military history, Muhammad emerges as the perfect strategist and tactitian who fought several battles against superior enemy forces and won them all. Muhammad Hamidullah quotes from the 1934 British War Office Training Regulations to prove that learning from history is essential because *"human nature and the underlying principles of war do not change, and it is for this reason that valuable lessons can be learned from EVEN THE MOST ANCIENT CAMPAIGNS"*. He goes on to describe Muhammad as the ideal military commander who was "practically always victorious", and analyses in some detail the battles in which Muhammad took part.[112]

Brigadier S.K. Malik also seeks to base the modern military strategy of Muslim armies on Muhammad's example:

> The military campaigns undertaken or initiated by the Holy Prophet (peace be upon him) are 'institutions' for learning the Quranic art of war. Time has only enhanced, not dimmed, their practical value for our training and mental and spiritual

development... At stake, in each of these campaigns, were decisions and actions of a magnitude that mankind has seldom faced before or since.[113]

Qur'an

Because of Muhammad's change of attitude when he moved from Mecca to Medina, the Qur'an is a contradictory mixture of the peaceable and the bellicose. The nineteenth century Islamic jurist Ibn Abidin highlighted the gradual stages by which the transition was made:

> Know thou that the command of fighting was revealed by degrees, for the Prophet was at first commanded to deliver his message, then to discuss and dispute and endeavour to convince the unbelievers by arguments, then the believers were permitted to fight, then they were commanded to fight at first at any time, except the sacred months, then absolutely, without any exception.[114]

According to the rule of abrogation (*naskh*), it is the harsher and more violent Medinan passages that apply today because they are later, while the earlier conciliatory passages dating from Muhammad's days in Mecca are not applicable. Mahmud Muhammad Taha summarised the situation in classical Islam:

> All the verses of persuasion, though they constitute the primary or original principle, were abrogated or repealed by the verses of compulsion (jihad).[115]

There are a considerable number of verses which speak of love, peace and forgiveness towards non-Muslims. Many of these are in sura (chapter) 2. For example:

> Quite a number of the People of the Book[116] wish they could turn you (people) back to infidelity after ye have believed, from selfish envy, after the Truth hath become manifest unto them: but forgive and overlook, till God accomplish his purpose: for God hath power over all things. Q 2:109

> Those who believe (in the Qur'an) and those who follow the Jewish (scriptures), and the Christians and the Sabians, – any

who believe in God and the Last Day, and work righteousness, shall have their reward with their Lord : on them shall be no fear, nor shall they grieve. Q 2:62

But most traditional Muslim scholars assert that all such verses are abrogated by the so-called "Sword Verse" (Q 9:5), which commands Muslims to fight anyone who refuses to convert to Islam.[117] This verse is a favourite of modern Islamic militants.[118]

But when the forbidden months are past, then fight them and slay the Pagans wherever ye find them, and seize them, beleaguer them, and lie in wait for them in every stratagem (of war); but if they repent, and establish regular prayers and practise regular charity, then open the way for them: for God is oft-forgiving, most merciful. Q 9:5

In addition to the Sword Verse, there are a plethora of other apparent Qur'anic injunctions to make war, particularly war against non-Muslims with the aim of converting them to Islam. Some occur even in sura 2, where so many peaceable verses are found.

Fight in the cause of God those that fight you, but do not transgress the limits; for God loveth not transgressors. And slay them wherever ye catch them, and turn them out from where they have turned you out; Q 2:190-191

And fight them on until there is no more tumult or oppression, and there prevail justice and faith in God; but if they cease, let there be no hostility except to those who practise oppression. Q 2:193

Fighting is prescribed for you, and ye dislike it. But it is possible that ye dislike a thing which is good for you, and that ye love a thing which is bad for you. Q 2:216

And fight them on until there is no more tumult or oppression, and there prevail justice and faith in God altogether and everywhere; but if they cease, verily God doth see all that they do. Q 8:39

Let not the unbelievers think that they can get the better (of the godly): They will never frustrate (them). Against them make ready your strength to the utmost of your power, including steeds of war, to strike terror into (the hearts of) the enemies, of God and your enemies, and others besides, whom ye may no know, but whom God doth know. Q 8:59-60

Fight those who believe not in God nor the Last day, nor hold that forbidden which hath been forbidden by God and His Apostle, nor acknowledge the Religion of Truth, (even if they are) of the People of the Book, until they pay the *jizya* with willing submission, and feel themselves subdued. Q 9:29

In the Qur'an, *jihad* is an all-encompassing struggle to make Islamic rule prevail. It includes offering one's time, property, health and life in the battle for Islam:

Not equal are those believers who sit (at home) and receive no hurt and those who strive and fight in the cause of Allah with their goods and their persons. Allah hath granted a grade higher to those who strive and fight with their goods and persons than to those who sit (at home): unto all (in faith) hath Allah promised good: but those who strive and fight hath He distinguished above those who sit (at home) by a special reward. (Q 4:95)

Those who believe and suffer exile and strive with might and main in Allah's cause with their goods and their persons have the highest rank in the sight of Allah: They are the people who will achieve (salvation). Q 9:20

Many other examples could be given of verses which can easily be understood to command or commend warfare (and especially to convince Muslims who were not keen to fight).[119] There are also other verses which speak of non-Muslims as the enemies of Muslims,[120] and about Islam's ultimate goal to establish Islamic authority over the whole world.[121]

Reuven Firestone distinguishes four kinds of war verses. He concludes from his analysis that the transition from pre-Islamic ideas about war to the fully-fledged Islamic doctrine of *jihad* was far from smooth, and that there must have been many early Muslims who were opposed to militancy and had to be persuaded to overcome their reluctance to fight.[122]

For further details of the development of *jihad* theology in the Qur'an see chapter 5.

Hadith

The accounts of what Muhammad said and did, allegedly reported by his closest companions, gained such authority that they came to be regarded as divinely inspired. Thousands of these traditions, called *hadith*, were collected in the ninth and tenth centuries into official volumes, by various scholars. Six such collections are considered authoritative, the best known being those of Bukhari and of Muslim. For most Muslims, *hadith* are second only to the Qur'an as a source of divine guidance. In practice they often take precedence over the literal Qur'anic statements, as they explain and interpret the Qur'an's sometimes obscure meaning and are heavily used to establish legal rulings. It is clear from the *hadith* that Muhammad and the first Muslims understood *jihad* to include physical warfare and literal killing.[123]

In the *hadith* collections, especially those of Bukhari and Muslim, military *jihad* takes up almost all the space of the chapters devoted to *jihad*. Muhammad's military expeditions (*ghazawat*) are treated as *jihad* and Muhammad's companions are seen as very much concerned with the offensive military activities of the Muslim community.[124]

Recorded in the *hadith* are many statements commanding or commending violence. One of the most often quoted (though less clear than many) is:

> Allah's Apostle said, "Know that Paradise is under the shades of swords." *Sahih Bukhari Volume 4, Book 52, Number 73: Narrated by 'Abdullah bin Abi Aufa*[125]

Another *hadith* of Muhammad's clearly states:

> The Prophet said: 'I was sent by the sword preceding the judgment day and my livelihood is in the shadow of my spear

and humiliation and submission are on those who disobey me.
Musnad Imam Ahmad, Volume 2, p. 50: Narrated by Ibn Omar

Others are more specific about the enemy and the aim of *jihad*, apparently indicating that Muslims must fight non-Muslims until they are willing to convert to Islam.

Allah's Apostle said, "I have been ordered to fight with the people till they say, 'None has the right to be worshipped but Allah,' and whoever says, 'None has the right to be worshipped but Allah,' his life and property will be saved by me except for Islamic law, and his accounts will be with Allah, (either to punish him or to forgive him.)" *Sahih Bukhari Volume 4, Book 52, Number 196: Narrated by Abu Huraira*

Some are concerned with fighting particular named categories of non-Muslims, for example polytheists.

The Apostle of Allah (peace_be_upon_him) appointed Abu Bakr our commander and we fought with some people who were polytheists, and we attacked them at night, killing them. Our war cry that night was "put to death; put to death". Salamah said: "I killed that night with my hand polytheists belonging to seven houses." *Sunan Abu Dawud Book 14, Number 2632: Narrated by Salamah ibn al-Akwa'*

Some very chilling *hadith*, which describe inanimate nature rising up to betray the Jews, are quoted in the literature of certain radical Islamic groups today. For example:

Allah's Apostle said, "You (i.e. Muslims) will fight with the Jews till some of them will hide behind stones. The stones will (betray them) saying, 'O 'Abdullah (i.e. slave of Allah)! There is a Jew hiding behind me; so kill him." *Sahih Bukhari Volume 4, Book 52, Number 176: Narrated by 'Abdullah bin 'Umar*

Examples of the assassination of individuals also occur in the *hadith*.

Allah's Apostle sent a group of the Ansar to Abu Rafi. Abdullah bin Atik entered his house at night and killed him while he was sleeping. *Sahih Bukhari Volume 4, Book 52, Number 265: Narrated by Al-Bara bin Azib*

The Prophet said, "Who is ready to kill Ka'b bin Al-Ashraf who has really hurt Allah and His Apostle?" Muhammad bin Maslama said, "O Allah's Apostle! Do you like me to kill him?" He replied in the affirmative. So, Muhammad bin Maslama went to him (i.e. Ka'b) and said, "This person (i.e. the Prophet) has put us to task and asked us for charity." Ka'b replied, "By Allah, you will get tired of him." Muhammad said to him, "We have followed him, so we dislike to leave him till we see the end of his affair." Muhammad bin Maslama went on talking to him in this way till he got the chance to kill him. *Sahih Bukhari Volume 4, Book 52, Number 270: Narrated by Jabir bin 'Abdullah*

Ka'b bin al-Ashraf, who was Jewish on his mother's side, was a poet who wrote verse satirising and lampooning Muhammad and some of his close companions. This incident was the result – the hurt which Muhammad refers to had been inflicted by Ka'b's pen.

Muhammad's decision to ethnically cleanse all non-Muslims from the Arabian Peninsula is recorded in the *hadith*.

Umar heard the Messenger of Allah (may peace be upon him) say: "I will expel the Jews and Christians from the Arabian Peninsula and will not leave any but Muslims." *Sahih Muslim Book 19, Number 4366: Narrated by Umar ibn al-Khattab*

Jihad fighters were promised sure rewards in Paradise:

The Apostle of Allah (peace_be_upon_him) said: If anyone fights in Allah's path as long as the time between two milkings of a she-camel, Paradise will be assured for him. If anyone sincerely asks Allah for being killed and then dies or is killed, there will be a reward of a martyr for him. Ibn al-Musaffa added from here: If anyone is wounded in Allah's path, or suffers a misfortune, it will come on the Day of resurrection as copious as possible, its colour saffron, and its odour musk; and if anyone suffers from ulcers while in Allah's path, he will have on him the stamp of the martyrs. *Sunan Abu Dawud Book 14, Number 2535: Narrated by Mu'adh ibn Jabal*

Jihad was instituted to convert all people to Islam:

The Prophet (peace_be_upon_him) said: I am commanded to fight with men till they testify that there is no god but Allah, and that Muhammad is His servant and His Apostle, face our qibla, eat what we slaughter, and pray like us. When they do that, their life and property are unlawful for us except what is due to them. They will have the same rights as the Muslims have, and have the same responsibilities as the Muslims have. *Sunan Abu Dawud Book 14, Number 2635: Narrated by Anas ibn Malik*

The Verse: "You (true Muslims) are the best of peoples ever raised up for mankind," means, the best of peoples for the people, as you bring them with chains on their necks till they embrace Islam. *Sahih Bukhari Volume 6, Book 60, Number 80: Narrated by Abu Huraira*

The *hadith* also records Muhammad's famous statement that *jihad* goes on beyond his time and would last until the eschatological end of time:

The Prophet (peace_be_upon_him) said: "A section of my community will continue to fight for the right and overcome their opponents till the last of them fights with the Antichrist." *Sunan Abu Dawud Book 14, Number 2478: Narrated by Imran ibn Husayn*

The Prophet (peace_be_upon_him) said: "Three things are the roots of faith: to refrain from (killing) a person who utters, 'There is no god but Allah' and not to declare him unbeliever whatever sin he commits, and not to excommunicate him from Islam for his any action; and *jihad* will be performed continuously since the day Allah sent me as a prophet until the day the last member of my community will fight with the Dajjal (Antichrist). The tyranny of any tyrant and the justice of any just (ruler) will not invalidate it. One must have faith in

Divine decree." *Sunan Abu Dawud Book 14, Number 2526: Narrated by Anas ibn Malik*

Shari'a[126]

Not only does *shari'a* (Islamic law) cover the personal, family and devotional life of an individual Muslim but also it lays down how an Islamic state should be governed. Reflecting the political and military ascendancy of Islam in the eighth and ninth centuries when it was compiled, the *shari'a* assumes that power lies in the hands of Muslims.

It is natural, given the sources used and the context in which it was created, that the *shari'a* should contain a set of rules specifically governing the manner in which Muslims are to wage war. These very practical, earthy and militarily relevant instructions leave no doubt that the writers of the *shari'a* believed *jihad* to encompass actual warfare. Moreover, *shari'a* clearly lays down *jihad* as one of the most basic religious duties. There is little difference between Sunni and Shi'a law concerning war.[127]

Linked to the concept of *jihad* is the division of the world into two domains: the House of Islam (*Dar al-Islam*) and the House of War (*Dar al-Harb*). Muslims are supposed to wage *jihad* to change the House of War (where non-Muslims are politically dominant) into the House of Islam, politically dominated by Muslims.

A number of practical handbooks and other forms of written guidance on the conduct of war were produced by scholars from the various schools of law. The general consensus was that the participants must be adult male Muslims, able-bodied and free (not slaves). They should also be without debt, have spiritual motives and their parents' permission. Opinion on other aspects of the conduct of the war varied, for example, whether non-combatants should be spared, whether crops and animals should be destroyed.[128] (For more details see chapter 7.)

Shaybani (750-804), *Siyar*

An important work, which is available in English translation, is Shaybani's *Siyar*.[129] Shaybani lived during the days of the 'Abbasid dynasty, centred on Baghdad. Born in Iraq, Shaybani was only fourteen when he joined the circle of Abu Hanifa, the founder of the Hanafi school of *shari'a*. Although Abu Hanifa himself died some three years later in 767, Shaybani continued as a follower of Abu Hanifa's disciple Abu Yousuf, and went on to become a teacher, a judge and an adviser to the caliph as well as a prolific author.

Siyar is the branch of Islamic law concerned with international relations, and Shaybani's was the first major work on this subject. Literally "motion", *siyar* had come to mean by Shaybani's time the conduct of the Islamic state in its relationships with non-Muslim communities. Interestingly, the early Muslim jurists used to deal with *siyar* under the general heading of *jihad*. Shaybani's *Siyar* begins with a citation of *hadiths* about war and then goes on to a systematic study (in the form of a dialogue) on how Muslims should relate to non-Muslims, including chapters on the following subjects: the conduct of the army in enemy territory, the spoils of war, relationships between Muslim territories and non-Muslim territories, peace treaties, and safe-conducts.

The detail which Shaybani covers is fascinating. In the following extract he considers what to do when confronted with a human shield as well as the issue of killing non-combatants.

> I asked: If the Muslims besieged a city, and its people [in their defence] from behind the walls shielded themselves with Muslim children, would it be permissible for the Muslim [warriors] to attack them with arrows and mangonels?
>
> He replied: Yes, but the warriors should aim at the inhabitants of the territory of war and not the Muslim children.
>
> I asked: Would it be permissible for the Muslims to attack them with swords and lances if the children were not intentionally aimed at?
>
> He replied: Yes.
>
> I asked: If the Muslim [warriors] attack [a place] with mangonels and arrows, flood it with water, and burn it with fire, thereby killing

or wounding Muslim children or men, or enemy women, old men, blind, crippled or lunatic persons, would the [Muslim warriors] be liable for the *diya* [blood money] or the *kaffara* [atonement] ?

He replied: They would be liable neither for the *diya* nor for the *kaffara*.[130]

The fact that Shaybani permits an attack on a place known to have Muslims within it is pertinent to the suicide plane attack on the World Trade Centre on September 11th 2001; it negates the argument that the attack could not have been the work of Islamic terrorists since there were Muslims in the building who were killed in the attack. Other jurists take a range of positions on this issue, some agreeing with Shaybani, others advising that only limited violence should be used if Muslims might be endangered. Al-Awza'i advised that no attack should be made at all, unless individual enemy soldiers showed themselves and could be picked off.[131]

Shaybani states clearly that Muhammad gave Arab polytheists the stark choice of either accepting Islam or being killed:

The Apostle of God gave Arab polytheists no alternative than conversion to Islam or execution. Abu Hanifa, Abu Yusuf, and Muhammad [b. al-Hasan] accepted this ruling.

I asked: If the Arab polytheists refused to adopt Islam, do you think that they would be allowed to make peace with the Muslims and become Dhimmis?[132]

He replied: They should never be allowed to do so, but they will be invited to accept Islam.[133]

For Shaybani the sword was a marker of the God-given Islamic government, given to deal with all possible forms of unbelief: polytheism, apostasy, People of the Book and Muslim dissenters from Islamic orthodoxy:

Allah gave the Prophet Muhammad four swords [for fighting unbelievers]: the first against the polytheists, which Muhammad himself fought with; the second against apostates, which Caliph Abu Bakr fought with; the third against the People of the Book, which Caliph 'Umar fought with; the fourth against dissenters which Caliph 'Ali fought with.[134]

Abu'l-Hasan al-Mawardi (972-1058), *Al-Ahkam al-Sultaniyya*

Abu'l-Hasan al-Mawardi, a jurist of the Shafi'i school of *shari'a* who served as *qadi* (judge) in Baghdad, wrote what is in effect an instruction manual for Islamic rulers entitled *al-Ahkam al-sultaniyya [The Ordinances of Government]* with detailed instructions on the ruler's duties and obligations in time of war. He defines the enemy in a *jihad* as those who refuse to convert to Islam:

The idolaters in enemy territory are of two classes. One, those who have received the call to Islam but rejected it and turned away from it... The other are those whom the call to Islam has not yet reached, who would be very few today on account of the victory the Almighty has accorded His Prophet's mission, unless there be nations unknown to us beyond the Turks and Greeks we meet in eastern deserts and remote western areas. We are forbidden to launch surprise attacks on such people and kill them or burn their property, for we may not initiate action against them before inviting them first to Islam, making the Prophet's miracles known to them, and informing them of such arguments as would make them respond favourably. Should they persist in their unbelief after such evidence is shown them, he [the commander] should fight them, for they are from his standpoint in the same class as those who have received the call.[135]

Al-Mawardi says that all idolaters in the enemy camp may be killed, whether they were actively engaged in fighting or not. He is uncertain as to whether old men can be killed in battle, but forbids the killing of women, children or young slaves. Date palms and other trees may be cut down in order to weaken the enemy. *Jihad* must be fought constantly:

He [the Muslim commander] should resume the attack every time he has the power to do so, never slackening in this under

normal circumstances, except to gain a rest. At the very least, he
must not let a year go by without holy fighting.[136]

Al-Mawardi stresses both earthly and heavenly rewards as
legitimate motivation for *jihad* warriors:

> To promise the hardy and valiant among them God's reward if
> they value the other world, and earthly reward and a share of the
> spoils if they value this one. As God, most High is He, has said:
> "And who desires reward in this world We will give him thereof,
> and whoso longs for reward in the hereafter, We will give him of
> it" (Qur'an 3:145). Reward of this world is booty; reward of the
> next, paradise. Thus God, most Exalted is He, has combined in
> his inducement two things to render His call more appealing to
> both categories.[137]

Al-Marghinani (1135-1197), the *Hedaya*

The Hanafi school of Shari'a[138] has a standard text book
written by the scholar Burhan al-Din al-Marghinani (born
at Marghian near Ferghana in today's Uzbekistan), known
as the *Hedaya*, which is available in English translation,
albeit eighteenth century English. Book IX contains chapters
called "On the Manner of waging War", "Of making Peace,
and concerning the Persons to whom it is lawful to grant
Protection", "Of Plunder, and the Division thereof", "Of the
Conquests of Infidels".

Some examples may indicate the level of detail involved in
the *Hedaya's* instructions. The important question of dividing
the plunder takes six pages. One fifth must go to the state and
the remaining four-fifths is allocated to the troops, with cavalry
getting more than the infantry. After this principle is laid down,
things become complicated. Should the cavalryman get double
or triple what the foot soldier has? What if he has more than
one horse? Is his share affected by the quality of his horse? What
if he mainly goes into battle on horseback but occasionally on
foot? What if his horse was killed or he sold it at the end of the
campaign? Then there is the question of what to give slaves,
women, children and non-Muslims, and what to do with the
fifth that was set aside for the state. All these issues are argued

in detail, referring to historical precedent, the example of Muhammad and the opinions of other Muslim scholars.[139]

A fascinating paragraph on the role of women in war is worth quoting in full:

> It is lawful for aged women to accompany an army, for the performance of such business as suits them, such as dressing victuals, administering water, and preparing medicines for the sick and wounded; - but with respect to *young* women, it is better that they stay at home, as this may prevent perplexity or disturbance. The women, however, must not engage in fight, as this argues *weakness* in the *Mussulmans* [Muslims]; women, therefore must not take any personal concern in battle unless in a case of *absolute necessity:* and it is not laudable to carry *young* women along with the army, either for the purpose of carnal gratification, or for service: if, however, the necessity be *very urgent, female slaves* may be taken, but not *wives*.[140]

With respect to the question of whether women can fight or not, it is interesting to note that Ayesha, one of Muhammad's wives, led troops into battle at the Battle of the Camel (656), but her army was defeated. In the Battle of Jabiya-Yarmuk (636), Muslim women in the camp played an important role by shaming any Muslims who fled the battlefield, sometimes even fighting against them.[141]

Ibn Rushd (Averroes, d. 1198), *Bidayat al-Mujtahid wa Nihayat al-Muqtasid*[142]

A famous Maliki scholar, the Spanish-born Ibn Rushd included the subject of *jihad* in his primer for Islamic jurists *Bidayat al-Mujtahid wa Nihayat al-Muqtasid*,[143] which quotes the opinions of a range of other scholars from various different schools. His book is intended as a starting point for *ijtihad* and he refrains from assessing the validity of the opinions he quotes. It covers a similar range of practical detail to other works, including for example the treatment of prisoners of war (whether or not they can be killed or only ransomed, enslaved or freed), whether or not monks and hermits may be killed, whether fire is a legitimate weapon, whether buildings, trees and cattle can be attacked, and facing what odds a Muslim soldier would be permitted to retreat rather than fight. Ibn Rushd also deals extensively with the laws of spoil and booty (*ghanima, fay', anfal*).

According to Ibn Rushd, there is a scholarly consensus that all polytheists (*mushrikun*) are to be fought and that that it is permissible to enslave them – men, women and children. Only monks are exempt from being enslaved, revealing that People of the Book are included in his definition of polytheists. There is also consensus that it is permissible in war to kill all adult male polytheist fighters, but once taken as prisoners there is some argument as to whether they may be executed and in what circumstances.[144]

Ibn Rushd also quotes disagreements between the schools of law as regarding land conquered by Muslims by use of force:

> Malik said that the land is not to be divided and stays as a trust
> *(waqf)* with its *kharaj* (revenue) being spent for the interest of the
> Muslims... Al-Shafi'i said that conquered lands are to be divided
> like spoils, that is into five parts. Abu Hanifa said that the *imam*
> has a choice of dividing it or imposing *kharaj* on its disbelieving
> tenants leaving it in their possession.[145]

Ibn Taymiyya (1263-1328)

Ibn Taymiyya was a scholar of the Hanbali school who lived in Damascus and whose extremist religious stance resulted in him spending several years in prison. Although he was not a mainstream scholar, it is useful to consider what he says of *jihad* as his teaching continues to be influential in certain sections of the Muslim world today. He was not only a prolific author but also himself participated in several military expeditions against heretics. His treatment of *jihad* in his *al-Siyasa al-Shar'iyya fi Islah al-Ra'i wa-al-Ra'iyya* (*Governance according to God's Law in Reforming both the Ruler and His Flock*) has less to say about the practical aspects of war than the other works described, but instead emphasises the religious justification for *jihad* (including war against rebellious Muslims) by quoting from the Qur'an and *hadith*.[146] According to Ibn Taymiyya, the aim of *jihad* is to make Islam dominant in the world, and all those who oppose this purpose must be fought:

> Since lawful warfare is essentially *jihad* and since its aim is that the
> religion is God's entirely and God's word is uppermost, therefore

according to all Muslims, those who stand in the way of this aim must be fought.[147]

God has provided both Qur'an and sword to win the world to his religion, Islam:

There are two things which can establish and sustain religion: the Qur'an and the sword.[148]

He advocates a permanent struggle between Islam and non-Muslims. Wherever Muslims are a weak minority they must endeavour by all possible means to become powerful and dominate the non-Muslims.[149]

Ibn Taymiyya exalts military *jihad* as the best religious act a man can perform, better than pilgrimage, prayer or fasting. *Jihad* implies "all kinds of worship, both in its inner and outer forms. More than any other act it implies love and devotion for God."[150] He says that women, children, monks, the elderly, disabled etc. are not to be killed unless they offer active help to the enemy's war effort such as by propaganda or espionage.[151]

Ibn Naqib al-Misri (d.1368), *'Umdat al-Salik* (Reliance of the Traveller)

This is an important Shafi'i text. According to Ibn-Naqib al-Misri, an Egyptian Hanafi jurist, *jihad* is fought against Jews, Christians, Zoroastrians and all other people, basically against all non-Muslims:

The caliph makes war upon Jews, Christians, and Zoroastrians until they become Muslims or else pay the non-Muslim poll tax... The caliph fights all other peoples until they become Muslim.[152]

His short section on the rules of warfare forbids the killing of women and children unless they are fighting against the Muslims. As to adult male captives, the caliph decides whether to kill, enslave, ransom or free them according to the best interest of Islam and the Muslims. Ibn Naqib al-Misri allows the killing of old men (i.e. over 40) and monks, but neither the killing of animals (unless they are being ridden into battle "or if killing them will help defeat the enemy") nor the cutting down of trees nor the destruction of the enemy's houses is permitted. He says it is unlawful to kill a non-Muslim to whom a Muslim has given his guarantee of protection, but then adds various conditions.[153] He deals with the various types of spoils of battle, personal and collective. His comments on prisoners of war are quoted in chapter 7.

Ibn Khaldun (1332-1406), *The Muqaddima*

The North African philosopher-historian Ibn Khaldun defined *jihad* as:

> A religious duty, because of the universalism of the (Muslim) mission and (the obligation to) convert everybody to Islam either by persuasion or force.[154]

He contrasts this with the doctrine of Christians and Jews, asserting that

> The other religious groups did not have a universal mission, and the holy war was not a religious duty to them, save only for purposes of defence.[155]

He recognised also that Christians and Jews were not "under obligation to gain power over other nations, as is the case with Islam".[156] Ibn Khaldun goes to some length in describing military and naval fighting techniques of the various Muslim dynasties and their enemies. His best known principle is the cyclical rise and fall of dynasties as the wild, uncivilised desert warriors fired by group kinship (*'asabiyya*) conquer new realms, only to decline as they give gradually give in to the luxuries of civilisation. They in turn are then conquered by fresh groups of desert warriors.

Shi'a Scholars
Abu Ja'far Muhammad ibn Hasan al-Tusi (955-1067),
al-Nihaya (The Conclusion)

For Twelver Shi'a Muslims the law on war was mainly laid down at the time of Abu Ja'far Muhammad ibn Hasan al-

Tusi who wrote an influential treatise called *al-Nihaya [The Conclusion]*. It is very similar to Sunni doctrines of war,[157] except for the requirement that *jihad* must be led by a divinely inspired imam (supreme Shi'a leader).[158]

Al-Muhaqiq al-Hilli (1206-1277), *Shara'i' al-Islam fi Masa'il al-Halal wal-Haram*[159]

Al-Hilli was another well-known Twelver Shi'a scholar whose book is an authoritative work on Imami law. Its title translated into English means: *The Laws of Islam in Matters of the Permitted and the Forbidden*. He defines the enemies whom it is obligatory to fight as:

1 Rebels who fight against the imam

2 *Dhimma* (Jews, Christians and other People of the Book) who breach the provisions of their pact with the Muslims

3 "All other kinds of infidels and non-believers"

Al-Hilli repeats the command to migrate *(hijra)* from a land where Muslims cannot practise the rituals of Islam. He also encourages Muslims to be active in safeguarding the frontiers of Islam (*ribat*). Priority should be given to fighting the near enemy rather than the one far away.[160]

An interesting paragraph deals with the question of using poisonous materials against the enemy in war. This is forbidden, except when victory cannot be obtained by any other means. As is usual in *shari'a*, necessity makes the forbidden permissible, and such exceptions can be used (and are used today) to legitimate all manner of atrocities including the suicide bombing of civilians.

The Mu'tazila Interlude

The *mu'tazila* were a rationalist school of theology who were dominant in the 'Abbasid Empire in the ninth century. They developed a theology of reason as a means of knowing God, and of God's justice as God binding himself to act in accordance with his essential attributes. Unlike other Muslims, they believed that the Qur'an was created in time (i.e. not existing eternally) and is open to interpretation by human reason. The laws of nature, created by a reasonable God, are open to human investigation and are predictable, including a clear link between cause and effect. Man is endowed with free will and is responsible for his actions. The *mu'tazila* used dialectic, logic and rational argument to develop their system. *Mu'tazila* thought led to a remarkable flourishing of Islamic sciences and culture and to a relaxation in relations between Muslims and non-Muslims.

However opposing views gained the upper hand and finally formed orthodox Sunni Islamic theology. According to the Ash'arites,[161] the victorious party, man cannot know God or understand him by his reason but must simply obey and accept God's inscrutable and arbitrary omnipotence and will. Divine predestination overrules man's free will and omnipotent power is God's main attribute. There is no link between cause and effect, as God in every moment creates all things anew according to his will. Creation is thus unpredictable and there is no need to study natural laws or to seek for causes of perceived effects. God is not accountable even to his own self and norms. The Qur'an is uncreated and has existed with God from eternity and as such is more an object of worship and of unquestioned obedience than of reasoned interpretations. Such views permeated Islamic doctrine and thinking stressing a totalitarian view of God and of his will for the world and strict obedience to *shari'a* and its injunctions, including *jihad* and the treatment of non-Muslims. These views also encouraged totalitarian forms of government. The Islamic ruler, as God's vice-regent (Sunni caliph or Shi'a imam) and delegate on earth, acts as God does: his will is not to be questioned but obeyed, he is not accountable to any human agency, only to God. The suppression of *mu'tazila* thought led inexorably to the "closing of the gates of *ijtihad*" when all further development of *shari'a* was banned.

The suppression of reason and of individual freedom of expression remains a characteristic of Islam that opposes efforts at free thought and real democracy. As Fatema Mernissi explains:

Democracy… [is] obliging us to face what we have been unable to contemplate up to now in our Muslim culture: *'aql* (reason) and *ra'y* (personal opinion or judgement). Since the beginning Muslims have given their lives to pose and solve the question that has remained an enigma up until the present: to obey or to reason, to believe or to think? The assertion that the individual and his freedom are not the sole property of the West is at the heart of our tradition, but it has been submerged in incessant bloodbaths.[162]

Mernissi sees the closing of the gates of *ijtihad* as part of the process of closing Islamic orthodoxy to the possibilities of freedom of thought under the "terror of the sword". Debate was always stifled by the political rulers (caliphs) and the religious establishment, and intellectual opposition was repressed. Dissidence henceforth was expressed by violent rebellions against totalitarian leaders, killing them and replacing them by other totalitarian leaders, not by questioning and changing the political system.[163]

Some observers see Ash'ari thought as imposing a fatalistic Islamic world-view in which the will to power remains the only absolute, because that is what God is. The believer can only surrender unconditionally to God's will, including a tyrannical political system akin to modern Fascism and communism. A system based on unreasonable pure will to power[164] inevitably leads to violence as the solution to all problems. Will must be imposed by force, as reason has no place in the system. Contemporary Islamism is dominated by this type of world-view, which is not only based on traditional Islamic orthodoxy but also consciously copied from Fascist and communist ideology. Islamist terrorism is a logical outcome of this development, which holds that the only way to reform Islam and set the world right is by *jihad* of the sword. God's omnipotence is transformed into a politics of unlimited power. The evil pagan world system (*jahiliyya*) must be totally destroyed so the pure original Islamic system of the caliphate can be re-established on its ruins.[165]

Later Scholars
Sheikh Ahmad Sirhindi (1564-1624)
Ahmad Sirhindi initiated a Sunni revival movement in Muslim India as a reaction to the syncretistic tendencies of several Mughal

rulers, including Akbar and Jahangir. While reforming Sufism through the Naqshbandiyya-Mujaddidiyya order he founded, he also stressed the importance of a full implementation of *shari'a* in government and society. He was given the accolade *mujaddid al-alf al-thani* (renewer of the second millennium). He argued forcibly against any accommodation with Hinduism, describing Hindus with the insulting term for a non-Muslim, *kafir*. He sought to revive the earlier *jihadi* spirit of the Islamic state, arguing that "*Shariat* can be fostered through the sword":[166]

> *Kufr* and Islam are opposed to each other. The progress of one is possible only at the expense of the other and co-existence between these two contradictory faiths is unthinkable. The honour of Islam lies in insulting *kufr* and *kafirs*. One who respects *kafirs*, dishonours the Muslims... They should be kept at an arms' length like dogs... The real purpose in levying *jizya* on them (the non-Muslims) is to humiliate them to such an extent that, on account of fear of *jizya*, they may not be able to dress well and to live in grandeur. They should constantly remain terrified and trembling. It is intended to hold them under contempt and to uphold the honour and might of Islam.[167]

It was under Sirhindi's influence that the Emperor Aurangzeb rescinded concessions made to the Hindus by his predecessors, reinstituted the classic Islamic *jizya* tax on non-Muslims, and renewed the *jihad* in India.

Sirhindi considered Shi'a Muslims to be even worse than *kafirs*. He was appalled at the influence they wielded at the Mughal court and argued that showing them honour was tantamount to destroying Islam.[168] This hatred of the Shi'a is still apparent in contemporary Pakistan, where various radical Sunni groups, especially the Sipah-i-Sahaba are engaged in indiscriminate violent attacks on Shi'a men, women and children.

Shah Wali Allah of Delhi (1702-1762)

A forerunner of modern reform movements, Shah Wali Allah endeavoured to unite Muslims around a reapplication of *shari'a* applied to present circumstances through pious personal endeavour at reinterpretation *(ijtihad)*. Renewal meant a return to pristine Islam, a condemnation of simple imitation *(taqlid)*, and a reopening of the gates of *ijtihad*. His aim was to rediscover the forgotten original precepts of ideal Islam as preserved in its revealed pure sources.[169] As to *jihad,* fighting in God's way was the perfect implementation of *shari'a.* Leaders of non-Muslim communities who refused to accept Islam ought to be killed, and their followers forcibly converted to Islam.[170]

> It has become clear in my mind that the kingdom of heaven has predestined that *kafirs* should be reduced to a state of humiliation and treated with utter contempt. Should that repository of majesty and dauntless courage (Nizam al-Maluk) gird his loins and direct his attention to such a task he can conquer the world. Thus the faith will become more popular and his own power strengthened; a little effort will be profoundly rewarded... You should therefore not be negligent in fighting *jihad*... Oh Kings! *Mala a'la* urges you to draw swords and not put them back in their sheaths again until Allah has separated Muslims from the polytheists and the rebellious *kafirs* and the sinners are made absolutely feeble and helpless... We beseech you (Durrani) in the name of the Prophet to fight a *jihad* against the infidels of this region. This would entitle you to great rewards before God the Most High and your name would be included in the list of those who fought *jihad* for His sake. As far as worldly gains are concerned, incalculable booty would fall into the hands of the Islamic *ghazis* and the Muslims would be liberated from their bonds... *Jihad* should be their first priority, thereby ensuring the security of every Muslim.[171]

4
Jihad and the Sacralising of Territory

The doctrine of sacred space

Early Muslims categorised land on the basis of its degree of sacredness. The most basic classification was the division of the world into *Dar al-Islam* and *Dar al-Harb*. According to Majid Khadduri:

> The jurist-theologians, although recognising no division within dar al-Islam, have differentiated certain territories from others on the basis of sacredness and religious significance.[172]

One hierarchy of sanctity subdivided the sacred space of *Dar al-Islam* into three kinds, whose varying degrees of sanctity are reflected in rules of varying strictness concerning the presence of non-Muslims (dead or alive). Muslim jurists differ over some details but the consensus about the three subdivisions of *Dar al-Islam* is as follows: (1) The *Haramayn*, meaning Mecca and Medina – non-Muslims are completely banned (2) The Hijaz — this is generally considered to be an area in the north-west of the Arabian peninsula, about 250 miles long by 150 miles wide, containing Mecca, Medina and many other sites sacred in Islam. Non-Muslims may travel through it but not settle there permanently. Non-Muslims are also not allowed to be buried there, as this is considered permanent residence. (3) The rest of *Dar al-Islam*, where non-Muslims may live with the second-class status of *dhimmi*s.[173]

Shari'a provided various rules that applied to these different divisions. A main interest of the jurists was the taxation to be applied to the various types of land.

Al-Mawardi examines the regulations pertaining to land taken from infidels. Such lands, he says, are of three sorts:

1   Land "seized by force or coercion, its owners having left it because killed, captured or exiled." This is either divided among the victors or kept as state land for all Muslims.

2   Land acquired from them "accidentally, effortlessly, owing to their evacuating it in fear." This becomes public property as a *waqf* (religious trust) that may not be sold or mortgaged.

3   Land taken through treaty. The unbelievers can remain on it and work it while being protected by the Muslims, but must pay the *kharaj* tax. It is preferable to induce them to transfer it by treaty to Muslim ownership.[174]

Khadduri describes a four-fold division of Muslim lands outside the Arabian peninsula:[175]

1   Land whose original owners converted to Islam. This is called *'ushr* land.

2   Conquered land which was divided among Muslims and also became *'ushr* land.

3   Conquered land left in the hands of its original owners to farm, but they had to pay the *kharaj* tax.

4   Waste land which when developed by Muslims became *'ushr* land.

1. The Whole Earth Belongs to the Muslims and to the Islamic State

Islam teaches that all lands belong to Allah who has given them to the Muslims. Some they already possess, the rest are theirs in theory and will gradually become theirs in practice. This doctrine is based on several verses in the Qur'an:

Allah has promised to those among you who believe and work righteous deeds that He will of a surety grant them in the land inheritance (of power) as He granted it to those before them; that He will establish in authority their religion the one which He has chosen for them; and that He will change (their state) after the fear in which they (lived) to one of security and peace: 'They will worship Me (alone) and not associate aught with Me.' If any do reject faith after this they are rebellious and wicked. (Q 24:55)

Said Moses to his people: "Pray for help from Allah and (wait) in patience and constancy: for the earth is Allah's to give as a heritage to such of his servants as He pleaseth; and the end is (best) for the righteous. (Q 7:128)

Before this We wrote in the Psalms after the Message (given to Moses): My servants the righteous shall inherit the earth. (Q 21:105)

According to Ibn Taymiyya, lands conquered from non-Muslims are actually being restored by Allah to the Muslims, to whom they really belong:

These possessions received the name of *fay* since Allah had taken them away from the infidels in order to restore (*afa'a, radda*) them to the Muslims. In principle, Allah has created the things of this world only in order that they may contribute to serving Him, since He created man only in order to be ministered to. Consequently, the infidels forfeit their persons and their belongings which they do not use in Allah's service to the faithful believers who serve Allah and unto whom Allah restitutes what is theirs; thus is restored to a man the inheritance of which he was deprived, even if he had never before gained possession.[176]

2. The *Hijra* Model and Muhammad's Conquests

Most Muslims view the *hijra* as a paradigmatic model to be followed in all times. It is seen as a stage in the political quest for the establishment of the Islamic state modelled on Muhammad's practice. They argue that the first Muslim community developed in clearly defined stages which must be emulated today. First came the stage of weakness in which the message of Islam was proclaimed (*da'wa*) to an unbelieving society, then the stage of separation from the unbelievers and migration (*hijra*) to a safe place where Muslim strength could be built up, and finally the stage of the sacred fight (*jihad*) to reconquer lost territory, victoriously extend Muslim political dominion and implement God's ideal state on earth.

Since the *hijra* the gaining, retention and, when necessary, reconquest of territory has been an integral part of Islam. In classical Islam all land conquered by force from *Dar al-Harb* became the God-given property of the Muslim community for ever. Islamised and sacralised, it was cleansed from defiling non-Muslim influence and governed by Islamic law. The state, as the representative of the community, was the ultimate owner of the land. Lands once conquered by Islam, if subsequently lost to non-Muslims, remain holy to Islam and it is imperative that such lost lands be restored to the rightful rule of the *umma* by *jihad*.

Muhammad's treatment of the conquered Jewish lands of Khaibar served as a paradigm for future treatment of conquered lands. These lands in principle belonged to Allah, Muhammad and the Muslims. The lands were divided as spoil among the Muslim fighters, with a fifth going to Muhammad. The former owners could be left as tenants paying the *kharaj* tax, but were at the mercy of the Muslim rulers who could expel them at any time.

> Umar bin Al-Khattab expelled all the Jews and Christians from the land of Hijaz. Allah's Apostle after conquering Khaibar, thought of expelling the Jews from the land which, after he conquered it belonged to Allah, Allah's Apostle and the Muslims. But the Jews requested Allah's Apostle to leave them there on the condition that they would do the labour and get half of the fruits (the land would yield). Allah's Apostle said, "We shall keep you on these terms as long as we wish." Thus they stayed till the time of 'Umar's Caliphate when he expelled them to Taima and Ariha. *Sahih Bukhari, Hadith 4.380: Narrated by Ibn Umar.*

This model was followed in the conquest of Egypt and many other non-Muslim lands.[177]

3. The Initial Expansion of Islam

During the first swift expansion of Islam after Muhammad's death, the caliphs further developed the concept of sacred space, deciding that conquered land should not be privatised as many wished, but turned into a trust for the whole Muslim community.

> It is true that at the outset, there was a feeling amongst the Arabs that they should acquire the lands, which would then be liable only to the voluntary precept (zakat) paid by the Muslim to the Islamic community; but the first caliphs assured the victory of the principle of the fay', the collective plunder made into a kind of pious or beneficial trust for the benefit of the whole community, present and future... All land conquered by force became the property of the Muslim community as a whole and not only of the combatants. It could not be sold, constituted into waqf or given away. Its administration belonged to the imam alone. Its proceeds were to be used for the public good.[178]

There was some argument between the various Muslim scholars on the status of the conquered lands. Ibn Rushd states that:

> They disagreed about the land that is conquered by the Muslims by the use of force. Malik said that the land is not to be divided and stays as a trust *waqf* with its *kharaj* (revenue) being spent for the interest of the Muslims, like the maintenance of those engaged in the defence of Islam, the construction of bridges and mosques, as well as other avenues of welfare.
>
> However al-Shafi'i and Abu Hanifa disagreed, claiming that the land could be divided like spoils (into five parts) or that the *imam* has the choice of dividing it or leaving it in the possession of its disbelieving tenants who must pay *kharaj*.[179]

Common to all classical scholars is the principle that all conquered lands belong in perpetuity to the Muslim *umma* whatever practical arrangements prevail (whether divided among the fighters or kept as state lands). The Muslim state, represented by the caliph and his governors, receives all the various taxes to be used for the benefit of the Muslims in perpetuity. Non-Muslim owners can at best remain only as tenants on their former lands; their tenancy rights can be abolished by the caliph if he considers it for the good of the Muslims.

4. Contemporary Muslim Scholars

The prominent Muslim scholar Sheikh Yusuf Al-Qaradhawi, the spiritual leader of the Muslim Brotherhood, states that lands once held by Muslims may never be given up to non-Muslims. Should they be lost in war, it is the duty of all Muslims to retake them, even if this process lasts until the end of the world:

> No Muslim, be he in authority or not, is allowed to abandon any of the lands of Muslims. The land of the Islamic world is not the property of any president, prince, minister or group of people. It is not up to anyone therefore to relinquish it under any circumstances.

> Conversely, it is the duty of individuals and groups to strive hard to liberate occupied territories and retrieve usurped land. The entire nation is jointly responsible for that and it is not up to the ruler or his subjects to choose to give up the land. If a particular generation lapses in idleness or is incapable of shouldering the responsibility, it has no right to force its idleness or incapacity on all the coming generations up till Judgement Day, by giving up what it has no right to. Therefore, I have issued a Fatwa indicating that it is unlawful for all homeless Palestinian refugees to accept damages in return for their lost land, even if they amount to billions. The land of Islam is not for sale; it is not to be relinquished, and no damages can possibly make up for its loss.[180]

For Al-Qaradhawi, contemporary *jihad* is focused on the retrieval of Muslim lands, and he quotes the Muslim Brotherhood founder, Hasan al-Banna, as saying:

> Our efforts and our *jihad* are focussed on two main axes – Islamic ideology and the Muslim land.[181]

Al-Qaradhawi states that the contemporary *jihad* against the Jews is in principle only over the problem of sacred land. The Jews have taken Muslim land in Palestine to set up the state of Israel. All schools of Islamic law agree that when Muslim land is occupied, *jihad* is obligatory to retake the land for Islam (the fact that Muslims first wrested these lands by force from non-Muslims is of course never mentioned):

> Our war with the Jews is over land, brothers. We must understand this. If they had not plundered our land, there wouldn't be a war between us... We are fighting them in the name of Islam, because Islam commands us to fight whoever plunders our land, and occupies our country. All the school of Islamic jurisprudence - the Sunni, the Shi'ite, the Ibadhiya - and all the ancient and modern schools of jurisprudence - agree that any invader who occupies even an inch of land of the Muslims must face resistance. The Muslims of that country must carry out the resistance, and the rest of the Muslims must help them. If the people of that country are incapable or reluctant, we must fight to defend the land of Islam, even if the local [Muslims] give it up... They must not allow anyone to take a single piece of land away from Islam. That is what we are fighting the Jews for.[182]

Many Muslims agree with Al-Qaradhawi that lands once possessed by Islam, if subsequently lost to an invader, remain holy to Islam and must be restored to its rule.

> For Muslims, no piece of land once added to the realm of Islam can ever be finally renounced.[183]

Historically, such lost lands include Israel, Spain, the Balkans, India and much of Central Asia. Hence the demand of terrorist groups for the reconquest of Israel, Spain, Kashmir, Chechnya and other lands finds a resonance in the wider Muslim world. At the same time, new lands settled by Muslims are added to the sacred space of Islam.

Isma'il Raji al-Faruqi, a renowned Palestinian-American Islamic scholar, defines the Islamic state as universal and all pervasive, aiming at controlling the whole earth in terms of territory and all human beings in terms of population. Even outer space should be under its control:

> Islam asserts that the territory of the Islamic state is the whole earth or, better, the whole cosmos since the possibility of space travel [is] not too remote. Part of the earth may be under direct rule of the Islamic state and the rest may yet have to be included; the Islamic state exists and functions regardless. Indeed its territory is ever expansive. So is its citizenry, for its aim is to include all humankind. If the Islamic state is at any time restricted to a few of the world's population, it does not matter as long as it wills to comprehend humanity.[184]

Kalim Siddiqui (1931-1996), founder of the Muslim Parliament of Great Britain, advocated emulating Muhammad's transition from Mecca to Medina as a necessary stage in the unification of the *umma* worldwide. Thus every Muslim enclave becomes a potential base for further expansion of Muslim rule, and Islam recognises no borders as it struggles to unite all Muslim enclaves everywhere to achieve the ultimate goal:

> The Islamic movement recognises no frontiers in the *Ummah*. The struggle for the liberation of any one part of the *Ummah* can be carried out from any other part of the *Ummah*. Every part of the *Ummah* is a potential asset for all other parts. This means that every obstacle in the path of the Islamic movement in one part of the *Ummah* is also an obstacle for the entire Islamic movement. Every Muslim engaged in the struggle in any part of the world, however remote or isolated, is engaged in a global struggle. Every group that is engaged in the struggle, however small or remote, is also part of the global struggle between Islam and *kufr.* The goal of the total transformation of the *Ummah* requires a total struggle. An important part of the method of Prophet Muhammad, upon whom be peace, was to acquire control over the environment around him.[185]

5. Implementation by Palestinian Movements

A contemporary example is the way Islamic movements in Palestine have moved away from the limited Palestinian nationalist discourse to stress increasingly the sanctity of Palestine as a holy Islamic land belonging to the whole Muslim *umma*. Palestine as a land conquered by Muslims is a holy *waqf* for all Muslims until the end of time; it cannot change its ownership and it cannot revert to non-Muslim rule.

According to the new discourse, any area associated with the initial revelation and the first conquest is a religious trust (*waqf*) and its Muslim occupants the guardians of this trust. The Islamic definition of such holy land prohibits the transfer of religious properties to non-Muslims.[186] Palestine is linked with Islamic revelation from Adam to Muhammad, it is the land of the prophets sent with the message of Islam. David and Solomon created what Muslims consider to have been Islamic states in Palestine. Therefore it must be ruled only by those who uphold Islam and its law.[187]

The Islamist Palestinian movement Hamas included in its Founding Charter the claim that Palestine is an Islamic *waqf* which can never be transferred to non-Muslims:

PART III STRATEGIES AND METHODS

The Strategy of Hamas: Palestine is an Islamic Waqf

Article Eleven

The Islamic Resistance Movement believes that the land of Palestine has been an Islamic Waqf throughout the generations and until the Day of Resurrection, no one can renounce it or part of it, or abandon it or part of it. No Arab country nor the aggregate of all Arab countries, and no Arab King or President nor all of them in the aggregate, have that right, nor has that right any organization or the aggregate of all organizations, be they Palestinian or Arab, because Palestine is an Islamic Waqf throughout all generations and to the Day or Resurrection. Who can presume to speak for all Islamic generations to the Day of Resurrection? This is the status [of the land] in Islamic Shari'a (20), and it is similar to all lands conquered by Islam by force, and made thereby Waqf lands upon their conquest, for all generations of Muslims until the Day of

Resurrection. This [norm] has prevailed since the commanders of the Muslim armies completed the conquest of Syria and Iraq, and they asked the Caliph of Muslims, 'Umar Ibn al-Khattab (21) for his view of the conquered land, whether it should be partitioned between the troops or left in the possession of its population, or otherwise. Following discussions and consultations between the Caliph of Islam, 'Umar Ibn al-Khattab, and the Companions of the Messenger of Allah, be peace and prayer upon him, they decided that the land should remain in the hands of its owners to benefit from it and from its wealth; but the control (22) of the land and the land itself ought to be endowed as a Waqf [in perpetuity] for all generations of Muslims until the Day of Resurrection. The ownership of the land by its owners is only one of usufruct, and this Waqf will endure as long as Heaven and earth last. Any demarche in violation of this law of Islam, with regard to Palestine, is baseless and reflects on its perpetrators.[188]

6. Sacralising Territory for Islam in the West

Sacralising new territory for Islam is an ongoing venture. Migrant Muslim communities in the West are constantly engaged in such sacralising activities. While first generation Muslim migrants sacralised the inner private spaces of their homes and mosques through the Islamic rituals performed there, the second generation took to the public sphere by organising processions, whether in honour of Muhammad's birthday or Sufi celebrations in honour of specific saints:

> Marching through Britain's city centres and immigrant neighbourhoods, the processions not only inscribe the name of Allah on the very spaces stretching between and connecting immigrant housing and mosques – city centre and immigrant periphery...[189]

This is part of the process of claiming territory for Islam, and placing it under *shari'a*. This would mean non-Muslims living in the area or visiting it would have to conform to *shari'a* regulations on dress, diet and behaviour.

For most Muslims in the West, adherence to *shari'a* is part of living in accordance to God's will.[190] While (for the most part) accepting that they must obey the non-Muslim laws of the land, they are nevertheless intent on constructing a Muslim infrastructure of institutions that will claim space for *shari'a*. The stronger the parallel network of mosques, *madrassas* (Islamic religious schools), Islamic centres, and *shari'a* councils becomes, the more pressure is exerted on Muslims to use these in preference to non-Muslim institutions. Within these networks the mosque plays a vital role.

A mosque is considered permanent for all eternity. Mosques, once built, become sacred spaces that may never be given up or demolished. The radical Islamist organisation Hizb ut-Tahrir comments on the demolition of a mosque (Arabic *masjid*) in Khartoum by the Sudanese government:

> This is one of the greatest evil. No one who believes in Allah and the Last Day, and believes that the masjids are the houses of Allah (swt) on the earth that are not allowed to be destroyed or demolished or violated under any pretext would undertake such an evil act. Not to mention the fact the reason given is groundless, for the land is the land of Allah (swt) and the Islamic state cannot own land in order to sell it to the people as we see happening in our country today, where the state is selling off land. In origin, the land belongs to Allah and it is owned by people through its seclusion or cultivation. The state intervenes only to organise and not to prevent. So imagine how much of an evil it is if the state takes this land which is being used as a masjid, which the Muslims have established in order to undertake one of the greatest of actions, ie the Salah! He (swt) says: "And who is more unjust than those who forbid that Allâh's Name be glorified and mentioned much (i.e. prayers and invocations, etc.) in Allâh's Mosques and strive for their ruin? It was not fitting that such should themselves enter them (Allâh's Mosques) except in fear. For them there is disgrace in this world, and they will have a great torment in the Hereafter." [Q 2:114]

> The 'Ulamaa' of the Ummah have agreed that when a part is designated for prayer by speech then it becomes excluded

from private ownership and it becomes public property for all Muslims... The Sharee'ah prohibits the destruction, sale or obstruction of a mosque even if the locality was ruined.[191]

The word mosque (*masjid* in Arabic) is derived from a root word meaning to prostrate, one of the postures of worship. Worship is considered to include not only acts of prayers and other devotions, but also the upholding and implementation of *shari'a*. With the mosque comes a community, as Muslim families settle around it. Soon a network of local Islamic institutions is established, such as *madrassas* and social, commercial and other systems, as well as political activity. (At certain periods and in certain places, for example under Western colonial rule, the political aspect of the mosque's function was very much reduced.) The mosque is the centre of authority for the local Muslim community. The schools of *shari'a* differ as to the relation and involvement of non-Muslims in the mosque and Muslim community. What is clear is that they must submit and conform to whatever the *shari'a* requires of them.

Another commonly used word for mosque is *jama'a*, derived from a root word meaning to gather or gathering. This emphasis on gathering or community links other mosques and communities of a similar theological persuasion across an area or country. In Pakistan such communities evolve a political wing with its accompanying militia whose primary purpose is the defence of the community. With the growing trend towards separate Muslim communities replicating the structures of their home countries, the real possibility of armed conflict could arise. This could be triggered by any perceived threat or damage to a mosque building in the West or to the developing autonomy of a Muslim minority community, perhaps even as a response to events affecting the *umma* elsewhere in the world. A further potential source of conflict is that of internal friction between the various sectarian and ideological movements within Islam. Such a conflict might not necessarily be between Muslims and the majority community, but could be between Muslims and another ethnic or religious minority. Mosques in some parts of the world have been used as the bases for insurgency, in particular to store weapons. The searching of mosques, particularly using non-Muslim personnel or dogs, can pose difficulties.

5
The Theology of War and Empire-Building

The Development of the Classical Theory of *Jihad*

According to classical Islam, *jihad* is the God-given method to expand Islam's political dominion.

> The *jihad* was therefore employed as an instrument both for the universalization of religion and the establishment of an imperial world state.[192]

The caliph was required to lead an army in *jihad* against unbelievers at least once a year. The classical manual of the Hanafi school of law, the *Hedaya*, clearly states that *jihad* is to be fought against infidels even if they are not the aggressors:

> The destruction of the sword is incurred by infidels, although they be not the first aggressors, as appears from various passages in the sacred writings which are generally received to this effect.[193]

The Shafi'i manual, *Reliance of the Traveller,* states:

> The caliph makes war upon Jews, Christians, and Zoroastrians (provided he has first invited them to enter Islam in faith and practice, and if they will not, then invited them to enter the social order of Islam by paying the non-Muslim poll tax... while remaining in their ancestral religion)... The caliph fights all other peoples until they become Muslim...[194]

The vast majority of contemporary Muslim scholars hold to this classical Islamic theory of war, a theory which presumes that war against non-Muslims would be essentially unrestricted. This was the policy of the Islamic empire under which the theory developed. The stages in the development of *jihad* are seen as necessary stages in the development of the power of the first Muslim community under Muhammad from weakness to overwhelming strength. According to the accepted doctrine of abrogation, it is the Qur'an's unconditional command to fight all unbelievers that is now valid until the end of time.[195]

The stages in the original development of *jihad*, seen as normative paradigms, were as follows:[196]

1 **Non-Confrontation:** verbal argument, not force, was used to protect the faith while the Islamic community was small and weak in Mecca. Patience and passive suffering were recommended in face of persecution. The early ban on fighting was seen by later Muslim scholars as a necessary protective tactic to avoid being destroyed by overwhelming force when the Muslim community was small and weak. This was followed by Muhammad's migration to Medina, which was necessary to save the weak community from extinction.

> Invite (all) to the way of thy Lord with wisdom and beautiful preaching; and argue with them in ways that are best and most gracious... but if ye show patience that is indeed the best (course) for those who are patient. And do thou be patient for thy patience is but from Allah; nor grieve over them: and distress not thyself because of their plots. For Allah is with those who restrain themselves and those who do good. Q 16:125-128

2 **Defensive Fighting:** after Muhammad first arrived in Medina fighting became lawful, but only against attackers, and there were restrictions against fighting non-combatants. "Fight in the path of God those who fight you, but do not transgress limits, for God does not love transgressors" (Q 2:190).

3 **Initiating Attacks Allowed:** in the second Medinan stage, as the strength of the community grew, it was permitted to take the offensive against polytheists, but with restrictions as to times and places. "Kill them wherever you find them and turn them out from where they have turned you out, for *fitna* [rebellion] is worse than killing, but do not fight them at the sacred Mosque..." (Q 2:191).

4 **Unconditional Command to Fight all Unbelievers everywhere and at any time:** Finally the command for indiscriminate *jihad* against all unbelievers at all times and places was given, which has been accepted ever since as valid ever since until the Day of Judgement. "When the sacred months are past, kill the idolaters (*mushrikun*) wherever you find them, and seize them, besiege them, and lie in wait for them in every place of ambush..." (Q 9:5).[197] This, the "Sword Verse", is calculated to have abrogated no fewer than 124 less aggressive Qur'anic passages. The reference to the sacred months is usually interpreted as meaning that after this specific sacred month, Muslims need not respect sacred months any more, but can fight whenever it is convenient.

5 **Permission to attack Jews and Christians.** A special verse was given to permit attacking Jews and Christians: "Fight those who do not believe in God or the Last Day, and who do not forbid what has been forbidden by God and His Messenger, nor acknowledge the religion of truth from among the People of the Book, until they pay the poll tax (*jizya*) out of hand, having been brought low" (Q 9:29).

While unconditional *jihad* against all non-Muslims in *Dar al-Harb* is accepted as applicable today and until the end of time, many Muslim scholars see all the stages Muhammad went through as possible models for various Muslim communities at various times in their development, according to their relative weakness or strength. In times of great weakness Muslims are to suffer patiently, waiting for the time when their strength will increase, or to emigrate to another area under Muslim control were they can gather their strength for the victorious return and reconquest. As their power grows, they can defend themselves against aggression, and as their power is further consolidated, they can go on the aggressive *jihad* against all non-Muslim neighbours to expand the area under Islamic dominion *(Dar al-Islam)*.

The House of Islam and the House of War

We have already seen that classical Islam divides the world into two: the part where Muslims are in power *(Dar al-Islam,* the House of Islam) and the part where Muslims are not in power *(Dar al-Harb,* the House of war). *Jihad,* in its classical interpretation, is an obligatory duty imposed on Muslims to wage war against non-Muslims in the House of War with the aim of changing it into the House of Islam i.e. gaining political control for Muslims.

> Thus the *jihad,* reflecting the normal war relations existing between Muslims and non-Muslims, was the state's instrument for transforming the dar al-harb into the dar al-Islam.[198]

Sayyid Qutb defined the House of Islam and its relationship to the House of War in classical terms:

> Only one place on earth can be called the home of Islam (dar-al-Islam), and that is the place where the Islamic state is established and the Shari'ah is enforced and Allah's limits are observed, and where all Muslims administer the affairs of the community with mutual consultation. The rest of the world is the home of hostility (dar-al-harb). A Muslim can have only two possible relations with dar-al-harb: peace with a contractual agreement, or war.[199]

Ali Sina of Faith Freedom International maintains that, according to Muslim scholars, the Qur'anic verse 9:23 banning Muslims from taking infidels as their *awlia* (protectors, custodians, rulers) implies that Muslims should never accept the rule or governance of non-Muslims.

> Hence they are required to overthrow the non-Islamic governments, whenever they are able to and wherever they reside to establish

Islamic governments. Until then, that country is considered to be Dar al Harb (House of war). When the governance of the country is turned over to the Muslims, that country becomes Dar al Islam (House of Islam) and Sharia becomes the law of the land. This does not mean that everyone will be forced to convert to Islam. It means that everyone becomes subject to Sharia and those who are not believers will be classified as dhimmis, who will have to pay Jizyah and support the Ummah financially.[200]

As Sina explains, Islamic political rule did not mean that everyone living in the territory must become a Muslim. Although polytheists were forced to convert on pain of death, Jews, Christians and other People of the Book could keep their faith if they paid the *jizya* poll tax and submitted to various humiliating restrictions about clothes, houses, transport etc. This second-class status was described as *dhimma* (meaning protected – in the sense that *dhimmi* were not to be killed). However *dhimmi* were very much second-class citizens under Islamic rule, and the disadvantages and general contempt which they endured meant that it was likely many would choose to convert to Islam. Thus spreading Islamic political rule facilitated the spread of the Islamic faith.

As we have seen above, the final stage in the development of the theory of *jihad* was the concept of a permanent state of war between the House of Islam and the House of War. This war can be interrupted from time to time by a temporary truce (*hudna*), but only when it is advantageous to the Muslims, for example, if they are short of money, ammunition or troops. The Muslims can break a truce whenever they feel it wise to do so.

One way of implementing the *jihad* imperative for permanent war against the infidels, was the ruling, developed quite early, that the caliph should lead an attack on *Dar al-Harb* at least once a year, thus proving his obedience to Islamic doctrine.[201] In times of weakness, these raids (*ghazwa*) might be of little substance, but the annual raid kept the spirit of *jihad* alive and served to legitimate aggressive attacks against non-Muslim territories from Morocco to India. The *ghazi* doctrine was a main legitimator of the Muslim expansion into India and of the Ottoman expansion into Europe. In Muslim Spain it took on the form of biennial raids against neighbouring Christian states led by the caliph or the local *amir*.[202]

Modern Muslims may use many methods to try to achieve victory over the House of War, but Muhammad's way was by military conquest, *jihad*.[203] Hence there is a theological justification for the use of violence against the non-Muslim world.[204]

Islamic scholars debate how to define what is or is not *Dar al-Islam*,[205] a question which is far from academic as *Dar al-Islam* is exempt from war, while *Dar al-Harb* is not.

The Inbuilt Urge to Expand

The classical teaching on *Dar al-Islam* and *Dar al-Harb* was practised for many centuries. In the words of Kenneth Cragg:

> Historically, Islam has made good its capacity to belong with wide diversities of humankind. But always, traditionally, this universality was on the basis of surrender.[206]

It was to the revival of this essentially imperialist strand within traditional Islam in the world today that Samuel Huntington was pointing in his 1996 book *The Clash of Civilizations*[207] in which he described the Islamic world as having "bloody borders". A map in the 1999 edition of *The Times History of the World* depicting the revival of religious conflicts in the world highlights virtually every country in the Islamic world whilst only Northern Ireland and Myanmar (Burma) can be found as modern illustrations of religious conflicts in non-Islamic contexts.[208] Of course most Muslims would respond that these are mainly liberation struggles and argue, quite rightly, that Muslims have faced varying degrees of discrimination and hostility in many of these contexts.

Islam has an inbuilt theological urge at its very core towards empire-building i.e. the continual expansion of its political dominion. This is seen as obedience to the divine duty imposed on Muslims to spread Allah's rule and religion to the whole world. As we have seen this does not necessarily mean the forced conversion of all individuals to Islam (though in the early expansion polytheists only had the choice between conversion to Islam or death), it does mean Islamic domination of all political structures and the imposition of *shari'a*.

Jihad and the expansion of Islam through war are not seen by Muslims as aggression, but as the God-ordained method of attaining to the ultimate peace under the dominion of Islam. The wars to disseminate Islam are not described by the Arabic word for war, *harb*, but by *futuh*, literally opening (of the world to Islam). The non-Muslims who stand in the way of the spread of Islam, creating obstacles to its mission (*da'wa*), are held responsible for the resulting state of war. The obstinate refusal of non-Muslims to accept Islam is viewed as aggression, as they hinder Islam in its God-ordained path to victory.[209]

A modern comment from Dr Ali Othman, for some years adviser on education to the United Nations Relief and Works Agency, rejects any need to apologise for aggressive *jihad*:

> The spread of Islam was military. There is a tendency to apologise for this and we should not. It is one of the injunctions of the Koran that you must fight for the spreading of Islam.[210]

Muslim scholars argue that the initial aggressive Islamic *jihad* which led to the spectacular expansion of the Islamic state was justified because it liberated the people in *Dar al-Harb* from the oppression of illegitimate infidel rulers and opened them up to the Islamic message. Yusuf al-Qaradhawi argues that the initial Islamic conquests were:

> In reality a rescue of the oppressed and wronged people from the tyranny of wrongdoers and the injustice of oppressors, and a liberation of the people from the domination of Persian Monarchs and Roman Caesars.[211]

Implied in this justification for the first *jihad* is the claim that similar contemporary aggression would be perfectly acceptable by this interpretation of Islam, and could thus justify and legitimate any Muslim aggression against any non-Muslim state in the world today, as they are all considered by Islamists to be illegitimate and oppressive.

Islam accepts as natural that Muslims should rule non-Muslims, and considers it unnatural that non-Muslims should rule Muslims. Non-Muslim rule is regarded as a kind of blasphemy that leads to corruption of religion and morality. This is the great affront of the non-Muslim world against Islam. Richard Chartres, the Anglican Bishop of London, describes Islam's unwavering belief in its own superiority:

> There is an immense sense in Islam of the superiority of Islam to everything else – and this is in terrible full-frontal collision with the evident inferiority of Muslim societies, technically, politically, economically, militarily... The crisis in Islam (it's not so much a battle between East and West, Christians and Muslims, it's a battle in Islam) comes from the terrible collision of this sense of superiority with the evident inferiority in so many other ways, which causes bewilderment and fierce debate on how we are going to get out of this bind.[212]

The late Zaki Badawi, president of the Muslim College in London, affirms the Islamic requirement for political power, and Islam's inability to function as a minority:

> As we know the history of Islam as a faith is also the history of a state and a community of believers living by Divine law. The Muslims, jurists and theologians, have always expounded Islam as both a Government and a faith. This reflects the historical fact that Muslims, from the start, lived under their own law. Muslim theologians naturally produced a theology with this in view – it is a theology of the majority. Being a minority was not seriously considered or even contemplated. The theologians were divided in their attitude to minority status. Some declared that it should not take place; that is to say that a Muslim is forbidden to live for any lengthy period under non-Muslim rule. Others suggested that a Muslim living under non-Muslim rule is under no obligation to follow the law of Islam in matters of public law. Neither of these two extremes is satisfactory. Throughout the history of Islam some pockets of Muslims lived under the sway of non-Muslim rulers, often without an alternative. They nonetheless felt sufficiently committed to their faith to attempt to regulate their lives in accordance with its rules and regulations in so far as their circumstances permitted. In other words, the practice

of the community rather than the theories of the theologians provided a solution. Nevertheless Muslim theology offers, up to the present, no systematic formulation of the status of being a minority. The question is being examined. It is hoped that the matter will be brought into focus and that Muslim theologians from all over the world will delve into this thorny subject to allay the conscience of the many Muslims living in the West and also to chart a course for Islamic survival, even revival, in a secular society.[213]

The extension of the Islamic empire is very much an aim of radical Muslims today. For example, it was preached by Sheikh Ibrahim Mahdi (an employee of the Palestinian Authority) at the Sheikh 'Ijilin Mosque in Gaza City on 12 April 2002.

> But the rock and the tree will say: 'O Muslim, O servant of Allah, a Jew hides behind me, come and kill him.' Except for the Gharqad tree, which is the tree of the Jews." We believe in this *hadith*. We are convinced also that this *hadith* heralds the spread of Islam and its rule over all the land....
>
> O beloved, look to the east of the earth, find Japan and the ocean; look to the west of the earth, find [some] country and the ocean. Be assured that these will be owned by the Muslim nation, as the *hadith* says, "from the ocean to the ocean..."[214]

Other Motives for *Jihad*
Protecting God's honour

In Islam, honour in the sense of prestige, power and superior status, belongs to God, his prophet (Muhammad) and his community (the *umma*). This honour must be protected whenever it seems to be threatened, for example, by a threat to Muslim territory.

> In accordance with reason and with Islamic religious law, if the enemy raids the land of the Muslims, *jihad* becomes a personal imperative binding on every Muslim man and woman, because our Muslim nation will be subject to a new Crusader invasion targeting land, honour, belief, and homeland.[215]

But God's honour is also considered to be at risk when there is criticism of Islam in the media or mockery of Islam in the arts; hence the fact that such incidents provoke outrage and violent demonstrations in the same way as political and military attacks on Muslim societies and states. A slight to God, Muhammad or Muslims is as much a reason for *jihad* as is a threat to Muslim territory. The worldwide violence that followed the publication of cartoons of Muhammad in Denmark on 30th September 2005 shows how widespread is this sense of the importance of honour. In Pakistan there is a mandatory death sentence for "derogatory remarks" about Muhammad.[216]

Many Muslims believe that the restoration of honour can only be achieved by the shedding of blood. We have already seen (chapter 1) how Osama bin Laden believes this emphatically. Muslims of this persuasion feel themselves honour bound to remove all humiliations such as past oppression by imperialism; present dependency on the West; Zionist, Indian and Russian conquest of Muslim lands; and the Western cultural invasion.

Eradication of paganism

A concept often invoked by contemporary Islamists is that of *jahiliyya*, which was originally used to indicate the era of polytheistic ignorance and immorality which prevailed in Arabia before Muhammad. It was the duty of Islam to eradicate *jahiliyya* in all its forms and establish the true faith in one God - Islam. Today's Islamists judge that modern society (both Muslim and non-Muslim) has lapsed into this pagan state. Western neo-paganism is expressed in secularism, consumerism and moral laxity, which must be destroyed. As Sayyid Qutb explains:

> Any society is a *jahili* society if it does not dedicate itself to submission to Allah alone in its beliefs and ideas, in its observances of worship and in its legal norms .According to this definition, all the societies existing in the world today are *jahili*... All Jewish and Christian societies to day to some degree or other are also *jahili* societies . . Lastly, all the existing so-called "Muslim societies" are also *jahili* societies. We classify them among *jahili* societies not because they believe in other

gods beside Allah or because they worship anyone other than Him, but because their way of life is not based on submission to Allah alone... they have relegated the legislative attribute of Allah to others and submit to this authority.[217]

Jihad as a continuing duty

Because the whole world has not yet been turned into *Dar al-Islam*, the need for *jihad* logically remains. *Hadiths* that speak of continuous *jihad* have already been quoted, and we have seen that the caliph was required to lead a military expedition against *Dar al-Harb* at least once a year. There is a debate within Islam about to whom the duty of performing *jihad* applies, whether it is a collective responsibility or an individual responsibility.

Some Muslims hold *jihad* to be a sixth "pillar of Islam" along with the other compulsory duties ("pillars") of affirming the faith, praying, fasting, giving alms, and going on pilgrimage to Mecca. For example, Sheikh Muhammad Taher of the Leeds Grand Mosque, UK, has said that

> the real worship is not confined upon prayer and fasting only, in fact, the One who made fasting obligatory is the same One who made fighting obligatory, and the One who said: 'Fasting has been prescribed for you', is the same One who said: 'Fighting has been prescribed for you', so both are worship.[218]

Amongst those who take or took this line were the fierce, austere and fanatical Khariji sect,[219] of whom more later. Another was 'Abd al-Salam Faraj (1952-1982), the founder of the Egyptian militant group Al-Jihad, who wrote a popular book called *The Neglected Duty*. According to Faraj, *jihad* is the missing sixth pillar of Islam, suppressed by scholars but necessary for Islam to flourish. It is a major individual duty incumbent on every Muslim and must not be deferred by any excuse.[220]

In an appendix "The Call to Jihad in the Qur'an" to the Saudi-sponsored Qur'an translation into English, *The Interpretation of the Meanings of The Noble Qur'an in the English language, jihad* is linked to prayer and fasting, two of the obligatory pillars. *Jihad* is described as similar to these pillars, and all three are obligations ordained by God on the believers. These claims in effect place *jihad* as one of the obligatory pillars of Islam.[221] (See also chapter 15.)

Osama bin Laden takes the same line, asserting that jihad is an "individual duty for every Muslim". For example, in a *fatwa* entitled "*Jihad* Against Jews and Crusaders" issued jointly with four other Islamist leaders on 23rd February 1998[222] he began by quoting the Sword Verse (Q 9:5), then set out the Muslim grievances, and then told all Muslims:

> The ruling to kill all Americans and their allies – civilians and military – is an individual duty for every Muslim who can do it in any country where it is possible to do it...[223]

Other texts were then quoted to prove that this was God's command.

Elsewhere bin Laden says:

> There are people who say, and it is no secret, that the *jihad* does not require the [participation] of the entire nation; these words are true, but their intent is not. It is true that *jihad* cannot include the entire nation today, and that repelling the aggressive enemy is done by means of a very small part of this nation; but *jihad* continues to be a commandment incumbent personally upon every Muslim.[224]

However most Muslims consider *jihad* a collective obligation laid on the Muslim community as a whole, and hence not a pillar, the five standard pillars being duties required of each individual believer. According to Ibn Abi Zayd al-Qayrawani (922-966), a leading jurist of the Maliki school of *shari'a*, the fact that some Muslims are performing *jihad* excuses others from participation: "*jihad* is a precept of Divine institution. Its performance by certain individuals may release others from the obligation."[225] Generally *jihad* is considered the responsibility of the state led by the lawful caliph or imam; individual Muslims cannot wage their own *jihads* though they should be willing to participate in the communal *jihad*.[226] Furthermore, a time may come when *jihad* is no longer necessary i.e. if the whole world is under Islamic rule.[227]

According to the Grand Mufti of Saudi Arabia, Sheikh Abdul

Aziz Ibn Baz (Grand Mufti of Saudi Arabia 1993-1999), the collective obligation may also become an individual obligation in certain circumstances: if the imam calls people out to fight, if Muslim territory is attacked, and for soldiers in the Muslim ranks preparing to fight.[228] It is probably the same logic which is behind the *fatwa* issued by Sheikh Faysal Mawlawi, Deputy Chairman of the European Council for Fatwa and Research, on March 23rd 2003 concerning American military bases in Arab and Muslim countries. This *fatwa* ruled that the bases were "aggressive troops" and launching *jihad* against them is an individual obligation incumbent on every Muslim who is able to do so (provided that such attacks do not result in internal strife between the rulers and the people of the country concerned). Mawlawi added that "in individual obligation, a Muslim does not need to seek the permission of the imam or the Muslim ruler".[229]

According to Khadduri, when Muslim power began to decline in the tenth century AD, there was a tacit understanding that the obligation for permanent *jihad* was to be suspended or made dormant for a time. He quotes in his support Ibn Khaldun, asserting that Ibn Khaldun considered this was a process of evolution of the Muslim community from a warlike stage to a civilised stage.[230] However, it is important to realise that Ibn Khaldun viewed the evolution of desert-dwelling "savage groups" to people who "settle in the fertile plains and amass luxuries" as an undesirable development. The savage groups, says Ibn Khaldun, were braver and "therefore better able to achieve superiority and to take away the things that are in the hands of other nations". He praises the first Muslims because "their fortitude... was not corroded by education or authority".[231]

Over the centuries the religious duty of *jihad* sometimes served as a useful concept for certain Muslim rulers wishing to legitimise their wars against non-Muslims and against competing Muslims. While wars against non-Muslims in *Dar al-Harb* needed no additional explanations, wars against Muslims could be justified by labelling the adversary as heretics or apostates who had deviated from true Islam. All

110

that was needed was to find some *'ulama* (Islamic religious scholars) who were willing to issue a *fatwa* calling for *jihad* against them. Timurlane (or Tamerlane or Timur Lang, 1336-1405) the Mongol conqueror labelled all Muslims he attacked as heretics, whether Shi'a or Sunni. He described the reasons for his fighting *jihad* as a *ghazi*:

> About this time there arose in my heart the desire to lead an expedition against the infidels, and become a *ghazi*: for it had reached my ears that the slayer of infidels is a *ghazi*, and if he is slain he becomes a martyr... By the order of God and the Prophet it is incumbent upon me to make war upon these infidels and polytheists.[232]

History of Revivals and *Jihad*

Revivals have been part of Islamic history since its earliest days, with revivalists calling for a return to the early pure Islam of the Qur'an and *sunna*, and to the original ideal state model of Muhammad in Medina. Puritan revivalists argued that the cause of Muslim political, military, and economic weakness was the departure from the original pure "true" Islam. They rejected later traditions, superstitions and pagan practices and demanded the violent purging of the community from all such elements. Following Muhammad's model, they preached a separation from *jahiliyya* (which in their eyes included other less puritantical Muslims whom they labelled as *kuffar* and hence deserving death), practised migration (*hijra*), established a Muslim state under *shari'a* and launched aggressive *jihad* (against Muslims accused of compromising with paganism and against non-Muslims) in order to expand the dominion of Islam.[233]

Examples of this kind of *jihad* in the last few centuries are more numerous than might be supposed. Many were led by Sufis and resisted European invasion, implementing *shari'a* and proclaiming *jihad*.[234] Modern Islamists see themselves as part of this revivalist *jihadi* tradition in Islam, seeking to resist non-Muslim domination, purify the faith, establish an Islamic state under *shari'a* and expand its territory by *jihad*.

Some Historical *Jihadi* Movements
Muhammad ibn 'Abd al-Wahhab (1703-1792) and
the Wahhabi movement in the Arabian Peninsula

Muhammad ibn 'Abd al-Wahhab founded a puritanical and militant reform movement based on a strict and literalist interpretation of Muslim sources as taught by the Hanbali school of law. He ensured its survival by an alliance with the tribal leader of the house of Saud. He judged the Islam of his time to be a degenerate version of true Islam, corrupted by blind imitation of clerics, the Shi'a elevation of their imams to the role of mediators, and popular folk religious Sufi practices such as saint-worship and tomb visitation, which he condemned as idolatry. He compared the Arabian society of his time to the pagan pre-Islamic period of ignorance (*jahiliyya*), and declared his Muslim opponents to be non-Muslims or apostates (the process of declaring someone to be an apostate is called *takfir*), thus justifying *jihad* against them. The Wahhabi state he co-founded with ibn Sa'ud destroyed tombs and shrines in Mecca and Medina and throughout the Arabian Peninsula. It also destroyed Shi'a shrines in Karbala in modern Iraq). It expanded by a *jihad* in which it massacred many of its opponents. It was crushed by Muhammad 'Ali of Egypt acting for the Ottomans in 1818.

A second smaller Wahhabi Saudi state survived, based on al-Diriya and Riyadh, from 1824 to1891. The third Wahhabi state was founded by 'Abd al-'Aziz Ibn-Sa'ud in the early twentieth century and continues in contemporary Saudi Arabia, whose state religion is Wahhabi Islam.

Wahhabi influence spread across the Muslim world in the nineteenth century, as pilgrims returning from Mecca impacted reform movements in India, Africa and other regions.

Usuman dan Fodio (1754-1817) and the Fulani *jihad* in West Africa[235]

From 1804 to 1808 Usuman dan Fodio, a leader of the Fulani tribe in West Africa who was also a Sufi in the Qadiri order, led a *jihad* against the Muslim rulers of the Hausa tribe. He claimed that the Hausa were not true Muslims but had mixed their Islam with local pagan practices, thus turning the land into *Dar al-Harb* and justifying *jihad*. He also argued that it was obligatory for Muslims to emigrate *(hijra)* from regions ruled by non-Muslims so as to prepare for *jihad* and reconquer the land for Islam. He imposed strict *shari'a* observance in his state. Dan Fodio claimed he was a *mujaddid* (reformer) of the new Islamic millennium, sent to purify Islam, and warned that the *mahdi* would soon appear. The leaders accepted his call, gave him their oath of allegiance *(bay'a)* and joined his *jihad*. The *jihad* spread, integrating existing Muslim states and forcibly converting many pagans to Islam, creating the Sokoto Empire in 1803 in what is now northern Nigeria.[236] Memories of this pure Islamic Empire fuel contemporary demands in northern Nigerian states for the imposition of *shari'a* and for Muslim domination in Nigeria.

Imam Shamil (1796-1871) against the Russians in the Caucasus

An ethnic Avar (the largest ethnic group in Dagestan) and leader of the Naqshbandi Sufi order in Daghestan, Shamil proclaimed a *jihad* against the Russians. He managed to unite the many frequently quarrelling Caucasian tribes and made effective use of guerrilla warfare tactics. Shamil was proclaimed the third imam of Dagestan in 1834, when he founded the Imamate of Dagestan and Chechnya. He fought the Russians for 25 years, repeatedly defeating superior Russian forces, until his surrender in 1859 when he and his family were arrested and then exiled to the small Russian town of Kaluga. He died in 1871 on a pilgrimage to Mecca.

The areas under his control, which included most of Dagestan and the Chechen region, were organised as an Islamic state under *shari'a*. He serves as a model for contemporary Chechens and other Caucasian Muslims in their insurgency against Russian rule.[237]

Sayyid Ahmad Barelwi in British India (1786-1831)

A reformer of the Naqshbandi Sufi order who tried to purify Indian Islam and Sufism of excesses and innovations, Barelwi founded the Tariqa-i Muhammadiyya reform movement in 1818. He was regarded as a *mujaddid*, and by some as the *mahdi*. Following a *fatwa* by a renowned scholar, Shah 'Abd al-'Aziz (1746-1824), that India under British rule had become *Dar al-Harb,* he too declared most of India as a land of unbelief and the House of War and urged Muslims to emigrate (perform *hijra)* to northern India, establish a *Dar al-Islam* there and prepare for *jihad*. In 1826 he performed a *hijra* and launched a *jihad* against the Sikh Kingdom of Ranjit Singh in the Punjab. Many Pashtuns followed him. He was killed in battle against the Sikhs at Balakot in 1831. Followers, known as the Mujahidin Movement, kept the *jihad* alive until the Muslim-led Great Mutiny of 1857 and beyond.

The strength of the *hijra* doctrine in India can be gauged from the fact that in the mid-1920s, following the agitation of the *khilafa* movement against the British for their treatment of defeated Turkey following the First World War, thousands of Muslims from the Punjab and the North West Frontier sold their land and possessions and emigrated to Afghanistan, declaring that it was un-Islamic to remain under British rule which was equated with *Dar al-Harb*.[238]

Muhammad Ahmad ibn 'Abdallah (the *Mahdi* 1844-1885) in Sudan

A charismatic religious leader who founded his own Sufi order, he declared himself *mahdi* in 1881 and proclaimed *jihad* against Anglo-Egyptian rule in Sudan. He set up a state (1882-1898) under *shari'a*. Following his death in 1885, the *mahdi* state weakened and it was defeated and destroyed by a British force under Lord Kitchener in 1898. Mahdism, however, remained a strong influence in Sudan, and following independence in 1956 was part of the driving force in the long-lasting civil war against the non-Muslim southerners.

The Sanusiyya in Libya (1837-1931)

Muhammad ibn 'Ali al-Sanusi (1787-1859) founded the Sanusiyya order in what is now north-eastern Libya in 1841 as a Sufi brotherhood based on the Shadhili order. A large part of the Bedouin population of the area came to be identified with the order which also spread to western Libya. The Sanusiyya at first fought the French who were encroaching from the west, and later the Italians who invaded Libya in 1911. In 1912 the Sanusi leader Ahmad al-Sharif proclaimed a *jihad* against the Italians. The Italians were held at bay for a while, but gradually crushed the Sanusi resistance and destroyed their centres.

'Abd al-Qader (1808-1883) in North Africa against the French

Following the French invasion of Algeria in 1830, Sidi Muhyi al-Din proclaimed a *jihad* against the French in the region of Oran. Abd al-Qader, his son, led the attacks and became famous for his courage and leadership skills. Ill health forced Muhyi al-Din to abdicate in favour of 'Abd al-Qader, who in 1832 was proclaimed *amir al-mu'minin* (leader of the faithful, a title given to the caliph or imam) by a tribal coalition pledging their *bay'a* to him. 'Abd al-Qader was a leader in both the Qadiri and Naqshbandi Sufi orders. In the areas under his control he set up a state under *shari'a*. He fought the French with varied success until his surrender in 1847.

Some Modern Calls to *Jihad*
The Ottoman *jihad* during the First World War

At the beginning of the First World War, the Ottoman Empire declared a *jihad* against Russia, France and Britain. During November 1914 a *fatwa* (translated into five languages) was issued by the highest religious authority in Istanbul, the Sheikh al-Islam, called on Muslims everywhere to join in the war. But few responded to the call. The *fatwas* were immediately followed by a *beyanname-i cihad* (declaration of holy war) issued by Sultan Mehmed V Resad.[239] After the war, when Mustafa Kemal Atatürk was fighting to remove Greek and Allied forces from Anatolia, this too was seen as a *jihad*. In a proclamation calling on the Turkish nation to unite against the Greeks, Atatürk said:

> We call on the whole nation to come together in unity and rise against the Greeks in total determination. The *jihad,* once it is properly preached, will, with God's help, result quickly in the rout of the Greeks.[240]

On September 19[th]1921 Atatürk was voted the title of *ghazi* (*jihadi* fighter for the faith, literally "one who takes part in a *ghazwa*") by the Grand National Assembly for his victory over the Greeks at the Battle of Sakarya.[241]

The *jihad* in Afghanistan against the Soviet Union (1979-1989)

Following the Soviet invasion of Afghanistan in 1979, the Islamist groups whose leaders had fled to Pakistan declared a *jihad* against the Soviets and the communist regime in Kabul. They were supported by conservative clerics and the elites of the old regime. The defence of Afghanistan from Soviet invasion (1979-1989) was known in Pakistan as the *jihad-e-Afghanistan*. With Pakistani and Saudi Arabian aid, the Afghan *jihad* became a popular theme all over the Muslim world, generating an inflow of funds and volunteers to support the war. The US helped with funds and weapons channelled through the Pakistani Inter-Service Intelligence (ISI).

The Palestinian cause as a *jihad*

Since the beginnings of the Jewish return to the Holy Land under the auspices of the Zionist movement, Muslims have called for a *jihad* to stop them and restore Islamic dominance in Palestine. This was exacerbated by the founding of Israel in 1948 and its successive victories over Arab armies in 1948, 1956, 1967 and 1973 as well as its conquest of Jerusalem.

In 1935 'Izz al-Din al-Qassam proclaimed a *jihad* against the British for their perceived pro-Jewish policies. He was killed in a fight against British forces in November 1935, but his *jihad* was the precursor of the Arab Revolt against the British in Palestine (1936-1939) initiated by the Mufti of Jerusalem, Haj Amin al-Husseini, who called for a *jihad* against the British and the Jews. In 1941, on his way to Nazi Germany, he issued a *fatwa* calling for *jihad* against the British. In 1948, following the UN decision on the partition of Palestine into Arabic and Jewish states, al-Husseini and the Arab League proclaimed a *jihad*. Further calls for *jihad* against Israel were sporadically issued by various Arabic political and religious platforms, including the Palestine Liberation Organisation (PLO) and the prestigious al-Azhar University in Cairo. PLO leader Yasser Arafat repeatedly called for *jihad*, even after his signing of the Oslo Peace Treaty with Israel in 1993.[242]

The Organisation of the Islamic Conference (OIC) at its fourth Foreign Ministers Conference in Benghazi in 1973 declared *jihad* for the liberation of Jerusalem. The name of its Palestine fund was changed to '*Jihad* Fund for Palestine'. This was followed by a drive to delegitimise Israel in all world forums and the UN resolution equating Zionism with racism. In 1980 the OIC again called for a *jihad* to save Jerusalem by all means.[243]

Hamas, Hizbullah and Palestinian Islamic Jihad all see their struggle against Israel as a *jihad* to restore Islamic land and rule. According to the Hamas founding charter, *jihad* is the only way to solve the problem of Israel - by destroying and eliminating it. The struggle is in essence a religious one between Jews and Muslims, and there is no possibility of peace.[244]

Resistance to US-led invasions of Afghanistan (2001) and Iraq (2003) as *jihad*

Gulbuddin Hekmatyar, leader of the Afghan Islamist movement Hizb-i-Islami, announced in December 2002 that his militia had joined the Taliban and al-Qa'eda in a *jihad* against all international and peacekeeping forces in Afghanistan, especially the Americans:

> I pray to Allah to make my participation and share in the Jihad against the Americans much greater than in the Jihad against the Russians. I hope that Allah will consider me a participant in all the operations that have been carried out and will be carried out against the Americans.[245]

Hekmatyar repeated his call for a *jihad* against America in November 2004, when he claimed that the war in Afghanistan and Iraq was the "crusaders'" second war against Muslims. The first was the Soviet invasion of Afghanistan, the second is being led by America.[246]

Jalaluddin Haqqani, the recently appointed Taliban commander in Afghanistan, in August 2006 repeated the Taliban declaration of a large-scale *jihad* against American-led foreign forces in

Afghanistan. He dubbed the US-led coalition forces "invaders" and announced that he would continue to fight them until their final expulsion from Afghanistan.[247]

Leaders of Pakistani Islamist organisations also saw the US-led invasion of Afghanistan as a cause for a legitimate *jihad* against America. Taqi Usmani, a leader in the Deobandi movement, argued that according to *fatwas* given by Islamic scholars, the *jihad* of the Taliban against the US is a true *jihad,* and it is the duty of every Muslim to participate in it.[248]

A recorded message purporting to come from ousted Iraqi president Saddam Hussein in July 2003 described the Iraqi resistance to American forces as a *jihad*. A number of well-known Muslim scholars from across the traditional and Islamist spectrum, also declared the fight against the US-led invasion of Muslim lands as a *jihad* of individual duty.

On March 20th 2003 the Islamic Research Committee of the leading Sunni religious academic institution, Al-Azhar University in Cairo, called upon all Muslims to launch a *jihad* in response to the US invasion of Iraq:[249]

> *Jihad* is an individual duty for all Muslims if the U.S. launches a war against Iraq. Arabs and Muslims should be on high alert to defend themselves, their doctrine and lands... [Muslims] have to forget all internal differences so as not to surrender to prospective attacks. *Jihad* is an individual duty in case an enemy occupies Muslims' lands. Our Arab and Muslim nation will face new crusades that aim to deprive us of our homeland, doctrine and dignity.

The Sheikh of Al-Azhar, Dr Muhammad Sayyid Tantawi, convened a press conference on April 5th 2003, in which he called on the Iraqi people to engage in *jihad*:[250]

> Continue its *jihad* in defence of religion, faith, honour, and property, because *jihad* is a religious ruling of Islam aimed at opposing aggressors. It is the right of the Iraqis to carry out any operation in defence of their homeland, whether martyrdom operations or any other means.

He encouraged volunteers from Arab and Islamic countries to go to Iraq

> to support the *jihad* of their oppressed brethren there, because resistance to oppression is an Islamic obligation, whether the oppressor is Muslim or not... The gates of *jihad* are open until the Day of Judgement, and I say to the volunteer: Go in peace, and I wish you the best. I speak words of truth, but I cannot order any man.

During a Friday sermon at Al-Azhar on April 6th 2003, he added:

> The American aggression against Iraq is not acceptable to Islamic law, and to the [*shari'a*] law; The Iraqi people must defend itself, its land, and its homeland with all means of defense at its disposal, because it is a *jihad* that is permitted by Islamic law. *Jihad* is an obligation for every Muslim when Muslim countries are subject to aggression. The gates of *jihad* are open until the Day of Judgement, and he who denies this is an infidel or one who abandons his religion. This is an obligation applying to the nation now, in order to respond to the aggression.

Another prominent Sunni leader Yusuf al-Qaradhawi issued multiple calls for *jihad* against the US-led invasion. The Association of Muslim Scholars, led by al-Qaradhawi, issued a statement at its Beirut conference in November 2004 that:[251]

> The *jihad*-waging Iraqi people's resistance to the foreign occupation, which is aimed at liberating the [Iraqi] land and restoring its national sovereignty, is a Shari'a duty incumbent upon anyone belonging to the Muslim nation, within and outside Iraq, who is capable of carrying it out. Allah has permitted this by saying: 'Permission (to fight) is given to those upon whom war is made because they are oppressed [Koran 22:39],' and He said to the Muslims: ' Fight for the sake of Allah against those who fight against you [Koran 2:190].'

Taxonomy of *jihad*
Two basic types: offensive and defensive

Jihad is traditionally divided into two types, offensive and defensive, as Gilles Kepel explains:

> One (*al-jihad almubadahah*) aims at the armed conquest of new lands for Islam. It is mainly the business of the Islamic ruler and his troops. Another—and this covers the Afghan case—is a defensive struggle (*al-jihad al-dafa'ah*) that is proclaimed when infidels attack Islamic territory. Such a proclamation is supposed to result in a general mobilization of all good Muslims. Those who can fight should fight. Those who can't fight should pay. And those who can't pay should pray. Significantly, all other legal obligations - such as fasting during Ramadan - are suspended as guarding the community becomes the overriding concern.[252]

Sheikh Yusuf al-Qaradhawi agrees that *jihad* can be an offensive means of expanding the Muslim state as well as being defensive:

> A *jihad* which you seek [an attack], and a *jihad* in which you repulse an attack. In the *jihad* which you are seeking, you look for the enemy and invade him. This type of *jihad* takes place only when the Islamic state is invading other [countries] in order to spread the word of Islam and to remove obstacles standing in its way. The repulsing *jihad* takes place when your land is being invaded and conquered... [In that case you must] repulse [the invader] to the best of your ability. If you kill him he will end up in hell, and if he kills you, you become a martyr [Shahid].[253]

While progressive interpreters reject the aggressive stance, most Muslims agree that *jihad* includes a religious obligation to defend any Muslim territory and all Muslims from any form of aggression, leaving the door open to very different interpretations of what "defence" can encompass. It is only in more recent times that a sanitised presentation of *jihad* as consisting mainly of a non-violent struggle for moral perfection has been presented to Western audiences by Muslim apologists, often backing their claim with the statement "Islam is peace".

Types of *jihad* by its objectives

Muslim scholars have analysed *jihad* in different ways. One analysis is given by Khadduri as follows:[254]

1 *Jihad* against polytheists

Polytheists (*mushrikrun*) must be fought until they are willing to convert to Islam. The term refers to pagans who have no concept of a single supreme deity, of whom there were many in the Arabian Peninsula in the early days of Islam. Even larger numbers were encountered in later centuries when Islam expanded into Africa and Asia.

2 *Jihad against Muslims*

a *Against apostasy*

This *jihad* applies to groups of Muslims who renounced Islam and joined *Dar al-Harb,* for example, some of the Arab tribes who rebelled soon after Muhammad's death. Because of their treason against the Islamic state they were given no chance to make peace on any terms except their return to Islam. Apart from this, rules of engagement were similar to a war against *Dar al-Harb.*

b *Against dissension and rebellion*

Dissenters were those who had unorthodox religious ideas but still submitted to the authority of the imam or those who had a grievance unrelated to beliefs. If they moved on to disobedience to the imam they were to be fought. The rules of engagement in such a war were more generous than in wars against unbelievers, for example prisoners of war could not be killed and their property could not be expropriated. The more destructive methods of attack were only permitted as a last resort.

3 Jihad against the People of the Book
(Jews, Christians and Sabeans)

Ahl al-Kitab (the People of the Book)[255] had a threefold choice: conversion to Islam (and then full citizenship in the Islamic state), *dhimma* status i.e. second-class citizenship as non-Muslims within the Islamic state in return for submission and payment of *jizya* tax, or war with the Muslims.

4 Strengthening the frontiers (ribat)

This was a defensive type of *jihad* with the purpose of safeguarding the frontiers of *Dar al-Islam*. It was of particular significance in Islamic Spain when it was under attack by Christian European forces. The concept of *ribat* is supported by Q 8:60[256] and various *hadiths*.[257] However, the *ribat* often served as a base from which to renew the aggressive attack on *Dar al-Harb* when Muslim strength permitted it.

'Azzam's alternative categorisation

An alternative, modern analysis of *jihad* has been made by Sheikh 'Abdullah 'Azzam, the spiritual mentor of Osama bin Laden. He divides the worldwide *jihad* into the following three categories:

1 Within Muslim countries, with the goal of reinstating rule by *shari'a*.

2 In countries with Muslim minorities, situated on the "fault lines" with other cultures e.g. the Balkans, Chechnya, Kashmir.

3 The international cultural struggle, in which Islam takes on Western – especially American – civilisation.[258]

Da'wa and jihad

Intensive Muslim missionary activities are taking place around the non-Muslim world today, much of it funded by

Saudi Arabia, which has invested billions of dollars into *da'wa* work. *Da'wa* (Islamic mission) is not limited to efforts at converting individuals, but includes efforts at converting whole societies and at establishing Islamic states or enclaves to demonstrate to non-Muslims the power and benefits of Islamic rule. In other words the aims of *da'wa* include the aim of classical *jihad*.

Two quotations from modern Muslim writers illustrate this understanding of the purpose of *da'wa*. Isma'il Raji al-Faruqi sees Islamic states as responsible for converting non-Islamic states following the model of Muhammad:

> A verse of the Qur'an assigns the duty of converting the Arabs to the first ummah, to Muhammad. The first ummah, in turn, converted the other ummahs within the Islamic state. By logical extension, Muslims, including their Prophet, have understood the Islamic state to be assigned the same duty toward other states.[259]

For Kalim Siddiqui, the priority of *da'wa* at this time is the establishment of Islamic states under *shari'a* in Muslim countries, an aim which would entail "regime change" in most Muslim states.

> But the fact of the matter is that the first step in *da'wah* is to establish Islam as a working model of a civilization, of a system, and, therefore, we must use our stay in this country [the UK] not to convert the country to Islam, but to establish Islam in the house of Islam. And once it is established there, then you will be able to establish Islam anywhere. That is da'wah. So, if we mobilize our resources in this country in order to support an Islamic movement overseas, ultimately that is part of da'wah in the non-Muslim world... But the message of Allah came as a method. The method was delivered through the Sunnah of the Prophet. The Sunnah of the Prophet was, and shall always be, to establish a working civilization of Islam which will then emerge from wherever it is established, pressing everything else into retreat. It is the base of Islam that we do not have at this moment. We have to build it and once we have built it then da'wah will follow as surely as day follows night.[260]

If a secondary purpose of *da'wa* is to spread the rule of Islam, then a secondary purpose of *jihad* is to create new Muslim believers.

Hassan Khaled, Mufti of the Lebanese Republic, has spoken of the role of *jihad* in increasing the number of Muslims:

> So jihad consolidated the religion and increased the number of the worshippers of Allah and thus jihad is considered one of the main supports of Islam and the Believers pay much attention to adopt it and adhere to it to a great extent.[261]

Sheikh Abdullah Ghoshah, Supreme Judge of the Hashemite Kingdom of Jordan reiterates the classical notions that "*jihad* is the Islamic word which other nations use in the meaning of 'War'" and that "*jihad* is legislated as one of the means of propagating Islam. Non-Muslims ought to embrace Islam either willingly or unwillingly through fight and *jihad*."[262]

Abdullah 'Azzam saw *jihad* as God's ordained method for establishing Islam in the world, saying it is a

> battle...for the reformation of mankind, that the truth may be made dominant and good propagated.[263]

Khurram Murad, a leader in the Jama'at-i-Islami and former Director of the Islamic Foundation in Leicester, sees *da'wa* and *jihad* as based on Muhammad's role as final prophet for all humanity. All humans belong potentially to the Islamic *umma* and their membership of the *umma* must be made a reality using Muhammad's methods – *da'wa* and *jihad*.

> Muslims must understand that Muhammad (pbuh) was not appointed prophet (by Allah) for any particular nation or era. Rather, he was sent for whole humanity irrespective of time and space. No other prophet shall follow Muhammad (pbuh) till the Day of Judgment. From the 6th century till the 21st and even beyond, Muhammad (pbuh) shall remain as the only prophet. The whole mankind today is his disciple and belongs to his Ummah. This statement, although simple, has far reaching connotations. It is obligatory then that Muhammad (pbuh)'s message be continuously delivered in the manner done in his time.[264]

There are different understandings of the way in which *jihad* helps to facilitate the conversion of non-Muslims to Islam. One is simply that the establishing of Islamic rule in a certain area will mean that any hindrances to the peaceful propagation of the faith can be removed from that area. *Da'wa* is expected to be most effective when the state enforces Islam and *shari'a* and supports *da'wa* with all its resources. *Jihad* (if successful) creates the conditions in which conversion to Islam can easily take place supported by the state institutions and without opposition from powerful enemy forces. This view is held by Yusuf al-Qaradhawi:

> [*Jihad*] would be aimed at liberating Muslim lands, fighting the forces that oppose the Islamic *da'wah* and the Muslim Ummah...[265]

Likewise Sheikh Muhammad Abu Zahra, an Egyptian member of al-Azhar Academy of Islamic Research, stressed the role of *jihad* in preparing the way for *da'wa*:

> *Jihad*... has been decreed to repel aggression and to remove obstructions impeding the propagation of Islam in non-Muslim countries.[266]

Muhammad Taher claims that Muslims are required by *shari'a* to engage in *jihad* for their right to propagate Islam to all without any hindrance.

> Islam has made the protection and preservation of the deen [religion in its practice] obligatory, and this is done through prayer, fasting, charity (zakah), Hajj, and all the other acts of worship and obedience... It is also done through calling people to the deen, and explaining to them its beauties and advantages, loving guidance for mankind, that they believe in Allah and worship Him alone. That they rule by Allah, establish the law and implement its rulings, and for this we have legislation to fight *jihad* in the path of Allah to preserve the deen, checking and deterring those who stand in the way of calling people to Islam.[267]

Thus movements like the Muslim Brotherhood see themselves as committed to both *da'wa* and *jihad*, or rather see both as different stages in the same enterprise:

> It is a call for *jihad* since it calls for preparation for *jihad* by all its forms and means so that truth may have the force to protect it and that the Da'wah may be able to face the challenges and surmount the barriers... Force is the surest way to establish the truth and how beautiful it would be if truth and force went side by side. Thus *jihad* for the spread of Islam and the protection of the holy places of Islam is another obligation which Allah made compulsory o the Muslims...[268]

This mention by the Muslim Brotherhood of using force to "establish the truth" hints at another way in which *jihad* creates new Muslims. In classical Islam, polytheists were offered the choice of conversion or death. Thus many became Muslims in order to save their lives.

Ibn Taymiyya saw another kind of linkage between *da'wa* and *jihad*. He argued that the Qur'an precedes the sword, meaning that the call to Islam precedes the use of force. Muslim minorities must propagate their faith, he said, until they become powerful enough to take control of the state:

> That is why the Shari'ah has enjoined war against the infidels. However it is not obligatory until full preparations have been made to fight them.[269]

According to Ibn Taymiyya, *da'wa* and *jihad* must go together. Non-Muslims who reject the call to Islam, which is God's call, lose their right to freedom. The Muslims must fight against them and subdue them so as to make the whole world free for those who submit to the call, the Muslims.[270]

This calls to mind the rule in classical Islam that the Islamic state was required to issue a call (*da'wa*) to its enemies to submit to Islam by converting or becoming *dhimmis*. If they refused, *jihad* was waged against them. *Da'wa*, according to Bassam Tibi, was in effect an invitation to *jihad* against those who reject it and place obstacles in its way.[271]

At its core Islam is a religious mission to all humanity. Muslims are religiously obliged to disseminate the Islamic faith throughout the world: "we have sent you forth to all mankind" (Saba 34:28). If non-Muslims submit to conversion or subjugation, this call (da'wa) can be pursued peacefully. If they do not, Muslims are obliged to wage war against them. In Islam, peace requires that non-Muslims submit to the call of Islam, either by converting or by accepting the status of a religious minority (dhimmi) and paying the imposed tax, jizya. World peace, the final stage of the da'wa, is reached only with the conversion or submission of all mankind to Islam.[272]

Even though it later developed more peaceful missionary forms, da'wa was from early times inextricably linked to jihad, both preceding jihad and following it.

6
Jihad, Eschatology and Messianism

The early *jihad* was driven by a sense of apocalyptic urgency, as Muslims expected the imminent end of the world. Muhammad was viewed as the last prophet, sent before the Day of Judgement to warn humanity,[273] but much else in early Islamic eschatology was an Islamised version of pre-Islamic Jewish and Christian eschatology. Qur'an and *hadith* have much to say about the terrible events of the last days and many Muslims expect the appearance of an End-Time deliverer, the *mahdi*.[274]

Historically, self-proclaimed *mahdis* arose all over the Muslim world throughout its history, posing a danger to established rulers who tended to suppress them because they were causing *fitna* (civil strife).[275] Self-proclaimed *mahdis* also led resistance movements to Western imperialism in the nineteenth century, including the Sudanese Muhammad ibn 'Abdallah who set up an independent *shari'a* state (1882-1898). Mahdism is thus a concept with great power to mobilise Muslims at all times, but especially in times of crisis and weakness.

Islamists decry traditionalist Muslim passivity with its focus on the world to come; they demand activist engagement to solve contemporary problems in the Muslim world and prepare for the advent of the *mahdi*.[276]

Radical Islamists are glad to assume the role of God's weapon of wrath in the *jihad* against his unbelieving, rebellious, and immoral enemies at this stage of world history. Many see themselves part of God's End-Time scenario, preparing the way for the promised deliverer who will set up God's Kingdom of justice and peace. They believe that the terrorism they are engaged in is part of God's cleansing fire of wrath poured on a rebellious and apostate humanity.

Eschatology is coming to play an increasingly important part in Islamist discourse. Most Islamists accept the traditional Sunni or Shi'a eschatological teachings on the signs of the End Times: the appearance of the Antichrist (*al-Dajjal*), the coming of the *mahdi* or the return of the Hidden Imam to set up a righteous rule on earth.[277] However, some groups are more heavily influenced by Islamic eschatology and perceive their activities as part of the End-Time scenario. Jerusalem and its Muslim holy sites have become central to this discourse.

After the Six Day War in 1967, Islamists had to present a theological alternative to the secular discourse dealing with the Jewish state of Israel and its successes. While sharpening all the traditional Muslim anti-Jewish rhetoric, they moved to an apocalyptic view of how Israel will ultimately be overcome and defeated in the End Times. The new Islamist messianic apocalyptic End-Time discourse follows a linear eschatological programme. Israel's successes against Muslims are explained using an Islamic eschatological framework. This interprets the rise of Israel in apocalyptic terms as fulfilment of God's plan for the End Times while revealing that it will eventually be defeated. Current events and personalities are recognised to have been prophesied and are fitted into an End-Time scheme. Various scenarios are created in which Muslims fight and defeat Israel and there is much speculation on the appearance of the *mahdi*, the *Dajjal* and Jesus.

Numerous books, pamphlets and hundreds of Internet sites discuss these issues. Most Islamist radical groups (Algerian, Egyptian, Palestinian, Salafi,[278] etc.) use apocalyptic material. It appears in the Hamas Charter, in Palestinian Islamic Jihad pamphlets, and in Hizbullah and Salafi-Jihadi[279] materials. The Islamist apocalyptic discourse has also entered the Muslim mainstream and its religious establishment. While perhaps seeming strange to Western secular thought, this discourse is an important way in which Islamic militants are preparing the general Muslim public for the final onslaught on the infidel West.

The Egyptian Takfir wal-Hijra organisation active in the 1970s and 1980s was a *mahdist* movement with an eschatological world-view similar to Christian premillennialism. The world was considered to be close to its End Time, as evidenced by the signs of disbelief, oppression, immorality, famine, wars, earthquakes and hurricanes. Their leader, Shukri Mustafa was seen as the promised *mahdi* who would found the new Muslim community, conquer the world by *jihad*, and usher in God's final reign on earth.[280]

Faraj, the theorist of al-Jihad, the organisation which assassinated Egyptian President Sadat in 1981, accepted the traditions of the *mahdi* who will reveal himself at the end of time and establish justice in the whole world. He taught that Muslims should not wait passively for the *mahdi*, but be active in the meantime spreading Islam – a view similar to Christian postmillennialism.[281]

Juhayman al-'Utaybi led his 1979 failed revolt against the Saudi regime[282] in the name of a proclaimed *mahdi*, Muhammad ibn 'Abdallah al-Qahtani, a student at the Islamic University in Riyadh, whose *mahdi* status had been revealed in dreams to his wife and sister and coincided with the beginning of the fifteenth century in the Islamic calendar. It was claimed that he fulfilled the *hadith* that the *mahdi* would appear at the *ka'ba* at the turn of the Islamic century, as well as others stating he will have the same name as the Islamic Prophet and exhibit similar physical attributes. The movement's ideology was rooted in the belief that after a long period of deviation from true Islam the *mahdi* would appear to put an end to tyrannical kingship and set up a reign of justice and peace. The movement was convinced that once the *mahdi* had revealed himself, all Muslims would pay him allegiance and defeat the forces of the corrupt regimes who would be swallowed up by the earth itself.[283]

Muslim media across the world now consistently present al-Qa'eda, the US-led "war on terror" and the invasions of Iraq and Afghanistan in an eschatological perspective. "End of Time" scenarios on CD and DVD are sold across the Muslim world as well as being propagated in print and on the internet. These romanticise and glorify the Taliban, al-Qa'eda and other *jihadi* groups, thus adding to their popularity.[284]

The main message is that the present conflict is the harbinger of the final redemption, that Muslim victory is assured, that God and nature will fight on the Muslim side. Muslims, God's party, will prevail in the last battle and annihilate the satanic enemy. This apocalyptic discourse diminishes the negative impact of defeats which are seen in the overall eschatological context as only temporary setbacks. Despair at present humiliation is replaced by a triumphalism based on the predictions of an apocalyptic ultimate humiliation and destruction of the USA (likened to the Qur'anic city of 'Ad) and of Israel.[285] By globalising *jihad*, al-Qa'eda and Salafi-Jihadism have shifted *jihad* from a local limited struggle against hypocritical Muslim leaders and regimes, to an End-Time cosmic struggle against all satanic powers in the world led by the "Crusading" USA. In apocalyptic warfare there can be no compromise and no truce. It is the battle to end all battles, to annihilate the enemy once and for all, and to build the final Kingdom of God on the ruins of the former world order.[286]

As an example of the proliferation of apocalyptic Salafi-Jihadi groups, Moroccan authorities in July 2006 arrested some 56 members of a previously unknown group, the Ansar al-Mahdi (meaning "helpers of the Mahdi") led by Hassan al-Khattab, a known Salafi-Jihadi who had been sentenced to two years in prison in 2003 following the Casablanca bombings. The group included a mix of drug traffickers, wives of Air Maroc pilots and members of the armed forces. The very name indicates that this new Salafi-Jihadi group is apocalyptic in its worldview.[287]

Shi'a *Mahdism*

For Twelver Shi'a,[288] the *mahdi* is the returning Hidden Imam who disappeared into occultation in 874 in Samarra. Important titles given to the messianic figure in Shi'a Islam are the Hidden Imam, al-Qa'im (the Rising One), Sahib (or Imam) al-Zaman (Lord of the Ages). These titles emphasise his divinely ordained mission, his sudden appearance and his role as ruler of all times.[289] When he returns, all Shi'a will be able to hear and see the *mahdi* no matter where they are.

There is an anti-Sunni strand in traditional Shi'a *mahdism*. As the Shi'a have for most of their history suffered oppression and injustice at the hand of the Sunnis, they tend to stress the element of the *mahdi* filling the earth with justice and righteousness.[290] The *mahdi* will rectify all that went wrong in Muslim history from the moment the Companions of Muhammad refused to accept 'Ali as Muhammad's legitimate heir.[291] Hussein with his band of 72 followers slaughtered at Karbala will join the *mahdi* at the head of 12,000 believers.

Shi'a traditional apocalyptic also tends to be hostile to non-Shi'a Arabs. Also, in the Shi'a version *al-Dajjal* is not the main evil opponent of the *mahdi*. This role is reserved for the Sufyani, who turns up just before the appearance of the *mahdi*. He is a descendant of Abu-Sufyan, Muhammad's main opponent among the Quraish who later accepted Islam and whose son Mu'awiyya founded the Umayyad dynasty. Mu'awiyya's son, Yazid, had Hussein killed at Karbala. The Sufyani is the main enemy in the last days, as his ancestors were the main enemies of the Shi'a in the early days of Islam. The Arabs are the main supporters of the Sufyani, whose usurpation of power starts in Palestine/Jordan and then extends to the whole Middle East. The Sufyani appears outwardly pious but is actually the most evil man on earth. He will deceive many and gain control of Palestine, Damascus, Hims, Jordan and Qinisrin. He will totally destroy the 'Abbasids and kill many Shi'a. When the Sufyani hears of the emergence of the *mahdi* he sends an army to fight him, but his army will be swallowed up by the earth between Mecca and Medina.[292]

In Shi'a tradition, after *al-Dajjal* is killed, the Sunnis are massacred and the *mahdi* will destroy the most holy mosque including the *ka'ba* in Mecca. In the words of Al-Hurr al-'Amili, a seventeenth century Shi'a scholar:

> "When the Qa'im arises, he will destroy the mosque of the haram, return it to its foundations..."[293]

In the contemporary Shi'a world, the rise of Khomeini to power in the Islamic Revolution of 1979 resonated with Shi'a eschatological symbols and inspired many Iranians to see him either as the promised "Hidden Imam" himself, or at least as some eschatological manifestation and representative of the Hidden Imam sent to prepare the way for the end times.

Khomeini and his followers rejected the traditional passive Shi'a *mahdism* that advocates a patient waiting for the *mahdi* who will come at the appointed time with no need for human activity on his behalf. They replaced this with an activist *mahdism* which stressed that humans can help prepare for the *mahdi's* coming by Islamising society, implementing *shari'a* and setting up an Islamic state that will serve the *mahdi* as a tool for implementing his programme.

According to Khomeinist doctrine, the only way for the downtrodden to free themselves is by a revolution in thought and attitude that will overcome years of brainwashing by oppressive regimes and exploiters. Such a universal revolution to free humans from tyrants will be launched by the twelfth Imam, the *mahdi*, on his return. He will be helped by his true supporters in a just *jihad*. Islam will be spread in all the world, replacing all other religions. The *mahdi* and his followers will defeat all oppressors forever. The *mahdi* revolution will destroy all false gods created by human minds, including: borders, races, nations, creeds, political parties, and false prophets. Forces of disbelief and wickedness will be permanently destroyed, and the rule of justice and equity firmly established, the golden age of peace and harmony under the government of God. The *mahdi* will offer Islam to all non-believers. Those who accept will not be killed; those who refuse will be killed.

> The Mahdi's revolution aspires to found a global community under one God, one religion, and one ideal system of law, and to bring all other communities under the united flag of Islam.[294]

Warfare and bloodshed are the only way to crush the negative influence of those who oppose justice and truth. Warfare and bloodshed are inevitable. The *mahdi* will rise with the sword to wipe out tyrants. War and bloodshed are part of his official task to make Islam a universal faith and to confront injustice and tyranny. He might even create new weapons to overpower all known weaponry of his time.[295]

The *mahdi* will purify Islam by removing from it all innovations and wrong interpretations that accumulated over the ages.

He will institute the penal laws of classical Islam without any leniency. He will guide the people back to the original Islam which they have forgotten.

Mahmoud Ahmadinejad, current President of Iran, has an activist belief in the *mahdi's* imminent return and has placed this belief at the centre of Iran's domestic and foreign policy. *Mahdaviat* is the term used to describe the belief in the *mahdi* and the efforts made to prepare for his return. There is no doubt that *mahdaviat* is a central part of Ahmadinejad's world-view and that it influences his statements and policies.[296] It is alleged that as Mayor of Tehran he secretly instructed the city council in 2004 to build a grand avenue to prepare for the *mahdi*.[297]

President Ahmadinejad urges Iranians to work hard for the return of the hidden *mahdi*. In a speech to senior clerics on 16 November 2005 he stated that his government's main mission was to "pave the path for then glorious reappearance of Imam *mahdi* (may God hasten his reappearance)" He also warned that Iranians must "refrain from leaning toward any Western school of thought" and that Iran must be turned into a "mighty, advanced and model Islamic society" so as to prepare for the *mahdi*. Reports in Tehran also allege that after his accession to the presidency in 2005, Ahmadinejad told regime officials that the Hidden Imam would return in two years.[298]

There are also persistent rumours that Ahmadinejad's new cabinet had drawn up a contract with the *mahdi* promising to work for his return in exchange for his support. It was said that the Minister of Islamic Guidance, Mohammad-Hossein Saffar-Harandi had been sent to Jamkaran (near Qom) to deposit the contract in a well where the Imam is believed to be hiding and from which he will reappear, thus sealing the deal. A report claims that Parviz Davoudi, First Deputy President, submitted this pact to the cabinet which ratified it in a formal meeting.[300]

There are allegations that Ahmadinejad is linked to the Hojjatieh, the radical Shi'a anti-Sunni and anti-Bahai movement that was banned by Ayatollah Khomeini in 1983 because of its objections to his doctrine of *velayat-e faqih*. The Hojjatieh seem to believe that chaos must be created to hasten the coming of the *mahdi* who will establish the final genuine Islamic state.[301] Ahmadinejad too seems to believe that an apocalyptic conflagration will precede the return of the *mahdi* so that chaos on an international scale is a legitimate precursor to the return of the Hidden Imam.[302] Nuclear weapons in the hands of Iran would seem to be an ideal tool for encouraging such chaos and for proffering to the *mahdi* to ensure his victory. Ahmadinejad seems bent on confrontation with the West over Israel and over Iran's nuclear programme. Critics say this explains his reckless statements and policies as he seems to believe that a nuclear war with Israel and the USA would speed the return of the *mahdi*.[303]

Ahmadinejad seems to be a devout believer in the imminent return of the *mahdi* and considers it to be his and his government's responsibility to pave the way for this event. He has mentioned the twelfth Imam in almost every one of his public speeches. Constructing the perfect powerful Islamic state seems to be part of this preparation, a tool to be handed over to the *mahdi* on his return which he can then use to fulfil his programme. For him, the whole mission of the Iranian Revolution was to prepare the way for the *mahdi*.[304]

It does not seem that Ahmadinejad claims to be the *mahdi* himself. Rather he may see himself as one who prepares the way for the *mahdi*'s appearance, one who hastens his coming. This does not preclude the possibility that, as they did with Khomeini, devout Iranians may nurse the hope that Ahmedinejad is himself the promised and awaited *mahdi*.

Some characteristics of the *mahdi* according to Shi'a sources[305]

- He is a descendent of Muhammad, from the offspring of Muhammad's daughter, Fatima and her son Hussein.

- He was born in 868 and is still alive though invisible (in occultation).

- He went into occultation when he was five years old.

- His father is the 11th Shi'a Imam, Hasan al-'Askari.

- His mother is Narjis, a Byzantine princess.

- Twelver Shi'a Muslims believe that the *mahdi* is the 12th and last of the Shi'a Imams.

- His first name is Muhammad.

- He is tall.

- His facial features are similar to those of Muhammad.

- His character is like that of Muhammad.

- The *mahdi* is supposed to be 40 years old when he appears.

- A loud call from the sky signals the *mahdi's* appearance.

- He emerges during the last days of the world from Mecca.

- He and Jesus are two different individuals.

- He precedes the second appearance of Jesus.

- He establishes justice, peace and truth throughout the world by establishing Islam as the global religion.

- Upon his emergence, the young among his followers, without any prior appointment, reach Mecca that very night.

- Each of his soldiers has the power of forty strong men.

- A large number of non-believers will convert to Islam once they see that the signs which were prophesied have occurred.

- His physical appearance:

Abu Ja'far ibn Ali al-Baqir said, Imam Ali, may Allah be pleased with him, was asked about the physical appearance of the Mahdi and said: He is a well built youth with a handsome face whose hair reaches his shoulders. The light of his face is contrasted by the darkness of his hair and beard.[306]

Sunni *Mahdism*

Traditional Sunni teachings on the *mahdi*[307] state that he will appear towards the end of time. He will be slender, brown-skinned man of medium height, with a broad forehead, a high, hooked nose, finely arched eyebrows, clear, dark eyes, white teeth with gaps between them, and slightly bow-legged. One translation states that he is a little slow of speech. When he is delayed, he will strike his left thigh with his right and. He will be 40 years old, although one variant says that he will be between 30 and 40. He will be humble towards Allah.[308]

After the appearance of the *mahdi*, Jesus will appear and both will fight *al-Dajjal*. The *mahdi* will fight the enemies of Islam, establishes right and justice and eliminates evil and corruption.[309]

There will be increased *fitna* (civil strife), killings and idolatry. Many (in some versions, thirty) false prophets will arise. The Byzantines (or the Romans) will attack north Syria (the A'maq). Many will be killed, but the Muslims prevail and conquer Constantinople. *Al-Dajjal* (who is blind in his right eye, and has the word *kafir* written between his eyes) emerges to fight the Muslims. He makes Jerusalem his centre, but cannot take Mecca or Medina. Jesus appears and kills him.

The *mahdi* will come from Medina to Mecca, where he will stand between the *Rukn* (corner)[310] and the *Maqam*[311] to receive the pledge of allegiance. An army from Syria will be sent against him, but it will be swallowed up by the earth between Mecca and Medina. An army will come to help him from the east from beyond the river (Central Asia), or from Khurasan, carrying black banners. The *mahdi* will conquer Persia and Rome, then fight *al-Dajjal* and win. The *mahdi* will destroy ornate buildings, even mosques, and build simple structures in their place.[312] The *mahdi* will rule for seven years (or five or nine) and fill the land with justice and prosperity, then he will die.

Some *hadith* claim that the *mahdi* himself will come from the East. Some state that the *mahdi* and Jesus are the same person.

Sunnis believe that various "Signs of the Hour"[313] will happen at the end of time.

We have no doubt that the awaited Mahdee (or rightly-guided Imam) will come forth from among the *Ummah* of the Prophet at the end of time (on earth). We believe in the Signs of the Hour, the appearance of ad-Dajjal (false-Messiah or Antichrist), the descent from heaven of Isa, son of Mary, the sun rising from the West, the emergence of the Beast from the earth, and other signs mentioned in the Qur'an and the authentic Hadeeth of the Prophet.[314]

The Signs of the Hour are divided into two groups: the Lesser and the Greater Signs. The Lesser Signs are moral, cultural, political and natural events serving to warn people that the end is near. They include moral decay, crime, natural disasters, and wars. The Greater Signs are regarded as a map to the future, giving details of a series of events with ever-increasing severity preceding the end of the world. These include war between Byzantium and the Muslims, the conquest of Constantinople, the appearance of *al-Dajjal* to tempt and seduce the Muslims, the appearance of the *mahdi*, the descent of Jesus to kill *al-Dajjal* and Gog and Magog.

Some Differences Between Shi'a and Sunni *Mahdism*

Sunni *mahdism* has many similarities to Shi'a *mahdism*, but also some significant differences. Following are some of the traditions in Sunni eschatology that differ from Shi'a *mahdism*:

- For Sunnis, the *mahdi*, while a descendant of Muhammad and Fatima, will be a descendant of Hassan, not of Hussein as the Shi'a believe.

- here is far more material in Sunni eschatological teaching about *al-Dajjal* than about the *mahdi*. It also deals much more with Jesus and his role than does Shi'a teaching.

- In Sunni traditional apocalyptic the Sufyani is sometimes a positive hero in the region of Syria.[315] In Shi'a eschatology the Sufyani is always an evil anti-*mahdi* figure.[316]

- Sunni *mahdism* places Jerusalem at centre of the *mahdi* apocalyptic. Jerusalem, not Mecca or Medina, has always been accepted as the city most connected to al-Dajjal, Jesus and the *mahdi*.[317] According to some, al-Dajjal reigns in Jerusalem, the *mahdi* and Jesus defeat him there, the *ka'ba* will come from Mecca to Jerusalem, and Jerusalem is depicted as the site of the Last Judgement and the resurrection. In Shi'a eschatology, Kufa is the *mahdi's* capital.

- Sunni eschatology is more prone than the Shi'a version to speculate on the exact date of the end. Shi'a apocalyptic warns against attempts at determining the exact date: A Shi'a *hadith* attributed to the Imam Muhammad al-Baqir states: "Those that specify times lie",[318] or "Any one who fixes the time of the appearance is telling a falsehood".[319]

- Sunni apocalyptic has much to say about Jesus and the *Dajjal*. In Shi'a apocalyptic, the messianic figure of the *mahdi* is the primary focus, representing the collective hopes and dreams of the oppressed Shi'a throughout history.[320]

- In Sunni apocalyptic, Jerusalem is the capital of the *mahdi*. In Shi'a apocalyptic, the messianic capital is Kufa in Iraq, 'Ali's capital. The *mahdi* first destroys many buildings in Kufa before rebuilding the city.[321] All Shi'a will gather to Kufa, their lives will be lengthened and there will be plenty for all.

- Compared to the Sunni version, Shi'a apocalyptic relies more on supernatural help and heroes resurrected out of the tragic past. Also, there do not seem to be large disciplined armies as in Sunni apocalyptic.

7
The Practicalities of *Jihad*

The practical rules of *jihad* are laid down in the source texts and in the classical legal texts of Islam. As we have seen, Muhammad himself and his companions serve as examples of how to practise jihad, models to be emulated by the *umma*.

The call by Islamists of the twentieth and twenty-first centuries for a return to the source texts of Islam and to the model of the early Islamic state has led to a renewal of the cruel customs sanctified by the example of Muhammad and his companions. What in other cultures and religions (and in liberal Islam) can be explained as primitive cultural excesses of a distant past are accorded by Islamists the prestige of being holy precedents set by the founders of Islam and divinely approval. The apparently callous practices of various Islamic terrorist groups have their basis in this doctrinal view.

Just as *shari'a* in previous centuries often served the state through the *ulama* to control religious excesses and heresies, so *shari'a* also prevented worse military excesses which might otherwise have occurred without the existence of the *shari'a* regulations governing *jihad*.

Declarations of War

According to *shari'a* the Muslim aggressors must first invite the enemy to convert to Islam before attacking them. If the invitation is accepted there is no attack. This principle of giving an opportunity to avoid attack (on certain terms) is also to be found in antiquity.[322]

Ibn Abi Zayd al-Qayrawani wrote:

We Malikis maintain that it is preferable not to begin hostilities with the enemy before having invited the latter to embrace the religion of Allah except where the enemy attacks first. They have the alternative of either converting to Islam or paying the *jizya,* short of which war will be declared against them.[323]

The majority view is that only the lawful caliph can declare war,[324] giving the enemy the opportunity to convert to Islam (and perhaps a three day period in which to decide) before opening hostilities.[325] Al-Mawardi has already been quoted making it very plain that no attack must be launched until the enemy had been offered the opportunity to convert to Islam in as clear and attractive a way as possible (see chapter 3). Ibn Rushd attributes the necessity to invite the enemy to convert to Islam before attacking to God's own example recorded in the Qur'an.[326]

> Nor would We visit with Our Wrath until We had sent an apostle (to give warning). Q 17:15

There is also a clear instruction by Muhammad recorded in the *hadith*.

> It has been reported from Sulaiman b. Buraid through his father that when the Messenger of Allah appointed anyone as leader of any army or detachment he would exhort him to fear Allah and to be good to the Muslims who were with him. He would say: "… When you meet your enemies who are polytheists, invite them to three courses of action. If they respond to any one of these, you also accept it and withhold yourself from doing them any harm. Invite them to (accept) Islam; if they respond to you accept it from them and desist from fighting them…If they refuse to accept Islam, demand from them the *jizya.* If they agree to pay, accept it from them and hold off your hands. If they refuse to pay the tax, seek Allah's help and fight them… *Sahih Muslim Book 19, Number 4294*

A number of early texts provide us with examples of the actual words used to issue these ultimatums. Usually couched in diplomatic language rather than overtly threatening, it is important to recognise the true message within them i.e. "Convert to Islam or we will attack." The following example was supposedly sent by Muhammad to the Byzantine emperor Heraclius.[327]

> In the name of Allah, the Gracious, the Merciful. From Muhammad the servant of Allah and Apostle to Heraqle [Heraclius], the Grand Chief of Byzantines: Peace be unto those who followed the right path. Thence I call upon you with the call of Islam, submit [to Islam] and you will be safe, [if you do] God will reward you twice, if you decline, then you will be liable to the sins of peasants. 'O people of the book! Come to common terms as between us and you, that we worship none but God, that we associate no partner with Him; that we erect not, from among ourselves, lords and patrons other than God. If they turn back, say ye: Bear witness that we are Muslims [they who have surrendered].[328]

To another Christian leader, the Patriarch of the Egyptian Copts, Muhammad wrote in similar vein, inviting him to embrace Islam and promised him a two-fold reward by God for his acceptance and for those who would follow in his footsteps but warning him, if he declined, of being accountable for himself and for all the Copts. The letter continued:

> O people of the Book, come to the common terms between us and you, that we shall worship none but Allah, and that we shall ascribe no partner unto Him, and that none of us shall take others for lords beside Allah. And if they turn away, then say: Bear witness that we are they who have surrendered unto Him.[329]

In a letter to Juraij bin Matta, the Coptic viceregent of Egypt and Alexandria (called Muqawqas in the Arabic sources), Muhammad invites Muqawqas to accept Islam. If Muqawqas fails to respond to this invitation, Muhammad says, he will bear responsibility for the evil that will befall his people:

> Peace be upon him who follows true guidance. Thereafter, I invite you to accept Islam. Therefore, if you want security, accept Islam. If you accept Islam, Allah the Sublime, shall reward you doubly. But if you refuse to do so, you will bear the burden of the transgression of all the Copts.[330]

A slightly less subtle example was sent by one of Muhammad's commanders to the Persians. The phrase about "loving to be killed" is a typical Islamic warning of imminent attack. Often it is expressed as saying that Muslims love death.[331]

> Peace be to those who follow the guidance. To proceed: We summon you to Islam, but if you refuse then pay the *jizya* in submission feeling humbled. If you refuse to do that, I have with me people who love being killed in God's path as the Persians love wine. Peace to those who follow the guidance.

Shi'a Muslims face a difficulty over the need for the imam to declare war. The majority of them believe that their last imam disappeared in 873 and they are still waiting for his return as the *mahdi*.[332] Ayatollah Khomeini, who overthrew the Shah of Iran in 1979, managed to get around this by his doctrine of *velayat-e faqih*[333] which overcame Shi'a resistance to political action in the absence of the rightful imam.

Modern Muslims still declare *jihad*. While traditionalists ascribe the authority to declare *jihad* to their present rulers in lieu of the legitimate caliph, many Islamists arrogate this authority to the leaders of their organisations. Calls for *jihad* have thus proliferated in the Sunni world in recent years. While in Mecca in 1978 Yasser Arafat declared a *jihad* to liberate Palestine.[334] Osama bin Laden's "Declaration of war against the Americans occupying the land of the two holy places",[335] dated August 23rd 1996, runs to 22 pages.[336] It uses the traditional language of "loving death" to make its threat.

> I say to you William[337] that: These youths love death as you love life. They inherit dignity, pride, courage, generosity, truthfulness and sacrifice from father to father. They are most delivering and steadfast at war.[338]

The leader of Laskar Jihad, an Islamic terrorist group active in Indonesia, particularly in Maluku and Sulawesi, issued a declaration of war which, like many modern Islamic declarations of war, gloated over American military failures. The first part was addressed to Muslims, urging them to prepare for war. The second part was addressed to the enemy:

You listen to this. Woe to the pawns of America. You listen to this. Woe to the pawns of the World Council of Churches. You listen to this. Woe to the pawns of the Zionist Crusaders. You listen to this. Woe to the Jews and the Christians. We the Muslim people invite the army of America to prove their strength here in Maluku. Let us fight to the bitter end. Let us prove for the umpteenth time that the Muslim people cannot be defeated by the physical strength which is always boasted about. The events of the second Afghanistan will take place in Maluku when you are determined to carry out your threats. Woe to America. Now you! Woe to America who is now suffering various defeats, various awesome beatings in Afghanistan. Let us meet like men on the battlefield...[339]

An Indonesian *jihad* manual, published in 2001, states as a "military doctrine of Islam" that before attacking the enemy it is necessary to give them give warning and teaching so that they wake up and accept Islam as their religion and submit to Islamic power.[340]

Invitations to embrace Islam or face the consequences, closely modelled on the early examples quoted above, have been announced regularly by the British-based Islamist group al-Muhajiroun, often in London's Trafalgar Square. These statements could be interpreted (and probably are by those issuing them) as a traditional Islamic declaration of war on non-Muslims. In a press release preparing for the "Rally for Islam" on July 23rd 2000 at Trafalgar Square, al-Muhajiroun stated:

This Summer will once again witness an extraordinary public call to the British public, The Prime Minister and The Queen from Muslims in Britain to embrace Islam as a spiritual and as a political belief. Leaders from the Muslim community here and abroad will address the masses throughout a day on various issues affecting society not only in Britain but globally. The public invitation in Trafalgar Square in London on Sunday the 23rd of July 2000 will be the fourth time Al-Muhajiroun have brought converts to Islam from various backgrounds including Hindu, Sikh, Christian, Jew and atheist to come out openly and publicly declaring why they left their previous beliefs and have decided to embrace Islam. The above event has always attracted thousands of people and this year is another chance to see why Islam is the fastest growing religion in the West. An opportunity for everyone to discover more about Islam as an economic, ritual, social, judicial or ruling system will be on the agenda.[341]

In January 2005 Omar Bakri Muhammad, leader of al-Muhajiroun, issued a declaration clearly stating his understanding of being at war with Britain:

> I believe the whole of Britain has become Dar ul-Harb (land of war)... The kuffar (non-believer) has no sanctity for their own life or property.[342]

Rules of Engagement

The conduct of war was governed by detailed rules, which generally forbade the killing of women, children and other non-combatants. Caliph Abu Bakr (632-634), Muhammad's immediate successor as leader of the Muslim community, established the principle that there should be no unnecessary destruction of property. This is derived from Abu Bakr's address to the first expedition sent to the Syrian border.[343] However, variations on the rules occur amongst the different Islamic jurists, many of them taking a more ruthless line than Abu Bakr. Indeed, variations on the rules even occurred during the jurisdiction of Muhammad himself. For example, treachery and mutilation[344] were prohibited by Muhammad until the Muslims found themselves on the receiving end of such behaviour at the hands of the Meccans. He then changed his ruling and ordered his followers to retaliate in a similar way.[345]

Non-combatants

The Sunni jurists are agreed that in general non-combatants who did not participate in the fighting should be unharmed during the fighting. This included women, children, monks, the elderly, blind and insane. However, a certain branch of the

Kharijis did permit the killing of women and children.[346] When towns were taken by force, women and children were included in the captives who could be enslaved or ransomed.

Some Hanafi and Shafi'i Sunni jurists held that peasants and merchants who did not participate in the fighting should be unharmed.[347] If the elderly or monks did anything to assist the enemy they were no longer exempt from attack.[348]

A comment by Shaybani permitting attack on a city by mangonels, flooding or fire, despite the risk to enemy non-combatants has already been quoted (see chapter 3).[349] He also allowed the cutting of water supplies, the poisoning of water supplies, and the use of poisoned or burning arrows.[350] (Some jurists specifically banned the use of poisoned arrows.)[351]

We have already seen Shaybani's instructions for how Muslims should respond to the enemy's use of Muslim children as human shield (see chapter 3).

The spoils of war

Classical *jihad* theory had elaborate rules derived from the Qur'an and *hadith* on the division of spoils after *jihad*. The intricate detail of these rules is exemplified by the twelfth cenutry Hanafi scholar Al-Marghinani's consideration of the plunder due to a cavalryman in every conceivable situation, which was examined in chapter 3. The spoils of war are considered to include captives (men, women and children), immovables like land and buildings, and movables like livestock, gold, silver and precious stones. Every warrior received his prescribed share of the booty which included captured persons as slaves and concubines. A fifth of all booty was set aside for the caliph and the state; there are elaborate rules on how to dispose of this fifth of the spoils.

It would seem that the desire for booty was second only to the religious command of *jihad* as a motivating force in the early Muslim expansion. During one of the early Muslim raids into Armenia, Habib ibn Maslamah al-Fihri, who was in command of the army in Armenia wrote to the Caliph 'Uthman asking for reinforcements. 'Uthman responded by ordering the governor of Syria, Mu'awiyya, to help:

'Uthman wrote to Mu'awiyah asking him to send to Habib a body of men from Syria and Mesopotamia interested in "holy war" and booty.[352]

Booty is here seen on almost the same level as "holy war" (*jihad*) as motivating the troops being sent out.

Seven centuries later and thousands of miles away the Mongol conqueror Timurlane (1336-1405) made the same link between religious merit and acquisition of plunder as legitimate motivations:

My principal object in coming to Hindustan... has been to accomplish two things. The first was to war with the infidels, the enemies of the Mohammadan religion; and by this religious warfare to acquire some claim to reward in the life to come. The other was... that the army of Islam might gain something by plundering the wealth and valuables of the infidels: plunder in war is as lawful as their mothers' milk to Musalmans who war for their faith, and the consuming of that which is lawful is a means of grace.[353]

The early Muslim sources are replete with stories of immense quantities of plunder taken after every battle, and on how some of it was sent back to the caliph. For instance, after Muslim forces under Khalid ibn al-Walid took the fortress of Amghishiya in Iraq in 633, al-Tabari notes;

The victors took spoils in it the like of which they never obtained again... the share of a horseman reached one thousand five hundred [dirhams], aside from additional spoils allotted to those who had stood out.[354]

And on another occasion:

Khalid took the children captive, sent God's fifth to Abu Bakr with al-Nu'man b, 'Awt and al-Nu'man al-Shaybani, and divided the spoils and the captives [among the troops].[355]

Later Muslim sources continue the decription of the vast amounts of loot taken from conquered territories. India attracted continued raids over centuries because of its vast wealth. The sources repeatedly mention that the Muslim armies obtained unlimited riches as booty from the destroyed temples and sacred sites, as well as in tribute from the vanquished rulers. These included precious stones, rubies and pearls, gold and silver in coins and ingots or bullion, as well as gold and silver icons, which represented wealth accumulated over centuries. According to *Ta'rikh-i-Firishta*, after just one raid,

> Mahmud [of Ghazna] broke down or burned all the idols, and amassed a vast quantity of gold and silver, of which the idols were mainly composed... Then he went back to Ghazna with twenty millon dirhams worth of gold and silver bullion. And the private spoils of the army were no less than that which came into the royal treasury.[356]

In fact, the Muslim Ghaznavid and Ghurid conquests in North India in the eleventh and twelfth centuries have been likened to a gold rush, the amount of booty taken in gold and silver being staggering.[357]

There are two kinds of spoil:[358] *ghanima* is the booty taken in battle and by force of arms; *fay'* is the booty obtained without fighting and includes payments given as part of a truce agreement, the poll tax (*jizya*) on *dhimmis*, taxes on merchandise, and the land tax.

Ghanima is the wider category, and included prisoners of war, captured women and children, land and property. Money received as ransom payment for prisoners is added to the *ghanima*. A fifth of the *ghanima* is set aside for the caliph, the rest is divided among those who fought in the battle.

The fifth of the *fay'* set apart for the caliph was to be divided into five equal parts, one for the caliph himself, the other parts for Muhammad's nearest in kin (the Hashemites), for needy orphans, the poor and for travellers in need. Four-fifths of the *fay'* were to be used to cover army pay and other essential expenses.

The looting of captured towns for a specified number of days (usually three) was accepted as legitimate and regularly followed whenever a town that had militarily opposed the conquest was taken. Even the holy city of Medina was not spared the customary three days of pillage during the civil war between Yazid ibn-Mu'awiyya and 'Abdallah ibn al-Zubair. Yazid's commander, Muslim ibn 'Uqba, after defeating the Medinan forces supporting ibn al-Zubair in 683, allowed his forces to pillage Medina for three days:

> Muslim gave up Medina to pillage for three days, they killed the people and seized the goods.[359]

After every battle, Muslim warriors gathered all the spoil they could from the battlefield and from the bodies of the dead. Captives (men, women and children) were enslaved. Dionysius of Tel Mahre (818-845), the great Syriac historian, reports that after one of the first battles in Palestine:

> The Arabs switched their attention to the fortified camp of the Romans [Byzantines] and secured for themselves more gold, silver, expensive clothing, slaves and slave-girls than they could count. Rich men they became that day and much wealth they acquired.[360]

Following the capture of Constantinople in 1453, Sultan Mehmet II, the Conqueror, reduced the time allowed for pillaging and looting of the city to just one day, so great was his fear of the potential destruction of the city he intended to make his new capital. Even so, in addition to material loot, almost half the city's population was sold into slavery.

Destruction of property

Abu Bakr's principle of no unnecessary destruction was supported fully by al-Awza'i (d. 774) and al-Thawri (d. 778) but greatly limited by many other jurists, including the founders of the four schools of Sunni law.[361] For example Malik, who compiled the first collection of *hadiths* under the title *Muwatta'* (*Way Made Smooth*), permits the destruction of everything except the flock and beehives. Hanifa requires the destruction of everything that cannot be brought under the control of the Islamic forces; this includes houses, churches, trees, flocks and herds. Shafi'i allows the destruction of trees and all inanimate objects, but animals can only be killed if leaving them alive would strengthen the enemy.[362] Shaybani also permits the killing of animals, destruction of towns and cutting down of trees. Interestingly his reasons include not only the practical (preventing the enemy from using the destroyed items) but also the psychological (to humiliate and anger the enemy).

> I asked: If the believers in the territory of war capture spoil in which there are [animals such as] sheep, riding animals, cows which resist them and they are unable to drive them to the territory of Islam, or weapons which they are unable to carry away, what should they do [with them]?

> He replied: As to weapons and goods, they should be burned, but riding animals and sheep should be slaughtered and then burned.

> I asked: Why should not [the animals] be hamstrung?

> He replied: Because that is mutilation, which they should not do because it was prohibited by the Apostle of God. However, they should not leave anything that the inhabitants of the territory of war could make use of.

> I asked: Do you think that they should do the same with whatever [other] animals refuse to be driven away or with whatever weapons and goods are too heavy to carry?

> He replied: Yes.

> I asked: Do you think that it is objectionable for the believers to destroy whatever towns of the territory of war that they may encounter?

> He replied: No. Rather do I hold that this would be commendable. For do you not think that it is in accordance with God's saying, in His Book: "Whatever palm trees you have cut down or left standing upon their roots, has been by God's permission, in order that the ungodly ones might be

humiliated." So, I am in favour of whatever they did to deceive
and anger the enemy.[363]

Prisoners of war

The taking of prisoners of war (generally regarded in pre-Islamic
times as part of the booty and very cruelly treated) is a subject on
which the Qur'an gives some guidance:

> It is not fitting for an Apostle that he should have prisoners of
> war until he hath thoroughly subdued the land. Ye look for the
> temporal goods of this world; but God looketh to the Hereafter:
> And God is exalted in might, Wise. Had it not been for a previous
> ordainment from God, a severe penalty would have reached you
> for the (ransom) that ye took. But (now) enjoy what ye took in
> war, lawful and good. Q 8:67-9

According to A. Yusuf Ali's comment[364] this means that the
motive of worldly gain (by demanding a ransom) was not normally
approved, so prisoners should not normally be taken. If, however,
many lives had already been lost in battle it might be better to take
prisoners. On this principle, 70 prisoners were taken at the Battle
of Badr (624) and ransomed.

The first part of the above verse appears to indicate that prisoners
should not be taken in the early stages of a war, but once the
enemy is defeated, the loss of life can be reduced and prisoners
taken. In the *Interpretation of the Meanings of The Noble Qur'an
in the English language*, the Saudi-approved English translation of
the Qur'an by Al-Hilali and Khan, this verse is translated as:[365]

> It is not for a Prophet that he should have prisoners of war (and
> free them with ransom) until he has made a great slaughter
> (among his enemies) in the land. You desire the good of this
> world (i.e. the money of ransom for freeing the captives), but
> Allah desires (for you) the Hereafter. And Allah is All-Mighty,
> All-Wise. Q 8:67

This means that large numbers of enemy troops should first
be killed, and only in the later stages of battle can some be
taken prisoners as booty and for ransom. The human desire for
material gain from ransom and booty must be secondary to the

God-ordained tactic of beginning with a massive slaughter of the enemy. Abu'l A'la Mawdudi, the noted Islamist thinker, argued in his comments on this verse:

> Under no circumstances should the Muslim lose sight of this aim and start taking the enemy soldiers as captives. Captives should be taken after the enemy has been completely crushed.[366]

Historically, Muslim armies have frequently resorted to this method, and campaigns of mass killings of perceived enemies, combatants and civilians, are customary even in contemporary struggles and civil wars. The recent conflicts in Lebanon, Algeria, Afghanistan, and now in Iraq, offer many examples of indiscriminate slaughter, including that of men, women and children, with the psychological aim of striking terror in the hearts of the enemy and causing him to surrender.

Another verse states:

> So, when you meet (in fight – *Jihad* in Allah's Cause) those who disbelieve, smite (their) necks till when you have killed and wounded many of them, bind a bond firmly (on them, i.e. take term as captives). Thereafter (is the time) either for generosity (i.e. free them without ransom), or ransom (according to what benefits Islam), until the war lays down its burden. Q 47:4 (al-Hilali & Khan translation)

With such a variety of possibilities, it is small wonder that the issue of prisoners of war is one on which the various schools of *shari'a* differ considerably. Some jurists, following Q 47:4, completely forbid the execution of prisoners and permit them only to be ransomed or freed. Others permit the execution of prisoners, but often hedge this with provisos, for example, that they should be given the opportunity to convert to Islam instead, or that there should be a military need to reduce the strength of the enemy. Other options include not only ransoming or setting free for nothing, but also enslaving them or exchanging them for Muslim prisoners. There was general agreement that women and children prisoners should not be killed but enslaved (however, if they were not of the People of the Book, they could be killed).

The following is the guidance given by Ibn Naqib in *Reliance of the Traveller*:

> Whoever enters Islam before being captured may not be killed or his property confiscated, or his young children taken captive.

> When a child or a woman is taken captive, they become slaves by the fact of capture, and the woman's previous marriage is immediately annulled.

> When an adult male is taken captive, the caliph considers the interests (of Islam and the Muslims) and decides between the prisoner's death, slavery, release without paying anything, or ransoming himself in exchange for money or for a Muslim captive held by the enemy. If the prisoner becomes a Muslim (before the caliph chooses any of the four alternatives) then he may not be killed, and one of the other three alternatives is chosen.[367]

Abu Yusuf also held that the fate of the prisoners (death or ransom) should be decided on the basis of the interests of the Muslims.[368] Shaybani also affirmed this, clearly stating that male prisoners of war should be killed if that would be advantageous to the Muslims, unless they were willing to convert to Islam (in which case they would be enslaved) or had previously been granted a safe-conduct (in which case they would be freed).[369] Any blind, disabled or insane prisoners of war should not be killed.[370] However, elsewhere Shaybani says that male prisoners unable to walk were to be killed, whereas transport had to be hired for women and children prisoners unable to walk.[371] The Kharijis generally held that prisoners should be killed, but only extremist Kharijis such as the followers of Nafi' ibn al-Azraq always adhered to this rule.[372]

In practice, the slaughter of men and the enslavement of women and children of defeated towns became a common practice in the expanding Islamic empire.[373] Indeed, it came to be seen as a *shari'a* rule that could not be changed. Following a victory in battle by Subuktigin of Ghazna around the year 1000, in his second invasion of North India, the Muslim chronicler al-'Utbi commented that the orders God had given to the first generation of Muslims were still valid:

> It is the order of God respecting those who have passed away that
> infidels should be put to death; and the order of God is not changed
> respecting your execution of the same precept.[374]

Muslim prisoners captured by the enemy were under no
obligation to submit to or obey their captors; they could escape
(unless they had promised not to) or destroy enemy property if they
had opportunity.[375] Muslim prisoners were not to give any valuable
information to the enemy, must refuse to fight against Islam, and
must not renounce their faith unless forced to do so.[376]

Hostage-taking and kidnapping

In the last section, we saw that the taking hostages for ransom
was sanctioned both by Muhammad's example at the Battle of Badr
and by the Qur'an. Demanding ransom for captives taken in war
(or kidnapped in raids) became a customary practice and a source
of wealth to Muslim commanders. Hostage-taking is still a normal
way for tribes to secure concessions from central government in
contemporary Muslim states such as Yemen.

Those who seek to present Islam in the best light to Westerners
claim that kidnapping and hostage-taking are contrary to *shari'a*,
especially when the hostages are foreigners granted visas by a
Muslim government, and are thus categorised as under its protection
(*musta'minin*).[377] Also, it is forbidden to kidnap innocent people
or civilians. Yet even these apologists for Islam concede that such
practices are legitimate in times of war. Islamic radicals counter
that the *umma* is in a state of *jihad* against illegitimate and infidel
governments which justifies raiding and kidnapping according
to Muhammad's own example. Further, they say that in modern
warfare there are no innocent civilians; all civilians are combatants,
because they support the aggressive government by participation in
elections and by paying taxes. A Salafi-Jihadi ideologue, Hammoud
al-'Uqla al-Shuaybi, issued a *fatwa* following September 11th 2001
which ran:

> [W]e should know that whatever decision the non-Muslim state,
> America, takes - especially critical decisions which involve war - it
> is taken based on opinion polls and/or voting within the House

of Representatives and Senate, which represent directly, the exact opinion of the people they represent - the people of America - through their representatives in the Parliament [Congress]. Based on this, any American who voted for war is like a fighter, or at least a supporter.[378]

Osama bin Laden and al-Qaʿeda have used the same logic.

It is a fundamental principle of any democracy that the people choose their leaders, and as such, approve and are party to the actions of their elected leaders ... By electing these leaders, the American people have given their consent to the incarceration of the Palestinian people, the demolition of Palestinian homes and the slaughter of the children of Iraq. This is why theAmerican people are not innocent. The American people are active members in all these crimes.

Statement From Shaykh Usama Bin Ladin, May God Protect Him, and Al Qaeda Organization[379]

Radical Islamist groups not only find legitimacy for their taking of hostages in the Muslim sources, but also appreciate the enhanced psychological effect of such methods in the era of modern mass media. Hizbullah kidnapped many Western hostages in Lebanon in the 1980s. Radicals in Iraq have resorted to the same technique in recent years, together with the beheading of some hostages to increase the reaction of fear and terror. ʿAbd al-Aziz al-Muqrin, head of al-Qaʿeda in Saudi Arabia until he was killed by security forces in June 2004, wrote a guide on kidnapping which was published in the al-Qaʿeda online magazine, *Muʿaskar al-Battar* in May 2004. While stating that hostages should be treated according to *shariʿa*, he posited five goals for kidnapping:[380]

1 Force governments to fulfil specific demands.

2 Create problems for a government in its relations with the hostages' home country.

3 Obtain important information from the hostages.

4 Obtain ransom money to provide financial support for the organisation.

5 Draw attention to specific concerns.

Beheading and throat-slitting

Muslims often choose to kill their opponents by beheading, both in battle and when executing captives. Of course, this practice is far from unique to Islam, but Muslims are encouraged to use this method by the example of Muhammad, especially in his dealing with the Jewish tribe the Banu Qurayza. A more detailed account of this incident is given towards the end of this chapter, but in summary Muhammad ordered the beheading of 600 to 900 of their adult males even though they had surrendered:

> Then the apostle went out to the market of Medina (which is still its market today) and dug trenches in it. Then he sent for them and struck off their heads in those trenches as they were brought out to him in batches. Among them was the enemy of Allah Huyayy b. Akhtab and Ka'b b. Asad their chief. There were 600 or 700 in all, though some put the figure as high as 800 or 900... This went on until the apostle made an end of them.[381]

The Qur'an also encourages Muslims in *jihad* to decapitate their enemies:

> Therefore when ye meet the Unbelievers (in fight) smite at their necks. Q 47:4

> Remember thy Lord inspired the angels (with the message): "I am with you: give firmness to the believers: I will instil terror into the hearts of the unbelievers: smite ye above their necks and smite all their finger-tips off them." Q 8:12

In the battle of Ullays against Persians and Christian Arabs in Iraq in 633-634, Khalid Ibn al-Walid, the famous Muslim commander, ordered the beheading of numerous prisoners of war after they had been captured:

Khalid then commanded his herald to proclaim to the men: "Capture! Capture! Do not kill any except he who continues to resist". As a result, the cavalry brought prisoners in droves, driving them along the canal. Khalid had detailed certain men to cut off their heads in the canal. He did that to them for a day and a night. They pursued them the next day and the day after, until they reached al-Nahrayn and the like of that distance in every direction from Ullays. And Khalid cut of their heads.[382]

Khalid also beheaded all the men in the fortress of 'Ayn Tamr in Iraq who had surrendered to him.[383] On another occasion he upbraided soldiers in his army who did not behead some of their captives, saying:

> What is the matter between me and you? Do you keep the custom of the Jahiliyyah and neglect the commandment of Islam?[384]

Khalid thus expressed his belief that having mercy on prisoners of war was a pagan custom, abolished by Islam which was made of sterner stuff.

In the civil wars over the succession to Muhammad, beheading was a favourite method of dealing with Muslim enemies. A certain Hujr ibn 'Adi from Kufa, who supported 'Ali, was sent by the governor (Ziyad) in chains to Mu'awiyya, who commented:

> By God, I will not be addressed by you or consider speaking to you. Take him out and behead him... Then he was brought forth and his head cut off.[385]

After Hussein ibn 'Ali, Muhammad's grandson, was killed in the battle of Karbala (680) by Yazid's troops, his head and the heads of seventy of his companions killed with him were displayed in Kufa:

> No sooner had al-Husayn been killed than on the very same day his head was despatched with Khawali b. Yazid and Humayd b. Muslim al-Azdi to 'Ubaydullah to Ziyad... The heads of the rest were cut off and [these] seventy-two heads were sent with Shamir b. Dhi al-Jawshan, Qays b. al-Ash'ath, 'Amr b. al-Hajjaj,

and 'Azrah b. Qays. They journeyed until they brought them to 'Ubaydullah b. Ziyad.[386]

Hussein's head was then sent to the Caliph Yazid in Damascus, where it was put on show.[387]

Rebels were often decapitated (or crucified). In Islamic Spain the Caliph al-Hakam I ordered the decapitation of some seven hundred notables of Toledo, following a rebellion in 807. They were invited to the castle as guests to a feast of reconciliation:

> Next morning the guests thronged to the fortress. They were not allowed to enter in a body, but were admitted one by one, while their horses were led away to the postern-door to await their masters. Now in the courtyard there was a great trench, whence the clay used in construction of the castle had been dug. Beside this trench stood executioners, and as each guest entered, the sword fell. For several hours this butchery continued.[388]

Decapitated heads were also used as trophies of war. Heads of enemy leaders were often sent to the caliph as proof that they had indeed been vanquished and killed. They were then publicly displayed as a mark of contempt and as a warning to would-be rebels. After the Almoravid victory at Zallaqa in Spain (1086), piles of heads severed from the bodies of the defeated Christians were loaded onto carts and sent to various cities of Muslim Andalusia to proclaim the victory.[389]

In 1396, following a victory of the Ottoman Sultan Bayezid at Nicopolis in Bulgaria over a Christian force composed mainly of French knights, the sultan ordered the three thousand who had surrendered decapitated:

> The next morning they were paraded before him, naked and in groups of three or four. The mass beheadings began early in the morning and continued through the day.[390]

Execution by beheading is an accepted punishment in Islamic criminal law, and is regularly practised in Saudi Arabia. Some 121 Saudis and foreigners were beheaded in 2000; 75 in 2001 and more than 50 were sentenced to death and beheaded in 2003.[391]

Slitting the throat of enemies was also perceived as a ritual slaughter, a sacrifice offered up to Allah to propitiate him. When 8,000 Armenian Christians were killed by Ottoman Muslims in Urfa in December 1895 the young men were killed by the traditional ritual Islamic method for slaughtering animals. They were thrown on their backs, held by their hands and feet, and then their throats were slit while a prayer was recited.[392]

Sometimes perpetrators and victims undergo ritual slaughter ceremonies to underline the religious motivation - perpetrators often participate in videoed ceremonies of dedication before going out on their missions. A recent example is the four-page Arabic document found in the luggage and cars of the perpetrators of the September 11th 2001 plane hijackings. Among other things it states:

> If God grants you a slaughter, you should perform it as an offering on behalf of your father and mother, for they are owed by you.[393]

Passengers killed in the hijackings and plane crashes are viewed as ritual sacrifices provided by God to the hijackers.[394]

Throat-slitting was widespread during the civil war in Algeria in the 1990s, hundreds of innocent civilians - men, women and children - had their throats ritually slit by radicals of the GIA (Armed Islamic Group) and other groups. Journalists, teachers and schoolgirls were an especial target of such murders. Here is an example:

> At 8.15 in the morning, six men holding hatchets, sawn-off shotguns and knives burst into the classroom at Oued Djer, a small village 50km south-west of Algiers. They seized fourteen-year-old Fatima Ghodbane and tore from her head the Islamic scarf she had only recently started wearing. As Fatima's classmates watched, the men dragged her outside and bound her hands with wire. One of the guerrillas pulled her head back by the hair and stabbed her several times in the face. Then he slit her throat.
>
> 'This is what happens to girls who go to university,' the murderer then told Fatima's classmates and teachers, shaking the knife, which was still covered in Fatima's blood. 'This is what happens

to girls who talk to policemen. This is what happens to girls who don't wear the *hidjab* [Islamic head-covering for women].'

Before dumping Fatima's body in front of the school gates, the killers carved the symbol of the Armed Islamic Group (GIA) on her hand. Fatima's death, in March 1995, is not an isolated case. According to the last recorded government figures, 101 teachers and 41 students of both sexes were killed in 1994 by Islamic extremists who attack schools because they are a symbol of the government.[395]

The Dutch film maker Theo Van Gogh had his throat slit on the streets of Amsterdam by Mohammed Bouyeri, a Dutch-born dual Moroccan-Dutch citizen, on 11 November 2004. Van Gogh had produced a film, *Submission,* which criticised the way Islam treated women. Following the release of the film he received many death threats from Muslims. In his trial, Bouyeri declared that "the law compels me to chop off the head of anyone who insults Allah and the prophet".[396]

Torture

The permissibility of torture in certain circumstances is based on Muhammad's example, who had ordered a man to be tortured in order to find out where he had buried his treasure.

Kinanah b. al-Rabi', who had the custody of the treasure of B. al-Nadir, was brought to the apostle who asked him about it... The apostle gave orders to al-Zubayr b. al-'Awwam, 'Torture him until you extract what he has', so he kindled a fire with flint and steel on his chest until he was nearly dead. Then the apostle delivered him to Muhammad b. Maslama and he struck off his head in revenge for his brother Mahmud.[397]

A *hadith* by Al-Bukhari gives another account of Muhammad ordering torture.

A group of eight men from the tribe of 'Ukil came to the Prophet and then they found the climate of Medina unsuitable for them. So, they said, "O Allah's Apostle! Provide us with some milk."

Allah's Apostle said, "I recommend that you should join the herd of camels." So they went and drank the urine and the milk of the camels (as a medicine) till they became healthy and fat. Then they killed the shepherd and drove away the camels, and they became unbelievers after they were Muslims. When the Prophet was informed by a shouter for help, he sent some men in their pursuit, and before the sun rose high, they were brought, and he had their hands and feet cut off. Then he ordered for nails which were heated and passed over their eyes, and they were left in the Harra (i.e. rocky land in Medina). They asked for water, and nobody provided them with water till they died (Abu Qilaba, a sub-narrator said, "They committed murder and theft and fought against Allah and His Apostle, and spread evil in the land.") *Sahih Bukhari Volume 4, Book 52, Number 261: Narrated Anas bin Malik*

While the punishments and execution methods specified in *shari'a* criminal law are brutal enough (amputation, flogging, beheading, crucifixion[398]), Muhammad in this case went far beyond the legal requirements, thus legitimising torture in the eyes of his followers. In the early sources there are repeated examples of people being tortured to force them to reveal hidden treasure, to convert to Islam, or out of revenge.

The Muslim conqueror of Sind, Muhammad ibn Qasim, is said to have been tortured to death by the Umayyad governor of Iraq, Salih bin 'Abdurrahman, as an act of revenge for the killing of his brother by Muhammad's uncle, Hajaj, the former governor of Iraq:

Muhammad, son of Kasim, was sent back a prisoner with Mu'awiyah, son of Muhallab... He was imprisoned by Salih at Wasit. Salih put him to torture, together with other persons of the family of Abu 'Ukail, until they expired: for Hajjaj had put to death Adam, Salih's brother, who professed the creed of the Kharijis.[399]

Slavery
The Qur'an accepts slavery as legitimate and often mentions slaves. It does not condemn slavery, although it does commend the spending of money to ransom slaves as a good deed:

> It is righteousness to believe in Allah and the Last Day and the Angels and the Book and the Messengers; to spend of your substance out of love for Him for your kin for orphans for the needy for the wayfarer for those who ask and for the ransom of slaves. Q 2.177

Muhammad and his companions kept slaves, enslaved captives and traded in slaves. Captive women could be taken as concubines, special permission being granted to Muhammad to allow him to do this in a Qur'anic verse:

> O prophet! We have made lawful to thee thy wives to whom thou hast paid their dowers; and those whom thy right hand possesses out of the prisoners of war whom Allah has assigned to thee; and daughters of thy paternal uncles and aunts and daughters of thy maternal uncles and aunts who migrated (from Mecca) with thee; and any believing woman who dedicates her soul to the Prophet if the Prophet wishes to wed her this only for thee and not for the Believers (at large); We know what We have appointed for them as to their wives and the captives whom their right hands possess in order that there should be no difficulty for Thee. And Allah is Oft-Forgiving Most Merciful Q 33:50

This verse clearly shows that according to the Qur'an, taking slaves in war was a God-given right. These slaves were considered spoils of war, and the women were usually destined to be concubines of the victorious warriors. Muhammad received his share in enslaved women.

The *hadith* include many references to slaves. Here is one in which Muhammad, in his attack on the Jews of Khaibar, took captives and encouraged one of his companions to take any slave girl he wished from the captives. Muhammad then took the chosen girl for himself:

> Anas said, 'When Allah's Apostle invaded Khaibar, we offered the Fajr prayer there (early in the morning) when it was still dark. The Prophet rode and Abu Talha rode too and I was riding behind Abu Talha. The Prophet passed through the lane of Khaibar quickly and my knee was touching the thigh of the Prophet .

He uncovered his thigh and I saw the whiteness of the thigh of the Prophet. When he entered the town, he said, 'Allahu Akbar! Khaibar is ruined. Whenever we approach near a (hostile) nation (to fight) then evil will be the morning of those who have been warned.' He repeated this thrice. The people came out for their jobs and some of them said, 'Muhammad (has come).' (Some of our companions added, "With his army.") We conquered Khaibar, took the captives, and the booty was collected. Dihya came and said, 'O Allah's Prophet! Give me a slave girl from the captives.' The Prophet said, 'Go and take any slave girl.' He took Safiya bint Huyai. A man came to the Prophet and said, 'O Allah's Apostle! You gave Safiya bint Huyai to Dihya and she is the chief mistress of the tribes of Quraiza and An-Nadir and she befits none but you.' So the Prophet said, 'Bring him along with her.' So Dihya came with her and when the Prophet saw her, he said to Dihya, 'Take any slave girl other than her from the captives.' Anas added: The Prophet then manumitted her and married her."

Thabit asked Anas, "O Abu Hamza! What did the Prophet pay her (as Mahr)?" He said, "Her self was her Mahr for he manumitted her and then married her." Anas added, "While on the way, Um Sulaim dressed her for marriage (ceremony) and at night she sent her as a bride to the Prophet . So the Prophet was a bridegroom and he said, 'Whoever has anything (food) should bring it.' He spread out a leather sheet (for the food) and some brought dates and others cooking butter. (I think he (Anas) mentioned As-Sawaq). So they prepared a dish of Hais (a kind of meal). And that was Walima (the marriage banquet) of Allah's Apostle ." *Sahih Al-Bukhari Hadith 1.367 Narrated by Abdul Aziz*

Hadith collections and *shari'a* manuals devote considerable space to legal rulings on slavery. These include rulings on the acquisition of slaves, on the freeing of slaves, on the status of female slaves, and much more. The following *hadith*, on non-returnable deposits, shows that dealing in slaves was no different from dealing in animals:

Yahya related to me from Malik from a reliable source from Amr ibn Shuayb from his father from his father's father that the Messenger of Allah, may Allah bless him and grant him peace, forbade transactions in which nonrefundable deposits were paid.

Malik said, "That is, in our opinion, but Allah knows best, that for instance, a man buys a slave or slave-girl or rents an animal and then says to the person from whom he bought the slave or leased the animal, 'I will give you a dinar or a dirham or whatever on the condition that if I actually take the goods or ride what I have rented from you, then what I have given you already goes towards payment of the goods or hire of the animal. If I do not purchase the goods or hire the animal, then what I have given you is yours without liability on your part.'"

Malik said, "According to the way of doing things with us there is nothing wrong in bartering an Arabic speaking merchant slave for Abyssinian slaves or any other type that are not his equal in eloquence, trading, shrewdness, and know-how. There is nothing wrong in bartering one slave like this for two or more other slaves with a stated delay in the terms if he is clearly different. If there is no appreciable difference between the slaves, two should not be bartered for one with a stated delay in the terms even if their racial type is different."

Malik said, "There is nothing wrong in selling what has been bought in such a transaction before taking possession of all of it as long as you receive the price for it from some one other than the original owner."

Malik said, "An addition to the price must not be made for a foetus in the womb of its mother when she is sold because that is gharar (an uncertain transaction). It is not known whether the child will be male or female, good-looking or ugly, normal or handicapped, alive or dead. All these things will affect the price."

Malik said that in a transaction where a slave or slave-girl was bought for one hundred dinars with a stated credit period that if the seller regretted the sale there was nothing wrong in him asking the buyer to revoke it for ten dinars which he would pay him immediately or after a period and he would forgo his right to the hundred dinars which he was owed.

Malik said, "However, if the buyer regrets and asks the seller to revoke the sale of a slave or slave-girl in consideration of which he will pay an extra ten dinars immediately or on credit terms, extended beyond the original term, that should not be done. It is disapproved of because it is as if, for instance, the seller is buying the one hundred dinars which is not yet due on a year's credit term before the year expires for a slave-girl and ten dinars to be paid immediately or on credit term longer than the year. This falls into the category of selling gold for gold when delayed terms enter into it."

Malik said that it was not proper for a man to sell a slave-girl to another man for one hundred dinars on credit and then to buy her back for more than the original price or on a credit term longer than the original term for which he sold her. To understand why that was disapproved of in that case, the example of a man who sold a slave-girl on credit and then bought her back on a credit term longer than the original term was looked at. He might have sold her for thirty dinars with a month to pay and then buy her back for sixty dinars with a year or half a year to pay. The outcome would only be that his goods would have returned to him just like they were and the other party would have given him thirty dinars on a month's credit against sixty dinars on a year or half a year's credit. That was not to be done. *Al-Muwatta' 31.1*

The Islamic conquests were accompanied by a huge increase in the number of slaves taken in the military campaigns. A vast network of slave trading emerged, growing as the territory of Islam grew, constantly supplied by campaigns and raids into *Dar al-Harb*. Originally slaves were taken from all the subjugated people as war booty. With the Islamisation of the Empire, slaves were obtained mainly from sub-Saharan Africa, the Slav territories, Central Asia (Turks) and from India. These were all non-Muslim infidels taken from *Dar al-Harb,* and this was legitimate by *shari'a* rules. Next to its value as a source of gold, Africa was seen as primarily a source of slaves. The Arabs were the first invaders of India to have captured and removed a large number of its inhabitants as enslaved captives.[400] Every raid into Hindu territory yielded slaves as booty. It is recorded that following one such raid by the Sultan Subuktigin of Ghazni (942-997):

> The Sultan returned, marching in the rear of this immense booty, and slaves were so plentiful that they became very cheap; and men of respectability in their native land, were degraded by becoming slaves of common shopkeepers. But this is the goodness of God, who bestows honours on his own religion and degrades infidelity.[401]

Of the Sultan Firoz Shah Tughlaq (1351-1388) it is said that:[402]

> The Sultan was very diligent in providing slaves, and he carried his care so far as to command his great fief-holders and officers to capture slaves whenever they were at war, and to pick out and send the best for the services of the court.

This sultan had 180,000 slaves of whom 40,000 were guards in his palace, and he had a special minister and bureaucracy dedicated to dealing with his slaves.

Slavery became one of the strongest motivations for the perpetuation of *jihad*. In addition to the customary use of slaves for menial domestic duties, agriculture and concubinage, Islam developed the systematic use of slaves in the army and administration. Boys and young men were forcibly converted to Islam and trained as slave soldiers of the Muslim state. These included the Turkic Mamelukes, who eventually became a powerful force within Islam and set up their own states. The Ottoman Empire recruited slave soldiers by the notorious *devshirme* institution, in which children of *dhimmi* populations were seized, forcibly converted to Islam, and then trained as the future elite troops of the empire. In India constant *jihads* led by slave soldier generals expanded the Islamic area and created numerous sultanates, the best known being the Sultanate of Delhi.[403]

As Muslims and *dhimmis* under their protection could not be enslaved, there was an imperative to continually raid non-Muslim territories to procure slaves. Slave raiding became a way of life for many Muslim war lords on the frontiers of *Dar al-Islam*. Muslim corsairs based in North Africa raided as far as the English coasts for slaves into the seventeenth century. Sub-Saharan Africans were taken as slaves by Arab and Berber tribes from the north and used as labourers, concubines, slave soldiers and eunuchs. The slave trade became a great source of wealth and power to Muslim states, and remained an important part of the economy of parts of the Muslim world well into the twentieth century. Non-Muslim black Africans were still being enslaved in South Sudan as part of the *jihad* during the long civil war into the twenty-first century, a practice which was abolished in the 2005 peace treaty.[404] Slavery still exists in Mauritania, where in June 2006 the new President, Ely Ould Mohammed Vall, pledged to fight all forms of slavery in his country, thus giving official recognition to the fact that slavery still existed in Mauritania.[405] Most slaves are from the Harratin community (also known as Black Moors, in contrast to the White Moors or Berbers), the descendants of mainly black Africans enslaved by the Muslim Berbers.

Slavery and *jihad* were thus interlinked in a symbiotic relationship. *Jihad* provided profitable booty in slaves; indeed slave raids were often camouflaged as *jihad*.[406] Slaves furthermore were used as fighting troops, for example, the Mamelukes and the Janissaries. Contemporary Muslims often criticise Western slavery of Africans but ignore the problem in Islam both past and present. While they claim that slavery contravenes the precepts of Islam, regulations governing the practice of slavery are undeniably part of *shari'a* and as such unchangeable (in the eyes of Sunni Muslims).

Espionage, intelligence and propaganda

There is a phrase in the famous Sword Verse (Q 9:5) which is interpreted by some Muslims as encouragement to use espionage.

> ...Slay the Pagans wherever ye find them, and seize them,
> beleaguer them, and *lie in wait for them in every stratagem (of
> war)* [emphasis added].[407]

Muhammad himself made good use of spies. Hamidullah describes Muhammad's use of a "network of intelligence service, espionage and counter-espionage" and asserts that this played a large part in his successful conquest of the Arabian peninsula.[408] He reviews Muhammad's use of spies during the battles of Badr, Uhud and the Khandaq, the war of Khaibar, the conquest of Mecca and various other military expeditions.[409] It was also thanks to intelligence reports that Muhammad was able to thwart various assassination conspiracies and to facilitate assassination plans of his own. For example, on hearing that Ka'b bin al-Ashraf, a chief of the Jewish tribe of Bane al-Nadir, had come to Mecca to use his poetry to instigate the Meccans to take revenge on Muhammad for the Muslim victory at the Battle of Badr, Muhammad "sent a small detachment who succeeded in assassinating the chief in his own castle nipping the evil in the bud".[410]

One particular intelligence-gathering expedition is described by Kandhalvi in his popular compilation of *hadiths* under the title "Huzaifah Goes For Spying".[411] Huzaifah was ordered by Muhammad: "Go to the enemy camp and bring us their news. Return immediately after observing what they are doing." Huzaifah duly went to the camp of the enemy, who in this case were the Jews of Banu Qurayza in Medina. The Jews became aware of his presence and shouted, "There is a spy among us. Every one of us should catch the hand of the person next to him." With great presence of mind Huzaifah caught hold of a nearby hand and demanded loudly, "Who are you?" Thus he managed to escape detection. When he reported back to Muhammad, Huzaifah could "see his beautiful teeth shining" on hearing of his spy's narrow escape.

Propaganda was also a tactic used by Muhammad with great success in order to create suspicion and dissension amongst his enemies. Hamidullah describes in detail how Muhammad sent a new convert to Islam to plant doubts in the minds of two groups of his enemies – the Meccans and a Jewish tribe in Medina.[412] This convert first warned the Banu Qurayza Jews in Medina not to trust the Meccans and suggested they asked the Meccans for some hostages to ensure their loyalty. Then he told the Meccans that the Jews were conspiring with the Muslims and wanted to hand over the Meccan leaders to the Muslims. He also recommended that the Meccans should ask the Jews to attack on the Sabbath when the Muslims would not be expecting it – an idea that was sacrilegious to the Jews. The resulting hostility between the Jews and the Meccans can be imagined.

Punishment for foreign spies caught by the Muslims was severe. If a non-Muslim who had been granted a safe-conduct to enter Islamic territory was later discovered to be a spy, he was to be killed. Crucifixion could be used, in order to deter others, unless the spy were a woman.[413] In the case of child spies, they are not to be killed but would become *fay'*.[414]

The punishment for a Muslim caught spying for the enemy seems to have been less clear cut. According to the Shafi'i and Maliki schools of *shari'a* this can be left to the discretion of the commanding officer. The Hanafi school says he should be imprisoned until he repents. Al-Awza'i suggests exile.[415]

The early Muslims continued to practise espionage and propaganda. Infiltration was a particular speciality of the Isma'ilis (see chapter 12). Mention must be made of the medieval Shi'a Isma'ili Fatimid Empire (910-1171), that was one of the first political powers to develop a sophisticated ministry of propaganda employing secret agents in order to establish their reign in Sunni Egypt and later in the wider Muslim world. Information was disseminated through mosque prayers, by pre-arranged "spontaneous" arguments in public libraries, by declaration from minarets, government communiqués on stone tablets and paper placed at strategic public places, hired poets who eulogised the Fatimids, bribery, and neutralising potential dissidents by appointing them to high office.[416] There is a long tradition within Islamic societies of the deliberate use of propaganda to promote favoured interpretations of Islam to Muslim societies and the wider non-Muslim world which survives until today.

An analysis of the Muslim insurgency in southern Thailand

lists psychological warfare as a main element in the arsenal of the insurgency:

> The use of agitprop (agitation/propaganda) methods by Muslim clerics, similar to those used by communists in the past, to force confrontational situations with the security forces and provoke them to overreact, thereby leading to human-rights violations and alienation of the man in the street against the security forces and, ultimately, against the government. Such agitprop methods were put to action in Thailand during the incident outside a mosque in April, and again in the incident on October 25...

> A skilfully planned and executed psychological-warfare (psywar) campaign by the perpetrators of violence and the Muslim clerics supporting them to project serious incidents of violence or terrorism, which might shock the international community, as incidents stage-managed by the local security agencies in order to have the Muslims discredited as terrorists.

> One finds here a close resemblance between the psywar tactics used by the perpetrators of violence in southern Thailand and those used elsewhere in the world by the members of the IIF [International Islamic Front, organised by Bin Laden and al-Qa'eda]. Pakistani jihadi terrorist organizations, which are members of the IIF, often project serious incidents of terrorism by their followers in India's Jammu & Kashmir as stage-managed by the Indian intelligence and security agencies in order to discredit the Muslims. Until Osama bin Laden admitted to al-Qaeda's responsibility for the September 11, 2001, terrorist strikes in the United States, the IIF was projecting them as having been carried out by Mossad, Israel's external-intelligence agency.

> One saw the use of such psywar tactics by some clerics and others after the violent incidents of January and April in Thailand's southern provinces. After the incidents of January, one Abdullah Ahamad, a religious teacher in Pattani, accused the police of selling the firearms issued to them to smugglers and blaming the Muslims for allegedly looting them. He

alleged: "The arms were stolen not by Muslim mujahideen or by separatists, but with the help of the soldiers in the camps, and the schools were burnt by pro-government elements." In an interview to the Agence-France Presse news agency after the January incidents, Yapa Barahaeng, a retired teacher, alleged: "Muslim groups haven't done this. It seems the government itself or the police or military have done it." There have been numerous instances of such false propaganda by Muslim activists to create a divide between the security forces and the local Muslim population. We in India are all too familiar with such psywar tactics used by the Pakistani members of the IIF and should, therefore, be able to understand the dilemma faced by the Thai security agencies in the face of externally instigated psywar attempts to have them demonized in the eyes of the Muslim population.[417]

Naval Warfare

The early Muslims, being desert-dwelling Arabs, were reluctant to go to sea (a fact which helped the Byzantine Empire to hold out against continued Muslim aggression). The most that Muhammad himself did in terms of naval warfare was, firstly, to send some auxiliary forces by sea to Aqaba to lend support to Muslims engaged in a land battle[418] and, secondly, to send 300 troops in pursuit of some Africans sighted in boats off the Arabian coast near Mecca. The Muslim troops reached an island, the Africans fled, and the Muslims returned to the mainland.[419]

Eventually the Muslim forces became more active at sea, occupying Cyprus in 648.[420] Many churches of the Byzantine era on Cyprus became mosques. By the tenth century Muslims had gained control of much of the Mediterranean, and their pirates were becoming a serious menace to Europeans. They became a major sea-power again in the fifteenth century when the Ottoman Turks controlled much of the eastern Mediterranean and African coasts, though they suffered a crushing defeat off Lepanto in 1571.

It is striking how little is written by Islamic jurists about the conduct of a war at sea, in contrast to the vast amounts of literature dealing with land-based warfare. So great was the general antipathy towards the sea that various *hadiths* report Muhammad promising that anyone who died in *jihad* at sea would have double the reward of a martyr who died on land.[421] One *hadith* records that Muhammad said, "Paradise is granted to the first batch of my followers who will undertake a naval expedition."[422] Shaybani states that as soon as a *jihad* fighter sets foot on a ship all his sins will be forgiven.[423]

Most of the rules of maritime warfare were derived by analogy with land warfare, a ship being seen as equivalent to a castle. Thus a ship could be attacked by hurling stones at it, by cutting it off from outside support, by fire or by sinking. Other tactics were designed to create panic, for example, throwing on to the ship such things as snakes, scorpions and harmful powders.[424] If the enemy tried to protect themselves by taking Muslims on board as human shields, their ship could still be attacked.[425]

The division of spoils – always an important topic in classical Islamic writings about war – was as on land.[426] However, there were special rules about prisoners of war which related to the fact that ships overloaded with booty and prisoners might sink. If the Muslims feared they would sink, they were permitted to throw into the sea not only the property they had taken but also the prisoners they had taken including women and children.[427] They were not, however, allowed to throw overboard any Muslim women or children who might happen to be on the ship,[428] nor any *dhimmis* on board, nor any non-Muslims who had been granted a safe-conduct.[429]

The Barbary corsairs[430]

An important chapter in the history of Muslim naval warfare concerns the Barbary corsairs, the Muslim pirates based in the ports of North Africa who terrorised European commerce in the Mediterranean and beyond for several centuries. Raids by Barbary pirates on western Europe did not cease until well into the nineteenth century, when they were subdued by Western naval power.

These pirates operated out of Tunis, Tripoli, Algiers, Sale and other ports in the Maghrib, preying on shipping in the western Mediterranean from the time of the Crusades. Later they attacked ships on their way to Asia around Africa. Their stronghold was the stretch of North Africa known as the Barbary Coast (a medieval European term for the Maghreb after its Berber inhabitants). Some of their predatory expeditions are said to have reached as far north as Iceland and far south along West Africa's Atlantic seaboard. As well as preying on shipping, they often raided European coastal towns. They captured large numbers of Christian slaves from Western Europe, who were sold in slave markets in North African coastal cities.

The *hijra* of many Spanish Muslims in the sixteenth century following the Reconquista by Ferdinand and Isabella and the final expulsion of all Muslims in 1609 was the impetus behind a resurgence of Muslim naval activities against the Christian states of Europe. The pirates built several fortresses to defend the Barbary ports of Algiers, Tripoli and Tunis, and paid the sultan of Tunis one fifth of their booty to use Tunis as pirate headquarters. The corsairs, as pirate captains, belonged to a highly valued and organised profession in Muslim North Africa. They were organised into guilds (*ta'ifas*) for their mutual benefit. Many of them were Europeans who had converted to Islam, and they played a prominent role in the governments of Algiers, Tunis, and Tripoli. The pirate governments were supported by selling Christians into slavery and by taking heavy tribute as protection money from other countries. Famous corsair admirals were Uruj Barbarossa (1504-1515) and his brother Kheir al-Din Barbarossa (1518-1530). They were strengthened by the expanding Ottoman naval and land power, and offered it their allegiance, thus extending Ottoman suzerainty to the Atlantic. Kheir al-Din Barbarossa was appointed admiral of the Ottoman fleet and took charge of Ottoman naval operations in the western Mediterranean. The corsairs legitimised their activities by describing them as a *jihad* against the infidels.

Algiers became the prosperous centre of an economy based primarily on state-sponsored piracy. Corsair wealth funded the development of the city with protective walls, a citadel (completed in 1590) and fine public buildings. The population grew from some 20,000 to about 100,000 by the seventeenth century and included a mix of Algerians, Turks, corsairs, and Jews. Thousands of Christian captives taken on raids were held in prisons called *bagnios*. They were sold, ransomed, or used as slaves.

In 1784 the Congress of the newly independent United States assigned $60,000 as tribute to the Barbary states to prevent attacks on American ships. But continued corsair attacks prompted the building of the US navy which attacked the Barbary pirates in a series of wars along the North African coast, starting in 1801. It was not until 1815 that naval victories ended tribute payments by the US, although some European nations continued annual payments until the 1830s. In 1816, a British Royal Navy raid, assisted by six Dutch vessels, destroyed the port of Algiers and its fleet of Barbary ships.

Seeing their piracy as a part of *jihad* against the infidels, the Barbary corsairs in many ways resemble modern Islamic terrorism and its methods, in which profitable criminal activities (such as drug-trafficking, kidnapping for ransom, fraud and robbery) are allied to religious Islamic *jihadi* goals. These are supported by Muslim merchants, politicians, governments and *'ulama*, all for their different reasons but under the general *jihad* umbrella.

Alliances with Non-Muslims
1 In theory and in history

According to classical *jihad* law, alliances with non-Muslims are to be avoided, though they are permissible in times of great need as a utilitarian measure:

> Muslims may not seek help from non-Muslim allies unless the Muslims are considerably outnumbered and the allies are of goodwill towards the Muslims.[431]

Non-Muslims who have fought alongside the Muslim armies are mentioned as being among those entitled to a token payment from the spoils of battle.[432]

Some contemporary Islamic scholars see the Qur'an as allowing alliances with non-Muslims:

> The Qur'an itself mentions about treaties with unbelievers and according to the Qur'an and hadith it is the duty of all Muslims

to honour all treaties and alliances with non-believers. The Muslims must respect all such alliances until non-Muslims dishonour these.[433]

Others cite the verse cite the Qur'an to claim such alliances are not permitted:

O ye who believe! take not the Jews and the Christians for your friends and protectors: they are but friends and protectors to each other. And he amongst you that turns to them (for friendship) is of them. Verily Allah guideth not a people unjust. Q 5:51

In historical practice there have been many occasions when Muslims formed alliances with non-Muslims against common enemies, even when those enemies were other Muslims. During the Crusades there were several such alliances. For instance in 1139 Muslim Damascus under its regent Mu'in al-Din Unur asked King Fulk of Jerusalem for aid against an attack by Imad al-Din Zengi ruler of Mosul and Aleppo. Fulk agreed and led a Crusader army north, forcing Zengi to withdraw. Following this success, another treaty was signed between Damascus and Jerusalem for their mutual protection against Zengi.

2 Current alliances

As current Islamism strives for victory over Western power and civilisation, it has formed a utilitarian alliance with Western hard left movements and personalities.[434]

The demise of Soviet communism and Maoism weakened the Western hard left in its various forms and ideologies, forcing it to look for other allies. In radical Islam it has found an unlikely ally who, despite in other respects being a natural ideological enemy, shares the hard left's hatred of Western liberal capitalism and Christianity. Following the fall of Marxism and Maoism, the Western far left remained as the (almost) sole proponent of radical egalitarianism. Through this ideological prism it sees Western states and societies as racist, class-based, imperialist and neo-colonial. This ideology uses post-modern politically correct terms to campaign for the diminishing of all differences between people in the spheres of income, gender, race, sexual preferences, and political power.[435] They thus consider that all white Westerners (except themselves) are reactionary oppressors[436] while all members of minority groups in the West are victims. On the one hand they argue for full equality, on the other when it comes to religion they denigrate Christianity whilst supporting the Islamic cause.

The alliance is beneficial to the Islamists in that Islam is promoted by leftist intellectuals in an attractively bowdlerised form which effectively conceals the violent aspects of Islamic sources, law and historical practice. For Islamists such an alliance is therefore fully justified in terms of Islamic law and the *exigencies* of jihad. The alliance gives them a secure foothold within Western states and societies (an ideological *ribat* line) from which they can pursue their strategy of long-term *jihad* "by all means possible".

Left-leaning intellectuals seem happy to ignore the failure of most Muslims in the West to integrate and turn a blind eye to the terrorist ideologies being propagated in some of these communities, blaming them on either Western foreign policy or alienated youth. Likewise they turn a blind eye to human rights abuses and dictatorial autocratic leadership in Muslim-majority states. While as secularists they pour contempt on the vestiges of Christianity in the West, calling them irrational, fundamentalist and obscurantist, they have no criticism to make of similar phenomena in Muslim societies and Islam the religion. Some would go as far as to deny that terrorism has any basis in Islam, seeing it rather as a phenomenon borne out of social alienation and/or in response to Western policies. This discourse has infiltrated and influenced most Western centres of power, inhibiting leaders from facing up to the reality of both Islamo-fascism and the development of Islamism in their societies.

Radical imams as well as Muslim governments have willingly adopted the idiom of the European left, accusing all who critique contemporary Islamic problems as racist, islamophobic, orientalist and imperialist. Under this protective ideological umbrella, many young Muslims in the West are being radicalised and turned to terrorism.[437]

Were the Rules Followed?

How were the rules of *jihad* put into practice by the first Muslims? The answer would seem to be that their practice was variable, and even Muhammad himself did not always follow the rules. Because Muhammad is seen as the model for all other Muslims to follow, his lapses from the established norm set a particularly significant precedent.

As has been seen, Caliph Abu Bakr gave strict orders that the civilian population and the livestock were to be spared, when the Muslims conquered new territory.[438] The aim of putting all Arabs under Muslim control drove his successor Caliph 'Umar (634-644) to demand the return of some Arabs[439] who had fled to Byzantine-controlled areas. He threatened that if they were not returned to him he would retaliate against the Christians within his territory, breaking the treaties made with them for their protection. According to the Muslim historian al-Tabari, 'Umar's threat ran as follows:

> It has come to my notice that a certain group of Arab tribesmen has left our territory and has sought residence in your territory; by God, if you do not drive them back, we will surely dissolve our covenants with the Christians living under Arab sovereignty, and expel them.[440]

The Banu Taghlib, a Christian tribe, were unwilling to pay the demeaning *jizya* and insisted on paying the *sadaqa* tax like Muslim Arabs. According to the rules, they could not do this and remain Christians. Caliph 'Umar, afraid that they too might defect to the Byzantines, made a treaty with them whereby the Taghlib were charged *sadaqa* at double the rate paid by Muslims and forbidden to baptise their children. It appears, however, that the Taghlib continued to baptise their children regardless, for Caliph 'Ali (656-661) later said that if he had time he would like to kill their fighting men and take captive the children because they had broken the treaty by baptising their children, thus forfeiting their right to protection.[441] (For more details see chapter 10.)

While Christians were supposed to be allowed to keep both their faith and their lives under Islamic rule, the 60-strong garrison of

Gaza were killed in 637 for refusing to convert to Islam.[442] This appears to have been an exceptional event. Some reports say that this may have been as a result of the anger of the Muslim commander, 'Amr, whom the Byzantines had treacherously tried to murder during negotiations. The wives and children of the garrison were spared, as were the civilian inhabitants of Gaza.[443]

Another apparent case of Muslims breaking their rules of engagement to get revenge for treachery was the murder of one Sergios who had spoiled the Arabs' trade. He is reported to have been killed by being suffocated in a drying camel stomach.[444]

At the hard-fought Battle of Jabiya-Yarmuk in 636, in which the Muslims suffered heavy losses but eventually won, they did not take prisoners on the battlefield, though afterwards they captured some of the Byzantine enemy who had fled.[445]

With regard to prisoners of war, the infamous example of brutality set by Muhammad in 627 against the Banu Qurayza, a Jewish tribe who lived in Medina, has already been mentioned. Muhammad besieged them because he feared they would join his enemies. The Qurayza offered to pay tribute, but Muhammad refused. He demanded that they embrace Islam, which the Qurayza refused. Finally Muhammad accepted their unconditional surrender. The Aws, a Medinan clan who were allies of the Banu Qurayza, pleaded with Muhammad to be lenient with them. Muhammad asked if they would accept a decision from one of their own, which they readily agreed to. Muhammad then sent for Sa'd ibn Mu'adh, a member of the Aws clan who had converted to Islam some time previously. Sa'd was dying from a wound he received fighting in defence of Medina, and his sentence on the Banu Qurayza was that the men should be killed and the women enslaved. Muhammad did not demur – the word of a dying man was considered doubly honourable by Arabs – and indeed responded that Sa'd's judgement was the judgement of God. The next day the men were beheaded one by one, and their bodies thrown into specially dug trenches. The process took all day, the last decapitations being performed by torchlight. The number killed is estimated at 700 by some sources[446] or even up to 900 by others.[447] Women and children were enslaved, and all the possessions of the tribe seized.[448]

Muslims have generally justified this massacre (which sent shock waves throughout Arabia, and after which the tribe ceased to exist) as specially sanctioned by God. This was the view of al-Mawardi (d.1072) who wrote "... it was not permitted [for Muhammad] to forgive [in a case of] God's injunction incumbent upon them; he could merely forgive [transgressions, offences etc.] in matters concerning his own person."[449] Hamidullah defends the massacre in a different way describing it as being "a decision of the arbitrator of [the Banu Qurayza's] own choice who applied to them their own Biblical law" and cites Deuteronomy 20:13-14. But many non-Muslim historians have condemned it as completely unjustified – "a barbarous deed... an act of monstrous cruelty" in the words of Sir William Muir whose biography of Muhammad was based entirely on Muslim sources.[451] The military imperative was certainly clear, in that the Banu Qurayza were the last of three Jewish tribes in Medina to be dealt with by Muhammad. The first had been allowed to leave with all their possessions, while the second just managed to escape with their lives. Unsurprisingly both had become staunch allies of Muhammad's enemies. It would seem Muhammad did not want to make the same mistake again.

The "rightly-guided" caliphs - Muhammad's first four successors - had their own preferences on prisoners of war. For example, Abu Bakr was against ransoms,[452] preferring that prisoners taken by the Muslims should either convert to Islam or be killed.[453] Umar liked to kill at least some of the prisoners he had taken,[454] but to buy back Muslims taken prisoner by the enemy.[455]

Despite their rules of engagement the Muslim Arabs gained a reputation for ferocity, possibly indicating that they may not always have followed them closely. This may be in accordance with the *shari'a* concept that necessity makes the forbidden permissible. Ibn Hudayl, a fourteenth century author of an important treatise on *jihad*, explains:

> It is permissible to set fire to the lands of the enemy, his stores of grain, his beasts of burden – if it is not possible for the Muslims to take possession of them – as well as to cut down his trees, to raze his cities, in a word, to do everything that might ruin and discourage

him, provided that the imam (i.e. the religious "guide" of the community of believers) deems these measures appropriate.[456]

There are few documented cases of mutilation, so it may have been chiefly their ferocity in battle that was feared, as indicated by Patriarch Sophronius of Jerusalem, writing in 634.[457] But the Oath of Justus for Jacob in the *Doctrina Iacobi nuper baptizati* (an anti-Jewish document written in about 634) stated that even if Jews and Saracens cut him into pieces, piece by piece, he would not deny Jesus Christ, which might indicate that the author of this oath thought it a possibility.[458]

Christian sources repeatedly mention the proclivity of the Arab armies to ravage the countryside. Thus, in their advance into Syria in 636,

> They went to the region of Baalbek, destroying and sacking everything in their path.[459]

Later, while taking Busra on the east of the Jordan River, they "destroyed the rest of the villages and cities".[460]

In another region they killed monks despite the order not to do so:

> These Arabs went up into the Mardin mountains and there they killed many monks and excellent ascetics, especially in the great and famous abbey on the mountain above Rhesaina, which is called 'The Abbey of Benotho', i.e. of the eggs.[461]

It would seem that the contingencies of war, the policy of terrorizing the adversary, and the desire for loot often prevailed. Legitimacy could always be claimed retrospectively by citing the principle of necessity.

Adapting *Jihad* for Modern Times

Various contemporary Muslim authors have tackled the subject of rules for the conduct of *jihad* in modern times. Many of these works appear to be designed primarily to defend the image of Islam to Westerners. They discuss the subject of international relations not only in wartime (as did the classical authors) but also in peacetime (an innovation). Generally the authors select the most humane regulations to be found in the classical Islamic works on *jihad* and present them as the norm (rather than as one end of the spectrum). In Peters' summary, "The classical doctrine of *jihad* has been stripped of its militancy and is represented as an adequate legal system for maintaining peace in the domain of international relations." Furthermore the best of Islamic principles are often contrasted with the worst of contemporary international practice. For example, the Western practice of surprise attacks is contrasted unfavourably with the classical Islamic requirement to offer the enemy the chance to convert to Islam or pay *jizya* before launching the attack.[462]

Writings perhaps not intended for non-Muslim readers sometimes take a different stance. For example, an article in a Kuwaiti Arabic-language newspaper *Al-Watan*, discussed the issue of killing non-combatants. It argued that "in the modern age" an army is supported by a whole range of complementary activities and all the people engaged in those activities are legitimate targets "especially on occupied Muslim lands such as Palestine"; indeed everyone in Israel who pays taxes or voted Ariel Sharon into power was a legitimate target. It also argued that civilians could be killed "when Muslims must launch a comprehensive attack against their enemies or shoot them from afar" as Muhammad shot at the people of Taif with a catapult when he was besieging their city. Enemy civilians, women and children as well as Muslims could be accidentally killed in such attacks (for example, suicide attacks) without incurring blame. The only exception was that "places that are designated for children and frequented only by them are not to be targeted".[463]

A comment from Mahathir Mohamad, then Malaysian prime minister, is interesting not least because Malaysia is generally thought of as a moderate Muslim country. Mahathir urged an international conference of young Muslims to acquire the skills and technology needed to create modern weapons in order to "strike fear into the hearts of our enemies and defend us". He listed as examples tanks, battleships, fighter planes and rockets, and said that matching western development in these areas would "prevent Islam from being humiliated, looked down upon and regarded as a religion of terrorists".[464]

Weapons of mass destruction

In terms of the conduct of modern warfare, the Islamic rule that non-combatants should not become involved would exclude the use of weapons of mass destruction.[465] One modern Islamic authority,[466] however, considers that nuclear weapons are a legitimate deterrent, reasoning from the following Qur'anic verse:

> Against them make ready your strength to the utmost of your power, including steeds of war, to strike terror into (the hearts of) the enemies of God and your enemies, and others besides, whom ye may not know, but whom God doth know. Q 8:60

Based on another verse from the Qur'an he asserts they could be used in retaliation or defence if the enemy has already used them.

> If then any one transgresses the prohibition against you, transgress ye likewise against him. Q 2:194

Following the Iraq war of March-April 2003, Dr Ahmed Omar Hashim, the president of Al-Azhar, also referred to Q 8:60 and called on Arab nations to obtain weapons of mass destruction so as to have the power God orders them to have in order to combat aggression. He stated that "the notion of ability [in this verse] is absolute. In other words, Muslims should fight their enemies with the same weapons, and even try to exceed them.[467]

Abdul Rahman Bilal, a major in the Pakistani Army, has argued that the Islamic world should acquire nuclear capability to serve as a deterrent "whenever its existence is threatened". He does not permit the use of chemical and biological weapons by Muslim countries, but urges that research should be done to find suitable antidotes.[468] Since Bilal wrote this, Pakistan has declared itself a nuclear power, with its so-called "Islamic bomb" acclaimed by many Muslims as a morale booster for the Islamic world:

> There has always been a tacit understanding that Pakistan's bomb will be used to regain the glory of Islam and defend the "rights" of the Muslims wherever they are persecuted by infidel powers. This

was truly an Islamic bomb. On the one hand it strengthened the autocratic hands of the oligarchy and allowed Pakistan's armed forces to rehabilitate themselves after the humiliating defeat in 1971 and on the other hand it allowed Pakistan to gain a very profitable position within the Muslim world. It was felt that Pakistan's nuclear capability served as a morale booster for the entire Islamic world. Foreign Minister of Iran expressed his joy and pride and said that the nuclear test by Pakistan has strengthened the confidence of the Muslim world in the face of the nuclear threat from Israel.[469]

Pakistan's radical Jammaat ud-Daawa organisation supports the use of "atomic weapons" in *jihad*, and their leader has praised the scientist who shared Pakistan's nuclear technology with Libya, Iran and North Korea, calling him a hero and saying: "He shared the technology for the supremacy of Islam and he acted on Allah's command."[470]

Iran is believed to have a nuclear programme being developed already. Certainly, Iran's then chairman of the Expediency Council, Akbar Hashemi Rafsanjani, has said that Iran must acquire nuclear technology.[471] While Iran claims it is only developing nuclear technology for peaceful purposes, obvious lies, omissions and evasions in the face of the inquiries held by the International Atomic Energy Agency (IAEA) and much circumstantial evidence has convinced most independent analysts that Iran has been trying to build, or at least has the capacity to build, a nuclear bomb in violation of the Nuclear Non-Proliferation Treaty it is signed up to.[472] In September 2005 the IAEA Board of Governors declared Iran to be in "non-compliance" with its obligations under the Nuclear Nonproliferation Treaty (NPT), thereby allowing the issue of Iran's nuclear program to be transferred to the UN Security Council.[473] In August 2006 Iran's supreme leader Ayatollah Ali Khamenei declared that Iran would continue to pursue nuclear technology despite the UN Security Council decision demanding it suspend uranium enrichment by the end of the month:

> The Islamic Republic of Iran has made its own decision and in the nuclear case, God willing, with patience and power, will continue its path.[474]

On December 23rd 2006 the UN Security Council unanimously adopted Resolution 1737 which demanded that Iran should immediately suspend its nuclear proliferation activities. The Resolution also demanded that all states should prevent the supply, sale or transfer to Iran of any equipment and that could contribute to its nuclear enrichment, reprocessing or heavy-water activities, or to the development of nuclear weapon delivery systems.[475]

Saudi Arabia, which sees Iran as its main regional competitor, is also thought to be considering acquiring nuclear capability as a deterrent.[476]

While the Iranian authorities continue to asset that the nuclear programme is intended only for peaceful purposes, a radical Iranian cleric in Qom, Mohsen Gharavian (a disciple of Ayatollah Mesbah Yazdi, President Ahmadinejad's spiritual mentor) has issued a *fatwa* stating that the *shari'a* does not forbid the use of nuclear weapons.

> One must say that when the entire world is armed with nuclear weapons, it is only natural that, as a counter-measure, it is necessary to be able to use these weapons. However, what is important is what goal they may be used for.[477]

Peter Probst, an expert on terrorism at the Pentagon, has noted that religiously motivated terrorists are generally more willing to cause mass casualties than are secular terrorists, and may even actively seek mass casualties. Marvin Centron, president of the American organisation Forecasting International, concurs, stating that that "new groups, such as Osama bin Laden's, have fewer restrictions on the use of weapons of mass destruction".[478] Centron's statement was borne out when evidence came to light in January 2004 that Osama bin Laden's Al-Qa'eda had indeed been seeking to develop chemical and biological weapons in Kandahar, southern Afghanistan, until interrupted by the US-led invasion of Afghanistan in October 2001. The programme was headed by a Malaysian called Yazid Sufaat, who had studied biochemistry in the US and had been an officer in the Malaysian army. He was under the direction of Hambali, an Indonesian accused of heading Al-Qa'eda's operations in south-east Asia and also known as Riduan Isamuddin.[479]

Prisoners of war

Modern Islamic apologists forbid the killing of prisoners of war. They base all their POW theory on a phrase in Q 47:4[480] which offers the alternatives of freeing the prisoners with or without a ransom.[481] Enslavement they say was only valid when the enemy practised it also, based on Q 16:126

> And if ye do catch them out, catch them out no worse than they catch you out.

Prisoners must be treated well according to Q 76:8

> And they feed, for the love of God, the indigent, the orphan, and the captive.

During the first days of the Iraq war of March-April 2003, the Iraqi Foreign Minister Naji Sabri stated that the Iraqis would treat their coalition prisoners of war in accordance with the teachings of Islam. "We are committed first of all to the teachings of Islam, and second we are committed to the conventions of Geneva in dealing with the prisoners of war." This statement, made in the context of video footage of five American POWs being aired on Al-Jazeera TV in contravention of the Geneva Convention,[482] makes clear the Iraqi intention to be guided by Islam rather than the Geneva Convention in any conflict between the two.[483]

Terrorising the Enemy

Speaking of *jihad* in military terms, Brigadier S.K. Malik of the Pakistani army explains that the objective of *jihad* is to impose the will of the Muslims on the enemy. The means to achieve this goal is by instilling terror into their hearts.[484] This is based on the Qur'anic verse 8:12 which we have already quoted in the context of beheading.

> Remember thy Lord inspired the angels (with the message): "I am with you: give firmness to the believers: I will instil terror

into the hearts of the unbelievers: smite ye above their necks and smite all their finger-tips off them." Q 8:12

If Muslims observe the divine *jihadi* code of conduct, they have God's promise of casting terror into the hearts of their enemies:

Soon shall We cast terror into the hearts of the unbelievers for that they joined companions with Allah for which He had sent no authority: their abode will be the fire; and evil is the home of the wrong-doers! Q 3:151

Malik finds several other Qur'anic verses that speak of instilling terror into the hearts of the enemy, including:

And Allah turned back the Unbelievers for (all) their fury: no advantage did they gain; and enough is Allah for the Believers in their fight. And Allah is full of strength able to enforce his will. And those of the people of the Book who aided them - Allah did take them down from their strongholds and cast terror into their hearts. (so that) some ye slew and some ye made prisoners. Q 33:25-26

The Qur'anic military strategy involves a stage of intense preparation for war,

... *in order to strike terror into the hearts of the enemies, known or hidden, while guarding ourselves from being terror-stricken by the enemy.* In this strategy, guarding ourselves against terror is the 'Base'; preparation for war to the utmost is the 'Cause'; while striking terror into the hearts of the enemies is the 'Effect'.[485]

This is based on Q 8:60 which we have already looked at earlier in this chapter.

For Malik, these Qur'anic verses imply the importance of psychological warfare - breaking the enemy's will by terror - in attaining victory. The war of wills ought to be fought and won before the "war of muscles" begins. Striking terror into the hearts of the enemy is not just a means to an end, but the end itself, as once this is achieved hardly anything else needs to be done. The imposition of terror is both means and end. It is achieved by destroying the enemy's faith, for an invincible faith is immune to terror.[486]

Contemporary Islamic terrorists are well aware of these Qur'anic principles and are using brutal methods of mass killings of civilians, kidnappings and beheadings in their fight against the West and against Muslim regimes they define as apostates. The terror instilled in the states and populations targeted by their *jihad* is seen as a scriptural and effective tool for breaking their will. It fits in well with the Qur'anic *jihad* doctrine of terrorising your enemies. In modern terms this is also a very useful propaganda tool. A recent example of its effectiveness was the withdrawal of the Spanish troops from Iraq following the massive train bombings in Madrid in March 2004 which caused the death of over 190 civilians.

8
The Islamic Concept of Peace

Peace is generally dealt with in classical Islam under the heading of "war". Peace is seen as an interlude in the *jihad* process that must go on until the whole world is *Dar al-Islam*, under the rule of Islam. War, being ordained by God, is viewed as positive. Peace therefore stands in danger of being negative unless it can be justified.

Permanent peace can be justified only within *Dar al-Islam*. The Arabic words for "peace" and "submission" come from the same root, and this is indicative of the nuance which the term "peace" generally carries in Islam, that of peace as a result of submission. Permanent peace in Islam is something like the *pax Romana*, a peace which results from the imposition of Islamic power, thus preventing all dissension. It could be termed the *pax Islamica*.

Peace Treaties

Temporary peace (*hudna*)[487] can be achieved by making a treaty with the non-Muslim enemy, but this is only permissible if it is advantageous for the Muslims, and preferably should not last for more than ten years. This is based on the example of Muhammad.[488]

> If Muslims are weak, a truce may be made for ten years if necessary, for the Prophet made a truce with the Quraysh for that long, as is related by Abu Dawud.[489]

The Muslims made a three-year peace agreement with Byzantine-ruled Egypt which allowed the Muslims to concentrate on attacking Iraqand northern Syria. When the military situation became more favourable for attacking Egypt they did so (639).[491]

If Muslims were to make a peace treaty that was not in their own interests it would be tantamount to abandoning the war, and so disobeying God's command. Thus peace-making is justifiable only if it is seen as part of the long-term war effort. It is scarcely an exaggeration to say that in classical Islam peace is considered a specialised kind of war.

> Peace, moreover, is war in effect, where the interest of the Mussulmans [Muslims] requires it, since the design of war is the removal of evil and this is obtained by means of peace:[492]

When circumstances change so that it becomes advantageous to the Muslims to break the truce they must do so, having given due notice of their intention to the enemy and allowing time for this news to disseminate throughout the enemy's territory. If the Muslims fail to renew the war when it becomes advantageous to them to do so, they are considered deserters.[493]

The Qur'an is strict about Muslims keeping the terms agreed, as long as the enemy has not violated the treaty.

> (But the treaties are) not dissolved with those pagans with whom ye have entered into alliance and who have not subsequently failed you in aught; nor aided any one against you. So fulfil your engagements with them to the end of their term: for God loveth the righteous. Q 9:4

> ...break not your oaths after ye have confirmed them; Q 16:91[494]

However a *hadith* records an instruction by Muhammad to army commanders which appears to indicate that different kinds of promise or guarantee had different levels of sanctity. Some were less binding and could be broken more casually.

> ...When you lay siege to a fort and the besieged appeal to you for protection in the name of Allah and His Prophet, do not accord to them the guarantee of Allah and His Prophet, but accord to them your own guarantee and the guarantee of your companions, for it is a lesser sin that the security given by you or your companions be disregarded than that the security granted in

189

the name of Allah and His Prophet be violated... *Sahih Muslim Book 19, Number 4294*

According to Sheikh 'Abdul Rahman 'Abdul Khaliq, peace treaties with Jews are made to be broken. In response to a question about the duty of a Muslim with regard to peace treaties with Jews he writes:

The first duty is to firmly believe in their invalidity and that because they contain invalid conditions they were born dead the very day they were given birth to...

The second duty of the Muslim is to believe that these treaties do not bind him and that it is not lawful for him to give effect to any of their contents except under compulsion and necessity...

The third duty is to work towards overthrowing these treaties...

Four more duties follow: the duty to detest and fight Jews, the duty to unite the Muslim community in so doing, the duty to believe that the presence of Jews in the Arab world is because Arab governments were not sufficiently Islamic, and the duty to pray for Muslim unity and victory over the Jews.[495]

Saudi Arabia's former Grand Mufti, Sheikh Abdul Aziz Ibn Baz, also made it clear that any cessation of hostilities with Israel could only ever be a temporary measure, pending the time that Muslims became strong enough to gain possession of the whole land for themselves.

The peace between the leader of the Muslims in Palestine and the Jews does not mean that the Jews will permanently own the lands which they now possess. Rather it only means that they would be in possession of it for a period of time until either the truce comes to an end, or until the Muslims become strong enough to force them out of the Muslim lands – in the case of an unrestricted peace.[496]

Islamic jurists define a treaty as a form of *'aqd* (literally, a tie), meaning an agreement on a certain act which has the object of creating legal consequences. It has a broader meaning than the Western concept of a contract because it implies a meeting of minds which follows an offer being made by one party and accepted by the other. This meeting of minds is more important than any legal niceties of signatures, witnesses etc.[497] Muhammad himself made a number of treaties, which his successors considered models to be emulated.[498] Treaties were categorised as either temporary (with *Dar al-Harb)* or perpetual (arrangements with the People of the Book regarding their *dhimmi* status within an Islamic state). Treaties with *Dar al-Harb* could include agreements on the payment of tribute, cessation of fighting, safe travel for civilians and ransoming prisoners of war.

Another kind of agreement, discussed at great length by the traditional Muslim jurists, was the granting of a temporary safe-conduct *(aman)* to a non-Muslim who wanted to spend some time in Islamic territory, often a merchant or trader.[499]

Permanent peace treaties?

There are modern Muslim scholars who promote a change to the classical Islamic doctrine in the form of the possibility of making *permanent* peace treaties with non-Muslims.[500] Some of these however make permanent peace conditional on non-Muslims submitting to the Islamic state and paying *jizya,* which is really no different from classical Islam.[501] Others hold that the only condition necessary is that Islam may be propagated without hindrance in the other state.[502]

Historical Treaties

The early sources record many treaties made by the Muslims with those they had threatened or attacked. The following examples are from the period of the "rightly-guided caliphs", traditionally seen as a model for later Muslims to emulate.

After their decisive victory over the Byzantines at the Battle of Jabiya-Yarmuk in 636, part of the Muslim army pursued the fleeing Byzantines to Melitene (also called Malatya) which they captured. They made a treaty with its inhabitants requiring them to pay *jizya,* the Islamic tax on conquered Jews and Christians.

The furious response of Heraclius, the Byzantine emperor, was to send troops to burn Melitene.[503]

After the fall of Damascus in December 636, an agreement was made at Baalbek, which gave the Greeks who wanted to evacuate the Baalbek area a staged withdrawal.[504] It was apparently a deliberate Muslim strategy to allow non-Muslims to leave conquered territory, because "it was better to allow hard-core non-Arab opponents of the regime to depart, and avoid becoming a disgruntled fifth column behind Muslim lines".[505] This seems to indicate a Muslim expectation that non-Muslims and non-Arabs were unlikely to become contented citizens of an Islamic state.

Either one or two truces were made in 637 at the Syrian stronghold of Chalkis. The first was apparently for one year only, after which Chalkis and its environs were supposed to surrender to the Muslims.[506] The terms of the second were that the Byzantines would make an annual payment of gold to the Muslims in return for which the Muslims would refrain from crossing the Euphrates i.e. would not invade Mesopotamia.[507] These Chalkis truces did not postpone for very long the loss of Syria or Mesopotamia to the Muslims, though Kaegi thinks they may have ensured the survival of the Byzantine Empire by giving them time to prepare the defence of the empire's heartland, Anatolia.[508] In 639 the Muslims broke the truce(s) on the pretext that the Byzantines had failed to pay the agreed tribute. However, Kaegi speculates that the real reason was probably the Muslims' fear that the Byzantines were using the time to mobilise more troops for a counter-offensive.[509] If so the Muslims were acting exactly in line with the Islamic teaching when they broke the truce because they feared it was becoming disadvantageous for them.

A later treaty was made with the Byzantine governor of Cyprus in 648 or 649 – peace in exchange for an annual payment of 7,000 dinars and the passing on of information to the Muslims about any Byzantine activities. The unfortunate Cypriots also had to pay tribute to the Byzantines and give them information about the Muslims.[510]

Some peace treaties with European countries in the seventeenth to nineteenth centuries are mentioned in chapter 10.

Pacifism

Pacifism is not completely unknown in Islam, though as will be seen there are very few groups whose commitment to pacifism on principle is absolute. Some Shi'as believe that nothing can be done to defend their community until the return of the Twelfth Imam, who went into hiding in 873. When he returns as the *mahdi* he will call the community to arm itself in order to restore pristine Islam and establish universal justice. They therefore adopt a quietist posture with almost fatalistic resignation. Mehdi Abedi and Gary Legenhausen have termed this "provisional pacifism".[511] However, the same theology inspires other Shi'as to respond in the opposite way by taking an activist political posture, calling on their fellow-believers to be alert and ready for revolution;[512] an example of this has already been described in chapter 6.

More often the approach to pacifism is by means of emphasising the spiritual understanding of *jihad*, that is, the battle with self against sinful habits, desires and actions. Those who take the line of emphasising the spiritual *jihad* often quote a *hadith* in which Muhammad described physical battle as "the lesser *jihad* (*jihad-e-asghar*)" i.e. inferior to the struggle for personal purity which he called "the greater *jihad* (*jihad-e akbar*)". One version runs:

> A group of Muslim soldiers came to the Holy Prophet [from a battle]. He said: Welcome, you have come from the lesser *jihad* to the greater *jihad*. It was said: What is the greater *jihad*? He said: The striving of a servant against his low desires. *Al-Tasharraf, Part I, p.70*

However, these *hadiths* are not included in the most important collections and are not very well attested (for example, the first narrator being known to have fabricated some *hadiths*). They are therefore discounted by radicals and militants.

The spiritual understanding of *jihad* is especially prevalent among Sufis. Thus for example a movement known as the Muridiyya,[513] which developed in Senegal under the leadership of the Sufi Ahmadu Bamba in the late nineteenth century, responded to French colonialism first by passive resistance and then by compromise and cooperation.[514]

However, not all the mystics of Islam have been inclined towards pacifism. Some have initiated movements of religious and social revolt against non-Muslim powers. Sufi-led rebellions against Western colonial powers may be said to have begun in the Caucasus in the late eighteenth century under the Sufi leader Sheikh Mansur Ushurma who led a violent resistance against the Russians.[515] In the 1810s Naqshbandiyya Sufism became established in the region under Sheikh Khalid al-Shahrazuri, who was strongly antagonistic to what he called "the enemies of religion, the cursed Christians".[516] A particular cause of Muslim resentment was the Russian ban on slave trading and raiding. The capture of Christian Armenians and Georgians for sale as slaves in the Middle East had been a significant source of income for the Muslims of the region and they believed the Russian prohibition violated their Islamic legal rights to enslave non-Muslims. Other causes of bitterness towards the Russians were heavy taxes, the introduction of alcohol and gambling, the abuse of Muslim women, and the cruelty of the Russian military.[517] The Sufi militant opposition to Russia was centred on the militant Naqshbandi-Muridiyya order which from 1834 was led by Imam Shamil.[518]

Some other examples of Sufi-led rebellions against Western colonialism have already been described in chapter 5. They include Sayyid Ahmad Barelwi (d.1831) who resisted British colonisation of the Mughal Empire in India, the Mahdist revolution of Sudan where many of the earliest Muslim missionaries and teachers were Sufis[519] (1882-1898), the Sanusiyya movement in Libya (1837-1931) and 'Abd al-Qader in the Maghreb (1808-1883). Examples of Sufi-led rebellions against Muslim regimes considered not Islamic enough include Usuman dan Fodio in West Africa and also the dervish-led rebellion of Kurds under Sheikh Said, the hereditary chief of the powerful Naqshbandi Sufi order, against the newly formed Turkish Republic in 1925.[520]

It is also interesting to note the very close links that had developed between some Sindhi *pirs* (Sufi "saints" – spiritual guides) and the Deobandi[521] by the early twentieth century.[522] Some *pirs* became very committed to the pan-Islamic cause and some were given senior ranks in Maulana Ubaidullah Sindhi's "Army of God" which he set up in 1915 in Afghanistan with the intention of invading India in rebellion against British rule. Others were involved in the Khilafat movement (1919-1924) which tried to preserve the status of the Sultan of Turkey as caliph.[523]

One very remarkable example of non-violent action occurred amongst the Pathans of north-west India. The Pathans are one of the most warlike peoples of the world, who normally despise the very idea of peace, and no government has yet been able to control them, whether British, Russian, Pakistani or Afghan. Yet a Puritan reformer called Abdul Ghaffar Khan[524] (1890-1988) managed to persuade the Pathans of the power of non-violence. In the struggle for a political voice for the Pathans, his party had a uniformed but *unarmed* wing called the *Khudai Khidmatgaran* (Servants of God) whose clothes were dyed a plum colour leading to their nickname the *Surkhposhan* or Red-Shirts. The Red-Shirt movement was at its height in 1930 and by 1932 the North-West Frontier was granted the same political rights and institutions as the rest of the sub-continent had.[525] They held to their policy of non-violence for many years, despite persecution, imprisonment and executions. Well does Abdul Ghaffar Khan deserve his nickname "the Gandhi of the frontier provinces".[526] However, unlike Gandhi, Abdul Ghaffar Khan's non-violence was pragmatic rather than principled – he did not believe that violence against the British could be effective. He managed to find a basis for his ideas of non-violence in both Islam and the traditional Pathan code of *Pukhtunwali.*[527]

A generally non-violent interpretation of *jihad* is held by the Ahmadiyya sect (considered apostates by other Muslims, and regarded as non-Muslims in Pakistan where they are severely persecuted). Their founder Mirza Ghulam Ahmad (1835-1908) rejected violent *jihad* as unnecessary in "a time of peace and security" such as India was enjoying under British rule.[528] However they do permit fighting in self-defence, to punish aggressors, and to ensure freedom to convert to Islam[529] – hence the raising of a volunteer corps of Ahmadis to fight in Kashmir alongside the Pakistani army after Pakistan's independence in 1947.[530]

9
Taqiyya

It is important for non-Muslims to be aware that in classical Islam Muslims are permitted to lie in certain situations, one of which is war.[531] This kind of permitted deception is called *taqiyya*. Generally translated in English as "dissimulation" or "concealment" the Arabic word derives from a root meaning to "shield" or "guard" oneself.

Shi'as, a minority amongst Muslims who have faced prolonged persecution by the majority Sunnis, were especially involved in the development of the doctrine of *taqiyya,* which is included in almost every classical work of Shi'a jurisprudence, permitting a person to deny their true beliefs in order to save themselves from harm. Shi'as often passed themselves off as Sunnis, while secretly maintaining their Shi'a beliefs. Among the Isma'ilis *taqiyya* reached its most radical form, as the whole movement at times operated in secret and adherents had to promise under oath not to reveal anything about the faith and its organisation.[532] The doctrine and practice of *taqiyya* is however not limited to the Shi'a, as many of the texts supporting it are from sources accepted by Sunnis, including the Qur'an.

> One of the teachings of the Qur'an is that a Muslim is permitted to conceal his belief in situations wherein, as a result of expressing it, his life, honour or property would be endangered.[533]

Although supposedly only for emergencies, *taqiyya* has "in practice become the norm of public behaviour among all Muslims – both Sunni and Shi'a - whenever there is a conflict between faith and expediency".[534] It is also a useful device in times of conflict and war, and has obvious relevance in the context of peace treaties and negotiations.

The sources justifying *taqiyya* include passages from the Qur'an, *hadith* and the various commentaries and manuals of the schools of law. A key Qur'an verse on which this doctrine is based states:

> Anyone who after accepting faith in Allah utters unbelief, - except under compulsion, his heart remaining firm in faith, - but such as open their breast to unbelief on them is Wrath from Allah and theirs will be a dreadful Penalty. Q 16:106

This verse indicates that the "dreadful penalty" will not be applied to someone who denied their faith *under compulsion*. It is backed up by another verse which occurs in the Qur'anic story of Moses, in which a man who "concealed his faith" questions the wisdom of killing someone for the sake of his faith:

> A believer, a man from among the people of Pharaoh, who had concealed his faith, said: "Will ye slay a man because he says, 'My Lord is God'? Q 40:28

A general warning against friendship with non-Muslims is also seen as lending support to the doctrine of *taqiyya* because of the phrase "by way of precaution" which can be interpreted as pretending friendship.

> Let not the believers take for friends or helpers unbelievers rather than believers; if any do that, in nothing will there be help from God: except by way of precaution, that ye may guard yourselves from them. Q 3:28

There is also support from the *hadith* which permits lying in three situations: to one's wife, in war, and for the purpose of reconciliation.

> Allah's Messenger (peace be upon him) said, "Lying is allowed in only three cases: falsehood spoken by a man to his wife to please her, falsehood in war, and falsehood to put things right between people. *Al-Tirmidhi Number 5033: Narrated by Asma', daughter of Yazid*

Muslim gives a slight variation on this:

> ... Ibn Shihab said he did not hear that exemption was granted in anything what the people speak as lie but in three cases: in battle, for bringing reconciliation amongst persons and the narration of the words of the husband to wife, and the narration of the words of a wife to her husband (in a twisted form in order to bring reconciliation between them). *Sahih Muslim Book 32, Number 6303*

Variations on this *hadith* are also recorded in the collections of Bukhari, Abu Dawud and an-Nasa'i. It is also quoted by the respected Egyptian *hadith* scholar Sheikh Mansur Ali Nasif.[535]

A somewhat different *hadith* reports Muhammad giving permission to lie in order to kill someone. It is an alternative telling of the story of the assassination of the poet who lampooned Muhammad which we have already considered in chapter 3, and begins as follows:

> Allah's Apostle said, "Who is willing to kill Ka'b bin Al-Ashraf who has hurt Allah and His Apostle?" Thereupon Muhammad bin Maslama got up saying, "O Allah's Apostle! Would you like that I kill him?" The Prophet said, "Yes." Muhammad bin Maslama said, "Then allow me to say a (false) thing (i.e. to deceive Ka'b)." The Prophet said, "You may say it."... *Sahih Bukhari Volume 5, Book 54, Number 369: Narrated by Jabir bin Abdullah*

The rest of this rather long *hadith* goes on to tell the story of how Muhammad bin Maslama duly lied to Ka'b and thus managed to kill him.

A *hadith* permitting lying under compulsion states:

> Allah's Messenger (peace be upon him) said, "Allah has overlooked my people's mistakes and forgetfulness, and what they are forced to do against their will." Ibn Majah and Bayhaqi transmitted it. *Al-Tirmidhi Number 6284: Narrated by Abdullah ibn Abbas*

Taqiyya is necessary even when dealing with Muslims, from whom some truths are best kept secret, as this *hadith* testifies:

I have memorized two kinds of knowledge from Allah's Apostle. I have propagated one of them to you and if I propagated the second, then my pharynx (throat) would be cut (i.e. killed). *Sahih Al-Bukhari, Hadith 1.121 Narrated by Abu Huraira*

As to the enduring validity of *taqiyya*, a *hadith* in Bukhari's collection states clearly:

Al-Hasan said: At-taqiyya (i.e., speaking against one's own beliefs lest his opponents put him in great danger) will remain till the day of Resurrection.[536]

The Shi'a imams repeatedly affirmed the doctrine of *taqiyya*, the sixth imam Ja'far as-Sadiq (699-765) deeming it the essence of religion with remarks such as "He who has no *taqiyya* has no religion" and "The *taqiyya* is [a mark of] my religion, and that of my forefathers."[537]

One underlying justification for the doctrine of *taqiyya* is the view that belief and faith are mainly matters of the heart. The declaration by word of mouth is secondary, the heart intention is all-important. God accepts belief without declaration, but declaration without belief is unacceptable. Mere words cannot extinguish the true flame of faith in a Muslim's heart.

Another justification is the sanctity of a Muslim's life which should be saved by all means possible. The following Qur'an verse is often used to justify *taqiyya*:

And make not your own hands contribute to your destruction but do good. Q 2:195

It is interpreted as laying a duty on all Muslims to save life, honour and property from danger and unlawful destruction by any means possible. There is a great deal of emphasis in writings about *taqiyya* on the special circumstances in which *taqiyya* is permissible. The doctrine is also justified by the claim that when faced with several evil choices, a Muslim should choose the least evil. Ibn Taymiyya stated that, while Muslims are forbidden from following non-Muslim laws and customs in a society where they are dominant, Muslims under non-Muslim rule may do so. Indeed, it is at times obligatory on such Muslims to copy their infidel rulers in order to protect themselves from harm, summon unbelievers to Islam, or gain information of benefit to Muslims.[538]

In a *fatwa* published on the popular Islam Online website in answer to a question concerning alleged Iraqi prisoners in Abu Ghreib prison who when tortured by American guards denounced Islam, the scholars use the case of 'Ammar ibn Yasir to justify *taqiyya* when under pressure:

> In his exegesis of the Qur'an, Imam Ar-Razi recorded that when the polytheists persecuted and tortured 'Ammar Ibn Yasir, he could not stand the torment and thus was forced to utter the words of *kufr*. Thereupon, it was said to the Prophet (peace and blessings be upon him): "O Messenger of Allah! 'Ammar has turned a disbeliever." The Prophet said: "No! 'Ammar is filled with faith; and faith has become his flesh and blood." 'Ammar came to the Prophet while shedding tears, whereupon, the Prophet (peace and blessings be upon him) wiped his tears and comforted him saying: "If they returned to their deed (i.e. torturing you), then return to your saying (i.e. the words of disbelief)."
>
> According to the exegetes, uttering the words of disbelief when one is under extreme pain and unbearable torture (while faith is reposed in one's heart) does not take one out of the fold of Islam…
>
> By way of analogy, as long as there is definite danger which cannot be avoided and against which there is no hope of a successful struggle and victory, one may utter the words of disbelief and drink or eat prohibited things. This may be danger facing one's own life or the life of one's family, or the possibility of the loss of the honor and virtue of one's wife or other female members of the family. It may also be the loss of one's material belongings to such an extent as to cause complete destitution.[539]

According to some scholars a further reason for the institution of *taqiyya* was that the Shi'a imams held that religious truths were not to be debased by dissemination to the general public but should be reserved for those capable of understanding them.[540]

Modern Shiʻa scholarship has defined four distinct categories of *taqiyya:*

1 Enforced *(ikrahiyya):* yielding to the instructions of an oppressor in order to save one's life.

2 Precautionary or apprehensive *(khawfiyya):* Shiʻa Muslims performing acts and rituals authorised by the *fatwas* of Sunni religious leaders in Sunni countries.

3 Arcane *(kitmaniyya):* to conceal one's beliefs as well as the number and strength of one's co-religionists, and to carry out clandestine activities to further religious goals. This is applicable in times of weakness when normal open propagation of one's beliefs *(idhaʻah)* cannot be carried out.

4 Symbiotic *(mudarati):* co-existence with the Sunni majority, participating with them in social and religious congregations in order to maintain Islamic unity and establish a powerful state comprising all Muslims.[541]

Contemporary Usage of *Taqiyya*

The *taqiyya* practice of deceiving enemies appears to be behind the activities of many contemporary Islamists who expend much energy to convince non-Muslims that Islam is and has always been peaceful and tolerant. Presumably the aim is that non-Muslims should be off their guard, and unprepared for the final onslaught to be launched when the *umma* has grown strong enough. Another motive is apologetic, wanting to defend Islam's image and win any comparison between Islam and other religions and ideologies. This includes the development of what appears to be an ambitious project of rewriting texts dealing with Islam.

A study published in 2003 by the American Textbook Council about history textbooks used in state schools revealed several aspects of this rewriting project and its impact on Western academics and educators who now tend to use self-censorship in their writings on Islam:

On controversial subjects, world history textbooks make an effort to circumvent unsavory facts that might cast Islam past or present in anything but a positive light. Islamic achievements are reported with robust enthusiasm. When any dark side surfaces, textbooks run and hide. Subjects such as jihad and the advocacy of violence among militant Islamists to attain worldly ends, the imposition of sharia law, the record of Muslim enslavement, and the brutal subjection of women are glossed over. Textbooks use language and concepts so similar to Islamic content guides that it appears they are lifting content broadly and uncritically from them. Either they or ignorant staff writers are taking these guides to be authoritative and factually correct... World history textbooks hold Islam and other non-Western civilizations to different standards than those that apply to the West. Domestic educational activists, Muslim and non-Muslim, who call themselves multiculturalists, seek a revised world history curriculum. They insist on harsh perspectives for the West while gilding the record of non-Western civilizations. For Islamists, the kind of cultural criticism and analysis that enchants American academics is unimaginable: indeed, it seems to activate rage and loathing. These academics ignore the dire consequences for any Muslims living in Islamic states who speak critically of their government or religion. Their allies are academic historians, first amendment organizations, educational associations and social studies experts that entertain romantic views of the Third World and skeptical views of the U.S. But above all, their collaborators are a handful of textbook editors in social studies and world history who determine what basic instructional materials used in classrooms nationwide say about Islamic history and its significance for the twenty-first century. During the last two decades, world history textbooks and the social studies editors who oversee their development have moved from the neglect of Islamic history to self-censorship. Any textbook negatives about Islam have been erased, replaced by fulsome praise and generalities designed to quell complaints from Islamists and their allies.[542]

Contemporary Muslim leaders often make contradictory statements. One way of interpreting such paradoxes is by acknowledging what scholars of Islam have identified as the permissibility of using different discourses for different audiences. This fits well with the *taqiyya* tradition that allows dissimulation not only in time of danger but when necessary in the interest of the Muslim community.[543]

There is a wide range of opinions amongst Muslims and much discussion and controversy between various Muslim factions and movements. But when Muslims discuss their beliefs with non-Muslims the *taqiyya* factor often comes into play.

The London-based Arabic newspaper, *al-Sharq al-Awsat*, commenting on the BBC Panorama programme "A question of leadership", broadcast on August 21ˢᵗ 2005, stated concerning Muslim leaders being interviewed by non-Muslim media:

> These very people, however, will use different terminology when speaking in English on foreign television networks. For this reason, when they are confronted with what they have previously argued in Arabic, they seem confused and frantically search for other arguments, which was the case on the Panorama special.[544]

On the Panorama programme Dr Taj Hargey, Chairman of the Muslim Education Centre, Oxford explained that Muslims have different discourses for different audiences – one for inner Muslim audiences and the other for the external public domain. Those in the public domain, including journalists, simply do not get to hear the inner discourse which is limited to Muslim-only circles.

> We have one vocabulary in private and we have another vocabulary for the public domain and that's why you don't hear it because you're the public domain.[545]

Discussing the Islamic Foundation in Leicester, UK Dr Hargey highlighted its double message:

> This Foundation has done some sterling work in many ways. But I think it has a double message. It has a public persona and it's got a private persona, and the public persona talks about bridge building, talks about interfaith relations, talks about integration

and so forth and so forth. But the real inner core is quite a different message. It's intolerant, it's rigid, it's exclusive. So I think we have a schizophrenic movement here.[546]

In the same BBC Panorama special report, Dr Azzam Tamimi, spokesman for the Muslim Association of Britain, argued that a declaration by Mohammad Shahid Raze, President of the World Islamic Mission of Europe, which stated that any Muslim targeting civilians by suicide bombing anywhere in the world is forbidden (*haram*), was not to be taken at face value because it was made under pressure.

That's a political statement produced under duress, under pressure.[547]

Dr Tamimi implies that it is accepted practice to issue different statements to different audiences, and that public statements made to the media or the authorities can be quite different from the real policy and beliefs as expressed in Muslim-only circles. His use of the phrase "under duress, under pressure" points to the doctrine of *taqiyya*, even though the nature of the "duress" and "pressure" was surely more to do with defending the international image of Islam than with any kind of other pressure applied to Mr Raze.

Muqtedar Khan, Chair of the Department of Political Science and Director of International Studies at Adrian College, USA, has called on moderate Muslims to take a clear stand against extremists in their midst. He accused some of hypocritical double talk especially in their demands for human rights for Muslims while ignoring or suppressing Muslim violations of human rights:

Many Muslims have become hypocritical in our advocacy of human rights in our struggles for justice. We protest against the discriminatory practices of Israel, India, and other non-Muslim nations, but are mostly silent against the discriminatory practices in Muslim states... But our silence at the way many Muslim nations have treated the same Palestinians really questions our commitment and concern for them... It is time that we faced these hypocritical practices and struggle to transcend them. For decades we have watched as Muslims in the name of Islam have committed violence against other Muslims...[548]

The Egyptian intellectual Sayyid al-Qimni accused many Muslim leaders of denying specific Islamic traditions when talking to Western audiences, although they are fully aware of their existence in Muslim sources. He offered several examples to support his claim:[549]

1 The Saudi Foreign Minister, in an interview with the American broadcaster Barbara Walters in November 2004, denied the existence of the *hadith* about trees calling to Muslims to kill Jews hiding behind them:

> Allah's Apostle (peace be upon him) said: The Last Hour would not come unless the Muslims will fight against the Jews and the Muslims would kill them until the Jews would hide themselves behind a stone or a tree and a stone or a tree would say: Muslim, or the servant of Allah, there is a Jew behind me; come and kill him; but the tree Gharqad would not say, for it is the tree of the Jews. *Sahih Muslim, Book 41, Number 6985: Narrated by Abu Huraira.*

The Minister expressed amazement, as if he had heard the *hadith* for the first time, denied it existed, and said it was incompatible with Islam. According to al-Qimni, the denial of a *hadith* amounts to apostasy, but no doubt the minister considered it *taqiyya*.

2 The American Muslim organisation, Council on American Islamic Relations (CAIR), took an American publisher to court for publishing in a school textbook on religions the (true) story about Muhammad marrying a Jewish captive woman, Safiyya bint Huyayy ibn Akhtab, after her father, brother, and all members of her tribe had been killed by Muhammad. According to al-Qimni, CAIR denied the incident

had ever occurred, and used a lie to have the passage excised from the school book. CAIR won the case and had the text of the story removed from the book. Yet the story (which we have already considered in chapter 7) is part of the Muslim source texts on the life of Muhammad well known to most Muslims.

As a result of his frankness, Sayyid al-Qimni received death threats to himself and his children from Islamist radicals and felt forced to retract his life's work to save himself and his family.

Sheikh Sayyid Tantawi, Grand Imam of al-Azhar University, and *taqiyya*

Sayyid Tantawi, Grand Imam of al-Azhar in Cairo since the 17 March 1996, is seen as the highest spiritual authority by most Sunnis worldwide. Under pressure from various sides, including the Egyptian government, al-Azhar scholars, Islamists and the non-Muslim world,[550] his statements are often contradictory and vacillating on issues ranging from female genital mutilation and the wearing of *hijab* (the Islamic headscarf for women) to *jihad* and suicide bombings.[551]

When addressing Western and international audiences, Tantawi tends to condemn all suicide bombings as un-Islamic and contrary to *shari'a*. In 1998, following the attacks on the US embassies in Kenya and Tanzania, Tantawi stated that

> Any explosion that leads to the death of innocent women and children is a criminal act, carried out only by people who are base, cowards and traitors, because a rational man with just a bit of respect and manliness, refrains from such operations altogether.[552]

After the September 11th 2001 attacks on the Twin Towers, Tantawi condemned the killing of civilians as a gruesome act denounced by the three monotheistic religions.[553] On December 3rd 2001, following a wave of suicide attacks against Israel, Tantawi condemned terrorism in all its forms and declared that *shari'a*, rejects all attempts on human life, and in the name of shari'a we condemn all attacks on civilians, whatever their community or state responsible for such an attack.

Tantawi clarified that he did not agree with the view that all Israelis were legitimate targets because this contradicted Muhammad's orders to his soldiers not to kill women or young boys.[554]

In 2002 at the opening session of a Cairo conference on "Media and the Arab/Muslim Image", Tantawi said the September 11th attacks the previous year were criminal.[555]

In 2003 at an international conference for Islamic scholars in Kuala Lumpur, Malaysia, Tantawi said that groups which carried out suicide bombings were the enemies of Islam. Suicide attacks, including those against Israel, were wrong and could not be justified.[556]

In a 2004 interview with the Italian daily *Avennire*, Tantawi condemned any one who deliberately harms the innocent and claimed that suicide bombers were not motivated by religion. They were pursuing "atrocious objectives" not acceptable to Islam.[557]

However in statements made to Arab and other non-Western audiences and media, Tantawi seems to take a hardline position, totally opposite to those cited above

Following calls by Israeli rabbis for him to condemn suicide attacks on civilian targets, Tantawi in 1997 declared such operations legal, blaming Israel for fuelling the violence. He told the Arabic daily *al-Hayat* that the Palestinian suicide bombers acted in self defence against aggressors and their actions were justified under Islamic *shari'a*.[558] In 1998 Tantawi, in another interview with *al-Hayat*, declared that Palestinian suicide attacks are legal under *shari'a*, stating that: "It is every Muslim, Palestinian and Arab's right to blow himself up in the heart of Israel".[559] In April 2001, Tantawi was quoted by Arabic newspapers *Saut al-Ama* (Egypt) and *al-Hayat* (London-Beirut) as stating that,

> Suicide operations are of self-defense and a kind of martyrdom, as long as the intention behind them is to kill the enemy's soldiers, and not women and children.[560]

In 2002 he went further, declaring at a reception for the leader of the Arab Democratic Party of Israel, Abd al-Wahhab Darawsheh, that suicide operations and the killing of Israeli civilians, even women and children, were permitted and should be intensified. He stated that "every martyrdom operation against any Israeli, including children, women and teenagers, is a legitimate act according to [Islamic] religious law, and an Islamic commandment, until the people of Palestine regain their land..."[561] In April 2002, speaking to 15,000 demonstrators at al-Azhar mosque after Friday prayers, Tantawi declared the door open for a Muslim *jihad* in Palestine, stating that those who carry out suicide bombings were not terrorists but martyrs.[562]

In 2004, following the new phenomenon of Palestinian women perpetrating suicide bombings, Tantawi was quoted in the Arabic press as confirming that Palestinian suicide bombings were acts of martyrdom, whether carried out by males or females. He also ruled that female suicide bombers are allowed to take off their *hijab* or wear a wider covering veil to hide their bombs in order to ensure the success of their operations.[563]

As far back as 1998, Tantawi had called for a Muslim *jihad* to support Iraq in the case of an American attack on Baghdad.[564] Tantawi called the 2003 US-led invasion of Iraq an act by terrorists, and gave his blessing to volunteers wishing to help the Iraqis fight against their "invaders". He stated that in the face of such aggression, martyr operations (suicide attacks) to prevent the overthrow of Saddam Hussein's regime were permitted by *shari'a*. Attempts to stop the US invasion of Iraq were legitimate *jihad*, and resisting the attack was a binding Islamic duty:

> Whoever wants to head for Iraq to support the Iraqi people, the door is open, and I say the door of *jihad* is open until the day of judgement.[565]

In January 2002 Tantawi co-chaired the First Alexandria Declaration of the Religious Leaders of the Holy Land with Anglican Archbishop George Carey, in which key Muslim, Christian and Jewish leaders committed themselves to supporting the peace process in the Middle East and condemned incitement to hatred and the use of violence against innocents.[566] Three months later, in a sermon in April 2002, Tantawi described Jews as "the enemies of Allah, descendants of pigs and apes", a comment that is clearly an incitement to hatred.[567]

Tantawi's contradictory statements illustrate the great difficulties faced by Westerners in their interactions with Muslim leaders who use *taqiyya*. It is clear that Tantawi, when addressing Arab and Muslim audiences, expresses approval of suicide bombings that target civilians both in the case of the Palestinian uprising and in the Iraqi resistance. He has legitimised such acts as prescribed by *shari'a* in cases he defines as defensive *jihad*. However to non-Muslim audiences he presents a much more moderate discourse. This raises the question of how many apparently moderate Muslim leaders are doing the same thing.

10
History: Muhammad and his Successors

Contemporary proponents of violent *jihad* consider the actions of Muhammad and the early history of the Muslim community under the *rashidun* (rightly-guided) caliphs to be models for all generations. The paradigm of these early conflicts in Islam shapes the violence of today and offers the justification for it. For example, the Sunni-Shi'a violence in Iraq is based on the early strife over the succession to Muhammad during 'Ali's caliphate.

Muhammad and Violence

Some liberal Muslim apologists today concede that Muhammad did use violence but claim that this was merely a defensive response in the face of extreme provocation. However, as we have seen, both the Qur'an and the *hadith* contain texts which, taken at face value, seem to indicate that Muhammad also took the initiative in engaging in offensive warfare.

Of course it can be argued that Muhammad lived in a very different time from our own and that it is unfair to judge him by modern standards of human rights and military conduct. Similarly the point could be made that Muhammad was merely a man and his belligerent actions and statements are examples of his human failings rather than divine guidance. However, traditionally Islam, whilst understanding Muhammad to be merely human, has also viewed him as effectively perfect and infallible, a timeless model for the Muslim community. Thus all but the most liberal or secular of modern Muslims, however uncomfortable they may feel about some of Muhammad's actions, must view them as not only good and just, but divinely sanctioned. In using extreme violence then,

Islamic militants are only following the perfect Islamic model of Muhammad. They are simply taking Islamic dogma to its ultimate logical conclusion.

It is interesting to see that some modern Muslim officers extol Muhammad's method of total *jihad* as a model for contemporary Muslim states and their military forces. Brigadier S.K. Malik of the Pakistani Army has this to say:

> The war [Muhammad] planned and conducted was total to the infinite degree. It was waged on all fronts: internal and external, political and diplomatic, spiritual and psychological, economic and military. Here was an ideal situation in which the military strategy, operating as an integral component of 'Jehad', the total strategy, produced spectacular results. By virtue of the application of their total power, the Muslims succeeded in turning the scales upon their enemies barely five years after the commencement of the war.[568]

We have already seen that in Muhammad's time there was a great deal of inter-tribal raiding amongst the Arabs, with the aim of stealing camels or sometimes women. Early in 623, the year after the Muslims migrated to Medina, Muhammad began to send his followers out on *ghazwas*, later in the year leading them himself. The targets were always trade caravans from Mecca, the place where he had been rejected and persecuted. Thus in their earliest military efforts the Muslims were taking the offensive. Muhammad forbade Muslims to engage in *ghazwas* within the *umma,* but allowed them to attack other tribes so long as their targets were not Muslims. By replacing tribal loyalty with religious loyalty, Muhammad transformed the *ghazwa* into the *jihad*[569] benefitting the whole Muslim *umma,* instead of the individual or tribe. The final stage of this transformation is described by Reuven Firestone as "the total declaration of war against all groups, whether kin or not, who did not accept the truth or the hegemony of Islam".[570] The result of this was that non-Muslim tribes found themselves facing a choice between converting to Islam or being attacked by the increasing military power of the Muslim community at Medina. As the more local tribes one by one accepted Islam, the

Muslims gradually had to move their field of war further away, so as to engage with non-Muslims.[571]

By the time of Muhammad's death in 632 virtually the whole Arabian peninsula had been subjugated to Islamic control. The degree of control varied.[572] Some parts were fully incorporated into the Medinan Islamic state, had converted to Islam and paid tax. In other areas most of the tribes but not all had converted and paid tax, while in areas remote from Medina they paid tax to the Islamic state but had not converted to Islam. Some tribes were politically allied with Medina but never paid taxes or acknowledged Muhammad's religious role.[573]

In considering the implications of the shift from allegiance based on kinship to allegiance based on a shared religion, it is important to understand just how powerful a force was tribal loyalty (*'asabiyya*). Writers have struggled to convey its overriding importance in pre-Islamic Arabia.

> Tribal spirit was no doubt the fountainhead of all cardinal moral ideas on which Arab society was built. To respect the bond of kinship by blood more than anything else in the world, and to act for the glory of the tribe – this was by common consent a sacred duty imposed on every man i.e. every individual member of the group.[574]

> It is difficult to give an adequately vivid and distinct idea of this *'asabiyya* as it is called - this deep, limitless and steadfast fidelity of the Arab to his fellow-clansmen; this absolute devotion to the interests, the prosperity, the honour and glory of the community wherein he was born and will die. The sentiment is not paralleled by Patriotism, as we understand that term – for that is an emotion which appears to the fiery Bedawy but lukewarm – it is a fierce and overpowering passion, and at the same time the first and most sacred of duties; in a word, it is the true religion of the desert.[575]

The closest ties were within the clan, the smallest genealogical unit. This kinship has been described as "tantamount to blood solidarity in a virtually legal sense of the word".[576] While there could be war between brother tribes or even between two branches of the same tribe, the clan was an indivisible unit. Retaliation for the death of any member of a clan is incumbent on all its members. Conversely anyone from the clan of the slayer can be killed in revenge if the slayer himself is not to be found.[577] While loyalty to one's comrades and equals within the kinship group was paramount, there was no equivalent loyalty to one's superiors outside of the kinship group.[578]

It was this allegiance and loyalty which Muhammad redirected from blood relatives to co-religionists, from the tribe or clan to the *umma*. He can also be said to have moderated the more barbarous elements of the *ghazwa* by introducing the concept of *dhimma*.[579]

According to Ibn Khaldun, *jihad* served to promote tribal unity within the *umma* (fighting a common enemy) as well as courage and self-reliance. He distinguished four kinds of warfare: (1) feuding between tribes and families (2) raiding among savage desert peoples i.e. those who earned their livelihood by war (3) *jihad* against external enemies (4) dynastic wars against seceders and those who are disobedient, which he considered were wars of "justice". The first two types of war he called wars of rebellion and sedition and considered them unjustifiable. The latter two types of war he called wars of holiness and justice, and considered them justifiable.[580]

The Four Rightly Guided Caliphs

Muhammad's immediate successors were the four "rightly-guided" caliphs whose rule covered the period 632 to 661. This period is often presented as the golden age of Islam. It is interesting to note that of these first four caliphs, so revered by Muslims, three were assassinated and the reigns of all were attended by great violence.

The caliphs expanded Islamic political and military domination into Palestine, Syria, Mesopotamia and Egypt. By no means all of those in the newly conquered territories converted to Islam, but many chose to do so because non-Muslims living under Islam suffered discrimination and various legal disabilities. In addition to the wars of expansion, there were rebellions which had to be put down, frequent rivalries between contenders for the top job, and many assassinations. This period of Islamic history is traditionally regarded by Muslims as a paradigm to which they should aspire, second only in importance to the example of Muhammad himself, yet at its very core is a history of assassinations, wars and rebellions brutally crushed. Much of the future development of Islam was a response to this early stage of which has provided models for radical groups throughout Muslim history.

There are many historical sources concerning this period, which have been subjected to painstaking scholarly examination. Some of these were written at the very time the events were taking place, for example a 634 Christmas sermon by Patriarch Sophronius of Jerusalem. Byzantine sources in general are relatively few. The most important are a brief history by Nicephorus (late eighth century) and a chronicle traditionally attributed to the Greek writer Theophanes from the ninth century. One particularly reliable source is that of Eutychius (876-940), a Christian Arab historian from Alexandria.

Muslim Arab histories are more plentiful and usually much lengthier than the other sources. Some of the best sources on the Muslim conquests are Ahmad b. Yahya al-Baladhuri (d.892) who wrote a work entitled *Kitab Futuh al-Buldan* (*Book of the Conquests of the Countries*), al-Tabari (839-923) who wrote *Ta'rikh al-Rusul wa'l-Muluk* (*History of Prophets and Kings*), al-Ya'qubi (d. late ninth or early tenth century) who wrote both a history (*Ta'rikh*) and a geography, Abu Muhammad Amad b. A'tham al-Kufi who wrote his *Kitab al-Futuh* (*Book of Conquests*) around 819, and Ibn Sa'd (ninth century) who wrote *Kitab al-Tabaqat* (*Book of Classes*). Al-Azdi al-Basri's *Ta'rikh Futuh al-Sham* (*History of the Conquest of Syria*) has details not found elsewhere but needs to be read critically. Various other sources will be mentioned in the following pages.[581]

Rebellion and internal dissension

As soon as Muhammad died various groups of Arabs rebelled against their new Islamic rulers.[582] Some refused to pay tax any more, but were willing to stay Muslims. Others refused to pay tax and gave no commitment that they would continue to adhere to Islam.[583] Certain groups who had always opposed alliance with the Muslims took advantage of the situation to rise against the pro-Muslim factions. The fighting that followed was known as *hurub al-ridda* (the wars of apostasy) although some scholars assert that many of the rebels had never converted to Islam in the first place.[584] It was however a name that stuck, and some Muslim authors describe the rebellion very much in terms of new converts abandoning the faith[585] with a great number of stubborn apostates being burned to death by the renowned general Khalid ibn al-Walid for refusing to return to Islam.[586] Although partly political, there was also a religious character to the rebellions in that four of the six uprisings were led by men who claimed to be prophets.[587] The *ridda* wars occupied most of the reign of the first caliph, Abu Bakr (632-4). It was Abu Bakr himself who insisted on dealing ruthlessly with the rebels, following the example of the deceased Muhammad, despite the hesitation of many others in Medina.[588]

The first group to be defeated were the Najd tribes who had asked if they could stop paying tax while remaining Muslims. The Banu Hanifa, a partly pagan, partly Christian tribe who had never paid taxes or converted to Islam, sought independence from Muslim rule under their "prophet" Musaylima; they were similarly defeated in the battle of Yamama and had to submit again to the control of Medina. It is reported that thirty-nine of Muhammad's companions and almost seven hundred Muslims were killed at Yamama, along with over fourteen thousand of the Banu Hanifa. This was violence on a much larger scale than normally occurred in inter-tribal feuds and raids in pre-Islamic Arabia.[589]

The rebellious tribes in Bahrain, Oman and Yemen were fought in turn until all had renewed their former alliances with Medina. Eventually the whole Arabian Peninsula was subdued, and what was effectively a standing army had been created because of the constant warfare and the number of new allies who had joined the victorious Muslims along the way.[590]

The overwhelming Muslim victory in the *ridda* wars seems to have been due to the unity and religious fervour of the Muslim forces. The rebels were mainly motivated by a desire for local independence, a love of old traditions, or an antipathy to paying taxes. Only the Banu Hanifa had had a specifically religious objection to Muslim rule. Another important factor was the collapse of the Persian Empire causing its former allies in Bahrain, Oman and Yemen to seek a new powerful ally such as Medina.[591]

The Muslim community divides into Sunni, Shi'a and Khariji

The *ridda* wars were followed by two civil wars (656-661 and 680-692). The first civil war (the Great *Fitna*) was triggered by the assassination of the third caliph, 'Uthman ibn 'Affan, in 656. It resulted in the first division of the Muslim community. At the Battle of the Camel (656), Muhammad's best loved wife, 'A'isha, with two of his companions (Zubair ibn al 'Awwam and Talha ibn 'Ubaidullah) fought against 'Ali ibn Abi Talib, Muhammad's cousin and son-in-law, who had been declared fourth caliph. They demanded that he hand over 'Uthman's assassins to be punished. 'Ali was victorious and Zubair and Talha were killed along with reportedly ten thousand other Muslims. The Umayyad Mu'awiyya ibn Abi Sufyan, 'Uthman's cousin and governor of Syria, then challenged 'Ali for the caliphate.

Following the inconclusive Battle of Siffin in 657, the permanent division of the Muslim community into three distinct sects took place: the Shi'as who followed 'Ali, the Kharijis who repudiated both Mu'awiyya and 'Ali, and Mu'awiyya's followers who became the main body who would later be called Sunnis. The basis of the dispute was over the succession to the caliphate. The Sunnis, who today form the great majority of Muslims (at least 80%) and are dominant in most Muslim states, accept the historical sequence of the first four caliphs and their successors (Umayyads and 'Abbasids) as legitimate. Their position was that any suitable person from Muhammad's tribe, the Quraish, was eligible to be elected as caliph. The Shi'a, who today comprise some 10-20% of all Muslims, believe that only 'Ali and his male descendants through Muhammad's daughter, Fatima, are the legal successors to Muhammad and should be the rulers (imams) of the Muslim world. The Kharijis rejected both Sunni and Shi'a claims, arguing that the position of caliph should be open to any suitable Muslim. The three sects all had the same attitude to war, but differed not only on the leadership issue, but also on the definition of a true Muslim i.e. who the enemy was.[592] The puritanical Kharijis took the most extreme stance, deeming that every Muslim who committed a major sin was an apostate and therefore an enemy.

Caliph 'Ali was assassinated in 661 by a Khariji in revenge for the defeat inflicted by 'Ali on the Kharijis (who had seceded from his forces) at the Battle of Nahrawan (658).[593] The leadership dispute was then continued by 'Ali's sons, Hassan and Hussein. Shi'as believe that the elder son Hassan was poisoned on the orders of Mu'awiyya. (It seems that actually he renounced his claim to the caliphate in return for a handsome stipend). The second civil war (680-692) was triggered by the rebellion of the younger son Hussein who claimed the caliphate after the death of Mu'awiyya in 680. Hussein and his small band of family and followers (including women and children) were massacred by soldiers of Mu'awiyya's son Yazid, the new Umayyad caliph, at the Battle of Karbala (680).

The shocking event at Karbala rallied many to the Shi'a cause, including Persian Muslims who welcomed an alternative to the Arab arrogance which gave Persian converts to Islam a subordinate position amongst the Arab tribes.

Following Hussein's death, 'Abdullah ibn al-Zubair proclaimed himself caliph in Medina. Yazid sent an army from Syria to depose him. At the Battle of al-Harra (683) outside Medina, the Syrians were victorious and looted Medina for several days. This victory established the Umayyad caliphate based in Damascus as rulers of the early Islamic state.[594] However, both the Umayyads and the next dynasty, the 'Abbasids, were constantly dealing with rebellions sparked by Shi'a or Khariji groups.

Another source of violence between the various groups of Arab Muslims was a historic rivalry between the northern (Qaysi) tribes and the southern (Qahtani, Yemeni, Kalbi) tribes.[595] Qaysi tribes had settled mainly in the northern parts of Syria and Iraq (Qinnasrin and the Jazira). Qahtani tribes had settled in southern Syria around Homs, in Palestine and in Transjordan. The Kalb, Tanukh, Judhan, Azd and Taghlib tribes were Qahtani southerners, while the Sulaym, Kalb, Tamim, Rabi'a and 'Uqayl tribes were

Qaysi northerners. Some southern tribes had been Monophysite Christian who converted to Islam in 629.

Under Mu'awiyya, the first Umayyad caliph (661-680), the Kalb tribe became particularly influential in Syria. Mu'awiyya was married to the daughter of a Kalbi aristocrat, and he relied on their support in his conflict with 'Ali; Mu'awiyya's son, Yazid, was also married to a Kalbi woman.

The Qays were a collection of clans with common genealogies. In the new garrison cites they developed into something like a political party. Because of Mu'awiyya and Yazid's reliance on the Kalb, the Qaysi tribes supported the anti-caliph Ibn al-Zubair during his revolt (682-692). Upon the death of Mu'awiyya II in 684, civil war broke out between the two groups in Syria. The two sides met in battle at Marj Rahit near Damascus in 684, and the Yemenis were victorious, installing a new Umayyad caliph. The conflict between the parties continued for centuries and was transferred to other territories, such as Africa, Spain, India and Sicily. Hostilities recurred under the reign of the Umayyad caliphs Abd al-Malik (685-705), Yazid II (720-724) who openly favoured the Qays, Walid II (743-744), Yazid III (744), and Ibrahim (744). When the 'Abbasids rebelled and attacked the Umayyads in 750, some 2,000 Kalbis defected to the 'Abbasids, because of the Umayyad Caliph Marwan II's reliance on the Qaysi tribes. In the reign of the famous 'Abbasid caliph Harun al-Rashid (786-809), the main problem in the Sind was the rivalry between Qays and Yemen.[596]

The battle at Marj Rahit thus proved disastrous for the Arabs, as it divided them permanently into two rival tribal confederations. The inherent tribal loyalties continued to plague the Arab Middle East well into modern times. As late as the nineteenth century, battles were still being fought in Palestine and Lebanon between groups calling themselves Qaysi and Yemeni.

Expansion beyond the Arabian Peninsula – "wars of conquest" in the Islamic terminology of the time

Immediately after Muhammad's death, while the Muslims were engaged on the one hand fighting the *ridda* wars within the Arabian peninsula, they simultaneously began a campaign to conquer the neighbouring lands of the Byzantine Empire, beginning with Syria. The expedition to Syria had in fact been planned by Muhammad before his death, and Caliph Abu Bakr ensured that it was carried out according to Muhammad's wishes.[597] Some scholars speculate that it may also have served the purpose of keeping happy the peripheral Arab tribes who wanted to go raiding but could not attack their fellow Muslims.[598]

The local populations of Palestine and Syria were taken completely by surprise at the Muslim attack, though the top echelons of Byzantine leadership may have been somewhat less surprised.[599] Emperor Heraclius tried to stir up the people to defend themselves, but in most cases the response was passivity and apathy,[600] perhaps due to the imposition of new military commanders from outside or to the financial cost of defence, which had to be borne by the local people. In addition they were not in the habit of fighting since the imperial government, in an effort to ensure public order, had banned private individuals from owning weapons. [601]

The turning point was the Battle of Jabiya-Yarmuk in Syria in 636, which saw the virtual destruction of the Byzantine army (though not the Byzantine Empire). This battle is analysed in detail by Kaegi, [602] whose opinion is that the military dimension was the primary factor in the Muslim conquests of this region.[603] He rejects the hypothesis that Christian sectarianism made many inhabitants of that part of the Byzantine empire disloyal. In fact many Christian Arab tribes of Syria wanted to remain part of the Byzantine Empire, albeit differing from the Emperor in theology, rather than be subject to the Muslim conquerors.[604]

While attacking Byzantine Syria, the Muslim Arab armies also attacked Sassanid Persia. The victory of Qadisiyya (636) ensured the conquest of Sassanid Mesopotamia, while the victory of Nihavand (642) brought all of Persia under their control. The conquest of the Sassanid Empire opened the gates to further conquests in Central Asia (Transoxania, Soghdania, Khurasan) and India.[605]

After Mesopotamia and Egypt had fallen to the Muslims, the next part of the Byzantine Empire to be targeted was Armenia (640-654). Caliph 'Uthman sent Muslim armies into Armenia who "made captives and plundered".[606] Unlike the earlier conquests, the Muslim victory in Armenia was not primarily due to military causes for the Armenians were better armed and more self-reliant than any other part of the empire. The Armenians' lack of resistance to the Muslim invasion was mainly due to local ethnic antagonisms and to their antipathy towards the Byzantine Empire from whom they differed on some Christological and ecclesiological issues. Some Armenian leaders and their followers defected to the Muslims (though without converting). Nevertheless, the Muslim invasion, which was violent and destructive, was seen by the chroniclers[607] not as liberation but as a catastrophe.[608] Even in Muslim sources there is sporadic mention of slaughter, taking captives, plundering churches, forced resettlement of Armenians, and settlement of Muslims in their lands.[609] Of the first raid into Armenia during the caliphate of 'Uthman, carried out by Salman b. Rabi'a al-Bahili under orders of al-Walid b. 'Uqba, the governor of Kufa, it is said:

> He went into the land of Armenia killing and taking prisoners and booty. Then, his hands laden [with plunder] he left and returned to al-Walid.[610]

Armenia was different from Palestine, Syria, Mesopotamia and Egypt in that the general population did not convert to Islam nor become assimilated to Islamic Arabic culture. They remained Christian and distinctively Armenian, and indeed rebelled when the Muslims later pressured them to convert to Islam and imposed higher taxes. On the other hand when Emperor Constans II managed temporarily to restore Byzantine authority over Armenia (652-3), he found Armenians who preferred Muslim rule.[611]

Armenian suffering increased with the invasions by the Turkmen under the Muslim Seljuk dynasty, and was exacerbated by the Crusades during which many Armenians sided with the Western Crusaders and the pagan Mongols against the Muslims.

Reasons for Byzantine collapse

The Byzantine army was the most efficient military machine of the time, a status it held for many centuries. It was due to its army that the Byzantine Empire managed to resist the Islamic onslaught in the seventh century (though losing the important provinces of

Palestine, Syria and Egypt) and survive for another 800 years until the fall of Constantinople in 1458. The Byzantine army was the product of superior discipline, organisation, armament and tactical methods. The Byzantines laid great emphasis on analysing themselves, their enemies and the geophysical environment. The results of this analysis were written down in their military manuals, especially the *Strategikon* of Maurice which was a comprehensive manual on all aspects of warfare and military leadership.[612] The Byzantines also had a strong navy and possessed the mysterious weapon known as Greek fire which was very effective in destroying enemy ships.

Following the Muslim attacks, the Byzantines reorganised the remaining Anatolian provinces under a civil-military administrative system. Each district was called a *theme* and placed under a *strategos* responsible for its defence and commanding an army corps called a *thema* of some 10,000 men. These standing forces were kept up to strength by selective recruitment among the local inhabitants. By the end of the seventh century there were thirteen themes: seven in Anatolia, three in the Balkans and three in the islands and coastal regions of the Mediterranean and Aegean seas. The standing army was kept at a strength of some 120,000-150,000 divided equally between cavalry and footmen.[613]

The main Byzantine strategy was defensive, its goal being the preservation of the Empire's territory and resources. It developed a sophisticated concept of deterrence based on the desire to avoid war as much as possible. When war was unavoidable, the Empire fought with the minimum possible expenditure of manpower and resources. The Byzantine strategy was to push any invaders back against defended mountain passes or river crossings where they would be destroyed in coordinated concentric attacks by Byzantine forces. The Byzantines also used economic, political and psychological warfare. They fomented dissension among their enemies, formed various useful temporary alliances, gave subsidies to allies and to barbarian chiefs to attack their enemies. The Byzantines also developed an efficient and widespread intelligence network with well paid agents in key positions in both hostile and friendly courts.[614]

There has been much scholarly debate about why the Byzantine Empire should have succumbed so quickly to the armies of the Muslim Arabs in the 630s despite the fact that the Byzantines had better organisation, better strategic thinking, better weapons and more funds. Their defeat was so surprising that several contemporary Christian sources saw it as God's judgement on the immorality and debauchery of Christians at the time, and particularly on Emperor Heraclius who had married his niece and supported a compromise theology called Monotheletism which was rejected by both sides (Chalcedonians and Monophysites) in the Christological debate of the time. These sources include Fredegarius in late 650s Gaul, the late seventh century Coptic historian John the Bishop of Nikiou, the late seventh century Armenian historian Sebeos, John Bar Penkaye from north Mesopotamia also in the late seventh century, and various seventh century Monophysite reactions recorded by the twelfth century Syrian Jacobite bishop Michael the Syrian.[615]

However there are many other factors which can be cited as causes.

1   Exhaustion of the Empire due to the long drawn out war (603-628) against the Sassanid Persians, even though the Byzantines had been ultimately successful. Byzantium did not have enough time to repair its finances and its frontier defences devastated by the Persians before the new Arab-Islamic onslaught of 632. It had serious problems paying its professional troops and its Arab auxiliaries on which the Empire had traditionally relied for the defence of the frontier.[616]

2   Serious internal political and religious unrest especially in the outlying provinces. Byzantine Greek-Orthodox (Melkite) persecution of non-Chalcedonians (Copts, Nestorians, Jacobites, Armenians) led to resentment and hostility that made it easier for the Muslims to penetrate, divide, and win some to their side especially among the non-Hellenistic populations. The Christians thus were divided and lacked a religious motivation comparable to that of the Muslim invaders.[617]

3 The Arab Ghassanids were allies of Byzantium and helped defend its frontier in eastern Syria and Palestine. They were however Monophysites, and Byzantine attempts to suppress their faith as a heresy alienated the Ghassanids and sparked unrest in their desert frontiers just as the Muslim armies started their invasions.

4 The fanaticism inspired by the new religion of Islam, especially its stress on *jihad* and the material and eternal benefits it offers. The Muslim fighters were heedless of death and of personal danger. The Byzantines underestimated the religious motivation of the Muslim Arabs. They failed to realise the significance of the fact that their Arab enemies – a familiar foe from the past – were now Muslim and strongly motivated by their new faith which gave them a loyalty and a cohesion that made them very resistant to Byzantine efforts to get them to betray, desert or change sides.[618]

5 Poor intelligence on the Muslims, poor communications and failure to react quickly and decisively. The population of Syria and Palestine had little inkling of how serious an onslaught they were to face from the Muslims.[619] Sophronius, writing in 634, states that the Muslims attacked "unexpectedly".[620]

6 Concurrent attacks on Byzantium by Slavs and Avars from the Balkans. The Byzantines were thus fighting on two fronts simultaneously.

Following the initial setback in the seventh century, the Byzantine Empire gradually recovered and reached a new peak of power under the Macedonian emperors between the late ninth and early eleventh centuries. By 1025 Byzantium was again the greatest power in the Mediterranean. It had recovered much lost territory and stretched from Azerbaijan and Armenia in the east to southern Italy in the west. However a new Muslim wave of attacks, this time by newly converted migratory Turkic tribes from Central Asia, brought about its final decline.

The Sassanid collapse

While Byzantium managed to survive the initial Muslim Arab onslaught, although with the loss of important provinces, the Persian Sassanid Empire collapsed totally in the face of the Muslim attacks. Most of the country was conquered from 643 to 650. The last resistance from the remnants of the Sassanid dynasty ended two years later.

The first Muslim expedition attacked the Nestorian Christian Lakhmid Arab allies of the Sassanids and captured their capital Hira in 633. Following a Sassanid victory at the Battle of the Bridge in 634 new Muslim forces were dispatched to the eastern front and these won a crucial victory in 636 at the battle of Qadisiyya on the Euphrates River near the Sassanid capital of Ctesiphon (near modern Baghdad). The Arabs quickly pushed further east, and within a short time defeated a major Sassanid counter-attack. They now controlled all of Mesopotamia, including the area now known as Khuzestan. Arab raiding parties then pushed over the Zagros mountains separating Mesopotamia and the Iranian plateau. Yazdegerd, the last Sassanid king, raised a new force but was decisively defeated in 642 in the important battle of Nahavand (some forty miles south of Hamadan in modern Iran) which completed the Muslim Arab conquest of the Sassanid Empire.

Reasons for the Sassanid collapse

Some of the causes cited for the Sassanid collapse are similar to those given for the Byzantine failures:

1 Military and economic exhaustion of the Sassanid Empire due to the long drawn out war (603-628) against the Byzantines.

2 Serious internal dynastic and religious unrest. Khusrau II (591-628) was murdered by his followers, and over a period of fourteen years there were twelve successive kings. Power passed into the hands of the generals, weakening central authority and paving the way for the Arab conquest.

3 A failure to realise the seriousness of the Muslim invasion,

mistaking it at first for customary raids by Arab nomads. The Sassanids did not understand the fanaticism inspired by the new religion of Islam, especially its stress on the physical and spiritual benefits of *jihad*.

4 The Nestorian Arab Lakhmids served as a buffer for the Sassanids on their western desert frontier. However in 602 the Lakhmid king was deposed and executed by the Sassanid Khusrau II on suspicion of treason and the Lakhmid kingdom was annexed. Lakhmid disaffection weakened the frontier at the crucial time of the Muslim Arab invasion.

Arab settlement in conquered areas

The Arab Muslim conquest of vast areas in the Fertile Crescent was followed by a major migration of tribes from all parts of the Arabian Peninsula into the new regions. This was a population movement involving not just fighting men, but whole tribes with their women and children. The families were lodged in the new military bases that were built on the edges of the deserts. The tribesmen provided the manpower needed for new advances into non-Muslim territories.[621]

The Growth and Decline of the Early Islamic Empire

When the power base of the Islamic empire shifted from Medina to Damascus in 661 an immense expansion of territory followed. Under the Damascus-based Umayyads, the first hereditary dynasty of caliphs, Islamic armies conquered east as far as northern India and central Asia (Tashkent 712) and west through North Africa (670), Sicily, Spain (711) and southern France (c.715). The advance across the Straits of Gibraltar was explicitly justified as part of the *jihad*.[622] In the midst of gaining these new territories, the Muslims continued to hammer away at the Byzantines, repeatedly besieging Constantinople (669, 674-80, 717) and making frequent incursions into Anatolia.

Then in the early eighth century the tide turned, and the armies of the caliphate suffered an unprecedented series of disastrous defeats in several, widely spread, theatres of war.[623] The result was not only a loss of territory but also a loss of morale amongst the Muslim troops. This was exacerbated by the fact that in many battles the senior commander was himself killed. Dramatic failures of this kind were not anticipated in Islamic theology and the resulting demoralisation was that much greater.

These defeats occurred in Sijistan (in modern Afghanistan) where the army was virtually annihilated (728), Ardabil in the Caucasus when only a few hundred Muslim troops survived of an army estimated at 25,000 (730), India where the Indians rebelled and the Muslim troops fled and refused ever to go back (731 or perhaps earlier), and a colossal defeat at the Battle of the Defile near Samarkand in Transoxania (731). Even on the Byzantine front, the Muslims experienced a defeat in 731. Finally, the Muslims were defeated in France at a battle between Poitiers and Tours (732).

Some of the reasons offered for this setback include:[624]

1 Internal dissension in the weakened Umayyad dynasty, including the dismissal and execution of its best generals.

2 Overextension which drained Muslim resources.

3 The unexpected resilience of the Byzantine Empire.

4 The vitality of the Franks united under Charles Martel.

5 The fierce resistance of the Khazars along the line of the Caucasus Mountains.

Despite all these defeats the caliphate continued with its policy of expansion on many fronts simultaneously, still suffering frequent – if less disastrous – defeats. This eventually weakened the Damascus-based Umayyad caliphate so much[625] that it paved the way for the rise of the 'Abbasid caliphate in Baghdad in 750 which took over from Damascus as the centre of the Islamic state.

The 'Abbasid dynasty continued in Baghdad until 1258 (when Baghdad was conquered by the Mongols), but various other independent caliphates arose in other places during this period, reducing the authority of the 'Abbasid caliphate. In Spain there was an emirate founded by the Umayyads (after they had been deposed in Damascus by the 'Abbasids) from 755, then in 912 a caliphate which lasted until its capital at Cordova fell to the Christian forces in 1236. Thereafter the centre of Spanish Islam became Granada. An Isma'ili Shi'a caliphate known as the Fatimids ruled North Africa (910-1171), making their power base in Egypt from 969 onwards. Another Shi'a group, the Buyids, exercised effective control in Baghdad from 945 to 1031 while retaining the nominal Sunni caliph.

Other regional dynasties in the medieval Muslim world included the Arab Hamdanids in Syria and the Persian Samanids in Transoxania. Three Turkish dynasties vied for power, with the Seljuks ultimately triumphing in the early twelfth century.

Turks and Mongols

In its eastward expansion, the Islamic Empire collided with Turkic tribes of Central Asia who were constantly migrating westward towards the regions of the Middle East. Many of these tribes converted to Islam and became front-line soldiers (*ghazis*) of the Muslim expansion into the Byzantine Empire, leading to the rise of the Seljuk sultanate. The Seljuks penetrated Byzantine Anatolia and under Alp Arslan (1064-1072) won the important battle of Manzikert in 1071 which was a disaster for the Byzantines. Manzikert opened up the Byzantine heartland to Turkmen settlement and Seljuk state-building. Armenia was conquered, and within a decade of Manzikert the Seljuks controlled three-quarters of Asia Minor. The Byzantine core territory gradually shrank after that to the coastlands of Asia Minor and the region around Constantinople.[626]

Turkic slave soldiers (Mamelukes) were also increasingly used to strengthen the empire's armies, and their commanders (sultans) gradually became influentiul political players. Mamelukes became a powerful force within Islam and set up their own states, the Mameluke Sultanate of Egypt being the most conspicuous example. During the Crusades, the Mameluke sultans of Egypt played a major role in defeating the Crusader armies and re-establishing Muslim rule in the areas once held by them.

Following the rise of Genghis Khan as ruler of all Mongols, his armies invaded Muslim areas in Central Asia and Iran and destroyed Baghdad in 1258, marking the end of the 'Abbasid caliphate. The Mongols were stopped in Syria by an Egyptian Mameluke army. They set up Mongol states in the vast areas they had conquered that later converted to Islam – the Golden Horde in Central Asia and Russia, and the Ilkhanid Empire in Iran and its environs.

Timurlane (ruled 1370-1405), a Muslim Turkic-Mongol ruler claiming descent from Genghis Khan, temporarily created a vast empire with its capital in Samarkand in the fourteenth century. He campaigned in all directions: Anatolia and Syria, Central Asia and North India, and crushed the last vestiges of Nestorian and Jacobite Christianity in Central Asia. He labelled all Muslims he attacked as heretics, whether Shi'a or Sunni. His conquests in India he justified with the words:

> My object in the invasion of Hindustan is to lead an expedition against the infidels that, according to the law of Muhammad (upon whom and his family be the blessing and peace of God), we may convert to the true faith the people of that country, and purify the land itself from the filth of infidelity and polytheism; and that we may overthrow their temples and idols and become *ghazis* and *mujtahids* before God.[627]

Timurlane died as he was preparing to invade China. The Timurid Empire he founded lasted until 1506.

By the seventeenth century three large Muslim empires dominated the Muslim world: the Sunni Ottoman Empire in Asia Minor, the Middle East, North Africa and Europe; the Shi'a Safavid Empire in the Iranian heartland, parts of Central Asia and the Caucasus; and the Sunni Mughal Empire in northern India.

The Crusades (1050-1291)

The Crusades were a delayed Christian reaction to the initial Muslim *jihad* of the seventh and eighth centuries that had overrun many Christian provinces including Palestine, Syria, Egypt, North Africa and Spain. The loss of the Holy Land to Muslim armies in the initial Islamic *jihad* was deeply mourned across the Christian world. This long history of losing Christian territories to Islam created a powerful motive to to recapture lands lost to Islam, especially the most important site for Christians, Jerusalem.

The Crusades were also a response to the continual *jihad* against Christian Byzantium, especially the Seljuk onslaught on the Byzantine Empire in the eleventh century. At the Battle of Manzikert in 1071 the Byzantine Empire suffered a humiliating defeat at the hands of the Seljuks that led to the loss of most of its Anatolian lands except for the coastlands of Asia Minor. The Byzantine Emperor Michael VII issued a plea for help to Pope Gregory VII in 1074, and this was renewed by Emperor Alexius I Comnenus to Pope Urban II in 1095.

Christian Europe also felt that it was being threatened by a Muslim encirclement from the south-west (Spain), from the south (Fatimid North Africa) and from the east (the Seljuk attack on Byzantium).[628]

Then there was the growing Seljuk and Fatimid harassment of Christian pilgrims to the Holy Land[629] as well as the Fatimid destruction of Christian holy sites in Jerusalem. In 1009, the Fatimid caliph al-Hakim (996-1021) sacked the pilgrimage hospice in Jerusalem and destroyed the Church of the Holy Sepulchre. He also persecuted the Christians under his rule, confiscating church property and destroying some 30,000 churches.[630]

In the late eleventh century European Christians, urged on by the Pope, launched a project of reconquest, the Crusades, that was to last for 250 years. After initial success, Christian states were set up in Syria and Palestine. The famous Sultan Saladin marked the turning of the tide against the Crusaders when he reconquered Jerusalem for Islam in 1187. In all there were nine Crusades between 1050 and 1271, but the new Mameluke dynasty in Egypt (1250-1516) delivered the final *coup de grace* to Crusader ambitions under Sultan Baybars (1260-1277), who conquered and destroyed the last Crusader strongholds on the coast. Many Christians in the fallen cities were massacred and enslaved. Following the fall of Antioch in 1268, the city was razed and its inhabitants either killed or enslaved. Baybars himself wrote a letter to its former Christian ruler, Count Bohemund, describing the horrors of its taking:

> Hadst thou but seen thy knights trodden under horses' hooves, thy palaces invaded and ransacked for booty, thy ladies bought and sold at four to the dinar of thine own money! Hadst thou seen any churches demolished, the crosses sawn in sunder, thy garbled gospels hawked about before the sun, the tombs of thy nobles cast to the ground...then thou wouldst have said, 'Would God that I were dust!'...This letter holds happy tiding for thee! It tells thee that God watches over thee, inasmuch as in these latter days thou was not in Antioch! As not a man has escaped to tell thee the tale, we tell it thee: as no soul could apprize thee that thou art safe, while all the rest have perished, we apprise thee![631]

The Muslims, initially divided among themselves and prone to infighting and even to arranging alliances with Crusaders against Muslim rivals, were gradually united under the Zengid (1146-1171) and later Ayyubid (1171-1250) dynasties. These used a revival of the *jihad* doctrine as a motivating and unifying tool and this led to a hardening of Muslim attitudes to Christians, including the Eastern Christians within Muslim lands. For most Muslim rulers of the time, the wars against the Crusaders were secondary to their wars against each other, and later against the greater threat to the Islamic commonwealth emerging from the East, the Mongols under Genghis Khan.[632]

Muslims in the twentieth and twenty-first centuries have made effective use of the Crusades to stir up guilt within modern Westerners, already uneasy about the evils of imperialism, colonialism, cultural insensitivity, and two world wars. Muslims fail to mention the initial *jihad* which wrested these areas from Christian rule in the first place, as well as the subsequent ill treatment of Christians and the destruction of churches which were the catalyst for the European counterattack.

For contemporary *jihadis* the Crusades have become the paradigm of the eternal battle between true Islam and the evil Western Christian enemy for domination of the whole world, a battle which they believe can only end with the final victory of Islam and the destruction of its Christian enemies and their allies, especially the Jews. The term "Crusaders" is used to imply all they hate in the West: secularism, materialism, immorality, corruption and decadence. Western imperialism and neo-imperialism (including the US-led invasions of Afghanistan and Iraq) are considered part of the eternal Crusade of the Christian West against true Islam. Not only Westerners but all Christians are now termed "Crusaders" thus legitimising a *jihad* against them. In this battle there are no neutrals and no innocents. Al-Qa'eda's founding manifesto in 1998 was called "Jihad against Jews and Crusaders". While all Western nations and their citizens are designated Crusaders, the term is especially prevalent in designating the perceived leader of the West, the USA and its citizens and soldiers.[633]

The Ottoman Empire

Having gained power, the Seljuks soon divided into independent principalities. The Ottoman dynasty was founded by Osman (pronounced Othman in Arabic, hence the European term Ottoman) who declared his independence of Seljuk rule in Anatolia around 1300. At this time the Ottoman state was a small frontier warrior state, "a small principality on the borders of the Islamic world, dedicated to Gazâ, the holy war against infidel Christianity".[634] Thus began the long and powerful reign of the Ottoman caliphate.

The Ottomans saw themselves as a *ghazi* Islamic state, perpetually involved in fighting the *jihad* against the infidels of *Dar al-Harb. Jihad* was the *raison d'être* of the Ottoman state, giving it religious legitimacy. Muslim *jihad* fighters, *ghazis,* were the spearhead of the Ottoman conquests. They constantly flocked to the Ottoman frontiers with *Dar al-Harb,* to raid the infidels and gain eternal merit as well as worldly booty.

The Ottomans invited masses of Turkic *ghazi* warriors to strengthen their *jihad* drive into the Balkans, where they soon occupied northern Greece, Macedonia and Bulgaria. At the Battle of Kosovo (1389) they defeated the Serbs and gradually established firm control over the western Balkans. The Ottomans captured Constantinople from the Byzantines in 1453, a turning point in history which fuelled their ambitions to conquer Christian Europe. They conquered Syria and Egypt in 1517. They brought all of Anatolia and Mesopotamia under their control, and renewed their drive into Central Europe, twice reaching the gates of Vienna (1529 and 1683). North Africa with the exception of Morocco, was also incorporated during the sixteenth century, which was the period of the most aggressive expansion. The Ottoman Empire continued as the chief Muslim power for about six hundred years.[635]

The Ottomans gradually replaced their independent tribal fighters with disciplined slave troops, first organised by Murad I (1360-1389) and known as *kapikullari*. Later they developed an elite slave fighting force known as the Janissaries (*Yenicheri*). Originally prisoners of war, the Janissaries were later kept up to number by means of a forced levy (*devshirme*) which occurred every few years. In these levies, instituted by Murad II (1421-51), a certain proportion of Christian boys were forcibly taken from their families and communities in the Balkans, forced to become Muslims, and trained for war. There was no justification for this within the *shari'a* but it may have arisen from the concept of Christians paying a tax to their Muslim overlords, in this case making the payment in children rather than in money.[636]

The Ottomans introduced a system of forced relocation of populations (*surgun*) in their empire. It served to remove recalcitrant communities from their historical environment, populate underdeveloped areas and cities, and introduce Ottoman-friendly populations into hostile areas. There were forced migrations of Turkmen tribes from eastern Anatolia into the Balkans, where they were used as *ghazi* warriors on the Hungarian and Austrian frontiers. Turkmen were also forcibly settled in Cyprus, Greece and Serbia to strengthen Ottoman control of their hostile Christian populations. *Surgun* was also used to forcibly resettle Armenian Christians, Orthodox Greeks and Jews into depopulated Constantinople after its conquest in 1453.[637] Turkmen were also settled in the Levant areas taken from the Mamelukes in the sixteenth century. Later, in the nineteenth century, Circassians and Abkhazians, driven from their Caucasus homelands by the Russian invasion, were settled first in the Balkans and then in the Levant.

As the military and economic strength of Muslim countries began to decline in comparison with European nations, it became more difficult to adhere to the doctrine of continued expansion into non-Muslim territory and ongoing *jihad*. Muslim governments had to abandon traditional teaching and, as a matter of sheer practicality, enter into permanent peace treaties with European governments. One such was the Treaty of Zsitivatorok (1606) between the Ottoman sultan and the Holy Roman emperor. A later sultan joined the Concert of Europe by signing the 1856 Paris Peace Treaty, thus effectively submitting to European international relations.[638]

Islamic Expansion in the Indian Sub-Continent[639]

The first Islamic invasion of India was ordered by Hajjaj bin Yusuf, the Umayyad governor of Iraq, in 708. Following two failed expeditions, he sent another force in 711, under the command of his nephew Muhammad bin Qasim, which proved successful and conquered large parts of Sind.[640]

Turco-Afghan-Mongol slave soldier groups displaced from Central Asia and operating on the eastern margins of Iran (Afghanistan) consolidated Muslim rule in North India in intermittent invasions over a long period. They established themselves in Khurasan, especially in Kabul and Ghazni in what is now Afghanistan.

The second large-scale Muslim invasion of India occurred in the eleventh century when Mahmud of Ghazni (997-1030), a slave (Mameluke) sultan, conducted seventeen raids in northern India over the course of his 33-year reign). He had vowed to the Caliph of Baghdad that he would undertake at least one *jihad* campaign per year against the pagans of India.[641] The Ghaznavids captured Lahore in 1030 and plundered north India.

The third invasion of India was by Mahmud Ghuri (d. 1206), who led his first expedition (to Multan and Gujarat) in 1175. The Ghurids had replaced the Ghaznavids, and began a systematic conquest of India, taking Delhi where they founded the Delhi Sultanate (1206-1526).[642]

The fourth wave of Islamic invasion was by Timurlane (1370-1405). In 1398 Timurlane crossed the Indus River and marched toward Delhi, ravaging the country as he went. His capture of towns and villages was usually accompanied by their destruction and the massacre of their inhabitants. Overcoming fierce resistance by the Governor of Meerut, he then defeated the armies of the Tughlaq Sultan Nasir al-Din Mahmud. Timurlane then entered Delhi and the city was sacked, destroyed and left in ruins. Before the battle for Delhi, Timurlane executed more than 50,000 (some say 80,000) captives. After the sack of Delhi most of the surviving inhabitants were captured and deported. Timurlane left Delhi in January 1399 loaded with an immense quantity of spoil.

The fifth wave of Islamic invasion was led by Babur, founder of the Mughal Empire, and continued under his successors.

The Turco-Afghan elites in India used Persian as the preferred language of court, bureaucracy and culture. Some Hindus were forcibly converted to Islam in the aftermath of the main battles, while others gradually converted to Islam through the efforts of the mystical Sufi orders. While many Hindus were massacred as pagans during the campaigns, the sheer size of the Hindu population forced Muslim *'ulama* to agree to redefine them as *dhimmis*.

The Mughal Empire

This was founded by Babur, a descendant of Genghis Khan and Timurlane, in 1526. It was consolidated by his grandson Akbar (1556-1605). The emperors extended the empire until at its apex in 1707 it embraced most of India except for the far south. The ruling elite was mainly of Turkic, Afghan and Iranian origin, but later Hindus, mainly Rajputs and Marathas, were included and formed some 20 percent of the aristocracy. The aristocracy was composed of lineage groups (denoted *biradari, jati, qawm* in various ethnic and linguistic communities) serving as clients of the emperor and ensuring the obedience of their supporters. The ruling elite was organised in the *mansabdar* system, in which each office holder held a rank that defined the number of troops he had to lead into battle. Beneath the *mansabdars* were numerous local notables called *zamindars*.

The Mughal Empire saw a flourishing of the arts which can still be appreciated in the architecture of the beautiful Taj Mahal.

Some Mughal rulers, like Akbar, were fairly tolerant towards their non-Muslim (mainly Hindu) subjects seeing them as essential to their empire's stability, economy and power. Others however strictly implemented *shari'a* doctrines on *jihad, dhimmis* and *jizya*. Destruction of Hindu temples in conquered areas and the construction of mosques in their place continued under all the Mughal rulers. Babur saw his campaign of conquest in India as a *jihad* against the infidel Hindus. Jahangir (1605-1627) destroyed Hindu temples (76 in the district of Benares alone).[643] Under Aurangzeb (1658-1707), many Hindu temples were razed,[644] non-Muslims in public offices were replaced by Muslims, *dhimmi* status, including the *jizya*, was harshly reimposed.[645] Aurangzeb's continuous wars (*jihads*) to expand his empire weakened it and after his death its power rapidly waned. The British stepped into the power vacuum and became de facto masters of the Muslim state, finally deposing the last emperor in 1858 and integrating it with their other Indian possessions.

See Chapter 11 for more information on Mughal attitudes to their non-Muslim populations.

Islam in South-East Asia[646]

Islam spread from various parts of southern Arabia and India to the Malay peninsula and to the Indonesian archipelago in the twelfth to fifteenth centuries. At the same time Islam also reached the coastlines of what are now Myanmar and Thailand.

While Islam established itself in most other regions by conquest, it was introduced into maritime South-East Asia mainly by traders and Sufis. In contrast to other regions where Muslim states were founded by the invading Muslim military elites, in South-East Asia existing dynasties converted to Islam, gradually converting the vast majority of the population to Islam.

A special element in the Islam of South-East Asia is its intimate link to the Malay people, the indigenous population of this vast region, who are spread from southern Thailand to the southern Philippines, transcending the boundaries of the nation-states within it.[647] Islam first entered the Malay world in the twelfth to thirteenth centuries and gradually superimposed itself on the local political culture, creating a network of sultanates bound by blood and marriage across the region. From its bases in Sumatra and Java, Islam spread further eastward to the Moluccas (1495) and reached the Philippines shortly after. The hereditary sultans of the various states saw themselves as protectors of Islam. Interestingly, modern Indonesia, which has the largest Muslim population in the world, is a secular democracy.

Contemporary Muslim minorities in South-East Asia

The integration of religious/ethnic minorities poses a challenge to many states around the world. In South-East Asia most Muslim minorities are also ethnically different from the majority population, creating an especially sensitive and inflammable situation. The Muslims of Thailand, Myanmar and the Philippines have long resisted assimilation into the majority culture and demanded some form of autonomy or independence for their respective areas. While many Muslims in these minority communities accept the legitimacy of majority non-Muslim rule as long as the basic freedoms of practising Islam are guaranteed, a growing radical minority see non-Muslim rule and efforts at assimilating and integrating Muslims into the national structures as having changed the status of their territories from *Dar-al-Islam* to *Dar al-Harb*, justifying armed resistance.[648]

Islam in Sub-Saharan Africa[649]

The Arab conquest of North Africa was achieved rapidly in the first era of Islam. It initiated the twin processes of Islamisation and Arabisation of the indigenous Berber population that have remained relevant in Africa ever since.

There were two directions of Islamic expansion: from north to south into the Sahel mainly by Berber conquerors and traders across the Sahara caravan routes (from Tripoli towards Fezzan in south-west Libya and from the Sous in southern Morocco); and east to west from the East African coastline (Kenya and Tanzania of today) as Muslim Arab traders and conquerors arrived by sea from southern Arabian regions such as Yemen, Oman and the Hadramaut.

Islam in sub-Saharan Africa was spread by several means:

1 Conquest (from Morocco into West Africa, from Egypt into the Sudan, from Oman into Zanzibar).

2 Trade across the Sahara and across the Indian ocean.

3 Migration and settlement (especially in East Africa).

4 Purposeful missionary work *(da'wa)* especially by Sufis.

5 Periodic revival movements that included a purification of Islam from pagan elements, the establishment of Islamic states under *shari'a* and their expansion though *jihad*.

The expansion of Islam south of Egypt was blocked for a while by the three Nubian Christian kingdoms that flourished along the Nile for some 600 years: Nobatia, Makuria, and Alodia. Trade agreements were made between Muslim Egypt and these kingdoms, but the relentless Muslim drive south finally caused their fall between the fourteenth and sixteenth centuries.[650] This opened the way for further expansion into present day Sudan south along the Nile valley and west to Darfur and Wadai.

There was also a thrust by Bedouin tribes from Arabia across the Red Sea to the Horn of Africa – eastern Sudan, Somalia and southern Ethiopia.

Colonial Era

European colonial expansion resulted in the effective subjugation of much of the Muslim world. By the early twentieth century the British, French, Russian and Dutch Empires controlled most Muslim lands, creating a theological crisis for Muslims as to the reasons for their humiliation at the hands of infidels. While there were *jihadi* flare-ups, the general consensus came to see the period as a time of Muslim weakness in which *jihad* was postponed until God would again strengthen the Muslim *umma*.

Independence

When, in the mid-twentieth century, Muslims were able to shake off the colonial yoke and gain their independence again, they did not on the whole revert to practising the traditional Islamic doctrine of war. Rather, they recognised public international law, for example, joining the United Nations. Even the charter of the Organisation of the Islamic Conference, an international body to which Muslim countries belong, affirms its members' commitment to the UN charter.[651] There have been, however, some very prominent exceptions to this generalisation.[652] Perhaps unsurprisingly Ayatollah Khomeini, the architect of the 1979 Islamic revolution in Iran, stated that he was opposed to treaties that contradicted Islamic law.[653] More surprisingly, Mahmud Shaltut (1893-1963), the Sheikh of Al-Azhar who insisted on a defence-only interpretation of *jihad*, affirmed the classical teaching that Muslims are free to denounce a treaty that has become disadvantageous to them.[654]

Muslims who have signed international agreements face a painful dilemma when such agreements prevent them from assisting their fellow-Muslims whom they see to be oppressed, for example, in Bosnia and Palestine, since under Islamic law they have an obligation to come to their aid.[655]

11
The Negative Impact of Islamic *Jihad* on Vanquished Populations

It is clear from the documents of the time that *jihad* in the Middle Ages brought in its wake destruction and misery to the conquered people. Muslim writers often claim that the Islamic conquests brought liberation to oppressed people and tolerance to all religious communities. But the accounts of the Christians and Jews who were on the receiving end are very different, and even Muslim historians often record large-scale brutality. It seems that *jihad* was all too frequently accompanied by destruction of cities, the killing of soldiers and the massacre of civilians, looting, widespread slavery, forced conversion, expropriation of lands for the victors and heavy taxation (*jizya, kharaj*). In a violent age, *jihad* was waged little differently from any other contemporary wars, despite the Islamic injunctions which should have limited the violence somewhat. (See also chapter 7.)

Forced Conversions to Islam

The issue of religious conversions during the expansion of the Islamic empire is a vexed point. Modern Muslim apologists deny there were any forced conversions to Islam during the early *jihad*. Many Muslim soldiers were undoubtedly strongly motivated by their religion, and some Muslim sources record religious polemics that might have been intended to convert. Writing about the aftermath of the Battle of Jabiya-Yarmuk (636), Kaegi says there is no evidence of the forced conversion of captured Byzantine prisoners.[656] There are *Muslim* reports of the Byzantines killing some of their own number who *voluntarily* converted to Islam. The earliest of these was Farwa b. 'Amr al-Judhami, governor of Ma'an in southern Palestine, whose conversion appears to have been part of his zealous attempts to develop good personal relations with the Muslims. According to Muslim reports he was executed by the Byzantines in 636.[657] Another early convert from Christianity to Islam, Ziyad b. 'Amr Nuqil, is alleged by Muslim sources to have been unofficially murdered by Christians at Mayfa'a, east of the Dead Sea.[658] Kaegi states that there is no evidence that the Byzantines tried to convert any Muslims to Christianity.[659]

However there can be no doubt that incidents of *forced* conversion to Islam did occur. While more sporadic in the Middle East where the enemies were mainly "People of the Book" and therefore had the option of choosing *dhimma* status, in the Muslim conquest of India and other areas deemed to contain pagan idolaters (not eligible for *dhimma* status), many of those who surrendered were given the stark choice of conversion to Islam or death.

Even Christian Arab tribes seen as potential allies in the war against the Byzantines, sometimes faced efforts at forced conversion by zealous Muslim commanders. One example concerns the Banu Taghlib Christians whose experience we have already considered from another perspective in chapter 7. 'Umair ibn-Sa'd, known for his antipathy to Christians, tried to forcibly convert the Banu Taghlib Christian tribes when he invaded their territories along the Euphrates River. When they refused he consulted Caliph 'Umar about how to handle this unexpected situation.

> 'Umair ibn-Sa'd wrote to 'Umar ibn-al-Khattab informing him that he had come to the regions on the Syrian slope of the Euphrates and captured 'Anat and the other forts of [i.e. along the course of] the Euphrates; and that when he wished to constrain the banu-Taghlib of that region to accept Islam, they refused and were on the point of leaving for some Byzantine territory; no one on the Syrian slope of the Euphrates whom he wished to constrain to Islam had before the banu-Taghlib showed such tenacity and asked permission to emigrate. 'Umair asked 'Umar's advice on this matter. 'Umar wrote back ordering him to double on all their pasturing cattle and land the amount of *sadakah* ordinarily taken from Moslems; and if they should refuse to pay that, he ought to war with them until he annihilates them or they

accept Islam. They accepted to pay double *sadakah* saying: "So long as it is not the tax of the 'uncircumcized', we shall pay it and retain our faith".[660]

From this record it is clear that 'Umair ibn Sa'd was in the habit of forcing Christian Arab tribes to convert to Islam, and was surprised at the firmness of the refusal of the Banu Taghlib. The Banu Taghlib were a special case, in that they were too proud to pay the humiliating *jizya,* and preferred to pay a double *sadaqa* tax instead.[661] However this report indicates that others had been "constrained" to accept Islam and complied. The exception made for the Banu Taghlib apparently continued to rankle with Muslim rulers. The Caliph 'Ali is reported to have said:

> If I should have the time to deal with the banu-Taghlib, I would have my own way with them. Their fighters I would surely put to death, and their children I would take as captives, because by christening their children they violated their covenant and are no more in our trust [dhimmah].[662]

Bar Hebraeus (1226-1286), a scholarly bishop of the Syrian Orthodox Church and a prolific writer, reports that the Umayyad Caliph al-Walid I (668 - 715). Al-Walid I tried to coerce the tribal chief of the Banu Taghlib to convert to Islam, and tortured him when he refused:

> And Walid said to Sham'ala, the chief of the Christian Arabs of Taghlib, 'Inasmuch as thou art chief of the Arabs, thou disgracest all of them when thou dost worship the cross. Therefore do what I wish and become a Muslim'. And he replied, 'Because I am chief of all the Arabs of Taghlib, I am afraid lest I may become the cause of the destruction of all of them; [for if] I deny Christ they will deny [Him also]'. When Walid heard these words, he commanded [his slaves] and they dragged him along face downwards and cast him out. And Walid sent him a message in which he swore saying, 'If he really will not agree [to what I say], I will make him eat his own flesh'. And when Sham'ala did not give way, even under this threat, Walid commanded and one cut off a slice of Sham'ala's thigh and roasted it in the fire, and

they thrust it into his mouth. And when Sham'ala persisted in his refusal even after this, Walid dismissed him, and he continued to live, the wound being visible in his flesh.[663]

Bar Hebraeus also reports that under the 'Abbasid Caliph al-Mahdi, Christian Arabs of the Tannukh tribe were forcibly converted to Islam:

> And in the year one thousand and ninety of the Greeks (A.D. 779) Mahdi came to Aleppo, and the Tannukh who lived in tents round about Aleppo went forth to meet him; and they were riding Arab horses, and were decked out with ornaments. Then it was said to him,' All these are Christians'. And he boiled with anger and compelled them to become Muslims, and about five thousand men became Muslims, but the women were saved [from this].[664]

In the various Muslim conquests in India, forced conversions of Hindus (and Buddhists) are mentioned. In one instance, during the campaigns of Mahmud of Ghazni in 1013-1014, it is claimed (relying on Muslim sources) that he forced Islam on the inhabitants of the hills bordering on Kashmir.[665] Jalal-ud-Din of Bengal (1414-1430) forcibly converted hundreds of his Hindu subjects to Islam and persecuted those who refused to convert.[666] In the early years of the tolerant Mughal Emperor, Akbar, some Hindus were forcibly converted to Islam.[667] Shah Jahan, (1628-1658) sporadically forced Hindus to convert to Islam on pain of death in times of war.[668]

During the reign of the Mughal Emperor Aurangzeb (1658-1707) special efforts were made to induce non-Muslims to convert to Islam. In addition to the reimposition of the *jizya* tax, all penalties for crimes and debts were annulled for converts, many of whom were also rewarded by high position and wealth. Some were forced to convert on pain of death, as happened to inhabitants of a region in the North-West Frontier some forty miles from Jalalabad who were converted at the point of the bayonet. Hindus in Surat were also forcibly converted, causing many to plan to migrate to Bombay, but the British turned down their request.[669]

Forced conversion of Christians and Jews occurred under the Almohads in North Africa and Spain where both communities were offered the choice between death or conversion.[670]

The Ottomans continued from time to time to practise forced conversions to Islam of conquered populations, especially during and after the seventeenth century. Efforts at forced conversion among the populations in the Rodope and Pirin mountains from 1666 to 1670 created a new population group named Pomaks (Christian Bulgarian Slavs converted to Islam). Some individual sultans were particularly zealous for their faith and instituted conversion campaigns, such as conversions of the Bulgarians by Selim I (1512-1520).[671]

There were also repeated forcible conversions of Jews to Islam in Shi'a Safavid Persia. The first was under Shah Abbas II (1642-1666), who in 1656 ordered all Jews in his kingdom to become Muslims. The newly converted Jews where known as *jadid al-Islam* (literally, the new of Islam). Forced conversions continued as late as 1839 where they are known to have occurred in the city of Mashad.[672]

Negative Impact in Various Regions
Palestine and Syria

In the initial invasion of Palestine, after a battle east of Gaza in 634, the Muslim armies killed four thousand peasants, Christian, Jewish and Samaritan and ravaged the whole countryside.[673]

After Mu'awiyya bin Abi Sufyan became governor of Syria in 640:

> He took Antioch by siege and plundered the villages around, leading the people away as slaves.[674]

Mu'awiyya was also ruthless in his treatment of Caesarea:

> Mu'awiyya besieged Caesarea with vigorous assaults, taking captives from the surrounding country and laying it waste. He sustained the hostilities by night and day for a long time until he conquered it by the sword. All those in the city, including the 7,000 Romans sent there to guard it, were put to death. The city was plundered of vast quantities of gold and silver and then abandoned to its grief.[675]

In another city, Euchaita, Mu'awiyya and his forces massacred the inhabitants though the city was open and had not resisted them:

> The Arabs found the gates of the unhappy city open and the people sitting around without the slightest fear. The next moment they were entering it, plundering it, piling up great mounds of booty. They seized the women, the boys and the girls to take back home as slaves. Even the city-governor was taken prisoner. Euchaita lay ravaged and deserted, while the Arabs returned exulting, to their country.[676]

Centuries later, when Palestine and Syria were again a battlefield during the Crusader era, 'Imad al-Din Zangi, Atabeg of Mosul, attacked and captured Edessa (1144). Bar Hebraeus reports that:[677]

> The Turks pushed in with drawn swords, which drank the blood of old men and young men, of strong men and women, of priests and deacons, of monks and anchorites, of nuns and virgins, of children of tender years, and of bridegrooms and brides. O what a bitter history! The city of Abghar, the friend of Christ, had become a thing to be trampled under foot because of our iniquity. Sons denied their fathers, and fathers their sons! The mother forgot to show mercy to her children! And every man ran to the top of the mountain. And when the aged priests who were carrying the coffins of the martyrs saw the wrath... they neither fled nor did they cease to pray until the sword silenced them.

Michael the Syrian, Patriarch of Antioch (1166-1199), also describes the scene which included the massacre of non-combatants:

> The Turks descended from the citadel upon those who had remained in the churches or in other places, whether because of old age, or as a result of some other infirmity, and they tortured them, showing no pity. Those who had escaped from being suffocated or trampled [in the crush] and had left the city with the Franks were surrounded by the Turks, who rained down upon them a hail of arrows which cruelly pierced them through.

O cloud of wrath and day without mercy! In which the scourge of violent wrath once again struck the unfortunate Edessenians. O night of death, morning of hell, day of perdition! which arose against the citizens of that excellent city. Alas, my brethren! Who could recount or hear without tears how the mother and the infant that she carried in her arms were pierced through by the same arrow, without anyone to lift them up or to remove the arrow! And soon, [as they lay] in that state, the hooves of the horses of those who were pursuing them pounded them furiously! That whole night they had been pierced by arrows, and at daybreak, which was for them even darker, they were struck by the swords and the lances!... And then the earth shivered with horror at the massacre that took place: like the sickle on the stalks of grain, or like fire among wood chips, the sword carried off the Christians. The corpses of priests, deacons, monks, noblemen and the poor were abandoned pell-mell. Yet, although their death was cruel, they nevertheless did not have as much to suffer as those who remained alive; for when the latter fell in the midst of the fire and the wrath of the Turks, [those barbarians] stripped them of their clothing and of their footwear. Striking them with rods, they forced them – men and women, naked and with their hands tied behind their backs – to run with the horses; those perverts pierced the belly of anyone who grew faint and fell to the ground, and left him to die along the road. And so they became the prey of wild beasts, and then they expired, or else the food of birds of prey, in which case they were tortured. The air was poisoned with the stench of the corpses; Assyria was filled with captives.[678]

Cyprus

Mu'awiyya ibn Abi-Sufyan was the first Muslim commander to invade Cyprus in 649 during Uthman's caliphate. According to Muslim sources, he accepted the capitulation of the Cypriot leaders and imposed a heavy tax on them.[679] However, Christian sources give a different picture:

When the Arabs reached the coast, they dropped anchor, moored their ships, armed themselves powerfully and came ashore. They scattered throughout the island, spoiling, enslaving, killing without pity... The barbarian force had scattered throughout the land, as I said before, to collect gold, slaves and expensive clothing and to bring it to Mu'awiyya at Constantina, who was absolutely delighted, as were his companions, at the quantity of the accumulated loot and of the captives, male and female of every age.[680]

Following news that Cypriots had sent ships to aid the Byzantine war effort, Mu'awiyya invaded the island a second time in 655. According to al-Baladhuri:

He took Cyprus by force, slaughtering and taking prisoners.[681]

He also settled 12,000 Muslim fighters on the island and had mosques built for them. According to Christian sources, Mu'awiyya sent a commander called Abu al-A'war to punish Cyprus:

As soon as the ships were ashore, the invaders filled all the mountains and the plains, intent on plunder and slaves. They winkled the natives out of the cracks in the ground, like eggs abandoned in the nest.[682]

Egypt

Most Muslims have been taught to view Egyptian history as a long, peaceful coexistence between the two religious communities, Muslim and Christian. They believe that the history of Egypt illustrates the tolerance of Islam and that Copts (Egyptian Christians) have always been well treated by Egyptian rulers who allowed them to play an important role in Egypt's administration. In this view the *jizya* tax was a just price for protection by the Muslim state, while other discriminatory practices are explained as legitimate means to visibly demarcate the communities.[683]

On the other hand, Copts see their history as a long series of persecutions, massacres, forced conversions, and destroyed churches. They feel themselves to be a subjugated people precariously surviving among a dominant and hostile majority. Martyrdom and suffering have a high symbolic meaning for Copts as they perceive themselves facing a constant threat to their existence.[684]

The seventh century chronicler John of Nikiou describes the *jihad* conquest of Fayyum and Nikiou in Egypt, including the massacre of non-combatant women and children:

> [In Fayyum] The Ishmaelites attacked, killed the commandant, massacred all his troops and immediately seized the town... Whoever approached them was massacred; they spared neither old men, nor women, nor children...Then the Muslims arrived in Nikiou. There was not one single soldier to resist them. They seized the town and slaughtered everyone they met in the street and in the churches – men, women and children, sparing nobody. Then they went to other places, pillaged and killed all the inhabitants they found... But let us now say no more, for it is impossible to describe the horrors the Muslims committed when they occupied the island of Nikiou, on Sunday, the eighteenth day of the month of Guenbot, in the fifteenth year of the lunar cycle, as well as the terrible scenes which took place in Cesarea in Palestine... Amr [b. al-'As] oppressed Egypt... He took considerable booty from this country and a large number of prisoners... 'Amr... showed no mercy in his treatment of the Egyptians and did not fulfill the covenants which had been agreed with him... He raised the tax to as much as twenty batr of gold, with the result that the inhabitants, crushed down by the burden and in no position to pay it, went into hiding... But it is impossible to describe the lamentable position of the inhabitants of this town, who came to the point of offering their children in exchange for the enormous sums that they had to pay each month...[685]

North Africa

The Muslim sources mention the taking of much booty, the killing and capture of many during the invasion, including the beheading of those who had surrendered. Many Berbers were enslaved and sent to the caliph.[686]

Non-Muslim prisoners were beheaded during a *jihad* campaign against Tripoli in the mid-seventh century, as chronicled by Ibn Khaldun in his *History of the Berbers and the Moslem Dynasties of Northern Africa*:

Abd-Allah set siege to the city [Tripoli]; but later, unwilling to let himself be diverted from the goal that he had in mind, he gave the order to break camp. While we were making our preparations, we spied some vessels that had just landed on the shore; immediately we attacked them and threw into the water anyone who was aboard. They put up some resistance, but then surrendered, and we tied their hands behind their backs. They were four hundred in number. Abd-Allah then joined us, and he had their heads cut off.[687]

'Abd al-Mu'min, the first Caliph of the Almohad dynasty (1094-1163), on conquering the province of Ifriqiyya (Tunisia of today) offered Jews and Christians the choice between conversion to Islam or death.[688] Apparently he failed to offer them the option of protected but subordinate *dhimma* status, as described in the *shari'a*. Similar policies were pursued in other areas that came under Almohad control. A contemporary Jewish account describes the Almohad ravages in North Africa and Spain:

Abd al-Mumin...the leader of the Almohads after the death of Muhammad Ibn Tumart the Mahdi...captured Tlemcen [in the Maghreb] and killed all those who were in it, including the Jews, except those who embraced Islam...[In Sijilmasa] One hundred and fifty persons were killed for clinging to their [Jewish] faith... All the cities in the Almoravid [dynastic rulers of North Africa and Spain prior to the Almohads] state were conquered by the Almohads. One hundred thousand persons were killed in Fez on that occasion, and 120,000 in Marrakesh. The Jews in all [Maghreb] localities [conquered]...groaned under the heavy yoke of the Almohads; many had been killed, many others converted; none were able to appear in public as Jews... Large areas between Seville and Tortosa [in Spain] had likewise fallen into Almohad hands.[689]

Sub-Saharan Africa

An important motivation for Islamic expansion into sub-Saharan Africa (*bilad al-Sudan* i.e. lands of the blacks) was the slave trade. Slave raiding continued for many centuries to obtain African slaves for the slave trade network that covered the Islamic world. It is estimated that the number of black African slaves exported by Arabs across the trans-Saharan trade route in the period 900–1100 exceeded 1,700,000. During this period, some 10,000 African slaves per annum were shipped across the Red Sea and the Indian Ocean to India and Islamic Asia. Some African slaves were used in the military as slave soldiers, but most were used for menial labour, for sexual services and as eunuchs in the harems of Islamic rulers.[690]

During the conquest of Egypt by 'Amr ibn al-'As, Nubia was also attacked but not conquered. The Nubians finally asked for a truce, which included among its conditions the payment of an annual tribute of three hundred (or four hundred) slaves to the Muslims.[691]

The Zanj slave rebellion (869–883) against the 'Abbasids in the Sawad region of Iraq was conducted by tens of thousands of African slaves forced to work in extremely harsh conditions in the salt marshes of south-west Iraq. In the extremely hot and humid climate, the Zanj slaves, who were given only minimal subsistence, had to drain the marshes, dig up and drag away tons of topsoil, and then plant labour-intensive crops like sugarcane on the less saline soil below. It is no wonder they revolted on at least three occasions. Encouraged by Khariji and Shi'a doctrines, they built their own capital, Mukhtara, in the salt marshes, occupied most of south Iraq and raided Basra. Al-Muwaffaq, a brother of the 'Abbasid caliph, al-Mu'tamid (870–892), finally defeated them in 883 after many battles.

Spain

The Muslim conquest of Spain was initiated in 711 by a Berber commander, Tarik ibn Ziyad, sent by Musa ibn Nusayr, the Umayyad governor of Muslim North Africa. Tarik, with 7,000 troops, crossed the Straits of Gibraltar and at the Battle of Guadalete defeated the Visigoth King Roderic. In an eight-year campaign most of Spain, except for small areas in the north, was conquered by the Muslim armies. Christian Spain became Muslim al-Andalus and was added to the expanding Umayyad Empire. The initial conquest was accompanied by much looting and the killing of Christian notables, soldiers and non-combatants, including children.[692]

The Umayyad caliphate was inconsistent in its treatment of non-Muslims. There was a long period of tolerance beginning in 912, with the reign of Abd al-Rahman III and his son, Al-Hakam II, in which the Jews and Christians of Al-Andalus prospered.

Some Christians appear to have deliberately sought martyrdom, even during the tolerant periods. For example, forty-eight Christians, known as the Martyrs of Cordoba, were executed by decapitation for blasphemy against Muhammad and Islam over a period of several years (850-859). They had publicly denounced Islam outside churches and in Islamic courts and mosques, insulted Muhammad and publicly asserted Christian beliefs considered blasphemous in Islam.[693]

With the death of al-Hakam III in 976, the situation of Jews and Christians deteriorated. The first major persecution occurred in December 1066, when the Jews were expelled from Granada and fifteen hundred families were killed when they did not leave. Starting in 1090 with the invasion of the Almoravids, the situation worsened further. Jews were forced to convert to Islam, and Christians were expelled, many to North Africa. With the defeat of the Almoravids in 1148 by the puritanical Almohads, Jews were again forced to convert to Islam; the conquerors confiscated their property and sold many into slavery. Famous Jewish educational institutions were closed, and synagogues everywhere destroyed.[694]

During these successive waves of violence, many Jewish and even Muslim scholars left the Muslim-controlled portion of Spain for Toledo, which had been reconquered in 1085 by Christian forces and was still relatively tolerant of both Jews and Muslims.

Persia

The conquest of the Sassanid Empire brought the main centre of the Zoroastrian religion under Islamic control. Originally the Zoroastrians were not included among the people of the Book and were treated as idolaters. However, the doctrine was soon adapted to extend the *dhimmi* status to the Zoroastrian communities as well. *Hadith* containing decisions made by the Prophet in favour of the Zoroastrians in Bahrein and Yemen were used in support of this new interpretation.

While nominally accepting Zoroastrians as a People of the Book, the Muslims were more severe with them than with Christians and Jews, destroying their fire temples and confiscating their treasures and books. 'Ubaidullah bin Abi Bakra, the Muslim general sent by Al-Hajjaj, governor of Iraq, made great efforts to suppress Zoroastrianism. As a result, many Zoroastrians fled to India. Further persecution of Zoroastrians in Iran over the centuries produced in repeated waves of migration to India. The result of these migrations is the small Parsee community in India.[695] It is estimated that some 50,000 Zoroastrians survive in Iran at the turn of the twenty-first century.[696]

While reports of forced conversions are rare in Muslim sources, in Zoroastrian memory, the Islamic conquest was an ongoing calamity that all but destroyed their culture and religion. The initial conquest meant massacres, enslavement and forced conversion to Islam of many who had fought against the Muslim invaders. In addition was the cultural catastrophe:

> The cultural calamity was disastrous. Books were burned, scholars slain and schools and libraries were destroyed because the invaders regarded the Koran as the last book that nullified the existing ones.[697]

Under the Safavids, the remnants of the Zoroastrians came under renewed severe persecution. Shah Abbas I (1587-1629) executed many Zoroastrians under the pretext that they were *kafirs*, not People of the Book. A letter sent from Safavid Persia to the Parsees in India claims that:

> In the year 977 Yazdgardi (987 Hijri) the agents of Shah Abbas came to Yazd to confiscate our religious books. They murdered two Mobeds who refused to surrender them. In Turkabad many Mobeds who refused to surrender the books were killed. The agents plundered and destroyed many scriptures here.[698]

Shah Abbas also dispatched troops to the Caspian province of Mazandaran, which had remained largely Zoroastrian and was ruled by the Zoroastrian Padouspanian dynasty, to forcefully convert them to Islam. He also forcefully deported many Zoroastrians to a ghetto town near Isfahan, named Gabrabad.

At the turn of the eighteenth century there were still several hundred thousand Zoroastrians left in Iran. The worst blow was delivered by the Safavid Shah Sultan Hossein (1694-1722) who issued a decree that all Zoroastrians should convert to Islam or face the consequences. Many were slaughtered, others converted to Islam, and some found refuge in Yazd and Kerman. The entire population of Gabrabad was massacred. Zoroastrian sources estimate the numbers killed at hundreds of thousands.[699]

In the twentieth century, Ayatollah Khomeini did not hide his contempt for Zoroastrians, and he regularly referred to them by the derogatory term *gabr*.[700] In 1993 and 1994, during Zoroastrian celebrations of the Chaharshanbeh Soori festival, security forces attacked the celebrating youths following Khamenei's orders not to allow the "atheist celebrations". Reports estimated a dozen killed and five hundred wounded.[701]

Byzantium – Asia Minor

Following their conquest of Syria the Muslims made frequent raids into Asia Minor, also mounting several campaigns for the conquest of Constantinople. Christian sources give a glimpse of these raids during the Umayyad caliphate and their consequences for the local population:

> As soon as the Arabs had left Leo's territory, they began to do all sorts of mischief and to commit all kinds of outrage in Roman [Byzantine] territory, burning down churches and houses, looting, shedding the blood of men and taking children captive. Many cities in the region of Asia fell to them that summer and they ruined them and took captives and looted, slaughtering the men and sending the children and the women back as slaves to their own country. That winter the Arabs spent in Asia. And Maslama sent Sulayman b. Mu'awid with 12,000 men to lay siege to the city of Chalcedon, to cut off

supplies from that approach to Constantinople and to lay waste and pillage Roman territory in general.[702]

The Seljuk, Turcoman and Ottomans continued the custom of raiding Christian territories. Christian and Ottoman chroniclers provide graphic evidence of the pillage and slaughter of non-combatants following the Ottoman *jihad* conquest of Constantinople in 1453. First, two Ottoman Muslim sources:[703]

> Sultan Mehmed (in order to) arouse greater zeal for the way of God issued an order (that the city was to be) plundered. And from all directions they (gazis) came forcefully and violently (to join) the army. They entered the city, they passed the infidels over the sword (i.e. slew them) and…they pillage and looted, they took captive the youths and maidens, and they took their goods and valuables whatever there was of them…

> The gazis entered the city, cut off the head of the emperor, captured Kyr Loukas and his family…and they slew the miserable common people…They placed people and families in chains and placed metal rings on their necks.

Ottoman sources include the key contents of letters sent by Sultan Mehmed himself to various Muslim rulers:[704]

> In his letter to the sultan of Egypt, Mehmed writes that his army killed many of the inhabitants, enslaved many others (those that remained), plundered the treasures of the city, 'cleaned out' the priests and took over the churches…To the Sherif of Mecca he writes that they killed the ruler of Constantinople, they killed the 'pagan' inhabitants and destroyed their houses. The soldiers smashed the crosses, looted the wealth and properties and enslaved their children and youths. 'They cleared these places of their monkish filth and Christian impurity'…In yet another letter he informs Cihan Shah Mirza of Iran that the inhabitants of the city have become food for the swords and arrows of the gazis; that they plundered their children, possessions and houses; that those men and women who survived the massacre were thrown into chains.

Two Christian sources, gathered from eyewitness accounts:[705]

(Then) the Turks arrived at the church [the great church of St. Sophia], pillaging, slaughtering, and enslaving. They enslaved all those that survived. They smashed the icons in the church, took their adornments as well as all that was moveable in the church...Those of (the Greeks) who went off to their houses were captured before arriving there. Others upon reaching their houses found them empty of children, wives, and possessions and before (they began) wailing and weeping were themselves bound with their hands behind them. Others coming to their houses and having found their wife and children being led off, were tied and bound with their most beloved...They (the Turks) slew mercilessly all the elderly, both men and women, in (their) homes, who were not able to leave their homes because of illness or old age. The newborn infants were thrown into the streets... And as many of the (Greek) aristocrats and nobles of the officials of the palace that he (Mehmed) ransomed, sending them all to the 'speculatora' he executed them. He selected their wives and children, the beautiful daughters and shapely youths and turned them over to the head eunuch to guard them, and the remaining captives he turned over to others to guard over them...And the entire city was to be seen in the tents of the army, and the city lay deserted, naked, mute, having neither form nor beauty.

Then a great slaughter occurred of those who happened to be there: some of them were on the streets, for they had already left the houses and were running toward the tumult when they fell unexpectedly on the swords of the soldiers; others were in their own homes and fell victims to the violence of the Janissaries and other soldiers, without any rhyme or reason; others were resisting relying on their own courage; still others were fleeing to the churches and making supplication- men, women, and children, everyone, for there was no quarter given...The soldiers fell on them with anger and great wrath...Now in general they killed so as to frighten all the City, and terrorize and enslave all by the slaughter.

It was in the context of the inexorable pressure of the Ottomans on the shrinking Byzantine state, that the Byzantine Emperor Manuel II (1391-1425) recorded his conversations with a Persian Muslim scholar (Dialogue 7, *Twenty-Six Dialogues with a Persian*) in which the Emperor stated:

> Show me just what Muhammad brought that was new and there you will find things only evil and inhuman, such as his command to spread by the sword the faith he preached... God is not pleased by blood - and not acting reasonably is contrary to God's nature. Faith is born of the soul, not the body. Whoever would lead someone to faith needs the ability to speak well and to reason properly, without violence and threats... To convince a reasonable soul, one does not need a strong arm, or weapons of any kind, or any other means of threatening a person with death...

These words were quoted by Pope Benedict XVI on September 12th 2006 at the University of Regensburg in Germany during a lecture dealing with the relationship between faith and reason. This quote caused a furore in the Muslim world as many Muslim leaders claimed the Pope had denigrated Muhammad and Islam by linking them to violence, and demanded an apology. Large demonstrations, some violent, erupted across the Muslim world and Christians and their churches were attacked in Iraq, Palestine, Nigeria and Somalia.[706]

Armenia

Sebeos reports on one of the first Arab incursions into Armenia and the taking of the major city of Dvin (640):

> Then, crossing by the bridge of the Metsamawr they inflicted the whole land with raiding, and gathered very much booty and many captives... On the fifth day they attacked the city. It was delivered into their hands because they surrounded it with smoke... The enemy army rushed within and put the multitude of the city's population to the sword. Having plundered the city, they came out and camped in the same encampment... After staying a few days, they left by the same route they had come, leading away the host of their captives, 35,000 souls.[707]

In 642-643 the Arabs returned to Armenia:

> When the next year came around, the Ishmaelite army came to Atrpatakan and split into three. One division went to Ayrarat, one division the region of *Sephakan gund,* and one division to Aluank'. Now those in *Sephakan gund* spread raids over that entire region with the sword, and took plunder and captives... Then the army which was in the region of Ayrarat struck with the sword as far as Tak', Iberia, and Aluank', taking booty and prisoners. It moved on to Nakhchawan to [join] the army which was attacking the fortress of Nakhchawan. However they were unable to take it. The did take the fortress of Khram; they slaughtered [its garrison] with the sword and they took captive the women and children.[708]

In 655, following a rebellion by leading Armenians, another Arab army ravaged Armenia:

> Then the army of Ishmael... besieged the city of Karin, and attacked its [inhabitants]. The latter, unable to offer military resistance, opened the gates of the city and submitted. Having entered the city, they collected gold and silver and all the large amount of the city's wealth. They ravaged all the land of Armenia, Aluank', and Siwnik', and stripped all the churches. They seized as hostages the leading princes of the country, and the wives, sons and daughters of many people.[709]

The migration of the Turks into the Anatolian highlands in the eleventh century marked the end of Armenian autonomy and the devastating chapter in their long history of suffering until modern times. According to Vahan M. Kurkjian in his *History of Armenia*:[710]

> The conquest of Armenia by the Turks was not easily accomplished, however. From 1048 to 1054 Toghrul Beg hurled his hordes at the eastern provinces of the Byzantine Empire. His cousin Koutulmish and his nephew Hassan were defeated, but his brother Ibrahim ravaged Vaspourakan, then marching northward, took Ardzen, a city of 800 churches and of immense wealth. They gave the city over to flames, after plundering it and

taking from the district 150,000 persons into virtual slavery. In 1054 Toghrul Beg led his troops into the Van district and spread devastation everywhere. The King, Gagik-Abas, was defeated in battle and took refuge behind his city walls. The Turkish chief then turned northwestward and laid siege to the city of Manazkert, but that place was saved through a heroic resistance led by Vassil, the son of the city's Armenian governor. Toghrul took revenge by pillaging the city of Ardzké, north of the Lake of Van. Kars had been taken and half destroyed by Ibrahim, but its King Gagik-Koriké was safe in the Kars citadel, built upon an impregnable rock...

However, Toghrul captured Sivas in the following summer (1059), reduced it to ruins and slaughtered the major part of the population. The survivors were carried away into slavery, and the Seljuk army recrossed the Halys River (Kizil Irmak) with an immense train of booty, including wagons loaded with gold, silver and rich fabrics — for Sivas had been a commercial center of great importance.

One of the greatest disasters that befell the Armenians was the capture of their capital Ani by Alp Arslan, the Seljuk sultan, in 1064.

And in this year 'Alb 'Arslan, the Sultan, went against the city of 'Ani, which was the first city of the Rhomaye, on the quarter of Armenia, and he captured it and made a great slaughter therein.[711]

And again according to Kurkjian:[712]

Alp-Arslan ("Bold Lion"), nephew and successor of Toghrul, was even more cruel than his uncle. He devastated the entire area of the Armenian plateau and the Lesser Caucasus. The city of Ani alone closed its gates against him with a courage born of despair. Bagrat, the duke, an Armenian, was then in command in behalf of the Emperor. Tired of fruitless assaults, Alp-Arslan was about to retire when the governor, fearing a new and more violent attack, ensconced himself in the citadel. Deserted by the Greek troops, the population began to flee along the valley of the Akhurian (Arpa-tchai). The Turks thereupon climbed over the undefended ramparts and entered the city on June 6, 1064. A frightful butchery followed, blood flowed in torrents in the streets, and in public places thousands fell by the sword. Those who had taken refuge in the churches perished and were buried in the ruins of the burnt edifices. Such survivors as were believed to be wealthy were tortured in an effort to force them to reveal the hiding places of their treasure.

"Men were slaughtered in the streets," says Aristakes of Lastivert, "women were carried away, infants crushed on the pavements; the comely faces of the young were disfigured, virgins were violated in public, young boys murdered before the eyes of the aged, whose venerable white hairs then became bloody and whose corpses rolled on the earth."

The dreadful holocaust continued for several days until the knight conqueror withdrew, leaving all in ruins behind him. Bagrat, the duke, and the Greek soldiers, had fled under cover of a storm. Alp-Arslan replaced them by a Moslem governor and garrison, and passed on towards Nakitchévan, followed by a caravan of booty and a multitude of slaves. Among the treasures seized from the Bagratid capital was the great silver cross which rose above the dome of the Cathedral. Alp-Arslan wanted to place it on the threshold of his mosque at Nakhitchévan, so that the "true believers" might enjoy the satisfaction of trampling upon the emblem of Christ every time they entered their sanctuary.

Armenian suffering reached its climax in the genocidal campaigns of 1894-1922, in which over 1.5 million Armenians were killed. Angered by Ottoman weakness and defeat, as well as by the rising nationalism and clamour for independence among its Christian subjects, Turkey determined to "resolve its Armenian question by the destruction of the Armenian race".[713] *Jihad* ideology and modern total war doctrine were combined in the effort to eliminate a whole indigenous people group deemed friendly to Turkey's enemies, especially Russia. The 1894-1896 massacres were carried out by a Kurdish irregular force, the Hamidiyye, set up and armed by the Sultan Abdul Hamid II

(1876-1909). Aided and coordinated by regular troops, they attacked Armenian villages, especially in the Sassun district, massacring the inhabitants.[714] During the First World War, the Young Turk government developed a plan to deport the entire Armenian population from Anatolia to Mesopotamia. The forced expulsion and deportation was accompanied by massacres, rape, kidnapping and looting which turned it into a machinery of death. Those walking towards Mesopotamia in the long "Death March" were reduced by constant attacks, starvation and illness. Many women committed suicide. Very few reached safety.[715] Numerous eye-witness accounts corroborate the charge of genocide which Turkish authorities continue to deny, claiming that Armenian deaths were only some 300,000 and were due to civil unrest in which many Turks had also been killed. Konstantinos Kaloyeridis, a Greek inhabitant of Erzinjan, was an eye witness who recalled:

> On 29 May [1915], the orders went out that not a single Armenian was to remain in the town. The policemen and gendarmes rushed into the Armenian quarters and with blows from sticks and rifle butts forced all Armenians to flee... The Armenians filled the road out of the town, moving towards the Kemah Boghazi pass. All you could hear was a general lamentation accompanied by burning tears. The Turkish gendarmes who went with them, and the Turkish inhabitants too, beat them and jeered... Shortly, the gendarmes withdrew to the mountainside and, together with the *chetes* [irregulars] and the Kurds, began a hail of rifle fire. As soon as the first Armenian fell dead, the throng went into turmoil and turned back with screams of pain. But then they came upon the Turks of Erzinjan, who were following them with rifles and sabres and who now fell upon them without mercy. Before the situation got this far, all the beautiful Armenian women had jumped into the river [Euphrates]. The whole surface of the river was covered with them... The Turks were slaughtering in great numbers, but the Armenians were many, and by rushing upon them they managed to break through the line of Turks and reach the plain. For several days afterwards a pitiless hunt went on... wherever they found an Armenian, they killed him... A few days

later there was a mopping-up operation: since many little children were still alive and wandering about beside their dead parents, the *chetes* were sent... to round them up and kill them. They collected thousands of children and brought them to the banks of the Euphrates, where, seizing them by the feet, they dashed their heads against the rocks. And while a child was still in its death throes, they would throw it into the river...[716]

India

During the many Muslim *jihads* into India, Hindu combatants captured during the campaigns were often massacred, as documented by Muslim chroniclers. The first invasion of India was ordered by Hajjaj bin Yusuf, the Umayyad governor of Iraq, in 708. Following two failed expeditions, he sent another force in 711, under the command of his nephew Muhammad bin Qasim, which proved successful and conquered large parts of Sind.[717] Hajjaj ordered bin Qasim to "behave in such a way that no enemy of the true faith is left in that country".[718] During the capture of Debal, when the inhabitants asked for mercy,

Muhammad Kasim replied that he had no order to spare anyone in the town and that the armed men had to do slaughtering for 3 days.[719]

When Muhammad bin Qasim took the fort of Brahmanabad in Sindh following a six-month siege (711-712), some six thousand Hindu captives were slain:

When the plunder and the prisoners of war were brought before Qasim, and enquiries were made about every captive, it was found that Ladi, the wife of Dahir, was in the fort with two daughters of his by his other wives. Veils were put on their faces, and they were delivered to a servant to keep them apart. One-fifth of all the prisoners were chosen and set aside; they were counted as amounting to twenty thousand in number, and the rest were given to the soldiers...(Qasim) sat on the seat of cruelty, and put all those who had fought to the sword. It is said that about six thousand fighting men were slain, but according to some, sixteen thousand were killed...[720]

Following another victory over a Hindu King (Dahar), bin Qasim "issued a mandate to the effect that all the prisoners of war should be put to death".[721] Hindu temples were looted, their idols destroyed and mosques built in their place. The wealth in spoils (captives, gold and other valuables) sent back to the governor in Iraq and the caliph in Damascus was enormous.

When Mahmud of Ghazni raided northern India in the eleventh century, he destroyed Hindu temples and idols, plundered their wealth, killed prisoners of war and forcibly converted Hindus to Islam. There are many accounts of Hindu temples being converted into mosques. For instance after the capture of Mirat by the Ghaznavid Sultan Qutb al-Din Aybak, it is stated that:

> All the idol temples were converted into mosques.[722]

Following the conquest of Delhi by this same Sultan:

> The city and its vicinity was freed from idols and idol-worship, and in the sanctuaries of the images of the gods, mosques were raised by the worshippers of one God.[723]

On conquering Benares:

> They destroyed nearly one thousand temples and raised mosques on their foundations.[724]

During Babur's conquests many Hindu temples were destroyed, including the temple at Ayodha where a mosque was built in its place.[725] These facts put in perspective the contemporary Hindu desire to reconvert the Ayodha mosque to a Hindu temple. While loudly denounced as sacrilege by Muslims around the world, Hindus see it as a just recompense for the desecration of thousands of Hindu temples by Muslims over the centuries.

Mahmud Ghuri's military campaigns in India, which began in 1175, were accompanied by ruthless slaughter, the destruction of temples and their replacement by mosques.[726] The chronicles of that period contain many accounts of slaughter and plunder. One sample runs:

> The army of the Sultan kept moving on, and committing slaughter and pillage.[727]

Timurlane conducted mass slaughter of prisoners during his *jihad* campaigns in northern India (1397-99):

> At this Court Amir Jahan Shah and Amir Sulaiman Shah and other amirs of experience, brought to my notice that, from the time of entering Hindustan up to the present time, we had taken more than 100,000 infidels and Hindus prisoners, and that they were all in my camp... I asked their advice about the prisoners, and they said that on the great day of battle these 100,000 prisoners could not be left with the baggage, and that it would be entirely opposed to the [Islamic] rules of war to set these idolaters and foes of Islam at liberty. In fact, no other course remained but that of making them all food for the sword. When I heard these words I found them in accordance with the rules of war, and I directly gave my command for the *Tawachis* [drumbeaters] to proclaim throughout the camp that every man who had infidel prisoners was to put them to death... When this order became known to the *ghazis* of Islam, they drew their swords and put their prisoners to death. 100,000 infidels, impious idolaters, were on that day slain. Maulana Nasiru-d-din 'Umar, a counselor and man of learning, who, in all his life, had never killed a sparrow, now, in execution of my order, slew with his sword fifteen idolatrous Hindus, who were his captives...[728]

Ibn Battuta (1304-1368 or 1377), the famous Muslim traveller, witnessed a display of brutality towards Hindu prisoners and their non-combatant wives and children, during a *jihad* campaign in southern India conducted by the Sultan Ghayasuddin (Ghiyath al-Din):

> Any infidel found in the jungle they took prisoner. They made wooden stakes sharpened at both ends and put them on the prisoners' shoulders to carry. Their wives and children were with them and they brought them to the camp. The stakes they had carried the day before were fixed in them and driven through them. Their women were killed and tied by the hair to the stakes. The little children were killed in their laps and left there... In the end the infidels were disastrously routed. Their leader was eighty ears old, and Nasir al-Din, the son of the sultan's brother, seized

him and took him to his uncle, who treated him with apparent respect until he had extracted from him his wealth, elephants and his horses. He was promising to set him at liberty, but when he had extorted everything he possessed, he killed and flayed him, stuffed his skin with straw, and hung it on the wall of Mutrah, where I saw it hanging.[729]

Alauddin Shah Bahmani, a Muslim ruler in the Deccan (1435-57), expressed the general antipathy of Muslim rulers to their Hindu subjects (Akbar and Jahangir were exceptions to the rule). His attitude is described by Muhammad Kasim Hindu Shah:

Therefore, as it was a rule with the princes of his family to slay a hundred thousand Hindoos in revenge for the death of a single Mussulman, he [Alauddin Shah Bahmani] swore, should Dew Raj take away the lives of the two captive officers, he would revenge the death of each by the slaughter of a hundred thousand Hindoos.[730]

Babur (1483-1530), founder of the Mughal Empire, revered as a model of Muslim tolerance by some modern historians, recorded the following concerning Hindu captives of a *jihad* campaign he was leading:

Those who were brought in alive [having surrendered] were ordered beheaded, after which a tower of skulls was erected in the camp.[731]

Akbar (1556-1605), famous for his religious tolerance, nevertheless continued the Mughal conquests of Hindu territories. It was said of him that:

His Majesty's mind was always intent upon clearing the land of Hindustan from the troubles and disturbances created by infidels and evil men.[732]

His generals ravaged and plundered the Hindu countryside:

Asaf Khan went under orders to take Rampur. He took the place, and having plundered and ravaged the country, he returned victorious. Husain Khuli Khan went to attack Udipur, the capital of the Rana and of his ancestors. He ravaged the country with fire and sword, and returned bringing great spoil and numerous prisoners from the fastnesses of the mountains.[733]

At the taking of the great Hindu fortress of Chitor after a long siege, it is related that:

> At early dawn the Emperor [Akbar] went in mounted on an elephant attended by his nobles and chiefs on foot. The order was given for a general massacre of the infidels as a punishment... By mid-day, nearly 2000 had been slain... those of the fortress who escaped the sword, men and women, were made prisoners, and their property came into the hands of the Musulmans. The place being cleared of the infidels, His Majesty remained there three days.[734]

This terrible punishment was meted out because the Hindus had tried to resist the Muslim *jihad* and invasion of their country. In the early years of Akbar's reign, Hindu temples and idols continued to be destroyed and Hindus had to wear patches of different colours on their sleeves to distinguish them from Muslims. As we have already seen, some Hindus were forcibly converted to Islam.[735]

Aurangzeb (1658-1707) treated non-Muslims with great severity while setting out to conquer the remaining Hindu parts of India, especially in the south. During a campaign against the Rajputs, his generals:

> employed themselves in laying waste the country, destroying temples and buildings, cutting down fruit trees, and making prisoners of the women and children of the infidels who had take refuge in holes and ruined places.[736]

Under the Mughal Furrukhsiyar (1713-1719) the Sikh fortress of Gurdaspur in the Punjab was besieged and the Sikhs finally surrendered.

> Their chief Guru, with his son of seven became prisoners, and received the predestined recompense for their deeds. 'Abdu-s Samad had three or four thousand of them put to the sword, and he filled that extensive plain with blood as if it had been a dish. Their heads were stuffed with hay and stuck upon spears.

Those who escaped the sword were sent in collars and chains to the Emperor... As to the rest of the prisoners, it was ordered that two or three hundred of the miserable wretches should be put to death every day before the *kotwal's* office and in the streets of the *bazaar*... After all the Guru's companions had been killed, an order was given that his son should be slain in his presence, or rather that the boy should be killed by his own hands, in requital for the cruelty which that one had shown in the slaughter of the sons of others. Afterwards, he himself was killed.[737]

Greece and the Balkans

John Cameniates provided an eyewitness account of the capture and pillage of Thessaloniki in 904. Cameniates, his father and brother, were taken prisoner while they tried to escape. Their lives were spared because they promised their captors a large amount of money. They were marched as prisoners through the city, and thus witnessed the terrible carnage of their fellow townspeople, including those who had sought refuge in the church. A summary and excerpts from Cameniates narrative reveals that:

The Thessalonians tried to escape through the streets, pursued by the Saracens, who were unleashed like wild beasts. In their panic, men. women, the elderly, and children, 'fell into each other's arms to give each other one last kiss.' The enemy hit with no mercy. Parents were killed while trying to defend their children. No one was spared: women, children, the elderly, all were immediately pierced by the sword. The poor wretches ran through the town, or tried to hide inside the caves; some of them, believing they could find refuge inside a church, would seek shelter inside, while others tried to scale the walls of the ramparts, from where they jumped into the void and crashed to the ground. Nuns, petrified with fear, with their hair dishevelled, tried to escape, and ended up by the thousands in the hands of the barbarians, who killed the older ones, and sent the younger and more attractive ones into captivity and dishonor... The Saracens also massacred the unfortunate people who had sought refuge inside churches." "The church [of Saint George] was full of wretches who had sought safety within it. There were about three hundred of them, as we learned later. A great number of murderous enemies came in. Immediately their leader bounced onto the holy altar, where the divine offices are held by the priests: there, crouching down with his legs crossed, in the manner of the barbarians, he sat, full of rage and arrogance, looking at the crowd of those people, full of the evil spirit of what he intended to commit. After grabbing my father and my brother with his hands, and after ordering that we be guarded in an area near the entrance by some of his men whom he had chosen, he gave a sign to his men to do away with the crowd. Like wild wolves when they meet their prey, they began to massacre the poor creatures quickly and mercilessly, and, overflowing with rage, they inquired with their eyes as to what the terrible judge wished to do with us: but he stopped them from doing anything against us, for the moment... After the end of the massacre of those poor people, the entire floor was covered with bodies, with a lake of blood in the middle. Then, as the murderer could not get out, he ordered that they pile up the bodies one on top of the other, on the two sides of the church; then he quickly jumped down from the altar, came up to us, and grabbed my father and my brother with his hands.[738]

Following the fall of Constantinople in 1453, the Ottomans moved to gain possession of Greece itself (the Peloponnesus). Towns that resisted experienced pillage and massacres. In 1460, when the towns of Gardiki and Kastrisi were taken, some 6,000 inhabitants were massacred.[739]

The ever-changing borders between the Ottoman Empire and Christian Europe during the Ottoman expansion became a region where *ghazis* terrorised the local population. The warriors received lands and tax exemptions in return for conducting raids into enemy territory and ensuring a constant flow of captives (slaves) for the Ottoman army and slave markets. In 1432 a Burgundian, Bertrandon de la Brocquiere, saw in the Maritsa valley in Bulgaria:

about twenty-five men and ten women, tied together with heavy chains about their necks. They had recently been captured in the Kingdom of Bosnia during a raid by the Turks, and were being taken to Adrianople by two Turks to be sold.[740]

Franciscan monks in Constantinople estimated that 60,000 Serbs were enslaved and transferred to Anatolia during 1438 alone. Other sources suggest that some 400,000 people were seized in the Balkans between 1436 and 1442. Some 160,000 were captured during the wars of 1439-1440. Many of the captives died in forced marches towards Anatolia.[741]

As late as the nineteenth century, travellers in the Balkans noted the extreme discrimination against the local Christian population. Arthur John Evans, travelling through Bosnia in 1875 notes:

> The truth is that outside Serajevo and a few larger towns where there are Consuls or resident 'Europeans', neither the honour, property, nor the lives of Christians are safe. Gross outrages against the person – murder itself – can be committed in the rural districts with impunity. The authorities are blind; and it is quite a common thing for the gendarmes to let the perpetrator of the grossest outrage, if a Mussulman, escape before their eyes... in the Medjliss, the only court where Christian evidence is even legally admitted, 'the evidence of twenty Christians would be outweighed by two Mussulmans'... If such complaint is made to a Consul, so surely is the complaining rayah [Ottoman subject] more cruelly oppressed than before; nor is consular authority so omnipresent as to save him and his family from ruin.[742]

Similar conditions prevailed throughout the Balkans, and indeed, throughout the Ottoman Empire wherever *dhimmis* lived.

12
Violent Sects and Movements: Past and Present

Once the legitimate use of violence to produce change had been established within the Islamic tradition, certain consequences followed. Violence was not just the prerogative of the Islamic state, but could also be claimed as valid by any Islamic rebel movement which might spring up. Many of these movements held that violence could be directed against civilians as well as against the state's armed forces despite the fact that mainstream teaching tended to forbid attacks on non-combatants.

However, to modern radicals whose aim is to return to the original sources and early model to purify Islam and reclaim its original glory and power, later limiting traditions are not authoritative. As they cast away the restrictions and limits set on *jihad* by establishment scholars over the centuries, they come face to face with the original texts and models. Sometimes they rediscover early concepts and interpretations which they understand to legitimise indiscriminate violence against diverse enemies. Thus contemporary Muslims wishing to re-enact the methodology of the early Muslims have examples of force, espionage, assassination etc. on which to model their own methods if they so choose.

Early Sects
Shi'a

As we have already seen (chapter 10), the main split in Islam occurred as a result of a leadership dispute when the Shi'as and Kharijis separated from the Sunnis during the Great *Fitna* of 656-661.

The Shi'a (the name is derived from *Shi'at 'Ali* i.e. the party or faction of 'Ali) initiated many bloody rebellions which ravaged large regions of the early Islamic empire. Although the first such uprisings were put down by the Sunni majority, the Shi'as eventually played an important part in the downfall of the Umayyad dynasty, only to find power taken not by a descendant of 'Ali but by the descendants of 'Abbas, Muhammad's uncle. Under the 'Abbasid dynasty the Shi'as became a vast secret community, who rebelled from time to time, but were gradually weakened by their own internal divisions, mainly on the vexed question of the succession to the position of supreme leader, the imam. Most of the Shi'a sub-sects believed that the imam was infused with a kind of divine light-substance which made him sinless and infallible. Most sub-sects also believed in the *mahdi*, i.e. that one or other of the imams (sub-sects would differ as to which particular imam) would return one day, since he had not actually died but merely gone into hiding.

Shi'a Islam, which is predominant in Iran today and whose adherents also form the majority in Iraq, has a strongly developed theology of death and in particular martyrdom. They are inspired by the martyrdom of Hussein at the Battle of Karbala on the tenth day of the Muslim month of Muharram 680. Millions of Shi'as make the annual pilgrimage to his shrine in Karbala, and commemorate his death in the annual 'Ashore festival of mourning and self-flagellation.

Kharijis[743]

At the same time that the Shi'as split away from the main body of Islam, so did another group – the Kharijis. Their most significant distinguishing feature was that they declared other Muslims to be apostates (and therefore deserving of the death sentence), and thus legitimised *jihad* against them. Indeed, they held that any Muslim committing a major sin was an apostate. The term for labelling someone as an apostate is *takfir*. The Kharijis believed that in order to exterminate evil and re-establish justice the apostates must be either forced to believe or killed.

It will be recalled that during the Great *Fitna* about who should be caliph, a battle was fought at Siffin in northern Iraq (657). After this battle Caliph 'Ali agreed to accept arbitration on the leadership dispute. Some of his followers were angered by this decision. They believed that the assassination of his predecessor Caliph 'Uthman had been just, given that 'Uthman had sinned. Quoting the Qur'anic motto "Judgement belongs to God alone", they held that the question of who should be caliph was not an appropriate subject for human arbitration. They withdrew from 'Ali's camp, stating that he had lost the right to the caliphate by making this concession to sinners, and that he and his followers were therefore no longer Muslims. Because they had withdrawn they were called Kharijis (meaning "seceders"). The following year 'Ali defeated the Kharijis at the Battle of Nahrawan, but was himself assassinated by a Khariji in 661. The Kharijis dispersed to other countries, though many remained in Iraq for a long time afterwards.

The Kharijis held that the appointment of both 'Uthman and 'Ali to the caliphate had been valid, but that each had forfeited their right to the position by later sinning and therefore – in the eyes of the Kharijis – becoming apostates. They considered that all Muslims who supported either 'Uthman or 'Ali were likewise apostates.

The Kharijis rebelled almost constantly for two centuries against first the Umayyad and then the 'Abbasid Sunni Islamic regimes, with battles being fought in Persia, Iraq and North Africa. They were brutal and ruthless in war. Despite many defeats, the Kharijis managed to establish states in the Arabian peninsula and in North Africa which survived for varying lengths of time. While the Kharijis themselves were eventually suppressed and exterminated by about 900, small remnant communities of a more moderate sub-sect of the Kharijis called the 'Ibadis survive in Oman, East Africa and North Africa. The Berber-speaking 'Ibadis in Algeria are called Mzabis after the desert region in which they are concentrated.

The Kharijis were extremely puritanical and legalistic. They forbade all luxuries such as music, games and ornaments. This strictness fitted with their doctrine that Muslims who committed major sins had effectively left the faith, i.e. apostatised, and were therefore liable to be killed. Unlike the other sects, they did not accept an oral profession of faith as sufficient to assure a person's status as a Muslim but believed that a life of righteousness and good works was also necessary. Their rebellions were motivated by the belief that any caliph who sinned must be deposed by force (unless he repented). The goal of the Kharijis was to create an Islamic community in which no one could deviate from the duties of Islam. *Jihad* by the sword was a vital part of their faith, a duty which they considered to be so binding that it was a "pillar of Islam" on a par with fasting, praying etc.

They stressed that all Muslims were equal and that the position of caliph should be held by the most pious Muslim in every generation, whether Arab, non-Arab, slave or even a woman. They rejected the Shi'a argument that the imam must be a descendant of 'Ali, and also rejected the Sunni practice of appointing to the caliphate (and all the main government posts) only those from Muhammad's tribe, the city-dwelling Quraish. This egalitarianism appealed particularly to non-Arab Muslims and also to the desert-dwelling Bedouin Arabs, whose warriors had done much of the fighting but felt they had not received a fair share of the spoils of war.

Apart from the equating of sin with apostasy, Khariji doctrines were based firmly on the Qur'an and on the words and example of Muhammad. They cannot therefore be regarded as heretical, but should be seen as a valid mainstream sect alongside Sunnis and Shi'as. In many ways they were simply taking literally what other Muslims found more convenient to interpret non-literally. Furthermore, the Khariji attacks were on other Muslim sects and regimes; they did not attack people who called themselves non-Muslims. Because they considered other Muslims to be apostates from Islam (and therefore to be killed on sight) these other Muslims were far worse in Khariji eyes than, for example, Jews and Christians, the People of the Book. In this way they differ very importantly from modern radical Islamic groups.

The Khariji doctrine of *takfir* – labelling other Muslims as infidels worthy of the death sentence for any perceived violation of the *shari'a* – has been revived in various modern groups of Islamic radicals including the Wahhabis, the Salafiyya movement, and many violent groups in Egypt, Jordan, Yemen, Algeria and Pakistan. These groups include al-Jihad and al-Jama'a al-Islamiyya in Egypt, the Armed Islamic Group (GIA) in Algeria and Al-Qa'eda. It is thus that they justify their *jihad* against Muslim regimes which they consider insufficiently Islamic. Unlike the Kharijis, these modern groups attack not only Muslims but also non-Muslims.

Isma'ilis

The Isma'ili sect began to be differentiated from the main body of Shi'as at the time of Imam Ja'far as-Sadiq (d. 765). They trace their imamate through one of his sons, Isma'il, and await the return of Isma'il's son Muhammad ibn Isma'il as the *mahdi*. Also known as "Seveners", they focus on the seventh imam, (whom some Isma'ilis consider to be Isma'il, although other Isma'ili sub-sects identify other individuals as the seventh imam). The Isma'ilis carried the Shi'a concept of secret (*batini*) teaching to great extremes, believing that only 'Ali and his descendants knew the real meaning of religious truth.

They developed what could be termed an intelligence service (i.e. the secret infiltration of normal society and the regime establishment) as a way to prepare for the final onslaught on the corrupt state power, and practised *taqiyya* to a high degree. The emissaries they sent out across the Muslim world tried to nurture any anti-government feeling and social unrest whether based on racial antipathies, economic discontent or any other the cause. They would create doubt, stress the need for an authoritative leader and impose an oath of secrecy and obedience. They would represent their own beliefs as Khariji to the Kharijis, as Shi'a to the Shi'as, as anti-Arab to the Persian nationalists etc. What they actually believed – apparently revealed only to the higher echelons of the movement – seems to have been a kind of mystic philosophy far removed from orthodox Islam.[744]

In the tenth century the Isma'ili message culminated in the appearance in North Africa of a certain 'Ubaydullah, who claimed to be the *mahdi* and the legitimate ruler of all Muslims by virtue of his descent from Muhammad's daughter Fatima through Muhammad ibn Isma'il. He established the Fatimid caliphate in Egypt.

Today Isma'ilis are found mainly in India and Pakistan, with smaller numbers in Yemen, Syria, Central Asia and Iran. Many have emigrated from the Indian sub-continent to East Africa and some to Europe and America.

Assassins

Amongst the many divisions and sub-sects of the Isma'ilis were the Assassins, based at Alamut in Persia, who were active for nearly two centuries starting around 1090.

The Assassins developed political killings (i.e. assassinations) by suicide devotees (*fida'iyun*) as the most effective tool to spread terror in the general populace and deter enemies from attacking them. They targeted only the great and powerful, and never harmed ordinary people. They always killed with a dagger since this was more likely to lead to capture and execution i.e. martyrdom, which would take the believer directly to paradise. More discreet methods, such as poison or killing from a safer distance with a bow and arrow, ran the "risk" of the Assassin getting away with it.[745]

The Assassins terrorised Syria and Iraq from their fortresses during the time of the Crusades. They were also a constant challenge to the Sunni rulers of Persia. Their power continued until 1256 when the Mongols attacked their fortress at Alamut in such overwhelming numbers that the Grand Master surrendered and was executed. The present Aga Khan traces his descent from this last Grand Master of Alamut.

Almoravids (*al-Murabitun*) 1056-1147

This puritanical reform movement arose among the Sanhaja (a Berber tribal federation) in the *ribats* (border fortresses) of the south-western Maghreb. It implemented an extremely strict version of the *shari'a* and was inspired by a militant and expansionist *jihad* ideology. Under Yusuf ibn Tashufin the Almoravids conquered Morocco in 1061 (founding Marakesh as their capital in 1062) and Muslim Spain in 1086. The Almoravids ensured the dominance of the Maliki school of law in the Maghreb. They were typical of many Islamic revivalist movements, seeking to purify the faith from pagan influences, establish strict *shari'a* and expand by *jihad*.

Almohads (*al-Muwahidun*) 1145-1269

The Almohads were a mahdist revival movement founded by Ibn Tumart (believed by his followers to be the *mahdi*) among the Berber Masmuda tribes of the high Atlas. They aimed to purify and revive Islam in the Maghreb by returning to the Qur'an and *hadith*. Ibn Tumart proclaimed himself as both *mahdi* and infallible imam.[746] The Almohads overthrew the Almoravids and established an empire which included North Africa from Morocco to the Egyptian border as well as Muslim Spain. Stressing the doctrine of *tawhid*, the Almohads were intolerant of other Muslims whom they considered apostates and therefore persecuted, killing many of them. They also severely persecuted Jews and Christians. Jews were forcibly converted to Islam, many were massacred and many synagogues destroyed. The Almohads exemplify a revivalist puritan mahdist movement, using *takfir* against other Muslims and so hostile to Jews and Christians that they were treated like polytheists, being offered only the choice between death or conversion to Islam without the possibility of *dhimma* status.

Later Reform Movements

Islam has seen a cycle of puritanical reform movements in the pre-modern era, which were a reaction to cultural, religious, political and economic decline at a time when Muslim states were under pressure from Western imperialism. Typically their leaders would seek to purge Islam of the various accretions it had accumulated over the centuries and to return to the fundamentals of the Qur'an and *hadith* and the first Islamic state established in Medina. Many of these movements had a messianic element in that their leaders claimed to be the long-awaited *mahdi* come to bring deliverance to Muslims and restore their glory.

Wahhabism

One of the most enduring of these movements was that founded in the Arabian peninsula by 'Abd al-Wahhab (1703-1792) who linked his movement to the House of Saud. Al-Wahhab considered Muslim society at the time to be little better than paganism, and he revived the Khariji practice of *takfir,* i.e. condemning all Muslims he disagreed with as apostates in order to justify *jihad* against them. The strictly puritanical Wahhabism remains today the predominant Islamic movement within Saudi Arabia.

In 1979 Juhayman al-'Utaybi (1943-1979), a strict Wahhabi who was disillusioned by the profligate lifestyle of the Saudi royal family, attempted to revolt against the Saudi regime in the name of Muhammad ibn 'Abdallah al-Qahtani, a student at the Islamic University in Riyadh, believed to be the *mahdi.* Qahtani's *mahdi* status had been revealed in dreams to his wife and sister. He fulfilled many of the predictions about the *mahdi* which occur in the *hadith:* the *mahdi* was to appear at the *ka'ba* at the turn of the Islamic century (1979 overlapped with the year 1400 in the Islamic calendar), and was to have the same name as the Prophet and similar physical characteristics. Juhayman and his followers believed that after a long period of deviation from true Islam, the *mahdi* would appear and put an end to corrupt, tyrannical regimes. They seized the Grand Mosque in Mecca but were eventually dislodged by the Saudi security forces after a violent siege.[747]

Salafiyya (neo-Wahhabism)

Wahhabism was a key factor in the development of the Salafiyya movement which became widely influential across the Muslim world, shaping the activist ideology of Islamic radicals from Morocco to Indonesia. Founded by Rashid Rida (1865-1935),[748] Salafiyya sought to return to the example of the "pious ancestors" (*salaf*) i.e. Muhammad, his companions, and the "rightly-guided" caliphs. Like Wahhabism it looked back for inspiration to the Kharijis in the early days of Islam and followed their example in the use of *takfir,* condemning secular Muslim society as heretical and apostate. Salafiyya added to Wahhabi puritanism an element of reinterpreting the origins of Islam in order to face the modern world. Another source of inspiration were the writings of Ibn Taymiyya in the thirteenth and fourteenth centuries.

277

Its organisational principles are those of the Saudi Ikhwan movement – a movement of radically extremist settlers who were sent in the 1920s and 1930s by the Saudis to found settlements on the Saudi borders. (Ironically they subsequently became a real danger for the Saudi regime.)

Since the 1950s the Saudi religious establishment has been active in disseminating Salafiyya, also known as neo-Wahhabism. In the 1990s it was the Salafiyya trend that caused various different Islamic radical groups to strengthen their links with each other.

The term "neo-Salafi" is now often heard, but seems to be used in a variety of different senses so it is difficult to try to define it.

Deobandi

The Deobandi movement grew out of the Indian Mutiny against the British in 1857, an event of major significance to the Muslim community in India. The Dar-ul-Uloom Deoband Islamic school was founded in 1867 in Peshawar. The Deobandi school taught a complete rejection of Western influence and values and a return to classical, conservative Islam. So successful was the Deobandi movement that by the time of its centenary in 1967 there were over 9,000 Deobandi schools and *madrassas* across South Asia. Today the Deobandi movement remains extremely influential amongst Muslims in India, Pakistan and Afghanistan and has helped to shape a distinctly South Asian, as opposed to Middle Eastern, brand of conservative Islam.

In recent years the Deobandi movement has become much more involved with Islamic militancy as a result of the *jihad* in Afghanistan against the Soviet Union in the 1980s, as they sought to defend their fellow-Muslims whose land had been occupied by non-Muslims.

The movement has come to the attention of the West because of its close connection with the Taliban and several key Pakistan-based Islamic militant groups. The Taliban emerged as a religious movement amongst ethnic Pathans very much growing out of Deobandi mosques and *madrassas* in Pakistan. During their rule in Afghanistan they continued to receive massive support and backing from the Deobandi school in Pakistan and even after the disintegration of their rule in 2001 the various Taliban and Al-Qa'eda cells left in Pakistan's North West Frontier Province are believed still to receive close support from the Deobandi school. In Pakistan itself the Islamist group Jamiat Ulema-e-Islam, which has links to Islamic militants fighting across Asia, is also firmly embedded within the Deobandi tradition.

Tablighi Jama'at

The Tablighi Jama'at was established in 1926 in what was then British India under the leadership of a Deobandi-associated Sufi scholar, Mawlana Muhammad Ilyas. Like the Deobandi school itself the Tablighi Jama'at is a movement which began as basically non-violent but later developed a violent element. In the case of the Tablighi Jama'at this change was a result of infiltration. The organisation, which is based near Delhi, is hugely influential with branches all over the Islamic world. Gatherings of supporters near Lahore, Pakistan, constitute the second largest assembly of Muslims in the world, surpassed in numbers only by the annual pilgrimage to Mecca. Tablighi Jama'at is very popular amongst Muslims from all sections of society, but particularly amongst educated, Westernised elites.

The Tablighi Jama'at considers that the most valuable kind of *jihad* is moral self-improvement. It stresses that Islam should be spread and promoted amongst nominal Muslims and unbelievers, not through force and compulsion, but through persuasion and peaceful means. They see physical *jihad* as secondary and inferior. However, during the 1980s the ISI (Pakistan's intelligence agency) and the CIA worked to infiltrate this hugely influential, and until then largely peaceful, Islamic organisation in order to recruit individuals to fight in the *jihad* against Soviet troops in Afghanistan. This helped to generate a violent element within the movement. The organisation is extremely large and diverse, and there is little interaction between different cells, making it difficult to gauge the extent to which this hugely influential and ostensibly peaceful organisation may now be linked to groups involved in violent activity.

Hasan al-Banna (1906-1949) and the Muslim Brotherhood

Out of the Salafiyya movement emerged the Muslim Brotherhood. This Egyptian group, founded by Hasan al-Banna in 1928, was the first grass-roots Islamic militant movement in modern times, the first of the groups who are often termed "fundamentalist" or "Islamist". Al-Banna, who had connections to Sufism, glorified active defensive *jihad*:

> The supreme martyrdom is only conferred on those who slay or are slain in the way of God. As death is inevitable and can happen only once, partaking in *jihad* is profitable in this world and the next. [749]

Banna saw Islam as an integrated, self-sufficient, and comprehensive social and political system which must be implemented in the context of an Islamic state - there could be no separation between state and religion. It was the implementation of *shari'a* which made a government truly Islamic, and such implementation was a primary goal of the movement.

The main objective of the Muslim Brotherhood is the establishment of an Islamic state under *shari'a* in Egypt, in all Muslim states and in all states in the world. This is a prelude to the re-establishment of a world-wide Islamic caliphate which will dominate the whole globe.

The movement early on developed branches in Syria, Palestine and Sudan. It then spread to most Arab and Muslim countries and established itself also in the West. Suppressed and persecuted by President Nasser in Egypt, many members fled to Saudi Arabia where they formed an alliance with the Wahhabi state against secular Arab regimes. The Syrian Branch revolted against the Ba'ath regime of President Hafiz al-Assad and was brutally suppressed in 1982.

The Muslim Brotherhood claims to be committed to non-violence and the use of legitimate political and other means to achieve its objective. In reality it has resorted to force and terrorism sporadically through its secret armed wings. It supports violent defensive *jihad* whenever Muslims are attacked. The Muslim Brotherhood has spawned numerous violent terrorist organisations.

The Muslim Brotherhood maintains a worldwide network of affiliated organisations, many of them viewed as mainstream by Western governments. Yusuf al-Qaradhawi is acknowledged as the current spiritual leader of all Muslim Brotherhood networks in Europe.

Mawdudi (1903-79) and Jama'at-i Islami

On the Indian subcontinent Abu'l A'la Mawdudi (1903-1979), influenced by al-Banna, founded the Jama'at-i Islami in 1941 as an elitist vanguard organisation aimed at establishing an Islamic order. His goal was the complete transformation of individual, society and politics in line with Islamic ideology, a transformation that should be attained gradually through the efforts of a highly motivated vanguard of enlightened Muslims acting as catalysts of the revolution. An Islamic state ruled by *shari'a* was seen as the panacea for all the problems Muslims faced worldwide. He defined *jihad* as primarily individual exertion "in the way of Allah" to alter the ideology and social order. While embracing the classic military understanding of Islam, he also considered *jihad* to cover non-violent means such as campaigning by speech and writing.[750]

Both the Muslim Brotherhood and the Jama'at-i Islami claim that Islam is a total ideological system that must dominate all public life (political, societal, economic), as well as personal matters and private worship. It is not enough for society to be composed of Muslims – it must also be Islamic in its basic structures.

Movements in the Post-Colonial Period

Following independence, most Muslim-majority nations did not deliver the promised improvements in social conditions. Their political, social, and economic failures contributed to the rise of radical Islam as a mass movement demanding a return to Islam as an authentic alternative political ideology. (See Appendix 3 on Various Networks of Radical Islam.)

Sayyid Qutb (1907-66)

Sayyid Qutb, the main ideologue of the Muslim Brotherhood in Egypt, was greatly influenced by Mawdudi. Qutb's writings (especially *Ma'alim fi al-Tariq,* translated as *Signposts on the Road* or *Milestones)* became the primary ideological source of contemporary radical Islamic movements, providing them with the criteria by which to judge contemporary regimes and societies. In this work he promoted the Khariji doctrine of *takfir,* the process of judging Muslims (individuals, regimes, societies and states) to be apostates or infidels if they do not wholly conform to the *shari'a.*

Qutb transformed the meaning of the Islamic term *hijra* (emigration) from a simple description of Muhammad's migration from Mecca to Medina to a distinct stage in the development of all true Islamic societies. *Hijra,* in Qutb's terminology, should be the response of true Muslims to the state of ignorance and immorality prevalent in their society. Following the example of Mawdudi, he employed a term originally reserved for the paganism of pre-Islamic Arabia and called this ignorance and immorality *jahiliyya.*[751] Qutb identified the enemy as all *jahili* societies, thus supplying a specific focus for revolutionary action. *Jahiliyya* is always evil in whatever form it manifests itself, always seeking to crush true Islam, he asserted, and therefore *jihad* by force must be used to annihilate *jahili* regimes and replace them by true Muslim ones.[752] He put an emphasis on the *qital* (fighting) aspect of *jihad*[753] and strongly rejected the defence-only interpretation.[754] He saw *jihad* as a method for actively seeking to free all peoples on earth from non-Islamic authority.[755]

Once Qutb had initiated the concept of condemning modern Muslim societies and states as *jahiliyya,* a whole area of controversy between mainstream and more radical Islamist movements was opened up. The central question for Islamists is the extent of *jahiliyya*: does it apply to society as a whole or only to the ruling regime? Does it include the bureaucracy and the military? The *ulama* establishment? If the entire society, not just the government, is *jahili,* then this legitimises attacks on civilians who are effectively apostates. There is no neutral ground.[756] For most Islamists, *jahiliyya* is the present condition of a society that by its non-implementation of full *shari'a* reveals its rebellion against God's sovereignty. All Western society and the international organisations dominated by it are considered *jahili* as were all the Muslim regimes of Qutb's day. For the more extreme radicals, all Muslim societies are *jahili* as well, justifying violent attacks against Muslim civilians everywhere.

Al-Jama'a al-Islamiyya (also al-Gama'a al-Islamiyya) in Egypt[757]

A radical offshoot of the Muslim Brotherhood, its roots lie in the Islamic Associations (*jama'at*) that appeared in the Egyptian universities in the early 1970s after President Sadat released the imprisoned Muslim Brothers and encouraged Islamic organisations as a counterweight to leftist-Nasserist groups. These associations organised summer camps where militants and sympathisers were initiated into the Islamist lifestyle of regular prayers, ideological training, preaching and proselytism. They followed Muslim Brotherhood doctrines as interpreted by Sayyid Qutb. A core network of activists was created that would eventually make the *jama'at* the dominant Islamic voice in the universities of the Arab world. In 1977 the associations won a majority in the Egyptian Students Union.

Following Sadat's peace initiative with Israel, al-Jama'a strategy moved to militant opposition to the regime and they organised clandestine actions in the slums of Egypt's great cities. The regime and its agencies were now seen as apostates and *jihad* was therefore legitimate against them. The Jama'a's primary goal was to overthrow the Egyptian government and replace it with an Islamic state under *shari'a*. The organisation conducted armed attacks against Egyptian security and government officials, Coptic Christians, and secular opponents of Islamism. Its support was based mainly in Upper Egypt in the Al-Minya, Asyut, Qina, and Sohaj governorates. It also found support in Cairo, Alexandria, and other urban locations, particularly among unemployed graduates and students. From 1993 onward al-Jama'a launched attacks on tourists in Egypt, most notably the attack in November 1997 at Luxor that killed 58 foreign tourists. It also claimed responsibility for the attempt in June 1995 to assassinate Egyptian President Hosni Mubarak in Addis Ababa, Ethiopia.

Its spiritual leader is the blind Sheikh 'Umar Abd al-Rahman, sentenced to life imprisonment in the US in January 1996 for his involvement in the 1993 World Trade Centre bombing. Among its main leaders are Hamdi Abdel-Rahman, Rifa'i Ahmed Taha, Fouad el-Dawalibi, Aboud al-Zomor, Ibrahim Nageh and Karam Zuhdi. The Jama'a has an external wing with supporters in several countries.

Under intense pressure from the state security services, the group declared a cease-fire in March 1999 and has not conducted an attack inside Egypt since August 1998.

Group leaders have recently published a series of books known as the "Concept Correction Series" in which they renounced their indiscriminate violence and extremist interpretations of Islam and apologise for their doctrinal mistakes that led to terrorism and the killing of many civilians as well as security forces.[758]

Muhammad 'Abd al-Salam Faraj (1952–1982) and Egyptian Al-Jihad

Muhammad Faraj was a former Muslim Brotherhood member (and disciple of Qutb) who founded Tanzim Al-Jihad because he was dissatisfied with the passivity of the Brotherhood. He laid the ideological base of his organisation in a short book he wrote, *al-Farida al-Gha'iba*, translated as *The Forgotten Obligation* or *The Neglected Duty*. The establishment of an Islamic state, said Faraj, had been decreed by God, and was therefore a compulsory duty for all Muslims. *Jihad* was the forgotten sixth pillar of Islam which had to be implemented at all times and places; there was no valid excuse for postponing it. Using Ibn Taymiyya's rulings against the Mongols as a basis, Faraj considered the situation in Egypt similar to that of the Muslims under the Mongols: the rulers are infidels and apostates who must be opposed and deposed, but the population was a mixture of true Muslims and infidels.

Faraj accepted the tradition of waiting for the *mahdi*, but believed this should not lead to passivity. He held that lack of messianic leadership was no reason to postpone the struggle, as leadership can be given in the interim by the best Muslim in the community. Therefore true Muslims should be active in fulfilling God's mandate to spread Islam to the whole world before the End Times and the appearance of the *mahdi*.[759]

Faraj managed to recruit many to his cause. The group was organised in a cellular structure, and used a *shura* (consultative committee) to decide matters of strategy. With branches in Cairo and Upper Egypt, the group pursued attacks against the government and promoted sectarian conflict. Al-Jihad tried to infiltrate the military, security services and government institutions so as to wage an immediate *jihad* which was initiated in 1981 with the assassination of President Sadat and three days of fighting in which they tried in vain to launch a revolution. Four people including Faraj were executed, and others given lengthy prison sentences.

Shukri Mustafa (1942-1978) and Takfir wal-Hijra

Shukri Mustafa (1942-1978) was a disciple of Qutb who took his teachings on separation from *jahiliyya* to their logical extreme, interpreting them to mean that all true Muslims in all generations must emulate Muhammad's model of *hijra* from Mecca to Medina. Therefore there must be physical separation from unbelieving society, withdrawal to a new location to establish a new alternative society (at one stage of their development they withdrew to live in caves in the Egyptian desert), and prepare for the stage of *tamakkun* (strength) and ultimate victory. Total separation (*mufassala kamila*) is compulsory during the temporary stage of weakness which ends when the alternative *umma* becomes strong enough to challenge the regime, return to conquer and establish the true Islamic state. Until that stage, passive separation, non-violence, and escape to safe areas to reduce contact with the apostate world were recommended.

All of Egyptian society – government and people - were considered apostate and as such legitimate targets for violent *jihad*. True Muslims must withdraw from them in a physical *hijra*. Mustafa interpreted separation as meaning that in case of war members of his organisation (officially called Jama'at al-Muslimin but more often known as Takfir wal-Hijra, a name given to them by the Egyptian authorities, based on their ideology) must not fight in the ranks of the Egyptian army, but should flee to secure positions. Takfir wal-Hijra members did indeed refuse to be conscripted to the army. They felt no allegiance to the Egyptian state, rejecting anything that might serve its interests. They did not recognise state education, uniforms, marriage or the legal system, since all were deemed *jahili*. The organisation did not allow its members to be state employees, and those who were changed jobs on joining Takfir wal-Hijra.[760]

Shukri Mustafa was a charismatic leader, seen by his followers as the promised *mahdi* who would found a new Muslim community, conquer the world, and usher in God's final reign on earth.[761] The movement had an eschatological world-view. They saw signs of the End Times in disbelief, oppression, immorality, famines, wars, earthquakes and hurricanes.

Takfir wal-Hijra hoped to gain the support of a large portion of the Egyptian population before it would consider itself to have reached the stage of power, when it was strong enough for the final assault on *jahili* society. However, although they did spread the concept of *takfir*, the organisation never reached the stage of power – it was still in its stage of weakness when it was destroyed by the Egyptian authorities. In 1978 Takfir wal-Hijra kidnapped and murdered the Egyptian Minister of Endowments Hasan al-Dhahabi. As a result of this, most of the group were tried and jailed, leaving Takfir wal-Hijra unable to act as an organised entity in Egypt.

Abdullah 'Azzam (1941–1989) and Maktab al-Khidmat

Abdullah 'Azzam, a Palestinian graduate of al-Azhar, was a member of the Muslim Brotherhood and a prominent *jihad* fighter in Afghanistan in the 1980s. He established the Afghan Service Bureau (*Maktab al-Khidmat*) to coordinate the efforts of the foreign fighters who came to Afghanistan. 'Azzam was considered by many to be Osama bin Laden's mentor.

'Azzam created a synthesis of classical *jihad* and Qutbist doctrine. He saw *jihad* as the greatest religious obligation after faith (*iman*). It is God's ordained method for establishing Islam in the world, a "battle... for the reformation of mankind, that the truth may be made dominant and good propagated."[762] 'Azzam claimed that *jihad* is the apex of a staged process that includes *hijra*, preparation, and *ribat* (frontline defence). Only the ill, the disabled, children, women who cannot emigrate and the aged are excused from this duty, which is an act of communal worship of God conducted under a recognised leader.[763]

Following Faraj, 'Azzam claimed that this obligation has been forgotten, and its neglect is the cause of contemporary Muslim humiliation. When not under direct attack by unbelievers, *jihad* is a communal obligation (*fard kifaya*) for which it is sufficient that the armed forces protect the borders and the imam sends out an army at least once a year "to terrorise the enemies of Allah".[764] However, when unbelievers occupy Muslim land, *jihad* becomes a compulsory individual obligation on every Muslim (*fard 'ayn*) and remains so until the liberation of the last occupied piece of Muslim land. 'Azzam offers quotes from the four Sunni *madhabs* (schools of law) to support this view.[765] He stresses the doctrine of sacred space which obliges all Muslims to fight the enemy who has enters an Islamic land or a land that was once part of the Islamic lands.[766] He argues that in the modern world, infidels occupy Muslim lands in Palestine, Afghanistan (in the 1980s), Kashmir, and other places, so it is clear that at present *jihad* is a personal duty for every Muslim as an individual.[767]

'Azzam also calls for Muslims to give up narrow nationalism and let their vision extend beyond national borders "that have been drawn up for us by the Kuffar." He rejects all arguments against the immediate implementation of *jihad*, such as the lack of a qualified leader, internal squabbles among Muslims, or insufficient manpower. On the contrary, he asserts that conducting *jihad* is part of the process of uniting Muslims and establishing the real caliphate.[768]

Hizb ut-Tahrir, HT (Hizb al-Tahrir al-Islami)[769]

Hizb ut-Tahrir is a radical Islamist organisation founded in 1953 in Jerusalem by Taqi al-Din al-Nabhani (1909-1977) who split from the Muslim Brotherhood. Its goal is the revival of the Islamic *umma* by creating a single Islamic state under a caliph implementing *shari'a* on the ruins of existing regimes in Muslim lands. Hizb ut-Tahrir has drafted a constitution detailing the political, economic and social systems of the Islamic state.

Executive and legislative powers are vested in an elected caliph (*khalifa*) in whom most functions of state are centralised. Nationalism and democracy are rejected as Western imports. Hizb ut-Tahrir claims to be a political party with Islam as its ideology. By politicising Muslims it aims at creating an extensive "fifth column" everywhere to prepare for the Islamic state. It refuses to be involved in social, religious or educational programmes, concentrating on political activity aimed at radicalising and mobilising Muslims. It has developed a staged programme for achieving its goals. Nominating an agreed-upon caliph will be the signal for implementing its radical vision using *jihad.*[770]

Early on Hizb ut-Tahrir established branches in Syria, Lebanon, Kuwait and Iraq. In 1968 and 1969 it was involved in attempted *coups d'etats* in Amman coordinated with simultaneous arrangements in Baghdad and Damascus. Further plots took place in Baghdad (1972), Cairo (1974) and Damascus (1976). Its plots, confrontational rhetoric and style caused it to be suppressed in most of the Middle East. The organisation has more recently gone international opening branches in many Western countries (where it is particuarltly active recruiting on university campuses) Central Asia and the Indian subcontinent. It was banned by the Pakistani government in November 2003 for involvement in extremist policies, preaching armed militancy, and spreading religious hatred. It is also banned in Egypt, Jordan, Germany and several other countries of the Muslim world and the West.

Contemporary Movements[771]

The various contemporary Islamic terrorist groups are closely enmeshed with each other, networked and interwoven, providing recruits and funds for each other, offering safe houses and serving as clearing houses for funds, arms and fighters. They have established a large array of front organisations such as legal businesses, charities, trusts, welfare, educational and other institutions to bankroll and whitewash their activities while raising large amounts of funds and many recruits for their cause. Some of the fund-raising is by drug-trafficking, hostage-taking and other criminal activities. Individuals who do not engage directly in violence nevertheless provide vital help to those who do engage in violence.

Further strands were added to the mesh in the 1990s when many extremist movements had to move from their country of origin, where radical militants were being repressed, to the West (especially Western Europe and North America), where they found freedom to continue their operations. Global communication technologies meant that such re-location did not hinder their work, but rather gave them a new pool of local Western Muslims from which to draw financial support and recruit new members.

Western attempts to focus exclusively on Al-Qaʻeda and isolate it from the mainstream Islamic tradition fail to understand the nature of Islamic terrorist networks. A good comparison would be the multitude of western NGOs or anti-globalisation groups. These organisations have a great deal of interaction and overlap with each other; they support each other, evolve coalitions on issues of common interest, and combine their causes together. The boundaries between them are not clearly defined. In addition key individuals can be involved as trustees or directors of several different groups at once. Another feature of this comparison is the way different groups merge and split, or close themselves down only to reappear under a new name or as several different new groups. Contemporary Islamic terrorism is manifested in the same kind of fluid, complex, ever-shifting networks, closely linked to and resourced by mainstream Muslim society, not as isolated, clearly defined entities.[772]

As we have seen in chapter 6, an eschatological world-view continues to be an important influence on today's radical groups, many of whom believe themselves to be living in the End Times and await the return of the *mahdi* or the Hidden Imam. This mindset also results in abundant conspiracy theories. They view Muslim history as a prelude to the End and the various battles as End-Time battles or at least dress-rehearsals for them. They perceive a series of cycles of victory and defeat, and are therefore not dismayed by defeat as this is only to be expected periodically, while ultimately God will bring them victory. This final victory, achieved by God himself when the Muslims face overwhelming odds, will be superior to the victories which the Muslims themselves have gained in the past by their own strength.[773]

Osama bin Laden is in many ways a *mahdi*-like figure, who has achieved an almost mythical status. His austere and devout lifestyle, zeal for Islam, reported exploits, legendary wealth, and international renown fit the classical *mahdi* picture and have increased his popular appeal to Muslims around the world.[774]

Ali Shariati (1933-1977), the main ideologue of the Iranian Islamic Revolution, reinterpreted the Shi'a concept of *intizar*, the waiting for the return of the Hidden Imam, as an active accelerating of his coming – a struggle towards the goal of revolution.[775] Many of the more bizarre statements and policies of the current Iranian president, Mahmoud Ahmadinejad, are a result of his conviction that because the *mahdi* will appear very soon it is possible to take great risks, seeing that the sure and final victory of Islam is imminent.

Having recognised how fluid and interlinked the various groups are, there is nevertheless some value in trying to characterise them individually and analyse their relationships with each other.

A classification of Arab terrorist groups

Many violent extreme groups in the Arab world of today, like al-Jama'a al-Islamiyya, Hamas, Hizb ut-Tahrir, the GIA of Algeria and many more, were born out of the Muslim Brotherhood as reinterpreted by Qutb. They have developed in two general trends excellently defined by Reuven Paz, academic director of the International Policy Institute for Counter-Terrorism, in his January 2000 paper on *The Heritage of the Sunni Militant Groups: An Islamic internacionale?*.[776]

1 *Islamic jihad groups*: These groups hold that the leaders of their countries are not true Muslims and therefore legitimate the use of violence against them, if not against the wider populace. In general terms they are better integrated with society at large than are the more isolationist *takfir* groups (see below), they do not consider their leaders to be sent by God in any exceptional way, and they accept the teaching of later Islamic scholars and leaders as authoritative alongside the earlier sources of Islam. Egyptian groups which fall into this category include Al-*Jihad*, now led by bin Laden's second-in-command Ayman al-Zawahiri, and al-Jama'a al-Islamiyya with its own various groups.

In the Levant this category includes the faction of the Palestinian Islamic Jihad led by Sheikh As'ad Bayoud al-Tamimi (as opposed to the Shqaqi faction which was primarily affiliated with the Islamic revolution in Iran), al-Tali'a al-Islamiyya in Syria, and two groups in Lebanon: al-Tawhid in Tripoli and al-Jama'a al-Islamiyya in Sidon.

2 *Takfir groups*: In general terms the Takfir groups are much more isolationist than the Jihadists. They withdraw from wider Muslim society, the members of which they consider to be apostates, and by this interpretation they justify the indiscriminate murder of civilians to achieve their aims. Their leaders are sometimes seen as being exceptional, even *mahdis*. They accept as authoritative the Qur'an, the teachings of Muhammad in the *hadith* and the rulings of the first four caliphs, and reject all later Islamic traditions.

Paz describes some offshoots of the Takfir trend including:

- **Egyptian Takfir groups:** Al-Najoun min al-Nar (Survivors of the Fire/Hell), comprised of remaining Egyptian members of Takfir wal-Hijra, was active in Bosnia and later Albania. They have a small number of Palestinian followers in the Gaza Strip. This group considers their main enemy to be the secular Arab regimes (not Israel). They therefore took no part in the Palestinian *intifada* and have no links with Hamas or Palestinian Islamic Jihad. They are considered by the latter two groups to be deviant.

- **The Jordanian Takfir:** Other Takfir groups have spread, by means of Saudi guidance and finance, to Jordan and the Palestinian Territories. They were present in the Gaza Strip until 1986 when they lost their identity by merging into the developing groups of Palestinian Islamic Jihad. In Jordan they have faced strong opposition from the authorities which has obliged them to keep on the move. In recent years the

Jordanian Takfir has acquired a large following of various nationalities but including many Egyptians. In April 1996 the Egyptian authorities demanded the extradition of 57 members of the Egyptian Takfir group who had fled to Jordan.

- **Others: The Salafi Group for Call and Combat (GSPC)** is an Algerian group with a mainly Takfiri ideology, which split off from the larger Armed Islamic Group (GIA) in 1996. It has emerged as a major source of recruiting for al-Qaeda operations in Europe. The GSPC is engaged in organising high-profile attacks against Western interests. The GSPC is now the biggest and best organised as well as the most hard-line and effective of Algeria's Islamist groups. It operates mainly in the Boumerdes and Kabyle regions, with many of its fighters based in the mountainous terrain. In the late 1990s the group carried out a number of attacks on government and military targets in the rural areas of Algeria. By 2000, the GSPC had taken over the GIA's external networks across Europe and North Africa and was active in establishing an "Islamic International" linked to al-Qaeda. Authorities have uncovered cells linked to the GSPC in Germany, Italy, Spain, France, Belgium, the Netherlands, and Britain. In 2003 the GSPC kidnapped a group of western (mainly German) tourists trekking in the Sahara. In 2004 the GSPC clashed with Niger and Chad army troops on the Niger/Chad border. The group was reportedly working with local Niger bandits and using bases left over from the Tuareg nomad rebellion in the country in the 1990s.

Salafi-Jihadi Groups[777]

We have already seen, earlier in this chapter, the origins of Salafiyya movement, also known as neo-Wahhabism. Salafism is now an international movement seeking a return to the perceived purest form of original Islam as practised by Muhammad and the two generations that followed him. Salafis reject perceived innovations (*bid'a*) in Islamic doctrine and practice, including the four Sunni schools of law, in favour of a direct and literal interpretation of Qur'an and *hadith*. Salafism and Wahhabism are often used interchangeably, but Salafis see themselves as more radical purifiers of Islam further than the Wahhabis.

Salafis enforce a rigid dress and behavioural codes: men are required to grow beards and women to cover themselves from head to foot. Most Salafis ban modern inventions such as photography, music, conventional banking and elections. Other modern phenomena like television, radio and the Internet are accepted by some Salafi scholars if they are used to propagate Salafi teachings.

Salafis are divided into three movements:

1 Purists, who reject political or organisational activism that divide the Muslim community and divert attention from the study of Islam and the propagation of Salafism. They see *jihad* in defensive terms and accept a *jihad* only when led by a legal Muslim government. They argue that it is forbidden to revolt against a Muslim government, no matter how oppressive or unjust.

2 Activists, who agree with the Muslim Brotherhood and similar movements that political activism is the best method for achieving the goal of an Islamic state under *shari'a*.

3 Salafi-Jihadists, who advocate violence and terror and actively promote rebellion against the state and all perceived enemies of Islam. This third movement is the main current carrier of Islamic terrorism around the world. It emerged during the anti-Soviet *jihad* in Afghanistan when *jihadi*, Wahhabi, Deobandi and other groups cooperated and intermingled in their fight against the common enemy. It was strengthened during the Gulf War of 1991 when the more radical Saudi Salafis rejected the reliance on US troops in the Arabian Peninsula to protect Saudi Arabia from Iraqi aggression.[778]

Osama bin Laden and Al-Qa'eda (the Base)[779]

Al-Qa'eda is a global Sunni Islamist Salafi-Jihadi umbrella network founded by Osama bin Laden in 1989 in Afghanistan where he had set up a base to finance, recruit, transport and train Islamist recruits for the Afghan resistance. Following the withdrawal of the Soviets from Afghanistan this organisation turned to international terrorism aimed at the US, Western states and interests, other non-Muslim states ruling Muslim minorities, and Muslim regimes it deemed apostate. Its chief ideologue is Ayman al-Zawahiri, leader of Egyptian al-Jihad who has become bin Laden's deputy. Al-Qa'eda facilitates and orchestrates the operations of Islamic militants around the globe, distributing information, resources and people and interconnecting them by serving as the hub.

Al-Qa'eda integrates Salafi-Wahhabi teachings with *jihad* and *takfir* doctrines. Its various elements are united by their hatred of the West (especially the US) and of the "illegitimate" regimes in Muslim states. The goal of al-Qaeda is to establish a pan-Islamic caliphate throughout the world by working with allied Islamist extremist groups to overthrow regimes it deems non-Islamic and to expel Westerners and non-Muslims from Muslim countries. A main aim is the expulsion of US forces from Muslim lands, especially Afghanistan, Iraq, Saudi Arabia, and the Gulf. The US is seen as the primary enemy of Islam at this time. The end of all Western influence in the Muslim world and the destruction of Israel are further aims, as is the support of all *jihad* groups around the world including Chechnya, Bosnia, Eritrea, Algeria, Sudan, Somalia, Indonesia, Thailand, and the Philippines. Bin Laden claims it is the duty of every Muslim to fight for the establishment of Islamic states in all areas that have ever been under Muslim control at any time in history.

Al-Qa'eda organised the 1993 bombing attack on the World Trade Centre in New York; the August 1998 American embassy bombings in Kenya and Tanzania; the bombing of the US navy ship *Cole* in Aden in October 2000, and many other suicide and other attacks worldwide. By far the most dramatic and destructive attack so far was the suicide plane bombing of the World Trade Centre and the Pentagon on September 11th 2001. Since then it has been involved through subsidiaries in the Bali (2002), Madrid, and London (2005) bombings among many more.

In Iraq Al-Qa'eda integrated Abu-Mus'ab al-Zarqawi and his militant group Al-Tawhid wal-Jihad into its network. This group is behind the most devastating suicide bombings and brutal kidnappings and beheadings in Iraq. Al-Zarqawi himself was killed in a US strike in Iraq in May 2006.

It is worth looking briefly at the infrastructure of Al-Qa'eda. It emerged from the organisation Maktab al-Khidmat, which was established by Abdullah 'Azzam to help the Afghani Mujahidin by recruiting and funding Arab volunteers. In 1987 'Azzam developed the ideological basis, composition and aims of what Bin Laden later set up as Al-Qaeda; indeed it was 'Azzam who coined the name Al-Qa'eda al-Sulba (The Solid Base). Thus Abdullah 'Azzam can be considered the ideological father of Al-Qa'eda. With a network of its own cells as well as associated terrorist groups and other affiliated organisations, Al-Qa'eda has links in some 55 countries. This makes it robust, flexible and quick to regenerate after suffering damage. According to the CIA, Al-Qa'eda can draw on the support of 6-7 million radical Muslims, of whom 120,000 are willing to take up arms.

Under the headship of Osama bin Laden is a pyramidical structure for strategic direction. The *majlis al-shura* (consultative council) is at the top, making major policy decisions on terrorist operations and issuing *fatwas*. Reporting to the *majlis al-shura* are four operational committees with the following responsibilities: (1) military (2) financial (3) *fatwa* and Islamic study (4) media and publicity. There is also a travel office. The global terrorist network is de-centralised into regional groupings called "families". Each nationality or ethnic group is assigned a particular geographical region as their responsibility. Some also have other responsibilities e.g. Libyans ran the documentation and passport office in Afghanistan, Algerians run the fraudulent credit card operations in Europe, and Egyptians have run most of the training facilities worldwide. Individuals may sometimes be sent on special missions outside their normal area.

The bulk of Al-Qa'eda's funding originally came from Osama bin Laden's personal fortune but donations are also received from around the world amounting to tens of millions of dollars.

It has a global financial network with a multiplicity of bank accounts and "front" organisations. It also raises funds through investments, business, Islamic charities and financial crime.[780] It is proving difficult for Western governments to curtail the cash-flow to Al-Qa'eda.

Developments in al-Qa'eda since the Afghanistan and Iraq invasions

Since the downfall of the Taliban in 2001 and the consequent loss of its safe base in Afghanistan, al-Qa'eda has had to adapt to the new situation in which its main leaders are on the run and many of its operatives captured or killed. It has responded by implementing a much greater degree of decentralisation and networking, skilfully manipulating the mass media and the internet, and encouraging many semi-independent proxy groups across the globe.

While Muslim governments have come out against its activities, it has won much sympathy among ordinary Muslims. Its leaders have been glorified as true leaders of *jihad,* creating a personality cult around bin Laden who is often revered as a "renewer or reformer (*mujaddid*) of our times."[781]

A main goal of Osama bin Laden has been to trap US forces in Muslim territory where the population could be mobilised to fight them in an asymmetrical insurgency which would balance out the American superiority in conventional forces and equipment.

> "We want to bring the Americans to fight us on Muslim land," he said as we walked through the woods in the high mountains at Tora Bora. "If we can fight them on our own territory we will beat them, because the battle will be on our terms in a land they neither know nor understand."[782]

The 2003 US-led invasion of Iraq gave al-Qa'eda this opportunity.

While al-Zawahiri remains its main ideologue, there has been a marked shift to Saudi al-Qa'eda thinkers formulating its new discourse on strategy and tactics. Among these are Abu-Hajir Abd-al-Aziz al-Muqrin, Abu Ubayd al-Qureshi, Abu Ayman al-Hilali, Abd al-Hadi and Seif al-Din Al-Ansari. This was in tandem with a shift from the global strategy to a focus on activity in the Arab Middle East, especially in Iraq, Saudi Arabia and Egypt. The hope is that in the Arab heartlands of Islam it will be finally possible to defeat the US and establish an Islamic state which will gradually spread across the whole area and then across the Muslim world.

Thus the ultimate inflexible goal of Al-Qaʿeda remains complete victory over infidel powers and the establishment of the Islamic caliphate. This strategic goal is considered so self-evident that it needs no discussion. No half-solutions or bargaining are permitted. To achieve this goal Muslims should not act on their own individually, but in unity with others, according to the overarching plan. However, such collective activity must be flexible and adapt to circumstances, keeping the enemy guessing.

At the tactical level,[783] Al-Qaʿeda holds that the *jihad* must address all aspects of country and society in which war is fought. Military, political and media actions must be integrated, the basic belief being that God will help the *jihadi* believers, in alliance with some West-hating infidel states (South America, Russia, China) and the Muslim acquisition of nuclear and other "dirty" technology to finally tip the balance and usher in the final victory.[784]

The insurgency doctrine of al-Qaʿeda has been evolving over time and is designed to defeat conventional Western military forces using terrorism and guerrilla tactics. It calls for insurgency action everywhere: in the deserts, mountains, sea and in urban areas.

In Iraq and Afghanistan the tactics are those of a long war of attrition. Al-Qaʿeda commanders must be psychologically prepared for the worst, and build a cellular organisation so that if one link falls, the organisation as a whole does not suffer a lethal blow. The war must be prolonged so as to exhaust the enemy by a "one-thousand wound" policy in which Muslim patience is pitted against Western demands for a quick fix. Set-piece battles and attacks on hardened targets that are too costly in terms of *mujahidin* casualties should be avoided. The key to victory lies in the reality that American bases and forces are known and immovable, while the *mujahidin* are light and mobile.

Some tactical principles:

1 Learn from experience, incorporate lessons into new tactics.

2 Small groups, small arms: small cell groups spare big losses. Limit fighting group to 6-10 men. Mobile, well supplied, multi-tasked, able to engage in reconnaissance, ambushes, raids, surveillance, kidnappings, and urban operations. The small group limits the ability of enemy airpower to fix its position and eliminate it. Procure small, cheap, easily available and reliable weapons, especially from the former Soviet Union. The Kalashnikov and its ammunition, grenades, RPGs, mortars, Improvised Explosive Devices (IEDs), tank mines, etc.

3 Create secure logistics to ensure the constant flow of men, weapons, food and equipment. Collect ordnance and hide in small caches across the country. Provide several logistics cells for each fighting group.

Military action must be combined with excellence in media action to gain support among ordinary Muslims and weaken the Western enemy. The essential interconnectedness of the military and media dimensions of the insurgency, which must all be pursued simultaneously, has been promoted in particular by Abu-Hajir Abd-al-Aziz al-Muqrin.[785] The aim is to create the impression that the insurgents are operating everywhere to prove their power, humiliate the enemy, encourage new recruitment and stimulate financial contributions to the costly business of *jihad*. Widespread activity gets media attention and places the enemy public opinion under pressure to tell their governments to pull put.

Al-Qa'eda has shown a remarkable organisational ability. While decentralising, it has maintained an image of a coherent leadership with a strategic plan and presents an image of an undefeatable monolith.[786] It has spread its ideology widely on the internet and the electronic media, using these tools for recruiting, training, expanding, and manipulating events. Its own websites include the internet journals *al-Ansar, al-Nida,* and *Mu'askar al-Battar.*

As a direct contact and command framework became more difficult to sustain, it has used refinements and changes in ideology to control developments and create new groups and new actions while keeping followers loyal to its central ideology.

Impact of the Iraq conflict on Salafi-Jihadi thinking

Since 2003 Iraq has developed as the central pole of attraction for global *jihad*, gaining new recruits to Salafi-Jihadism from all over the Muslim world as well as diverting *jihadists* from other fronts. It has become the main front in the global war, commanding the attention and resources of radical Muslims from around the world. Its insurgency techniques and tactical innovations are copied elsewhere, as in Afghanistan, and it serves as a training ground for *jihadists* who will later implement what they learned in other regions.[787]

The struggle in Iraq has strengthened the *jihadi* concept of the total struggle, in which politics and media are as important as the military battle. It has also encouraged their psychological warfare doctrine, whose aim is to dominate the enemy's imagination and mould the way he thinks about the war. They realise that the main battlefield is in the minds of the Western public and the weakening of resolve in Europe and in part of the American public has vindicated their strategies and encouraged them to redouble their efforts in Iraq, Afghanistan and elsewhere. They have become convinced that the very ferocity and barbarity of their actions, the powerful imagery of Muslims as victims and as victors now broadcast on all the modern media channels, furthers their cause, weakens the enemy and gains them sympathisers and recruits in the Muslim world.[788]

Some current Salafi-Jihadi leaders, thinkers and their writings
Ayman al-Zawahiri[789]

Al-Zawahiri, leader of the Egyptian Al-Jihad group, repudiated the Egyptian *jihadi* notion of dealing first with the enemy near at hand (i.e. the "apostate" regime in Egypt) when he joined al-Qa'eda, opting instead for the concept of a global *jihad* against the further enemies such as the US. However, more than other

Salafi-Jihadi leaders, he retains the Qutbist heritage and returns to it to some degree as he adapts his ideology and tactics to changing circumstances. This very prominent and influential leader is therefore not typical of Salafi-Jihadis.

Al-Zawahiri believes that the *jihadi* movement needs an arena that can act like an incubator to help the movement flourish and gain experience in military combat, politics and organisational matters. This was the role of Afghanistan during the anti-Soviet *jihad* in the 1980s, and he believes Iraq currently fills the niche.[790]

Following the fall of the Taliban in Afghanistan and the unfolding of the US-led war against terror, he has again focused on the Arab Middle East as the main arena for the decisive battle against the enemies of Islam. In a letter to Abu Mus'ab al-Zarqawi, leader of the Iraqi al-Qa'eda of the Land of the Two Rivers, he sets out many of his beliefs and draws a distinction between the strongly Salafi attitudes and practices of al-Zarqawi and al-Zawahiri's own ideology, which retain much of the non-Salafi thinking of Egyptian Al-Jihad.[791]

1 In the letter, Al-Zawahiri states his belief that a first step toward the ultimate goal of establishing a worldwide caliphate is the establishment of an Islamic state in the Middle East, the "heart of the Islamic world". This was the original strategy of Egyptian Al-Jihad which tried to initiate an Islamic revolution in Egypt when it assassinated President Sadat in 1981. It was later Salafi-Jihadi groups like al-Qa'eda that shifted the struggle to the global sphere and especially to the fight against the US. While al-Zawahiri agreed to this widening of the scope of *jihad*, it was mainly because there seemed to be no other practical option, since Middle East regimes had successfully clamped down on the radical Islamic groups in their countries, thus forcing them to seek other locations. Al-Zawahiri is still convinced of the primacy of the Middle East and has gladly taken the opportunity to initiate a *jihad* struggle in Iraq which he sees as part of the historic heartland of Islam. This explains the focus on Iraq in *jihadi* circles and the willingness to pour into it the maximum available resources of manpower and weapons to try and gain an Islamist victory there.

2 Al-Zawahiri states that the ultimate goal for him is the establishment of the world wide caliphate "in the manner of the Prophet". This again was a main goal of the original Egyptian Al-Jihad movement and the establishment of an Islamic state in Egypt was seen as a necessary first step in that direction. The national Islamic state would then gradually extend its power and rule and join with similar states until the world-wide caliphate was established.

3 Al-Zawahiri encourages the extension of the successful Iraqi struggle to neighbouring secular countries, again congruent with the Egyptian Jihad principle of fighting first the enemy nearby rather than the enemy far away.

4 Al-Zawahiri stresses the importance of public support for the *jihad* effort and encourages al-Zarqawi not to be isolated from the general Muslim public. This again was a characteristic of the early Egyptian Al-Jihad which wanted to emulate the success of the Iranian Islamic Revolution in gaining mass support for its struggle. Egyptian Al-Jihad rejected the isolationist *takfiri* position of total separation from society, and sought to infiltrate society and the regime at all levels in order to initiate a popular revolution when appropriate. Al-Zawahiri often speaks on the lack of reform, freedom, and justice in Muslim states: *jihad* will deliver the expected freedom and justice to the oppressed Muslim populations. Al-Zawahiri aims much of his discourse at convincing Muslim public opinion and gaining its sympathy for his movement and its aims.[792]

5 Al-Zawahiri criticises the growing brutality of al-Zarqawi seen in beheadings and in indiscriminate slaughter of Shi'a Muslims. This again highlights the ideological differences between the two. Egyptian Al-Jihad did not follow the line of Takfir wal-Hijra which proclaimed the whole of society to be non-Muslim infidels, and therefore possible targets of *jihad*. Rather it limited its takfir only to the government and

its employees and targeted only them. Al-Zarqawi follows the more extreme *takfiri* line which has been accepted by most radical Salafi-Jihadis.

6 There is another factor which also helps to create the difference between Al-Zawahiri and al-Zarqawi in their attitude to Shi'a. The Salafiyya movement holds that Shi'a Muslims are the worst enemies of true Islam, worse even than Jews and Christians. Their deep hatred for Shi'as has been inherited from Wahhabism, which had historically held that Shi'as were the main infidel enemy. (Wahhabis invaded the Shi'a holy sites in Iraq in the nineteenth century destroying them and massacring many Shi'as.) This is why contemporary Salafis feel justified in the indiscriminate slaughter of Shi'as. However Egyptian Al-Jihad has a more ambiguous attitude to the Shi'a, and does not see them as the main enemy. The main enemies identified by Egyptian Al-Jihad are, first, the infidel rulers in Sunni Muslim states, then their allies (perceived to be Western "Christian" countries and Israel).

7 Al-Zawahiri encouraged al-Zarqawi to befriend *ulama* from the various Sunni schools of thought and schools of law so as to gain their support for the *jihadi* struggle. Here again we see the difference between the Egyptian Al-Jihad which accepted the Sunni *madhabs* as authoritative as against the Salafis who dismiss them as an innovative deviation from original pure Islam and rely only on Qur'an and *hadith*.

Abu Bakr Naji, *The Management of Barbarism*, 2004[793]
This book first appeared on a website, the al-Ikhlas *jihadi* forum (http://ekhlas.com/forum) and was published by the al-Qa'eda affiliate, the Center of Islamic Studies and Research. Its subtitle is "The phase of transition to the Islamic state". The author Abu Bakr Naji is a regular contributor to the *Sawt al-Jihad* online magazine. In this book he attempts to map the stages of a strategic programme towards empowerment. By "management of barbarism" the author refers to the period ushered in by the desired collapse of the superpower. This will be a period of savage

chaos which must be well managed by the *jihadis* if they are to achieve their ultimate goal.

Naji defines three stages in implementing the *jihad*:

1 The disruption and exhaustion phase. In this phase the *jihadis* exhaust the enemy's forces by stretching them through a dispersal of targets. They also attract and recruit Muslim youth through spectacular attacks like the bombing in Bali.

2 The management of barbarism phase. In this phase the *jihadis* establish internal security, ensure food and medical supplies, defend their zone from external attack, establish *shari'a* justice, build up their armed forces and intelligence capabilities and ally themselves to neighbouring elements sympathetic to their cause.

3 The empowerment phase. This is a continuation of phase two in which *jihadi*-controlled regions are united and expanded while delivering knock-out blows to the enemy.

Naji urges *jihadis* to make a careful study of Western management, military principles, political theory and sociology so as borrow successful strategies and recognise inherent weaknesses which can be exploited to defeat the US and its allies. He recommends trying to provoke the superpower into invading the Middle East directly (as happened when the US invaded Iraq). This constitutes a great propaganda victory for the *jihad* movement for the following reasons:[794]

1 All Muslims are outraged at the invasion of a Muslim land by an infidel power.

2 Muslims are impressed by the *jihadis* taking on a superpower.

3 The insurgency proves that the superpower is not invincible.

4 Muslims will despise the proxy government allied to the infidel invader.

5   The fight will drain the superpower's economy and military resources.

6   This will lead to social unrest in the US and the ultimate defeat of the superpower.

The asymmetrical clash with the US will gradually wear it down, fracture its society and lead to its inevitable demise.

Naji offers a three stage programme for establishing the caliphate, following Muhammad's model:

1   Bomb sensitive local targets such as oil facilities and tourist sites, forcing the local regime to build up security around these targets.

2   This spreading of the regime's security forces will open security vacuums in other regions and urban areas which must be attacked. The growing chaos will result in the general population welcoming *jihadi* administrators to manage their basic necessities.

3   Once in control of these regions, the "administrators of barbarism" can network with each other and organise a caliphate for the whole state.

Naji is concerned at potential weaknesses of the *jihadi* movement. While individual small-scale initiatives are welcome, large-scale operations must be left to the High Command to organise and approve. There is a danger that targeting the wrong people, especially when the victims are Muslims, could turn the Muslim general public against the movement.

At the same time, Naji is clear that it is violence that will force the Muslims at large to choose sides, creating the chaotic conditions necessary for the *jihad* to succeed. Brutal violence must therefore be continued and increased.

Abu Qatada, *Between Two Methods*, 1994[795]

Abu Qatada is a Jordanian of Palestinian origin who studied law in Saudi Arabia, fought in the Afghan *jihad* and in 1993 was granted political asylum in the UK in spite of having been twice convicted in Jordan on terrorist charges. In Britain he served as a key recruiter for Islamic terrorist groups including al-Qa'eda and the GIA and was known as "al-Qa'eda's spiritual ambassador in Europe".[796] He specialised in defining enemies of the *jihad* movement, including non-jihadi Salafis i.e. Salafis who reject political and organisational activism.

Abu Qatada wrote the following definition of global *jihad* movement:

> Those groups and organizations that were established in order to eliminate the evil (Taghutiyyah) heretic (Kafirah) regimes in the apostate countries (Bilad al-Riddah), and to revive the Islamic government that will gather the nation under the Islamic Caliphate.[797]

He argues that true *jihad* movements differ from other Islamic groups that merely seek political legitimacy from heretical regimes. The *jihad* movement does not seek to reform the existing regimes but to eliminate them. The main thing is not the armed struggle in itself, but the comprehensive world-view that comes from the perception of God's true unity *(tawhid)* and of total submission and obedience to it. His vision is of a future world totally controlled by Islam.

Abu Qatada coined the term *the Jihad movement of future hope,* which he defined as "a movement of Salafi world-view, perceptions, doctrines, and way... totally cleansed from any remains of the wrong Sufi doctrine; does not belong to any school or trend besides that of the Qur'an and Sunnah." The existing *jihad* movements had not yet achieved this goal, he said, but were on the right path. Their duty is now to open new arenas for *jihad* outside of their own countries. The many-pronged battle must be waged by all forces united under a single commander, whom all other leaders should serve.[798]

Since October 2002 Abu Qatada has been detained under the Terrorism Act for alleged involvement in the preparation, commission and instigation of terrorist activity and its support through fundraising.

Abu Mus'ab al-Suri, *Observations Concerning the Jihadi Experience in Syria* (no date)[799]

Al-Suri is a Syrian Salafi-Jihadi ideologue and activist with roots in the Muslim Brotherhood; his real name is Mustafa Setmariam Nasar. He has written several books on the present evil world order and the illegitimacy of modern democratic systems. He also authored a number of tactical works focusing on guerrilla warfare and the use of terrorist cell structures. Many of his books deal with the *jihad* culture and others focus on the history and development of Islamic political systems.[800]

Al-Suri is a careful student of failed modern *jihads* and of Western counterterrorism strategy. He has listed several main causes for the failures of *jihad* in the recent past, so that these can be avoided and rectified to ensure success:

1 Local regimes cooperated against the *jihadis*, their security apparatuses helping each other. The solution is to mount many attacks all over the world and establish bases of operation in every country so as to weaken regime cooperation as each regime is stretched to the limit trying to defend itself.

2 *Jihadis* ignored local ethnic minorities and tribes, enabling regimes to mobilise them in the fight against the *jihadis*. As an example he mentions that Syria used both Beduin and Kurds against the *jihadis*. The solution is that *jihad* movements must pay attention to these groups and co-opt them as much as possible.

3 Lack of connection between lower-rank *jihadis* and their leaders. This tempts lower ranking fighters to settle down, marry and pursue their own interests. Al-Suri stresses the importance of the foot soldiers of *jihad* and the need to give them the best possible training and strategic understanding while developing their loyalty and relationship with the top leadership.

4 Insufficient popular support. The *jihad* movement must communicate its goals and methods better to the general

Muslim population, seeing them as an integral part of the project and giving them a stake in the *jihad*. Propaganda is vital, but lies and exaggerations must be avoided, as they are counterproductive.

5   Too few religious scholars and clerics supportive of their cause to grant them legitimacy, indeed some clerics were alienated from the cause. Al-Suri stresses the need to recruit many clerics to the cause, getting them involved in the actual fighting. With their help to teach the new *jihadi* generation, a self-sustaining and growing movement will sweep away the old order and establish the global caliphate in its place.

His most recent book, *The Call for a Global Islamic Resistance,* was posted on the internet in January 2005.[801] In it he advocates a decentralised system of *jihad* waged by many local autonomous units across the world. He also stresses the importance of waging a truly global war simultaneously in both Muslim and Western states.

Al-Suri was arrested in Quetta, Pakistan by Pakistani security forces in October 2005.

Abu Muhammad Al-Maqdisi[802]

Abu Muhammad Al-Maqdisi is a Palestinian born in Nablus in 1959, whose real name is Issam Muhammad Taher Al-Burqawi. He became the spiritual teacher of the Salafi-Jihadi movement in Jordan and the spiritual mentor of Abu Mus'ab al-Zarqawi, who led several Islamic terrorist groups and eventually became the *amir* of al-Qa'eda in Iraq. Al-Maqdisi combined radical Wahhabi Salafism with Abdullah 'Azzam's teaching on global *jihad* to create the contemporary brand of Salafi-Jihadism. He rejected the quietist traditional Salafis, preaching violent *jihad* and the need to overthrow the apostate regimes in Muslim lands.

Maqdisi wrote many Islamist works that condemn democracy as the greatest threat to God's sovereignty. Muslims must fight against it and destroy it. All who believe in democracy and practise it are to be treated as enemies and fought by *jihad*. He also attacked Arab regimes (including Jordan and Saudi Arabia) for their apostasy using Ibn Taymiyya's limited doctrine of *takfir*, and provided ideological guidance to global *jihadis*. His proposed strategy is a long-term struggle that will mobilise the whole *umma* to achieve the ultimate goal. Al-Maqdisi has criticised some of al-Zarqawi's brutal activities, especially against Shi'a civilians, as counter-productive and damaging to the *jihadi* cause.[803]

Maqdisi stresses two main Islamic principles:

1 *Tawhid*, the belief in the oneness and absolute indivisibility of God and the religious obligation to worship Him alone.

2 The obligation to struggle against polytheism *(shirk, jahiliyya)* in all its manifestations. Muslims must demonstrate enmity and hatred to all polytheists until the polytheists renounce their ways and enter the true path of Islam.

Implementing these twin principles is the main duty of every Muslim, more important than daily prayer, almsgiving or any other Islamic obligation. For Maqdisi, as for other Salafi-Jihadists, the combination of these twin religious obligations translates into a desire for radical political change through *jihad*.

Some of his main points are:

1 *Jihad* is an act of worship. As such it is obligatory at all times and in all circumstances until the Day of Judgement. Nothing invalidates it.

2 It is permissible to ally oneself with disbelievers to fight other disbelievers in order to repel the greater of two evils.

3 It is obligatory to rebel against rulers who have apostatised from Islam by replacing *shari'a* with non-Muslim legislation or have allied themselves with enemies of Allah and of Muslims.

4 Fighting such apostate Muslim rulers takes priority over fighting non-Muslim infidels, as apostasy is worse than *kufr*. It is the most urgent and serious obligation under all circumstances to fight them and replace them with true Muslims.

5 Defensive *jihad* has priority over offensive *jihad*, and *jihad* against the near enemy has priority over *jihad* against the enemy far way.

6 *Jihad* is the school in which strong bonds are formed between the various groups of fighters, enhancing unity and laying a good base for Islam's final victory.

7 In every age there is a group of faithful Muslims engaged in *jihad* against God's enemies.

A recent innovative study on contemporary Salafi-Jihadi thinkers

An important study on the relative importance of various thinkers in the Salafi-Jihadi movement has recently been published by the Combating Terrorism Center.[804] The report uses the methodology of statistical "citation analysis" to identify the most influential *jihadi* authors, medieval and modern. It looked at *jihadi* websites and at the books cited there. As expected, among the medieval scholars Ibn Taymiyya ranks first, followed by his disciple Ibn al-Qayyim al-Jawziyya. These are followed by Ibn Hajar al-'Asqalani (1372-1449), Al-Qurtubi (died 1273) and Ibn Kathir (1301-1373).

Among the modern Salafi-Jihadi authors, Sayyid Qutb ranks first, followed by Ahmad Shakir (an Egyptian who died in 1958), Abu Muhammad al-Maqdisi, al-Shinqiti (a Mauritanian who died in 1973), Abdel-Aziz Ibn Baz (Grand Mufti of Saudi Arabia 1993-1999), 'Abdullah 'Azzam, the Egyptian 'Abd al-Qadir bin 'Abd al-'Aziz and Yusuf al-'Uyayri (a Saudi who was killed in 2003),

The study notes that modern Salafi thinkers are of three types:

1 Conservative scholars, most of them Wahhabi, whose conservative and narrow doctrines provide *jihadis* with legitimacy.

2 Saudi establishment clerics who are politically quietist and support the Saudi regime. They also represent classical themes

of *jihad* but teach that only the Muslim ruler (caliph, Imam) has the right to proclaim *jihad*; that it is sinful to rebel against a Muslim ruler, even if he is sinful; and that it is wrong to accuse other Muslims of being non-Muslims. *Jihadis* disagree with them on who has the right to proclaim *jihad*, who can excommunicate Muslims, and whether violent revolt against a Muslim ruler is legitimate.

3 *Jihadi* theorists who call for *jihad* against non-Muslims and the overthrow of apostate regimes. Qutb is the first in this category, followed by al-Maqdisi. Al-Maqdisi is defined as the key living ideologue of the *jihadi* movement.

The study also reveals a new trend among the *jihadis*: a shift in ideological influence from Egyptian laymen (Qutb, al-Zawahiri) to formally trained clerics from Saudi Arabia and the Levant.

Surprisingly, Osama bin Laden does not appear at the top of the list of influential ideologues, while his lieutenant, al-Zawahiri seems to be insignificant in the *jihadi* intellectual world.[805]

Jihadi strategists, thinkers who mainly offer secular analytical studies of the strengths and weaknesses of the *jihadi* movement, include Yususf al-'Uyayri and Abu Ubayd al-Qureshi.

The study concludes with the following recommendations:

1 Label the *jihadi* movement "Qutbism" rather than *jihadi* or Salafi-Jihadi. *Jihadis* hate this appellation as it suggests that they follow a mere human rather than God and that they are a deviant sect.

2 Publish statements by influential Saudi *salafi* clerics that denounce *jihadi* terrorism.

3 Encourage *jihadi* intellectuals to renounce specific targets and methods (as happened in al Tartusi's renunciation of the London bombings or al-Maqdisi's renunciation of al-Zarqawi's brutal methods).

4 Disseminate negative facets of *jihadism*, such as violence

against civilians, goal of a totalitarian state, mistreatment of women and *takfir*.

Classification of Violent Radical Sunni Organisations

Most violent Sunni Islamist organisations can be classified by the ideological sources from which they emerged as well as their regional base. For the Sunni groups (there are of course many more groups than the ones mentioned here as examples) these are defined as:

Arab world
Muslim Brotherhood affiliates–Hamas
Muslim Brotherhood offshoots–Hizb ut-Tahrir
Qutbist Jihadi–Tanzim al-Jihad, al-Jama'a al-Islamiyya
Qutbist Takfiri–Takfir wal Hijra, Salafist Group for Call and
    Combat (GSPC)
Salafi-Wahhabi–al-Tawhid wal Jihad, Laskar Jihad (Indonesia),
Indian sub-continent
Deobandi - Harakat-ul Mujahideen (HUM), Harakat-ul-Jihad-Al-Islami (HUJI), Taliban, Jaish-e-Mohammed (JEM), Sipah-i-Sahaba
Jama'at-i-Islami - Hizb-ul Mujahideen (HM)
Ahl-i-Hadith - Lashkar-e-Tayyiba

Global
Salafi-Jihadi – al-Qa'eda, Jema'ah Islamiyah
Many other organisations which began in a particular country or region are now becoming global, in particular the Muslim Brotherhood and Hizb ut-Tahrir.

Following the intermingling of these various groups in the Afghan *jihad* against the Soviet Union in the 1980s, most groups now reveal mixed doctrinal orientations, fusing Deobandi, Jama'at-i-Islami, Muslim Brotherhood and radical Wahhabi-Salafi doctrines with different weightings accorded to the various ideologies. The global Salafi-Jihadi orientation as seen in al-Qaeda arose out of such a mixture of Salafi, Jihadi and Takfiri doctrines.

Shi'a Movements
Hizb al-Da'wa al-Islamiyya (Islamic Da'wa Party)[806]

This is the oldest and most important of the activist Shi'a organisations in Iraq that opposed Saddam Hussein's Ba'ath regime. The party was established in Najaf in 1957 by the young Shi'a cleric Muhammad Baqir al-Sadr with a group of junior Shi'a clergy. Al-Sadr was concerned that Islam was on the decline in secularist Iraq and he founded the organisation as a "party of God" (in Arabic *hizb Allah*) to call people back to Islam while giving a voice to the Shi'as of Iraq who felt discriminated by the Sunni regime. The Da'wa was active in the universities and among the poor Shi'a communities.

Da'wa demands an Islamic Republic in Iraq based on *shari'a*. Da'wa posited a preparatory stage during which the general population would be educated, to be followed by the stage of activism. Any organisational form was legitimate if it could spread the call more effectively. The party has a pyramidical hierarchical structure with a General Leadership Council at the top. At the bottom are the basic units known as the Family (*al-usrah*) or the Ring (*al-halaqa*). Inside Iraq under Saddam great secrecy was mandated and an ordinary member knew only the members of his own unit. The structure was strongly influenced by that of the communist and Ba'athist party structures.

Da'wa was Saddam's most feared opposition. Under the influence of Iranian Ayatollah Khomeini the party's main political and guerrilla thrust occurred in 1979 when it engaged in mass anti-Ba'ath demonstrations and in armed attacks against Ba'ath party members and internal security centres in an attempt to topple the regime and replace it with an Iranian-style Islamic government. The Iraqi regime responded by arresting thousands and executing hundreds, including al-Sadr. During the Iran-Iraq war (1980-1988) the party sporadically hit at Ba'ath targets inside Iraq. It also had a small regular unit that fought alongside Iran against Iraq, and it carried out terrorist attacks against pro-Iraqi regimes in the Middle East (Kuwait) and against Western targets.

Da'wa was involved in an assassination plot against Saddam in 1982 and an attack on his motorcade in 1987. It was harshly repressed (the Iraqi authorities executed 96 of its members in 1980 alone) causing it to become more militant and eventually to split into several factions. Regime repression caused it to become more militant. Based in Tehran for many years, Da'wa was supported by Iran though it tried to preserve some autonomy. Following the US-led invasion of Iraq in 2003, Da'wa returned to Iraq in an attempt to re-establish the party after its many years of clandestine existence.

The contemporary Shi'a Iraqi Islamist movements, SCIRI and the Muqtada al-Sadr group are spin-offs from Da'wa.

Da'wa has recently taken a moderate pragmatic stance. It has spoken out against other groups wanting to impose strict Islamic codes of dress and behaviour on the population. It is now led by Ibrahim Ja'afari, who has served as prime minister of Iraq 2005-2006.

Hizbullah (Iran)[807]

This is a Shi'a vigilante militia serving as the unofficial watchdog of the Iranian Islamist regime.

Hizbullah traces its ancestry to the extreme Islamist organisations that were active in Iran in the 1940s and 1950s like the Fida'iyan-i Islam. Hizbullah founders were followers of Ayatollah Ruhollah Khomeini, and their slogan was: "Only one party, the party of Allah (*hizb Allah*). Only one leader, Ruhollah."

Hizbullah has an extreme politicised interpretation of Shi'a Islam, which includes anti-Zionist and anti-Western attitudes, and is willing to use violence to attain its goals. It is fanatically loyal to Khomeini's principles and to the conservative clerics who are his successors.

Hizbullah entered Iranian politics during the 1978-1979 upheavals in Iran, recruiting mainly from among the urban poor and the bazaaris (the merchants, shopkeepers, and artisans organised around Iran's traditional marketplaces). It played an important role in organising the massive demonstrations and strikes that led to the downfall of the shah. Its members served as unofficial enforcers of the new clerically dominated Islamic Republican Party established by Khomeini in 1979 and played a significant role in the consolidation of the new Islamist regime. Hizbullah also supplied the regime with a pool of fighters for the war against Iraq.

Its main leader was the cleric Hujjat al-Islam Hadi Ghaffari, who served as a minister in Khomeini's government and also was responsible for cooperating with the Lebanese branch of Hizbullah founded in 1982. In post-1979 Iran, Hizbullah activists employed clubs, chains, knives, and guns to disrupt the rallies of opposition parties, beat their members, and ransack their offices. They were instrumental in the downfall of President Abol-Hasan Bani Sadr, the closing of the universities, the enforcement of veiling, the suppression of the press, and the cowing of the population into silence.

Hizbullah has not developed into a political party. In recent years some of its squads have become the personal militias of powerful clerics. It has links with like-minded groups in Lebanon and other Middle Eastern countries. In Iran it is closely linked to other radical Shi'a militias serving the regime such as the Revolutionary Guards and the Basij.

Hizbullah in Lebanon[808]

Hizbullah in Lebanon is not only a political party but also a military, political and social organisation. This radical Shi'a Islamist group is one of the most powerful terrorist organisations in the Middle East, and has perpetrated many attacks on Israel and on Western targets. It emerged in Shi'a-dominated south Lebanon in response to the Iranian Islamic Revolution. Hizbullah was created by Iran in the 1980s to project its power in the Arab Sunni world at a time when most Sunni Arab states sided with Saddam Hussein's Iraq in his long war against Iran (1980-1988). Hizbullah was also supported by Iran's sole Arab ally, Syria, as a useful proxy in its war against Israel.

The origins of Hizbullah lie in the close ties (including family relationships) between Shi'a *ulama* of Iran, Iraq and Lebanon. The Shi'a academies of Najaf and Karbala in Iraq have traditionally been the training ground for both Iranian and Lebanese *ulama*, and the radicalisation of these Shi'a centres under Muhammad

Baqir al-Sadr and later Ayatollah Ruhollah Khomeini impacted the Lebanese scholars and through them the Lebanese Shi'a community which shifted from a quietist to an activist mode in the 1970s and 1980s.

The spiritual leader of Hizbullah in Lebanon is Sayyid Muhammad Husayn Fadlallah,[809] the son of a scholar from south Lebanon. Fadlallah was born and studied in Najaf where he imbibed the new spirit of Islamist activism. In the 1970s he was joined by many Lebanese theology students expelled from Iraq by the Ba'ath authorities. These became the core of the future Hizbullah.

The declared objective of Hizbullah is the transformation of Lebanon into an Islamic state on the Iranian model, the liquidation of Israel, and the liberation of all occupied Arab lands, including Jerusalem. To achieve this it proclaimed *jihad* against Israel, the US, and their perceived allies in Lebanon. Hizbullah conducted its struggle on three levels: open, semi-clandestine, and secret.

In 1982 Syria decided to permit the Shi'a Islamist government in Iran to dispatch a thousand members of the Revolutionary Guards to Lebanon's Beqa'a Valley, which was occupied by Syrian forces. The Iranian delegation, consisting of both military and religious instructors, recruited a number of young, militant Lebanese clerics affiliated with the Lebanese branch of Hizb al-Da'wa al-Islamiyya, Fadlallah's group and Islamic Amal (a breakaway faction of the Amal movement led by Husayn al-Musawi). The Iranian ambassador to Damascus, 'Ali Akbar Muhtashimi, established a council to govern the new movement which included himself, Shi'a *ulama*, and security personnel responsible for the militia. Iranian funds and training led to the rapid growth of Hizbullah's military wing, which devoted itself primarily to the expulsion of the American and European multi-national force (MNF) in Beirut and the defeat of occupying Israeli forces. The Organisation of the Islamic Jihad, the movement's secret branch led by 'Imad Mughniyeh, operated against Western targets, assassinating and kidnapping Westerners in Lebanon, and blowing up the American Embassy in 1983 and the barracks of French and American forces in Beirut as well as Israeli army barracks in the south in 1984. Hundreds died in these attacks and the US and France withdrew their forces from Lebanon. Israel, facing pressure from Hizbullah and other groups in Lebanon, withdrew from central Lebanon in 1985. According to one informed estimate, between 1984 and 1993, Hizbullah was responsible for around 90% of all armed attacks against Israeli forces in Lebanon.[810] Baalbek, capital of the Beqa'a province, became an autonomous zone for Hizbullah.

Hizbullah gained world public attention following the violence of its Organisation of Islamic Jihad, which operated not only in Lebanon but also in Europe (e.g. bombings in Paris in 1986) and later in Latin America against Israeli Jewish targets (e.g. the Israeli Embassy in Argentina in 1992 and the Israeli cultural centre in Buenos Aires in 1994).

In addition to its incessant attacks on Israeli targets in southern Lebanon, Hizbullah developed a wide network of welfare services for the Shi'a inhabitants of the south, the Beqa'a and the slums of Beirut. These included hospitals, pharmacies, small-scale factories to offer employment, scholarships, and development projects. Hizbullah also founded its own "scout" movement for youth, summer camps and soccer league. It published a weekly newspaper and operates its own radio and TV stations.

Wary of the new peace initiatives following the 1990-1991 Gulf War, Hizbullah re-organised itself as a political party and participated in the 1992 elections winning eight parliamentary seats. Its political option was especially important following the Israeli withdrawal from southern Lebanon in 2000 which deprived it of its justification for continuing to operate as an independent militia force. Fadlallah and the movement's political leadership temporarily abandoned their goal of establishing an Islamic state and tried to maximise their influence in post-war Lebanon.

Syria continued to use Hizbullah as a proxy for attacks against Israel. Only Hizbullah was allowed to systematically recruit, train and deploy a highly structured military apparatus in south Lebanon. It constantly attacked Israeli soldiers in the security zone Israel occupied in southern Lebanon until Israel withdrew from south Lebanon in May 2000. Israel retaliated against Hizbullah attacks by targeting Hizbullah leaders in Lebanon.

After the withdrawal of Israeli forces from south Lebanon, many observers expected Hizbullah to end its war against Israel and focus its energies on much-needed economic reconstruction in the south. However, after an initial lull, the group launched a new war, this time against Israeli soldiers stationed in the Sheba'a Farms area of the Golan Heights which it claimed is Lebanese. The start of the Palestinian *intifada* in September 2000 also stimulated Hizbullah to renew its attacks against Israel and to get involved in supporting various Palestinian terror groups as well as building up its own network within the Palestinian areas. In the autumn of 2000 it captured three Israeli soldiers in the Sheba'a Farms and kidnapped an Israeli non-combatant whom it may have lured to Lebanon under false pretences. By early 2001, the attacks severely worried Prime Minister Hariri who claimed there was a clear agreement with Syria to end Hizbullah provocations in the security zone.

Hizbullah receives substantial amounts of financial, training, weapons, explosives, political, diplomatic, and organisational aid from Iran and receives diplomatic, political, and logistical support from Syria. Funding for Hizbullah has come under increased scrutiny since 11th September 2001. An estimated $60-100 million dollars a year comes from Iran but this may be exceeded by donations from the Shi'a Lebanese Diaspora in West Africa, the US and the so-called Triple Frontier Area along the junction of Paraguay, Argentina and Brazil. It also raises revenue from its own array of commercial businesses in Lebanon.

Hizbullah has established cells in Europe, Africa, South America, North America, and Asia. It continues to have extensive links to the Iranian Hizbullah and the Iranian Revolutionary Guards as well as close links with the Iraqi Da'wa organisation and with Palestinian Jihad. It also has close links to the Syrian security and intelligence services. It is linked too with many Shi'a (and Sunni) radical organisations across the Muslim world. Iran undoubtedly remains the group's supreme ideological mentor as well as an important source of funding.

Hizbullah's links with the Iraqi Da'wa go back to Fadlallah's student years in Najaf, where he developed a friendship with Muhammad Baqir al-Sadr and was involved in the founding of the Iraqi Da'wa.[811] Muqtada al-Sadr, current leader of the Sadrist movement in Iraq, is a nephew of Muhammad Baqir al-Sadr.

With help from Iran and Syria, Hizbullah developed to become the strongest Shi'a organisation in Lebanon, given a privileged status of maintaining its own armed militia, trained symmetrically but fighting asymmetrically, and controlling its own territory when all other Lebanese militias were disarmed. It became in effect a state-within-a-state. Following Israel's total withdrawal from Lebanon in 2000, Hizbullah continued to amass sophisticated weapons from Iran and Syria (experts estimate over 12,000 rockets and missiles). It also developed an ideology of seeking the total destruction of the state of Israel (coupled with blatant anti-Semitism) as justification for its continued existence as a liberation movement. It thus allied itself to Palestinian Hamas and Islamic Jihad, who also do not accept Israel's right of existence in any borders.

It would seem likely that Iran, feeling the growing pressure of American encirclement, encouraged the July 12th, 2006 Hizbullah attacks against Israel, knowingly inviting Israeli reaction in order to divert world attention from its nuclear programme. The fierce Israeli attacks on Lebanon weakened Hizbullah, but did not eliminate it, and Hizbullah is expected to emerge ultimately as a stronger force because of their proven ability and enhanced reputation. Hizbullah's resistance to Israeli attacks and its continued rocketing of cities in northern Israel won it many admirers in Lebanon and across the Arab and Muslim worlds.

Moderate Sunni Arab states (most of whom have Shi'a minorities within their borders) are fearful of the newly emerging Shi'a power in the region under Iran's tutelage and view it with deep apprehension. They fear that traditional Sunni political domination of the area and its oil wealth is now under real threat, and resent Hizbullah as an Iranian proxy destabilising the region. King Abdullah of Jordan voiced the common fear of Arab Sunni rulers about the danger of a "Shi'a crescent" based on Iran with the western wing running through Iraq to Lebanon and the southern wing running through Iraq to the Shi'a populations of Bahrain and Saudi Arabia. Such a Shi'a sphere of influence, protected by a future Iranian nuclear capability, would control the oil of Iran, Iraq, Saudi Arabia and the Gulf states – more than half of the world's known reserves.[812] Sunni regimes in Riyadh, Cairo, Amman, Kuwait and the Gulf worry openly about the possible emergence of a Shi'a axis linking Tehran with Baghdad, Damascus, and Beirut.[813]

At the same time, pro-Hizbullah sympathies have swept the Muslim masses across the world as the emotional satisfaction of regaining lost Muslim honour against Israel has filtered down.

Use of Psychological Warfare by Islamic Radicals

Islamic radicals, and especially al-Qa'eda, have become expert in the use of psychological warfare in their asymmetrical battle against the US and the West. They have learned to use innovative and untraditional means and tactics, as well as unexpected weapons and technologies. Abu Jandal al-Azdi, a leading ideologue of al-Qa'eda in Saudi Arabia (killed in November 2004 by Saudi security forces), published an article in March 2004 ("The Al-Qaeda Organization and the Asymmetric War"[814]) in which he described how al-Qa'eda has taken advantage of the American psychological propensity to be easily provoked. He claims that the United States reacts like a cowboy taking revenge instead of having the patience to study the problem before retaliation. According to al-Azdi, Al-Qa'eda has managed to make America serve as its public relations agent. It has succeeded in making the United States look as if it was waging a global war against the whole Islamic world, thus enhancing Muslim perceptions of the urgency of a defensive *jihad* and recruiting many against America.[815]

One aim of Islamic radical organisations is to terrorise the civilian populations in the West by constant threats (including the nuclear threat) and acts of barbaric brutality. Islamic radicals have become very skilful in manipulating modern media including TV stations, the internet, videos, CD-ROMs and DVDs in their psychological warfare. These are aimed both at the enemy to shock and frighten peaceful Western societies by showing the brutality of the terrorist methods (hostage taking, beheading, etc.) and at mainline Muslim societies with the aim of gaining sympathisers, raising funds and enhancing recruitment.[816]

We have already seen in chapter 7 how radical Islamists encourage conspiracy theories and make skilful use of agitprop methods. By deliberately contriving confrontational situations, the radical Islamists provoke the security forces to overreact. This leads to human rights violations, which make the Muslim population hostile to the security forces and governments. There is also the possibility of shocking the international community. It has even been alleged[817] that the 2003 Iraq war was engineered by radical Islamists, who wanted the US to attack a Muslim country. As an added twist they may seek to present the violent incidents as having been stage-managed by the local security forces in order to try to discredit the Muslims as terrorists. (Examples from Thailand and India have been given in chapter 7.)[818]

Countering the terrorist psychological warfare methods calls for professional handling by the security forces and the political leadership. A carefully researched and developed counter-terrorism strategy is necessary, including the setting up of joint psywar centres to counter the psywar propaganda of the terrorists, disseminate correct information to the populations and encourage civil society to counter the activities of the extremists.[819]

The Pentagon has gradually realised the importance of psychological warfare in its war against terror, and is reported to have funded a special programme of psychological operations to help it win hearts and minds in the Muslim world.[820] It has also added an extra 3,700 personnel to its psychological operations and civil affairs units - an increase of 33%.[821]

13
The Motivation of Terrorists and Suicide Bombers

The primary motivation of terrorists and suicide bombers is theological, compounded mainly of duty and reward. But there are also other reasons which serve to inspire them. Martyrdom has a very special position in Shi'a Islam because Hassan and Hussein, the martyrs, are seen as models to be emulated, and suffering is sought after.

1 Duty to God and obedience to his command in the Qur'an

It is important to realise that most Islamic terrorists are devout and sincere in their faith. They can speak without irony of the "holy bomb" that killed nearly 200 non-Muslims in Bali, Indonesia on 12 October 2002.[822] They are men and women of religion, who consider themselves to be following the example of the founder of their faith, no matter what the personal cost.

They look back to the original sources of Islam and interpret them as justification for violence. A Pentagon study came to the conclusion that, in spite of other suggested motivations, most Muslim suicide bombers are motivated mainly by the commands of the Qur'an.[823] An example of this logic could be seen on the Chechen website www.qoqaz.com (now removed) where articles appeared which directly used verses in the Qur'an and incidents from the life of Muhammad to legitimise the execution of non-Muslim prisoners and hostages. For example:

In an article titled "A Guide to the Perplexed Regarding the Permissibility of Killing Prisoners" which appeared in the column "Jihad News from the Land of the Caucasus" the author suggests that the Islamic religious scholars present five different alternatives, drawn from the various interpretations of the Qur'an:

1 A polytheist prisoner must be killed. No amnesty may be granted to him, nor can he be ransomed.

2 All infidel polytheists and the People of the Book (i.e. Jews and Christians) are to be killed. They may not be granted amnesty, nor can they be ransomed.

3 Amnesty and ransom are the only two ways to deal with prisoners.

4 Amnesty and ransom are possible only after the killing of a large number of prisoners.

5 The Imam, or someone acting on his behalf, can choose between killing, amnesty, ransom or enslaving the prisoner.[824]

Mention has already been made in chapter 7 of an article in the Kuwaiti newspaper *Al-Watan* which used examples from Muhammad's life to legitimise the killing of non-combatants (including women and children) if they are citizens of countries with which Muslims are at war and if their actions are connected even in the most remote sense to any war effort. Referring to Israel the author states:

> It is common knowledge that the Zionist society is a military society, and every one of them takes part in warfare, whether as a soldier in the army, as a reservist, by paying taxes to the Jewish state and its army which kills Muslims, or by voting to put Sharon in a position to give the orders to kill Al-Dura and other Palestinian children.[825]

The same kind of argument was expressed by a failed suicide bomber interviewed on British television.[826] According to this logic American and British citizens would also be legitimate targets merely because they pay taxes or vote for a government which sends troops to fight in Islamic countries.

In another example Suleiman Abu Gheith, an Al-Qa'eda spokesman, states that,

> Allah said: 'He who attacked you, attack him as he attacked you,' and also, 'The reward of evil is a similar evil,' and also, 'When you are punished, punish as you have been punished.'

He cites the *hadith* collections of Ibn Taymiyya, Ibn al-Qayim and others to argue from this for the use of weapons of mass destruction on the basis of reciprocity of punishment. By estimating the number of Muslim deaths caused by America's intervention and foreign policy in Afghanistan, Iraq, Somalia, Palestine, Sudan, the Philippines, Bosnia, Kashmir, Chechnya etc. Abu Gheith calculates how many American deaths can be legitimately sought in return:

> We have not reached parity with them. We have the right to kill four million Americans – two million of them children – and to exile twice as many and wound and cripple hundreds of thousands. Furthermore, it is our right to fight them with chemical and biological weapons, so as to afflict them with the fatal maladies that have afflicted the Muslims because of the [Americans'] chemical and biological weapons."[827]

Of course many Muslims would reject Abu Gheith's method of reasoning.

Although there are abundant arguments to demonstrate that *jihad* in general is a duty, there is a debate within contemporary Islam as to whether suicide killings are also a duty, or even legitimate. Some extreme radicals have revived the Khariji and Assassin traditions of suicide killings as a legitimate weapon in their contemporary *jihad*. In order to do this, a theological distinction previously drawn in Islam between deliberately going to one's certain death at the hands of an overwhelmingly strong enemy (as the Assassins did) and dying by one's own hand (as modern suicide bombers do) had to be blurred.[828]

Another interesting comment on this issue comes from Shaybani in an imagined scenario whereby a Muslim pierced by a (long-handled) lance would have to deepen his own wound in order to reach his opponent with his own (much shorter) sword.

> I asked: if a [Muslim] warrior is run through by a lance, would you disapprove if he advances – though the lance be piercing him – in order to kill his adversary with the sword?

> He replied: No.

> I asked: Do you not think that he helped against his own life by so doing [i.e. that he committed suicide, which is forbidden]?

> He replied: No.[829]

Suicide killings are described as martyrdom (*istishad*). To fight for Islam, and more particularly to die in *jihad*, is considered a testimony (*shahada*), a term more normally used of the Islamic creed as verbally professed: hence the use of the term *shahid* to mean a martyr.[830] The cult of martyrdom has always been strong amongst Shiʻa extremists, but the concept has now spread also to Sunni groups, motivating their members to acts of violent martyrdom.[831] Suicide bombings are an important component in their arsenal of weapons as demonstrated by Hamas, Islamic Jihad and other Palestinian groups in Israel and the suicidal plane attacks on the World Trade Centre in New York by Al-Qaʻeda members.

The debate within contemporary Islam about the legitimacy of suicide attacks arises from the fact that suicide *per se* is regarded as a serious sin.[832] However, the evidence for this from the Qur'an is somewhat tenuous.

> And spend of your substance in the cause of God, and make not your own hands contribute to (your) destruction; but do good; for God loveth those who do good. Q 2:195

Although this is a Qur'anic verse often cited as forbidding suicide, A. Yusuf Ali's comment[833] interprets the verse as concerned not with suicide but with the use of one's wealth. He sees it as a command to give generously in support of a just war in the cause of God and a warning that those who are reluctant to give freely may be "helping in their own self-destruction". Alternatively if they spend their money on something other than "the cause of God" the enemy may gain an advantage and thus they will have contributed to their own self-destruction. The word "your" before "destruction" does not appear in the Arabic original, but Ali has inserted it in his translation.

> O ye who believe! Eat not up your property among yourselves in vanities: but let there be amongst you traffic and trade by mutual good-will: nor kill (or destroy) yourselves: for verily God hath been to you most merciful! Q 4:29

Asra Rasheed sees this as a prohibition on suicide,[834] but A. Yusuf Ali interprets it as a command not to kill fellow-believers and not to destroy oneself by squandering one's wealth.[835]

As so often, the *hadith* are less ambiguous, and some record clear-cut condemnations by Muhammad of suicide:

> The Prophet said, "A man was inflicted with wounds and he committed suicide, and so Allah said, "My slave has caused death on himself hurriedly, so I forbid Paradise for him." *Sahih Bukhari Volume 2, Book 23, Number 445: Narrated by Thabit bin Ad-Dahhak*

> ... if someone commits suicide with anything in this world, he will be tortured with that very thing on the Day of Resurrection... *Sahih Bukhari Volume 8, Book 73, Number 72: Narrated by Thabit bin Ad-Dahhak*

Others too long to quote here in full describe those who commit suicide as "disobedient"[836] and as "dwellers of hellfire".[837]

It is important to note that Islamic radical groups involved in suicide attacks do not use the phrase "suicide bombers" but instead refer to *shahids* (martyrs or witnesses, Arabic plural *shuhada)* making it clear that they view the bombers as noble victims who have sacrificed their lives in *jihad*, not as suicides. In the selection and training of bombers, any suicidal individuals are weeded out so that the motives of the *shahids* are kept pure.

The concept of suicide killings has received support not only from radicals but from many mainstream Islamic leaders as well. It was noticeable that following September 11th 2001, no *fatwa* condemning suicide attacks was issued.[838] A number of public statements by Sheikh Muhammad Sayyid Tantawi, Grand Imam of Al-Azhar, commending Palestinian suicide operations and permitting suicide attacks in Iraq have been mentioned in chapter 9. The Mufti of Egypt, Sheikh Dr Ahmad Al-Tayyeb, has expressed support for suicide attacks in the Palestinian context too.[839] A congress of 50 Islamic scholars from seven countries, meeting in Lebanon in January 2002, also affirmed the legitimacy of suicide attacks against Israel.[840] Three months later a meeting of the Organisation of the Islamic Conference in Kuala Lumpur, representing all the Muslim nations, refused to condemn suicide bombings.[841] Likewise Sheikh Yusuf al-Qaradhawi, in his capacity as head of the European Council for Fatwa and Research, gave a report to the Council at their meeting in Stockholm in July 2003, which approved suicide attacks in Palestine on the basis that it was a situation of extreme necessity and thus normal prohibitions became irrelevant.

> What weapon can harm their enemy, can prevent him from sleeping, and can strip him of a sense of security and stability, except for these human bombs – a young man or woman who blows himself or herself up amongst their enemy? This is a weapon the likes of which the enemy cannot obtain, even if the U.S. provides it with billions [of dollars] and the most powerful weapons, because it is a unique weapon that Allah has placed only in the hands of the men of belief. It is a type of divine justice on the face of the earth... it is the weapon of the wretched weak in the face of the powerful tyrant...[842]

He also argued that suicide attacks were not suicide as such but martyrdom, because of the different motives – advance and attack by self-sacrifice for a higher goal, or escape and retreat by fleeing life because of failure and weakness.[843]

Because of the debate about the validity of suicide bombings, it is essential for any particular suicide bomber that his death is declared to be a martyrdom.[844] Without the confidence that this will happen he will be reluctant to go ahead with the suicide. He also needs to be sure that any debts he may have will be promptly paid off after his death, because there is a belief that the martyr will not go to heaven if he is in debt.[845]

Another belief of Palestinian suicide bombers is that the bomber must repeat the Islamic creed just before he dies. If he fails to do that he will be questioned by two angels about his motives for suicide, and if he cannot truthfully say he died in the cause of God he will go to hell.

2 Heavenly reward

To die in *jihad* is to die a glorious and noble martyr and to ensure oneself an immediate place in paradise, with all sins forgiven. A martyr will not have to face examination in the grave by the two "interrogating angels" or any temporary punishment in hell. He will be given the highest of the various ranks in paradise, nearest the throne of God, a crown of glory, seventy or seventy-two virgins and other heavenly delights. Many would-be martyrs speak of their hope of being kept alive and sustained by God. Furthermore a martyr's intercession will be accepted for up to seventy of his relatives so that they too can go straight to paradise.[846] Female martyrs expect to find themselves given a prestigious place in paradise, close to Muhammad[847] or to become one of the heavenly virgins.[848] One woman caught before she could blow herself up had expected to become after martyrdom "the purest and most beautiful form of angel at the highest level possible in heaven".[849]

These various rewards and honours in the afterlife are stressed by the groups who recruit *shahids*. However, since dying in *jihad* is generally considered the only guaranteed way to gain immediate access to paradise[850] it is probably this – the certainty of going straight to paradise - more than the seventy virgins, which motivates most suicide bombers. Indeed, Esposito asserts that the belief that a *shahid* goes directly to paradise is the "main motivator" for Muslims in war against non-Muslims.[851]

> Think not of those who are slain in God's way as dead. Nay, they live, finding their sustenance in the presence of their Lord. Q 3:169

The rewards for dying in *jihad* are promised in both the Qur'an and the *hadith*. Examples from the Qur'an include:

> Let those fight in the cause of God who sell the life of this world for the Hereafter. To him who fighteth in the cause of God, - whether he is slain or gets victory – soon shall we give him a reward of great (value). Q 4:74

> But the Apostle, and those who believe with him, strive and fight with their wealth and their persons: for them are (all) good things: and it is they who will prosper. God hath prepared for them gardens (paradise) under which rivers flow, to dwell therein: that is the supreme felicity. Q 9:88-89

A relevant *hadith* runs as follows:

> The Apostle of Allah (peace_be_upon_him) said: If anyone fights in Allah's path as long as the time between two milkings of a she camel, Paradise will be assured for him. If anyone sincerely asks Allah for being killed and then dies or is killed, there will be a reward of a martyr for him. Ibn al-Musaffa added from here: If anyone is wounded in Allah's path, or suffers a misfortune, it will come on the Day of resurrection as copious as possible, its colour saffron, and its odour musk; and if anyone suffers from ulcers while in Allah's path, he will have on him the stamp of the martyrs. *Sunan Abu Dawud Book 14, Number 2535: Narrated Mu'adh ibn Jabal*

We have already seen how the Assassins made sure of being captured after completing their killing, so that they too would be killed and go to paradise as a martyr. Similarly one of the Muslim troops at the Battle of Badr (624), 'Auf b. Harith, was so inspired by Muhammad's talk of martyrdom for those slain in battle that he removed his armour and fought until he was killed.[852]

According to Osama bin Laden there is an extra reward for killing Americans, or perhaps all Jews and Christians (People of the Book).

> These youths know that their rewards in fighting you, the USA, is double than their rewards *(sic)* in fighting some one else not from

the people of the book. They have no intention except to enter paradise by killing you.[853]

Someone who dies in *jihad* on the battlefield is buried in a different way from other Muslims. Instead of ceremonial preparation – being washed and dressed carefully as if to go to the mosque – the martyr is left just as they are in their bloodstained clothes. Traditionally they were buried where they fell.[854] This follows the example of what Muhammad ordered for Muslims who were killed in the Battle of Uhud (625):

> .... He ordered them to be buried with their blood on their bodies and they were neither washed nor was a funeral offered for them. *Sahih Bukhari Book 23, chapter 37, number 676 narrated by Jabir bin 'Abdullah*[855]

So great is the honour of being a martyr that often the relatives will not express grief at the death but rather gratitude for the martyrdom. (This was particularly true of the mothers of the Iranian soldiers killed in the Iran-Iraq war of 1980-88.)[856]

This emphasis on the heavenly rewards which Muslim suicide bombers can expect to receive contrasts sharply with the psychology of the suicide bombers of the Tamil Tigers. In Sri Lanka the cause of the Tamils is overwhelmingly political and the religious dimension is not emphasised. For the Tamil Tigers the ethos of suicide bombing is one of sacrifice rather than heavenly reward. The individual sacrifices himself or herself for a political cause which is greater than the life of one man or woman. It is the suffering of their fellow Tamils and the value of their sacrifice, rather than any reward in the afterlife, which are stressed during their training.

The Tigers carry cyanide pills around their necks, in order to ensure they are not captured alive and forced to divulge information. This indicates another key difference from Islamic suicide bombers who would view the use of a suicide pill as genuine suicide and not martyrdom. Suicide in the Tamil tradition is not viewed with the same abhorrence. (Other differences from the Islamic tradition include the greater use of female suicide bombers, and the institutional taking and training of bombers from a very young age.)

3 Response to humiliation

One of the characteristics of Islam is its emphasis on shame, as opposed to the traditional Western emphasis on guilt borne out of a Judaeo-Christian heritage. Shame is to be avoided at all costs, and honour, which includes the concept of pwer for the Muslim community, is to be sought and safeguarded. True faith – Islam – based on God's final revelation must be protected from insult and abuse. (Other faiths, being false or incomplete in Muslim opinion, have no right to such protection.) When Baghdad fell to the US-led coalition forces in April 2003 many Muslims around the world, particularly Arabs, were in shock and denial; the defeat of a Muslim leader by non-Muslims caused enormous anguish.

Shame and humiliation cannot be borne and are considered legitimate justification for a violent response. Muslim statements of outrage concerning the imposition of non-Muslims on their territory or rights are often phrased in terms of "humiliation", with the unspoken assumption that this is the greatest grievance possible. Many Islamic terrorists and suicide bombers see their task as contributing to the vital process of redeeming Islam's honour from the humiliation imposed on it by the West.

In the words of Osama bin Laden,

> The walls of oppression and humiliation cannot be demolished except in a rain of bullets...Death is better than life in humiliation! Some scandals and shames will never be otherwise eradicated.[857]

Saad al-Fagih, a Saudi dissident and director of the Movement for Islamic Reform in Arabia, commenting on the presence of American troops in Iraq after the ousting of President Saddam Hussein said:

> The sight of US tanks in Baghdad is the most humiliating event for Muslims and Arabs since 1967. Baghdad, the capital of the Islamic Caliphate for 600 years, occupies a central place in the Muslim memory and means more even than Riyadh or Cairo."[858]

The following quotation comes from an Indonesian manual on *jihad*. Gaining dignity is placed on a par with spreading Islamic power as fuel for the "spirit of *jihad*".

> Let the spirit of jihad burn among the Muslims at all times and situations because *jihad* is the fortress of defence for Islam and the way to improve the dignity of the Muslims from the scorn and contempt heaped on it. The jihad may not cease until all the world is free from the oppression/cruelty and bows to the power of Islam.[859]

Even Sheikh Tantawi of Al-Azhar University teaches that it is permissible for Muslims to fight non-Muslims in other countries for no greater injury than that the non-Muslims are "actively condemning or belittling" Muslims or the religion of Islam.[860]

4 The importance of history

Islamic terrorists have a highly developed and clear sense of history. The humiliations of the Crusades,[861] the loss of Islamic Spain to Ferdinand and Isabella in the fifteenth century Reconquista, Western colonialism, and the end of the last Islamic caliphate with the collapse of the Ottomans following the First World War are all still keenly felt by Islamic militants. For many extremists these events, which happened decades and even hundreds of years ago, carry a sense of immediacy and urgency, a burden of humiliation at the hands of the West which has lost none of its potency with the passage of time. This characteristic is described with proud sarcasm as a "fault" by the radical Saudi sheikh, famed for his anti-Americanism, Sheikh Safar bin Abdur-Rahman Al-Hawali. In his *Open Letter to President Bush* he appears to despise Germany and Japan for not still holding a grudge against the US for their defeat in the Second World War.

> Mr President, don't suppose that I want to recount your few faults and forget our own (in your eyes) very many faults. No, I will mention to you a serious fault of us Muslims: we don't forget our tragedies no matter how much time has passed. Imagine, Mr President, we still weep over Andalusia and remember what Ferdinand and Isabella did there to our religious, culture and honor! We dream of regaining it. Nor will we forget the destruction of Baghdad, or the fall of Jerusalem at the hands of your Crusader ancestors. That is, we are not (in your opinion)

at the level of civilisation enjoyed by the Germans and Japanese who support your hostilities and forget your past treatment of them. Moreover, the African Muslims who embraced Islam after the fall of Andalusia cry along with the Arabs, just as the Indonesians do who only recently heard about Andalusia. It may be a problem for us, but who will pay the price after a while?[862]

5 Identification with heroes

Shahids are heroes. They are honoured and admired and held up as ideals to be imitated and followed. In India *shahids* of old are worshipped, and the devout seek their intercession.[863] Self-denying leaders such as bin Laden, who abandoned a wealthy lifestyle for one of austerity, are also heroes. Many who volunteer to be *shahids* are inspired by such examples.

A Palestinian suicide bomber is given a large, prestigious funeral. His family (who would have known nothing about his mission until he was dead) are fêted and honoured in public testimonials from groups like Hamas and Islamic Jihad. They are generally proud and delighted at what has happened.[864] The organisation which recruited, trained and sent the bomber provides his family with ongoing financial support. King Fahd of Saudi Arabia also sends funds to the families of martyrs, as did the former Iraqi president Saddam Hussein. Gifts may also come from Arab charities. A bomber's family can receive in the region of $25,000 in cash.

The Palestinian Authority runs summer camps for children at which talks and activities are used to present terrorists as role models and heroes for the children. Some of the camps are named after individual terrorists or suicide bombers, and others are simply called *"shahid"*.[865] The first female Palestinian suicide bomber, Wafa Idris (who has had educational programmes as well as summer camps named after her), was celebrated in song on Palestinian Authority TV.[866]

6 Training

The training given to potential terrorists and suicide bombers involves a deliberate process of imbuing the students with a fanatical hatred of the West and a perception that the West is responsible for all the woes of the Muslim world. Those who have been through this process emerge highly motivated to expend their lives in *jihad* against the West. Furthermore, if the training process is violent, as it sometimes is, those who have been brutalised by it may lose all compunction or compassion for their future victims, and emerge absolutely single-minded and ruthless. (See chapter 14 for more on the training of Islamic terrorists in general.)

7 *Bay'a*

An important concept in Islam is that of *bay'a,* the swearing of an oath of allegiance and obedience to a religious or political leader. When Muhammad died the Muslim community made their *bay'a* to his successor Abu Bakr, the first caliph. In posters for the referendum on extending Saddam Hussein's presidency held in Iraq on October 15th 2002 (naturally a foregone conclusion) the word *bay'a* was used, and the day described as the "day of the oath of allegiance". As such the Iraqi people were swearing their oath of allegiance to Saddam Hussein as their caliph. For Islamic terrorist groups the concept has particular significance. Many Islamic militants have performed *bay'a* to their leaders such as Osama bin Laden, as the title *Sheikh,* often used to refer to him, indicates. Interestingly, Western converts to Islam are often encouraged to perform *bay'a* as well. *Bay'a* can be passed on by a leader to his successor or can be distributed to a number of his followers, thus creating a network, as for example the network of Islamic centres created in nineteenth century India when various *pirs* passed *bay'a* to each other.[867]

Bay'a, which is a lifelong and personal commitment, indicates the intensely strong nature of the bonds of loyalty and co-operation which can exist within and between Islamic terrorist networks. Western intelligence agencies have found it correspondingly difficult to infiltrate or establish informers amongst such networks.

A distinction needs to be drawn between an oath of allegiance to a leader such as Saddam Hussein who is political, and one to a much more overtly religious leader like Osama bin Laden.

Allegiances to the former can shift very easily and quickly depending on the varying circumstances and fortunes of the political leader. However, an oath of allegiance to a religious leader is far more binding since it is a matter of faith. In seeking out potential terrorist movements, one could therefore examine where *bay'a* is made, and to whom.

8 Specific grievances

All radical Islamic movements share a common hostility to Western influences and their perceived corruption of Islamic societies; such influences are viewed as a continuation of colonialism and imperialism by other means. The West is held responsible for the decline and loss of the Islamic empires such as the Mughals, the Ottomans and Safavi Iran i.e. for blasphemously spoiling the God-ordained order of the world in which Muslims rule over non-Muslims. Western civilization is blamed for the corruption of all that is good in the world and for encouraging the evils of secularism, atheism, alcohol, drugs, sexual permissiveness, family breakdown etc. Globalisation, capitalism, secularism, materialism and consumerism are other Western characteristics which are condemned. It is interesting to remember that Muhammad was strongly opposed to commerce and trade in Arabia, believing them to be the cause of social ills. Islamists hold that Western values must be rejected as they lead to moral chaos and threaten Muslim identity and self-esteem.

The US is seen as the leading Western power, imposing its immoral and secular values by means of its economic superiority, cultural hegemony etc. and thus humiliating Muslims and robbing them of their culture and dignity. Islamic revival has come to focus on the USA as the enemy of God, the incarnation of evil, a diabolical opponent of all that is good. Israel is seen as a "dagger in the heart of the Arab world", a Western creation which is causing suffering to Palestinian Muslims. American support for Israel is perceived as one-sided.

Dependency, failure, powerlessness, humiliation and jealousy all lead to a search for scapegoats for the ills of Muslim society and thus to conspiracy theories. Christianity, the West, the US, Jews,

Freemasons etc. are thought to be conspiring against Islam in some kind of a global cultural war, whose battlefields include Palestine, Iraq, Lebanon, Tajikistan, Kashmir, the Philippines, Somalia, Eritrea, Chechnya, Bosnia and elsewhere. Sayyid Qutb thought that Marxists were participating in a conspiracy against Islam with the Christian West and with Jews.[868] Taqiuddin an-Nabhani (1909-1977), founder of Hizb ut-Tahrir, believed that Orientalists and Christian missionaries were conspiring with Western states to get revenge on Islam for Christendom's defeat in the Crusades; he saw Western colonialism and the military conquest of Arab lands in the First World War as part of this conspiracy.[869] Ayatollah Khomeini expressed his fears as follows:

> The hands of the missionaries, the orientalists and of the information media — all of whom are in the service of the colonialist countries — have cooperated to distort the facts of Islam in a manner that has caused many people, especially the educated among them, to steer away from Islam and to be unable to find a way to reach Islam.

> Islam is the religion of the strugglers who want right and justice, the religion of those demanding freedom and independence and those who do not want to allow the infidels to dominate the believers.

> But the enemies have portrayed Islam in a different light. They have drawn from the minds of the ordinary people a distorted picture of Islam and implanted this picture even in the religious academies. The enemies' aim behind this was to extinguish the flame of Islam and to cause its vital revolutionary character to be lost, so that Muslims would not think of seeking to liberate themselves...

> The colonialists and their lackeys have made these statements [that Islam has nothing to do with society or government] to isolate religion from the affairs of life and society and to tacitly keep the 'ulama of Islam away from the people, and drive people away from the 'ulama because the 'ulama struggle for the liberation and independence of the Muslims. When their wish

of separation and isolation is realized, the colonialists and their lackeys can take away our resources and rule us.[870]

The car accident which killed Britain's Princess Diana and her Egyptian Muslim boyfriend Dodi Al-Fayed in 1997 is believed by many Muslims to have been arranged by the British intelligence service to ensure that no Muslim could enter the senior levels of the monarchy. The suicide attacks on the World Trade Centre on September 11th 2001 are considered to have been organised by Jews with the intention of throwing the blame on to Muslims. Malaysian Prime Minister Mahathir Mohamad claimed in a speech to the Organisation of the Islamic Conference in October 2003 that "the Jews rule this world by proxy. They get others to fight and die for them."[871]

Coupled with anti-Westernism is a nostalgia for Islam's glorious past. Modern ideologies such as nationalism and socialism are deemed to have failed to deliver, more or less wherever they have been tried. The solution is therefore seen as a return to traditional, conservative Islam.[872]

Various specific aims have been adopted by different contemporary groups over the course of time:

8a Fighting their own governments

The plethora of twentieth century extremist Islamic groups, differing from each other in the details of their theology and methodology, would at first each focus their violent activities on destabilising and destroying the "infidel" regimes in their own countries. As we have seen this was in obedience to the Islamic command to fight the enemies near at hand before dealing with enemies further afield.[873] Examples include Mawdudi in the Indian subcontinent, Qutb in Egypt[874] and Khomeini in Iran.

Sheikh Omar Abdul Rahman in his book *The Present Rulers and Islam: Are they Muslims or Not?* promotes the view that the *umma* is justified in removing the country's leader by force if he or she is not ruling according to the *shari'a*. While many other Islamic authorities, working on the principle of the lesser of two evils, say this should only be done if it does not lead to *fitna* (disorder and conflict), Rahman prefers to overthrow the regime even if *fitna* results.[875]

8b Fighting repression of Muslims

The disparate groups were brought together in the 1980s and especially in the 1990s by common causes around the world. These causes were those where Muslims perceive their coreligionists to be under threat from non-Muslims. A classic example is Afghanistan, where thousands of volunteers from across the Muslim world joined the *jihad* against the Soviet Union in the 1980s. Under Afghan influence a "brotherhood of the persecuted" developed among the groups, leading them to cooperation and mutual assistance despite their differences. This cooperation was accompanied by a spread of the ideas of the *takfir* groups to the *jihad* groups, especially in regard to the struggle in the Arab world against rulers perceived as collaborators with the "Western infidel culture".

Many Afghan veterans returning home after the Soviet withdrawal instigated a radicalisation of Islamist groups and a marked increase in violence in their home countries, especially in Algeria and Egypt. Others however found new sponsors and moved to other flashpoints where they sensed infidel attacks on Muslim communities, such as Kashmir, Bosnia, Chechnya, Daghestan, Kosovo and the Philippines. They have been instrumental in intensifying the militancy of Islamist movements in Indonesia and in sub-Saharan Africa.

8c Fighting the US

The Gulf War of 1990-1 further radicalised these groups by endorsing their perception of the West as aiming to re-colonise Muslim states. Their sensibilities were especially outraged by the permanent stationing of American troops in Saudi Arabia. The polluting presence of *kafir* (infidel) soldiers near Islam's holiest places, Mecca and Medina, was perceived as an aggressive act aimed at dominating the Muslim heartland.[876] The US thus became an "enemy near at hand" and therefore a focus of attention for groups such as al-Jama'at al-Islamiyya.

338

One of the consequences of the influence of *takfir* ideology on the Egyptian group Al-Jihad was the anti-American extremism that led them to carry out the bombing of the World Trade Centre in 1993, and several other bombing attempts in the US. Prior to the early 1990s Al-Jihad had confined their terrorist operations to Egypt.

Osama bin Laden's Al-Qa'eda was in the forefront of those who encouraged interaction and networking between a wide variety of such movements around the world, preparing for assaults that would really hurt and humiliate America. Petty squabbles and enmity towards corrupt regimes in Muslim lands became secondary in the light of this *jihad* against the greater *kufr* (unbelief). The results of this shift have now been seen, among others, in the bombings of the American embassies in Nairobi and Dar-es-Salaam in 1998 and in the suicide plane attacks on the World Trade Centre and the Pentagon in the US on September 11th 2001.

Such apparently "senseless" attacks in fact fit perfectly the classical terrorist strategy defined by the Brazilian guerrilla Carlos Marighella as "turning political crisis into armed conflict by performing violent actions that will force those in power" into a military response "that will alienate the masses."[877] The response of the West to September 11th 2001 in Afghanistan and Iraq did indeed lead to a hardening of public opinion across the Islamic world and growing support for Osama bin Laden and others like him. A similar policy can be seen in other contexts such as Kosovo and Macedonia where violence has provoked military responses which in turn have led to international intervention, ultimately producing results favourable to the terrorist groups which began the cycle. This may also be the strategy in Palestine and Kashmir.

9 Personal grudges

Some terrorists and suicide bombers have the additional motivation of seeking to avenge a personal hurt or insult they have suffered. One such was a Palestinian interviewed on a British television programme who explained that as a boy of twelve he had been slapped by an Israeli border guard for no reason. He said that, being a Muslim his principle, was, "If you slap me once, I will slap you twice,"[878] and viewed the suicide attacks he was helping to organise as the retaliatory double slapping.[879]

Basic requirements for the motivation of suicide bombers

The multiplicity of motives which go to create suicide bombers can be summarised as five main requirements:

- a political cause worth dying for

- a theology which affirms the legitimacy of suicide martyrdom

- the assurance that after death he/she will be authoritatively declared a martyr

- economic and financial support for the martyr and his family after death

- media involvement – a martyr must also be a public hero

If one or more of these is missing there is likely to be a scarcity of recruits for suicide missions.

Recognising a suicide bomber

Although a suicide bomber does not normally inform his family of his intentions, there is a pattern of behaviour which might be spotted by those who know him. He will develop a new circle of friends, and drop old friends. He will probably stop going to the local mosque and start attending another one. He will be quiet and polite, yet outspoken about issues of faith with an uncompromising attitude. He will avoid places and situations where women are likely to be present, so as not to meet women whose heads are uncovered or non-Muslim women. He will refuse to associate with women (apart from close relatives), even if he has known them for a long time.

In Muslim contexts he will grow a beard and begin to dress very conservatively, with long sleeves and high necklines. He will be devout and reluctant to socialise or take part in any non-religious gatherings. However, in Western contexts he may deliberately adopt the opposite behaviour, in an attempt to conceal how he is thinking. In the latter case, he would dress in casual Western clothing, take care to be seen at nightclubs, leave tell-tale beer cans around etc. Shortly before the date of the attack, the suicide bomber may indulge in unusual extravagances, such as taking family and friends out to meals, which in retrospect are recognised to have been farewells.

The next generation of suicide bombers is expected to prove well nigh impossible to detect. Practising *taqiyya* to a high degree, they will effectively blend into the society in which they are living. In a Western context they would be clean-shaven, will avoid visiting radical mosques or meeting in person with anyone publicly known as an extremist. Communication with their radical colleagues will be conducted by a variety of secure means. They will avoid travelling to places such as Afghanistan or any other theatre of armed conflict but rather will go on holiday to expensive resorts. They will consort with non-Muslims of the opposite sex, drink alcohol and eat pork, and generally participate in popular culture e.g. sport, music etc. Many would be likely to have good jobs in industry and commerce, probably involving IT and communication skills. They will not use traditional "handlers" or follow the classic cell patterns. This will make detection and monitoring by the security forces extremely difficult.

Further comments on the Islamic theology of martyrdom

There are two main categories of martyr[880] – those who die on the battlefield and those who do not.

1 Martyrs both in this world and the next

The battlefield martyrs are called "martyrs both in this world and the next", their martyrdom in this world being recognised by the special burial rites described above which – according to most Islamic authorities – do not include washing the body. There are many detailed rules concerning the purpose of the battle and how long a time may pass between injury and death in order to qualify as a battlefield martyr.

Perhaps most important is the intention of the martyr. Someone who went into battle for the wrong reason, for example to show off or in the hope of spoils, would not be a true battlefield martyr. However, since only God knows the intentions of the heart, all who die on the battlefield will be buried as if they were true battlefield martyrs. Those who did not go with the right intentions or with true belief will not receive a martyr's reward in heaven, and may even go to hell. They are therefore known as "martyrs in this world only".

2 Martyrs in the next world only

This includes all those who fail to qualify as battlefield martyrs. Examples would be someone who accidentally wounds themselves fatally with their own weapon on the battlefield, someone who dies in battle against Muslims, or who dies defending their family against Muslim brigands or highway robbers. Within this category are many different types of martyrs:

a *Those who died violently or prematurely*

i) Those murdered while in the service of God. This is sometimes taken to include Muhammad himself since his death was supposedly precipitated by tasting a piece of poisoned mutton he was offered by Zaynab bt. al-Harith.

ii) Those killed for their beliefs, i.e. Muslims killed by non-Muslims because they adhered to Islam. John the Baptist and various other pre-Islamic prophets are also included here.

iii) Those who die from disease or accident. Early *hadith* collections mention victims of plague and pleurisy as well as those who drowned or burned to death, and women who died in childbirth. The logic is that elevation to the rank of martyr is divine compensation for the painful deaths they suffered.

iv) The "martyrs of love". These are people who fell in love, remained chaste, concealed their secret and died.

v) The "martyrs who died far from home". These are Muslims who fled their homeland in time of persecution in order to preserve their faith, and died in a foreign country.

b Those who died a natural death

i) while engaged in a meritorious act such as pilgrimage or prayer or a journey in search of knowledge.[881]

ii) after leading a virtuous life – i.e. who had waged successfully the "greater *jihad*" against their soul. This is particularly strong amongst Shi'as.

c Living martyrs

Those who are engaged in successful war against their own souls i.e. are living according to Islamic teaching. This concept was promoted by the Sufi scholar Abu 'Abd al-Rahman al-Sulami (d. 1021) who held that a battlefield martyr is only a *shahid* externally, whereas someone who kills his own soul while living in accordance with Sufi teaching is a true martyr.

14
The Making of an Islamic Terrorist

Of the many Muslims who would acknowledge the continuing validity of the classical teachings of Islam on war and expansion of Islamic territory, only a small number put their beliefs into practice in the most literal way and become active terrorists. This chapter seeks to examine the psychology, selection and training of Islamic militants, with special reference to suicide bombers.

Psychology

Most terrorists are extremely devout Muslims, who regularly say prayers and attend mosques. A good proportion have come to Islam from another faith; they have the zeal of the convert and may feel the need to prove themselves worthy Muslims.[882] All are motivated with a sense of intense rage, hatred and revenge towards those they see as their oppressors who have humiliated their religion and their people. They feel they are breaking out of a state of impotency and striking back from their position of humiliation. Suicide bombers within the Islamic tradition are almost all young and single.[883] In most contexts they are commonly men, except in Chechnya where, as we shall see later in this chapter, there are many women (including widows) amongst the suicide bombers. Also the Palestinian Fatah, Tanzim, al-Aqsa Martyr Brigades as well as Palestinian Islamic Jihad have used women as suicide bombers in their attacks on Israeli targets since the start of the second intifada in 2000.[884] A few months before his assassination Sheikh Ahmed Yassin, the leader of Hamas, reversed the former policy of his organisation by issuing a *fatwa* permitting women to carry out suicide attacks. Soon after his *fatwa*, a Palestinian mother of two from Gaza blew herself up at the Israeli military checkpoint at the Erez crossing on January 15th 2004.[885]

Studies show that most tend to be introverts.[886] However, there is no indication that they are mentally ill in any medical sense. Far from being lone individuals, Islamic suicide bombers are recruited, trained, supported and backed up by Islamic militant groups at every level. In addition, in Palestine, suicide bombers come from a background where they are venerated and treated as heroes after their death on television, on the radio, in the newspapers, in the mosques, in public murals and at every conceivable level.

Recruits may be involved with such organisations for some time before they become suicide bombers themselves, sometimes forming close, intense friendships with their comrades. Those who volunteer to be suicide bombers – and are accepted – undergo a period of rigorous training from which there is no turning back.

Rather than being spontaneous acts of pure emotion and frustration, almost all suicide bombings are the result of deliberate, reasoned planning over some time; in the case of the September 11th 2001 attacks years had been spent in planning and preparation. Palestinian suicide bombers settle their debts if they can,[887] write farewell letters and record videos for their families before leaving home for the last time. A typical video will consist of a prayer, a speech asserting the Palestinians' resolve never to be crushed by Israel, and then family messages.

It seems highly unlikely that the phenomenon of Islamic suicide bombing could exist on anything like the same scale, if at all, without this overwhelming institutionalisation of the idea in the prevailing culture. Likewise lone Islamists striking at international targets are likely to be amateurish and ineffective without groups like Al-Qa'eda to train them and back them up.

Socio-economic deprivation

It is generally held that communities struggling to survive in grinding poverty, with few educational opportunities, widespread unemployment and little prospect of change are good breeding grounds for terrorism. The logic is that frustrated young men, who have no other way to change their situation and no other purpose to motivate them, are likely to find terrorism an attractive option. They have nothing to lose and potentially could gain personal glory and play a part in ushering in the true Islamic state which they see as the solution to all their ills.

Lack of education, it is argued, makes them more susceptible to the rhetoric and persuasion of terrorist organisations. Some failed Palestinian suicide bombers interviewed for television described themselves as young and ignorant, and indicated that, because of this, they were content simply to do what they were told by those who recruited and trained them, without questioning.[888]

While there is surely truth in this, it must be remembered that many Islamic terrorists are both affluent and well educated. Indeed many have been educated up to tertiary level in the West. So poverty and deprivation can be a contributory factor to the making of an Islamic terrorist, but would rarely be the only factor.

Selection and recruitment

Individuals with the right predisposition to become terrorists or suicide bombers are usually spotted and recruited at mosques, schools and religious institutions.

There has been an explosive growth in the number of *madrassas* all around the world and particularly, since the Soviet-Afghan War of 1979-89, in the Pakistan-Afghanistan region. Many of these schools are less concerned with education than with military training for young Muslims to wage *jihad*. Funding comes mainly from Saudi Arabia, either direct or through a network of charities. Ironically Saudi Arabia was originally encouraged in this endeavour by the US, in the hope that it would provide a bulwark against extremist Shi'a Islam.

Pakistan's Ministry for Religious Affairs estimates that more than 1.5 million Pakistani children attend *madrassas,* while the Brussels-based think tank, International Crisis Group, believes that nearly one-third of school-going children in Pakistan are getting their education at a *madrassa*.[889] They are often from the poorest families, who cannot afford to give their children any other kind of education. The *madrassas* provide not only a free education, but also free board and lodging. In addition there are students at the *madrassas* from all across the Muslim world, for example, Malaysia, Thailand, Nigeria, Philippines, Indonesia and the Gulf.

The students, who may be as young as nine or ten, are taught the Qur'an interpreted according to Wahhabi Islam. Very little if any other education is provided. Treatment can be brutal. Some students go on to become a new generation of imams and Muslim clerics all around the world, while others become *jihad* fighters in various different countries. The Taliban (a term which means "students") trained in these *madrassas*. In 1997 the Haqqania School near Peshawar closed down and sent all its pupils (who numbered more than 2,800) to Afghanistan to fight for the Taliban against the Northern Alliance.[890]

In Turkey the *madrassas* were abolished by Atatürk after his proclamation of the republic. In the 1950s and 1960s the state established schools for imams and preachers. However in the later decades of the twentieth century they formed a base for newly emergent Islamist political parties, which in turn produced the first non-secular Turkish prime minister, Necmettin Erbakan, who came to power in 1996.[891]

Malaysia's privately run religious schools, known as Sekolah Agama Rakyat (SAR, School of the People's Religion), are a breeding ground for future Muslim terrorists, according to the independent Malaysian think-tank, the Malaysian Strategic Research Centre. Its director, Abdul Razak Baginda, warned in January 2003, "The government must now watch these SARs more closely to ensure their students are not recruited by terrorist groups.... We have to take strong action or else we are finished." The SARs are run by individuals and groups aligned to the opposition political party the Parti Islam SeMalaysia.[892]

An appallingly brutal Islamic school in Kenya, the Khadija Islamic Institute for Discipline and Education in Eastleigh, Nairobi, was attended by teenage boys from Kenya, Ethiopia, Sweden and the UK. They were taught the Qur'an, English, Arabic and Maths. According to one former pupil, the killing of Christians was glorified. "They told us it's called *jihad*. They said if you enter a church with bombs and kill yourself you will go to heaven."[893]

Singaporean Muslims are recruited to the Jemaah Islamiyah terrorist group at religious classes offered for a general mass audience. From amongst those recommended for consideration, the Jemaah Islamiyah leaders seek to identify those who are interested to know more about the plight of oppressed Muslims around the world. The recruitment process usually takes about eighteen months.[894]

Jemaah Islamiyah in Indonesia uses women to lure men to join its ranks. The women seduce the men, then marry them. Neither husband nor wife can be sure that the other is not reporting back to Jemaah Islamiyah, so the loyalty of both to the organisation is assured. Female madrassas have been created to train the women for this role.[895]

In the UK young Muslims are recruited from the mosques by recruiting agents who stand outside giving away leaflets, get chatting and invite potential recruits for a meal. Recruits are often social misfits, perhaps fresh from prison and without money or friends. They may be given pocket money and somewhere to live. Gradually the meetings they attend become more political and they are taught to despise moderation and tolerance. Many are converts to Islam, and their ignorance of Arabic can be exploited by giving them the most extreme possible interpretations. Without Muslim relatives to give them a different interpretation of Islam, they may hear no other form of Islamic teaching but what their recruiters give them. Promising individuals are sent on training camps where they are taught horse-riding and how to handle guns.[896]

While British recruits often have a criminal record, it appears that a different strategy was employed by Assirat al-Moustaqim (The Straight Path), the Moroccan Islamist group responsible for the bombing in Casablanca on May 16th 2003. Assirat al-Moustaqim recruited operatives who lived in Casablanca and had no police records or previous involvement with radical Islam.[897]

An Indonesian *jihad* manual describes how to select individuals to serve in the "martyr brigades", defined as elite troops whose role is to engage in terrorism, sabotage, propaganda and psychological warfare. This is a somewhat different job description from that of the suicide bomber, but the willingness to die is emphasised throughout. The chosen men must have a strong faith and a true love of martyrdom. They must be courageous, skilled and always ready to sacrifice themselves if the conditions require it. They are chosen from among the strong and brave Muslims who no longer think of this earthly life and are supported with weaponry suitable to their tasks.[898]

In Chechnya those recruited as suicide bombers are often women, particularly women who have lost husbands and brothers to the Russians, who tend to target young men for arrest, torture and disappearance. The bereaved women are encouraged to offer themselves for suicide missions in order to get their revenge. Shamil Beno, who was the Chechen foreign minister during the republic's brief self-proclaimed independence in the 1990s, estimates that there are 30,000 families "that could produce *shahids,* families that have suffered terribly and see no alternative". Interestingly he sees the suicide response as not so much religiously motivated but the only practical way in which women can retaliate.[899]

Al-Qa'eda has fourteen mandatory qualifications for membership: knowledge of Islam, ideological commitment, maturity, self-sacrifice, discipline, secrecy and concealment of information, good health, patience, imperturbability, intelligence and insight, caution and prudence, truthfulness and wisdom, the ability to observe and analyse, and the ability to act.[900]

Recently recruitment of Islamic terrorists by means of Internet message boards has become popular. For example a Malaysian posted a message on an Arabic-language message board as follows: "Dear Brothers, I have already succeeded with the grace of Allah and his help, to go to Kurdistan for *jihad* through one of the brothers in this forum. Praise be to Allah, I have fought there, by the grace of God and his bounty. But martyrdom was not granted to me, and therefore I ask Allah to give me more lifetime and to make my deeds good. I ask anyone who has capacity to organise for me to go to another *jihad* front to correspond with me." There are reported to be hundreds of such message boards.[901]

Training

Once they become involved with Islamic militant groups the recruits enter a world where their rage is directed, channelled, and given a sense of purpose and an outlet. They are shown videos of Muslims suffering and are taught to demonise their future targets. They learn to consider their targets as utterly dehumanised - they are to be sacrificed for God without a hint of pity. An example of this kind of thinking comes from a columnist identified as Seif Al-Din Al-Ansari, writing in the online magazine *Al-Ansar*, which is affiliated with Al-Qa'eda:

> Regardless of the norms of "humanist" belief, which see destroying the infidel countries as a tragedy requiring us to show some conscientious empathy and... an atmosphere of sadness for the loss that is to be caused to human civilisation – an approach that does not distinguish between believer and infidel... - I would like to stress that annihilating the infidels is an inarguable fact, as this is the [divine] decree of fate...[902]

According to Iraqi police, not only "brainwashing" but also drugs are used on young Iraqis being recruited for suicide missions. The main drug involved is said to be Artane, an antipsychotic drug which can give a sense of invulnerability.[903]

Palestinian suicide bombers are trained within a small cell of activists who between them cover the following functions: recruiter, bomb-maker, trainer, transport of the suicide bomber to the target area, and the bomber himself or herself. The cell chooses the target and carefully guides the bomber in the making of the farewell video.[904] Suicide bombers are not taken to reconnoitre their target areas beforehand lest they should begin to feel compassion for their future victims.[905]

The Jemaah Islamiyah in Singapore give their new recruits a strong sense of exclusivity and self-esteem. They are told they will be martyrs if they die for the cause, and also that any who leave the organisation are infidels.[906]

An Indonesian *jihad* manual lists thirty "military doctrines of Islam". These are a mixture of spiritual exhortation and practical advice, tactics and rules of engagement, each one backed up with a selection of quotations from the Qur'an and *hadith*. Some examples are:

> Plant the goal of jihad in the way of Allah as to die a martyr, fall in the way of Allah, or gain victory by establishing Islam on the face of the earth.

> Love jihad more than anything else other than Allah and His apostle.

> In planning to attack the enemy or during an attack, do not argue a lot, something that will cause you to lose strength and boldness as a result of division.

> Know clearly and in detail where the enemy is that must be attacked so that you don't make any mistakes and attack your own side.

> Do not feel proud and boastful when you see that the enemy forces are smaller than yours. Large numbers do not necessarily defeat small numbers, if there is pride.

> In making an attack the first priority must be to kill all the leaders/commanders of the enemy because that will cause chaos among their followers.

> Have faith to the fullest extent; life and death are in the hands of Allah. There is no one who can be killed except with His permission. From all of this, do not retreat because of fear of death in the face of a strong and powerful enemy.

> If you hear rumours, news of peace etc. do not be caught up and spread them, but examine them first, then tell them to the leader/commander.

> Be just towards your enemies who surrender. Do not kill them. So too with women and children unless they fight against you.

Give shelter (amnesty) to the heathen and idolater who are reluctant to fight against the Muslims.[907]

Another section describes how "martyr brigades" should operate.

> They must be organised according to a tight system with a secret network that the enemy will have difficulty in analyzing. The commando structure must be complex with small teams which consist of a few members according to the need. Each of them must be expert in the field of arms. It would be excellent if every team had their own experts, in weapons, explosives etc. They will use special codes and will be very secretive in their operations, and will have all the supplies necessary to support the success of the martyr brigades.
>
> Control of the field: it is necessary to evaluate the targets that will be destroyed. The first choice is the facilities vital to the enemy so that they will be weakened. The principle, "strike once, destroy the enemy" must be implanted in these troops.
>
> Control of guerrilla tactics, both jungle, mountain and especially city guerrilla tactics vital to enemies in the city.
>
> These troops will not disclose the secrets of their troops even though they have to die, for the sake of the security and the continuation of the struggle.[908]

Al-Qa'eda's terrorists are amongst the best trained and most disciplined. It has several training manuals, the main one being a multi-volume work, running to 7,000 pages, called *Encyclopaedia of the Afghan jihad*. Much of the material was culled from American and British military manuals and it was put together by Egyptians and Saudis who had been educated in the US and UK. It is written simply and clearly so the instructions on weapons, tanks, explosives, intelligence, first aid etc. could be followed easily by someone who was not highly educated. First published in book form in Arabic in 1996, a CD version appeared in 1999.[909] Another of Al-Qa'eda's military training manuals is called *Declaration of Jihad Against the Country's Tyrants*. It presents an interpretation of Islamic teaching that justifies kidnapping for ransom, torture, killing and the exchange of hostages, especially if the victim is non-Muslim.

> We find permission to interrogate the hostage for the purpose of obtaining information. It is permitted to strike the non-believer who has no covenant until he reveals the news, information and secrets of his people... The religious scholars have also permitted the killing of a hostage if he insists on withholding information from Muslims. They permitted his killing so that he would not inform his people of what he learnt about the Muslim condition, number, and secrets.... The scholars have also permitted the exchange of hostages for money, services, expertise and secrets of the enemy's army, plans and numbers.[910]

Al Qa'eda runs training camps at which three standard courses are taught. Basic training involves guerrilla warfare and *shari'a*. Advanced training covers explosives, assassination techniques and heavy weapons. Specialised training includes surveillance and counter-surveillance, forging identity documents and conducting suicide attacks by vehicle or at sea.[911]

Al-Qa'eda have also launched an online magazine called *Al-Battar Training Camp*,[912] whose aim is to "spread military culture among the [Muslim] youth" by means of basic lessons in "sports training, through types of light weapons and guerrilla group actions in the cities and mountains, and [including] important points in security and intelligence". The introduction of the first issue (December 2003 or January 2004?) bemoans the fact that "many of Islam's young people" do not yet know how to bear arms, not to mention use them" and urges that preparing for *jihad* is a personal commandment that applies to every Muslim. The magazine finishes by saying "O Mujahid brother, in order to join the great training camps you don't have to travel to other lands. Alone, in your home, or with a group of your brothers, you too can begin to execute the training programme."[913]

However Al-Qa'eda considers that the most important form of training is psychological preparation, chiefly by religious indoctrination. The subjects covered include Islamic law, Islamic history, contemporary Islamic politics, how to preserve one's faith when interacting with non-Muslims, how to wage *jihad*, the life of Muhammad.[914] The hijackers of the September 11th 2001 planes had had little military training but were chosen because of their psychological state and their willingness to be martyrs.[915]

While hardly classified as "training", Hizbullah's computer game *Special Force* shows the kind of attitudes imbued by real training procedures. It begins with target practice at a boot camp, shooting at the faces of Israeli leaders. This is followed by replications of actual Hizbullah operations. Finally there is a gallery of fallen Hizbullah heroes. Hizbullah claimed to have sold more than 7,000 copies in the first two months of the game's launch and say that it allows a form of participation for the "thousands" of would-be volunteers that they have to turn away.[916] Mahmoud Rayya, an official from the Hizbullah bureau, commented, "In a way, Special Force offers a mental and personal training for those who play it, allowing them to feel that they are in the shoes of the resistance fighters."[917] A helper at Champions computer arcade in Beirut, where *Special Force* can be played, makes clear that he understands the intention of the game to be training: "It serves a certain goal. It's not just for fun. It's a way to teach youngsters to know their enemy better and be patriotic".[918]

15
Contemporary Muslim Debate on *Jihad*

Currently Islamic teaching on war is in a state of flux. The Muslim press, in particular Muslim cyberspace, is filled with debate and discussion about the Islamic doctrine of war. Although the traditional doctrine is no longer all-pervasive and unquestioned, it is nevertheless still very influential – as President Sadat of Egypt found to his cost.[919] Before making a peace treaty with Israel, he took the precaution of obtaining a ruling from the respected Al-Azhar University to say that the treaty did not violate the *shari'a*. Many Muslims however remained unconvinced, including those who assassinated him for neglecting what they asserted was the Islamic duty to fight non-Muslims.[920]

Parts of the traditional Islamic doctrine of war clearly run counter to modern international agreements such as the Geneva conventions and protocols and UN General Assembly resolutions. Even Sobhi Mahmassani, a renowned Lebanese legal expert whose general stance is that Islamic and international principles are compatible, admitted that rules about war are an exception to this.[921]

Some Modern Arguments Against the Classical Islamic Doctrine of War

Having looked in detail at the classical Islamic doctrine of war, it is helpful to consider briefly some of the main threads of argument offered by contemporary Muslims who have a more pacific faith than historical Islam. A useful discussion from this viewpoint can be found in the chapter "War and Peace in Islamic Law" by Harfiyah Haleem and Abdul Haleem in *The Crescent and the Cross*.[922] Like other Muslims with a peaceable perspective, the authors tackle a range of points found in the classical Islamic scholars' doctrine of war and offer alternative interpretations. Clearly it is sometimes a struggle to maintain respect for the revered scholars of the past whose classical interpretations are now being so radically revised. For example, Shafi'i is described as confused, and opinions are attributed to him with phrases like "as Shafi'i himself probably realised" or "this does not necessarily mean that Shafi'i thought non-combatants could be killed".[923]

War is only justified for self-defence[924] or pre-empting an imminent attack.

The first Muslims suffered ten years of persecution in Mecca before they fought back.[925] When self defence is required, war becomes not only justifiable but an obligation, as the Qur'an commands, "Fight in the cause of God those who fight you." (Q 2:190). One of the great exponents of the defensive nature of *jihad* was Mahmud Shaltut.[926] Another was Sir Sayyid Ahmed Khan (1817-1898) who tried to persuade his fellow Indian Muslims that they were only justified in fighting the British powers if the British *actively* prevented them from exercising their Islamic faith.[927] A contemporary exponent is Dr Abdel Mo'ti Bayoumi, a member of the Islamic Research Institute at Al-Azhar University. [928]This is the line of argument in Fatoohi's book *Jihad in the Qur'an* which he wrote after September 11th 2001 for Muslims, for those considering converting to Islam, and to convince other non-Muslims of the peaceful nature of Islam. Louay Fatoohi holds that armed *jihad* is a temporary measure for self-defence but peaceful *jihad*, in the sense of self-improvement and preaching Islam and working for good, is permanent.[929]

War is only justified if the aim is to stop evil and oppression.

Haleem et al. quote from the Qur'an in support of this, to indicate that God has set one group of people against another in order to prevent the earth from becoming "full of mischief" (Q 2:251).[930] Dr Kamal Boraiq'a Abd es-Salam of Al-Azhar, using another Qur'anic verse for support (Q 2:193),[931] states that:

> The purpose of war in Islam is to suppress tyranny, ensure the right of man to his home and freedom within his nation, prevent persecution in religion and guarantee freedom of belief to all people.[932]

Interestingly both Haleem et al. and Abd es-Salam confound the two justifications – self-defence and the elimination of oppression – and treat these two ideas as if they were one. Perhaps this is indicative of a preferential concern for oppressed Muslims rather than for oppressed people in general.[933] Another important contemporary voice who takes the line that *jihad* is primarily to rescue the weak from persecution is Ali Asghar Engineer.[934]

Qur'anic commands to make war were applicable only in their specific contexts.

Classical doctrine taught that Jews and Christians should be fought until they submitted and paid the *jizya* tax (Q 9:29, quoted in chapter 3) but Shaltut asserts that this referred to a particular group of treacherous, oath-breaking non-Muslims described in Q 9:7-13 and was not a general command.[935] Haleem et al. use the same Qur'anic passage and the same argument to deny the classical teaching that Muslims should fight pagans (i.e. polytheists) until the pagans are either killed or have converted to Islam.[936]

A different kind of contextual argument is used by Shaltut with reference to the Qur'anic command "Fight the unbelievers who gird you about, and let them find firmness in you" (Q 9:123). This Shaltut interprets as a tactical directive for application once legitimate fighting has broken out; it is a war plan which tells the Muslims that "when enemies are manifold, it is imperative to fight the nearest first of all, then the nearest but one and so on, in order to clear the road from enemies and to facilitate the victory."[937]

The same reasoning is applied by some scholars to sections of other Islamic teaching on war, not found in the Qur'an. In the words of Dr Bayoumi such legislation is "situation-related" or "time-related"[938] and therefore not universally applicable.

Some of the early Muslim scholars were misguided in the deductions they made from the Qur'an and the *hadith*.

Examples of this include the suggestion that the normal concept of *Dar al-Harb* is erroneous,[939] and that Shaybani's pivotal work on *siyar* is mostly his personal opinion based on expediency rather than the *hadith*.[940] A particularly important aspect of this argument concerns the traditional method of weighting the relative importance of individual Qur'anic verses. This is what produced the aggressive stance of classical Islamic doctrine, but some modern scholars have rejected the method, including the eminent Mahmud Shaltut.[941]

Fresh interpretation of Arabic terminology.

Some arguments under this heading include the following. (i) The Arabic word "*jihad*" should not be taken to include "fighting" for which there is another term, *qital,* in the Qur'an. It should only mean the striving for personal improvement.[942] (ii) The Qur'anic command "Fighting *[qital]* is prescribed for you" (Q 2:216) comes soon after a verse about enduring trials and adversity (Q 2:214). It is argued that the Arabic could just as well mean "Being fought against is prescribed for you" i.e. a statement that the Muslims would have to endure the affliction of being attacked.[943] (iii) Although *jihad* is an obligation (*fard*), an obligation is not the same as a compulsion.[944]

Scholars who argue as above are also usually at pains to emphasise that when war becomes necessary it should be fought justly and without recourse to excessive violence. For example, non-combatants should not be harmed, neither should crops, animals or the environment.[945] There is also an emphasis on the fact that those who go to war should have the right motives – not for personal glory or for personal gain but what the Qur'an calls *fi sabil Allah* (in the way of God).[946]

Other Contemporary Debate

Much of the contemporary debate centres on the justification for war, in contrast to the pre-modern debate in which jurists focused mainly on devising rules for the conduct of war, the treatment of prisoners etc. Some argue for a stricter interpretation than classical Islam, others for a more lenient interpretation. A few examples will give a sample of the debate.

Is *jihad* defensive only?

Some Al-Azhar scholars have tried to reinterpret *jihad* as purely defensive, including not only war but all areas of human endeavour, trying to adapt it to international realities and treaties without altering the classical categories. This effort has failed as in recent years. Following the Afghanistan *jihad* and Western penetration into Musim states such as Afghanistan and Iraq, al-Azhar scholars have called for active *jihad* against the "occupation forces" and justified the use of terrorism and suicide bombings.

Dr Muhammad Ma'ruf al-Dawalibi, a counsellor to the King of Saudi Arabia and formerly a professor in the Faculty of Law at Damascus University, wrote an article in the Arab press[947] outlining (amongst other things) many of the usual arguments of modern liberal Muslims against a militaristic and aggressive interpretation of *jihad* which we have just considered. Four weeks later the same daily newspaper printed an article by Ahmad Naser al-Rajihi containing a point-by-point rebuttal of each of al-Dawalibi's arguments, and asserting that *jihad* does indeed mean literal fighting of non-Muslims and that this is by no means limited to self-defence.[948]

Must Muslims engage in warfare?

Another area of discussion centres on whether Muslims must engage in *jihad* (the classical Islamic understanding) or whether they can refrain on the basis that God has already promised to annihilate the infidels so that Muslims themselves need not take responsibility for ensuring this annihilation. The Qur'anic verse which presents this possible get-out clause runs:

> ... we can expect for you either that God will send His punishment from Himself, or by our hands. Q 9:52

Seif al-Din al-Ansari[949] argues strongly for the classical position i.e. that Muslims must engage in warfare. He agrees that "the elements of the collapse of Western civilisation are proliferating" anyway, but disagrees that this absolves Muslims from working for the annihilation of the infidels. He argues that unless Muslims get involved in the annihilation of an "infidel country", it might simply be replaced by another infidel regime, rather than by the Islamic state.

Does the end justify the means?

The respected Saudi Salafi Sheikh Ibn 'Uthaymeen has condemned the activities of Palestinian suicide bombers, declaring that they "have wrongfully committed suicide", they are not martyrs and they will go to hell. Unusually, his reasoning is wholly pragmatic: such suicide killings do not benefit Islam because (1) they do not result in conversions to Islam but tend rather to make the enemy more strongly anti-Muslim (2) the Israeli response to a suicide bombing usually kills more Muslims than the number of Jews killed by the bomber.[950] Presumably he would feel suicide bombers were justified if the results were more positive.

Jihad is to preserve pluralism and variety?

Sheikh 'Abd al-Hamid al-Ansari, dean of the faculty of *shari'a* at Qatar University, is renowned for his liberal views. Writing in the London-based Arabic daily, *Al-Hayat*,[951] he puts forward a very unusual understanding of *jihad*.

> *Jihad*, in its real meaning, is a means of preserving the right of pluralism and variety and guaranteeing freedom of choice for all, because diversity is considered a natural and universal truth...

This is of course the exact opposite of the classical Islamic doctrine of *jihad* which is intended to spread Islamic power, not to preserve pluralism and diversity.

Sheikh al-Ansari is also unusual in that he calls for dialogue with non-Muslims, urging Muslims to forget past wrongs done to them by the West, to put aside conspiracy theories, and to engage in some self-criticism. The opposite position was taken by a prestigious group of Islamic scholars in Saudi Arabia, headed by the Grand Mufti, Sheikh Ibn Baz, who issued a *fatwa* condemning "debates, meetings and dialogue" with non-Muslims as "invalid" and "rejected by Allah". Their reasoning was apparently that such dialogue might enable the non-Muslims "in achieving their desires, fulfilling their aims, breaking the bonds of Islam, and bending the fundamentals of Islamic faith".[952]

Suicide or martyrdom?

The London-based Saudi daily *Al-Sharq Al-Awsat* abandons normal Islamic vocabulary and refers in its news reporting to "suicide attackers" instead of "martyrs". The paper defends its action on the basis of journalistic professionalism and neutrality, and points out that its editorials (as opposed to news reports) do use the term "martyrdom".[953]

Are Jews and Christians allowed to live?

The London daily newspaper *Al-Hayat* published an article on October 21st 2001 by Khaled Muhammad Batrafi, a regular columnist on the paper.[954] Batrafi, a Saudi, was reporting an argument he had had with a friend, following a sermon he had heard at the mosque which called for the annihilation of Christians and Jews. As we have seen, classical Islam teaches that Christians and Jews, as "People of the Book", are not to be killed or forced to become Muslims, but may live in an Islamic state albeit with an inferior status to the Muslim citizens. Batrafi therefore said the preacher's words were heresy and quoted to his friend some Qur'anic verses in support of humane treatment of Christians and Jews (Q 3:64; Q 60:8). His friend however, quoted other texts in support of the preacher's stance, and the two of them discussed the various possible interpretations, their historical contexts and how to apply them to Christians and Jews today.

Discerning Trends

Amidst the diversity of opinion about war amongst contemporary Muslims, Ann Elizabeth Mayer detects the emergence of certain trends. One trend seeks to prove the essential compatibility of *shari'a* with international law in order to justify Muslims adhering to public international law. The most common way of approaching this is to argue that international law is actually derived from Islamic law. This is completely contrary to the findings of scholarly research, where the prevailing opinion at present is that international law derives primarily from European thought.[955] Muslim scholars argue that European thought came under the influence of Islam during the Crusades and in Islamic Spain.[956]

However, as Mayer points out, "Regardless of the strength of its scholarly underpinnings, the theory that international law derives from Islam can function like a benign fiction that facilitates the reception of international law in the Muslim world."[957]

Another trend is to abandon the traditional division of the world into *Dar al-Harb* and *Dar al-Islam*;[958] some do this by replacing *Dar al-Harb* with various alternative categories of territory e.g. *Dar al-Sulh* (House of Truce)[959] and *Dar al-'Ahd* (House of Treaty)[960] indicating peaceful co-operation with the non-Muslim world, or *Dar al-Shahada* (House of Testimony) meaning that Muslims can freely practise their faith there. The validity of these alternatives has always been a subject of debate amongst Muslim jurists, and the distinctions between them are difficult to define.[961] A further position is that a country which was once *Dar al-Islam* and is now ruled by non-Muslims remains *Dar al-Islam* and only lapses into *Dar al-Harb* when most or all of the requirements of Islam are no longer possible.[962] Sir Sayyid Ahmad Khan believed that India under the British Raj could be considered *Dar al-Islam* because the Muslims were free to pursue their religious and social duties.[963] Moulvi Abu Said Mohammed Husain likewise held that

> The city or country wherein Mohammedans are freely allowed to perform their religious duties is not called *Dar-ul-Harab*. If that place be actually the kingdom of Mohammedans, and other nations have conquered it (as India), then as long as these enjoy liberty to perform their religious duties therein, it is called the *Dar-ul-Islam* in virtue of its being originally a *Dar-ul-Islam*; and if it has ever been in the possession and under the government of any other nation, and Mohammedans are allowed by them to perform their religious duties, then also it is *Dar-ul-Islam* : or at least it may be called *Darus-Salam-wal-Aman* (place of safety). In both these cases Mohammedans are not allowed to wage war against them, or to regard any war as a religious war...[964]

The issue of whether or not a truce or treaty is believed to be in place is of great practical significance. Anjem Choudhary, the head of the British Islamist organisation Al-Muhajiroun, has said that his organisation does not encourage its followers in Britain to carry out attacks in Britain because they were living under a "covenant of security" that required them not to strike at the host country where they lived. Yet his organisation heaped praise on the suicide attackers who killed over 3,000 people on September 11th 2001 and said that any Muslims who condemned the attack were apostates whose opinion should carry no weight.[965]

A further trend is to consider certain features of traditional teaching on *jihad* in the light of international law and concepts of a just war. Since armed aggression (as in classical Islamic law) is forbidden in Article 2(4) of the UN Charter, *jihad* must therefore be re-defined as for defence only. For example, Hasan Moinuddin argues that Muslims must not begin hostilities.[966] Others however may have definitions of "self-defence" which are not quite the same as those of international law. Sobhi Mahmassani's definition includes "to protect freedom of religion, to repel aggression, to prevent injustice and to protect social order"[967]– a much broader definition than in international law, which permits anticipatory self-defence only when the need to attack is immediate, overwhelming and leaves no other option.[968] To some Muslims, "self-defence" can even include ridding a society of polytheism and destroying anything that obstructs the propagation of Islam.[969]

Similarly, Ala' Eddin Kharofa, an Iraqi professor of Islamic law, seems to extend the definition of "self-defence" to include fighting all non-Muslims so that they cannot plot against Muslims:

> The Qur'an also carries the command to the Muslims to fight all disbelievers so as they would not be able to plot against them. See al-Baqara [i.e. Surah 2 of the Qur'an]: 190-193 and al-Tauba [i.e. Surah 9 of the Qur'an]:36).[970]

A similar position is taken by Mohammed al-Asi, the elected Imam of the Islamic Centre in Washington DC, a senior member of the UK-based Institute of Contemporary Islamic Thought, and advisor to another UK-based organisation, the Islamic Human Rights Commission. Writing in the British periodical *Crescent International,* he looks at Q 2:193, and argues that Muslims cannot at present "enjoy freedom of conscience and will, and a truly independent state" so therefore our understanding of the Qur'an and Sunnah obliges us to carry the burden of *jihad* to deter all forms of persecution, discrimination, and hurt and injury premeditated by inimical forces. Muslims, like all other people, are entitled to security: security for their lives, their possessions and their faith.[971]

He condemns all, whether Muslims or non-Muslims, who try to argue that *jihad* is no longer an obligation for Muslims. He also condemns

those who try to deceive the Muslim public into believing that self-determination (Islamic self-determination) is obtainable through international forums, American patronage or Zionist channels. [i.e. those who say] Anything will do provided that it is not *jihad* and *qital* for the cause of Allah.

Al-Asi appears to consider that anything less than Islamic self-determination amounts to persecution of Muslims, and thus *jihad* is necessary. His inclusion of the word *qital* emphasises his belief in the need for physical warfare. (He does not, however, permit the forcible conversion of non-Muslims to Islam.)

Another modern variation on traditional Islamic teaching on *jihad* is to redefine it so as to legitimise the use of force on behalf of liberation struggles against oppressors in the developing world. One of these struggles is the Palestinian cause. Numerous calls have been made for a *jihad* to liberate Palestine and Jerusalem from Israeli control, and even before Israel existed there were calls for *jihad* against the Jewish settlers in Palestine. In the case of Palestine *jihad* has been so re-defined by some Muslims as to make it an obligation even on non-Muslims![972] Mayer believes that the existence of the Palestinian issue, which is so prominent in Muslim consciousness around the globe, may have hampered progress towards bringing Islamic law on war in line with public international law.[973]

In a similar vein, Mawdudi pictured true Islam and its past and present leaders as a modern-style revolutionary party engaged in a revolutionary struggle (*jihad*) to reshape the world:

Islam is a revolutionary ideology which seeks to alter the social order of the entire world and rebuild it in conformity with its own tenets and ideals. 'Muslims' is the title of that 'International Revolutionary Party' organized by Islam to carry out its revolutionary program. *'jihad'* refers to that revolutionary struggle and utmost exertion which the Islamic Nation/Party brings into play in order to achieve this objective....There is no doubt that all the Prophets of Allah, without exception, were Revolutionary Leaders, and the illustrious Prophet Muhammad was the greatest Revolutionary Leader of all.[974]

Likewise Azzam Tamimi has described *jihad* in terms of a struggle against all political or economic oppression or tyranny, a sort of permanent revolution against any and all evil. Interestingly Tamimi repeats the traditional teaching on martyrdom in *jihad* carrying the promise of great reward in the hereafter.

One of the basic features of the Islamic faith is that it generates within the believer a passion for freedom... it liberates man from servitude and renders him un-slaveable... This is where the concept of *jihad* lies. *Jihad* is the constant endeavour to struggle against all forms of political or economic tyranny; for life has no value in the shade of despotism. Islam wages war against despotism using the weapon of al-amr bilma'ruf wan-nahyu 'anil-munkar (enjoining good and forbidding evil) through a series of actions the minimum of which is by the heart, that is by boycotting evil and disliking it. This may then progress, depending on ability and resources, to condemning evil through the use of various means of non-violent expression, such as speaking up, writing or demonstrating, or eventually to the use of force. What matters here is that oppression should never be given a chance to establish itself in society... Not only does the Islamic faith permit a Muslim to resist despotism and rebel against it, but it makes it incumbent upon him to do so with whatever means available to him. It is understandable that a Muslim may lose his life struggling against oppression, and for this he or she is promised a great reward in the life after death. In other words the effort made is not wasted and the sacrifice is not in vain.[975]

A rather complex issue which some Muslim thinkers are tackling is the question of what entity can conduct a *jihad*. In classical Islam it was the *umma,* the entire Muslim community, but in today's world of nation-states that is impractical. Yet the goal of every liberation struggle is a nation-state. According to Hassan Hanafi, an Egyptian intellectual, Islam supports the idea that every people deserves its own nation-state,[976] a position that seems to be gaining adherents. Further support comes from the Organisation of the Islamic Conference, implicitly by its very structure and explicitly in its 1972 Charter, which recognises the right of "all peoples" to self-determination (especially Muslims and most particularly the people of Palestine).[977]

Any attempt to determine trends in current Muslim thinking on *jihad* may be complicated by political rhetoric. For example in the Iran-Iraq war of the 1980s, each side justified the war as a *jihad* against the other, surely an impossibility under any definition of *jihad*.[978]

Furthermore, the doctrine of *taqiyya* (see chapter 9) must not be forgotten. *Taqiyya* adds to the complications of the debate on *jihad* since there is often a difference between statements addressed to the West and statements intended for a Muslim audience as illustrated by the survey of statements by Tantawi in chapter 9. Another prominent figure, Ayatollah Khomeini, provides a further illustration. On one occasion Khomeini stated that *jihad* was nothing to do with defence but meant "expansion and the taking over of other countries" and that Muslims are obliged "to fight and to spread Islamic laws throughout the world", whereas another time he denied any intent to use armed force or wars of aggression to achieve his objectives which were to be accomplished by spiritual means.[979] It should not be forgotten that the doctrine of *taqiyya* is particularly strong amongst Shi'as like Khomeini.

Westerners and other non-Muslims should always bear in mind that some comments they hear or read on *jihad* may well be a case of being "given what they want to hear" rather than the true opinion of the speaker or writer. A phrase used by Professor Kharofa concerning a fellow-Muslim is revealing. Kharofa writes that he finds himself "having to remind him of the linguistic and Islamic idiomatic meanings of the word [*jihad*], and how Muslims understand it *without any misrepresentation to gain the pleasure of Westerners.*"[980]

Many Muslims assert that Islamic international law is superior to modern international law. Their argument is based on the fact that Islamic international law was formulated thirteen centuries ago, whereas the present system of international law came into being only about four centuries ago. For example, they say that the Islamic requirement to warn the enemy of an impending attack pre-dates by many centuries the 1907 Hague Convention's ruling on the opening of hostilities. They also argue that Islamic international law was more humane than other systems at the time it was created.[981] They claim that it enshrined the principles of equality, reciprocity and peace long before these were recognised internationally,[982] (a claim that seems impossible to justify if these terms are understood in their normal Western sense). Another reason given for the superiority of Islamic law is that it is based on religion and therefore has a moral sanction.[983]

Contemporary Methods of *Jihad*

Classical *jihad* methodologies are now being supplemented by a range of other strategies and tactics, seen as part of a broad *jihad* complex with the ultimate aim of making Islam dominant worldwide. These additional modern methods include the following:

Weakening of the West in image and in fact

A main goal of Islamist groups is to attack Western (especially American) interests and symbols of power. They seek to weaken Western economies and those of Muslim states friendly to the West by targeting airports and planes, oil installations and tankers, Western tourists, etc. Some groups have investigated the use of poison gas in imitation of the Japanese sect that used it in the Tokyo underground, and of poisoning water supplies in Western cities. They have also attacked Western military installations and military personnel and their families (as in Saudi Arabia). As security services tighten their protection on one set of targets, terrorists look for softer types of targets of unexpected type and in unexpected places.

Infiltration of Western systems

This effort is subsidised by vast amounts of money from oil-rich Muslim states, Muslim businessmen and Muslim charities. Islamic lobbying groups are founded to put pressure on state ministries and bureaucracies, the media and political parties. Huge investments in the West underpin demands for the introduction of Islamic financial tools. Governments are put under pressure to follow Muslim-friendly internal and external policies or forego economic benefits. In education school textbooks, especially those teaching history and Islam, are being rewritten so as to depict Islamic history and doctrine as non-violent and tolerant. "Politically correct" views on Islam are fostered and any critique of Islam is attacked as Islamophobic. In some countries legal action is taken against those criticising aspects of Islam, alleging they are inciting religious hatred.

The Islamisation of knowledge

By funding academic chairs and encouraging and funding Muslim academics to take up lecturing posts in Western universities it is hoped to influence students and the teaching of academic subjects by Islamist concepts of science, knowledge and religion. Another method is the founding of Islamic think tanks, research and academic institutions particularly in the West, using them to disseminate Islamic views. Some of these institutions are linked to Islamist movements while presenting a moderate face to their Western audiences. The Virginia-based International Institute of Islamic Thought is very active in this field.[984]

Active *da'wa*

Missionary outreach using print, audio-visual, internet and other materials is resulting in the conversion of Westerners to Islam. The conversion of celebrities is especially effective in making Islam acceptable to general public opinion. However, the ultimate goal of Islamist *da'wa* is the establishment of Muslim dominion – Islamic states – in every country of the world.

Demographic changes

The rapid population growth in Muslim countries and in Muslim minorities in the West, coupled to the growth in the number of Muslims immigrating into Western states, is seen as being in God's providence, tilting the balance decisively in favour of Islam, and giving Muslims a more effective political lobby worldwide and within the Western democracies. The hope is that this will effect legal changes in favour of Muslims.

Destabilisation of states with large Muslim minorities

This is practised particularly in states on the fringes of Islam e.g. Nigeria, Ivory Coast, Kenya, the Philippines and India. One method is by demanding the implementation of *shari'a* in Muslim-majority regions even when Muslims are a minority in the country as a whole. This is seen as a prelude to imposing *shari'a* on all the population. The northern and central federal states of Nigeria offer a good example of this trend. Another method is to support Muslim demands for independence or autonomy as well as for outright rebellions against central governments. This is practised in Kashmir and the Philippines. As Yusuf al-Qaradhawi has stated:

> The Islamic Movement should consider itself at the 'beck and call' of every Islamic Cause and respond to every cry for help wherever that cry may come from. It should stand with Eritrea in its *jihad* against the unjust Marxist Christian regime...by Sudan against the treacherous Christian racist rebellion... It should support the Muslims of the Philippines against the biased Christian regime... it should also help the Muslims of Kashmir... support the Muslims of Somalia... mobilise the Muslims of the world for the Palestine Cause...[985]

A growing persecution of non-Muslim minorities in Muslim states

The methods used include discrimination, violence against individuals and whole communities, forced conversions, ethnic cleansing and in some places enslavement. Violence has been especially marked in recent years in Sudan, Indonesia, Nigeria, Egypt and Pakistan to name but a few. Indigenous non-Muslim (especially Christian) minorities in Muslim states are increasingly viewed as having repudiated their God-ordained subordinate *dhimma* status as set out in *shari'a* by their demands for equality before the law and their support of secular governments. They are also assumed to be allies of the Western "Christian" enemy. They thus become legitimate targets of *jihad* and increasingly suffer violent attacks. Whenever tensions increase between the West and Islam there is a backlash against Christians in Muslim states. Apart from violence, there are many other human rights abuses against non-Muslims in Muslim states, particuarly those where *shari'a* has an important role in the constitution and/or legislation, such as Saudi Arabia, Sudan, Pakistan and Iran. (This continues to happen despite Muslim minorities in the West making good use of the Western concept of human rights and equality on their own behalf.)

A Contemporary Example of Radicalism within Mainstream Islam

A good example is the official English translation of the Qur'an, financed and supported by the Saudi establishment: *Interpretation of the Meanings of the Noble Qur'an* by Muhammad Taqi-ud-Din Hilali and Muhammad Muhsin Khan (Riyadh: Maktaba Darussalam, 1996). The translators are both on the staff of the Islamic University in Medina. This version was certified by the late Sheikh 'Abdul 'Aziz bin 'Abdullah Ibn Baz of the Presidency of Islamic Research, Ifta, Call and propagation in Riyadh, which is part of the Saudi Ministry of Islamic Affairs, Endowments, Propagation and Guidance. It includes interpretations from classical Islamic sources, especially al-Tabari, al-Qurtubi, Ibn Kathir and al-Bukhari. In the eyes of most Muslims it would therefore represent a mainstream orthodox version. It has allegedly become the most widely disseminated Qur'an in Islamic bookstores and Sunni mosques throughout the English-speaking world.

This version, in its interpolations, footnotes and appendices carries a clear anti-Jewish and anti-Christian bias. Right in the first sura, the *fatiha* it has interpolated the words "(such as the Jews)" and "(such as the Christians)" in verse 7 thus implying this is part of the text itself concerning those who are under God's wrath and those who went astray.

As we have already seen (chapter 5), this translation promotes the view that *jihad* is one of the "pillars" of Islam, like the obligatory duties of prayer, fasting, alms-giving etc. The footnote to Q 2:190, "And fight in the way of Allah those who fight against you, but transgress not the limits…" explains that *jihad* is one of the pillars of Islam given to propagate Islam:[986]

> Al-Jihad (holy fighting) in Allah's Cause (with full force of numbers and weaponry) is given the utmost importance in Islam and is one of its pillars (on which it stands). By Jihad Islam is established, Allah's Word is made superior… And His religion (Islam) is propagated. By abandoning Jihad (may Allah protect from that) Islam is destroyed and the Muslims fall into an inferior position; their honour is lost, their lands are stolen, their rule and authority vanish. Jihad is an obligatory duty in Islam on every Muslim, and he who tries to escape from this duty, or does not in his innermost heart wish to fulfil this duty, dies with one of the qualities of the hypocrite.

The footnote to Q 2:193 "Fight them until there is no more Fitnah…", presents a *hadith* from Bukhari (Vol. 1, No. 24) narrated by Ibn 'Umar,

> "I have been ordered (by Allah) to fight against all the people till they testify that *La ilaha illallah wa Anna Muhammada-ur-Rasul Allah* (none has the right to be worshiped but Allah and that Muhammad is the Messenger of Allah), and perform *As-Salat (Iqamat-as-Salat)* and give *Zakat*, so if they perform all that, then they save their lives, and properties from me except for Islamic laws, and their reckoning (accounts) will be done by Allah.[987]

This clearly implies a *jihad* against all non-Muslims until they accept Islam.

In Q 47:4 this version interpolates in brackets: "Thus [you are ordered by Allah to continue in carrying on Jihad against disbelievers till they embrace Islam and are saved from the punishment in the Hell-fire or at least come under your protection]"…[988]

In Appendix III, "The Call to Jihad" (pp.845-864), it presents the traditional view of the development of *jihad* by Muhammad:

As it is now obvious, at first "the fighting" was forbidden, then it was permitted and after that it was made obligatory – (1) against them who start "the fighting" against you (Muslims)... (2) and against all those who worship other along with Allah... as mentioned in *Surat Al-Baqarah (II), Al-Imran (III)* and *Taubah (IX)...* and other *Surah* (Chapters of the Qur'an). Allah made the fighting (Jihad) obligatory for the Muslims and gave importance to the subject matter of *Jihad* in all the *Surah* (Chapters of the Qur'an) which were revealed at Al-Medina) as in Allah's Statement:..."[989]

The whole appendix glorifies violent *jihad* against non-Muslims and could read as a manifesto of the most radical Islamist groups such as al-Qa'eda. According to this appendix, the main reason for present Muslim weakness is that they have neglected *jihad* and befriended disbelievers. The remedy is to return to the original practice of *da'wa* and *jihad* which included "... and they subjected others to its (Islam's) teachings".[990] These examples - and there are many more - reveal the aggressive tenor of this version of the Qur'an. Trying to differentiate between radical Islamist rhetoric and such mainstream versions of Islam is thus obviously a very difficult, if not impossible task.

16
Muslims Against Violence: Progressive Reformers

The word "reform" carries two distinct meanings in the context of Islam, meanings which are diametrically opposed to each other, linked only by the fact that each has been derived from returning to the sources of Islam. Most often "reform" refers to a puritanical and usually violent interpretation of Islam, such as is followed by Islamists and Islamic militants of today. Less often it means a progressive, liberal and modernist interpretation of Islam. It is the latter meaning which is the subject of this chapter.

Progressive reformers of orthodox Islam are offering some really new interpretations of their faith, but in most Muslim societies they are a small minority and face determined and often violent opposition by the dominant traditionalist and Islamist forces.[991] Progressive reformers represent a wide variety of approaches to the challenges of modernity, and are characterised by a peaceful approach to Western and other non-Muslim cultures. Most see themselves as good Muslims who oppose secularism as an atheistic ideology but embrace the separation of religion from state and politics. They accept what they consider to be a core of basic Islamic values, distilled from the Islamic source texts, as spiritual and moral norms that override coercive political and social interpretations. However, they are willing to ignore traditional Islamic concepts and interpretations which contradict modern values of freedom and equality. They see a need to radically change traditional orthodox Islam in such a way as to integrate liberal humanistic values at its very core.[992]

Progressive reformers are so few in number and their ideas are so opposed to the mainstream of traditional Islam, let alone to

Islamism, that they put themselves at considerable risk when they publish. They are often accused by Islamists of the serious crimes of apostasy (*irtidad*), blasphemy and unbelief (*kufr*), and heresy (*ilhad*) – all of which are crimes under *shari'a* that incur the death penalty. Radicals also issue death threats against progressives and attack them physically.

For example, Yusuf al-Qaradhawi rejects the call for separation of state and religion as apostasy from Islam:

> Since Islam is a comprehensive system of 'Ibadah (worship) and Shari'ah (legislation), the acceptance of secularism means abandonment of Shari'ah, a denial of the Divine guidance and a rejection of Allah's injunctions. (...) the call for secularism among Muslims is atheism and a rejection of Islam. Its acceptance as a basis for rule in place of Shari'ah is a downright apostasy.[993]

One UK-based reformer Ehsan Masood admits that Muslims advocating such reform are at present mainly living in the West – they could not articulate such ideas in Muslim states. He recognises that reformers will face fierce opposition from both traditionalists and Islamists who will accuse the reformers of trying to modify Islam to please the West.

> History is on the side of the opponents of reform. Reformers have hitherto failed to reach Islam's masses, whether in the 2nd century of Islam or in the 19th and early 20th centuries. They have, at best, remained a minority, elite voice.[994]

However, there are reformers living in the Muslim world as well, but they do indeed put their lives at risk by articulating their ideas. Ulil Abshar-Abdalla of the Liberal Islam Network, based in Jakarta, Indonesia, argues for a contextualised interpretation of Islam for the modern day by means of *ijtihad* to "seek a new formula" to translate the universal values of Islam into the context of contemporary life. He considers that the type of Islam established by Muhammad at Medina "was one possible translation of the universal Islam... But there are possibilities of translating Islam in other ways, in different contexts." Amongst other recommendations, he urges that "all those legal products of classical Islam which discriminate between Muslims and non-Muslims should be amended on the basis of the universal principle of human equality" and that religion should be separated from public life and political power. When his article on this subject was published in *Kompas,* an Indonesian daily newspaper, it resulted in a death sentence being passed on him by certain Islamic groups in Indonesia.[995]

Sir Sayyid Ahmad Khan (1817-1898), India[996]

Sir Sayyid Ahmad Khan was an Indian Muslim reformer who, following the failure of the Indian Mutiny against British rule in India, sought to reform Islam in the light of Western scientific ideals and education so as to ensure its survival against Hindu competition. Muslims, he believed, must assimilate all that is best in Western civilisation and discard their own "backward" and "superstitious" traditions. They must reject the blind following of religious tradition (*taqlid*), re-open the gates of *ijtihad* and return to the Qur'an itself. He encouraged Muslims to learn English, enter the British bureaucracy and became junior partners of the British in the exercise of power. He founded the Muslim College in Aligarh in 1875 which offered a modernist curriculum with the aim of producing an educated elite of Muslims able to compete successfully with Hindus for jobs in the Indian administration.

Khan founded his thinking on scientific rationalism, asserting that Islam conforms to reason and to nature. Only the Qur'an was the revealed legitimate source of doctrine, many *hadith* being fabricated and not authentic. *Shari'a* was partly corrupted over the centuries by foreign influences and Islamic institutions. Everything that came after the Qur'an was subsidiary and of secondary importance. Khan differentiated between essential basic principles in the Qur'an (*usul*) and secondary details *(furu')*. He also dismissed the miraculous elements in the Qur'an. Khan argued that Muslims are obliged to follow Muhammad only in strictly religious matters, but not necessarily in worldly issues.

Khan was thus able to reduce the authority of the *sunna*, *shari'a* and *madhabs*, and reinterpret *jihad* in purely defensive terms, to be implemented only in the most dire necessity. He also condemned the concepts of *dhimma*, slavery and concubinage.

Muhammad 'Abduh (1849-1905), Egypt[997]

'Abduh is regarded as the architect of Islamic modernism and most prominent reformer of the nineteenth century. Following a period as an anti-imperialist activist alongside Jamal al-Din al-Afghani (1838-1897), 'Abduh made his peace with the British in Egypt and was appointed rector of al-Azhar and Mufti (chief *shari'a* judge) of Egypt.

He tried to make Islam compatible with the modern age by reinterpreting traditional Islamic concepts in modern terms. He developed criteria for selectively borrowing from the West and creating a synthesis of Islam and modernity. 'Abduh claimed that through *ijtihad* a Muslim is able to apply Qur'an and *sunna* to modern conditions. *Shura, ijma'* and *maslaha* were constituted to limit the caliph's powers and can thus be seen as democratic principles: *shura* is equivalent to the legislative assembly, *ijma'* is equivalent to public opinion, and *maslaha* is the common good, which all in positions of power are bound to serve.

'Abduh, however, advocated a return to Qur'an and *sunna* as the true sources of Islam, in order to escape from the stultifying effects of traditional *taqlid,* the principle of following the chain of great Islamic scholars through the ages and the claim that anything not covered by them is a heretical innovation (*bid'a*) that must be opposed.

'Abduh wanted to reform Islam by selectively adapting the best of Western scientific, political, philosophical and cultural thought. He saw no contradiction between revelation and reason and used *mu'tazili* thought to emphasise the role of reason in Islam. He saw Islam as the pre-eminent religion of reason, totally in harmony with science, but weakened by centuries of blind imitation and superstitions. In order to revive Islam, it was necessary to use *ijtihad*, and distinguish between the immutable core of Islam (*'ibadat*) and the flexible and changeable social rules (*mu'amalat*).

'Abduh rejected the notion that Islam is a religion of violence and war. He argued that *jihad* in the sense of military combat was required by God only to defend the truth and its adherents and to keep intact the message of Islam. It is thus purely defensive. Acts of aggression are illegitimate and detested by God.

'Abduh's critique of traditional Islam and acceptance of Western thought opened the doors to secularism. Ironically, however, his call to a return to the pure Muslim source texts as the only legitimate source caused some of his disciples to follow the path to Salafi literalistic fundamentalism.

'Abduh argued that the intent of the Islamic fundamental principles should guide interpretation and legislation and the process of necessary change in Muslim societies. Using the principle of public welfare he issued legal decrees reforming polygamy and the status of women and legitimating bank interest.

Mahmud Muhammad Taha (1910-1985), Sudan[998]

The Sudanese scholar and religious leader Mahmud Muhammad Taha saw two different messages in the Qur'an: (1) the Meccan revelation which he defined as the essential, eternal and unchangeable principles of Islam, valid for all times, and (2) the Medinan revelation which consisted of temporal rules suitable for the context of tribal Arabia in the seventh century. He held that the Medinan passages were simply concessions to the primitive society of the time and therefore irrelevant for the modern age. This included the Medinan teaching on *jihad* which was only given because the Arabs at the time were not mature enough to live according to the superior Meccan principles of freedom and peace. The Meccan verses of peaceful persuasion were temporarily abrogated by the Medinan verses on *jihad*. The sword was given for a time to curb the abuses of freedom and help spread Islam. The sword was however suspended once the new community matured and was stabilised and brought under the rule of law (*shari'a*). However, many aspects of contemporary *shari'a* are not the original principles of Meccan Islam, but a descent from their moral height as a temporary adaptation to specific contexts. *Shari'a* ought to develop from its contextualised more primitive level towards the original universal peak of the Meccan revelation in which *jihad* did not exist.[999]

Taha emphasised that the Meccan message taught the inherent dignity of all humans regardless of gender, religion, or race. It demanded equality between men and women, and freedom of choice in matters of religion. He saw the *shari'a* as able to evolve endlessly. In contrast to reformers like 'Abduh, Taha rejected both the *sunna* and the Medinan passages of the Qur'an, advocating the development of *shari'a* based solely on the universal principles of the Meccan passages of the Qur'an. He did not advocate a return to the model of the early Muslim community, but a forward move to a future community shaped by his message. His *ijtihad* relied both on rational thought and on mystical reflection aimed at understanding the metaphorical meanings of the Qur'an. He called for a total revision of *shari'a* and was executed as an apostate by the Nimeiri regime in 1985.

Fazlur Rahman (1919-1988), Pakistan[1000]

Rahman, a Pakistani scholar and long-time professor at the University of Chicago, was Director of the Islamic Research Institute in Pakistan until forced to leave by pressure from conservative elements. His book *Major Themes of the Qur'an* uses his method of interpreting the text not literally but by looking for the moral intention behind it. In order to interpret the Qur'an meaningfully for modern times, Rahman said that a double movement of thought is needed:

1 From the present situation to Qur'anic times – understanding the meaning of the Qur'an as a whole, as well as its specific tenets that were responses to specific contextual situation of its time.

2 From Qur'anic times to the present – generalise the specific answers as universal and apply them to present realities and contexts.

Rahman also differentiated between legal and moral regulations. He held that legal rulings are mostly binding in their moral sense, not in their literal wording.

He believed that much of classical Islamic commentary and law was wrong because the jurists had ignored the moral imperative behind the text, viewing the text as unchangeable literal legal enactments. He considered that Muslims have failed to understand the true meaning of the Qur'an because of the traditional methods applied to it, creating the traditional sciences of the Qur'an and the legal framework of *shari'a*, and rejecting Islamic philosophy. The Qur'an lost its vibrancy and revolutionary import as it was buried under the "debris of grammar and rhetoric" and the many commentaries on commentaries on Qur'an and *hadith* written by scholars of the past.

Rahman asserted that Muslims can free themselves from the burden of the past by studying history critically, understanding the historical processes by which Islam assumed the form it has today, and differentiating the essentials of the faith from all unnecessary or outmoded additions.[1001]

Fazlur Rahman argued that *jihad* exists so that Islam can accomplish its social and political goals of justice and equality:

> There is no doubt that the Qur'an wanted Muslims to establish a political order on earth for the sake of creating an egalitarian and just moral-social order. Jihad is the instrument for doing so.[1002]

Bassam Tibi (1944-), Germany

Bassam Tibi, Professor of International Relations at the University of Göttingen, Germany and formerly Bosch Fellow and Research Associate at Harvard University, appeals for Muslims to "revise their understanding of peace and tolerance by accepting pluralism". Furthermore, he said, Muslim leaders should give up the notion of *jihad* in the sense of conquest, as opposed to *jihad* as an internal struggle of the individual.[1003]

Tibi argues for a "cultural accommodation" of Islamic religious doctrine to the changed social and historical contexts of the modern world. This entails a reform of religious concepts and their cultural underpinnings allowing Muslims to accept equality and mutual respect between themselves and non-Muslims.[1004]

Tibi also argues for a separation between religion and politics. Religion should be restricted to belief and ethics. Islam should be reconciled with cultural modernity.[1005]

> What is needed in the world of Islam are religious reforms maintaining the spirit of religion as an ethics, but smoothing the way to its de-politicisation.[1006]

Tibi recommends that European Muslims give up *jihad* and *shari'a* since they are incompatible with Western concepts of human rights and with Western constitutions.

> Muslims have to give up three things if they want to become Europeans: They have to bid farewell to the idea of converting others, and renounce the Jihad. The Jihad is not just a way of testing yourself but also means using violence to spread Islam. The third thing they need to give up is the Shariah, which is the Islamic legal system. This is incompatible with the German constitution.[1007]

Ziauddin Sardar (1951-), UK[1008]

Ziauddin Sardar is a British Muslim scholar born in 1951 in Pakistan. He is a cultural critic, journalist and writer calling for a serious rethinking of Islam to make it compatible with modernity.

According to Sardar, Islam has acquired a "pathological strain" because of relying on old interpretations that do not fit contemporary contexts. Muslims tend to blame all their problems on outside forces rather than examining and reforming Islam. Islam's source texts have been frozen in past history, so they can have no meaning for today:

> Historic interpretations constantly drag us back to history, to frozen and ossified contexts of long ago; worse, to perceived and romanticized contexts that have not even existed in history.[1009]

Sardar argues that this freezing of Islam has had devastating effects, causing:

Three metaphysical catastrophes: the elevation of the Shariah to the level of the Divine, with the consequent removal of agency from the believers, and the equation of Islam with the state.[1010]

Sardar claims that only the Qur'an can be considered as divine in Islam. There is nothing divine about the *shari'a,* which is simply

a human construction, an attempt to understand the divine will in a particular context... wherever the Shariah is imposed... Muslim societies acquire a medieval feel.[1011]

Sardar argues that *shari'a* is a set of guiding principles for Muslim societies that should be constantly and dynamically changing to produce solutions to new problems Muslims face. The Qur'an itself has to be constantly reinterpreted in changing contexts – only its text remains constant.

Sardar accuses Islamism of reducing Islam to a "totalitarian" ideology that leads to a totalitarian state order as exemplified by the Taliban, Iran, Sudan, and Saudi Arabia:

The transformation of Islam into a state-based political ideology not only deprives it of all moral and ethical content, it also debunks most Muslim history as un-Islamic. Invariably when Islamists rediscover a 'golden past', they do so only in order to disdain the present and mock the future. All we are left with is messianic chaos, as we saw so vividly in the Taliban regime, where all politics as the domain of action is paralyzed and meaningless pieties become the foundational truth of the state.[1012]

In Islamic history, clerics and religious scholars gradually prevented the people from having any say, and authoritarianism, theocracy and despotism became supreme. Traditional Muslims and Islamists today dispense with moral reasoning and ethics as they defend despots like Saddam Hussein simply because they are Muslims and reduce *jihad* to a violent holy war against anyone identified as an enemy. For Sardar, *jihad* must be understood as a multifaceted spiritual, intellectual and social concept. It includes personal struggle, intellectual endeavour, and social construction as well as the non-violent struggle for peace and justice for all people everywhere.[1013]

Sardar acknowledges the difficulty in motivating Muslims to examine themselves and their religion.

> The most significant answers to the contemporary plight of the Muslim people are buried deep within the history, social practice and intellectual and political inertia of Muslims themselves. Muslims, on the whole, are very reluctant to look at themselves or to examine the process through which they have transformed Islam into a suffocating and oppressive ideology.[1014]

He also accepts that in recent decades the debates within Islam

> produced a narrow, intolerant, obscurantist, illiberal, brutal and confrontational interpretation of Islam.[1015]

He hopes that new trends within Islam will result in a reinterpretation of *shari'a,* which will be viewed not as divine and immutable but open to be modified or reformulated in its entirety. He also hopes to see the separation of religion from state to ensure an Islam that is authentic, moderate, liberal, tolerant, open and democratic.

Free Muslims Coalition (FMC), US[1016]

This is an American Muslim organisation that wants to reform Islam by promoting a modern interpretation compatible with other faiths and characterised by a commitment to democracy and peace. It believes the Qur'an provides basic principles which Muslims can flexibly interpret to adapt Islam to modernity. It accepts the secular separation of religion from the state as a positive factor that guarantees democracy. The organisation opposes Islamism and is worried by the broad support among the Muslim community for Islamist extremism and terrorism. It has called on Muslim leaders to fully reject and condemn religious violence and terrorism, and on Muslims to unreservedly apologise for the September 11th 2001 atrocities and other terrorist attacks implemented in the name of Islam.

Rather than viewing radical Islamism as a marginal movement, it accepts that it has deep roots within Muslim communities and states around the world. It calls for a critical examination of

Islam that will eliminate aspects such as its "victim culture";
the teachings of hatred, intolerance, and violent *jihad*; and the
conspiracy theories blaming Jews for all Muslim problems.

Finally it calls on "moderate" Muslims to break their silence
and passivity and unite to defeat the forces of extremist Islam.
It has published a statement of its beliefs:

> We believe in the re-interpretation of Islam for the 21st century
> where terrorism is not justified under any circumstances.
>
> We believe in the separation of religion and state.
>
> We believe that democracy is the best form of government.
>
> We believe in the promotion of secularism in all forms of
> political activity.
>
> We believe that equality for women is an inalienable right.
>
> We believe that religion is a personal relationship between
> the individual and his or her God and is not to be forced on
> anyone.[1017]

Ehsan Masood, UK

Ehsan Masood, Project Director for Gateway Trust in
Woking, argues for a revision and reinterpretation of Muslim
sources.[1018] He wants to see a revision of aspects of *shari'a* to
keep up with modern times, especially in the areas of human
rights and the rights of children and minorities. He also calls
for a reinterpretation of the meaning of Qur'an and *hadith*.
The Qur'an especially must be read in its historical context,
meaning that not all passages are relevant for contemporary
Muslims. Masood would also like to see a reform in the role of
authority in Islam.

As we have seen, Masood recognises the extreme opposition
which progressive reformers face, but he hopes that recent
atrocities by Muslim terrorists, the emergence of Islamic reformers
in the West and the availability of modern communications will

carry the message or progressive reform across the Muslim world and finally initiate the desired reform.

Soheib Bencheikh, France[1019]

Bencheikh, the Grand Mufti of Marseille, is a typical liberal Muslim intellectual, pious but not Islamist. He opposes the hegemonic tendencies of the Islamists. His message is that Islam in the West needs to develop a theology that accepts minority status:

> Islam has always developed the theology of a majority faith sovereign in its territory. In France, it is crucial to create a minority theology.

In doing so, he believes, Muslims will discover an Islam that does not impose itself by force.

Muslims must be prepared to make radical changes in order to live in the modern West:

> If I live in the West, I will interpret Islam in a way that does not marginalize me in the West.

Unlike Islamists who dream of establishing Islamic states in the West, Bencheikh accepts that secularism is a non-negotiable component of Western culture, a value that French Muslims must claim as their own.

Sisters in Islam (SIS), Malaysia[1020]

This is a group of Muslim professional women in Malaysia deeply concerned at the injustice women suffer in states where *shari‘a* has been implemented. They define themselves as believing Muslims with a right to participate in the contemporary processes of reinterpreting, redefining and implementing Islam. They believe that the Qur'an teaches a few universal and eternal principles that include equality, justice and freedom. These core values must override all lesser and seemingly contradictory rules and interpretations.

Sisters in Islam reject the doctrine of abrogation. In their view, verses such as "Let there be no compulsion in religion" (Q 2:256) are valid today and affirm freedom of religion - so the death penalty for apostasy is un-Islamic. They hold that the traditional allocation in *shari'a* of different rights to men and women, to Muslims and non-Muslims contradicts the core teachings of equality and justice.

Like other reformers, the Sisters in Islam call for the doors of *ijtihad* to be reopened. Interpretation of the source texts must not be left in the hands of an exclusive elite group (Islamic scholars, *ulama*) that isolates the text from its original historical as well as from contemporary contexts. While the Qur'an is a divine revelation, its interpretation is a human effort that inevitably leads to diverse opinions. Sisters in Islam believe that this diversity is a positive phenomenon that has enabled Islam to survive in a variety of cultures and societies while preserving its universalist message. Only such an enlightened interpretation of Qur'an and *hadith* can provide solutions to the real problems Muslim face today and make Islam truly relevant to their lives. The Islamist rejection of this diversity, expressed in the condemnation of differing views as apostasy, presents a real danger to the survival of Islam in the modern age.

Their approach to interpreting Muslim source texts (including their opposition to abrogation) opens the way for a peaceful interpretation of *jihad*, understood only in its spiritual and moral sense.

Sisters in Islam believe that the Islamist version of Islam goes against the fundamental principles of the Qur'an, promoting an intolerant vision of an Islamic state as a dictatorial, theocratic, and inherently unequal political system. This system condemns those who dare challenge its authority as apostates and then imposes the death sentence on them, thus silencing all opposition.[1021]

Islam Hadhari, Malaysia[1022]

This is a progressive type of Islam promoted by former Malaysian prime Minister Mahathir Mohammad and the present Prime Minister Abdullah Ahmad Badawi. It focuses not so much on *shari'a* as on Islam as a whole. Badawi argues that because contemporary Islam is associated with violence and extremism it needs to be formulated anew. He called his new concept "Islam Hadhari", or cultural (progressive) Islam. It was pitted against the "conservative Islam" of the main opposition political party, the Islamic PAS.

According to Badawi, Islam Hadhari emphasises economic development, civil society and cultural progress. It does not simply hark back to the past, to Muhammad's time, but gives equal emphasis to the present and the future. It emphasises wisdom, practicality and harmony. Islam Hadhari also stresses the central role of knowledge in Islam. It preaches hard work, honesty, good administration and efficiency. It also appeals to Muslims to be inclusive, tolerant and outward-looking and encourages moderation or a balanced approach to life. At the same time it does not stray from the fundamentals of the Qur'an and *sunna*. It advocates that Muslims should attend secular rather than religious schools. Committees have been set up in Malaysia to spread its message, and mullahs have been instructed to preach it during Friday sermons.[1023]

As to *jihad,* Badawi explains it as a sustained effort to discipline the individual's self and as an endeavour to uphold social justice and peace. It is also the quest for improved quality in knowledge, science, economics and all areas of life. He blames Muslims for having narrowed down the meaning of *jihad* to fighting and that this has become the only meaning commonly understood by the general public.[1024]

Islam and Reform Workshop, 2004, Egypt

A conference of progressive intellectuals and researchers from Arab and other Islamic countries was held in Cairo, October 5th – 7th 2004. It discussed the issue of reform within Islam, as well as the possibility of "moderate" Islamist movements participating in democratic systems. The conference published a final statement listing ten recommendations. The most important of these was a call for a radical revision of Islamic jurisprudence and its relationship to the *sunna,* based on the principle of ongoing *ijtihad* and the primacy of the Qur'an over *hadith*. Another important point was a call to break the monopoly of religious establishments on the interpretation of Islam, stressing the full right of individual Muslims to develop their own contextualised interpretations.[1025]

Although the final communiqué did not refer to *jihad*, it was mentioned by Dr. Sa'ad Al-Din Ibrahim, Chairman of the Ibn Khaldun Center For Development Studies in Cairo (the main sponsors of the conference), in his opening speech. For him *jihad* is the intellectual struggle to keep the gates of *ijtihad* wide open until Judgement Day, in order to protect freedom of thought and expression in all matters. This struggle includes the efforts to prevent the marginalisation of the Muslim intellectuals by their own governments, by official religious institutions and by extremists, radicals, and zealots who have turned Islam into a means of intimidation and terror all over the world.[1026]

Amir Taheri[1027]

Taheri, who is of Iranian origin but now living in the West, represents those Muslims who accept the Western secular divide between religion and politics. For Taheri, contemporary Islamism is simply a political movement masquerading as a religious movement, "a secular wolf disguised as a religious lamb". He alleges that making use of Islam for political ambitions began long ago with the Umayyads who used religion to legitimise their dynastic rule, and similar manipulations continued throughout Islamic history. Taheri claims that this contradicted Muhammad's teachings.

In modern times, he traces this manipulation to Jamal al-Din al-Afghani through al-Banna and Mawdudi. This type of Islam divides the world into Muslim against non-Muslim rather than between good and evil. It is a Muslim variant of Marxism and Fascism that destroys individual freedoms.

Amir Taheri sees the only solution in a revival of Muslim theology that emphasises the unity of God in its spiritual aspects as the only absolute and immutable truth. Qur'an and *shari'a* are relative and open to infinite interpretations. Islam must become a religion separate from politics. While Muslims can be involved in politics, they must recognise that political conflicts are not about religion but about territory, borders and statehood.

Abdurrahman Wahid, often called Gus Dur (1940-), Indonesia[1028]

Indonesia developed a tolerant and non-violent form of Islam, and in the mid-twentieth century was perhaps the only Muslim-majority context in which Muslims and non-Muslims were equal. Its concept of "Pancasila" allowed Indonesian citizens a choice of several faiths. Since then it has gradually moved, with the rest of the Muslim world, towards radicalism, accompanied by discrimination and violence towards non-Muslims.

Abdurrahman Wahid, former leader of Indonesia's Nahdatul Ulama and former president of Indonesia (1999-2001), argues that religion and politics must be separate. He rejects the notion that Islam should form the basis for the nation state's political or legal system, which he calls a Middle Eastern tradition, alien to Indonesia.

Wahid has fiercely critiqued Islamist, Wahhabi, Salafi and *jihadi* forms of Islam, which he calls a minority fundamentalist religious cult fuelled by petrodollars. He is painfully aware of the danger they pose to the world at large and to Islam in particular.

Wahid argues for a multifaceted alternative Islam capable of responding to the realities of modern life and able to withstand the onslaught of Islamism. Its building blocks are:

1 Human dignity, free will and tolerance.

2 The right of all Muslims to perpetual reinterpretation of Qur'an and *sunna* in the light of ever-changing human situations.

3 Islamic spirituality (Sufism) as well as a diverse local folk Islamic cultural traditions.

4 Sexual equality.

5 Acceptance of modernity and the good it offers to Muslims.

While he does not specifically mention *jihad*, Gus Dur is committed to non-violence on the Gandhi and Martin Luther King model. Universal Islamic concepts and doctrines, based on unabrogated Qur'anic statements, are for him the binding rules of contemporary Islam. These cannot be displaced by Arab traditions of an ancient specific context. Among these basic universal doctrines he stresses the following:[1029]

1 Establishing justice, leading to prosperity both economic and spiritual

2 Diversity and mutual understanding

3 Tolerance to other religions

4 Unity and peaceful co-existence

5 Non-violence

Conclusion

These reformers have shown immense courage in grappling with the thorny issue of the place of violence within the Islamic texts and within Islamic societies. The place of reason and its relation to violence in religion has been considered but it has often brought threats, intimidation and even death for some. Yet it is a process which must continue.

The secular Muslim state paradigm

Two Muslim states ventured beyond reform and reinterpretation to impose radical secularisation in order to marginalise Islamic radicalism. These are Turkey under Mustafa Kemal Atatürk and Tunisia under Habib Bourguiba.

Turkey[1030]

The modern secular Turkish republic was born in 1923 as the first secular state in the Muslim world. Its founding father, Mustafa Kemal Atatürk (1881-1938), pushed through a radical programme of secularisation. Atatürk believed that Western-type secular nationalism was essential for modernity and progress and that the traditional religious establishment was a hindrance to achieving these goals. He imposed a clear separation between the state and religion while dismantling the structure of the Ottoman religious establishment. The caliphate was abolished in 1924. The *shari'a* was replaced by a secular legal system based on Western models. In 1928 the clause about Islam as the state religion was removed from the constitution. Islamic *madrassas* were closed and all educational institutions were placed under the Ministry for Public Instructions. Official Islam was placed under the Directorate of Religious Affairs, a government department directly responsible to the prime minister. The officially tolerated form of Islam thus became part of the government structure under strict government control and no other type of Islam was tolerated. Islam effectively became an instrument of the state, mobilised to further its national goals. It was valued for its cultural heritage and its cohesive utility in unifying the new nation, but was not allowed any leverage on power. The Sufi orders were banned and all shrines shut down. External symbols of Islam such as the hat for males and the headscarf for women were outlawed. The Gregorian calendar was introduced. Latin script replaced the Arabic script and Turkish replaced Arabic as the liturgical language: the Qur'an was read in Turkish and the call to prayer was issued in Turkish too.

In the 1930s Ataturk's secular thought was codified into the official state ideology known as Kemalism which was written into the constitution in 1937. At its core were six basic principles:

1 Republicanism

2 Nationalism

3 Populism

4 Statism

5 Secularism

6 Revolutionism

Following Ataturk's death in 1938, a relaxation of militant secularism gradually emerged, especially after the introduction of multiparty politics in 1945. The military became the self-appointed guardians of Atatürk's secular legacy and several times intervened to ensure its survival. The last example of such military intervention occurred in 1997 when the country's first Islamist prime minister, Necmettin Erbakan, was removed from power after only a year in office. The military view the current prime minister, Recep Tayyip Erdogan, as an Islamist in disguise.

Turkish society remains polarised between a large section of traditional religious Muslims and a fairly large secular urban elite. Islam has been manipulated by the political parties and government who saw it as a tool in the fight against the radical left. Concessions were made to religious sentiments: the pilgrimage to Mecca was permitted in 1948, courses to train prayer-leaders in mosques were opened in 1949 and religious education in schools was allowed in the same year. Arabic was restored to the prayer call in 1950. With political liberalisation religious sentiments re-emerged as mosque attendance grew and new mosques were built.

Since the 1970s a series of Muslim political parties have been formed, the latest of which, Justice and Development, came to power with a large majority in 2002. Justice and Development rejects the Islamist label, claiming that it accepts the secular state, and that it is a Muslim Democratic party similar to Christian Democratic parties in Europe.

But the issue of religion refuses to go away, and is a visible or invisible factor in both domestic and foreign policy in Turkey. One sign of this polarisation is the periodic controversy over how women should dress. Some women argue that wearing a headscarf is a human right and a religious duty. Secularists see the headscarf as a provocative political symbol, and have managed to get it banned from universities, state schools and government ministries.

Optimists see Turkey as a model for other Muslim societies - a pro-Western state, practising multi-party democracy, which has turned its back on Muslim radicalism. Others believe the Turks have yet to resolve a deep-seated crisis of identity. It is noteworthy how strong Islamism is amongst the people of a country whose leaders were resolutely secular for eight decades.

Tunisia[1031]

Following independence in 1956, the new president, Habib Bourguiba (1903-2000) instituted various reforms aimed at modernising Tunisia. Bourguiba was a moderate moderniser and secularist who wanted to build a progressive and Westernised Tunisia. He saw traditional Islam as a hindrance to the achievement of his goals and embarked on a programme of reforming Islam. While he tried to legitimise his policies in Islamic modernist terms, his initiatives brought more secularisation than in any other Arab country.

Bourguiba's broad strategy was to weaken all independent sources of power within the traditional religious establishment: the 'ulama, shari'a courts, schools and religious foundations (hubus). He portrayed himself as a reformer in the tradition of Muhammad 'Abduh. The basic tenets of Islam needed to be reinterpreted to make them more compatible with modernisation. Nationalism, not Islam, was the central element of Tunisian identity. Bourguiba in effect nationalised Islam, making it subservient to the secular state and part of the government apparatus under its control. The religious apparatus became an administrative part of the government and strictly under its control, manipulated by it to further its goals of modernisation and economic development.

Bourguiba suppressed the traditional Islamic educational system of the Zaytunah college, the traditional centre of Islam in Tunisia making it part of the University of Tunis and secularised the state educational system. A new family law called the Personal Status Code was enacted which replaced shari'a in the areas of marriage, divorce and childcare. This code granted women far more extensive rights than anywhere else in the Arab world. It abolished polygamy and repudiation (divorce by the husband merely repeating the words "I divorce you" without going to court) and required the consent of both partners prior to marriage.[1032] Tunisia was the first Arab country to outlaw polygamy and declare equality between men and women. Bourguiba's reforms were less radical than Atatürk's in Turkey, but nevertheless significant.

Shari'a courts were abolished in 1956 and the *hubus* (*waqf*) land was nationalised. This deprived the *ulama* of an important independent source of income and made them dependent on the government, which gradually brought the religious establishment under its control. Popular Islam, especially the Sufi orders, were weakened and some shrines closed.

In 1960 Bourguiba attacked the practice of Ramadan fasting by stating as his *fatwa* that the *jihad* for economic development and against underdevelopment suspended the command to fast. Bourguiba made Islam subservient to the secular Tunisian state, limiting its role in society, although the constitution declares Islam the state religion.

Islamist groups influenced by the Egyptian Muslim Brotherhood appeared in the1970s and 1980s, the largest being the al-Nahda movement led by Rashid al-Ghannoushi. The Islamists succeeded in creating a parallel society, anti-secular and anti-state in its orientation. The new president, Zine El-Abidine Ben Ali, who had replaced the ailing Bourguiba in 1987, first tried to accommodate the Islamists by ordering various policy changes to give Islam a more prominent role in public life and to portray the government as the protector of Islam. The call to prayer was broadcast on television, Islamic calendar dates appeared on official documents, and the Zaytunah was accorded the status of a university. This was followed by a crackdown on the Islamists and the suppression of their political structures. The army and police were purged of Islamists and hundreds of activists were arrested. Al-Nahda was refused recognition as a party, and Ghannoushi was forced into exile. To gain the support of Tunisia's women, a whole range of reforms affecting the status of women was introduced and several women were admitted to the party central committee and one woman to the political bureau. The regime proclaimed itself the defender of women's rights against the Islamists.[1033]

The 1988 Tunisian National Charter contained a ban on political parties based on religion and supported reforms that would emphasise Islamic modernism while keeping mosques out of politics.[1034] However, Ben Ali's regime became less democratic as shown by President Ben Ali in 1994 and 1999 winning re-election with 99% of the vote. After Tunisia's constitution was amended in 2002 to extend the term of the president, Ben Ali was again re-elected in 2004 with more than 90% of the vote.

Tunisia was the first Arab country to adopt a specific family planning policy which includes birth control. It has succeeded in educating its women and bringing them into the work force. Men and schoolchildren are taught about contraception. As a result, the fertility rate has been reduced to 2.08.[1035]

Conclusion

The models of secular Muslim-majority states in Turkey and Tunisia have succeeded in containing and marginalising Islamism so far. There is no doubt that these two states also offer greater equality and freedom than most other Muslim states. While Tunisia is more repressive in dealing with opposition to the regime, Turkey has actually liberalised its democracy in recent years as it tries to gain access to the European Union. Both countries have achieved a certain degree of economic development. However Islamist tendencies are present and continual alertness is required by the governments to avoid Islamist infiltration of the power centres as well as to prevent Islamist terrorist activities. Turkey and Tunisia serve as a beacon of hope for secularists in the Middle East and in the wider Muslim world while attracting the wrath of Islamists who condemn them as infidel and apostate. There are other models of state governance within the Muslim world which have safeguards against Islam, such as Indonesia's Pancasila,[1036] although this has not proved to be as resilient as the secular models.

17
Responses to Islamic Terrorism

Military strategists recognise the importance of "knowing your enemy". Yet following September 11th 2001 it appeared that American and British political leaders went to great lengths to deny any connection between Al-Qa'eda and mainstream Islam i.e. to consider Al-Qa'eda as mindless extremists, motivated by a pointless blind fanatical hatred of the West. They were referred to as "enemies of civilisation", "enemies of our way of life" or simply "terrorists". Seen as such, it is a struggle to comprehend what can have possibl y motivated them to carry out such apparently senseless acts of violence.

However in the context of radical Islamists' understanding of Islam, with its historical teaching of *jihad*, *Dar al-Islam* and *Dar al-Harb*, together with the historical development of a theology of violence amongst sects and *jihad* groups through the ages, their actions are far from senseless but rather are guided by a clear logic. With this understanding one can begin to look seriously at how to address them.

Islamic terrorists do not function in isolation. Not only are they networked to each other but also they are linked to the Muslim community at large, from which they draw funds and new recruits to enable their continued operation. The interconnections resemble a multiplicity of spiders' webs. To remove a single individual, for example Osama bin Laden, from this scenario would have relatively little effect on the overall position. It is the networking of groups which gives them their great strength, so efforts should be made to isolate the groups from each other, and prevent the flow of funds, personnel and expertise.

In order to begin to tackle Islamic terrorism effectively, greater surveillance and penetration of these networks is vital. However, it is particularly difficult to infiltrate Muslim groups, as Muslims are very unwilling to act as agents for the non-Muslim world and non-Muslims find it difficult to pass themselves off convincingly as Muslims. Also the cellular structure makes penetration from outside difficult, in particular where such groups are ethnic-, tribal- or even family-based. As well as current terrorist activities it is important to research all matters relating to Islamic theology, history, interpretation and practices and to analyse the findings in terms of their influence on the terrorist networks and individuals. A spider weaves its web in secret in a dark corner, and cannot be tackled until a light is shone upon it. Similarly, a light must be shone on the network of Islamic groups and interconnections to reveal the true complexity of the situation.

World War IV and Fourth Generation Warfare?

Military experts have defined four generations of warfare types in the modern history of warfare. Each succeeding stage is marked by a greater dispersion on the battlefield.[1037]

1 First generation warfare reflected the tactics of the era of the smoothbore musket using line and column. A good example is the French revolutionary armies characterised by low training levels of conscripted troops and their revolutionary zeal.

2 Second generation warfare was based on fire and movement, and remained essentially linear. It was a response to the invention of the rifled musket, breechloaders, barbed wire, the machinegun, and indirect fire. There was a heavy reliance on indirect fire. Massed firepower replaced massed manpower.

3 Third generation warfare was driven by new ideas developed by the German army in World War I. Because of their weaker industrial base, the Germans developed radically new tactics based on manoeuvre rather than attrition. These were the first non-linear tactics. The attack relied on infiltration to bypass and collapse the enemy's combat forces rather than seeking

to close with and destroy them. The defence was in depth and often invited penetration, which set the enemy up for a counterattack. The addition of the tank as a new technological element caused the development of the blitzkrieg in which the basis of the operational art shifted from place to time.

4 The fourth generation battlefield is the most recent development and includes all of society as part of the battlefield. It is asymmetrical warfare characterised by an increased importance of actions by very small groups of combatants and a decreasing dependence on centralised logistics. There is more emphasis on manoeuvre. Small, highly manoeuvrable and flexible forces dominate. The goal has changed from destroying the enemy physically to collapsing him internally and psychologically. Targets now include the population's support for the war and the enemy's culture. Fourth generation warfare seems likely to be widely dispersed and largely undefined, the distinction between war and peace becoming blurred. It is a non-linear warfare having no definable battlefields or fronts. The distinction between "civilian" and "military" is disappearing. Actions occur concurrently throughout all participants' depth including their society as a cultural, not just a physical, entity.

The new global war against terror is seen in terms of fourth generation warfare which has been adopted by the Islamist terrorist organisations, especially those linked to al-Qaʿeda. It has also been described as a fourth World War.[1038] Following the first and second World Wars, the Cold War between the West and the Communist world is seen as the third World War, and the contemporary war against terror as the fourth.

Fourth generation warfare is marked by the end of the state's monopoly on war. A variety of entities, not just formal armies, are fighting using many different means such as terrorism, immigration and the media. State militaries, designed to fight other state militaries, find most of their equipment, tactics and training inadequate or even counterproductive when fighting against non-state enemies. Fourth generation warfare is characterised by conflicts between cultures (including religions) rather than between specific states.[1039] Globalisation and modern technology enable military operations anywhere at any time while making societies more vulnerable to attack. New technologies have dramatically increased the potential destructive force of small groups of militants. Global media saturation has made possible a high level of manipulation. Finally, non-hierarchical networked organisational types, made possible by improvements in technology, are very effective in recruiting, training, surviving and acting. A basic premise of fourth generation warfare is that superior political will can defeat greater military and economic power. Its strategy is to change the minds of the enemy's decision makers, convincing them that their strategic goals are too costly and unachievable.[1040]

It is important to recognise that a global Islamic totalitarian movement characterised by an asymmetric mode of operation is currently at war with the rest of the world. It is a long term global war that cannot be contained in separate individual local pockets. The global *jihad* targets the enemy's political will rather than just its military forces, and terrorism is just one tactic among many it uses. The most successful networks combine urban warfare, relief work and hate media as a three-pronged *jihad*. The need exists to develop a multidisciplinary long-term strategic plan to deal with this threat.

The global *jihad* operates at different levels:[1041]

1   A traditional religious holy war in which it is absolutely vital to understand the religious dimension and concepts of the enemy. It should be countered by efforts at religion-shaping and knowledge-building within the Muslim world.

2   A post-modern net-war in which the enemy is organised as a network rather than a hierarchy and in which media networks are both observers and participants. Media networks act as weapon platforms and systems, front lines and theatres of operations.

3   A manifestation of warlordism and piracy in the age of globalisation.

According to this view, global *jihad* rests on five bases:[1042]

1　Wahhabi Saudi Arabia which in the past three decades has used its oil money and influence to alter the balance of power in the Muslim world using Muslim international organisations and non-governmental organisations as force multipliers (i.e. to dramatically increase the effectiveness of a military force). It has concurrently used its money to influence Western media, think tanks and academic institutions.

2　Al-Azhar University, the highest authority in the Sunni world, has been altered by Saudi money and influence to adopt an ideology similar to that of the Muslim Brotherhood,[1043] thus legitimising Islamist discourse all over the Muslim world.

3　Al-Qa'eda, which has managed to become the recruiting, training and franchise base for the global *jihad* network

4　Islamic media, for example, Al-Jazeera and Al-Manar (the Hizbullah TV station) which have become very effective in disseminating the global *jihad* message

5　Sections of Western academia, who can be considered as an unwitting fifth column, are providing conceptual ammunition and academic immunity to secret jihadists.

Possible ways of dealing with the Islamic terrorist threat

Given these precautionary and preparatory tactics, what broad strategies are available for dealing with Islamic terrorism?

1 Elimination

At one end of the spectrum of responses is the elimination of all individuals involved in terrorist activities by killing them, as for example in the elimination of the Kharijis by mainstream Muslims. This is also how the Assassins were dealt with in the Middle Ages when their main centre at Alamut in Persia was wiped out by the Mongols under

Hulagu in 1256. Those based in Syria were subjugated by the Mameluke Sultan Baybars, who had captured all their castles by 1273.[1044]

In one sense the US's determined pursuit of Islamic terrorists could evolve into such a response. Because of the way in which terrorists are interlinked, to remove just the perceived "ringleaders" is very unlikely to have any effect on the movement as a whole. The Americans may therefore go on to extend their targeting more broadly resulting in a spiralling with unpredictable consequences. Without making a conscious or deliberate policy of mass elimination, their actions could thus develop in that direction.

Even if this method were considered acceptable, it could not be permanently effective. Sooner or later terrorism would re-emerge, as individual Muslims examined the roots of Islam, gave them a particular interpretation, and made their own decisions to return to the violence of the early days of their faith. Given the theological character of Islam, the non-violent Muslim masses are bound to give rise to violent individuals from time to time. The removal of the Assassins centuries ago has not prevented the development of Palestinian suicide bombers now. Non-violent Islam is like a cone balanced on its point; it cannot exist in that state indefinitely but is bound to fall i.e. to give rise to violent elements.

2 Military defeat

History shows that until now the advance of Islam has only ever been stopped by military defeat. We have already seen how Kaegi's analysis indicates that it was military factors that were the primary cause of the success of the early Muslim invasions of the Levant. In western Europe it was only Christendom's military might which reversed the Muslim advance into France at the battle of Tours (732, also known as the battle of Poitiers) and drove Islam out of Spain in the Reconquista (culminating in the fall of Granada in 1492). Similarly in eastern Europe militant Christendom turned back the Muslim advance in Austria at the siege of Vienna (1683).

Historically Europe was attacked by Muslim armies and could be defended by conventional warfare. Now it is faced with terrorist activities, and it is not clear how to defeat these militarily. Even finding the enemy can prove virtually impossible e.g. in Afghanistan. However, a modern example illustrating that the likelihood or otherwise of a strong physical response can still be an important motivation for Islamic terrorists is described by Bernard Lewis.

> One of the most surprising revelations of those who held the American Embassy in Teheran from 1979 to 1981 was that their original intention had been to hold the building and the hostages for only a few days. They changed their minds when statements from Washington made it clear that there was no danger of serious action against them. They finally released the hostages, they explained, only because they feared that the new President, Ronald Reagan, might approach the problem "like a cowboy".[1045]

3 Colonialism

It is noteworthy that Islamic terrorism was in abeyance throughout the eighteenth and nineteenth centuries when European colonial powers ruled most of the Muslim world. It was only in the mid-twentieth century, when the colonial yoke was being thrown off all around the world, that radical Islam re-appeared on the scene. It would seem that strong Western colonial rule prevented the rise of active militants within Islam. For example, in 1921 the British arrested and tried for conspiracy Pir Ghulam Mujaddid Sirhindi who made inflammatory anti-British speeches and denounced the presence of Muslims in the British army.[1046] This particular *pir* was willing to endure the discomforts of prison, but many others were not and also felt that the humiliation and disgrace of prison endangered their special status in society. Many therefore quickly gave in when punishment loomed.[1047] One such Khilafat supporter, Maulvi Muhammad Sadiq of Nawabshah, had served only a week of his one-year sentence for refusing to furnish security for good behaviour when he changed his mind and acceded to the authorities' demands. He justified this with a verse from the Qur'an:[1048]

> He who takes up a burden which he has not the power to bear commits a sin.[1049]

Abdul Ghaffar Khan felt that *jihads* against the British were of no use, serving only to provoke them into greater violence and ruthlessness. He considered that the British presence in the North-West Frontier was so firmly established that it was not possible to oust them by violence. "Earlier, violence had seemed to me the best way to revolution... but experience taught me that it was futile to dig a well after the house was on fire."[1050] We have already seen how the Muridiyya movement in Senegal responded to French colonialism with passive resistance and eventually cooperation (chapter 8).

A separate reason why colonialism helped to contain Islamic terrorism was the theology adopted by some Indian Muslims that so long as the British government allowed Muslims to practise their faith freely they should not be attacked (see chapter 15).

However, colonial rule does not necessarily prevent the rise of the ideas, as for example in Egypt where the Muslim Brotherhood came into existence during a period of British military and political influence in the country (albeit not full colonialism).

4 Brutal repression

The majority of Muslim governments today face opposition from Islamist movements who seek to topple the existing regime by terrorism and replace it with their own, more Islamic, system. Many of these countries respond to the threat with brutal repression. Terrorists and suspected terrorists are arrested, tortured, imprisoned without trial etc. Some may be formally executed or surreptitiously murdered. Countries which fall into this category include Egypt, Syria, Tunisia, Algeria and Saudi Arabia.

It is noteworthy that in Egypt the Muslim Brotherhood have now abandoned their policy of violence and are pursuing their goals by political means. A similar thing seems to be happening in Algeria and Syria. These moves however, are more tactical than ideological. Given changed circumstances, the Muslim Brotherhood might encourage violence, as it did in Sudan in 1989 even though it was fully involved in the democratic process. If the movements seeking to reform society change only their methods and not their aims, the question remains as to what they will do once they have attained power through the political processes. Will they continue to allow some form of democracy or will they install a totalitarian regime?

5 Denial of human rights

In Western democracies the method of brutal repression is not an option, hence the flourishing centres of radical Islam which now exist in the western world, directing and funding the activities of the terrorists. The most the West can do to control or limit these activities is a suspension of certain human rights to permit, for example, the detention of suspects without trial. This is difficult to sustain because of the protests of human rights activists, as has been seen with regard to both American and British actions against terrorists since September 11th 2001. For such a method to be workable it requires overwhelming public support which in turn requires a public awareness of the threat of Islamic terrorism.

6 Financial restrictions

A more acceptable way might be to stem the flow of funds to terrorist organisations. The sums involved are vast. Steven Stalinsky's well documented report[1051] on Saudi donations to Palestinian *jihad* fighters concludes that the Saudi royal family has been their main financial supporter for decades. He calculates that in a period of five and a half years (January 1998 – June 2003), over US$4 billion was donated. Much of this was specifically designated for the families of martyrs. King Fahd himself gave a pledge to support a thousand Palestinian families of martyrs. Money continues to flow to terrorist groups from donations all around the Muslim world, often collected in mosques and diverted through seemingly innocent charities. This is in addition to criminal activities including the drug trade, kidnapping for ransom, fraud and robbery. If these funds could be prevented from reaching the terrorists it is likely that their activities would have to be severely curtailed.

7 Economic uplift

Many have suggested that Islamic terrorism is the expression of frustrated impoverished young Muslim men, without education or employment, who have no earthly hope. It has therefore been suggested that a massive injection of aid into the poorest Muslim regions to enable development and economic transformation would see an end to militant Islam. The US in particular has developed the concept of economic transformation as part of the overall war against terror intended to complement the military component. General John Abizaid, former head of the US Central Command, used American troops in the Horn of Africa to build schools and clinics and dig wells in an effort to counter sympathy for the terrorists. The idea is for local governments then to run the facilities, thus bolstering their appeal to the impoverished population. Abizaid's concept calls for dealing with the perceived root causes of terror over a long period of time. The US military has been implementing similar policies in Indonesia, the Philippines, North Africa and Yemen.[1052] The UK armed forces also have a similar approach.

President Musharraf of Pakistan has been encouraged to accelerate the economic development of the tribal areas in the Northwest of Pakistan. An elaborate plan for the reconstruction and development of the tribal region has been drawn up that envisages boosting agriculture, irrigation, livestock and industry.[1053]

Unfortunately this theory is belied by the fact that many Islamic terrorists, particularly in the Gulf and Middle East, are neither poor nor uneducated. A good proportion, especially those in leadership, is from the comfortable, cultivated middle classes. Osama bin Laden is immensely wealthy and has used his own money to fund much of Al-Qa'eda's activity. The terrorists' motivation is theological, not just psychological. Sadly the theory of paying Islamic terrorism to disappear seems to be more wishful thinking than grounded in reality.

8 Yield to the terrorists' requests

In theory terrorist activity should cease if the terrorists are given what they want. This was the analysis of the BBC's World Affairs Editor, John Simpson, citing the examples of the IRA in Northern Ireland and ETA in Spain:

> There is only one method of defeating political violence. It begins by mobilising the support of governments who might otherwise be quietly sympathetic to extremists, and goes on to

isolate those responsible for the violence *by reducing the causes of discontent.*[1054]

In the case of Islamic terrorists their immediate goal is to rule the Muslim world according to the strictest forms of Islam. Some might argue that the non-Muslim world should withdraw from any involvement in Muslim regions, should cede Palestine, Chechnya, Kashmir, south Thailand, Mindanao in the Philippines, and all the other areas where Muslims are seeking to establish Muslim or Islamic states, and put up an "Islamic curtain" between the Muslim and the non-Muslim world. It is relevant to remark that whilst Samuel Huntington's thesis of a "clash of civilisations" may at first have seemed an extreme position, there is now some recognition of the validity of his argument.

But would this permanently satisfy the terrorists? Or is it possible that, because of their ultimate global agenda i.e. to change all the remaining *Dar al-Harb* to *Dar al-Islam,* they would break through the "Islamic curtain" and continue the struggle for dominance?

9 Peace treaty

As we have seen, the traditional Islamic doctrine of war has much to say about when and how Muslims are permitted to make peace with the enemy. This suggests the possibility of the non-Muslim world making some kind of formal peace with the Muslim community worldwide. However, there are a number of serious difficulties with this, not least the fact that peace treaties in classical Islam are supposed to be only temporary, in effect, merely truces. Another problem is that there is no single Islamic authority accepted by all Muslims with whom to negotiate. Thirdly, there are sections of the Muslim community who believe that Muslims may freely break any agreement made with non-Muslims.

10 Co-opt terrorist groups into a peace process[1055]

Alastair Crooke, a former senior British intelligence officer, has been active in advocating that Western governments engage in dialogue with Islamic terror groups, get to understand them better, and induce them to participate in a peace process along the lines of South Africa and Northern Ireland. He has set up the "Conflict

Forum" think tank to further these efforts. Patrick Seale defined this as "the first systematic attempt by a new western institution to challenge the view propagated by Washington neo-conservatives that the West is engaged in a life-and-death struggle with militant Islam".[1056] Since 2004 Crooke has headed delegations that have met with Hizbullah leaders in Lebanon and with Hamas leaders in the Palestinian Territories, among others, in an effort to understand them better and learn to see things from their perspectives. He stresses that it is important to listen to these movements, which does not necessarily mean agreeing to their claims. Some sources think he is acting on behalf of the British government in seeking to establish non-official ties to these organisations.

Crooke argues that Western governments and their intelligence services simply do not understand Islamic terrorists, are unwilling to engage with them in dialogue, and therefore continually offer warped analysis that is often based on wrong information. As examples he cites the US administration's expectations that Iyad Allawi's secular party would do well in the December 2005 elections in Iraq, and that Hamas would not gain a majority in the Palestinian elections in January 2006. Both these predictions were proved wrong and the real outcomes caused deep problems for the American strategies and plans in Iraq and Palestine. The West, says Crooke, seems unable to predict, shape or even understand the ongoing processes in the Middle East, largely because of its ideological position not to talk with Islamist movements such as the Muslim Brotherhood, Jama'at-i-Islami, Hamas and Hizbullah. (He does exclude the *takfiri* groups from such talks.) He thinks it is imperative that Western governments recognise these "moderate" Islamist movements that have a political wing, have entered the democratic process in their countries and have gained legitimacy from large constituencies within their own societies.

Crooke advances a pragmatic argument, namely, that violent movements have always influenced world history, and that states finally had to deal with terrorists who later became leaders of their new nations or of political parties within their states.

While it is certainly important to have a good understanding of what motivates Islamist groups that engage in terrorism,

Crooke's methodology seem to have several flaws. First, it ignores the problem of *taqiyya*, appearing to assume that by talking to Islamists one will become informed of their real opinions. As we have seen it is not likely that Islamists will knowingly convey to a Westerner their true aims and motives. Second, it equates Islamist terrorism with Western governments' responses to it, and blames neo-colonialism and aggression for the problems of the Muslim world. Third, such efforts could marginalise Muslim moderates, liberals, secularists and democrats who are already under tremendous pressure from Islamists. The method implies that only radicals can deliver the wished-for peace. Fourth, it ignores the fact that successful peace processes, such as in Northern Ireland, often occur only when the radical groups realise they are critically weakened, lose hope of gaining their goals by violence, and lose much of their popular support. This only happens after a long process of conflict in which a determined state and its security forces inflict real damage on the terrorists. Finally, Crooke's method accepts almost intuitively that the radical terrorist groups are the only true representatives of their societies and nations, ignoring the many other powerful forces within them. This seems to be a Marxist point of view prevalent in Western hard left circles.

11 Theological undermining

An ingenious method is reported to have been employed on various occasions. According to the stories, dead Islamic terrorists are buried with pig body-parts. Because the pig is considered unclean,[1057] some Muslims believe that this kind of treatment will prevent the deceased from going to paradise. If the certainty of going immediately to paradise is the main motivation of terrorists and suicide bombers, then this relatively cheap and easy response might possibly prove to be an effective deterrent.

Places and times where this method is reported to have been used include:

1 Peshawar in British India in 1882. A British Officer was shot by an Afghan who believed he would go to paradise for killing an infidel. The assassin was killed by soldiers, and his body was burnt in a pig skin. The authorities claimed that

Muslims believed this would prevent his entering paradise, and that this action would act as a deterrent to other would-be assassins.[1058]

2 The Philippines in the early twentieth century.[1059] In one case in 1911, following numerous terrorist attacks by Muslim insurgents, General John J. Pershing ordered his men to catch the perpetrators and teach them a lesson. The captured terrorists were forced to dig their own graves and were tied to posts. The American soldiers then slaughtered pigs in their view and rubbed their bullets in the pigs' blood and fat. When the terrorists saw that they would be contaminated with pig blood they were aghast, believing that as a result they could not enter paradise even if they died as martyrs. All but one were shot, their bodies dumped into the grave with the pig guts spread over them. The lone survivor was allowed to escape back to the terrorist camp to tell his companions what had happened. It is reported that this action brought a stop to terrorism in the Philippines for the next 50 years.[1060]

3 In the Gaza Strip in 2002.[1061] Some Jewish settlers in the Gush Katif area of the Gaza Strip claimed to have defiled the body of a dead Palestinian with pigskin and lard. Residents of Efrat in the West Bank said they did the same to a Palestinian who tried to blow up their supermarket. This method was also suggested by the deputy Israeli police minister Gideon Esra in the Israeli newspaper *Yediot Aharonot,* a few weeks before September 11th 2001,[1062] and again by an Israeli rabbi in 2004 who proposed hanging bags of pig fat in Israeli buses as a deterrent to Palestinian suicide bombers, who frequently target buses.[1063]

Whether or not this method has ever actually been used, the logic behind it would be hard to defy, if Muslims really do believe that contact with pig parts will stop a martyr going to paradise. However there does not appear to be any warrant for this belief in Islamic theology and Philps reports that Palestinian Muslims scorned the idea.[1064] Raeed Tayeh, public affairs director of the Muslim American Society Freedom Foundation, has also denied that Muslims would be barred from heaven by such treatment.[1065] Furthermore, even if the method were workable, its very offensiveness raises the question of whether it could ever really be recommended.

Nevertheless there are other ways in which the theological basis for suicide bombers could be undermined. Since no individual suicide attack is a martyrdom unless Islamic leaders say it is, there is the possibility of an Islamic leader declaring that a particular suicide attack was not martyrdom. This means the bomber will not go straight to paradise. The bomber will also have been relying on a financial pay-out for his family (that will also clear his own debts if any, a necessary pre-requisite for going to paradise) which might not be forthcoming. If militants begin to fear that they may not be "covered" by this kind of theological and financial support, they will be less willing to kill themselves in suicide attacks.

So if at least some Islamic leaders could be persuaded to publicly condemn at least some suicide bombings, not just to Western audiences, but also in the relevant religious terminology for their own community, this particular method of terrorist attack, which is so hard to deal with militarily, might lose its popularity. An example of this occurred when Saudi Arabia's Crown Prince Abdullah made a rare televised statement after three suicide attacks in Riyadh in May 2003 which killed 34 people including some Saudi civilians. He warned that the terrorists who committed the atrocity "have a destiny that is very harsh in hellfire".[1066] In other words, he proclaimed that the suicide bombers were not martyrs going to heaven but murderers going to hell.

Similarly Saudi Arabia's Council of Senior Clerics, headed by Grand Mufti Sheikh Abdul-Aziz al-Sheikh, issued a *fatwa* in August 2003 stating that acts of sabotage, bombing and murder in their country were not a part of "*jihad* for the sake of God". It stated that those who assisted or sheltered the perpetrators were guilty of "great sin".[1067] It appears that this condemnation may have been limited only to terrorist attacks within the boundaries of Saudi Arabia.

Similarly if the Islamic media were to refrain from making heroes of the suicide bombers, it is possible that fewer young men would be motivated to follow in their footsteps. Perhaps a small beginning was made when the Italian branch of the Muslim World League dismissed the newly appointed imam of Rome's Grand Mosque, the largest mosque in Europe, for having praised Palestinian suicide bombers in his sermon at Friday prayers on 6 June 2003 and having called on Allah "to annihilate the enemies of Islam".[1068]

However this proposed method is complicated by the fact that the bombers usually look chiefly to their own militant group for backing, affirmation and the assurance of heaven. Statements by those outside the group, even if they are respected Islamic religious leaders, may carry little weight with the bomber in comparison with statements by the leaders of his or her own small group. The statements of more prominent leaders may, for example, be dismissed as merely designed to please Western governments.

Historically there was a great difference of opinion between the Kharijis, who considered that death in battle against "unrighteous" governments was martyrdom, and Sunni theologians who considered that rebellion against the government was not a *jihad* and therefore could not lead to martyrdom.[1069]

12 Empowering of Islamism

In their very understandable desire to find a peaceful solution to the problems posed by large restive Muslim minorities, some Western governments have responded by empowering those they perceive as moderate Islamists within the Muslim community, turning them into the officially recognised representatives of all Muslims within the state. However, this strategy is more difficult to pursue than its proponents seem to realise. The two greatest challenges are (1) the fact that radical Islamists are actively seeking to take control of moderate Muslim organisations, and (2) the problem which non-Muslims have in understanding the true stance of Islamists who may be practising *taqiyya* or, at the very least, using phrases such as "Islamic revivalism" whose implications are not well understood by most non-Muslims. .

411

A good case study of what is likely to happen is the Muslim Council of Britain (MCB), created in 1997 at the instigation of the British government who wanted to have a Muslim umbrella organisation that could give moderate mainstream Muslims a national voice and act as the representative of the whole Muslim community in the UK to the government and the British public. The MCB draws its support from a network of mosques and community groups and has some 400 affiliated bodies. Its original leadership grew out of the anti-Rushdie campaign and has now been taken over by Jama'at-i Islami[1070] and Muslim Brotherhood activists. It has been criticised by British Muslims as not being representative of the variety within the British Muslim community.[1071] This illustrates how easily a handful of radical activists can infiltrate and take over a supposedly mainstream Muslim organisation.

While Islamists in the UK use moderate language when talking about internal UK affairs, they are radical in the rhetoric they use about events in the Muslim world, condemning as illegitimate all moderate and secular regimes in Muslim-majority countries and supporting all radical Islamist leaders and movements in Muslim states, justifying "defensive jihad", the imposition of *shari'a* and the establishment of Islamic states. If this is their agenda for Muslim states, what is their agenda for the UK and other Western states?

The French government, in spite of its radically secular attitude that precludes religion from any public forum, backed the establishment of a French Council for the Muslim Religion (CFCM) established in 2003 with almost 1,000 affiliated mosques. It hoped this would weaken the impact of radical Islam in France, what Interior Minister Nicolas Sarkozy described as "the Islam of cellars and garages that has fed extremism and the language of violence" and would create "an official Islam for France". However in the first elections to the CFCM, the Islamists affiliated to the Muslim Brotherhood won a majority.[1072] This should not have been as much of a surprise as it was to the French government as only about 10% of French Muslims pray at mosques regularly. The mosque-based CFCM thus was unlikely to be representative of all five million French Muslims.[1073]

Western governments must realise that attempts to create official representatives of Islam are likely to backfire due to the activism of the Islamists who are well funded by oil-rich states such as Saudi Arabia. Such Islamist activists are working hard to infiltrate and take over the leadership of all Muslim organisations and institutions in the West. The result is that governments are in effect empowering the most extreme Islamist forces while weakening the moderate and secular Muslims who are well disposed towards democracy, secularism and similar Western values.[1074]

13 Reform of Islam

If terrorism is going to be dealt with at its source, Islam has to change and undergo a transformation. In the long term it would appear that the only way to bring an end to Islamic terrorism is for a liberal reform of the teachings of Islam with regard to war and violence. Christianity underwent its own reformation in the fifteenth and sixteenth centuries (which included a growing move towards the separation of Church and state), but this has not happened to Islam, at least not yet. Such a reform of Islam would require a new *ijtihad* to reinterpret the original sources. The current debate within Islam as to whether or not a new *ijtihad* can take place at this stage has involved a number of individual Muslims who have embraced the concept of change and are calling for the origins of their faith to be reinterpreted in the light of modern standards of human rights, freedom, democracy etc. (see chapter 16). These lone voices do not have substantial followings as yet, but they are becoming more numerous. As long as they remain few in number they are at physical risk themselves.

Perhaps the ideal kind of reformed Islam would relegate the *hadith* to a minor source or ignore it altogether. A new *shari'a* would be formulated based on the Qur'an alone, interpreted for modern times. The theory of abrogation would be abandoned or preferably reversed giving the Meccan verses primacy over the Medinan verses in any case of contradiction. Traditional *shari'a* laws that deny universal human rights will be declared invalid.

The reformers mentioned in chapter 16 have come up with such suggestions, but the question is: do they stand a chance of evolving into a mainstream movement that can radically change Islam around the world?

Even calling for a new *ijtihad*, let alone opining on what conclusions it should reach, can be seen as hugely controversial in Islamic circles as the majority believe that "the gates of *ijtihad*" have been closed for a thousand years. Islamic societies have a long tradition of condemning as blasphemers, heretics and apostates, those who suggest ideas which differ from orthodoxy, and in Islam the penalty for apostasy is death. Groups like the *mu'tazila* in the eighth and ninth centuries suffered massive and rapid suppression when their theology fell out of favour with Islamic orthodoxy.

So for real, permanent and widespread change, the central institutions of Islam, both Sunni and Shi'a, need to be engaged so that they can bring about this reform. Following the suicide attacks in Saudi Arabia on May 12th 2003, in which Saudi civilians were killed, it was reported that Saudi Arabia intended to set up a commission to formally re-examine the concept of *jihad* in Islam.[1075] But the author is not aware of any other institutional efforts in this direction.

It may be possible for the West (and other non-Muslims) to assist this process by encouraging the individuals and by putting pressure on the leading Muslim institutions to bring about reform that would eliminate from Islam military *jihad*, suicide martyrdom, the empire-building thrust etc. This encouragement would need to be given with great care, perhaps behind the scenes, as overt Western support might lead to a loss of credibility with the Muslim public in general. A recent step in the right direction is the proposal by the Rand Center for Middle East Public Policy that the US government should "foster moderate Muslim networks... [that is] to bolster the capabilities of moderate Muslims resisting the spread of extremist ideologies".[1076]

Another reservation is that there is no way of guaranteeing that a new *ijtihad* will have the desired effect of producing a mainstream Islam which rejects the violent traditions of the past. When Sir Sayyid Ahmad Khan returned to the original sources of Islam he concluded that *jihad* could only be permitted in the direst necessity of self-defence. By contrast, when those like the *takfir* groups have sought to strip away later Islamic teaching and return to the very oldest sources of Islam, they have emerged more militant as a result. When Muhammad 'Abduh advocated a return to the Qur'an and *sunna*, abandoning centuries of traditional teaching, he wanted to open Islam to reason, science and the best of Western political and philosophical thought. Yet some of his followers, on abandoning traditional teaching, became Salafis. A new *ijtihad* could open up a Pandora's box.

14 Changing the language used to describe radical Islam

Following September 11ᵗʰ 2001 a new lexicon of Islamic terms has entered English and other Western languages. These include Islamic terms like *jihad, shari'a* and *burqa*.[1077] The European Union, in an effort to appease Muslim sensibilities, has been trying to compile another "new lexicon" of public communication which would remove derogatory terminology about Islam like "Islamic terrorism" and "fundamentalists".[1078]

Another twist to a new lexicon is the well intentioned response to Islamic terrorism proposed in the paper "Choosing Words Carefully: Language to Help Fight Islamic Terrorism" by Dr. Douglas E. Streusand and LTC Harry D. Tunnell IV of the US National Defense University, Center for Strategic Communications, Washington DC.[1079]

The authors of this paper are looking for a way to delegitimise Islamic terrorists in the eyes of other Muslims. They argue that the best way to do this is for Western politicians and media to define and describe Islamic terrorists and their ideologies not in the Islamic terms they themselves use to legitimise their cause among Muslims, but by using alternative Islamic terms with negative connotations in the eyes of most Muslims.

As an example, the paper calls for Westerners to cease using the word *jihad* to describe the main doctrine of the radical groups, and the word *mujahidin* to describe their members, as well as the word "caliphate" to describe their ultimate goal of a worldwide Islamic state under *shari'a*. Instead it recommends using terms like *haraba*,[1080] *fitna* and *mufsidun,* which in Islam denote illegitimate warfare and sinful activities such as rebellion, sedition and criminal activity punishable under *shari'a*.

This approach has some merit as a device to try to divide the radicals from mainstream Muslims. Moderate governments in the Muslim world and their establishment clerics have been doing some of this for decades, accusing the Islamist radicals of being Kharijis and of sowing *fitna* and *fasad* (corruption). However, it does not appear to have had much success in weakening the cause of the radicals, partly because it is often difficult to distinguish between radical and establishment Islamic rhetoric as they compete for the same constituency using similar terms.

Using alternative negative terms to describe the terrorists might be a small beginning in the long war against Islamic terrorism. Such efforts however, are only tactics and cannot be expected to substitute for an effective long-term strategy.

The suggested approach entails considerable risks. Islamic terrorists use most of their doctrinal terms in ways accepted as orthodox by early and classical Islam and true to a literal understanding of the Muslim source texts. The integration of religion and politics is part of orthodox Islam. This is part of their appeal to mainstream Muslims. It might be naïve to suppose that a clever use of alternative Islamic vocabulary by the West would negate this reality. There is therefore a real risk of a mainstream Muslim backlash at what they would perceive to be offensive infidel efforts at redefining Islam and dividing the Muslim world. This might further feed the anger and hatred against the West already widespread in Muslim societies and even help to recruit more radicals.

The current American policy of seeking to re-define typologies and terminology of Islamic warfare (as set out, for example, in *Islamic Rulings on Warfare* by Youssef H. Aboul-Enein and Sherifa Zuhur) has linked theology to psychological warfare.[1081] This could also be detrimental in the long term, for the Islamists have realised the strategy and may well develop tools to counter it.

15 Dialogue, counselling and deprogramming

Faced with many thousands of Islamist militants linked to radical terror groups, the government in Yemen developed a new approach to the war on terror based on dialogue with potential rank-and-file sympathisers and recruits to al-Qaʿeda and other Islamic terror organisations. In August 2002 Humud Abdulhameed al-Hittar, a religious judge *(qadi)* who is president of the Court of Appeal for Sanaʿa and al-Jawf Province, was named by Yemeni President Salih as "chairman of the Committee for Religious Dialogue with Al-Qaʿeda Supporters in Yemen". The committee's brief was to initiate dialogue on the subject of Islam and its true interpretation with young people who had returned from Afghanistan and with other young people in detention who were leaning to radical Islamist positions. The approach was one of respect and equality, leading to a conversation between the two sides. Common ground was to be stressed as well as the duty to speak the truth. Participation was voluntary. Discussions were to continue until some mutual agreement has been reached.[1082]

While most detainees were initially suspicious of the clerics' motives, gradually trust was built up as religious themes based on Qurʾan and *sunna* and their interpretation were discussed. It was stressed that if the clerics were persuaded by the radicals they would join them in *jihad*, but if the detainees were persuaded by the clerics, they would give up their ideology of armed struggle. It was claimed that in most cases the clerics were able to convince the detainees that the radical doctrine of *jihad* espoused by them did not stand up to close scrutiny using Islamic criteria and methodology. This method focused exclusively on Islam and its interpretation and ignored politics. Detainees came from various Islamic terror groups, including al-Qaʿeda, the Aden-Abyan Islamic Army,[1083] Takfir wal-Hijra and the Zaydi al-Houthi movement.[1084] According to the clerics, the al-Qaʿeda members were the most difficult to convince. The programme includes an unspecified period of surveillance after release from detention, and the former militants are helped to integrate into society, being provided with jobs or educational opportunities. By June 2005 some 350 suspects had been released through this programme.[1085]

The committee claimed excellent results, arguing that it had "eliminated 90 percent of the ideology that had formed the basis of terrorist operations in Yemen". As a result, Humud al-Hittar was invited to France to share his methods with French officials. However there has been no independent evaluation of the effectiveness of the method, and it is not clear whether the programme really was aimed at reducing terrorism, or was merely a ploy by the president to enhance his image among Islamists while he continued to harshly suppress the militant insurgents in Yemen.[1086]

Saudi Arabia has also initiated programmes to re-educate extremists.[1087] One is a counselling programme for Saudi security prisoners which is run by the Saudi Interior Ministry with the aim of encouraging them to renounce extremist beliefs. The committee involved includes over a hundred leading clerics and some 30 psychiatrists and psychologists. The clerics discuss religion within the detainees and seek to convince them from Islamic source texts of their errors of interpretation. The main concepts discussed are *jihad*, *takfir*, judging by man-made laws, and the expulsion of polytheists from the Arabian peninsula. Prisoners are given individual counselling as well as classes in small groups. The committee reported good progress and by January 2006 more than 400 prisoners had been released, based on the assessment of the programme counsellors.

Another Saudi initiative is the Al-Sakina Campaign for online dialogue with radicals, which is run by the Saudi Ministry for Religious Endowments and Islamic Affairs. Its aim is to prevent the spread of extremist views on the Internet. Some forty *ulama* with Internet skills and with psychiatric training visit extremist websites and forums to chat with participants, urging them to renounce their extremist ideas. The campaign information director Khaled al-Mushawwah said that they had examined and carefully studied 130 websites linked to al-Qaʿeda before engaging participants in discussions. He also claimed that they have succeeded in causing a decline of *takfir* ideology on the websites involved.

Choosing Options

Of these fifteen options, a number are difficult to contemplate because the end would not justify the means. Others, less drastic, are unlikely to succeed. Still others are irrelevant because they cannot be used unless the clock is put back to the days of colonialism or of a different style of warfare. Some are based on false premises and could therefore be counterproductive.

The best hope in the long term would seem to be the route of Islamic reform, a non-violent method which, despite its drawbacks, has the potential to permanently eliminate the threat of Islamic terrorism. This method is closely linked to that of undermining the terrorists' motivation by theological pronouncements. Without a theology to fuel it, Islamic terrorism would eventually shrivel and die. The cone of non-violent Islam would now be resting on its base, stable and very difficult to knock over. Consequently, individuals who interpreted the sources in the traditional way would have a problem trying to gain a following from the Muslim public at large. In seeking to promote a reform of Islam resulting in the removal of its violent tradition and the separation of religion from state, the West would be moving towards a strategy which begins to address the underlying ideology rather than merely combating the numerous individuals who will continue to emerge hydra-like from it. It is vital that the West should begin to give active support to Muslims seeking reform and to challenge the leaders of the Muslim world to take up this cause with urgency. Such a strategy could thus isolate remaining Muslim militants from their support base amongst wider Islamic society. This method however must be pursued with great care, as Western intervention in Muslim affairs, especially Muslim theology, would be seen by many Muslims as being itself a justification for violent *jihad*.

This could create space for more conventional tactical approaches of dealing with the current situation – structures and individuals – at an economic, political, intelligence and military level without such a widespread fear of popular backlash from the Islamic world. Of these more immediate methods the restriction of funding could well prove to be amongst the most effective. Theological arguments with terrorists or potential terrorists in detention could also convince some of alternative, less violent interpretations of Islamic teaching.

Such a multiple approach, coupled with going some way towards meeting certain Muslim grievances, could offer the possibility of a more peaceful future. Nevertheless, the real enemy must be identified, and it is not the terms used, but some doctrines and practices of orthodox Islam as implemented in the contemporary world. The main long-term effort must go towards supporting those Muslims who are engaged in a radical reform of classical orthodox Islam, helping them become the main dominant current in the Muslim world that can eventually assume political power in Muslim states and societies.

18
Conclusion

A vital aspect of what the Chinese general Sun Tzǔ described some two and a half thousand years ago as "the art of war" is the skill now termed "enemy recognition". It is essential for those engaged in war to be able to distinguish foe from friend. Much time in training is given, for example, learning to recognise the silhouette of an enemy tank, from any direction or angle.

Similarly, Sun Tzǔ endorsed the saying:

> If you know the enemy and know yourself, you need not fear the result of a hundred battles.[1088]

Knowing the enemy

Lack of knowledge of their enemy has often created difficulties for non-Muslims under attack by Muslims. Even in the earliest days the Byzantine forces failed to appreciate the nature of their Muslim Arab enemies, and the significance of the fact that they were no longer pagans. In Kaegi's analysis of the early defeats of the Byzantine Christian army by the Muslim Arabs he observes:

> Part of Byzantium's difficulties was generally poor intelligence on the Muslims and failure to act rapidly, properly and decisively on what intelligence they did acquire about the Muslims. Although some Byzantines were immediately aware of the Islamic component in the motivation of Arabs, Byzantines generally underestimated the religious motivation of Arabs as Muslims and understood very little about this new religion.[1089]

A variety of interpretations have been suggested with respect to contemporary Islamic violence. Huntington wrote of Islam's "bloody borders" and interpreted war in its contemporary expression in terms of a clash of civilisations. By contrast, Francis Fukuyama, following his idealistic predictions of a post-Cold War period characterised by liberal democracies, argues that current Islamic violence represents the death throes of a religion unable to compete and coexist with liberal democracy.[1090]

Following the attacks on September 11th 2001 and the US's subsequent overthrow of the Taliban in Afghanistan and Saddam Hussein in Iraq and its pursuit of Al-Qa'eda terrorists worldwide, the debate on the nature of the conflict has taken centre stage. Many Muslims interpret the situation in terms of the West waging war on Islam, while those in the West, particularly the American and British governments, have been at pains to assert that the West is at war only with terrorists and terrorism, not with the household of Islam.

The American government has shown a marked reluctance to define their enemy any more specifically than by such epithets as "criminals", "terrorists", "evildoers", or "a bunch of cold-blooded killers". This vagueness is a serious handicap, for it prevents them from knowing either their enemy or themselves. The careful omission of the word "Islamic" means that the enemy's motives remain a complete mystery as does the enemy's extent. For the activities of militant Muslims are nourished by a whole network of other traditionally-minded Muslims, whose interpretation of Islamic theology encourages them to become supporters of those who actively engage in this kind of violence. Yet President George W. Bush has been at pains to dissociate the recent terrorist attacks in Europe, Asia and the Middle East from Islam:

> Some call this evil Islamic radicalism; others, militant Jihadism; still others, Islamofascism. Whatever it's called, this ideology is very different from the religion of Islam.[1091]

A new lexicon which renames a table as a "chair" does not alter the form or function of the object which has been renamed, but rather is liable to cause confusion. As long as America's enemy remains so ill-defined, America will also find difficulty in identifying allies. The most important of these in the long term would be liberal Muslims who interpret the sources of their faith in a more peaceable manner and are willing to contemplate making adjustments appropriate for modern times and values.[1092] This would include the rejection of such Qur'ans as Hilali and Khan's *Interpretation and Meanings of the Noble Qur'an* with its radical interpretations of the text. (See below.)

A vaguely defined enemy means that war goals too can be no more than vague. Donald Rumsfeld, when he was US Secretary of Defence, declared that his aim was to prevent terrorists "from adversely affecting our way of life". But this is only to tackle the symptoms, not to get to the root of the matter. Unless the militant interpretation of Islamic sources is recognised as the basic cause of Islamic terrorist activities, there is little hope of a lasting solution.[1093] Thankfully this has now begun to happen, with the recent publication of the *Militant Ideology Atlas* by the US Pentagon's Comabating Terrorism Centre. It is an in-depth study of the *jihadi* movement's top thinkers and their most popular writings. This is regarded as the first systematic mapping of the ideology inspiring al-Qa'eda.[1094]

British Foreign Office Minister Mike O'Brien took a similar line to official US government policy by arguing that the conflict hinges on the Kharijis, whom he described as a radical heretical Islamic terrorist group, in contrast to Islam itself which he saw as essentially peaceful and lacking in war-like intentions.[1095]

Likewise, a United Nations initiative is based on the view that the causes of tensions and conflict between the West and the Muslim world are primarily political, not religious. A report issued on November 13th 2006 by a 20-member panel of leaders from a variety of cultural and religious backgrounds, setting out a framework for the new Alliance of Civilisations Initiative, emphasised this view. It was endorsed by the UN Secretary-General Kofi Annan, who said in a written statement, "The problem is not the Koran or the Torah or the Bible. Indeed, I have often said that the problem is never the faith, it is the faithful and how they behave to each other."[1096]

By contrast with the US, UK and UN, a NATO think-tank clearly and specifically named "Islamist terrorism" as "a new shared threat of a global nature that places the very existence of NATO's members at risk".[1097] A 2005 report by the think-tank states that "it is imperative to defend [our freedom and democracies] against Islamist extremism",[1098] indeed the report urges that NATO should "take on responsibility for defeating Islamic jihadism *as its key mission*".[1099]

"War" in Islamic thought

Wars continue to be fought in which the name of Islam as a religion is invoked along with the concept of *jihad*. As this work has sought to show, this reflects the mainstream interpretation of Islamic scholars in the classical period of Islam. Although many Muslim descriptions of their own faith in the context of war have painted a picture of peace and tolerance, denying that war is central to their faith, this does not reflect either mainstream Islamic doctrine or Muslim historical practice.

Throughout the history of Islam, there have been times when Muslims have sought to return back to the original Islam i.e. classical Islam. The institutionalisation of Islam, which saw Islam being controlled by the state authorities – whether the Abbasids, the Ottomans or modern-day Muslim regimes – has often produced a reaction in some Muslims who have sought to return Islam to its pristine origins. These "puritans" or revivalists have included Sunnis, Shi'as and Sufis. For the masses, Islam has more often than not taken on a traditional form, where people believe in God, concern themselves with prayer and with the other basic devotional duties of Islam but do not bother much with legal, political or military requirements. The puritan form has sought to draw such traditionalists back to the classical period by re-emphasising the Qur'an, the *hadith* and the *shari'a* and by instilling within them a sense of the importance of Arab holy history, that is, the first hundred years of Islam. Of course at times there have been rationalists who sought to reinterpret Islam in the light of reason, but they have been relatively few and more often than not have come to a sticky end. (Confusingly, terms like "reform" and "renewal" are used to describe not only liberal reform by rationalists but also puritanical reform by Islamists.)

It is always important to be clear which of these two opposite meanings is intended.) In the modern world, where there is neither caliph nor caliphate, where Muslim states now control Islam, and where the majority of Muslims are traditionalists, we are currently experiencing one of these periodic bouts of renewal and the inevitable accompanying violence. A twenty-first century imam, who feels strongly that Islam is oppressed by the tyrannous and unjust governments of the US and Europe, comments:

> We say it proudly that Islam recognizes the near-inevitability of recourse to war.[1100]

A new and widely disseminated version of the Qur'an makes sure, through footnotes, appendices and interpolations, that modern readers cannot interpret the texts on warfare in any way except literally. For example, the addition of modern equivalents for "steeds of war" in Q 8:60 in the 1996 translation quoted below can be compared with the 1975 translation quoted in chapter 7.

> And make ready against them all you can of power, including steeds of war (tanks, planes, missiles, artillery) to threaten the enemy of Allah and your enemy, and others besides whom, you may not know but Allah does know...[1101]

Islam in its classical interpretation finds it difficult to coexist with the modern world. Such coexistence will remain a challenge unless Islam can examine itself and make modifications. No matter how much is done to improve the socio-economic status of impoverished Muslim populations, no matter how carefully the West tries to avoid causing any kind of "humiliation" which might inflict psychological pain on Muslims, there will still remain theological reasons for Muslims to wage war on non-Muslims, unless Islam itself can change.[1102] This is true despite many Muslim claims to the contrary. It is essential that non-Muslims bear in mind the Islamic doctrine of *taqiyya* and its likely repercussions in terms of spurious claims about the peaceable nature of Islam made to non-Muslim audiences. For example, it is often claimed that *jihad* is limited to defensive war, yet in reality many *jihads* have been offensive, at least in the Western understanding of the word. Such claims are eagerly accepted by those who want to believe them true, and in this way are beginning to shape Western policies. Non-Muslims must listen carefully to Muslims, and distinguish between dissembling Muslims who say that "Islam is peaceful and always has been" and forthright Muslims who say that "Islam began as a violent faith, but we would like to see it become a peaceful one". Non-Muslims must also be able to interpret "coded" language used by some Muslims, where radical ideas are presented but not always recognised and understood as such be a Western audience.

How far the Islamic world is capable of coming to terms with its own history, theology and practice is hard to estimate or predict. As long as moderate Muslims do not acknowledge that there is a problem within Islam itself, not just with a small minority of Islamic radicals, there is little hope of change. Typically Islam finds great difficulty in admitting fault or the need for change. However, there are contemporary Muslims who are beginning to face this reality. Writing in the *Wall Street Journal* Hussain Haqqani, former adviser to Pakistan's prime ministers Benazir Bhutto and Nawaz Sharif, stated:

> Muslims have suffered a great deal from their tendency to shun discussion of ideas, especially those relating to history and religion and their impact on politics. Hard-liners won't tolerate questioning of their views that Islam has nothing to learn from "unbelievers" or that Muslims have a right to subdue other faiths, by force if necessary. The notion of an Islamic polity and state – supported by extremists, questioned by moderates – is also an issue which must be aired.[1103]

The same idea has been expressed by other Muslims, particularly in the Saudi press immediately after the suicide attacks there in May 2003.[1104] The following two examples were published in English-language Saudi periodicals.

> Crushing them [the terrorists] will not be enough. The environment that produced such terrorism has to change. The suicide bombers have been encouraged by the venom of anti-Westernism that has seeped through the Middle East's veins, and the Kingdom is no

less affected. Those who gloat over September 11, those who happily support suicide bombings in Israel and Russia, those who consider non-Muslims less human than Muslims and therefore somehow disposable, all bear part of the responsibility for the Riyadh bombs.[1105]

The time of pretending that radicalism does not exist in Saudi Arabia is long past. How can we expect others to believe that a majority of us are a peace-loving people who denounce extremism and terrorism when some preachers continue to call for the destruction of Jews and Christians, blaming them for all the misery in the Islamic world?[1106]

Similar sentiments appeared in the Arabic-language press as well. For example:

What many of the official sheikhs and columnists – who do not awaken until a catastrophe occurs – say about the phenomenon does not deal with the real causes and roots of the ideology of *jihad*... *jihad* groups find ideological cover in the religious message spread by the mosques and schools.[1107]

If Islamic theologians continue to argue a simple two-fold division of the world into *Dar al-Islam* and *Dar al-Harb*; if they continue to dehumanise the enemy;[1108] if a majority of Muslims continue meanwhile to deny that these things are happening; if Western politicians, media, church leaders and others continue to acquiesce with the assertion that religion is not a factor in terrorist violence and therefore that Islam need not change; it is difficult to see how peace can be achieved unless the whole world is under the rule of Islam.

Understanding the religious framework

Today's secular West often struggles to take religion seriously, and finds it difficult to believe there could be wars of religion in our time. There is a reluctance to take at face value the statements expressing religious commitment and the priority of religion which are made by many Muslim leaders, as for example, the following comment from Pakistan's former president, General Zia-ul-Haq.

The professional soldier in a Muslim army, pursuing the goals of a Muslim state CANNOT become "professional" if in all his activities he does not take on "the colour of Allah". The non-military citizen of a Muslim state must, likewise, be aware of the kind of soldier that his country must produce and the ONLY pattern of war that his country's armed forces may wage.[1109]

It is relevant to note that the institutional motto of the Pakistani army is "Iman, Taqwa and Jihad Fi Sabil-Lilah" [Faith, Piety and *jihad* in the way of God].

In this there is nothing new, as Islam has always emphasised the spiritual aspect of warfare. Ibn Khaldun asserted that military victory depended not only on military preparedness but also on spiritual insight, the latter meaning "the dedication of the commander, the morale of the army, the use of psychological warfare, and informed and inspired decision-making".[1110]

Wars of religion, for example Europe's Thirty Years War (1618-48), have often had appalling consequences, but to pretend that a religious war is not a religious war does nothing to ameliorate the situation. Denying reality is no more effective in dealing with danger than the ostrich's strategy of sticking its head in the sand. It is interesting to note that the analogy of the Thirty Years War has been used recently by a British army officer in the context of the US counter-offensive against al-Qa'eda.

> What is emerging from the counter-offensive is a new thirty years war in which extreme belief systems, old but massively destructive technologies, instable and intolerant societies, strategic crime and the globalisation of all commodities and communications combine to create, potentially at least, a multi-dimensional threat which transcends geography, function and capability.[1111]

It would be helpful if more in the West were to follow this lead and recognise that the "war on terror" is more accurately described as a religious war, for the chief motivation for the terror in question is undoubtedly some version of the religion of Islam.[1112] A deep understanding of the religious framework, world-view and thought processes of the enemy is therefore essential for an ultimate victory.

Following September 11th 2001, many Westerners were eager to make statements dissociating Islam from violence and terrorism, but discovered this argument could not be substantiated. They then tried to argue that although violence and terrorism do occur within Islam they are a mere aberration, not a part of true Islam. This argument likewise was revealed to be invalid. They then tried to distinguish between a moderate Islam and an extremist Islam, but it became apparent that – to echo the words of Jordan's King Abdullah II[1113] – there is no such thing as extremist Islam and no such thing as moderate Islam, for Islam is one. It has a classical formulation which can be regarded as "the standard" from which a range of variants has developed. Finally it has been acknowledged, at least implicitly by at least some,[1114] that violence and terrorism do form an intrinsic part of classical Islam.

Just as it is important to recognise that war-fighting is a central part of the classical understanding of *jihad*,[1115] so it is also important to recognise that physical warfare is **not** the only method now being used to turn *Dar al-Harb* into *Dar al-Islam*. Other methods include the (often deliberately) higher birth rate of Muslim communities in the West compared with their host communities; this could be seen as "demographic *jihad*" and opens up the possibility of, for example, major English cities becoming Islamic and a Kosovo-style conflict developing in the UK. Similarly one could speak of "*hijra jihad*" as Muslims migrate to the West, "economic *jihad*" as they buy Western businesses and encourage a growing *shari'a*-compliance in the banking and financial sectors of the West, and "information *jihad*" as they use media, school curricula and every method in between to re-shape Western thinking on the nature of Islam and Islamic history. It is interesting to note how closely this mirrors the statement quoted in chapter 10 by a Pakistani brigadier of the military being just one aspect of the total strategy of *jihad*.[1116] We have already seen in chapter 1 how Libya's Colonel Qadhafi, counting the growing number of Muslims in Europe, has predicted a victory for Islam in the continent "without swords, without guns, without conquests". He concluded his tally of European Muslim millions, by saying:

Europe is in a predicament, and so is America. They should agree to become Islamic in the course of time, or else declare war on the Muslims.[1117]

Although Islam is one, there is still an important distinction which must be drawn between Islam the ideology and Muslims the people who follow it. While Islam the ideology may cause great hardship and suffering to non-Muslims it also causes great hardship and suffering to many Muslims (particularly women). If an "enemy" is to be defined, then the enemy is not Muslims but the classical interpretation of Islam.

The cold war paradigm

When confronted with the communist threat in the cold war era, efforts at dividing moderate Marxists from radical Marxists were not really effective. Only the determination to face Marxism as a totalitarian expansionist ideology in all its manifestations, an ideology that needed to be defeated, eventually brought about the downfall of the communist threat.

In a similar way, Islam in its classical, orthodox form must be recognised as the seedbed of the radical phenomenon. Islamists believe that the time of Muslim weakness is past and the time of victory is at hand, a classical Islamic doctrine of *hijra* – based on Muhammad's example – that has fuelled the contemporary Islamic resurgence in all its various forms. The non-Muslim world must be clear as to the real identity of the enemy, and must give their support **not** to the orthodox Muslim majority who bear the seeds of radicalism within them, but to the progressive liberal Muslim minority who are calling for a root-and-branch reform of Islam. This minority faces enormous opposition from both radicals and mainstream orthodox, for they have recognised that it is mainstream Islam, as understood by most Muslims today, that needs to be reformed. Terms like *jihad* must be given a new content that clearly rejects traditional interpretations and focuses instead on an individual spiritual and moral struggle. Orthodox concepts of *shari'a* need to be reformed so as to remove their potential for violence and oppression.

The dangers of wishful thinking

Genuine Muslim reform of Islamic concepts must not be confused with non-Muslim wishful thinking. It seems that relativistic post-modern attitudes to norms and values are making it difficult for many Westerners to recognise the dangers of the *jihad* aspects of traditional Islamic theology and its Islamist expressions. Lewis Carroll, in *Through the Looking Glass*, humorously described this relativistic attitude to objective facts, words, texts and values.

> "When *I* use a word," Humpty Dumpty said, in rather a scornful tone, "it means just what I choose it to mean - neither more nor less."

> "The question is," said Alice, "whether you *can* make words mean different things."

> "The question is," said Humpty Dumpty, "which is to be master - that's all."

Words can mean whatever the speaker wants them to mean, irrespective of the generally understood meaning. Humpty Dumpty's attitude was a ludicrous joke for Carroll's first readers in the nineteenth century, but now in the twenty-first century it is not so very different from the mindset of many Westerners.

Another memorable quote from the same book illustrates another twenty-first century danger.

> "I can't believe *that!*" said Alice.

> "Can't you?" the Queen said in a pitying tone. "Try again: draw a long breath, and shut your eyes."

> Alice laughed. "There's no use trying," she said: "one *can't* believe impossible things."

> "I daresay you haven't had much practice," said the Queen. "When I was your age, I always did it for half-an-hour a day. Why, sometimes I've believed as many as six impossible things before breakfast..."

The skill of convincing oneself that the impossible is true does not provide a good starting point for analysing a problem and finding effective solutions. There is a real danger of substituting our wishful views for reality. It is worse than useless to pretend that Islam is like a post-modern contemporary Western-style religion limiting itself to the private sphere of ethics. Muslims understand the Western mind very well, and the West renders itself very vulnerable if it cannot or will not understand how Muslims think.

The West must also acknowledge that it does have power to effect change and not consider itself helpless in the face of the Islamic challenge. During the Cold War, President Ronald Reagan reversed his predecessors' policies and integrated "economic warfare" and "political wafare" into the military struggle with the Soviet Union.[1118] Like the Reagan doctrine, a line must now be drawn in the sand, using a combination of economic, political and military methods, to protect Western liberties and the Western way of life from Islamism. Very few Western governments have yet been willing to do this, although Denmark and Australia have recently taken bold steps in this direction.

Finding Solutions

Having identified the causes of Islamic terrorism, the question remains as to how best to work for peace. Islamic terrorists are soldier-politician-theologians, always attacking, using speed and surprise, fighting on a global "battlefield", keener to establish spiritual bases in people's minds than geographical bases, using subversion, with no code of conduct, attacking civilians as much as military targets, using propaganda, economics and politics as well as military means, and seeing "peace" only as an opportunity to change strategy. Fear is part of the arsenal of a terrorist and, following the precepts and examples of early Islam, one of the main strategies of the Islamic terrorists has been creating terror. In this they have been eminently successful, for a relatively small number of attacks on Western targets have had a strong psychological impact, making Western populations jittery, fearful and extremely anxious to please. The result is

that, through increasing anti-terror legislation and precautions
– understandable as this is -, Western societies are being "locked
down" to the point where the very freedoms which have made
the West unique are now being eroded.

Given the accessibility of the materials necessary to create
weapons of mass destruction (chemical, biological or nuclear),
the current growth in radical Islam, and the calls even by
moderate Muslim leaders such as Malaysia's then prime minister
Mahathir Mohamad for technological advance in weaponry, it is
imperative that violence in Islam be addressed. The probability
that Iran under President Mahmoud Ahmadinejad will have
nuclear weaponry in a few years' time is rightfully causing grave
alarm in the Western world.

No working with Islamists

Clearly there should be no more repetitions of Western powers
deliberately raising up Islamists for their own purposes, as the US
did in Afghanistan in the 1980s. The American mistake seems
to have been that they regarded religion as a neutral force and
thought that they could channel religious conviction to serve their
own agenda without realising how the Islamist agenda would
itself gather momentum from the impetus they had given it. This
fundamental mistake has been made by many other governments,
who believed that they could use or work with Islamists, not
realising the likely future effects of giving assistance to the Islamist
cause. The ongoing consequences continue to be seen in events
such as September 11th 2001.

The current British policy of accepting groups such as the
Muslim Brotherhood as legitimate and using them to defeat
those considered to be extremists is foolhardy, for in the end the
objectives of the Muslim Brotherhood are not dissimilar from
those of the extremists; it is only their methods which differ. Such
groups can often practise *taqiyya*; they feign non-violence and
democratic values when in fact these are just an interim measure
to gain acceptance and power after which they will be abandoned.
Furthermore such a policy pits the British and other Western

governments against Middle Eastern governments who recognise such groups for what they are and are seeking to suppress them. The West is therefore in the invidious position of wanting the Muslim world to embace the West's war against terror whilst at the same time the West itself is embracing those who are perceived by Muslim countries as potential terrorists.

Military and economic measures

In the short term, it is instructive to recall that force has in the past managed to reverse the Islamic expansion, when no other method has been effective. Sheikh Ibn Uthaymeen's reasoning that suicide bombing was not legitimate *because it did not help the Islamic cause* adds further weight to arguments for a physically strong response to Islamic terrorism.

A physical response would formerly have meant simply a military response, but in today's world another way physically to limit the activities of Islamic terrorists would be by financial restrictions to prevent the flow of funds to terrorist organisations. Economic power, in the form of trade sanctions or trade agreements, could be used to exert force indirectly by encouraging Muslim governments to curtail the activities of radicals and the promulgation of radical ideologies within their borders. Another possibility would be to make security treaties conditional on the protected government implementing certain policies, for example, promoting a more liberal kind of Islam. Furthermore, the dependence on oil which has led the West to turn a blind eye to Saudi Arabia's activities needs to be reconsidered. Saudi Arabia is using its vast oil wealth to promote Wahhabism worldwide, but it goes unchallenged by the West. Has the West the courage to confront Saudi Arabia on this? Should this be a further reason to develop alternative forms of energy so as to reduce the West's dependence on Middle Eastern oil?

The NATO think-tank report which acknowledges so clearly the Islamic nature of the threat to the West also recognises that a military response needs to be accompanied by other tactics:

> In our view, terrorism is only the war-like part of a much more far-reaching offensive against the liberal and democratic world.

> And it can be fought perfectly through military means, provided that the employment of military resources is set within the framework of a wider strategy, one that brings together other State and societal resources.[1119]

Former Spanish president José María Aznar, who headed the NATO think-tank, had the previous year listed "seven theses" for tackling Islamic terrorism. In these he indicates that the military is important but not the only approach: know the enemy, understand we are at war, pursue an active policy (not containment or appeasement), recognise that we are fighting against an ideology as well as against a group or movement, accept that the central front of the war is Iraq, international cooperation is essential, and continue to combat old forms of terrorism as well as the new ones.[1120]

Bearing in mind what we have described as demographic *jihad*, *hijra jihad*, economic *jihad*, information *jihad* and similar methods for Islamising the non-Muslim world, it is important to use not only counter-terrorism and other military methods, but also methods relevant to the other Islamic challenges to the West. These would include political warfare, economic warfare and psychological warfare.[1121]

Cutting the links between religion and violence

In the long term, however, the most realistic way to provide a permanent, solution to the problem of Islamic violence is the liberal reform of the Islamic doctrine of *jihad* i.e. for one of the peaceable non-classical variations to supersede the classical interpretation and to be acknowledged as the new norm. Such reform must also include a clear separation of religion from state. There are already the seeds of liberal reform within the Muslim world, and it is to be hoped that such reform will develop and come to maturity. While external factors (military, economic, political pressure from the non-Muslim world etc.) might help to speed this process, there is no intrinsic reason why such reform could not take place independently. The military defeat of Islam is not a necessary prerequisite for a liberal reform of the faith and ideology.

The United States Institute of Peace, which describes itself as "an independent, non-partisan, national institution established and funded by Congress" has recommended that the US support such "Islamic renewal". (It must be assumed that when the Institute uses the term "Islamic renewal" or "Islamic reform" it is a liberal progressive change which is referred to, rather than change in the other direction.)

> Current U.S. efforts to fight terrorism, promote democratic change, and improve America's image in Muslim countries are insufficient because they do not pay attention to the religious debate in the Muslim world. The United States could address these challenges by using the enormous, yet neglected, normative capital of Islamic reformist traditions in partnership with viable and credible Muslim partners.[1122]

It is unclear whether this institute's recognition of the role played by Islamic ideology in terrorism reflects a change in government policy or is simply a recommendation to them.

This type of reform of Islam would not, of course, mean a complete cessation of all violence from Islamic contexts, but it would mean a cutting of the link between religion and violence. The historic churches like the Church of England are often said to be built on scripture, tradition and reason. So too is Islam, built as it is on Qur'an, *hadith* and *ijtihad*. It is the third factor, reason, which is important in ameliorating the more strident aspects of scripture and particularly of tradition, and which must be encouraged within Islam, provided always that it leads to a more liberal interpretation of the sources.

Elements for reform

A liberal reform of Islam could begin by recognising that Islam has borrowed many elements from other traditions, which it then Islamised and claimed as its own. This would liberate Muslims from the hobbling belief that every element of their faith is unique and special to Islam, thus making it easier for them to be open to the possibility of change. It should also recognise that the Qur'an was written in an evolving context and its attitude reflects the changing situation of the first Muslims.

A liberal reform of Islam would need to find a new means of psychological resonance with the general Muslim public. Islamists have used terms like *hijra* and *umma* to enhance the sense of Islamic identity, to help Muslims to glory in their faith, to produce in the Muslim community a feeling of self-worth and of confidence that centuries of humiliation are now to be overturned with the rediscovery of the roots of their faith and the honour which is its due.

It would even be conceivable for Islam to reform on the one point of violence alone if other aspects of liberal Islam were unacceptable to the majority. Perhaps the Ahmadiyyas have shown the way in their total rejection of violent *jihad* while remaining true to their understanding of the tenets of Islam.

Islam takes great pride in the concept of the *umma,* the whole body of Muslims worldwide. The received wisdom is that Islam displays a unity and cohesion that gives it immense strength. This was certainly what the Byzantine armies experienced when they found to their surprise that their normal tactic of inducing some of their Arab enemies to defect no longer worked now that those Arabs had become Muslims. But the idea of Muslim unity continuing throughout the succeeding centuries is very much open to question. Modern Muslims tend to believe that any tensions within the *umma* are a result of Western conspiracy despite the fact that, as this work has sought to show, there is a huge range of theological differences within Islam, not to mention ethnic and national differences.[1123] Furthermore Islamic history contains many examples of distinctions drawn within the *umma* right from the beginning. Even during Muhammad's lifetime, there was a distinction made between the Muslims who had moved from Mecca to Medina with him (*muhajirun*) and the Muslims who were native-born Medinan (*ansar,* helpers).[1124] The *umma* was not so much a super-tribal loyalty but rather the domination of the other Arab tribes by the Quraish, the tribe to which Muhammad and the first Muslims belonged.[1125] Islamic history has been characterised by inter-ethnic (Arabs, Turks, Persians) and intersectarian (Sunni-Shi'a) conflicts. Indeed, some scholars, such as van Ess, assert that the *umma* concept had little significance in early Islam and has gained its current importance only in recent times.[1126] Even today many of these historical tensions still exist, as for example seen in the horrific Sunni-Shi'a conflict in Iraq. The growing development of a Shi'a arc is posing a severe threat to the Sunni parts of the Middle East, with possible global ramifications. This internecine conflict is itself producing a reaction in peaceable Muslims who are revolted by the daily carnage and are increasingly disillusioned with the religion which produces such hatred, cruelty and violence. The vicious sectarian conflict has not prevented the age-old ethnic hatreds from re-emerging, as for example, Arabs against Persians or Arabs against Kurds.

Arab Islam is dominant in the Muslim world today and is generally considered normative. This is due to the fact that the heavenly original of the Qur'an is believed to be written in Arabic and to the fact that Muhammad and the first Muslims were Arabs. Increasingly the issues facing the Arab world (such as the Palestinian issue) are shaping the non-Arab Muslim world as well, and arguably are reinforcing the classical doctrine of *jihad*. Left to its own devices, and without the constant stimulus of Arab grudges, non-Arab Islam might develop a more peaceable doctrine. Indonesian Islam did so, as manifested by the Indonesian doctrine of Pancasila which drew on China and India as well as the Middle East to provide a range of acceptable religious beliefs, both Muslim and non-Muslim. Current moves to impose Middle Eastern Islam (that is, classical Islam) as the standard in places like Indonesia are creating tensions with non-Muslim minorities in societies which had previously enjoyed inter-communal harmony. It is also creating tensions with those Muslims who reject the Arab Islamic norm.

For the first time in history the Muslim world itself has globalised to such an extent that its influence is no longer limited to *Dar al-Islam*, but through economic and trade agreements, business deals, financial products and other methods, it can exert great influence in the non-Muslim world. Yet at the same time its own internal divisions, whether sectarian, ethnic or ideological, threaten to bring it tumbling down. Ultimately Islamism poses a far greater threat to Islamic societies than it does to the rest of the world, at least in the short term. Where Islamism has been contained, such as Turkey, Tunisia or Syria, it has been by means of military or other forceful suppression. Democracy more often than not liberates Islamism and catapults it to power.

What the West can do – and what it cannot do

The year 1979, with the Iranian Revolution leading to the Iran-Iraq war, the Soviet invasion of Afghanistan, and Juhayman al-'Utaybi's attack on the Holy Mosque at Mecca, has proved to be a significant turning point in the modern development of Islamic radicalism. For Muslims this was no coincidence.[1127] This saw Muslim scholars looking back to Islam's original sources in order to reform their faith as well as looking forward to the End Times and the final battle.

> Terrible mistakes were made. We failed to stop the looting, failed to seal the borders, and we disbanded the Iraqi army. We were blind. We were strong but we weren't smart.[1128]

This failure is fundamentally a failure to understand, which has blighted statesmen, politicians, academics and soldiers alike. Donald Rumsfeld, towards the end of his tenure as US Secretary of Defence, conceded:

> If I were grading I would say we probably deserve a 'D' or a 'D-plus' as a country as to how well we're doing in the battle of ideas that's taking place in the world today.[1129]

The West must recognise the mistakes it has made, both in colonial and in present history, in the way we have fought wars and in the way in which we have sought to dominate the Muslim world. This humiliation of Muslims, which they feel so acutely in the present context, is due not only to the West's geo-political economic interests but also to military intervention in Iraq and Afghanistan and the pursuit of the "war on terror". This has resulted in Muslims reaching back to classical Islam as the basis of their core identity and has led to the development of radical

Islamism. It is with greater sensitivity and understanding that the West must now engage the world of Islam.

Whilst this book focuses on the theological basis of radicalisation, the wider political economic interests as described in chapter 1 should not be forgotten, for they play a major part in forming the basis for which classical Islam can be used as the justification for violence.

Yet the baby must not be thrown out with the bath water, as the chastened West seeks to atone for and learn from its mistakes. At present the West is too hesitant to assert its Judaeo-Christian culture or indeed to assert other non-Muslim cultures and traditions now found in the West, for example, Hindu and Buddhist. Whilst war-fighting will no doubt be necessary, the West must recognise that governance, economics and diplomatic skill will all play key roles in winning the long war against classical Islam. It must pay particular attention to the growing number of liberals in Islam. It must also pay attention to the other non-Muslim cultures and societies (particularly India, China, South America and the many parts of Africa) who are facing the challenge of Islam, just as the West is. Where war-fighting is necessary, it will not be by classical fixed battle formations but fourth generation warfare and asymmetrical fighting. It will be fighting an enemy that is defined by ideology and governed by rules of engagement which are very different from those of the West.

If the West wants to assist in the long-term solution of promoting a non-violent kind of Islam, it must do so with great care or its well-meant efforts could be counter-productive. When Mike O'Brien argued that Islamic violence is rooted in a radical heretical movement, the Kharijis, his comments were opposed by some in the Middle East who pleaded with him not to promote that interpretation. What O'Brien did not realise was that making culprits of the Kharijis has given them enormous credibility with certain sections of the Muslim community in the Muslim world. The Kharijis have become a focal point for dissent in the Middle East. The Khariji paradigm is now used by Wahhabis and others to justify violent opposition to legitimate Muslim rulers who are deemed to be autocratic, corrupt or in cahoots with the West.

441

Another potential pitfall for Western efforts to foster non-violent forms of Islam is exemplified by Sir Sayyid Ahmad Khan in India. While he was happy to cooperate with and submit to British rule in the nineteenth century, other Muslims have bitterly criticised him for this. For example Jamal al-Din al-Afghani (1838-97) wrote in his *Al-Urwah Al-Wuthqa*:

> The English authorities saw in Sir Sayyid Ahmad Khan a useful instrument to demoralize the Muslims so they began to praise and honour him and helped him build his college at Aligarh and called it the college of the Muslims in order that it be a trap to catch the sons of the believers and spread unbelief amongst them. Materialists like Sir Sayyid Ahmad Khan are even worse than the materialists in Europe for those in Western countries who abandon their religion still retain their patriotism and do not lack zeal to defend their fatherland while Sir Sayyid Ahmad Khan and his friends represent foreign despotism as acceptable.[1130]

It would be useful for Western governments to remember the strong resentment amongst some Muslims to British efforts to encourage Sir Sayyid Ahmad Khan's college in India.

The strategy of trying to enlist cooperative Muslims in promoting a submissive, non-violent type of Islam is in many ways similar to what the French authorities tried to do when they created a national council of Muslims in 2003. It is not unlike what the British did when they created the Muslim Council of Britain in 1997. But both organisations were quickly taken over by extremists. The mere fact of being a non-Muslim initiative can doom such a plan to failure from the start.

The part which the non-Muslim world can play in the reform of Islam can therefore never be more than indirect. Ultimately it is for the Muslim world to address the issues and consider what changes can be brought about. Reform cannot be imposed on Islam from outside. A Saudi security expert has stated clearly that it is not for the West to try to change the Muslim world; any movement for change must come from within Muslims themselves.[1131] His opinion is typical. But non-Muslims can, with great care, wisdom and diplomacy, help to create an atmosphere conducive to finding a solution. Part of this would be simply to refrain from undermining the stance of liberal Muslims i.e. to refrain from making statements to the effect that Islam is already wholly peaceable and does not need to be reformed. More positively, support could be given to the creation of liberal Muslim networks.[1132] Another possibility would be supporting efforts towards growth in mutual understanding: this would mean non-Muslims beginning to grasp the reality of Islam and how different it is from secular materialism as well as from Judaeo-Christian traditions, and Muslims beginning to understand the basis of democracy, individual freedom of conscience and other values which are so alien to classical Islam. The importance of non-Muslims using appropriate, sensitive and tactful language cannot be overestimated; great damage can and has been done by careless and insensitive comments and vocabulary, indicative of a lack of understanding of cultural and religious factors. (On the other hand, as has already been explained, a different kind of damage can be done by using inaccurate Islamic vocabulary as suggested by the proponents of the "new lexicon".)

Consideration of effective methodology to promote a new doctrine of *jihad* side-steps the most important question of all: what should that new doctrine be? At one extreme would be pacifism, but that would be to impose on Islam a restraint which mainstream Christianity has never imposed on itself in its standard teaching on just war. So where should the boundaries be drawn? Self-defence? But how would that be defined? Is there any place for the concept of *Dar al-Harb*? Can peace treaties with non-Muslims be permanent? What about the conduct of war? Civilian casualties seem to have become an intrinsic part of modern warfare, so what should Islam say about this today? It is the author's hope that the right use of force of various kinds, coupled with good diplomacy, may nudge the Islamic world forward into a debate on this subject, leading to a reformation of this area of Islamic teaching, and thus to a more peaceful and stable world.

Ultimately to gain victory over the Islamists will require the exercise of the will and a right understanding of the situation. Do those engaged in such a task have the necessary will to achieve the end required? Do they properly understand what they are up against? Furthermore do they have the spiritual, the moral and the cultural resources as well as the technological resources and the courage and perseverance to win what may well prove to be a very protracted war?

Appendix 1: Traditional Divisions in Islam

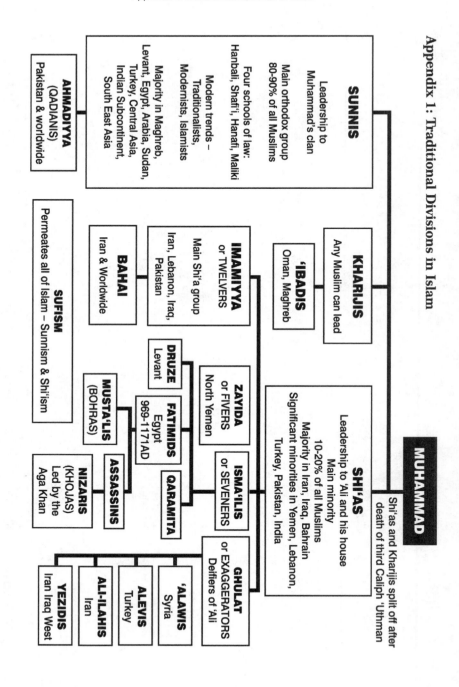

MUHAMMAD

Shi'as and Kharijis split off after death of third Caliph 'Uthman

SUNNIS

Leadership to Muhammad's clan

Main orthodox group 80-90% of all Muslims

Four schools of law: Hanbali, Shafi'i, Hanafi, Maliki

Modern trends – Traditionalists, Modernists, Islamists

Majority in Maghreb, Levant, Egypt, Arabia, Sudan, Turkey, Central Asia, Indian Subcontinent, South East Asia

AHMADIYYA (QADIANIS) Pakistan & worldwide

KHARIJIS

Any Muslim can lead

'IBADIS Oman, Maghreb

SHI'AS

Leadership to 'Ali and his house

Main minority 10-20% of all Muslims

Majority in Iran, Iraq, Bahrain Significant minorities in Yemen, Lebanon, Turkey, Pakistan, India

IMAMIYYA or TWELVERS

Main Shi'a group

Iran, Lebanon, Iraq, Pakistan

BAHAI Iran & Worldwide

ZAYDIA or FIVERS North Yemen

DRUZE Levant

ISMA'ILIS or SEVENERS

FATIMIDS Egypt 969-1171AD

MUSTA'LIS (BOHRAS)

QARAMITA

NIZARIS (KHOJAS) Led by the Aga Khan

ASSASSINS

GHULAT or EXAGGERATORS Deifiers of 'Ali

'ALAWIS Syria

ALEVIS Turkey

ALI-ILAHIS Iran

YEZIDIS Iran Iraq West

SUFISM Permeates all of Islam – Sunnism & Shi'ism

446

Appendix 2: Modern trends in Islam

Pre-modern revivals –
Sirihindi (India 1564-1624), 'Abd-Al-Wahhab (Arabia 1703-1792)

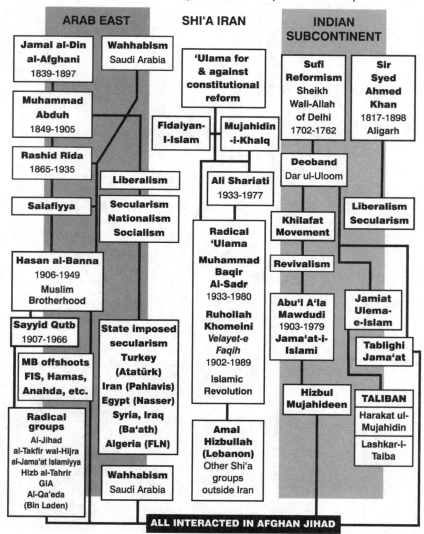

ARAB EAST		SHI'A IRAN	INDIAN SUBCONTINENT	
Jamal al-Din al-Afghani 1839-1897	**Wahhabism** Saudi Arabia	**'Ulama for & against constitutional reform**	**Sufi Reformism** Sheikh Wali-Allah of Delhi 1702-1762	**Sir Syed Ahmed Khan** 1817-1898 Aligarh
Muhammad Abduh 1849-1905		**Fidaiyan-I-Islam** / **Mujahidin-i-Khalq**		
Rashid Rida 1865-1935			**Deoband** Dar ul-Uloom	
Salafiyya	**Liberalism**	**Ali Shariati** 1933-1977		**Liberalism Secularism**
	Secularism Nationalism Socialism	**Radical 'Ulama**	**Khilafat Movement**	
Hasan al-Banna 1906-1949 Muslim Brotherhood		**Muhammad Baqir Al-Sadr** 1933-1980	**Revivalism**	
Sayyid Qutb 1907-1966	**State imposed secularism Turkey (Atatürk) Iran (Pahlavis) Egypt (Nasser) Syria, Iraq (Ba'ath) Algeria (FLN)**	**Ruhollah Khomeini** *Velayet-e Faqih* 1902-1989 Islamic Revolution	**Abu'l A'la Mawdudi** 1903-1979 **Jama'at-i-Islami**	**Jamiat Ulema-e-Islam** **Tablighi Jama'at**
MB offshoots FIS, Hamas, Anahda, etc.				
Radical groups Al-Jihad al-Takfir wal-Hijra al-Jama'at Islamiyya Hizb al-Tahrir GIA Al-Qa'eda (Bin Laden)		**Amal Hizbullah (Lebanon)** Other Shi'a groups outside Iran	**Hizbul Mujahideen**	**TALIBAN** Harakat ul-Mujahidin Lashkar-i-Taiba
	Wahhabism Saudi Arabia			

ALL INTERACTED IN AFGHAN JIHAD

447

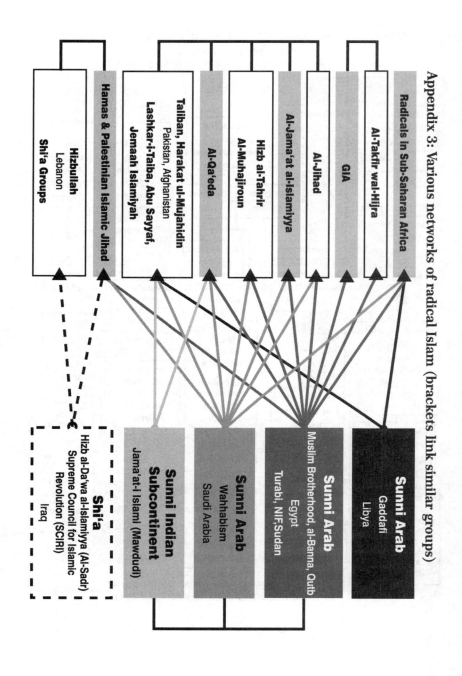

Appendix 3: Various networks of radical Islam (brackets link similar groups)

Appendix 4
"Bin Laden" audiotape

This is a translated transcript of an audiotape said to be of Osama bin Laden, aired by al-Jazeera satellite television channel on 4 January 2004, text published by BBC news.[1133]

From Osama Bin Laden to his brothers and sisters in the entire Islamic nation: May God's peace, mercy and blessings be upon you.

My message to you concerns inciting and continuing to urge for *jihad* to repulse the grand plots that have been hatched against our nation, especially since some of them have appeared clearly, such as the occupation of the Crusaders, with the help of the apostates, of Baghdad and the house of the caliphate, under the trick of weapons of mass destruction.

There is also the fierce attempt to destroy the al-Aqsa Mosque and destroy the *jihad* and the *mujahideen* in beloved Palestine by employing the trick of the roadmap and the Geneva peace initiative.

The Americans' intentions have also become clear in statements about the need to change the beliefs, curricula and morals of the Muslims to become more tolerant, as they put it.

In clearer terms, it is a religious-economic war.

The occupation of Iraq is a link in the Zionist-Crusader chain of evil.

Gulf states 'next'
Then comes the full occupation of the rest of the Gulf states to set the stage for controlling and dominating the whole world. For the big powers believe that the Gulf and the Gulf states are the

key to controlling the world due to the presence of the largest oil reserves there.

O Muslims: The situation is serious and the misfortune is momentous. By God, I am keen on safeguarding your religion and your worldly life. So, lend me your ears and open up your hearts to me so that we may examine these pitch-black misfortunes and so that we may consider how we can find a way out of these adversities and calamities.

The West's occupation of our countries is old, yet new. The struggle between us and them, the confrontation, and clashing began centuries ago, and will continue because the ground rules regarding the fight between right and falsehood will remain valid until Judgement Day.

Take note of this ground rule regarding this fight. There can be no dialogue with occupiers except through arms.

This is what we need today, and what we should seek. Islamic countries in the past century were not liberated from the Crusaders' military occupation except through *jihad* in the cause of God.

Under the pretext of fighting terrorism, the West today is doing its utmost to tarnish *jihad* and kill anyone seeking *jihad*. The West is supported in this endeavour by hypocrites. This is because they all know that *jihad* is the effective power to foil all their conspiracies.

Jihad is the path, so seek it. This is because if we seek to deter them with any means other than Islam, we would be like the one who goes round in circles. We would also be like our forefathers, the al-Ghasasinah [Arab people who lived in a state historically located in the north-west of the Persian empire]. The concern of their seniors was to be appointed officers for the Romans and to be named kings in order to safeguard the interests of the Romans by killing their brothers of the peninsula's Arabs. Such is the case of the new al-Ghasasinah; namely, Arab rulers.

Words of warning

Muslims: If you do not punish them for their sins in Jerusalem and Iraq, they shall defeat you because of your failure. They will also rob you of land of *al-Haramayn* [Mecca and Medina]. Today [they robbed you] of Baghdad and tomorrow they will rob you of Riyadh and so forth unless God deems otherwise.

Sufficient unto us is God.

What then is the means to stop this tremendous onslaught? In such hard times, some reformers maintain that all popular and official forces should unite and that all government forces should unite with all their peoples. Everyone would do what is needed from him in order to ward off this Crusader-Zionist onslaught.

The question strongly raised is: Are the governments in the Islamic world capable of pursuing this duty of defending the faith and nation and renouncing allegiance to the United States?

The calls by some reformers are strange. They say that the path to righteousness and defending the country and people passes though the doors of those rulers. I tell those reformers: If you have an excuse for not pursing *jihad*, it does not give you the right to depend on the unjust ones, thus becoming responsible for your sins as well as the sins of those who you misguide.

Fear God for your sake and for your nation's sake.

God does not need your flattery of dictators for the sake of God's religion.

Arabs 'succumbed to US pressure'

The Gulf states proved their total inability to resist the Iraqi forces. They sought help from the Crusaders, led by the United States, as is well known. How can these states stand up to the United States? In short, these states came to America's help and backed it in its attack against an Arab state which is bound to them with covenants of joint defence agreements. These covenants were reiterated at the Arab League just a few days before the US attack, only to violate them in full. This shows their positions on the nation's basic causes. These regimes wavered too much before taking a stand on using force and attacking Iraq. At times they absolutely rejected participation and at other times they linked this with UN agreement. Then they went back to their first option. In fact, the lack of participation was in line with the domestic desire of these states. However, they finally submitted and succumbed to US pressure and opened their air, land and sea bases to contribute toward the US campaign, despite the immense repercussions of this move.

Most important of these repercussions is that this is a sin against one of the Islamic tenets.

Saddam arrest

Most important and dangerous in their view was that they feared that the door would be open for bringing down

dictatorial regimes by armed forces from abroad, especially after they had seen the arrest of their former comrade in treason and agentry to the United States when it ordered him to ignite the first Gulf war against Iran, which rebelled against it.

The war consumed everything and plunged the area in a maze from which they have not emerged to this day. They are aware that their turn will come. They do not have the will to make the difficult decision to confront the aggression, in addition to their belief that they do not possess the material resources for that. Indeed, they were prevented from establishing a large military force when they were forced to sign secret pledges and documents long ago. In short, the ruler who believes in some of the above-mentioned deeds cannot defend the country. How can he do so if he believes in all of them and has done that time and again?

Those who believe in the principle of supporting the infidels over Muslims and leave the blood, honour and property of their brothers to be available to their enemy in order to remain safe, claiming that they love their brothers but are being forced to take such a path - of course this compulsion cannot be regarded as legitimate - are in fact qualified to take the same course against one another in the Gulf states. Indeed, this principle is liable to be embraced within the same state itself.

Those who read and understood the history of kings throughout history know that they are capable of committing more than these concessions, except those who enjoyed the mercy of God. Indeed, the rulers have practically started to sell out the sons of the land by pursuing and imprisoning them and by unjustly and wrongly accusing them of becoming like the *Khawarij* [Kharijis] sect who held Muslims to be infidels and by committing the excesses of killing them. We hold them to be martyrs and God will judge them.

All of this happened before the Riyadh explosions in Rabi al-Awwal of this year [around May 2003].

This campaign came within a drive to implement the US orders in the hope that they will win its blessings.

'Miserable situation'

Based on the above, the extent of the real danger, which the region in general and the Arabian Peninsula in particular, is being exposed to, has appeared. It has become clear that the rulers are not qualified to apply the religion and defend the Muslims. In fact, they have provided evidence that they are implementing the schemes of the enemies of the nation and religion and that they are qualified to abandon the countries and peoples.

Now, after we have known the situation of the rulers, we should examine the policy which they have been pursuing. Anyone who examines the policy of those rulers will easily see that they follow their whims and desires and their personal interests and Crusader loyalties.

Therefore, the flaw does not involve a secondary issue, such as personal corruption that is confined to the palace of the ruler. The flaw is in the very approach.

This happened when a malicious belief and destructive principle spread in most walks of life, to the effect that absolute supremacy and obedience were due to the ruler and not to the religion of God.

In other countries, they have used the guise of parliaments and democracy.

Thus, the situation of all Arab countries suffers from great deterioration in all walks of life, in religious and worldly matters.

We have reached this miserable situation because many of us lack the correct and comprehensive understanding of the religion of Islam. Many of us understand Islam to mean performing some acts of worship, such as prayer and fasting. Despite the great importance of these rituals, the religion of Islam encompasses all the affairs of life, including religious and worldly affairs, such as economic, military and political affairs, as well as the scales by which we weigh the actions of men - rulers, *'ulama* and others - and how to deal with the ruler in line with the rules set by God for him and which the ruler should not violate.

Therefore, it becomes clear to us that the solution lies in adhering to the religion of God, by which God granted us pride in the past centuries and installing a strong and faithful leadership that applies the Qur'an among us and raises the true banner of *jihad*.

The honest people who are concerned about this situation, such as the *'ulama*, leaders who are obeyed among their people, dignitaries, notables and merchants should get together and meet in a safe place away from the shadow of these suppressive regimes and form a council for *Ahl al-Hall wa al-'aqd* [literally those who loose and bind; reference to honest, wise and righteous people who can appoint or remove a ruler in Islamic tradition] to fill the vacuum caused by the religious invalidation of these regimes and their mental deficiency.

The right to appoint an imam [leader] is for the nation.

The nation also has the right to make him correct his course if he deviates from it and to remove him if he does something that warrants this, such as apostasy and treason.

This temporary council should be made up of the minimum number of available personnel, without [word indistinct] the rest of the nation, except what the religion allows in case of necessity, until the number is increased when the situation improves, God willing.

Their policy should be based on the book of God [the Qur'an] and the *sunna* [customs] of his Prophet [Muhammad], God's peace and blessings be upon him. They should start by directing the Muslims to the important priorities at this critical stage and lead them to a safe haven, provided that their top priority should be uniting opinions under the word of monotheism and defending Islam and its people and countries and declaring a general mobilisation in the nation to prepare for repulsing the raids of the Romans, which started in Iraq and no-one knows where they will end.

God suffices us and he is the best supporter.

Appendix 5
Editorial in *Al-Masaa*
(2 February 2004)

Al-Masaa is an Egyptian government daily newspaper. This editorial was published on 2 February 2004 and supports Palestinian suicide attacks, even if children are killed. The English translation is from MEMRI Special Dispatch No. 658 (6 February 2004)

We ask again, why do the various Palestinian organisations insist on publishing the name of everyone who carries out a martyrdom operation against the Zionist entity?

We have no argument regarding the question of the legitimacy of these operations, because they are considered a powerful weapon used by the Palestinians against an enemy with no morality or religion, [an enemy] who has deadly weapons prohibited by international law, that is not deterred from using them against the defenceless Palestinian people.

Even if during [a martyrdom operation] civilians or children are killed - the blame does not fall upon the Palestinians, but on those who forced them to turn to this modus operandi.

Ultimately, we should bless every Palestinian man or woman who goes calmly to carry out a martyrdom operation, in order to receive a reward in the Hereafter, sacrificing her life for her religion and her homeland and knowing that she will never return from this operation.

But at the same time, we wonder about the reason for publishing the names of those who carry out the [martyrdom] operations; [this publishing] is a valuable gift that the Palestinian resistance gives the Zionist entity, since as soon as it receives this gift, the armies of the [Zionist] entity hasten to the home of the martyr's family, wounded by the loss of its son, in order to multiply its pain by destroying its home. Moreover, the home of the martyr's family is always destroyed negligently, causing serious damage to or the collapse of the neighbour's home.

We ask the leaders of these organisations: Give us one good reason for publishing the names of the martyrs whom, it can be assumed, martyred themselves for the religion, the homeland, and the people, and not for any other reason. The Lebanese resistance published [the names of] those who took this path during the years of the Zionist occupation [in Lebanon] without any logical justification. We were surprised that the Palestinian resistance is employing the same method, also without any justification.

This is even though the situation is different, as the *shahids* in the case of Lebanon, such as Sanaa Muheidali and other women, lived in territories not under the control of the Zionist occupation, while in the Palestinian case, [they live under Zionist occupation].

Appendix 6
The Zarqawi Document

This document was captured in Baghdad and released by the US authorities, who believed it to have been written by Abu Musab al-Zarqawi, a Jordanian suspected of close ties with Al-Qa'eda and of involvement in terrorist attacks in Iraq (killed in 2006).

The document was initially obtained by a Kurdish militia, which had captured a courier named Hassan Ghul, who confessed that he was taking the document from Ansar al-Islam, a group affiliated with Al-Qa'eda that had been supported by Saddam Hussein, to Al-Qa'eda operatives.

The existence of the document was first reported by Dexter Filkins of The New York Times on 10 February 2004. The document itself is undated.

1 The foreign mujahidin

Their numbers continue to be small, compared to the large nature of the expected battle. We know that there are enough good groups and *jihad* is continuing, despite the negative rumours. What is preventing us from making a general call to arms is the fact that the country of Iraq has no mountains in which to seek refuge, or forest in which to hide. Our presence is apparent and our movement is out in the open. Eyes are everywhere. The enemy is before us and the sea is behind us. Many Iraqis would honour you as a guest and give you refuge, for you are a Muslim brother; however, they will not allow you to make their homes a base for operations or a safe house. People who will allow you to do such things are very rare, rarer than red sulphur. Therefore, it has been extremely difficult to lodge and keep safe a number of brothers, and also train new recruits. Praise be to Allah, however, with relentless effort and searching we have acquired some places and their numbers are increasing, to become base points for the brothers who will spark war and bring the people of this country into a real battle with God's will.

2 The present and future

There is no doubt that American losses were significant because they are spread thin amongst the people and because it is easy to get weapons. This is a fact that makes them easy targets, attractive for the believers. America, however, has no intention of leaving, no matter how many wounded nor how bloody it becomes. It is looking to a near future, when it will remain safe in its bases, while handing over control of Iraq to a bastard government with an army and police force that will bring back the time of [Saddam] Hussein and his cohorts. There is no doubt that our field of movement is shrinking and the grip around the throat of the *mujahidin* has begun to tighten. With the spread of the army and police, our future is becoming frightening.

3 So where are we?

Despite few supporters, lack of friends, and tough times, God has blessed us with victories against the enemy. We were involved in all the martyrdom operations – in terms of overseeing, preparing, and planning – that took place in this country except for the operations that took place in the north. Praise be to Allah, I have completed 25 of these operations, some of them against the Shi'a and their leaders, the Americans and their military, the police, the military, and the coalition forces. There will be more in the future, God willing. We did not want to publicly claim these operations until we become more powerful and were ready for the consequences. We need to show up strong and avoid getting hurt, now that we have made great strides and taken important steps forward. As we get closer to the decisive moment, we feel that our entity is spreading within the security void existing in Iraq, something that will allow us to secure bases on the ground; these bases that will be the jump start of a serious revival, God willing.

4 Plan of action

After much inquiry and discussion, we have narrowed our enemy to four groups:

A Americans

As you know, these are the biggest cowards that God has created and the easiest target. And we ask God to allow us to kill, and detain them, so that we can exchange them with our arrested sheikhs and brothers.

B Kurds

These are a pain and a thorn, and it is not time yet to deal with them. They are last on our list, even though we are trying to get to some of their leaders. God willing.

C The Iraqi troops, police, and agents

These are the eyes, ears, and hand of the occupier. With God's permission, we are determined to target them with force in the near future, before their power strengthens.

D The Shi'a

In our opinion, these are the key to change. Targeting and striking their religious, political and military symbols, will make them show their rage against the Sunnis and bare their inner vengeance. If we succeed in dragging them into a sectarian war, this will awaken the sleepy Sunnis who are fearful of destruction and death at the hands of these Sabeans, i.e., the Shi'a. Despite their weakness, the Sunnis are strong-willed and honest and different from the coward and deceitful Shi'a, who only attack the weak. Most of the Sunnis are aware of the danger of these people and they fear them. If it were not for those disappointing sheikhs, Sufis, and Muslim brothers, Sunnis would have a different attitude.

5. Way of action

As we have mentioned to you, our situation demands that we treat the issue with courage and clarity. So the solution, and God only knows, is that we need to bring the Shi'a into the battle because it is the only way to prolong the duration of the fight between the infidels and us. We need to do that because:

A The Shi'a have declared a subtle war against Islam. They are the close, dangerous enemy of the Sunnis. Even if the Americans are also an archenemy, the Shi'a are a greater danger and their harm more destructive to the nation than that of the Americans who are anyway the original enemy by consensus.

B They have supported the Americans, helped them, and stand with them against the *mujahidin*. They work and continue to work towards the destruction of the *mujahidin*.

C Fighting the Shi'a is the way to take the nation to battle. The Shi'a have taken on the dress of the army, police, and the Iraqi security forces, and have raised the banner of protecting the nation and the citizens. Under this banner, they have begun to assassinate the Sunnis under the pretence that they are saboteurs, vestiges of the Ba'ath, or terrorists who spread perversion in the country. This is being done with strong media support directed by the Governing Council and the Americans, and they have succeeded in splitting the regular Sunni from the *mujahidin*. For example, in what they call the Sunni triangle, the army and police are spreading out in these regions, putting in charge Sunnis from the same region. Therefore, the problem is you end up having an army and police connected by lineage, blood, and appearance to the people of the region. This region is our base of operations from where we depart and to where we return. When the Americans withdraw, and they have already started doing that, they get replaced by these agents who are intimately linked to the people of this region. What will happen to us, if we fight them, and we have to fight them, is one of only two choices:

i If we fight them, that will be difficult because there will be a schism between us and the people of the region. How can we kill their cousins and sons and under what pretext, after the Americans start withdrawing? The Americans will continue to control from their bases, but the sons of this land will be the authority. This is the democracy, we will have no pretext.

ii We can pack up and leave and look for another land, just like it has happened in so many lands of *jihad*. Our enemy is growing stronger day after day, and its intelligence information increases. By God, this is suffocation! We will be on the roads again.

iii People follow their leaders, their hearts may be with you, but their swords are with their kings. So I say again, the only solution is to strike the religious, military, and other cadres of the Shi'a so that they revolt against the Sunnis. Some people will say that this will be a reckless and irresponsible action that will bring the Islamic nation to a battle for which the Islamic nation is unprepared. Souls will perish and blood will be spilled. This is, however, exactly what we want, as there is nothing to win or lose in our situation. The Shi'a destroyed the balance, and the religion of God is worth more than lives. Until the majority stands up for the truth, we have to make sacrifices for this religion, and blood has to be spilled. For those who are good, we will speed up their trip to paradise, and the others, we will get rid of them. By God, the religion of God is more precious than anything else. We have many rounds, attacks, and black nights with the Shi'a, and we cannot delay this. Their menace is looming and this is a fact that we should not fear, because they are the most cowardly people God has created. Killing their leaders will weaken them and with the death of the head, the whole group dies. They are not like the Sunnis. If you knew the fear in the souls of the Sunnis and their people, you would weep in sadness. How many of the mosques have they have turned into Shi'a mosques ("husayniyas")? How many houses they have destroyed with their owners inside? How many brothers have they killed? How many sisters have been raped at the hands of those vile infidels? If we are able to deal them blow after painful blow so that they engage in a battle, we will be able to reshuffle the cards so there will remain no value or influence for the ruling council, or even for the Americans who will enter into a second battle with the Shi'a. This is what we want. Then the Sunni will have no choice but to support us in many of the Sunni regions.

When the mujahidin have secured a land they can use as a base to hit the Shi'a inside their own lands, with a directed media and a strategic action, there will be a continuation between the mujahidin inside and outside of Iraq. We are racing against time, in order to create squads of mujahidin who seek refuge in secure places, spy on neighbourhoods, and work on hunting down the enemies. The enemies are the Americans, police, and army. We have been training these people and augmenting their numbers. As far as the Shi'a, we will undertake suicide operations and use car bombs to harm them. We have been working on monitoring the area and choosing the right people, looking for those who are on the straight path, so we can cooperate with them.

We hope that we have made progress, and perhaps we will soon decide to go public – even if gradually – to display ourselves in full view. We have been hiding for a long time, and now we are seriously working on preparing a media outlet to reveal the truth, enflame zeal, and become an outlet for *jihad* in which the sword and the pen can turn into one. Along with this, we strive to illuminate the hindering errors of Islamic law and the clarifications of Islamic legal precepts by way of tapes, lessons, and courses which people will come to understand.

The suggested time for execution: we are hoping that we will soon start working on creating squads and brigades of individuals who have experience and expertise. We have to get to the zero-hour in order to openly begin controlling the land by night and after that by day, God willing. The zero-hour needs to be at least four months before the new government gets in place. As we see we are racing time, and if we succeed, which we are hoping, we will turn the tables on them and thwart their plan. If, God forbid, the government is successful and takes control of the country, we just have to pack up and go somewhere else again, where we can raise the flag again or die, if God chooses us.

6. What about you?

You, noble brothers, leaders of *jihad*, we do not consider ourselves those who would compete against you, nor would we ever aim to achieve glory for ourselves like you did. The only thing we want is to be the head of the spear, assisting and providing a bridge over which the Muslim nation can cross to promised victory and a better tomorrow.

As we have explained, this is our belief. So if you agree with it and are convinced of the idea of killing the perverse sects, we stand ready as an army for you, to work under your guidance and yield to your command. Indeed, we openly and publicly swear allegiance to you by using the media, in order to exasperate the infidels and confirm to the adherents of faith that one day, the believers will revel in God's victory. If you think otherwise, we will remain brothers, and disagreement will not destroy our cooperation and undermine our working together for what is best. We support *jihad* and wait for your response. May God keep for you the keys of goodness and preserve Islam and his people. Amen, amen.

Appendix 7
Fighting Terrorism:
Recommendations by Arab Reformists

Inquiry and Analysis Series - No. 232
July 28, 2005
No.232

Fighting Terrorism: Recommendations by Arab Reformists
By A. Dankowitz*

The question of how to fight Islamic terrorism preoccupies many Arab reformists who are working to denounce Islamist thought, to encourage independent and critical thinking, and to establish values of democracy and human rights in the Muslim world. For example, in February 2005, a group of reformists submitted to the U.N. a request that it establish an international court to judge Muslim clerics who incite to violence and bloodshed. The request was examined by the U.N. legal counsel and distributed to the U.N. Security Council. [1]

Following the July 7, 2005 London bombings, Arab reformists further expanded their criticism and honed their arguments, not only regarding Muslim extremists, but also regarding the European countries, particularly Britain, which allows extremist activity within its borders in the name of protecting individual rights. They also increased their criticism of the silent Muslim majority and moderate Muslim intellectuals, who capitulate to Islamist pressure and do not speak out decisively against it.

The following are some of the recommendations by reformist Arab writers.

Europe Must Change its Lenient Treatment of Muslim Extremists

One of the most salient reactions to the bombings was censure of Europe, particularly Britain, for its years-long policy of granting safe haven to Muslim extremists, enabling them to spread their ideas in schools, mosques, and the media, and giving them legal protection – in the name of protecting freedom of expression. Saudi intellectual Mashari Al-Dhaydi, columnist for the London daily *Al-Sharq Al-Awsat,* wrote: "The time has come for those who turn a blind eye to notice that the enemies of freedom have, unfortunately, exploited the atmosphere of freedom provided by the European countries, to destroy the foundations of freedom and to strangle any possibility that freedom would be born as a concept, and subsequently as a reality, in Arab and Muslim countries.

"They have used [European] freedom to spread religious fanaticism everywhere. People who disseminate the ideological and political platform of bin Laden ...are the greatest enemies of the freedom that the European countries defend...

"Fundamentalist terrorism knows no borders. Whoever thinks he can be comfortable near a wolf and can turn him into a domestic puppy will be astounded when one day it falls upon his flock. A wolf is a wolf, and can be nothing other than itself..." [2]

Abd Al-Rahman Al-Rashed, director-general of the Al-Arabiya TV channel and former editor of the London Arabic-language daily *Al-Sharq Al-Awsat,* called for the expulsion of Muslim extremists: "For over 10 years now, I myself and other Arab writers have warned against the dangers of leniency – not tolerance – in handling the extremism that is now spreading like a plague among Muslims in Britain and among those immigrating to Britain.

"We were never understood why British authorities gave safe haven to suspicious characters previously involved in crimes of terrorism. Why would Britain grant asylum to Arabs who have been convicted of political crimes or religious extremism, or even sentenced to death?...

" The battle we face is against the ideology, as opposed to against the terrorists themselves. The terrorist groups make the most of freedom of speech and movement, as reward [their benefactors] by spreading propaganda among neutral individuals and by frightening their opponents.

"Such leniency on behalf of the British government has allowed Arab and Muslim extremists to seek safe haven in Britain, away from their own countries, to the point that the extremists have overcome the moderates...

"The time has come for British authorities to be realistic and resolute regarding extremism, before complete chaos is unleashed onto British society. In the past, we told you: 'Stop them!' Today, we tell you: 'Expel them.'" [3]

In an article in the Saudi daily *Al-Jazeerah*, columnist Hamad bin Hamad Al-Salami mentioned by name bin Laden supporters residing in Britain who openly expressed their support for Al-Qaeda terrorist operations in the media – for example, on Al-Jazeera TV and in the Arabic daily *Al-Quds Al-Arabi*. "Those [who attacked] Saudi Arabia, [the new] Iraq, Egypt, and others have now risen against the country that hosts them and provides them with work and a livelihood. Among them are: [Muhammad] Al-Musa'ari, [Sa'ad] Al-Faqih, Abu Qatada, Abu Al-Muntazar, [Hani] Al-Siba'i, and [Abd Al-Bari] 'Atwan. They deceive millions when they appear with their robes and tarbooshes, and sometimes with [Islamic] decorations, claiming to possess knowledge in the ethics of Islam..." [4]

Incitement on the Internet Must Be Stopped

In another article, Al-Rashed singled out the Internet as "the preferred arena for extremists": "Most terrorist crimes are linked to the Internet... One terrorist group murders, and a group of extremists justifies the act, incites, and recruits [activists]." Al-Rashed explains that the Internet has become an effective tool for terrorists for several reasons: It is easy to use, messages reach the public quickly, it is cheap, and it is uncensored. He goes on to state that "the most important medium in corrupting young Muslims's thinking throughout the world is the Internet – not the schools – because young people use the Internet intensively and by means of it learn about incitement, recruitment, and terrorist education." In Al-Rashed's view, extremist websites must be censored, and it must be understood that "the source of intellectual danger today is the media, including the Internet." [5]

Arab Intellectuals Must Stop Speaking in Two Voices

Arab reformists also harshly criticized their intellectual colleagues. Egyptian commentator and *Al-Sharq Al-Awsat* columnist Muna Al-Tahawibrought up the issue of the aspirations of some intellectuals to please their target audience: "The time has come for us to declare resolutely that the claim heard whenever Muslims stage a terror attack – 'George Bush made me do it' – is a stupid one... The time has come for us to stop rebuking others. We all know the extent to which extremism has increased in our societies, but it is easy to ignore this fact and to say 'we aren't like that' instead of dealing with the matter...

"Much has been written and said about the extremist groups and extremists who found a safe haven in London. But not enough is said about the so-called intellectuals, who are in effect no more than justifiers of terrorism...

"Listening to the interviews with them on the Arab TV channels after the London attacks, one might think that George Bush and Tony Blair themselves went to Leeds, brought the group of young people to London, and pressed the button. The so-called intellectuals rejoiced that on July 7 George Bush and Tony Blair learned a lesson they wouldn't forget. Of course, all this was said in Arabic. The so-called intellectuals believe that this is what the Arab world wants to hear.

"But when one reads their commentaries in American newspapers, one might think that they had lost their memory and forgotten everything they'd said a few days before on Arab TV. Suddenly, those who hadn't uttered a single sentence on Arab TV without mentioning George Bush and Tony

Blair become cautious and sad. Instead of rebuking George Bush for everything, they tell *The Washington Post* or *The New York Times* that they're surprised and frightened, and cannot understand why young Muslims blow themselves up on London's public transportation...

"The time has come to talk in one single voice, and not in two voices – one addressed to the West [and the other to the Arabs]. The Arab world is fed up with violence, and has suffered greatly from it...

"Let us speak in one voice that takes responsibility, and let us begin discussing ways of emerging from this frightening chaos that will affect us all..." [6]

The Terrorists Must Be Separated from Their Sympathizers

Egyptian scholar and columnist Dr. Mamoun Fandy also focused on Arab intellectuals' hypocritical approach of to terrorism. He argued that the television stations' desire for cheap programming made them prefer showing the readily available extremist material to producing high-quality but expensive shows. Fandy wrote: "The terror events in London, the murder of the Egyptian ambassador to Iraq, and the Arab reaction point to a problem greater than terrorism – the problem of Arabs who identify with terrorism, whose numbers grow daily... In Egypt there is now a group of writers and editors and even politicians past the age of 50, who take political Viagra and feel intoxication and lust when they curse the U.S. and applaud the terrorists. They do not understand that they are fanning flames that will consume everyone, and that they themselves are committing suicide just like those with the car bombs...

"Since 9/11, I have been reading and hearing the Egyptian media, and I cannot name five writers who condemn terrorism unequivocally... Is Cairo such a failure that it contains not a single man or woman who says 'no' to terrorism?...

"The terrorist discourse is first and foremost cheap television [programming]... The sizeable increase in the number of Arab satellite channels, and their keen aspiration to fill airtime, are the main reason for the growth of the fundamentalist stream.

"When we compare, for example, production costs for a video film of [Lebanese singer] Nancy Ajram with the cost of broadcasting hours of one of our greatest sheikhs promoting terrorism, we find that the cost of the video film, or of an hour of quality programming, can reach $20,000 – while the price paid by television to one of the sheikhs for an hour [of material] is, at most, $1,000...

"Cheap television [programming] is the incubator of terrorism, and the workshop for the creation of a terror discourse... If the U.S. or the Arab countries want to fight terrorism, they must first of all begin by separating the terrorists from those who sympathize with terror... Unfortunately, all the big businessmen who trade with the U.S. and with the West identify with terrorism – if they didn't, why hasn't a single merchant among the friends of the U.S. and the West taken out a single ad in an Arab newspaper condemning terror?... Why do those who really profit from U.S. and Western dollars remain silent? Why are they the first ones to own cheap television stations that spread terror?..." [7]

Muslims Must Denounce the Terrorists; The West Must Stop Being Naive

In another article, written after the July 23 bombings at Sharm Al-Sheikh, Mamoun Fandy called upon the Muslims to issue religious edicts [*fatwa*] against terrorism, and further added: "Muslims worldwide must have the courage to reject terrorism... Just as bin Laden and his group describe moderate Muslims as followers of the West and as unbelievers, it is time for the Muslim leaders to proclaim bin Laden himself to be an unbeliever...

"Further, it is time to strip the title of 'mosque' from a place where firebombs are made...moderate Muslims can boycott such mosques, because they do not have the courage necessary to wrest them from the extremists. When a mosque becomes a place where firebombs are made, it ceases to be a mosque, and should be treated as the scene of a crime..."

Fandy also discussed the West's naiveté towards those it perceives as 'moderate Islamists': "I have met with and talked to a large number of Muslims, especially in the West, who denounce violence in public but say in private conversations that 'the West deserves [to suffer from terrorism].' In addition, they say in public that this is vengeance for what is happening in Palestine and Iraq. In their private conversations, all I have heard is blind hatred spurred by a sense of nihilistic destruction, which is a virus that has begun to take over many Muslims, particularly those living in the West.

"Many condemn bin Laden, but unfortunately many others have not condemned him in any way. Most of [the latter] live in Europe and the U.S. They are not sleeper cells, as the naïve in the West call them; they are cells that are wide awake, ready to strike at any moment.

"Of course, it is not helpful when a 'good' man like London Mayor Ken Livingstone invites Yousef Al-Qaradhawi [to London], just as it is not helpful when Tony Blair and George Bush invite people who are likely in the future to become terrorists to meetings in the British government and the White House. It is regrettable that Western media channels, particularly CNN and the BBC, host Islamist activists who support terrorism and treat them as experts and analysts...

"Only two things can stop terrorism:...issuing *fatwa* s removing bin Laden and his supporters from the fold of Islam, and the West ceasing to be naïve about 'moderate Islamists.' There is no such thing as 'moderate Islamists.' There are ordinary Muslims who lead ordinary lives, and there are terrorists and people who are likely to become terrorists in the future." [8]

Muslims Must Ban Suicide Bombings for Moral Reasons

Jamal Ahmad Khashoggi, former editor of the Saudi daily *Al-Watan,*called on Muslims to ban suicide operations: "The time has come for us to take a firm, clear stand that will come from the highest institutions of Islamic law and will ban, explicitly and without exception, all 'suicide operations.' Not because the West is demanding this of us, nor because the Arab governments have been burned by the fires of these operations, but because they run counter to the spirit and letter of Islam...

"We must return to the 'fundamentalist' position that adheres to the letter and spirit of Shari'a and not be influenced by politics or by interests. This is what the leading Saudi clerics, such as Sheikh

Abd Al'-Aziz bin Baz and Muhammad bin 'Athamin, did when they ruled firmly that suicide operations were forbidden. Current [Saudi] Mufti Sheikh Abd Al'-Aziz Aal Al-Sheikh has continued in the same path. Their position [against suicide bombing] preceded the 9/11 attack – thus there is no room to claim that this was due to American pressure [on Saudi Arabia].

"The call to encourage and support suicide operations was strongest in the 1990s, when we finally discovered the weapon that makes the Israelis' blood flow and spreads among them the horror they have caused us. Frightening suicide operations the length and breadth of Israel, in clubs, coffee shops, and buses, have targeted soldiers and civilians alike.

"We did not care about the children, the elderly, and the women who were cruelly killed. We were angry, and we remain angry, and we did not notice the treacherous nature of the attacks, and [the fact] that they violated the clear religious law against suicide. We did not heed the Prophet's explicit instruction that the Muslims must kill only combatants, not women and children.

"Anger blinded us, and we enjoyed the analyses that claimed Israel was facing its most difficult challenge since the October [1973] war. The newspapers published news of the fear in Israel, and of emigration from [the country]. And we believed it...

"The two sheikhs, [bin Baz and bin 'Athamin] belong to the Salafi school that bases itself on the clear text [of the Koran]. Therefore, they paid no heed to all the political justifications, as others did who claimed to 'better understand the situation and the strategic interest,' and who refused to rule that suicide operations were permitted.

"Sheikh bin 'Athamin was clear, even tough, when he told a man who sought his jurisprudent opinion regarding these [suicide] operations: 'In my view, [he who perpetrates such acts] is committing suicide, and will be punished in Hell'...

"If only we could sketch out a diagram of the suicide operations since they became the weapon of choice of the Jihad warriors, we would see how they have degraded morally, to the point of blowing up children in Baghdad and peaceful passengers on London's transportation... How wise it would be for all those who permit suicide attacks to go back to the religious fundamentalist position that prohibits them – even if they are a respected cleric such as Sheikh Yousef Al-Qaradhawi, or a movement with a just cause, such as the Hamas movement. Turning to these operations was a great moral mistake, and turning away from them is a good virtue…" [9]

The Religious Institutions Must Take Practical Measures Against the Terrorists

Sa'ad Allah Khalil, who writes for reformist websites, also criticized Muslim clerics: "How long will we continue to bury our heads in the sand and to think that the world is ignorant and knows nothing about us? How long will we deceive ourselves? How complacent we are if we imagine that we can, with declarations and telegrams [condemning terrorism], convince the world that our thought and culture are innocent of terror…

"It is true that not every Muslim is a terrorist. But since 9/11, hasn't every terrorist been a Muslim?… Is there a sheikh or an Islamic religious authority that denies these murderers' and their leaders' affiliation to Islam? Don't they give bin Laden the title of 'sheikh,' and sometimes the title 'the sheikh *mujahid* [Jihad warrior]'? Don't they always find an excuse and justification for these murderers?…

"The terrorists deliberately distort the precepts of Islam and the image of the Muslims, and thus are necessarily the enemies of Islam and the Muslims. Why, then, isn't a clear and honest religious position towards them taken… like the hostile positions that these sheikhs take against some of the Muslim schools of religious thought and their followers. Why not dry up all the sources of the terrorists, and demand an accounting from those who encourage them, from their followers, and from those who try to find justification for them? …

"The religious institutions, and the official and unofficial religious authorities, must take real, not formal, measures – in order to salvage what can be salvaged. If they will not do so, it won't be long until the world stands in a single rank against Islam and the Muslims." [10]

The Muslims Must Form a New Religious Culture

In addressing the religious dimension of terrorism, Iraqi researcher Majed Al-Gharbawi called for going beyond the issuing of new *fatwa* s against terrorism to form a new, clear-cut religious culture and to expose those who exploit religion for political purposes. He wrote:

"Terrorism in the name of religion and of Islam has become a real danger that threatens global security and the well-being of peoples... [I do not want] to detract from the importance of the psychological, political, and economic reasons [for terrorism], but they are secondary reasons.

"The driving reason is religious ideology... All the bloody acts that struck at Muslims were carried out in the name of the religion, and all the disasters from which the Muslim peoples suffered were in the name of Islam. In the name of religion, wars have broken out; blood has been let; murder has been legitimized; rights have been revoked; regimes have been taken over; those with different opinions have been accused of unbelief; and Muslims with different opinions have even been accused of heresy... Religion was and remains a cover for justifying acts of terror and for arbitrary policies...

"The religious discourse has reshaped the logic of the [Islamist] movements, based on mockery of life and love of death, hatred for the other and self-glorification, neglect of this world and [preparation] for the hereafter, satisfying Allah by means of sacrifice for any goal.

"The religious discourse has not educated the people of the Islamist movements to adopt leniency, mercy, and tolerance for the other – but rather has educated to hatred of the other and plans to murder and uproot the other... The individual in the Islamist movements was not created to settle the land and live his life, but rather for the sake of the world to come; [this individual] aspires daily for Allah to grant him martyrdom so that he will be freed of the burden of responsibility, and will gain Paradise and pleasing Allah forever... This culture is completely unconnected to the human values to which the Koran calls...

"How is it possible to deal with this way of thought? ... In my opinion, even *fatwa* s that prohibit this will not help, because [the clerics who would issue them] are denounced by the extremist Islamist movements ...

"There is a need to form a new religious culture that will lay out the borders of the *Shari'a* laws in the Koran, will set out what is characteristic of the life of the Prophet, and will clarify when and how the law is absolute for every time and place... Then, there is a need to discuss intensively the issue of abolishing chapters in the Koran [*naskh*] and [a need to examine] whether it is true that the verse of the sword [Koran 9:5] abolished all mercy, leniency, and forgiveness in the Koran... [Likewise,] there is a need to view the first Muslims as human beings with feelings, aspirations, and political goals [and not as divine]...

"We must uncover the shame of all those who have enlisted the religion and the religious text for their own political and social goals..." [11]

The Silent Majority Must Speak Out Against the Terrorists

Renowned columnist Amir Taheri called upon the silent and moderate majority of the Muslims in the world to speak out against the extremists who distort the image of Islam. He wrote: "What do we do about people who are prepared to court certain death in exchange for killing others? ... The first thing to do is not to be impressed by the fact that an individual who has been brainwashed out of his or her humanity is ready to die in order to kill others. The only reasonable way to treat such individuals is as a new form of weaponry.

" Just like all other weapons that impress when first introduced, these suicide-killers will continue to terrorize and fascinate until we find an antidote... like all other arms, this new weapon is designed by some people, financed by investors, manufactured somewhere, and deployed by leaders who can be identified and destroyed.

" These human weapons are designed and shaped by a constant flow of anti-Western propaganda from Arab satellite television, the so-called Islamic associations, and countless *madrassas* (Islamic schools) and mosques throughout the world, including London itself...

"The London attack is not the work of a small group of people.

It is the bitter fruit of a religion that has been hijacked by a minority of extremists, while the majority looks on in concern and amazement. Until we hear the voices of the Muslims condemning attacks of this kind with no words [of qualification] such as 'but' and 'if,' the suicide bombers and the murderers will have an excuse to think that they enjoy the support of all Muslims. The real battle against this enemy of mankind will begin when the 'silent majority' in the Islamic world makes its voice heard against the murderers, and against those who brainwash them, believe them, and fund them." [12]

The War on Terrorism Requires Extensive Intellectual, Political and Educational Activity

Iraqi commentator and human rights activist Dr. Kazem Habib pointed out a number of directions for the war on terror: "...The calls issued by the conferences and associations, and by the sheikhs and Muslim political forces, cannot stop the terror operations and bloodshed in various places of the world. Where there are extremist Muslims, there is no point in talking about how murdering a man who has committed no crime is forbidden by Islam – because most of the religious schools, the large majority of the imams in the world's mosques, and most of the preachers on the Arab TV channels educate to violence and spread hatred and animosity towards people of other religions and other streams of thought. They do not acknowledge the other; they do not show tolerance towards non-Muslims. Moreover, they disseminate hatred against Muslims who do not walk in their own path, treating them as unbelievers – distinguishing between murdering a Muslim and murdering a non-Muslim, and preaching that it is permitted to murder a non-Muslim but forbidden to murder a Muslim...

"Most of the Arab and non-Arab imams in the mosques in Europe are educating today to hatred of the West and of the other religions, because they see the people of the West as unbelievers who are of no use whatsoever to Islam... and also see them as 'parasites' that must be gotten rid of, or converted to Islam – that is, to transform *Dar al-Harb* into *Dar al-Islam* ... In the Muslim world, the education in the religious and public schools is no different from what is taking place in the mosques in Europe, only much worse. Every year, these schools produce a large group of terrorists that fans out across the globe…"

In order to fight terror, Dr. Habib proposes an international program for fighting backwardness and poverty in the world, as well as a struggle against totalitarian and tyrannical regimes in Arab and Muslim countries. He proposes to refrain from negotiating with the forces of political Islam, including the Muslim Brotherhood movement, because they seek to obtain the same goals as the forces of international terrorism, only their methods are different. He demands an accounting from governments that permit the dissemination of hatred of the other in their educational institutions, and he urges that practical solutions be found for the problems in various regions in the world – particularly the Middle East – as without them, extremist solutions will emerge and will lead to more bloodshed.

According to Dr. Habib, "the war on terror … requires intensive and ongoing intellectual, political, and educational activities, in order to fight the extremist and terrorist Islamic Salafi thought and the Salafi *da'wa* that calls to establish a fundamentalist Islamic regime …" [13]

A. Dankowitz is Director of MEMRI's Reform Project

[1] A few months after the submission of the request, signed by some 4,000 Arab and Kurdish intellectuals, Under-Secretary-General for Legal Affairs and U.N. Legal Counsel Nicolas Michel responded with a letter to the initiators of the request, Arab reformists Dr. Jawad Hashem, Dr. Shaker Al-Naboulsi, and Lafif Lakhdar. He explained that the establishment of a court depended on a U.N. Security Council resolution or on international agreement. He added that a copy of their request had been distributed to all Security Council members. www.metransparent.com, July 2, 2005.

[2] Al-Sharq Al-Awsat (London), July 12, 2005. The translation is based both on the Arabic original and Al-Sharq Al-Awsat 's own translation into English.

[3] Al-Sharq Al-Awsat (London), July 9, 2005.

[4] Al-Jazeerah (Saudi Arabia), July 10, 2005.

[5] Al-Sharq Al-Awsat (London), July 18, 2005.

[6] Al-Sharq Al-Awsat (London), July 18, 2005

[7] Al-Sharq Al-Awsat (London), July 11, 2005.

[8] Al-Sharq Al-Awsat (London), July 25, 2005.

[9] Al-Watan (Saudi Arabia), July 19, 2005.

[10] www.metransparent.com, July 13, 2005.

[11] www.elaph.com, July 8, 2005.

[12] Al-Sharq Al-Awsat (London), July 8, 2005.

[13] www.rezgar.com, July 16, 2005.

Glossary

'Abbasid – the second dynasty of Sunni caliphs, based in Baghdad. c.f. Umayyad

afa'a - restore

Ahl al-Kitab – literally "the People of the Book" i.e. those who have their own revealed scriptures. The term is applied to Jews, Christians, Sabeans [followers of John the Baptist] and sometimes Zoroastrians

Ahmadi – member of the Ahmadiyya sect

Ahmadiyya – a Muslim sect, originating in nineteenth century India, regarded as extremely heretical by other Muslims

aman – temporary safe-conduct granted to non-Muslims who want to enter *Dar al-Islam* e.g. to trade

amir al-mu'minin – prince of the believers, a title rserved to the caliph or imam.

ansar – literally "helpers". Native-born Medinan Muslims. c.f. *muhajirun*

'aqd - literally "tie". An agreement. A meeting of minds on a certain act with the object of creating legal consequences

Assassins – an Isma'ili sect (active 1090 - 1256) whose devotees practised suicide assassinations

al-Azhar University, Cairo – the leading scholarly institution of Sunni Islam

Banu an-Nadir – a Jewish tribe living in the Arabian peninsula in Muhammad's time

Banu Hanifa – an Arab tribe of Muhammad's time, partly pagan and partly Christian

Banu Qurayza – a Jewish tribe living in Medina who were exterminated when Muhammad had all the men killed

Banu Taghlib – a Christian Arab tribe of Muhammad's time

batini – inner, esoteric

bay'a – the act of swearing allegiance and obedience to a religious or political leader

beyanname-i cihad – declaration of war [Turkish]

biradari- group of male kin (patrilineage) among Pakistani Muslims

Byzantium – the city later known as Constantinople and now called Istanbul. The Byzantine Empire began in 330 as the Eastern Roman Empire and then evolved into a distinctive medieval Eurasian-Christian civilisation with Byzantium the centre of eastern Orthodox Christianity.

caliph – the Sunni title for the supreme ruler of the Muslim community c.f. imam

Chalcedonian – refers to the doctrine, affirmed at the Council of Chalcedon in 451, that the divine nature and the human nature are united in Christ unconfusedly but indivisibly. c.f. Monophysite and Monthelete

Dajjal – the Antichrist

Dar al-'Ahd – House of Treaty

Dar al-Harb – literally "House of War". Classical Islam's term for territory not under Islamic rule

Dar al-Islam – literally "House of Islam" i.e. territory under Islamic rule

Dar al-Sulh – House of Truce

Dar al-Shahada – House of Testimony

da'wa – call or invitation to Islam i.e. Islamic missionary work

Deobandi – radical movement very influential in south Asia and Afghanistan. Rejects all western influence and seeks to return to classical Islam. In recent years has become militant.

dervish – a member of one of many Sufi brotherhoods or orders. Their spirituality is characterised by seeking a state of ecstasy by dancing, whirling, repeating a name of God or other methods.

devshirme – the forced levy of Christian boys for the Janissaries

dhimma – literally "protected". The status of Jews, Christians and Sabeans in an Islamic state. They were permitted to live and keep their own faith, in return for payment of *jizya* and adherence to various demeaning regulations

dhimmi – those with *dhimma* status

diya – financial compensation for homicide or injury **fard** – obligation, duty

fasad – corruption, immorality

Fatimids – Isma'ili dynasty based in Cairo, ruling from 969 to 1171.

fatwa – an authoritative statement on a point of Islamic law

fay' – property taken from non-Muslims without fighting, which went to the state treasury

fida'iyun – literally "men of sacrifice", people who give up their life for a cause. This term was used for adherents of the Assassin sect who went on suicide missions.

fi sabil illah – in the way of God

fitna – rebellion, sedition, disorder, schism, civil strife. The "great *fitna*" was the period of conflict within the Muslim community (656-661) when it divided into three sects.

Gazâ – Turkish term for holy war on behalf of Islam

ghazi – literally "one who takes part in a *ghazwa*". Fighter for the faith

ghazwa – inter-tribal raid, much practised in pre-Islamic Arabia. Often called "razzia"

al-ghazw al-fikri – *intellectual raid or aggression, a term used by Islamists to signify the Western intellectual penetration of the Muslim world*

hadith – traditions recording what Muhammad and his early followers said and did. Some are considered more authentic and reliable than others. c.f. *sunna*

Hanafi – a Sunni school of Shari'ah, founded by Imam abu Hanifa (d.767)

Hanbali – a Sunni school of Shari'ah, founded by Imam Ahmad ibn Hanbal (d.855)

Haramayn – Mecca and Medina, the two sacred cities

harb – war

hedaya – guidance

Hidden Imam – according to Shi'a Islam, the twelfth Imam who went into hiding in 873 AD and is believed to be still alive, one day to return as the *Mahdi.*

hijra – emigration (of Muslims from Mecca to Medina in 622)

hubus – North African term for Islamic *waqf* (religious endowment)

hudna – temporary truce agreed with a non-Muslim nation. Sometimes translated ceasefire

hurub al-ridda – wars of apostasy (632-4)

'Ibadis – a modern-day sect descended from the Kharijis, found in Oman, East Africa and North Africa. Berber-speaking 'Ibadis in Algeria are called Mzabis.

idha'ah – open propagation of beliefs, the opposite of *taqiyya ijma'* – the consensus of Muslim scholars on any given subject. Used in *ijtihad*.

ijtihad – the process of logical deduction on a legal or theological question, using the Qur'an and *hadith* as sources, which created the Shari'ah

Ikhwan – brethren (plural of *akh* "brother"). In the context of Saudi Arabia refers to a religious and military brotherhood which played an important part in the unification of the Arabian Peninsula under Ibn Sa'ud in the early decades of the twentieth century. The Ikhwan were recruited from nomadic tribesmen and then, in order to break their tribal allegiances and force them to abandon their nomadic lifestyle, were settled in pan-tribal military cantonments around oases to farm the land.

ikrahiyya – enforced *taqiyya*, to save one's life

imam – the Shi'a term for the supreme ruler of the Muslim community (equivalent to the Sunni caliph). The same term is used by Sunni Muslims to mean the prayer leader at a local mosque, similar to a Christian parish priest.

intifada – literally "a throwing off". Used of the Palestinian uprising against Israeli occupation.

intizar – waiting for the Hidden Imam

'Isa – Jesus

Islamism – the term preferred by Muslims to describe what is often called by others "Islamic fundamentalism" or "political Islam". It denotes the view of Islam as a comprehensive political ideology that aims at establishing Islamic states under *shari'a* wherever possible by a variety of means (which may include violence). It is characterised by zeal, activism and a desire to follow the *shari'a* in minute detail.

Isma'ilis – a secretive Shi'a sect who infiltrated normal Muslim society. Also called "Seveners". Today they are found mainly in India and Pakistan.

istishad – martyrdom

jahiliyya – the time of ignorance (meaning before Islam), especially pre-Islamic Arabia

Janissaries – elite troops in the Ottoman Empire, comprised of young Christian boys who had been forcibly taken from their families, converted to Islam and trained for war

jama'a – group, organisation

jati – subcaste in the Hindu caste system, associated with a specific trade

jihad – literally "striving". The term has a variety of interpretations including (1) spiritual struggle for moral purity (2) trying to correct wrong and support right by voice and actions (3) military war against non-Muslims with the aim of spreading Islam

jihad almubadahah – aggressive *jihad*

jihad al-dafa'ah – defensive *jihad*

jihad-e-asghar – lesser *jihad*, often used to mean military *jihad*

jihad-e-akbar – greater *jihad*, often used to mean spiritual struggle

jizya – a tax payable by non-Muslims (Jews, Christians and Sabeans) within an Islamic state. Various practices designed to humiliate the payer were associated with this tax.

ka'ba – literally "cube". The large cubic stone which stands in the centre of the Grand Mosque at Mecca. Muslims face the *ka'ba* when praying.

kaffara – atonement, making amends

kafir – infidel i.e. non-Muslim. This is a term of gross insult. (pl. *kafirun* or *kuffar)* c.f. *kufr*

khandaq – trench or ditch

Kharijis – literally "seceders". A puritanical sect of Islam with a highly developed doctrine of sin. Sinners were considered apostates. The sect began in 657 as a result of disputes over the succession to the caliphate, and continued to rebel against the caliphate for two centuries. They survive today in a more moderate variant, the 'Ibadis. (Arabic sing. *khariji*, Arabic pl. *khawarij)*

khawfiyya – precautionary *taqiyya* e.g. Shi'a Muslims performing Sunni acts and rituals in Sunni countries

Khilafat movement – a movement which tried to preserve the status of the Sultan of Turkey as Caliph (1919-1924)

Khudai Khidmatgaran – literally "Servants of God". A nonviolent Pathan movement of the 1930s seeking a political voice in north-west British India. Nicknamed the "Red-Shirts"

kitmaniyya – arcane *taqiyya,* to conceal one's beliefs as well as the number and strength of one's co-religionists, and to carry out clandestine activities to further religious goals.

kufr – unbelief c.f. *kafir*

madrassa – Islamic religious school

Mahdi – the awaited End Time deliverer

Majalla – the Ottoman Civil Code, an 1877 compilation of rules and guidelines from the Hanafi School of Shari'ah, intended to be used as a reference text for state court judges untrained in "finding" the law in traditional Hanafi texts. Certain sections are still applicable in Palestinian courts today.

majlis al-shura – consultative council

Maliki – a Sunni school of Shari'ah, founded by Imam Malik ibn Anas (d. 795)

manakh – serious inter-tribal conflict in pre-Islamic Arabia. Compared with a *ghazwa,* a *manakh* was rare but much more violent.

mansabdars - the military-type ranking of all imperial officials in the Mughal empire. The mansabdars governed the empire and commanded its armies in the emperor's name

mansukh – that which is abrogated or superseded c.f. *nasikh* and *naskh*

masjid – mosque

maqam - *Maqam Ibrahim* is a stone situated a little distance from the north-east wall of the *ka'ba*

Mecca – the Arabian city where Muhammad lived until the age of 52, now the holiest city in Islam.

Medina – Muhammad and his first followers emigrated from Mecca to Medina in 622 because of persecution. At Medina Muhammad established and led the first Islamic state, where Islam developed into a more aggressive form.

Monophysite – refers to the doctrine that the incarnate Christ had only one nature (divine) c.f. Chalcedonian and Monothelete

Monothelete – The Monothelete heresy was a politically inspired compromise between the Chalcedonian and Monophysite positions, devised in the seventh century in an attempt to unite the Christians in the face of Persian and later Muslim invasions. Monotheletism asserts two natures in Christ but only one mode of activity.

mudarati – "symbiotic" *taqiyya,* the co-existence of Shi'as with Sunni for the sake of Islamic unity and power

Mughal – the Arabic and Persian form of "Mongol". Conventionally used to describe the Muslim dynasty that ruled large parts of India from the early sixteenth to the mideighteenth century. Also spelled "Mogul"

muhajirun – the Muslims who moved from Mecca to Medina with Muhammad c.f. *ansar mujahid* – a person who takes part in *jihad*. Plural *mujahidin* or *mujahidun*.

muqaddas – holy

murid – literally "one who desires", a disciple of a Sufi *pir*

Muridism – a term used for a pacifist Sufi movement in Senegal and also for a militant Sufi movement in the Caucasus

mushrikun – literally "associationists", those who associate another being with the one God, the worst sin in Islam

Mu'tazilites – literally "withdrawers". A rationalist school of Islam which originated in the second Islamic century. They held that someone who sins is neither a believer nor an unbeliever, and opposed the view that the Qur'an was eternal and uncreated. They also differed from orthodox Muslims in denying predestination and in believing that God must always act justly.

Mzabis – a name given to Berber-speaking 'Ibadis living in Algeria

Naqshbandiyya – a prominent Sufi order founded in the fourteenth century in Bukhara. It is widespread in the Caucasus and Central Asia, and is characterised by its use of silence and concentration.

nasikh – a Qur'anic verse that abrogates another verse c.f. *mansukh* and *naskh*

naskh – abrogation – the rule whereby an earlier-dated verse of the Qur'an is considered subordinate to a later-dated verse c.f. *mansukh* and *nasikh*

Ottomans – a Turkish clan who established a principality in Anatolia around 1300. By military conquest their territory expanded into the Ottoman empire, which was the dominant Muslim power for some six centuries. The Ottoman Sultanate was abolished in 1922 and the caliphate in 1924.

People of the Book – see *Ahl al-Kitab*

pir – Sufi "saint" or spiritual guide

Pukhtunwali – the Pathan code of honour, which governs all aspects of life. Its main features are hospitality, truce, vengeance and *nanawatey* (a kind of asylum by which feuds can be ended)

qawm – identity and solidarity group based on kinship, sometimes equivalent to tribe. It can also include residence and trade. The basic unit of social community in Afghanistan

qibla – direction faced during prayer (originally towards Jerusalem, later towards the *ka'ba* at Mecca) *qital* – fighting

qiyas - analogical reasoning, used in *ijtihad*

Qur'an – a series of "revelations" which Muhammad believed God gave him over the period 610 to 632

Quraish - the Arab tribe to which Muhammad and the first Muslims belonged

radda – return, restore

rashidun – the rightly guided ones, used of the first four caliphs following Muhammad

razzia – a European pronunciation of *ghazwa*

Red-Shirts – see *Khudai Khidmatgaran* and *Surkhposhan*

ribat – strengthening the frontiers of *Dar al-Islam,* a type of defensive *jihad*

ridda – apostasy

rightly-guided caliphs – the first four caliphs who succeeded in turn to the leadership of the Muslim community following Muhammad's death. Their rule covered the period 632 to 661.

Rukn - corner, either the Black Stone which is fixed in the south-east corner of the *ka'ba,* or the corner itself which contains the Stone

Sabeans (Sabians) – followers of John the Baptist. Considered in the Qur'an to have a revealed religion and thus to be in the same category as Jews and Christians, i.e. not pagans. There are still some Sabeans in modern Iraq. c.f. *Ahl al-Kitab*

sadaqa – voluntary alms-giving. Distinguished from *zakat* (compulsory alms-giving)

sahih – true. Used before the name of a compiler of a collection of *hadiths,* to indicate reliability

salaf – pious ancestors

Salafiyya – widespread radical movement, also called neo-Wahhabism

Sanusiyya – a Sufi-led rebel movement in Libya (1837-1931)

SAR – Sekolah Agama Rakyat, private Islamic schools in Malaysia (literally "School of the People's Religion)

Sassanid or Sassanian – a Persian dynasty founded in 224. It was destroyed by the Arab Muslims in 637-651.

Shafi'i – a Sunni school of Shari'ah, founded by Imam Muhammad bin Idris ash Shafi'i (d. 820)

shahada – testimony, particularly reciting the Islamic creed. Also legal testimony in a court of law. Also martyrdom.

shahid – martyr or witness

shari'a – Islamic law

shura – consultative assembly

Shi'a – a minority sect of Islam, which broke away from the main body in 657. It is a majority in Iran and Iraq.

sira – biography of Muhammad, usually referring to the authoritative early accounts (Ibn Ishaq, al-Tabari etc.)

siyar – literally "motion". This word came to mean the types of conduct of the Islamic state in its relationships with non-Muslim communities – statecraft or foreign policy. It was the title of a famous work by Shaybani on international relations.

Sufism – Islamic mysticism

sunna – literally "a trodden path". The actions and words of Muhammad as recorded in the *hadith*. Some Muslims also include the actions and words of Muhammad's early followers who know him personally.

Sunni – the largest sect of Islam, comprising 80-90% of the Muslims today.

sura – a chapter of the Qur'an

Surkhposhan – literally "Red-Shirts". A nickname for the *Khudai Khidmatgaran*

takfir – the process of declaring someone to be an apostate from Islam. This process began with the Kharijis, who applied it very broadly, as do some modern-day groups

Taliban - literally "students" or "seekers". The ultra-conservative Islamic movement which gained political power in Afghanistan 1996-2001

taqiyya – literally "shield" or "guard". To conceal one's real beliefs in situations of great danber or necessity in order to save one's life. A doctrine which is very strong in Shi'a Islam, but also present in Sunni Islam. c.f. *idha'ah*

'ulama – scholars, those learned in the study of Islam

umma – the whole body of Muslims worldwide

Umayyad – the first dynasty of Sunni caliphs, based in Damascus. They followed the rightly-guided caliphs and were succeeded in 750 by the 'Abbasid dynasty.

velayat-e faqih – vice-regency of the Islamic jurists i.e. government by the Islamic jurists, a doctrine devised by Ayatollah Khomeini (1900-89) the architect of the 1979 Islamic Revolution in Iran

Wahhabism – strictly puritanical form of Sunni Islam, predominant in Saudi Arabia

waqf - Islamic religious endowment (trust)

Yenicheri – Janissaries

zamindars - local landholders who acquired the right to collect revenues or taxes from an area of land. Instituted by the Mughal Empire

Zaydi – Fiver Shi'a sect that ruled North Yemen for many centuries

Zoroastrianism – the pre-Islamic religion of Persia, strongly ethical and with both monotheistic and dualistic aspects.

Bibliography

"A question of leadership", transcript, *BBC Panorama*, 21 August 2005, http://news.bbc.co.uk/1/hi/programmes/panorama/4171950. stm, viewed 22 August 2005.

Abbas, Tahir, (ed.), *Muslim Britain: Communities under Pressure,* (London & New York: Zed Books, 2005).

Abdelnasser, Walid M., *The Islamic Movement in Egypt* (London: Keegan Paul International, 1994).

Abd es-Salam, Kamal Boraiq'a, "Responding to Dr Bat Ye'or", 23 August 2002, in *Religious News Service from the Arab World,* 2 September 2002.

'Abdul Khaliq, Sheikh 'Abdul Rahman, *Verdict on the Treaties of Compromise and Peace the Jews,* reproduced at http://www.islaam. com/articles/treaty.htm, viewed 18 September 2001.

Abedi, Mehdi and Legenhausen, Gary (eds.), *Jihad and Shahadat: Struggle and Martyrdom in Islam* (Houston: Institute for Research and Islamic Studies, 1986).

Aboul-Enein, Youssef H. and Zuhur, Sherifa, "Islamic Rulings on Warfare" (Carlisle, Pennsylvania: Strategic Studies Institute, U.S. Army War College, October 2004)

"About SIS", http://www.geocities.com/wellesley/veranda/7502/about/ content1.htm, viewed 11 August 2005.

Abshar-Abdalla, Ulil, "Freshening Up Our Understanding of Islam", in *Kompas,* 18 November 2002. Quotations are an English translation from the Indonesian original.

Abu Gheith, Suleiman, "In the Shadow of the Lances", from the Center for Islamic Research and Studies website (originally www.alneda. com then changed to http://66.34.191.223. Reported by MEMRI

Special Dispatch Series No. 388, 12 June 2002.

Abu-Manneh, Butrus, "The Naqshabandiyya-Mujaddidiyya in the Ottoman Lands in the Early 19th Century", *Die Welt des Islams* Vol. 12 (1986), pp. 1-36.

Abu Sulayman, 'Abdul Hamid A., *Towards an Islamic Theory of International Relations: New Directions for Methodology and Thought,* (Herndon, Virginia: The International Institute for Islamic Thought, 1994).

Abu Sway, Mustafa, "Kidnapping Foreign nationals: An Islamic Perspective", *Christian Science Monitor,* 3 February 2006.

Abu Yusuf, Ya'qub b. Ibrahim al-Ansari, *Kitab al-Kharaj* (Cairo, 1933).

Abu Yusuf, Ya'qub b. Ibrahim al-Ansari, *Kitab al-Radd 'ala Siyar al-Awza'i,* (ed.) Abu al-Wafa al-Afghani (Cairo, 1938).

Abu Zahra, Muhammad, *Al-'Alaqat al-Dawliyya fi l-Islam* (Cairo: al-Dar al-Qawmiyya li-l-Tiba'a wa-l-Nashr, 1964).

Abu Zahra, Muhammad, "The Jihad (Strivings")), in D.F. Green, *Arab Theologians on Jews and Israel, Extracts from the Proceedings of the Fourth Conference of the Academy of Islamic Research* (Geneva: Editions de L'Avenir, 1976), pp. 61-63.

Abul-Fadl, Mona, *Where East Meets West: The West on the Agenda of the Islamic Revival*, Islamization of Knowledge Series (no. 10) (Herndon, Virginia: The International Institute of Islamic Thought, 1992).

'Afif, Shams-i Siraj, "Tarikh-i Firoz Shahi", in Elliot and Dawson, *A History of India As Told by Its Own Historians*, Vol. 2. (New Delhi: D K Publishers, reprinted 2001).

Ahmad, Hazrat Mirza Ghulam, *Jesus in India: Jesus' Escape from Death on the Cross and Journey to India* (London: The London Mosque, 1978). English version of *Masih Hindustan Mein* (1899) by Mirza Ghulam Ahmad.

Ahmad, Khurshid, "Muslim Ummah at the Threshold of 21st Century", *Tarjumanul Qur'an* (November 1997).

Ahmad, Mirza Ghulam, *Tohfah Golrviyah* (1902). Republished in Vol. 17 of *Ruhani Khaza'in,* the collected works of Ghulam Mirza Ahmad (Rabwa, 1965)

Ahmed, Akbar S., *Islam Under Siege: Living Dangerously in a Post-Honour World*, (Cambridge: Polity Press, 2003).

Ahsan, Muhammad, "Human Development in the Muslim World", *The Muslim World*, Vol. 94 (April 2004).

Akbar, M.J., *The Shade of Swords: Jihad and Conflict between Islam and Christianity* (London: Routledge, 2002).

Akhavi, Shahrough, "Elite Factionalism in the Islamic Republic of Iran", *Middle East Journal*, 41. 2 (Spring 1987), pp. 181-201.

Akhtar, Parveen, " '(Re)turn to Religion' and Radical Islam", in Tahir Abbas, (ed.), *Muslim Britain: Communities under Pressure*,(London & New York: Zed Books, 2005).

Alexander, Yonah and Swetnam, Michael S., *Usama bin Laden's al-Qaida: Profile of a Terrorist Network* (Ardsley, USA: Transnational Publishers, 2001).

Alexander, Yonah and Swetnam, Michael S., *Usama bin Laden's al-Qaida: Profile of a Terrorist Network*, (New Delhi: Aditya, 2002).

Ali, Abdullah Yusuf, *The Holy Qur'an: Text, Translation and Commentary* (Leicester: The Islamic Foundation, 1975).

al-Ali, Hamid Abdullah, "The Legality of Killing Jewish Women and Children in Palestine", *Al-Watan*, 31 August 2001. English translation by Shira Gutgold published in the *Jerusalem Post*, 5 September 2001.

Almascaty, Hilmy Bakar, *Panduan Jihad Untuk Aktivis Gerakan Islam [A Manual for jihad for Islamic Movement Activists]* (Jakarta: Gema Insani Press, May 2001).

Alsumaih, Abdulrahman Muhammad, *The Sunni Concept of Jihad in Classical Fiqh and Modern Islamic Thought,* unpublished PhD thesis, University of Newcastle upon Tyne, Faculty of Law, Environment and Social Sciences, Department of Politics, 1998.

Amini, Ayatollah Ibrahim, *Al-Imam al-Mahdi, the Just Leader of Humanity,* translated by Abdulaziz Sachedina, 2nd edition, (Qum: Ansariyan Publications, 1999).

Anderson, Norman (ed.), *The World's Religions,* 4th edition (Grand Rapids, Michigan: Eerdmans, 1975).

Anderson, Norman, *Islam in the Modern World: A Christian Perspective* (Leicester: Apollos, 1990).

al-Ansari, 'Abd al-Hamid, "Landmarks in Rational and Constructive Dialogue with the 'Other' ", *Al-Hayat* (London), 31 May 2002. Extracts in English translation in MEMRI Special Dispatch Series No. 386, 5 June 2002.

Ansari, Humayun, *The Infidel Within: Muslims in Britain Since 1800* (London: Hurst & Company, 2004).

Ansari, Sarah F.D., *Sufi Saints and State Power: The Pirs of Sind, 1843-1947* (Lahore: Vanguard Books, 1992) published by arrangement with Cambridge University Press.

al-Ansari, Seif Al-Din, writing in *Al-Ansar,* No. 16, 24 August 2002, www.jehad.net. Extracts in English translation in MEMRI Special Dispatch Series No. 418, 4 September 2002.

al-Aqqad, Abbas Mahmoud, *Haqa'iq al-Islam wa Abatil Khusumih* (Cairo: Dar al-Hilal, 1957).

Ardabili, *al-Anwar li-'Amal al-Abrar* (Cairo, no date).

Armanazi, Najib, *L'Islam et le Droit International* (thesis) (Paris: Librairie Picart, 1929).

Armstrong, Karen, *Holy War* (London and Basingstoke: Macmillan London Limited, 1988).

Arsu, Sebnem, "World Leaders Plan for Resolving East-West Rift", *The New York Times,* 14 November 2006.

Asculai, Ephraim, "Iran After The IAEA Vote: Still In The Driver's Seat", Jaffee Center for Strategic Studies, Tel Aviv Notes, No. 148, 30 September 2005.

Ashburn, Kristen, "The Suicide Bombers", *Telegraph Magazine,* 15 November 2003, pp. 24-33.

al-Asi, Mohammed, "Qur'anic Teaching on the Justification for *jihad* and Qital", *Crescent International* (1-15 June 2003), pp. 7, 11.

Atatürk'ün Tamim, Telgraf ve Beyannameleri (Circulars, Telegrams and Proclamations by Atatürk published as volume IV (1991) of Atatürk'ün Söylev ve Demeçleri (Ankara, 1989).

Atwan, Abdel Bari, "Total war: Inside the new Al-Qaeda", *The Sunday Times,* 26 February 2006.

Atwan, Abdel Beri, "The Pope has wronged [Muslims]... And should apologize", *Al-Quds al-Arabi,* 18 September 2006.

al-Azdi al-Basri, Muhammad b. 'Abdullah Abu Isma'il, *Ta'rikh Futuh al-Sham,* (ed.) 'Abd al-Mun'im 'Abdullah 'Amir (Cairo: Mu'assasat Sijill al-'Arab, 1970); (ed.) William Nassau Lees. Bibliotheca Indica (Calcutta, 1857).

Aznar, José María, *NATO: An Alliance for Freedom: How to transform the Atlantic Alliance to effectively defend our freedom and democracies* (Spain: Fundación para el Análisis y los Estudios Sociales, 20 October 2005).

Aznar, José María, "Seven Theses on Today's Terrorism" address at Georgetown University, 21 September 2004, http://www3. georgetown.edu/president/anzar/inauguraladdress.html, viewed 24 November 2006.

'Azzam, 'Abdullah, *Defense of the Muslim Lands,* (London: Ahle Sunna Wal Jama'at, nd).

'Azzam, 'Abdullah, *Join the Caravan,* (London: Azzam Publications, 1996).

Azzam, Maha, "Al-Qaeda: the misunderstood Wahhabi connection and the ideology of violence", The Royal Institute of International Affairs, Middle East Programme, Briefing No. 1, (February 2003).

Babur, *The Baburnama -Memoirs of Babur, Prince and Emperor,* translated and edited by Wheeler M. Thacktson, (Oxford University Press, 1996).

Badawi, Zaki M. A., *The Reformers of Egypt,* (London: Croom Helm, 1978).

Badawi, Zaki, M.A., *Islam in Britain* (London: Taha Publishers, 1981).

al-Baghdadi, 'Abd al-Qahir, *Mukhtasar Kitab al-Farq Bayn al-Firaq,* (ed.) Philip Hitti (Cairo, 1924).

Baghdadi, Abu Mansur 'Abd al-Qahir ibn Tahir, *Kitab Usul al-Din* (Istanbul, 1928).

Bajwa, Afzal, "Musharraf tells Abizaid where to get off", *The Nation,* 9 March 2006.

Bakhash, Shaul, *The Reign of the Ayatollahs: Iran and the Islamic Revolution* (New York, 1984).

al-Baladhuri, Ahmad b. Yahya, *Futuh al-Buldan [Conquests of the Countries]* (ed.) M.J. De Goeje (Leiden: Brill, 1866).

al-Baladhuri, Ahmad b. Yahya, *The Origins of the Islamic State,* a translation of *kitab futuh al-buldan,* translated by Philip Khuri Hitti (Piscataway, NJ: Gorgias Press, 2002).

Baljon, J.M.S., *The Reforms and Religious Ideas of Sir Sayyid Ahmad Khan* (Lahore: Shaikh Muhammad Ashraf, 1964).

Banerjee, Mukulika, *The Pathan Unarmed: Opposition and Memory in the North West Frontier* (Karachi: Oxford University Press, 2000).

Bangash, Zafar (ed.), *In Pursuit of the Power of Islam: Major Writings of Kalim Siddiqui* (London: The Open Press, 1996), pp. 253-255.

al-Banna, Hasan, *Five Tracts of Hasan al-Banna (1906-1949): A Selection from the Majmu'at Rasa'il al-Imam al-Shahid* (Berkeley, California: University of California Press, 1978).

Baram, Amaziah, "Two Roads in Revolutionary Shi'i Fundamentalism in Iraq: Hizb al-Da'wa al-Islamiyya and the Supreme Council of the Islamic Revolution of Iraq", in Martin E. Marty and R. Scott Appleby (eds.), *Accounting for Fundamentalisms: The Dynamic Character of Movements*, (Chicago: University of Chicago Press, 1994), pp. 531-586.

Bar Hebraeus, *The Chronography of Bar Hebraeus*, translated from the Syriac by Ernest A. Wallis Budge, Vol. I, (Piscataway, NJ: Gorgias Press, 2003).

Barghuthy, Omar Saleh, "A Ministry of Propaganda under the Fatimids", *Journal of the Middle East Society* (Spring 1947), pp. 57-59.

Barkey, Karen, "Ottoman Toleration: The Construction of Mechanisms of Inter-Religious, Inter-Ethnic Peace", Columbia University, Paper prepared for "Religion, Identity, and Empire", 16 & 17 April 2005, pp. 23-24, http://www.yale.edu/ycias/europeanstudies/empire/OE_Toleration_revised.pdf, viewed 3 May 2006.

bar Penkaye, John, *Ris Melle*. See Brock (1987).

Batrafi, Khaled Muhammad, "Why do we hate the People of the Book?" *Al-Hayat,* 21 October 2001. Extracts in English translation quoted in MEMRI Special Dispatch Series No. 295, 1 November 2001.

Bat Ye'or, *The Decline of Eastern Christianity under Islam: From Islam to Dhimmitude* (Cranbury, New Jersey / London: Farleigh Dickinson University Press and Associated University Presses, 1996).

Bat Ye'or, *Islam and Dhimitude: Where Civilizations Collide*, (Madison, NJ: Fairleigh Dickinson University Press, 2001).

Bayoumi, Dr Abdel-Mo'ti, "Wrong Zionist Perceptions of *jihad* in Islam via the Internet", *Al-Musawwar,* 23 August 2002. English translation in *Religious News Service from the Arab World,* 2 September 2002.

Bayoumi, Dr Abdel-Mo'ti, Dr Abdel Mo'ti Bayoumi interviewed by Cornelis Hulsman "Commenting on Bat Ye'or's article" in *Religious News Service from the Arab World,* 28 August 2002.

Bangash, Zafar, (ed.), *In Pursuit of the Power of Islam: Major Writings of Kalim Siddiqui* (London: The Open Press, 1996).

Bencheikh, Soheib, "Islam and Secularism", Interview with Soheib Bencheikh, Qantara.de, http://qantara.de/webcom/show_article.php?wc_c=478&wc_id=130&printmode=1, viewed 27 October 2006.

Berkes, Niyazi, *The Development of Secularism in Turkey*, (London: Hurst and Co. edition 1998).

Bewly, Aisha, "Introduction", in Muhammad Ibn Sa'd, *The Men of Madina* Vol. 2, a translation of Vol. 5 of *Kitab al-Tabaqat*) (London: Ta-Ha Publishers, 2000), pp. ix-x.

Bilal, Abdul Rahman, *Islamic Military Resurgence* (Lahore: Ferozsons (Pvt.) Ltd, 1991).

bin Laden, Osama, "Declaration of War Against the Americans Occupying the Land of the Two Holy Places", http://www.meij.or.jp/new/Osama%20bin%20Laden/jihad1.htm, viewed 6 September 2005.

bin Omar, Abdullah, "The Striving Sheik: Abdullah Azzam", translated by Mohammed Saeed in *Nida'ul Islam*, Issue 14, July-September 1996, http://www.islam.org.au/articles /14/AZZAM.HTM, viewed 28 September 2003.

Blair, John C., *The Sources of Islam: An Inquiry into the Sources of the Faith and the Practice of the Muhammadan Religion* (Madras: The Christian Literature Society for India, 1925).

Blair, Tony, "Why we fight on", transcript of a speech given by Mr Blair at the Foreign Policy Centre in London, 21 March 2006, *Real Clear Politics*, http://www.realclearpolitics.com/articles/2006/03/terrorism_must_be_tackled_head.html, viewed 24 November 2006.

Blanchard, Christopher M., *Al Qaeda: Statements and Evolving Ideology*, Congressional Research Service (CRS), Report for Congress, 16 November 2004, http://www.fas.org/irp/crs/RS21973.pdf, viewed 8 April 2005.

Blankinship, Khalid Yahya, *The End of the Jihad State: The Reign of Hisham Ibn 'Abd al-Malik and the Collapse of the Umayyads* (Albany: State University of New York Press, 1994).

Bonney, Richard, *Jihad: From Qur'an to bin Laden*, (Basingstoke: Palgrave Macmillan, 2004).

Borowiec, Andrew, "Tunisian leader advises on terror", *The Washington Times*, 16 February 2004.

Bos, Stefan J., "Christians Near Northern Iraq Persecuted", *Assist News Service,* 5 April 2003.

Bostom, Andrew G., "Muhammad, the Qurayza Massacre, and PBS", *FrontPageMagazine.com,* 20 December 2002.

Bostom, Andrew G. (ed.), *The Legacy of Jihad: Islamic Holy War and the Fate of Non-Muslims* (New York: Prometheus Books, 2005).

Boyle, J.A. (ed.), *The Cambridge History of Iran,* Vol. 5, (Cambridge: Cambridge University press, 1986).

Brachman, Jarret M. and McCants, William F., "Stealing Al-Qa'ida's Playbook", Combating Terrorism Center at West Point, CTC Report, (February 2006), pp. 15-17.

Breydy, Michael, *Corpus Scriptorum Christianorum Orientalium,* Vol. 471-2 Scriptores Arabici T.44-5 (Louvain: E. Peeters, 1985).

Bright, Martin, *When Progressives Treat with Reactionaries: The British State's Flirtation with Radical Islamists,* (London: Policy Exchange, 2006).

Brock, S.P., "North Mesopotamia in the Late Seventh Century. Book XV of John Bar Penkaye's *Ris Melle",* *Jerusalem Studies in Arabic and Islam,* Vol. 9 (1987), pp. 51-75.

Brooke, Steven, "The Preacher and the Jihadi", *Current Trends in Islamist Ideology,* Vol. 3, Hudson Institute, 16 February 2006, http://www.futureofmuslimworld.com/research/pubID.41/pub_detail.asp#, viewed 21 June 2006.

Brown, Judith M., *Modern India: The Origins of an Asian Democracy,* 2nd edition, in *The Short Oxford History of the Modern World* series (Oxford: Oxford University Press, 1995).

al-Bukhari, al-Imam Abu Abdillah Muhammed, *Sahih Al-Bukhari,* (ed.) Shaikh Qasem al-Rifaie (Beirut: Dar Al-Qalam, 1987).

Bush, George W., *Remarks by the President to the National Endowment for Democracy,* Ronald Reagan Building and International Trade Center, Washington D.C., 6 October 2005, http://www.ned.org/events/oct0605-Bush.html, viewed 7 March 2007.

Butterworth, Charles E. and Zartman, I. William, *Between the State and Islam,* (Cambridge: Cambridge University Press, 2001).

Carey, Andrew, "Islam's Confused Identity", *The Church of England Newspaper,* 28 August 2003, p. 8.

Caroe, Olaf, *The Pathans 550 B.C. – A.D. 1957* (London: Macmillan & Co. Ltd, 1965).

Carter, B.L., *The Copts In Egyptian Politics, 1918-1952* (London: Croom Helm, 1984).

Cassese, A. (ed.), *The Current Legal Regulation of the Use of Force* (Dordrecht: Martinus Nijhoff, 1986).

Catlos, Brian A., *The Victors and the Vanquished: Christians and Muslims of Catalonia and Aragon, 1050-1300* (Cambridge: Cambridge University Press, 2004).

Chebatoris, Matthew, "Islamist Infiltration of the Moroccan Armed Forces", *Terrorism Monitor*, Volume 5, Issue 3, 15 February 2007.

Chen, Joanna, "A Martyr or a Murderer", *Newsweek,* 23 February 2004.

Cirkovic, Sima M., *The Serbs,* (Oxford: Blackwell, 2004).

Cohen, Joshua and Chasman, Deborah, *Islam and the Challenge of Democracy: A Boston Review Book*, (Princeton & Oxford: Princeton University Press, 2004).

Cohen, Mark R., *Under Crescent and Cross: The Jews in the Middle Ages,* (Princeton, New Jersey: Princeton University Press, 1994).

Collins, Roger, *The Arab Conquest of Spain 710-797,* (Oxford: Blackwell, 1989).

Conesa, Pierre, "Background to Washington's War on Terror", *Le Monde Diplomatique,* January 2002.

"Conquered Land", Extract from the Encyclopaedia of Islam, CD-ROM Edition v. 1.0, © 1999 Koninklijke Brill NV, Leiden, The Netherlands.

Cook, David, *Contemporary Muslim Apocalyptic Literature,* (Syracuse, NY: Syracuse University Press, 2005).

Cook, David, *Understanding Jihad* (Berkeley, Los Angeles, London: University of California Press, 2005).

Cook, David, *Studies in Muslim Apocalyptic* (Princeton, New Jersey: The Darwin Press, 2002).

Cook, David, "America, the Second 'Ad: Prophecies About the Downfall of the United States," *Yale Center for International and Area Studies*, Vol. 5, The United States and the Middle East: Cultural Encounters (2002), pp. 150-93.

Corbin, Henri, *En Islam Iranien* (Paris: Gallimard, 1971).

Corn, Tony, "World War IV as Fourth-Generation Warfare", *Policy Review,* January 2006.

Cragg, Kenneth, *The House of Islam,* 2nd edition (California: Dickenson Publishing Co., 1978).

Cragg, Kenneth, "A Tale of Two Cities: Helping the Heirs of Mecca to Transform Medina", *Mission Frontiers* (December 2001).

Crane, Robert D., *Hirabah versus Jihad* Islamic Research Foundation Inc. (2006). http://www.irfi.org/articles/articles_301_350/hirabah_versus_jihad.htm, viewed 22 February 2007.

Crone, Patricia and Cook, Michael, *Hagarism: The Making of the Islamic World* (Cambridge: Cambridge University Press, 1977).

Crumley, Bruce, "*Jihad*'s Hidden Victim", *Time,* 2 June 2003, p. 48.

al-Daqs, Kamil Salama, *Ayat al -Jihad fi l-Qur'an al-Karim* (Kuwait: Dar al-Bayan, 1972).

ad-Damishqi, Ibn Katir, *Before & After the Last Hour,* (Karachi: Darul Ishaat, 2004)

Dankowitz, A., "Fighting Terrorism: Recommendations by Arab Reformists", *MEMRI Inquiry and Analysis Series*, No. 232, 28 July 2005

Daraz, Muhammad 'Abd Allah, "Mabadi' al-Qanun al-Dawli al-'Amm li-l-Islam", *Risalat al-Islam,* 2 (1950).

al-Dawalibi, Ma'ruf, "Islam and Nationalistic and Secularistic Trends", *Ash-Sharq al-Awsat,* 31 December 1989, reprinted in Kharofa (1994), pp. 1-17.

Dawoud, Khaled, "America's Most Wanted", *Al-Ahram Weekly Online,* Issue No. 552 (20-26 September 2001).

Declaration of Jihad Against the Country's Tyrants, Military Series, recovered by police in Manchester UK from the home of Nazihal Wadih Raghie, 10 May 2000.

Dekmejian, Hrair, *Islam in Revolution: Fundamentalism in the Arab World* (Syracuse, NY: Syracuse University Press, 1985).

Delehaye, Hipployte, "Passio sanctorum sexaginta martyrum", *Analecta Bollandiana: A Journal of Critical Hagiography,* Vol. 28 (1904), pp. 289-307.

Dennan, Shane and Black, Andrew, "Fourth generation warfare and the international jihad", *Jane's Intelligence Review,* October 2006, pp. 18-23.

Dentan, Robert C. (ed.), *Lectures of the Department of Near Eastern Languages and Literatures at Yale University*, American Oriental Series No. 38 (New Haven, Connecticut: Yale University Press, 1955).

Devenny, Patrick, "True Fanatic", *The American Spectator*, 15 December 2005.

Dionysius the Syrian, "Text No. 13: Dionysius Reconstituted", in *The Seventh Century in the West-Syrian Chronicles*, introduced, translated and annotated by Andrew Palmer (Liverpool: Liverpool University Press, 1993).

Doctrina Iacobi Nuper Baptizati, (ed.) N. Bonwetsch, *Abhandlungen der Königlichen. Gesellschaft der Wissenschaften zu Göttingen*, Philologisch-Historische Klasse. Neue Folge Vol.12, No. 3 (Berlin: Weidmannsche Buchh., 1910).

Donner, Fred M., "The Sources of Islamic Conceptions of War", in Kelsay and Johnson (1991), pp. 31-69.

Donohue, J.J. and Esposito, J.L. (eds.), *Islam in Transition: Muslim Perspectives* (New York: Oxford University Press, 1982).

Dozy, R., *Histoire des Musulmans d'Espagne*, 4 vols (Leiden: Brill, 1861).

Dozy, Reinhart, *Spanish Islam: A History of the Muslims in Spain*, translated by Francis Griffin Stokes (London: Goodward Books, 1913).

Drogin, Bob and Miller, Greg, "Spy Agencies Facing Questions of Tactics", *Los Angeles Times*, 29 October 2001.

Dupuy, R. Ernest and Dupuy, Trevor N., *The Collins Encyclopedia of Military History From 3500BC to the Present*, (New York: Harper Collins, 1993).

Dunn, Michael Collins, "Fundamentalism in Egypt", *Middle East Policy* Vol. 2, No. 3 (Summer, 1993)

"Egyptian Progressive Criticizes Muslim Intellectual Doublespeak", *MEMRI Special Dispatch Series*, No. 847, 14 January 2005.

Eibner, John, "My Career Redeeming Slaves", *Middle East Quarterly*, Vol. 4. No. 4, (December 1999).

Elliot and Dawson, *A History of India As Told by Its Own Historians*, 8 volumes (New Delhi: D K Publishers, reprinted 2001).

Ellis, Eric, "Mahathir Tirade at 'Jews Ruling World' ", *Times Online*, 17 October 2003, http://www.timesonline.co.uk /printFriendly/0,,1-3-857059,00.html, viewed 5 December 2003.

Emerson, Steven, "The American Connections to Islamic Terror", statement to Senate Judiciary Committee's Subcommittee on Terrorism, Technology, and Government Information, 24 February 1998; *Patterns of Global Terrorism*, 200, United States Department of State, May 2002, http://library.nps.navy.mil/home/tgp/hamas. htm, viewed 28 June 2005.

Enayat, Hamid, *Modern Islamic Political Thought* (Austin: University of Texas Press, 1982).

The Encyclopaedia of Islam, new edition, 11 vols (Leiden: Brill, 1979 onwards).

Engineer, Ali Asghar, "Islam and Non-violence", in Kumar (1995).

Esposito, John (ed.), *Voices of Resurgent Islam* (New York: Oxford University Press, 1983).

Esposito, John, *Islam: The Straight Path* (New York: Oxford University Press, 1988).

Esposito, John L. (ed.), *The Iranian Revolution: Its Global Impact,* (Miami: University of Florida Press, 1990).

Esposito, John (ed.), *The Oxford History of Islam* (Oxford: Oxford University Press, 1999).

Esposito, John (ed.), *The Oxford Encyclopedia of the Modern Islamic World,* 4 Volumes, (New York: Oxford University Press, 1995).

Esposito, John L., *Unholy War: Terror in the Name of Islam* (Oxford: Oxford University Press, 2002).

Esposito, John L., "Practice and Theory", in Joshua Cohen and Deborah Chasman, *Islam and the Challenge of Democracy: A Boston Review Book,* (Princeton & Oxford: Princeton University Press, 2004).

Eutychius, *Das Annalenwerk des Eutychios von Alexandrien,* edited and translated Michael Breydy *Corpus Scriptorum Christianorum Orientalium,* Vol. 471-2 Scriptores Arabici T.44-5 (Louvain: E. Peeters, 1985).

Evans, Arthur John, *Through Bosnia and the Hrzegovina on Foot during the Insurrection August and September 1875,* (Elibron Classics, originally published by Longmans Green, 1876).

el Fadl, Khaled Abou, *Rebellion and Violence in Islamic Law* (Cambridge: Cambridge University Press, 2001).

al-Fagih, Saad, "The War that Bin Laden is Winning", *The Guardian,* 13 May 2003.

Fandy, Mamoun, "Egypt's Islamic Group: regional revenge?" *Middle East Journal* Vol. 48, No. 4 (Autumn, 1994).

Faraj, Muhammad 'Abd al-Salam, *Al-Faridah al-Gha'ibah [The Neglected Duty]*. English translation in Jansen, Johannes J. G. *The Neglected Duty: The Creed of Sadat's Assassins and Islamic Resurgence in the Middle East* (New York: Macmillan, 1986), pp. 159-234.

al-Faruqi, Isma'il Raji, *Islam* (Brentwood, Maryland: International Graphics, 1984).

Fatoohi, Louay, *Jihad in the Qur'an: The Truth from the Source* (Kuala Lumpur: A. S. Noordeen, 2002).

Feldner, Yotam, "Sheikh Tantawi's Positions on Jihad Against Coalition Forces, Saddam's Resignation, and the War in Iraq", *MEMRI Inquiry and Analysis Series,* No. 130, 8 April 2003.

Ferguson, John, *War and Peace in the World's Religions* (London: Sheldon Press, 1977).

Fick, Nathaniel, *One Bullet Away: The Making of a Marine Officer* (Boston: Houghton Mifflin, 2005).

Fighel, Jonathan, "Sheikh Abdullah Azzam: Bin Laden's Spiritual Mentor", Institute for Counter Terrorism, 27 September 2001, http://www.ict.org.il/articles/articledet.cfm?articleid=388, viewed 28 September 2003.

"Final Declaration", Islam and Reform Workshop Cairo, 5-7 October 2004, Ibn Khaldun Centre for Development Studies (ICDS), NGO Events/News, Egypt, 7 October 2004, http://www.mengos.net/events/04newsevents/egypt/october/ibnkhaldun-English.htm, viewed 25 November 2005, also http://www.brookings.edu/fp/research/projects/islam/cairoclosing.pdf, viewed 25 November 2005.

Fine, John V.A. Jr., *The Late Medieval Balkans: A Critical Survey from the Late Twelfth Century to the Ottoman Conquest,* (Ann Arbor, MI: Michigan University Press, 1994).

Fisher, Humphrey J., *Slavery in the History of Muslim Black Africa,* (London: Hurst & Company, 2001).

Firestone, Reuven, *Jihad: The Origin of Holy War in Islam* (New York: Oxford University Press, 1999).

Fredegarius, *Chronicles,* (ed.) Bruno Krusch (Hanover: MGH Scriptores Rerum Merovingicarum T.2, 1888, repr. 1984).

Free Muslims Coalition website, www.freemuslims.org: "Our Positions: What we believe in"; "We are so sorry for 9-11"; "About FMCAT", viewed 22 October 2004.

Friedmann, Yohanan, *Tolerance and Coercion in Islam: Interfaith Relations in the Muslim Tradition*, (Cambridge: Cambridge University Press, 2003).

Friedman, Thomas L., "Defusing the Holy Bomb", *The New York Times*, 27 November 2002.

Fuller, Graham E., "The Youth Factor: The New Demographics of the Middle East and the Implications for U.S. Policy", The Saban Center for Middle East Policy at the Brookings Institution, Analysis Paper No. 3, June 2003.

Fundación para el Análisis y los Estudios Sociales (president of FAES, José María Aznar) *NATO: An Alliance for Freedom: How to transform the Atlantic Alliance to effectively defend our freedom and democracies*, 20 October 2005.

Furnish, Timothy, "Beheadings in the Name of Islam", *Middle East Quarterly*, Vol. 12, No. 2 (Spring 2005).

Furnish, Timothy, "Mahdism in the Sunni World Today", *ISIM Newsletter*, (4/99), p. 22.

Gaffney, Frank J., and colleagues, *War Footing: 10 Steps America Must Take to Prevail in the War for the Free World*, (Annapolis, Maryland: Naval Institute Press, 2006).

"Al-Gama'a Al-Islamiyya vs. Al-Qaeda", *MEMRI*, Special Dispatch Series, No. 1301, 27 September 2006.

Gambill, Gary C., and Abdelnour, Ziad K., "Hezbollah: Between Tehran and Damascus", *Middle East Intelligence Bulletin,* Vol. 4 , No. 2 (February 2002).

Gandhi, Rajmohan, *Understanding the Muslim Mind*, (New Delhi: Penguin Books India, 1987).

Ganor, Boaz, "Terror as a Strategy of Psychological Warfare", 15 July 2002, *Institute for Counter-Terrorism*, http://www.ict.org.il/articles/articledet.cfm?articleid=443, viewed 30 October 2006.

Gardner, Frank, "Grand Sheikh Condemns Suicide Bombings", *BBC News*, 4 December 2001. Available at www.bbc.co.uk/hi /english/ world/middle_east/newsid_1690000/1690624.stm, viewed 5 December 2001.

Gatsiounis, Ioannis, "Islam Hadhari in Malaysia", Center on Islam, Democracy and the Future of the Muslim World, Current Trends in Islamist Ideology, Vol. 3, 16 February 2006, www.futureofmuslimworld.com/research/pubID.43/pub_detail.asp, viewed 21 June 2006.

Gerholm, Thomas, "Two Muslim intellectuals in the postmodern West: Akbar Ahmed and Ziauddin Sardar", in Akbar Ahmed and Hastings Donnan, (eds.), *Islam, Globalization and Postmodernity* (London & New York: Routledge, 1994).

Ghannoushi, Soumaya, "The Erosion of the Arab State", *Aljazeera*, 26 September 2006.

Ghoshah, Abdullah, "The Jihad is the Way to Gain Victory", in D.F. Green, *Arab Theologians on Jews and Israel, Extracts from the Proceedings of the Fourth Conference of the Academy of Islamic Research*, pp. 67-68.

al Ghunaimi, Mohammad Talaat, *The Muslim Conception of International Law and the Western Approach* (The Hague: Martinus Nijhoff, 1968).

"GLOBAL TRENDS 2015: A Dialogue About the Future With Nongovernment Experts," National Intelligence Council, December 2000, http://www.dni.gov/nic/NIC_globaltrend2015.html#link8b, viewed 22 August 2006.

Godson, Dean, "Gone Native", *Prospect*, July 2006, pp. 12-14.

Goffman, Daniel, *The Ottoman Empire and Early Modern Europe,* (Cambridge: Cambridge University Press, 2002).

Gökay, Bülent, "Russia and Chechnia: A Long History of Conflict, Resistance and Oppression", *Alternatives: Turkish Journal of International Relations, ,* Vol. 3, Nos. 2 & 3, Sumer & Fall 2004.

Gold, Dore, *Hatred's Kingdom: How Saudi Arabia Supports the New Global Terrorism* (Washington DC: Regnery Publishing Inc., 2003).

Goldziher, Ignaz, *Introduction to Islamic Theology and Law* (Princeton, NJ: Princeton University Press, 1981).

Gowing, Peter G., "Moros and Khaek: The Position of Muslim Minorities in the Philippines and Thailand", in Ahmad Ibrahim et al., *Readings on Islam in Southeast Asia* (Singapore: ISEAS, 1985).

"The Great Divide: How Westerners and Muslims View Each Other", A 13-Nation Pew Global Attitudes Survey, (Washington DC: Pew Research Center), 22 June 2006.

Green, D.F., *Arab Theologians on Jews and Israel, Extracts from the Proceedings of the Fourth Conference of the Academy of Islamic Research* (Geneva: Editions de L'Avenir, 1976).

Grunebaum, Gustav E. Von, *Classical Islam: A History, 600-1258*, translated by Katherine Watson, 1st US (ed.) (Chicago: Aldine, 1970).

Guillaume, Alfred, *The Life of Muhammad: A Translation of Ibn Ishaq's Sirat Rasul Allah* (Karachi: Oxford University Press, 1955).

Gunaratna, Rohan, *Inside Al Qaeda : Global Network of Terror* (London: Hurst & Company, 2002).

Haddad, Y.Y., "The Quranic Justification for an Islamic Revolution: The View of Sayyid Qutb", *Middle East Journal* Vol. 37, No. 1 (Winter 1983).

Haddad, Y.Y., "Sayyid Qutb: Ideologue of Islamic Revival" in Esposito (ed.), (1983), pp. 67-98.

Halden, Philip, "Salafi in Virtual and Physical Reality", *ISIM Newsletter* No. 13 (December 2003).

Haleem, Harifyah Abdel, Oliver Ramsbotham, Saba Risaluddin and Brian Wicker (eds.) *The Crescent and the Cross:Muslim and Christian Approaches to War and Peace* (Basingstoke: Macmillan Press Ltd, 1998; New York: St Martin's Press, Inc., 1998).

Hall, John R., "Apocalypse 9/11", in Phillip Lucas and Thomas Robbins, (eds.), *NewReligious Movements in the Twenty-First Century: Political and Social Challenges in Global Perspective* (London: Routledge, 2004), pp. 265-282.

Halliday, Fred, "The Left and the Jihad", *OpenDemocracy*, 8 September 2006.

Halm, Heinz, *Shiism* translated by Janet Watson (Edinburgh: Edinburgh University Press, 1991)

Hamas, "Palestine in Islamic History", HAMASONLINE, www. hamasonline.com/indexx.php?page=Palestine/palestine_in_islamic_ history, viewed 17 March 2005.

Hamas, "The Charter of Allah: The Platform of the Islamic Resistance movement (Hamas)", translated and annotated by Raphael Israeli, Harry Truman Research Institute, The Hebrew University, Jerusalem, Israel, http://www.ict.org.il/articles/h_cov.htm, viewed 28 November 2005.

Hamid, Tawfik, *The Roots of Jihad* (USA: Top Executive Media, 2005).

Hamidullah, Muhammad, *Documents sur la Diplomatie Musulmane à l'époque du Prophete et des Khalifes Orthodoxes* (Paris: Librarie Oriental et Americane, Thesis, University of Paris, 1935).

Hamidullah, Muhammad, *Muslim Conduct of State,* 3rd edition (Lahore: Sh. Muhammad Ashraf, 1953).

Hamidullah, Muhammad, *The Battle Fields of the Prophet* (New Delhi: Kitab Bhavan, 1983).

Hammes, Thomas X., "Insurgency: Modern Warfare Evolves into a Fourth Generation", *Strategic Forum,* No. 214, January 2005.

Hammoud, Mirna, "Causes for Fundamentalist Popularity in Egypt" in Moussalli, Ahmad S. (ed.), 1998. *Islamic Fundamentalism: Myth and Realities,* pp. 322-323.

Haqqani, Hussain, "Where's the Muslim Debate?" *The Wall Street Journal,* 22 May 2003.

Harling, Peter and Guidère, Mathieu, " 'Withdraw, move on and rampage': Iraq's resistance evolves", *Le Monde Diplomatique* (May 2006).

Harnden, Toby, "Video Games Attract Young to Hizbollah", *The Daily Telegraph,* 21 February 2004, p. 18.

Hassiotis, Ioanis K., "The Armenian Genocide and the Greeks: Response and Records (1915-23)", in Richard G. Hovannisian, (ed.), *The Armenian Genocide: History, Politics, Ethics,* pp. 146-147.

al-Hawali, Sheikh Safar bin Abdur-Rahman, *Open Letter to President Bush,* 15 October 2001, Azzam Publications http://www.sunnahonline.com/ilm/contemporary/0025.htm, viewed 24 August 2007.

Hawting, G.R., *The First Dynasty of Islam: The Umayyad Caliphate AD 661-750,* (London: Routledge, 2000).

Hider, James, "Iraqis Drugged, Brainwashed and sent to die for Bin Laden", *The Times,* 22 March 2004.

Higgins, Rosalyn, "The Attitude of Western States towards Legal Aspects of the Use of Force", in Cassese (1986).

al-Hilali, Muhammad Taqi-ud-Din and Khan, Muhammad Muhsin, *Interpretation of the Meanings of the Noble Qur'an in the English Language: A Summarized Version of At-Tabari, Al-Qurtabi, and Ibn Kathir with Comments from Sahih Al-Bukhari,* 15th revised edition (Riyadh: Darussalam Publishers and Distibutors, December 1996).

al-Hilli, al-Muhaqqiq, *shara'i' al-Islam fi masa'il al halal wal-haram*, translated by Hasan M. Najafi, Vol. 1 (Qum: Ansariyan Publications, 2001).

Hilmi, Dr Tareq, "Amrika alati nabghad" (Arabic, America That We Hate), *Al-Sha'b*, 17 October 2003. See on-line at: http://alarabnews.com/alshaab/GIF/17-10-2003/tareq.htm , viewed 27 September 2006, English translation in Reuven Paz, "Islamism and Anti-Americanism", *Middle East Review of International Affairs*, Vol. 7, No. 4, (December 2003).

Hirschberg, H.Z., *The Jews of North Africa*, Vol. 1 (Leiden, 1974).

Hiskett, Mervyn, *The Sword of Truth: The Life and Times of the Shehu Usuman dan Fodio* (Evanston, IL: Northwestern University Press, 1994).

Hizb-ut-Tahrir, "They destroy the Houses of Allah", The Media Office of Hizb-ut-Tahrir in Sudan , 12 May 2005, http://www.hizb-ut-tahrir.info/english/sudan/2005/may1205.htm, viewed 28 November 2005.

Hodgson, Marshall G.S., *The Venture of Islam*, Vol. 1, *The Classical Age of Islam* (Chicago: University of Chicago Press, 1974).

Holt, P.M., *A Modern History of the Sudan*, 3rd edition (London: Weidenfeld and Nicolson, 1967).

Holt, P.M., Lambton, Ann K.S. and Lewis, Bernard (eds.), *The Cambridge History of Islam, Vol. 1A, The Central Islamic Lands from pre-Islamic Times to the First World War* (Cambridge: Cambridge University Press, 1970).

Holt, P.M., Lambton, Ann K.S. and Lewis, Bernard (eds.), *The Cambridge History of Islam, Vol. 2B, Islamic Socieiy and Civilizaton*, (Cambridge: Cambridge University Press, 1970).

Hookway, James, "How a Terrorist Proves his Faith", *Far Eastern Economic Review*, 14 November 2002.

Hooper, Charles, *Civil Law of Palestine and Transjordan* (Jerusalem: Azriel, 1933-6).

Hopwood, Derek, *Egypt: Politics and Society 1945-1990* (London: Harper Collins Academic, 1991).

Hopwood, Derek, *Habib Bourguiba of Tunisia*, (Basingstoke and London: The Macmillan Press, 1992).

Hosenball, Mark and Isikoff, Michael, "Al Qaeda Strikes Again", *Newsweek* (26 May – 2 June 2003), pp. 20-26.

Hourani, Albert, *Arabic Thought in the Liberal Age 1798-1939,* (Cambridge: Cambridge University Press, 1983).

Hovannisian, Richard G. (ed.), *The Armenian Genocide: History, Politics, Ethics,* (Basingstoke & New York: Palgrave, 1992).

Hughes, Thomas Patrick, *A Dictionary of Islam* (Lahore: Premier Book House, 1885).

Hulsman, Cornelis, "Commenting on Bat Ye'or's article" in *Religious News Service from the Arab World,* 28 August 2002.

"Human Rights in Saudi Arabia: A Deafening Silence", Human Rights Watch (December 2001) hrw.org/backgrounder/mena/saudi/, viewed 27 April 2006.

Huntington, Samuel P., *The Clash of Civilisations and the Remaking of the World Order* (New York: Simon and Schuster, 1996).

Hurley, Victor, *Jungle Patrol: The Story of the Philippine Constabulary* (New York: E.P. Dutton, 1938).

Husain, Moulvi Abu Said Mohammed, *A Treatise on Jihad (Iqtisad-fi-Masail-il-Jihad)* translated from Urdu (Lahore: Victoria Press, 1887).

Ibn 'Abd-Allah, Hasan, *Athar al-Uwal fi Tartib al-Duwal* (Cairo, 1878 or 1879). The original work dates from 1308 or 1309.

Ibn Abidin, Muhammad Amin, *Radd al-Muhtar 'ala al-durr al-Mukhtar,* 7 vols (Cairo, 1856 or 1857).

Ibn Abi Zayd al-Qayrawani, Abu Muhammad 'Abdullah, *La Risala (Epitre sur les éléments du dogme et de la loi del'Islam selon le rite malakite).* Arabic text with French translation by Leon Bercher, 4th edition (Algiers, 1951).

Ibn al-Atir, *al-Kamil fi al-Ta'rikh,*

Ibn A'tham al-Kufi, Abu Muhammad Ahmad, *Kitab al-Futuh,* (ed.) Muhammad 'Ali al-'Abbasi and Sayyid 'Abd al-Wahhab Bukhari, 8 vols, (Hyderabad: Da'irat al-Ma'arif al-'Uthmaniyya, 1968-75).

Ibn Battuta, *The Travels of Ibn Battutah,* edited by Tim Mackintosh-Smith (Basingstoke: Macmillan, 2002).

Ibn Baz, Abdul-Aziz; Abdullah, Abdul-Aziz Ibn Abdullah Al-Shaykh; Al-Fawzan, Salih Ibn Fawzan and Abu Zaid, Bakr Ibn Abdullah (The Permanent Committee for Academic Research and Ifta) *Unification of Religions,* Fatwa no. 19402, 2 June 1997 available at www.troid.org/articles/islaamicinfo/Islaamingeneral/whatisislaam/unificationofreligion, viewed 7 August 2003.

Ibn Baz, Shaykh and Uthaymeen, Shaykh, *Muslim Minorities: Fatawa Regarding Muslims Living as Minorities* (Hounslow: Message of Islam, 1998).

Ibn Hisham, 'Abd al-Malik *al-Sira al-Nabawiyya* (ed.) Heinrich Ferdinand Wüstenfeld *Sirat Rasul Allah [Das Leben Muhammeds]* 2 vols (Göttingen: Dieterischen Buchhandlung, 1858-60).

Ibn Hudayl, *L'ornement des âmes*, French translation by Louis Mercier, (Paris, 1939), p. 195; English translation by Michael J. Miller. Quoted in Andrew G. Bostom, (ed.), *The Legacy of Jihad: Islamic Holy War and the Fate of Non-Muslims* (New York: Prometheus Books, 2005).

Ibn 'Izzat, Muhammad and 'Arif, Muhammad, *Al-Mahdi and the End of Time*, (London: Dar Al Taqwa, 1997).

Ibn Khaldun, *The Muqaddimah: An Introduction To History*, translation Franz Rosenthal, 3 vols (London: Routledge & Kegan Paul, 1958).

Ibn Khaldun, *History of the Berbers and the Moslem Dynasties of Northern Africa*, translated from Arabic [into French] by Baron De Slane (Paris, 1925).

Ibn Naqib al-Misri, Ahmad, *Reliance of the Traveller: A Classic Manual of Sacred Islamic Law, 'Umdat al-Salik,* edited and translated Nuh Ha Mim Keller revised edition (Beltsville, Maryland: Amana Publications, 1997).

Ibn Qudama, Abu Muhammad 'Abd-Allah ibn Ahmad ibn Muhammad, *Kitab al-Mughni,* (ed.) M. Rashid Rida, 9 vols (Cairo, 1947 or 1948).

Ibn Rushd, Abu al-Walid Muhammad Ibn Muhammad (Averroes), *Bidyat al-Mujtahid wa-Nihayat al-Muqtasid [The Beginning for him who Interprets the Sources Indepently and the End for him who Wishes to Limit Himself]* Chapter on *jihad* in English translation in Peters (1996), pp. 29-42.

Ibn Rushd, *The Distinguished Jurist's Primer (Bidayat al-Mujtahid),* translated by Imran Ahsan Khan Nyazee, Vol. 1 (Reading: Garnet Publishing, 1994).

Ibn Sa'd, Muhammad, *Kitab al-Tabaqat al-Kabir,* (ed.) Eduard Sachau et al. 9 vols (Leiden: Brill, 1904-40).

Ibn Sallam, Abu 'Ubayd al-Qasim, *Kitab al-Amwal,* (ed.) Muhammad Khalil Haras (Cairo, 1968).

Ibn Sallam, *The Book of Revenue (Kitab al-Amwal)*, translated by Imran Ahsan Khan Nyazee, (Reading: Garnet, 2002).

Ibn Taymiyya, Taqi al-Din Ahmad, *al-Siyasa al-Shar'iyya fi Islah al-Ra'i wa-al-Ra'iyya [Governance according to God's Law in Reforming both the Ruler and his Flock]*. Section on *jihad* reproduced in Peters (1996), pp. 43-54.

Ibn Taymiyya, Taqi al-Din Ahmad, *Majmu'at al-fatawa li-Sheikh al-Islam Taqi al-Din Ahmad Bin Taymiyya al-Hurani*, (al-Mansourah: dar al-wafa' wal nashr wal tawzi', 1997).

Ibn Taymiyya, *Iqtida al-sirat al-mustaqim*, Vol. 1, 416, quoted in Yohanan Friedmann, *Tolerance and Coercion in Islam: Interfaith Relations in the Muslim Tradition*, (Cambridge: Cambridge University Press, 2003), p. 26.

Ibn 'Uthaymeen, Sheikh, *Riyaadhus-Saaliheen*, Vol.1, 165-166. Available at www.fatwa-online.com/fataawa/worship/jihaad/jih004/0010915_1.htm, viewed 12 August 2003.

Ibn Warraq, *Why I am not a Muslim* (New York: Prometheus Books, 1995).

Ibn Warraq, "Honest Intellectuals Must Shed their Spiritual Turbans", *The Guardian*, 10 November 2001.

Ibrahim, Ahmad, Sharon Siddique and Yasmin Hussain (eds.), *Readings on Islam in Southeast Asia* (Singapore: Institute of Southeast Asian Studies, 1985).

Ibrahim, Naajeh, Asim Abdul Majid and Darbaalah, Esaam-ud-Deen, *In Pursuit of Allah's Pleasure* (London: Al-Firdous Ltd, 1997).

Imber, Colin, *The Ottoman Empire, 1300-1650: The Structure of Power* (Basingstoke: Palgrave Macmillan, 2002).

"In the tent or out?", *The Economist*, 28 October 2004.

Inalcik, Halil, *The Ottoman Empire: the Classical Age 1300-1600* (London: Phoenix Press, 2000).

"Indonesia Backgrounder: Why Salafism and Terrorism Mostly Don't Mix", ICG Asia Report, No. 83, 13 September 2004.

International Crisis Group (ICG), Asia Report No. 43, "Indonesia Backgrounder: How the Jemaah Islamiyah Terrorist Network Operates", Jakarta/Brussels, 11 December 2002.

Interpretation of the Meanings of The Noble Qur'an in the English language, a summarised version of At-Tabari, Al-Qurtubi and Ibn Kathir with comments from Sahih Al-Bukhari, summarized in one volume, by Dr Muhammad Taqi-ud-Din Al-Hilali and Dr Muhammad Muhsin Khan of the Islamic University, Medina, (Riyadh: Darussalam, 1996).

"Interview With Afghan Islamist Leader On Jihad Against U.S.", *MEMRI, Special Dispatch Series* - No. 455, January 6, 2003.

Iqbal, Anwar, "Islamic schools create Pakistani dilemma", United Press International, 17 August 2002.

"Iraqi Detainees Forced to Denounce Islam: Disbelievers?", *Islam Online,* http://www.islamonline.net/servlet/Satellite?cid=1119503 548526&pagename=IslamOnline-English-Ask_Scholar/FatwaE/ FatwaEAskTheScholar, viewed 15 August 2005.

"Islam, Apostasy and PAS", *Resources@Sisters in Islam,* 22 July 1999, http://www.muslimtents.com/sistersinnislam/resources/1apostat.htm, viewed 14 November 2005.

"Islamic Perspectives on Peace and Violence", *United States Institute of Peace,* Special Report 82, 24 January 2002, www.usip.or/pubs/ specialreports/sr82.html, viewed 5 September 2005.

Ismail, Salwa, *Rethinking Islamist Politics: Culture, the State and Islamism,* (London: IB Tauris, 2003).

Istanbuli, Yasin, *Diplomacy and Diplomatic Practice in the Early Islamic Era* (Oxford: Oxford University Press, 2001).

Izutsu, Toshihiko, *The Structure of the Ethical Terms in the Koran* (Tokyo: Keio Institute of Philological Studies, 1959).

Jaber, Hala and Mahnaimi, Uzi, "Suicide Bombing was a Family Affair", *The Sunday Times,* 18 January 2004.

Jabbour, Nabeel T., *The Rumbling Volcano: Islamic Fundamentalism in Egypt,* (Pasadena, CA: William Carey Library, 1993).

Jackson, Roy, *Fifty Key Figures in Islam,* (London and New York: Routledge, 2006).

Jaffe, Greg, "A General's New Plan to Battle Radical Islam", *Wall Street Journal,* 2 September 2006.

Jahanian, Darius, "Islamic era histroy of Zoroastrians of Iran through political analysis and historical letters", http://www.vohuman.org/ Article/Islamic%20era%20histroy%20of%20Zoroastrians%20of%2 0Iran.htm, viewed 4 May 2006.

Jameelah, Maryam, *Islam and Modernism* (Sant Nagar, Lahore: Mohammad Yusuf Khan, 1968).

Jan, Abid Ullah, *A War on Islam?* (Birmingham: Maktabah Al Ansar, 2002).

Jan, Abid Ullah, "Palestine Is Both Religious And Muslim Issue", USA Media Monitors, Saturday 15 October 2005, http://usa.mediamonitors. net/content/view/full/21402, viewed 11 November 2005.

Jandora, John W., "Developments in Islamic Warfare: The Early Conquests", *Studia Islamica,* Vol. 64 (1986), pp. 101-113.

Jansen, Johannes J. G., *The Neglected Duty: The Creed of Sadat's Assassins and Islamic Resurgence in the Middle East* (New York: Macmillan, 1986).

Jenet, Christie and Stewart, Randal G., (eds.), *Politics of the Future: The Role of Social Movements,* (Melbourne: Macmillan, 1989).

Jaspert, Nikolas, *The Crusades,* translated by Phyllis G. Jestice, (New York and London: Routledge, 2006).

"Jihad in Cyberspace", *The Economist,* 15 March 2003.

John, Bishop of Nikiu, *Chronicle* translated R.H. Charles (London, Oxford, 1916).

John, Elizabeth and Chelvi, K.T., "The Chilling Jemaah Islamiyah Goal", *New Sunday Times,* 19 January 2003.

Johnson, James Turner, "Historical Roots and Sources of Just War Tradition in Western Culture" in Kelsay and Johnson (1991), pp. 3-30.

Johnson, James Turner and Kelsay, John (eds.), *Cross, Crescent and Sword: The Justification and Limitation of War in Western and Islamic Tradition* (Westport, Connecticut: Greenwood Press, 1990).

Johnson, Nels, *Islam and the Politics of Meaning in Palestinian Nationalism* (London: Kegan Paul, 1982).

Johnson, Paul, *The Birth of the Modern: World Society 1815-1830* (New York: Harper Collins, 1991).

Jomier, Jacques, *How to Understand Islam,* (London: SCM Press, 1989).

Jukes, Worthington, *Frontier Heroes: Reminiscences of Missionary Work in Amritsar 1872-1873 and on the Afghan Frontier in Peshawar 1873-1890* (manuscript dated Exmouth, 1925, re-typed Peshawar, 2000).

Juynboll, Gautier H.A., (translation), *The History of Al -Tabari Vol. XIII: The Conquest of Iraq, Southwestern Persia, and Egypt* (Albany: State University of New York Press, 1989).

Kaegi, Walter E., *Byzantium and the Early Islamic Conquests* (Cambridge: Cambridge University Press, 1992).

al-Kalbi, *Al-Hafz Al-Tashil Fi Ulum Al-Tanzil [The Easiest Revelation of Theology]*.

Kandhalvi, Muhammad Zakariyya, "Stories of Sahabah" in *Tablighi Nisab* (Dewsbury: Anjuman-e-Islahul Muslemeen of U.K., no date but probably soon after 1938).

Katz, Rita, "It's Real", 21 October 2005, *National Review Online*, http://www.nationalreview.com/comment/katz200510210928.asp, viewed 26 October 2005.

Kelsay, John and Johnson, James Turner (eds.) *Just War and Jihad: Historical and Theoretical Perspectives on War and Peace in Western and Islamic Traditions* (Westport, Connecticut: Greenwood Press, 1991).

Kennedy, Hugh, *The Prophet and the Age of the Caliphates: the Islamic Near East from the Sixth to the Eleventh Century* (Harlow: Pearson Education Limited (Longman), 1986).

Kepel, Gilles, *The Prophet and The Pharaoh: Muslim Extremism in Egypt,* (London: al-Saqi, 1985).

Kepel, Gilles, *Jihad: The Trail of Political Islam,* translated Anthony F. Roberts (London: I.B. Tauris, 2002).

Kepel, Gilles, "The Origins and Development of the Jihadist Movement: From Anti-Communism to Terrorism", translated Peter Clark in *Asian Affairs,* Vol. 34, No. 2 (July 2003), pp. 91-108.

Kepel, Gilles in "Political Islam: A Conversation with Gilles Kepel and Jeffrey Goldberg", *CENTER Conversations*, No. 22, July 2003, www.eppc.org/docLib/20030728_CenterConversation22.pdf, viewed 22 September 2005.

Khadduri, Majid, *War and Peace in the Law of Islam* (Baltimore: The Johns Hopkins Press, 1955).

Khadduri, Majid, (translated and annotated) *The Islamic Law of Nations: Shaybani's Siyar* (Baltimore: The Johns Hopkins Press, 1966).

Khaled, Hassan, "Jihad in the Cause of Allah", in D.F. Green, *Arab Theologians on Jews and Israel, Extracts from the Proceedings of the Fourth Conference of the Academy of Islamic Research*, pp. 63-66.

Khamenei, Ali, "No Need for Iran-US Negotiations," excerpts from a *khutbah* addressed to Tehran's Friday worshippers on 16th January 1998, *MSANEWS,* 27 January 1998.

Khan, Majid Ali, *The Pious Caliphs* (New Delhi: Millat Book Centre, 1976).

Khan, Qamaruddin, *The Political Thought of Ibn Taymiyah Taymiyah* (Delhi: Adam Publishers, 1982).

Khan, Sa'ad, Reasserting International Islam: A Focus on the Organization of the Islamic Conference and Other Islamic Institutions, (Oxford: Open University Press, 2001), pp. 107-108.

Khan, Sir Syed Ahmed, in *The Pioneer,* 23 November 1871 and in *Review on Dr Hunter's Indian Musulmans: Are They Bound in Conscience to Rebel Against the Queen?* (Benares: Medical Hall Press, 1872).

Kharofa, Ala'Eddin, "Muhammad the Messenger of God (PBUH) and Westerners", in Kharofa (1994), pp. 95-102.

Kharofa, Ala'Eddin, *Nationalism, Secularism, Apostasy and Usury in Islam* (Kuala Lumpur: A.S. Nordeen, 1994).

Khomeini, Ayatollah Ruhollah, "Islamic Government", in Donohue and Esposito (1982), pp. 314-322.

Khwaja, Maruf, "Muslims in Britain: generations, experiences, futures", *openDemocracy*, 2 August 2005.

King, Anthony, "One in four Muslims sympathises with motives of terrorists", *The Daily Telegraph*, 23 July 2005.

Kinross, Lord, *The Ottoman Centuries: The Rise and Fall of the Turkish Empire* (New York: Morrow Quill Paperbacks, 1979).

Kister, M.J., "The Massacre of the Banu Qurayza: A Re-examination of a Tradition", *Jerusalem Studies in Arabic and Islam,* Vol. 8 (1986), pp. 61-96. Also reproduced in Kister, M.J. *Society and Religion from Jahiliyya to Islam* (Aldershot: Variorum, 1990).

Klein, F.A., *The Religion of Islam* (London: Curzon Press Ltd and New York: Humanities Press Inc, 1906, reprinted 1971, 1979).

Kohlberg, Etan, "The Development of the Imami Shi'i Doctrine of Jihad" in *Zeitschrift der Deutschen Morgenlaendischen Gesellschaft,* Vol. 126 (1976).

Kraemer, Joel, "Apostates, Rebels and Brigands", *Israel Oriental Studies,* Vol. 10 (1980), pp. 34-73.

Kramer, Martin, *Islam Assembled: The Advent of the Muslim Congresses* (New York, Columbia University Press, 1986).

Kramer, Martin, *Hezbollah's Vision of the West* (Washington, D.C: The Washington Institute Policy Papers, No. 16, 1989).

Kramer, Martin, "Redeeming Jerusalem: The Pan-Islamic Premise of Hizballah", in David Menashri, (ed.), *The Iranian Revolution and the Muslim World* (Boulder: Westview, 1990), pp. 105-130.

Kramer, Martin, "Hizbullah: The Calculus of Jihad", in Martin E. Marty and R. Scott Appleby, (eds.), *Fundamentalisms and the State: Remaking Politics, Economies, and Militance*, (Chicago: University of Chicago Press, 1992), pp. 539-556.

Kramer, Martin, "The Moral Logic of Hizballah", in Walter Reich, (ed.), *Origins of Terrorism: Psychologies, Theologies, States of Mind* (Washington, DC: Woodrow Wilson Center Press, 2001), pp. 131-157.

Al-Kufi, *The Chachnamah, an Ancient History of Sind*, translated by Mirza Kalichbeg Fredunbeg, (Lahore: Vanguard Books, 1985).

Al-Kufi, *The Chachnama*, in Elliot and Dawson, *A History of India As Told by Its Own Historians*, Vol. 1, pp. 131-211.

Kumar, R. (ed.) *Khan Abdul Gaffar Khan: A Centennial Tribute* (New Delhi: Nehru Memorial Museum and Library, Har-Anand Publications, 1995).

Kuran, Timur, "The Religious Undercurrents of Muslim Economic Grievances", Social Science Research Council, http://www.ssrc.org/sept11/essays/kuran.htm, viewed 13 September 2006.

Kurkjian, Vahan M., *A History of Armenia* (The Armenian General Benevolent Union of America, 1958).

Lal, K.S., *The Legacy of Muslim Rule in India*, (New Delhi: Aditya Prakashan, 1992).

Lane-Poole, Stanley, *The Barbary Corsairs*, (London: Darf Publishers, 1984).

Lapidus, Ira M., *A History of Islamic Societies*, (Cambridge, New York and Melbourne: Cambridge University Press, 1988).

Laroui, Abdallah, "Western Orientalism and Liberal Islam: Mutual Distrust?", *Middle East Studies Association Bulletin*, Vol. 31, No. 1, July 1997.

"Leading Islamist Sheikh Yousef Al-Qaradhawi: We are Fighting in the Name of Islam...", MEMRI: Latest News, Special Dispatch Series No. 1102, February 28, 2006, http://memri.org/bin/articles.cgi?Page=subjects&Area=antisemitism&ID=SP110206, viewed 31 May 2006.

Le Tourneau, Roger, *The Almohad Movement in North Africa in the Twelfth and Thirteenth Centuries*, Princeton, NJ: Princeton University Press, 1969.

Lewis, Bernard, *The Assassins: A Radical Sect in Islam* (London: Phoenix, 2003). First published 1967.

Lewis, Bernard, *The Political Language of Islam* (Chicago and London: The University of Chicago Press, 1988).

Lewis, Bernard, "Roots of Muslim Rage", *The Atlantic Monthly*, Volume 266, No. 3, (September 1990), pp. 47-60.

Lewis, Bernard , "License to Kill: Usama bin Ladin's Declaration of Jihad", *Foreign Affairs,* (November/December 1998).

Lewis, Bernard, "The Revolt of Islam", *The New Yorker,* 19 November 2001.

Lewis, Bernard, *The Crisis of Islam: Holy War and Unholy Terror,* (London: Weidenfeld and Nicolson, 2003).

"Libyan Leader Mu'ammar Al-Qadhafi: Europe and the U.S. Should Agree to Become Islamic or Declare War on the Muslims", MEMRI, TV Monitor Project, Clip No. 1121, 10 April 2006, http://www.memritv.org/Transcript.asp?P1=1121, viewed 22 August 2006.

Lichtenthaler, Gerhard, "Muslih, Mystic and Martyr: The Vision of Mahmud Muhammad Taha and the Republican Brothers in the Sudan: Towards an Islamic Reformation?" MA dissertation (London: SOAS, 1993).

Lind, William S., Nightengale, Keith and Sutton, Joseph W., "The Changing Face of War: Into the Fourth Generation", *Marine Corps Gazette*, October 1989, pp. 22-26.

Lind, William S., "Understanding Fourth Generation War", AntiWar.com, 15 January 2004, http://antiwar.com/lind/index.php?articleid=1702, viewed 24 October 2006.

Lindley-French, Julian, *British Strategic Leadership: food for thought* The Shrivenham Papers No. 2 (October 2006) (Shrivenham, UK: The Defence Academy, 2006).

Lippman, Thomas W., *Inside The Mirage: America's Fragile Partnership with Saudi Arabia* (Boulder, Colorado: Westview, 2004).

Lucas, Phillip and Robbins, Thomas, (eds.), *New Religious Movements in the Twenty-First Century: Political and Social Challenges in Global Perspective* (London: Routledge, 2004).

MacAskill, Ewen and Traynor, Ian, "Saudis Consider Nuclear Bomb", *The Guardian,* 18 September 2003.

Maghraoui, Abdesalam M., *American Foreign Policy and Islamic*

Renewal, United States Institute of Peace Special Report 164 (July 2006)

Mahmasani, Sobhi, *al-Nazariyya al 'Amma Li'l-Mujibat wa'l-'Uqud* (Beirut, 1948).

Mahmassani, Sobhi, "International Law in the Light of Islamic Doctrine", *Academie de Droit International, Recueil des Cours*, Vol. 117 (1966).

Al-Majalla, translated Charles Hooper in *Civil Law of Palestine and Transjordan*, Vol. 1 (Jerusalem: Azriel, 1933-6).

Mallat, Chibli, *Shi'i Thought from the South of Lebanon*, (Oxford: Centre for Lebanese Studies, 1988).

Malfuzat-i-Timuri, in Elliot and Dawson, *A History of India As Told by Its Own Historians*, Vol. 3, (New Delhi: D K Publishers, reprinted 2001), pp. 394-395.

Malik, Aftab, "The state Muslims are in", *openDemocracy,* 15 August 2005.

Malik, Brigadier S.K., *The Quranic Concept of War,* Indian edition (New Delhi: Himalayan Books. 1986).

Mango, Andrew, *Atatürk* (London: John Murray, 1999).

Mansour, Mu'aadh, "The Importance of Military Preparedness in Shari'ah" in *Al-Battar Training Camp* issue 1 (December 2003 or January 2004?) www.hostinganime.com/battar/b1word.zip. Excerpts in English translation in MEMRI Special Dispatch Series No. 637, 6 January 2004.

Mansur, 'Ali , *Al-Shari'a al-Islamiyya wa-l-Qanun al-Dawli al-'Amm* (Cairo: al-Majlis al-A'la li-l-Shu'un al-Islamiyya, 1971).

Mansur, Salim, "Muslim on Muslim Violence: What Drives It?", Center for Security Policy, Occasional Papers Series , No. 1, June 2004.

al-Maqdisi, Abu Muhammad, "This is Our 'Aqeedah", Reviving Islam.com Research Team, http://www.revivingislam.com/aqeedah/thisisouraqeedah.html, viewed 27 January 2006.

Marcus, Itamar, "PA TV Glorifies First Woman Suicide Terrorist – Wafa Idris", *Palestinian Media Watch Bulletin,* 24 July 2003.

Marcus, Itamar, "UN is Funding Summer Camps Honoring Terrorists", *Palestinian Media Watch Bulletin,* 25 July 2003.

al-Marginani, 'Ali ibn Abi Bakr, *The Hedaya : Commentary on the Islamic laws* translated Charles Hamilton, 4 volumes (New Delhi:

Kitab Bhavan, 1985). This is a facsimile of a book originally published in 1791.

Marlowe, Lara, "Where girls are killed for going to school", written by Lara Marlowe for *Marie Claire, Amnesty International Press Awards,* http:// www.amnesty.org.uk/news/awards/period.html, viewed 28 April 2006.

Marty, Martin E. and Appleby, R. Scott (eds.), *Accounting for Fundamentalisms: The Dynamic Character of Movements,* The Fundamentalism Project Vol. 4 (Chicago and London: University of Chicago Press, 1994).

Marty, Martin E. and Appleby, R. Scott (eds.), *Fundamentalisms and the State: Remaking Polities, Economies and Militance,* The Fundamentalism Project, Vol. 3 (Chicago and London: University of Chicago Press, 1993).

Marty, Martin E. and Appleby, R. Scott (eds.), *Fundamentalisms Observed* The Fundamentalism Project Vol. 1 (Chicago and London: Chicago University Press, 1991).

Masmoudi, Radwan A., "The Silenced Majority", *Islam 21,* Issue No. 34 (May 2003), http://islam21.net/quarterly/Islam21-May03.pdf, viewed 11 August 2005.

Masood, Ehsan, "A Muslim Journey", *Prospect,* Issue 113 (August 2005).

Masriya, Y., "A Christian Community: The Copts In Egypt," in Veenhoven et al., *On Human Rights And Fundamental Freedoms, A World Survey,* Vol. 4, (The Hague: Martinus Nijhoff, 1976).

al-Matboli, Ahmed, "German Exhibition Promotes Peaceful Islam", *IslamOnline,* 27 April 2006, http://www.islamonline.net/English/ News/2006-04/27/article02.shtml, viewed 16 October 2006.

al-Mawardi, Abu'l Hasan, *The Ordinances of Government: al-Ahkam al-Sultaniyya w'al-Wilayat al-Diniyya* translated Wafaa H. Wahba, The Centre for Muslim Contribution to Civilization (Reading: Garnet Publishing Ltd, 1996).

Mawdudi, Sayyid Abul A'la, *Jihad fi Sabilillah (jihad in Islam),* translated Kurshid Ahmad, (ed.) Huda Khattab (Birmingham: Islamic Mission Dawah Centre, 1997).

Mawlawi, Faysal "Seeking Martyrdom by Attacking US Military Bases in the Gulf", *Islam Online,* http://www.islamonline.net/servlet/Satell ite?pagename=IslamOnline-English_Ask_Scholar/FatwaE/FatwaE& cid=1119503546700, viewed 25 June 2006.

Mayer, Ann Elizabeth, "War and Peace in the Islamic Tradition and International Law" in Kelsay and Johnson (1991), pp. 195-226.

McCants, William (ed.) and Brachman, Jarret, *Militant Ideology Atlas* (New York: Combating Terrorism Center, US Military Academy, 2007).

McGrory, Daniel, "Cleric's tape threat to destroy Rome", *The Times*, 3 April 2004.

McGrory, Daniel and Lister, Sam, "Prophets of Hate Prey on Rootless Misfits", *The Times*, 31 January 2003.

MEMRI The Middle East Media Research Institute, P.O. Box 27837, Washington DC 20038-7837, USA http://memri.org:

> "Egyptian Progressive Criticizes Muslim Intellectual Doublespeak", *MEMRI Special Dispatch Series*, No. 847, 14 January 2005.

> Feldner, Yotam, "Sheikh Tantawi's Positions on Jihad Against Coalition Forces, Saddam's Resignation, and the War in Iraq", *MEMRI Inquiry and Analysis Series*, No. 130, 8 April 2003.

> "Al-Gama'a Al-Islamiyya vs. Al-Qaeda", *MEMRI*, Special Dispatch Series, No. 1301, 27 September 2006.

> "Leading Islamist Sheikh Yousef Al-Qaradhawi: We are Fighting in the Name of Islam...", *MEMRI: Latest News, Special Dispatch Series*, No. 1102, 28 February 2006, http://memri.org/bin/articles.cgi?Page=subjects&Area=antisemitism&ID=SP110206, viewed 31 May 2006.

> Stalinksy, Steven, "Saudi Policy Statements on Support to the Palestinians", *MEMRI Special Report*, No. 17, 3 July 2003.

> Stalinsky, Steven, "Leading Egyptian Islamic Clerics on Jihad Against U.S. Troops in Iraq: March-August 2003", *MEMRI Inquiry and Analysis Series*, No. 145, 14 August 2003.

> Yehoshua, Y. "Reeducation of Extremists in Saudi Arabia", *MEMRI, Inquiry and Analysis Series*, No. 260, 18 January 2006.

> Yehoshua, Y. "A Cairo Conference Calling for Reform Raises the Ire of the Egyptian Religious Establishment", *MEMRI Inquiry and Analysis Series* - No. 192, 22 October 2006.

Menashri, David (ed.), *The Iranian Revolution and the Muslim World* (Boulder: Westview, 1990).

Merle, Renae, "Pentagon Funds Diplomacy Effort, Contracts Aim to Improve Foreign Opinion of United States", *Washington Post*, 11 June 2005.

Mernissi, Fatema, *Islam and Democracy: Fear of the Modern World* (Cambridge, MA: Perseus Publising, 1992).

"MI5 Chief Fears Dirty Bomb is Inevitable", *The Times,* 18 June 2003.

Michael the Syrian, *Chronique de Michel Le Syrien*, edited and translated from the Syriac by Jean-Baptiste Chabot, Paris, 1899-1905, Vol. 3, 235-236; quoted in Andrew G. Bostom, (ed.), *The Legacy of Jihad: Islamic Holy War and the Fate of Non-Muslims,* pp. 612-613.

Mikkelson, Barbara and David, "Pershing the Thought", Urban Legends Reference Pages at www.snopes.com/rumors/pershing.htm, 26 February 2002; viewed 11 December 2002.

Miles, Hugh, "Blogger is jailed for four years for insulting Islam and president", *The Daily Telegraph*, 23 February 2007.

Mishal, Shaul and Sela, Avraham, *"The Palestinian Hamas: Vision Violence and Coexistence"* (New York: Columbia University Press, 2000).

Mishkat al-Masabih, English translation with explanatory notes by James Robson, 2 vols (Lahore: Sh. Muhammad Ashraf, 1990).

al-Misri, Ahmad Ibn Naqib, *Reliance of the Traveller: A Classic Manual of Sacred Islamic Law ('Umdat al-Salik)* edited and translated Nuh Ha Mim Keller, revised edition (Beltsville, Maryland: Amana Publications, 1997).

Mneimneh, Hassan and Makiya, Kanan, "Maual for a Raid", *The New York Review of Books,* 17 January 2002.

Moinuddin, Hasan, *The Charter of the Islamic Conference and Legal Framework of Economic Co-operation among Its Member States* (Oxford: Clarendon Press, 1987).

Muhammad, Mahathir, "Dr Mahathir PM of Malaysia's Speech in Full to the OIC", 16 October 2003, http://www.mathaba.net/gci/news/mahathir.htm, viewed 22 June 2006.

Muir, Sir William, *Mahomet and Islam* (London: The Religious Tract Society, 1895).

Mujahid, Sobhi, "Resisting U.S. Aggression Islamic Duty: Al Azhar Grand Imam", *Islam Online,* 22 February 2003, www.islamonline.net/English/News/2003-02/22/article14.shtml, viewed 13 April 2003.

Mukalled, Diana, "The World is Closley Watching", *al-Sharq al-Awsat,* 30 August 2005, http://aawsat.com/english/news.

asp?section=2&id=1465, viewed 6 September 2005.

Murad, Khurram, "Prophethood: Root Cause of Islam-West Conflict", *Tarjuman al-Quran,* (July 1992), http://www.jamaat.org/Isharat/archive/792.html, viewed 8 September 2005.

Murawiec, Laurent, "The Saudi Takeover of Al-Azhar University," *Terrorism Monitor,* Volume 1, Issue 7, 4 December 2003.

Murphy, John, "Psychological warfare and the demise of the new millennium suicide-bomber" LLC White Paper Las Vegas: SusbloodLabs, 2006, http://www.susbloodlabs.com/PsychologicalWarfareandathedemiseofthesuicidebomber.pdf, viewed 28 November 2006.

Musharbash, Yassin, "The Al-Qaida Guide to Kidnapping", *Spiegel Online,* 1 December 2005, http//www.spiegel.de/international/0,1518,387888,00.html, viewed 27 April 2006.

"Muslim anger grows at Pope speech", *BBCNEWS,* 15 September 2006.

"Muslim Council of Britain: Much ado about nothing", *Q-News,* March-April 2002, pp. 22-23.

an-Nabhani, Taqiuddin, *The Islamic State* (London: Al-Khilafah Publications, no date).

Nadler, Daniel J., "Muslim Tolerance Post 9/11, Discourse or Dictation?", *The Harvard Salient,* 15 September 2006.

Nadwi, Syed Abul Hasan Ali, *Muslims in the West: The Message and the Mission,* (Leicester: The Islamic Foundation, 1983).

Nafziger, George E. and Walton, Mark W., *Islam at War: A History,* (Westport, CO & London: Praeger, 2003).

Naik, Gautam, "Tunisia Wins Population Battle, and Others See a Policy Model", *The Wall Street Journal,* 8 August 2003.

al-Na`im, Abdullahi, "Religious Freedom In Egypt: Under The Shadow Of The Dhimma System," in: Swidler, Leonard, (ed.), *Muslims In Dialogue* (Lewiston, New York: Edwin Mellen Press, 1992).

Naji, Abu Bakr *The Management of Barbarism* see English translation available as pdf under the name *The Management of Savagery*

Naji, Abu Bakr *The Management of Savagery: The Most Critical Stage through Which the Umma will Pass,* transl. William McCants (23 May 2006). Translation funded by John M. Olin Institute for Strategic Studies at Harvard University, http://www.ctc.usma.edu/Management_of_Savagery.pdf

Nasif, Sheikh Mansur Ali, *Al-Tajj al Jami lil-usul fi Ahadith al-Rasul* (Istanbul: Dar Ihya al-Kutub al-'Arabiyyah, 1961). Also published in Cairo by Matba'ah 'Isa al Babl al Halabi (no date).

NATO: An Alliance for Freedom: How to transform the Atlantic Alliance to effectively defend our freedom and democracies, a report by Fundación para el Análisis y los Estudios Sociales (president of FAES, José María Aznar), 20 October 2005.

Nicephorus, *Short History*, (ed.) C. Mango (Washington: Dumbarton Oaks, 1990).

Nicholson, Helen, *The Crusades*, (Westport, Connecticut: Greenwood Press, 2004).

Nettler, Ronald, "A Modern Islamic Confession of Faith and Conception of Religion: Sayyid Qutb's Introduction to *tafsir, Fi Zilal al-Quran"*, *British Journal of Middle Eastern Studies,* Vol. 21, No. 1 (1994).

Nevo, Yehuda D., and Koren, Judith, *Crosroads to Islam: The Origins of the Arab Religion and the Arab State* (London: Prometheus Books, 2003).

Nizami, Hasan, *Taju'l Maasir,* in Elliot and Dawson, *A History of India As Told by Its Own Historians*, Vol. 2, (New Delhi: D K Publishers, reprinted 2001).

Noble Qur'an, The, see al-Hilali and Khan

Norwich, John Julius, *Byzantium: The Apogee,* (London: BCA, 1991).

Noth, Albrecht, "Heiliger Kampf (Gihad) gegen die 'Franken': Zur Position der Kreuzzüge im Rahmen der Islamgeschichte", *Saeculum,* Vol. 37 (1986), pp. 240-259.

Novak, Michael "What the Islamists have Learned", *The Weekly Standard,* 22 November 2006.

Obermann, Julian, "Early Islam", *Lectures of the Department of Near Eastern Langages and Literatures at Yale University* (ed.) Robert C. Dentan, American Oriental Series No. 38 (Yale University Press, 1954).

O'Callaghan, Joseph F., *A History of Medieval Spain* (Ithaca, NY: Cornell University Press, 1975).

Omar, Rageh, *Only Half of Me: being a Muslim in Britain*. (Viking: London, 2006).

O'Neil, Sean and Lappin, Yaacov, "Britain's online imam declares war as he calls young to jihad", *The Times,* 17 January 2006.

Oren, Michael B., *Power, Faith and Fantasy: Amercia in the Middle East 1776 to the present* (New York and London: W.W. Norton & Company, 2007).

Overy, Richard (ed.), *The Times History of the World,* new edition (London: Times Books, Harper Collins Publishers, 1999).

The Pakistan Penal Code with Commentary and Shariat Criminal Laws (Lahore: PLD Publishers, 1998).

"Palestine in Islamic History", HAMASONLINE, www.hamasonline. com/indexx.php?page=Palestine/palestine_in_islamic_history, viewed 17 March 2005.

Palestinian Media Watch bulletins http://www.pmw.org.il.

Palmer, J.A.B., "The Origin of the Janissaries", *Bulletin of the John Rylands Library,* Manchester, Vol. 35, No. 1 (September 1952), pp. 448-481.

Pargoire, J., "Les LX Soldats Martyrs de Gaza", *Echos d'Orient: Revue de Théologie, de Droit Canonique, de Liturgie, d'Archaelogie, d'Histoire et de Géographie Orientales,* Vol. 8 (1905), pp. 40-43.

Park, Michael Y., "Sept. 11 Creates New Lexicon", Fox News, 11 September 2006, http://www.foxnews.com/story/0,2933,213240,00. html, viewed 16 October 2006.

Parry, Richard Lloyd, "Muslim nations defend use of suicide bombers", *The Independent,* 11 April 2002.

Patai, Raphael, *Jadid al-Islam: The Jewish "New Muslims" of Meshed,* (Detroit: Wayne State University Press, 1997).

Paz, Reuven, *The Heritage of the Sunni Militant Groups: An Islamic internacionale?,* 4 January 2000, http://www.ict.org.il/articles/ articledet.cfm?articleid=415, viewed 5 December 2003.

Paz, Reuven, "Middle East Islamism In The European Arena", *Middle East Review of International Affairs,* Vol. 6, No. 3, (September 2002).

Paz, Reuven, "Global Jihad and Wmd: Between Martyrdom and Mass Destruction", in Hillel Fradkin, Husain Haqqani and Eric Brown, (eds.), *Current Trends in Islamist ideology,* Vol. 2, (Washington, DC: Hudson Institute, Center on Islam, Democracy, and The Future of the Muslim World 2005), pp. 76-77.

Paz, Reuven, "Sawt al-Jihad: New Indoctrination of Qa'idat al-Jihad", Intelliegence and Terrorism Information Centre at the Center for Special Studies (CSS), www.intelligence.org.il/eng/g_j/rp_h_11_ 03.htm, viewed 12 June 2006.

Perkins, Kenneth J., *A History of Modern Tunisia,* (Cambridge: Cambridge University Press, 2004).

Perry, Mark and Crooke, Alastair, "How to lose the war on terror", *Asia Times Online,* Part 1: Talking with the 'terrorists' ", 31 March 2006; Part 2: "Handing victory to the extremists", 1 April 2006; Part 3: "An exchange of narratives", 3 June 2006.

Peters, Alan, "Mullah's Threat Not Sinking In", *FrontPageMagazine,* 4 November 2006, http://www.frontpagemag.com/Articles/ReadArticle.asp?ID=20065, viewed 14 February 2006.

Peters, Rudolph, *Islam and Colonialism: The Doctrine of jihad in Modern History* (The Hague: Mouton, 1979).

Peters, Rudolph, *Jihad in Classical and Modern Islam: a Reader* (Princeton: Markus Wiener Publishers, 1996).

Phillipson, Coleman, *The International Law and Custom of Ancient Greece and Rome,* 2 vols (London: Macmillan and Co. Ltd, 1911).

Philps, Alan, "Settlers Use Pigskin to Foil the Martyrs", *The Daily Telegraph,* 26 February 2002.

Pipes, Daniel, *Slave Soldiers and Islam: The Genesis of a Military System*, (New Haven and London: Yale University Press, 1981).

Pipes, Daniel, "Muslims Love Bin Laden", *New York Post,* 22 October 2001.

Pipes, Daniel, "Know Thy Terrorists", *New York Post,* 19 November 2002.

Pipes, Daniel, "The Mystical Menace of Mahmoud Ahmadinejad", *New York Sun,* 10 January 2006.

Pipes, Daniel, Book review of Soheib Bencheikh, "Marianne et le Prophète: L'Islam dans la France laïque", *Middle East Quarterly* (December 2000).

Piscatori, James, *Islam in a World of Nation States* (Cambridge: Cambridge University Press, 1986).

Piscatori, J.P., "The Shia of Lebanon and Hizbullah: The Party of God", in Christie Jenet and Randal G. Stewart, (eds.), *Politics of the Future: The Role of Social Movements*, (Melbourne: Macmillan, 1989), pp. 292-231.

Porteus, Tom, "Reading Iran", *Prospect,* Issue 118, 22 January 2006.

Price, Randall, *Unholy War* (Eugene, Oregon: Harvest House Publishers, 2001).

Puin, Gerd R., "Observations on Early Qur'an Manuscripts in Sana'a," in Stefan Wild, (ed.), *The Qur'an as Text,* (Leiden: E.J. Brill, 1996), pp.107-111.

Al-Qadhafi, Mu'ammar, excerpts from a speech given by Libyan leader Mu'ammar Al-Qadhafi, aired on Al-Jazeera TV on April 10, 2006, see "Libyan Leader Mu'ammar Al-Qadhafi: Europe and the U.S. Should Agree to Become Islamic or Declare War on the Muslims", MEMRI, TV Monitor Project, Clip No. 1121, 10 April 2006, http://www.memritv.org/Transcript.asp?P1=1121, viewed 22 August 2006.

al-Qaradawi, Yusuf, *Non-Muslims in the Islamic Society,* (Indianapolis: American Trust Publications, 1985).

al-Qaradawi, Yusuf, *Priorities of the Islamic Movement in the Coming Phase,* (Swansea: Awakening Publications, 2000).

al-Qaradawi, Yusuf, "The Sacred Duty of Defending Jerusalem", 23 August 2005, http://www.islamonline.net/servlet/Satellite?p agename=IslamOnline-English-ask_Scholar/FatwaE/FatwaE&ci d=1119503543558, viewed 28 November 2005.

al-Qaradawi, Yusuf, http://www.islamonline.net/fatwa/english/ FatwaDisplay.asp?hFatwaID=61551, viewed 10 August 2005.

"Quadrennial Defense Review Report", US Department of Defense, 6 February 2006, http://www.defenselink.mil/qdr/report/ Report20060203.pdf, viewed 13 October 2006.

al-Qurtuby, Sumanto, "Seeding Peace on Earth: Abdurrahman Wahid's Movements on Peace and Nonviolence", http://www.wahidinstitute. org/pdf-docs/Peace-on-The-Earth.pdf, viewed 3 September 2006.

Qutb, Sayyid, *Fi Zilal al-Quran* (Beirut: Dar al-Shuruq, 1987).

Qutb, Sayyid, *Islam and Peace* (Cairo: Dar al-Shuruq, 1988).

Qutb, Sayyid, *Milestones* (Lahore: Qazi Publications, no date). Also *Milestones [Ma'alem Fil Tariq]* (Indianapolis: American Trust Publications, 1990).

Qutb, Sayyid, "Social Justice in Islam", in Shepard, W. (ed.), *Sayyid Qutb and Islamic Activism: A Translation and Critical Analysis of 'Social Justice in Islam'* (Leiden: EJ Brill, 1996).

Qutb, Sayyid, *The Islamic Concept and its Characteristic* (Indianapolis: American Trust Publication, 1991).

Rabasa, Angela, Bernard, Cheryl, Schwartz, Lowell H. and Sickle, Peter,

Building Moderate Muslim Networks (Santa Monica, California: Rand Center for Middle East Public Policy, 2007).

Racius, Egdunas, *The Multiple Nature Of The Islamic Da'wa,* Academic Dissertation, The Faculty of Arts, University of Helsinki (Helsinki: Valopaino Oy, 2004).

Rahim, Abdur, *The Principles of Muhammadan Jurisprudence* (London: Luzac, printed Madras 1911).

Rahman, Fazlur, *Major Themes of the Qur'an* (Minneapolis: Bibliotheca Islamica, 1980).

Rahman, Shaykh Omar Abdul, *The Present Rulers and Islam. Are they Muslims or Not?* (London: Al-Firdous, 1990).

Rajaee, Farhang, *Islamic Values and World View: Khomeyni on Man, the State and International Politics* (Lanham, Maryland: University Press of America, 1983).

al-Rajihi, Ahmad Naser, "Heavenly Religions Encourage Legitimate War", *Ash-Sharq al-Awsat,* 28 January 1990, reprinted in Kharofa (1994), pp. 24-30.

Ramadan, Tariq, "The Contradictions of the Islamic World", *Qantara,* http://www.qantara.de/webcom/show_article.php/_c-476/_nr-88/i.html?PHPSESSID=5869, viewed 13 September 2006.

Raman, B., "Thai dilemma over Muslim anger", *Asia Times,* 3 November 2004.

Al-Rashed, Abdul Rahman, "Ministry of Interior's Advisors and the Wrong Advice", *Asharq Alawsat,* 16 January 2005.

Rasheed, Asra, *Death* (Birmingham: Al-Hidaayah Publishing and Distribution, 2001).

Reeve, Simon, *The New Jackals: Ramzi Yousef, Osama bin Laden and the Future of Terrorism* (London: André Deutsch, 1999).

"Reformist Iranian Internet Daily: A New Fatwa States That Religious Law Does Not Forbid Use of Nuclear Weapons", *MEMRI,* Special Dispatch Series, No. 1096, 17 February 2006.

Reich, Walter (ed.), *Origins of Terrorism: Psychologies, Theologies, States of Mind* (Washington, DC: Woodrow Wilson Center Press, 2001).

Reid, James J., "Total War, the Annihilation Ethic, and the Armenian Genocide, 1870-1918", in Richard G. Hovannisian, (ed.), *The Armenian Genocide: History, Politics, Ethics,* 37.

Reilly, Robert R., "The Roots of Islamist Ideology", (London: Centre for Research into Post-Communist Economies ,CRCE, February 2006).

Reynalds, Jeremy, "Radical Islamic Group Threatens Britain After Police Raid", *Assist News Service,* 30 July 2003.

Rizvi, Sayyid Athar Abbas, *Muslim Revivalist Movements in Northern India in the Sixteenth and Seventeenth Centuries* (New Delhi: Agra University Press, 1965).

Rizvi, Sayyid Athar Abbas, *Shah Wali-Allah and His Times* (Canberra: Ma'rifat Publishing House, 1980).

Roberts, Tom (writer and director), *Witness: Inside the Mind of the Suicide Bomber* (Channel 4, 10 November 2003).

Rogerson, Barnaby, *The Prophet Muhammad* (London: Little, Brown, 2003).

Rood, Judith Mendelsohn, "Why and How Should Christian Students Study World Religions?", *CCCU Advance* (Spring 2003).

Rose, Flemming , "Why I published the Muhammad cartoons", *Spiegel Online,* 31 May 2006, http://service.spiegel.de/cache/international/spiegel/0,1518,418930,00.html, viewed 6 June 2006.

Ross-Harrington, Jonathan, "Re-Examining Jemaah Islamiyah in the Wake of the Zawahiri Letter", *Terrorism Monitor,* Volume 3, Issue 21, 3 November 2005.

Roy, Olivier, *The Failure of Political Islam* (London: I.B. Tauris, 1994).

Rubin, Barry and Colp Rubin, Judith, (eds.), *Anti-American Terrorism and the Middle East* (New York: Oxford University Press, 2002).

Ruhollah, Khomeini, "Islamic Government", in John J. Donohue and John L. Esposito, (eds.), *Islam in Transition: Muslim Perspective,* (New York and Oxford: Oxford University Press, 1982).

Runciman, Steven, *A History of the Crusades, Vol. 1,* (Cambridge: Cambridge University Press, 1951).

Ruthven, Malise, *Islam in the World* (New York: Oxford University Press, 1984).

Sachedina, Abdulaziz, "The Development of *Jihad* in Islamic Revelation and History" in Johnson and Kelsay (1990).

Sachedina, Abdulaziz, "Justification for Violence in Islam", in *Journal of Lutheran Ethics,* 19 February 2003.

Sacranie, Iqbal, "The role of British Muslims in bringing justice to

Palestine", *Al Aqsa,* Vol. 3, No. 1, http://www.aqsa.org.uk/journals/vol3iss1/british.htm, viewed 22 July 2003.

al-Saidi, 'Abd al-Muta'ali, *Fi Maydan al-Ijtihad* (Helwan: Jam'iyyat al-thaqafa al-Islamiyya, no date).

Sajid, Abdul Jalil , "Islam and Ethics of War and Peace", 18 May 2002, http://www.preparingforpeace.org/sajid_islam_and_ethics_of_war_and_peace.htm, viewed 7 June 2006.

Salam, Sahid-Ivan, *Jihad and the Foreign Policy of the Khilafah State* (Khilafah Publications, 2001) http://www.challenging-islam.org/library/jihadpolicy.pdf, viewed 27 November 2006)

Salibi, Kamal S., *Syria Under Islam: Empire on Trial 634-1097* (Delmar, New York: Caravan Books, 1977).

Sanasarian, Eliz, *Religious Minorities in Iran* (Cambridge: Cambridge University Press, 2000).

Sankari, Jamal, *Fadlallah: The Making of a Radical Shi'ite Leader* (London: Saqi Books, 2005).

Sardar, Ziauddin, "Can Islam Change?", *New Statesman,* 13 September 2004. http://www.newstatesman.com/200409130016, viewed 20 September 2005.

Sardar, Ziauddin, "Viewpoint: The global voices reclaiming Islam", *BBC NEWS,* 6 September 2005.

Sardar, Ziauddin, "Rethinking Islam", June 2002, *Islam For Today*, http://www.islamfortoday.com.sardar01.htm, viewed 27 May 2005.

Sayyed, Tashbih, "The Islamic Bomb", *Pakistan Today,* 26 December 2003.

Schacht, Joseph, "Law and Justice", in P.M. Holt, Ann K.S. Lambton and Bernard Lewis, (eds.), *The Cambridge History of Islam,* Vol. 2B *Islamic Societiy and Civilizaton*, (Cambridge: Cambridge University Press, 1970), pp. 563-564.

Schacht, Joseph, *The Origins of Muhammadan Jursiprudence* (Oxford: Oxford University Press, 1950).

Scheuer, Michael, "Al-Qaeda's Insurgency Doctrine: Aiming for a "Long War", *Terrorism Focus*, Vol. 3, Issue 8, 28 February 2006.

Schleifer, Ron, *Psychological Warfare in the Intifada: Israeil and Palestinian Media Politics and Military Strategies,* (Brighton: Sussex Academic Press, 2006).

Schleifer, S. Abdullah, "Understanding JIHAD: Definition and Methodology - Part One", *The Islamic Quarterly*, London, (Third

Quarter, 1983), *Sal@m,* http://www.salaam.co.uk/knowledge/schleifer1.php, viewed 9 August 2005.

Sciolino, Elaine, "French Islam Wins Officially Recognized Voice", *The New York Times,* 14 April 2003.

Sciolino, Elaine, "French Threat to Militant Muslims After Council Vote", *The New York Times,* 15 April 2004.

Seale, Patrick, "Healing the Wounds between Islam and the West", *Al-Hayat,* 10 December 2004.

Sebeos, *Histoire d'Héraclius,* translated F. Macler (Paris: E. Leroux, 1904).

Sebeos, *History,* translated Robert Bedrosian (New York: Sources of the Armenian Tradition, 1985).

Sebeos, *The Armenian History attributed to Sebeos,* Part I. Translation and Notes by James Howard-Johnston, (Liverpool: Liverpool University Press, 1999).

Sebeos, *The Armenian History attributed to Sebeos,* Part II. Historical Commentary (Liverpool: Liverpool University Press, 1999).

Sewall, Gilbert T., *Islam and Textbooks,* A Report of the American Textbook Council, (New York, NY: American Textbook Council, 2003), http://www.historytextbooks.org/islamreport.pdf, viewed 18 August 2005.

Shah, Muhammad Kasim Hindu, *Ta'rikh-i-Firishta* (Lucknow, 1864).

Shah, Muhammad Kasim Hindu, *Ta'rikh-i-Firishta,* in Elliot and Dawson, A History of India As Told by Its Own Historians, Vol. 6, p. 233.

Shahid, Irfan, "Asrar al-nasr al-'arabi fi futuh al-Sham" in *Bildad al Sham Proceedings* (1985).

Shahrastani, Abu al-Fath Muhammad ibn 'Abd al-Karim, *Kitab al-Milal wa al-Nihal,* (ed.) Cureton (London, 1846).

Shahzad, Syed Saleem, "Armageddon: Bringing it on", *Asia Times Online,* 20 May 2005.

Shaltut, Mahmud, *Al-Qur'an wa al-Qital [The Qur'an and Fighting]* (Matba'at al-Nasr and Maktab Ittihad al-Sharq, 1948). English translation in Peters (1996), pp. 60-101.

Shaltut, Mahmud, *The Muslim Conception of International Law and the Western Approach* (The Hague: Martinus Nijhof, 1968).

Shapira, Shimon, "The Origin of Hizballah", *Jerusalem Quarterly,* 46 (Spring 1988), pp. 115-130.

Shariati, Ali, *On the Sociology of Islam* translated Hamid Algar (Berkeley: Mizan Press, 1979).

Shariati, Ali, "Intizar: The Religion of Protest and the Return to Self", in Donohue and Esposito (1982), pp. 98-304.

Sharma, Sri Ram, *The Religious Policy of the Mughal Emperors,* (New Delhi: Munshiram Manoharlal Publishers, 1988).

Shawkani, Abu al-Fath Muhammad ibn 'Abd al-Karim, *Nayl al-Awtar,* 8 vols, 2nd edition (Cairo, 1952).

Shaybani, Muhammad ibn al-Hasan, *Sharh Kitab al-Siyar al-Kabir,* with commentary by Shams al-Din Muhammad b. Ahmad b. Sahl Sarakhsi, 4 vols (Hyderabad, 1916-17).

Shaybani, *Siyar,* translated with an introduction, notes and appendices by Majid Khadduri as *The Islamic Law of Nations: Shaybani's Siyar* (Baltimore: The Johns Hopkins Press, 1966).

Shemesh, A. Ben, *Taxation in Islam,* Vol. 2 (Leiden: Brill, London: Luzac and Co. Ltd, 1965).

Shirbon, Estelle, "Rome Imam Suspended After Praising Suicide Bombers", Reuters, 13 June 2003. Available at http://www.reuters.com/newsArticle.jhtml?typetopNews&storyID = 2928250, viewed 19 June 2003.

al-Shishani, Murad, "Al-Zawahiri Addresses Reform in Muslim World", *Terrorism Focus,* Vol. 3, Issue 3, 25 January 2006.

al-Shishani, Murad, "Salafi-Jihadists in Jordan: From Prison Riots to Suicide Operation Cells", *Terrorism Focus,* Vol. 3, Issue 9, 7 March 2006.

Shultz, Richard H. Jr., and Beitler, Ruth Margolies, "Tactical Deception And Strategic Surprise In Al-Qai'da's Operations", *Middle East Review of International Affairs,* Vol. 8, No. 2, June 2004.

Sicker, Martin, *The Islamic World in Ascendancy: From the Arab Conquests to the Siege of Vienna* (Westport, Connecticut: Praeger Publishers, 2000).

Siddique, Sharon, "Conceptualizing Contemporary Islam: Religion or Ideology?" in Ahmad Ibrahim, Sharon Siddique and Yasmin Hussain, (eds.), *Readings on Islam in Southeast Asia,* (Singapore: Institute of Southeast Asian Studies, 1985).

Siddiqui, Kalim in Zafar Bengash (ed.), *In Pursuit of the Power of Islam: Major Writings of Kalim Siddiqui,* (London: The Open Press, 1996).

"Silencing voices of dissent", *Q-News*, March-April 2002, p. 26.

Simpson, John, "Why Tourists are Now the Ideal Targets", *The Sunday Telegraph*, 1 December 2002, p. 21.

Sina, Ali, "Can Islam be reformed?", http://www.faithfreedom.org/Articles/sina31119.htm, viewed 7 September 2005.

Sirriyeh, Elizabeth, *Sufis and Anti-Sufis: The Defence, Rethinking and Rejection of Sufism in the Modern World* (Richmond: Curzon Press, 1999).

Smith, Jane Idleman and Haddad, Yvonne Yazbeck, *The Islamic Understanding of Death and Resurrection* (Albany: State University of New York Press, 1981).

Sobhani, Ayatollah Ja'far, *Doctrines of Shi'i Islam: A Compendium of Imami Beliefs and Practices*, translated and edited by Reza Shah-Kazemi (London: I.B. Tauris, 2001).

Solihin, S.M., *Copts And Muslims In Egypt* (Leicester: The Islamic Foundation, 1991), pp. 7-8.

Solihin, S.M., *Studies on Sayyid Qutb's Fi Zilal al-Quran*, (unpublished thesis, Department of Theology, University of Birmingham, 1993).

Sophronius, *Sermones*. PG 87.3, pp. 3201-364 in "Weihnachspredigt des Sophronios" (ed.) H. Usener *Rheinisches Museum für Philologie* n.s. 41 (1886), pp. 500-516.

Special Correspondent, "Shi'ite supremacists emerge from Iran's shadows", *Asia Times Online*, 9 September 2005, http://www.atimes.com/atimes/Middle_East/GI09Ak01.html, viewed 17 January 2006.

Spengler, "Military destiny and madness in Iran", *Asia Times Online*, 6 June 2006.

Stalinksy, Steven, "Saudi Policy Statements on Support to the Palestinians", MEMRI Special Report No. 17, 3 July 2003.

Stalinsky, Steven, "Leading Egyptian Islamic Clerics on Jihad Against U.S. Troops in Iraq: March-August 2003", *MEMRI Inquiry and Analysis Series*, No. 145, 14 August 2003.

St Clair-Tisdall, W., *The Sources of Islam: A Persian Treatise*, translated and abridged by Sir William Muir (Edinburgh: T. and T. Clark, 1901).

Stemmann, Juan Jose Escobar, "Middle East Salafism's Influence and the Radicalization of Muslim Communities in Europe", *Middle East Review of International Affairs*, Vol. 10, No. 3, (September 2006).

Strawson, John, "Encountering Islamic Law," essay presented at the Critical Legal Conference, New College, Oxford, September 9 – 12, 1993. The World Wide Web Virtual Library: Islamic and Middle Eastern Law, http://www.uel.ac.uk/faculties/socsci/law/jsrps.html, p.11.

Streusand, Dr Douglas E. and Tunnell IV, LTC Harry D., "Choosing Words Carefully: Language to Help Fight Islamic Terrorism", US National Defense University, Center for Strategic Communications, 23 May 2006 , http://www.ndu.edu/csc/docs/Choosing%20Words%20Carefully--language%20to%20Help%20Fight%20Islamic%20Terrorism%2024%20May%2006.pdf, viewed 3 September 2006.

"Suicide bombers follow Quran, concludes Pentagon briefing", *WorldNetDaily,* 27 September 2006, http://www.worldnetdaily.com/news/article.asp?ARTICLE_ID=52184, viewed 30 October 2006

Suleiman, Mustafa, "The Rector of the Azhar University asks Arabs to Obtain Mass Destruction Weapons", *Al-Usbu',* 21 April 2003. English translation in *Arab-West Report* (17-23 April 2003).

Sun Tzŭ, *The Art of War,* Foreword by James Clavell (London: Hodder and Stoughton, 1981).

al-Suyuti, Jalal al-Din, *Al-Atkun Fi Ulum al-Qur'an [The perfection of Qur'anic theology].*

Swidler, Leonard (ed.), *Muslims In Dialogue* (Lewiston, New York: Edwin Mellen Press, 1992).

Synopsis of the seminar on The Impacts of Climate Change on the Islamic World", The Policy Foresight Programme and The Oxford Centre for Islamic Studies, Oxford Centre for Islamic Studies, 24 July 2006.

Taarnby, Michael, "Yemen's Committee for Dialogue: Can Jihadists Return to Society?", *Terrorism Monitor,* Vol. 3, Issue 14, 15 July 2005.

al-Tabari, Abu Ja'far Muhammad ibn Jarir, *Ta'rikh al-rusul wa'l muluk (Annales)* (ed.) M.J. De Goeje et al. 15 vols (Leiden: Brill, 1879-1901).

al-Tabari, Abu Ja'far Muhammad ibn Jarir, *Kitab al-Jihad wa Kitab al-Jizya wa Ahkam al-Muharibin min Kitab Ikhtilaf al-Fuqaha,* (ed.) J. Schacht (Leiden: Brill, 1933).

al-Tabari, Abu Ja'far Muhammad ibn Jarir, *The History of al-Tabari,* edited by Ehsan Yar-Shater , 39 volumes (Albany: New York: State University of New York Press, 1993).

Tafrali, O., *Thessalonique – Des Origines au XVI Siecle,* 1913.

Taha, Mahmoud Mohamed, *The Second Message of Islam,* translated Abdullah Ahmed An-Na'im (Syracuse, New York: Syracuse University Press, 1987).

Taher, Shaykh Muhammad, Friday Khutbah, "The Battle of Badr", 24 December 1999, Leeds Grand Mosque.

Taher, Shaykh Muhammad, Friday Khutbah, "Open Message", 26 March 2004, Leeds Grand Mosque, http://www.leedsgrandmosque.com/khutbahs/khutba-20050722.asp, viewed 8 September 2005.

Taher, Shaykh Muhammad, Friday Khutbah, "The objectives of the Islamic sacred law", 19 March 2004, Leeds Grand Mosque, http://www.leedsgrandmosque.org.uk/khutbahs/khutba-20040319.asp, viewed 8 September 2005.

Taher, Shaykh Muhammad, Friday Khutbah, "The objectives of the Islamic sacred law".

Taheri, Amir, "A deadly mix: Politics and Theology", World Net Daily, February 21, 2003, http://www.benadorassociates.com/article/248, viewed 6 April 2005.

Taheri, Amir, "Tantawi's Tantrum", *National Review Online,* 16 May 2003.

Taheri, Amir, "Hijacking Islam", *New York Post,* 12 February 2006.

Tahir-ul-Qadri, *The Awaited Imam* (Lahore: Minhaj-ul-Quran Publications, 2003)

"Taking our religion back one Muslim at a time", Free Muslims Coalition,

http://www.freemuslims.org/, viewed 2 November 2005.

Talhami, Ghada Hashem, "The Modern History of Islamic Jerusalem: Academic Myths and Propaganda", *Middle East Policy,* Vol. VII, No. 2 (February 2000).

'Takiyya' in *The Encyclopedia of Islam,* CD-ROM Edition, Leiden: Koninklijke Brill NV, 2003.

Tamimi, Azzam, "Concepts of Life Beyond Death: Martyrdom, Resurrection, Heaven and Hell", Institute of Islamic Political Thought, 26 March 2004, http://www.ii-pt.com/web/papers/concept.htm, viewed 8 September 2005.

Tantawi, Sheikh Muhammad Sayyid – a summary of his teachings can be found at http://www.sunnah.org/history /Scholars/mashaykh_azhar.htm, viewed 25 January 2002.

Thalib, Ustadz Ja'far Umar, Ahlus Sunnah wal Jama'ah, address broadcast on Radio SPMM [The voice of struggle of the Maluku Muslims] (1-3 May 2002). Excerpts at www.persecution.org/news/report2002-05-15.html, viewed 20 May 2002.

The Chachnamah, an Ancient History of Sind, translated by Mirza Kalichbeg Fredunbeg, (Lahore: Vanguard Books, 1985):

"The Charter of Allah: The Platform of the Islamic Resistance movement (Hamas)", Translated and annotated by Raphael Israeli , Harry Truman Research Institute, The Hebrew University, Jerusalem, Israel, http://www.ict.org.il/articles/h_cov.htm, viewed 28 November 2005.

"The Great Divide: How Westerners and Muslims View Each Other", A 13-Nation Pew Global Attitudes Survey, (Washington DC: Pew Research Center), 22 June 2006.

"The Role of Palestinian Women in Suicide Terrorism", Israel Ministry of foreign Affairs, 30 January 2003, http://www.mfa.gov.il/MFA/MFAArchive/2000_2009/2003/1/The+Role+of+Palestinian+Women+in+Suicide+Terrorism.htm, viewed 1 September 2006.

Theophanes, *Theophanis Chronographia,* (ed.) C. De Boor, 2 vols (Leipzig, 1883-5).

"They destroy the Houses of Allah", The Media Office of Hizb-ut-Tahrir in Sudan, 12 May 2005, http://www.hizb-ut-tahrir.info/english/sudan/2005/may1205.htm, viewed 28 November 2005.

Tibi, Bassam, "War and Peace in Islam", in Terry Nardin, (ed.), *The Ethics of War and Peace: Religious and Secular Perspectives,* (Princeton, NJ: Princeton University Press, 1996).

Tibi, Bassam, "The Renewed Role of Islam in the Political and Social Development of the Middle East", *The Middle East Journal, Vol. 37,* No.1, 1983.

Tibi, Bassam, *Arab Nationalism: Between Islam and the Nation-State,* 3rd edition (Basingstoke: Macmillan Press Ltd, 1997).

Tibi, Bassam, *Islam between Culture and Politics,* (Basingstoke: Palgrave Macmillan, 2005).

Tibi, Bassam, *Conflict and War in the Middle East: From Interstate War to New Security,* 2nd edition (Basingstoke and London: Macmillan Press Ltd, 1998).

Timmerman, Kenneth R., "Iran's Nuclear Zealot", *Project*

Syndicate, http://www.project-syndicate.org/print_commentary/ timmerman2/English, viewed 13 February 2006.

Tisdall, Simon and MacAskill, Ewen, "America's Long War", *The Guardian,* 15 February 2006.

Troll, C.W., *Sayyid Ahmad Khan: A Reinterpretation of Muslim Theology,* (Karachi Oxford University Press, 1979).

"UK foreign policy 'key' to tackling terror, say Muslim advisors", *The Muslim News,* 10 November 2005.

Ulph, Stephen, "New Online Book Lays Out Al-Qaeda's Military Strategy", *Terrorism Focus,* Vol. 2, Issue 6, 17 March 2005.

Ulph, Stephen, "Islamist Ideologues Struggle to Raise Morale", *Terrorism Focus,* Vol.3, Issue 6, 14 February 2006.

Ulph, Stephen, "Setmariam Nasar: Background on al-Qaeda's Arrested Strategist", *Terrorism Focus,* Vol. 3, Issue 12, 28 March 2006.

The United Nations Development Programme, "Arab Human Development Report 2004", Regional Bureau for Arab States (RBAS) (New York: United Nations Publications, 2005).

al-'Utbi, *Tarikh Yamini,* in Elliot and Dawson, *A History of India As Told by Its Own Historians,* Vol. 2 (New Delhi: D K Publishers, reprinted 2001).

Van Ess, Josef, *Theologie und Gesellschaft im 2. und 3. Jahrhundert Hidschra. Eine Geschicthe des religiösen Denkens im frühen Islam,* 6 vols (Berlin: de Bruyter, 1991-5).

Vasiliev, A.A., *A History of the Byzantine Empire,* 2 vols (Madison: University of Wisconsin Press, 1958).

Veliankode, Sidheeque M.A., *Doomsday: Portents and Prophecies,* (Toronto: Al-Attique Publishers, 1999).

Voll, John O., "Fundamentalism in the Sunni Arab World: Egypt and the Sudan", in Marty and Appleby, *Fundamentalisms Observed,* (Chicago: Chicago University Press, 1991).

Vryonis, S. Jr., "A Critical Analysis of Stanford J. Shaw's, History of the Ottoman Empire and Modern Turkey. Volume 1. "Empire of the Gazis: The Rise and Decline of the Ottoman Empire", 1280-1808, off print from Balkan Studies, Vol. 24, (1983).

Waddy, Charis, *The Muslim Mind,* 2nd edition (Longmans, 1976).

Wahid, Abdurrahman, "Right Islam vs. Wrong Islam", *The Wall Street Journal,* 30 December 2005.

Walker, Martin, "The coming of the Shiʻa Empire", *Middle East Times,* 3 February 2005.

Walsh, Duncan, "Boys Rescued from Kenya's Islamic School of Torture", *The Times,* 30 January 2003.

Wansbrough, John, *Quranic Studies: Sources and Methods of Scriptural Interpretation,* (Oxford: Oxford University Press, 1977).

Waqidi, Abu ʻAbd-Allah Muhammad ibn ʻUmar ,*Kitab al-Maghazi,* (ed.) Alfred von Kremer (Calcutta, 1856).

Watkins, Eric, "Yemen's Innovative Approach to the War on Terror", *Terrorism Monitor,* Vol. 3, Issue 4 (24 February 2005).

Watt, W. Montgomery, *Muhammad Prophet and Statesman* (Oxford: Oxford University Press, 1961).

Watt, William Montgomery, *The Formative Period of Islamic Thought* (Oxford: Oneworld Publication, 1998).

Werbner, Pnina, *Imagined Diasporas Among Manchester Muslims* (Oxford: James Currey, 2002).

"What can the U.S. do in Iraq?" *International Crisis Group (ICG),* Middle East Report No. 34, 22 December 2004.

"What is Progressive Islam?" *ISIM Newsletter,* No. 13 (December 2003).

Whitaker, Raymond, "Mahmoud Ahmadinejad: The Nuclear Prophet", *The Independent,* 3 February 2006.

"Whoever Wants to Go to Iraq to Fight , Can Go: Tantawi", *Islam Online,* News Section, IslamOnline.net, http://www.islamonline. net/english/news/2003-04/05/article15.shtml, viewed 23 November 2005.

Wiktorowicz, Quintan and John Kaltner, "Killing in the Name of Islam: Al-Qaeda's Justification for September 11", *Middle East Policy,* Volume X, No. 2 (Summer 2003).

Wild, Stefan (ed.), *The Qur'an as Text,* (Leiden: E.J. Brill, 1996).

Wink, Andre, *Al-Hind: The Making of the Indo-Islamic World,* Vol. I, "Early Medieval India and the Expansion of Islam 7th-11th Centuries", (Leiden: Brill, 1990).

Wink, Andre, *Al-Hind: The Making of the Indo-Islamic World,* Vol. II, "The Slave Kings and the Islamic Conquest 11th-13th Centuries", (Leiden: Brill, 1997).

Wood, Rick, "Wahhabism: Out of Control?" *Mission Frontiers* (December 2001).

Woolacott, Martin, "The Bali Bomb may Deal a Fatal Blow to the Islamists", *The Guardian,* 18 October 2002.

Yahya, Harun, *Signs of the Last Day,* (Istanbul: Global Publishing, 2004).

Yakan, Fathi, *Problems Faced by the Da'wah and the Da'iya,* (Singapore: International Islamic Federation of Student Organizations, 1985).

al-Ya'qubi, Ahmad b. Abi Ya'qub, *Ta'rikh,* (ed.) M. Th. Houtsma 2 vols, (Leiden: Brill, 1883).

al-Yassini, Ayman, *Religion and State in the Kingdom of Saudi Arabia* (Boulder, Colorado: Westview Press, 1985).

Yehoshua, Y., "Reeducation of Extremists in Saudi Arabia", *MEMRI,* Inquiry and Analysis Series, No. 260, 18 January 2006.

Yehoshua, Y., "A Cairo Conference Calling for Reform Raises the Ire of the Egyptian Religious Establishment", MEMRI Inquiry and Analysis Series, No. 192, 22 October 2006.

Youssef, Roxanne, "Tantawi still isn't as vitriolic as Gad Al-Haq", *Middle East Times,* issue 20, pp. 1-4. Quoted in Desmond Wiggins, University of South Australia, "Islamic Texts and Circumcision", *Africa Update,* Vol. VIII, Issue 4 (Fall 2001): Conversations on AIDS, viewed 1 June 2006.

Zakaria, Fareed, "Now, Saudis See the Enemy", *Newsweek* (26 May – 2 June 2003), p.19.

Zakaria, Fareed, "Suicide Bombers Can be Stopped", *Newsweek* (25 August – 1 September 2003), p.15.

Zambelis, Chris, "Egyptian Gama'a al-Islamiyya's Public Relations Campaign", *Terrorism Monitor,* Volume 3, Issue 35, 12 September 2006.

al-Zawahiri, Ayman, in "Serialized Excerpts from Egyptian Al-Jihad Organization Leader Ayman al-Zawahiri's Book 'Knights Under the Prophet's Banner' ", London: *Al-Sharq al-Awsat* in Arabic, 2 December 2001, http://www.fas.org/irp/world/para/ayman_bk.html, viewed 12 November 2004.

Zebiri, Kate, "Musim Anti-Secularist Discourse in the Context of Muslim Christian Relations", *Islam and Christian-Muslim Relations,* Vol. 9, No. 1 (1998).

Zeidan, David, "The Islamist View of Life as a Perennial Battle", in Barry Rubin and Judith Colp Rubin, (eds.), *Anti-American Terrorism and the Middle East* (New York: Oxford University Press, 2002), pp. 11-26.

Zeidan, David, "The Islamic Fundamentalist View of Life As a Perennial Battle", *Middle East Review of International Affairs,* Volume 5, No. 4, (December 2001).

Zeidan, David, "The Copts: Equal, Protected, Or Persecuted? The Impact of Islamisation on Muslim-Christian Relations in Modern Egypt", *Islam and Christian-Muslim Relations,* Vol. 10, No. 1, (1999). pp. 53-67.

az-Zubaidi, Al-Imam Zain-ud-Din Ahmad bin Abdul-Lateef, (compiler) *The Translation of the Meanings of summarized Sahih Al-Bukhari Arabic-English,* translation Dr Muhammad Muhsin Khan (Riyadh: Maktaba Dar-us-Salam Publishers, 1994).

Zuhayli, Wahba, *Athar al-Harb fi al-Fiqh al-Islami. Dirasa muqarina.* (Beirut: Dar al-Fikr, 1965).

Zwemer, S.M., *Arabia: The Cradle of Islam* (Edinburgh and London: Oliphant Anderson and Ferrier, 1900).

References and Notes

Please note that material on websites is often removed after a short period, and websites themselves may also disappear.

1   In his preface to Majid Khadduri, *The Islamic Law of Nations: Shabyani's Siyar* (Baltimore, Maryland: The Johns Hopkins Press, 1966), p. xi.

2   M.J. Akbar, *The Shade of Swords: Jihad and Conflict between Islam and Christianity* (London: Routledge, 2002), pp. xvi.

3   Abdullah Ghoshah, "The Jihad is the Way to Gain Victory", in D.F. Green, *Arab Theologians on Jews and Israel, Extracts from the Proceedings of the Fourth Conference of the Academy of Islamic Research* (Geneva: Editions de L'Avenir, 1976), pp. 67-68.

4   Hugh Miles, "Blogger is jailed for four years for insulting Islam and president", *The Daily Telegraph*, 23 February 2007.

5   Simon Tisdall and Ewen MacAskill, "America's Long War", *The Guardian*, 15 February 2006.

6   "Quadrennial Defense Review Report", US Department of Defense, 6 February 2006, http://www.defenselink.mil/qdr/report/Report20060203.pdf, viewed 13 October 2006.

7   Greg Jaffe, "A General's New Plan to Battle Radical Islam", *Wall Street Journal*, 2 September 2006.

8   *NATO: An Alliance for Freedom: How to transform the Atlantic Alliance to effectively defend our freedom and democracies*, a report by Fundación para el Análisis y los Estudios Sociales (president of FAES, José María Aznar), 20 October 2005, p. 15.

9   **Note on Jihad as foreign policy of Muslim state**

Majid Khadduri in his study of Shaybani's *Siyar* explains how the early scholars of Islam saw *jihad* as the framework of Islam's relationship with non-Muslims:

> The early jurists treated the subject matter of the siyar either under the general heading of the jihad, or under such particular subjects as the maghazi (campaigns), ghanina (spoil), ridda (apostasy), and aman (safe-conduct); but almost all confined their treatment to the law of war. (Majid Khadduri, "Introduction", in Majid Khadduri, *The Islamic Law of Nations: Shaybani's Siyar*, (Baltimore: The Johns Hopkins Press, 1966), p. 39).

> We have seen how Abu Hanifa and his disciples, especially Shaybani, laid down general rules and principles governing Islam's external relations, based on the assumption that a normal state of war existed between Islamic and non-Islamic territories. (Khadduri, "Introduction", in Majid Khadduri, *The Islamic Law of Nations: Shaybani's Siyar*, p. 57).

> "...the Jihad was regarded as the permanent basis of Islam's relations with its neighbours..." (Khadduri, *War and Peace in the Law of Islam*, p. 64)

A statement made by Jordan's Supreme Judge in 1968 also makes clear that *jihad* is the normal basis for relationships with non-Muslims.

> Jihad is an Islamic word which other nations use in the meaning of "War"... Scholars have disputed about the reason for which jihad is legislated. Some of them said: Jihad is legislated in order to be one of the means of propagating Islam. Consequently Non-Muslims ought to embrace Islam either willingly or through wisdom and good advice or unwillingly through fight and Jihad... War is the basis of the relationship between Muslims and their opponents unless there are justifiable reasons for peace, such as adopting Islam or making an agreement with them to keep peaceful. (Sheikh Abdullah Ghoshah, Supreme

Judge of the Hashemite Kingdom of Jordan, "The Jihad is the Way to Gain Victory", in D.F. Green, *Arab Theologians on Jews and Israel, Extracts from the Proceedings of the Fourth Conference of the Academy of Islamic Research*, p. 67.

A Hizb ut-Tahrir publication revives the classical concept of *jihad* as the main method of the foreign policy of the Islamic state as a preparation for the reinstatement of the caliphate and a reimplementation of the classical *jihad* doctrine:

The foreign policy objectives of the Islamic Ummah were practically carried out by the Khilafah State that represents the message of mercy, Islam, and it is not concerned with the blood or the money of the people... The Khilafah State was and will be upon its re-establishment, a state that serves to bring the truth to the peoples and to deliver guidance to humanity. However, the return of the Khilafah and the defining of its foreign policy objective, would not in itself, practically project its message to the whole world without some kind of practical assistance or vehicle. In other words, although the Messenger of Allah had received these revelations from Allah, it did not mean that Islam would be transferred to the world automatically by itself without some material action from the Muslims. Islam has defined the material action. This action will remove all physical obstacles to the attainment of the noble foreign policy objectives of the Khilafah State. This is Jihad.... Jihad is the practical method through which the Islamic Creed is conveyed to the world and the manner in which the Foreign Policy Objectives are achieved. (Zahid-Ivan Salam, *Jihad and the Foreign Policy of the Khilafah State*, (Khilafah Publications, 2001), p. 51, http://www.challenging-islam.org/library/jihadpolicy.pdf, viewed 17 November 2006).

So from here we can clearly see that the conveyance and spread of the Islamic message and the spreading of its creed (*'aqeedah*) is the basis upon which the Islamic Ummah defines their relationship with all other peoples of the world... This conveyance to the whole of mankind actually forms the basis of the Islamic foreign policy, which would lead the Islamic

Ummah to be internationally effective... In fact the Islamic ideology did not only define the foreign policy, but it also demonstrated the method by which this foreign policy was to be practically executed and therefore carried to the whole world. This demonstration is in the guidance of the Messenger and it is al-Jihad... (Zahid-Ivan Salam, *Jihad and the Foreign Policy of the Khilafah State*, (Khilafah Publications, 2001), pp. 42-43, http://www.challenging-islam.org/library/jihadpolicy. pdf, viewed 17 November 2006)

Indeed, it was these foreign policy objectives that propelled them at the speed of light and gave them the ability to command and conquer for the sake of Allah _ through Jihad and that Jihad never stopped. Indeed, the Islamic Ummah was alive due to it. It gave life, power, dignity and influence to the Muslims. Indeed, it was the Jihad by the Khilafah State that caused all of this and it was the Jihad that gave the Muslims life. Without it the Islamic Ummah would be like an empty shell. (Zahid-Ivan Salam, *Jihad and the Foreign Policy of the Khilafah State*, (Khilafah Publications, 2001), p. 86, http://www.challenging-islam.org/library/jihadpolicy. pdf, viewed 17 November 2006).

10   Thomas W. Lippman, *Inside The Mirage: America's Fragile Partnership with Saudi Arabia* (Boulder, Colorado: Westview, 2004), p. 303.

11   Arabic singular *khariji*, Arabic plural *khawarij*.

12   Brigadier S.K. Malik, *The Quranic Concept of War*, Indian edition (New Delhi: Himalayan Books, 1986), p. 142

13   Brigadier S.K. Malik, *The Quranic Concept of War*, Indian edition (New Delhi: Himalayan Books, 1986), p. 143

14   General M. Zia-ul-Haq in Brigadier S.K. Malik, *The Quranic Concept of War*, Indian edition (New Delhi: Himalayan Books, 1986), no page number.

15   Islamism is a term used to denote the view of Islam as a comprehensive political ideology that aims at establishing Islamic states under *shari'a* wherever possible by a variety of means.

16   Ibn Warraq, "Honest Intellectuals Must Shed their Spiritual Turbans", *The Guardian*, 10 November 2001.

17   It is becoming increasingly difficult to establish the truth about Islam as these biases gradually find their way into the textbooks of schools and universities. A 2003 report by Gilbert T. Sewall on American textbooks states that "on significant Islam-related subjects, textbooks omit, flatter, embellish, and resort to happy talk, suspending criticism or harsh judgements that would raise provocative or even alarming questions." Sewall cites *jihad* as an example which is "defanged or oversimplified". Gilbert T. Sewall, *Islam and Textbooks*, A Report of the American Textbook Council (New York, NY: American Textbook Council, 2003), http://www.Historytextbooks.org/islamreport.pdf, viewed 18 August 2005.

18   Youssef H. Aboul-Enein and Sherifa Zuhur "Islamic Rulings on Warfare", (Carlisle, Pennsylvania: Strategic Studies Institute, US Army War College, October 2004), p. vii.

19   Tony Blair, "Why we fight on", transcript of a speech given by Mr Blair at the Foreign Policy Centre in London, 21 March 2006, *Real Clear Politics*, http://www.realclearpolitics.com/articles/2006/03/terrorism_must_be_tackled_head.html, viewed 24 November 2006.

20   Najeh Ibrahim, Asim Abdul-Maajid and Esaam ud-Din Darbaalah, *In Pursuit of Allah's Pleasure* (London: Al-Firdous, 1997), p. 55.

21   Abul A'la Mawdudi, *Jihad fi Sabilillah"* (Birmingham: U.K.I.M, 1997), pp. 12-13.

22   "Dr Mahathir PM of Malaysia's Speech in Full to the OIC", 16 October 2003, http://www.mathaba.net/gci/news/mahathir.htm, viewed 22 June 2006.

23   Bernard Lewis, "Roots of Muslim Rage", *The Atlantic Monthly*, Volume 266, No. 3, (September 1990), pp. 47-60.

24   Fathi Yakan, *Problems Faced by the Da'wah and the Da'iyah*, (Singapore: International Islamic Federation of Student Organizations, 1985), pp. 214-215.

25   Fathi Yakan, *Problems Faced by the Da'wah and the Da'iyah*, pp. 154-155.

26   Shaykh Muhammad Taher, Friday Khutbah, "The Battle of Badr", 24 December 1999, Leeds Grand Mosque.

27   'Abdul Hamid A. Abu Sulayman, *Towards an Islamic Theory of International Relations: New Directions for Methodology and Thought,* (Herndon, Virginia: The International Institute for Islamic Thought, 1994), p. 1.

28   The FSI is calculated by *Foreign Policy* journal and the Fund for Peace, an independent research organisation, considering the following factors:

   1   Mounting Demographic Pressures

   2   Massive Movement of Refugees and Internally Dispaced Persons

   3   Legacy of Vengeance - Seeking Group Grievance

   4   Chronic and Sustained Human Flight

   5   Uneven Economic Development along Group Lines

   6   Sharp and/or Severe Economic Decline

   7   Criminalisation or Delegitimisation of the State

   8   Progressive Deterioration of Public Services

   9   Widespread Violation of Human Rights

   10   Security Apparatus as "State within a State"

   11   Rise of Factionalised Elites

   12   Intervention of Other States or External Actors

29   Muhammad Ahsan, "Human Development in the Muslim World", *The Muslim World*, Vol. 94 (April 2004).

30   Abu Sulayman, *Towards an Islamic Theory of International Relations: New Directions for Methodology and Thought,* p. 1.

31 Khurshid Ahmad, "Muslim Ummah at the Threshold of 21st. Century", *Tarjumanul Qur'an* (November 1997).

32 Abid Ullah Jan, *A War on Islam?* (Birmingham: Maktabah Al Ansar, 2002), p. 43.

33 Khomeini Ruhollah, "Islamic Government", in John J. Donohue and John L. Esposito, (eds.), *Islam in Transition: Muslim Perspective*, (New York and Oxford: Oxford University Press, 1982), pp. 314-315.

34 Tariq Ramadan, "The Contradictions of the Islamic World", *Qantara*, http://www.qantara.de/webcom/show_article.php/_c-476/_nr-88/i.html?PHPSESSID=5869, viewed 13 September 2006.

35 The United Nations Development Programme, "Arab Human Development Report 2004", Regional Bureau for Arab States (RBAS) (New York: United Nations Publications, 2005), p. 95.

36 Andrew Borowiec, "Tunisian leader advises on terror", *The Washington Times*, 16 February 2004.

37 Abdul Rahman Al-Rashed, "Ministry of Interior's Advisors and the Wrong Advice", *Asharq Alawsat*, 16 January 2005.

38 Timur Kuran, "The Religious Undercurrents of Muslim Economic Grievances", Social Science Research Council, http://www.ssrc.org/sept11/essays/kuran.htm, viewed 13 September 2006.

39 Pierre Conesa, "Background to Washington's War on Terror", *Le Monde Diplomatique*, January 2002.

40 Fred Halliday, "The Left and the Jihad", *openDemocracy*, 8 September 2006.

41 "GLOBAL TRENDS 2015: A Dialogue About the Future With Nongovernment Experts," National Intelligence Council, December 2000, http://www.dni.gov/nic/NIC_globaltrend2015.html#link8b, viewed 22 August 2006.

42 "GLOBAL TRENDS 2015: A Dialogue About the Future With Nongovernment Experts," National Intelligence Council, December 2000, http://www.dni.gov/nic/NIC_globaltrend2015.html#link8b, viewed 22 August 2006.

43   Graham E. Fuller, "The Youth Factor: The New Demographics of the Middle East and the Implications for U.S. Policy", The Saban Center for Middle East Policy at the Brookings Institution, Analysis Paper No. 3 (June 2003).

44   Salim Mansur, "Muslim on Muslim Violence: What Drives It? ", Center for Security Policy, Occasional Papers Series , No. 1 (June 2004).

45   "The Arab Human Development Report 2004", United Nations Development Programme, Regional Bureau for Arab States (RBAS), (New York: United Nations Publications, 2005), p. 83.

46   Iqbal Sacranie, "The role of British Muslims in bringing justice to Palestine", Al Aqsa, Vol. 3, No. 1, http://www.aqsa.org.uk/journals/vol3iss1/british.htm, viewed 22 July 2003.

47   Abid Ullah Jan, "Palestine Is Both Religious And Muslim Issue", USA Media Monitors, Saturday 15 October 2005, http://usa.mediamonitors.net/content/view/full/21402, viewed 11 November 2005.

48   Sa'ad Khan, Reasserting International Islam: A Focus on the Organization of the Islamic Conference and Other Islamic Institutions, (Oxford: Open University Press, 2001), pp. 107-108.

49   John O. Voll, "Fundamentalism in the Sunni Arab World: Egypt and the Sudan", in Martin E. Marty and R. Scott Appleby, (eds.), Fundamentalisms Observed, The Fundamentalism Project Vol. 1 (Chicago and London: Chicago University Press, 1991), p. 347.

50   John Esposito, (ed.), Voices of Resurgent Islam, (New York: Oxford University Press, 1983), pp. 12-13.

51   Hrair Dekmejian, Islam in Revolution: Fundamentalism in the Arab World, (Syracuse, New York: Syracuse University Press, 1985), pp. 29-36.

52   Bassam Tibi, "The Renewed Role of Islam in the Political and Social Development of the Middle East", The Middle East Journal, Vol. 37, No.1 (1983), p. 7.

53   Maruf Khwaja, "Muslims in Britain: generations, experiences, futures", openDemocracy, 2 August 2005.

54   Akbar S. Ahmed, *Islam Under Siege: Living Dangerously in a Post-Honour World*, (Cambridge: Polity Press, 2003), p. 59.

55   Osama bin Laden, "Declaration of War Against the Americans Occupying the Land of the Two Holy Places", http://www.meij.or.jp/new/Osama%20bin%20Laden/jihad1.htm, viewed 6 September 2005.

56   Ehsan Masood, "A Muslim Journey", *Prospect*, Issue 113, 28 August 2005.

57   Aftab Malik, "The State Muslims are in", *openDemocracy*, 15 August 2005.

58   Parveen Akhtar, " '(Re)turn to Religion' and Radical Islam", in Tahir Abbas, (ed.), *Muslim Britain: Communities under Pressure*, (London & New York: Zed Books, 2005), p. 176.

59   "UK Foreign Policy 'Key' to Tackling Terror, say Muslim Advisors", *The Muslim News*, 10 November 2005.

60   Kate Zebiri, "Musim Anti-Secularist Discourse in the Context of Muslim Christian Relations", *Islam and Christian-Muslim Relations*, Vol. 9, No. 1, (1998), pp. 47-50.

61   Sayyid Qutb, "Social Justice in Islam" in W. Shepard, (ed.), *Sayyid Qutb and Islamic Activism: A Translation and Critical Analysis of 'Social Justice in Islam'* (Leiden: EJ Brill, 1996), pp. 292-293.

62   Qutb, "Social Justice in Islam", pp. 292-293.

63   Syed Abul Hasan Ali Nadwi, *Muslims in the West: The Message and the Mission*, (Leicester: The Islamic Foundation, 1983), p. 177.

64   Anthony King, "One in Four Muslims Sympathises with Motives of Terrorists", *The Daily Telegraph*, 23 July 2005.

65   Abdel Beri Atwan, "The Pope has Wronged [Muslims]... And Should Apologize", *Al-Quds al-Arabi*, 18 September 2006.

66   Amir Taheri, "A deadly mix: Politics and Theology", World Net Daily, 21 February 2003, http://www.benadorassociates.com/article/248, viewed 6 April 2005.

67 Olivier Roy, *The Failure of Political Islam*, (London: IB Tauris, 1994), pp. x-xi.

68 Mirna Hammoud, "Causes for Fundamentalist Popularity in Egypt" in Ahmad S. Moussalli, (ed.), *Islamic Fundamentalism: Myth and Realities*, (Reading: Garnet Publishing, 1983), pp. 322-323.

69 R. Hrair Dekmejian, *Islam in Revolution: Fundamentalism in the Arab World*, (Syracuse, New York: Syracuse University Press, 1985), p. 29.

70 Soumaya Ghannoushi , "The Erosion of the Arab State", *Aljazeera*, 26 September 2006.

71 Ali Khamenei, "No Need for Iran-US Negotiations," excerpts from a *khutbah* addressed to Tehran's Friday worshippers on 16th January 1998, published in *MSANEWS*, 27 January 1998.

72 Ali Khamenei, "No Need for Iran-US Negotiations," excerpts from a *khutbah* addressed to Tehran's Friday worshippers on 16th January 1998, published in *MSANEWS*, 27 January 1998.

73 Dr Tareq Hilmi, "Amrika alati nabghad" (Arabic, America That We Hate), *Al-Sha'b*, 17 October 2003, http://alarabnews. com/alshaab/GIF/17-10-2003/tareq.htm, viewed 27 September 2006. English translation in Reuven Paz, "Islamism and Anti-Americanism", *Middle East Review of International Affairs*, Vol. 7, No. 4 (December 2003).

74 "GLOBAL TRENDS 2015: A Dialogue About the Future With Nongovernment Experts," National Intelligence Council, December 2000, http://www.dni.gov/nic/NIC_globaltrend2015. html#link8b, viewed 22 August 2006.

75 "Synopsis of the seminar on The Impacts of Climate Change on the Islamic World", The Policy Foresight Programme and The Oxford Centre for Islamic Studies, Oxford Centre for Islamic Studies, 24 July 2006.

76 Harun Yahya, *Signs of the Last Day*, (Istanbul: Global Publishing, 2004), pp. 43-45.

77 Taqiuddin al-Nabhani, *The Islamic State*, (London: Al-Khilafah Publications, no date), pp. 188-192.

78   Ruhollah Khomeini, "Islamic Government", in Donohue and Esposito, (eds.), *Islam in Transition: Muslim Perspectives*, (New York: Oxford University Press, 1982), pp. 314-315.

79   Aftab Malik, "The State Muslims are in", *openDemocracy*, 15 August 2005.

80   "The Great Divide: How Westerners and Muslims View Each Other", A 13-Nation Pew Global Attitudes Survey, (Washington DC: Pew Research Center), 22 June 2006.

81   Rageh Omar, *Only Half of Me: Being a Muslim in Britain*, (Viking: London, 2006), p. 13.

82   Excerpts from a speech given by Libyan leader Mu'ammar Al-Qadhafi, aired on Al-Jazeera TV on 10 April 2006, see "Libyan Leader Mu'ammar Al-Qadhafi: Europe and the U.S. Should Agree to Become Islamic or Declare War on the Muslims", MEMRI, TV Monitor Project, Clip No. 1121, 10 April 2006, http://www. MEMRItv.org/Transcript.asp?P1=1121, viewed 22 August 2006.

83   Yehuda D. Nevo and Judith Koren, *Crossroads to Islam: The Origins of the Arab Religion and the Arab State* (London: Prometheus Books, 2003), p. 1.

84   Harfiyah Abdel Haleem, et al., *The Crescent and the Cross* (London: Palgrave Macmillan, 1998), p. 98.

85   Qur'anic references are given as the surah (chapter) number followed by the number of the verse within the surah. All are from A. Yusuf Ali's *The Holy Qur'an: Text, Translation and Commentary* (Leicester: The Islamic Foundation, 1975) unless otherwise stated. Verse numbers vary slightly between different translations of the Qur'an so if using another version it may be necessary to search in the verses just preceding or just following the number given here to find the verse cited.

86   Gustav E. Von Grunebaum, *Classical Islam: A History, 600-1258*, translated by Katherine Watson, 1st US edition (Chicago: Aldine, 1970), p. 84.

87   Ignaz Goldziher, *Introduction to Islamic Theology and Law* (Princeton, NJ: Princeton University Press, 1981), pp. 37-44;

Ibn Warraq, *Why I am not a Muslim* (New York: Prometheus Books, 1995), pp. 68-71.

88 Patricia Crone and Michael Cook, *Hagarism: The Making of the Islamic World* (Cambridge: Cambridge University Press, 1977), pp. 3-9, 12-15, 21-28.

89 Warraq, *Why I am not a Muslim*, pp. 75-85.

90 Malise Ruthven, *Islam in the World* (New York: Oxford University Press, 1984), pp. 80-81.

91 Gerd R. Puin, "Observations on Early Qur'an Manuscripts in Sana'a," in Stefan Wild, (ed.), *The Qur'an as Text*, (Leiden: E.J. Brill, 1996), pp. 107-111.

92 John Wansbrough, *Quranic Studies: Sources and Methods of Scriptural Interpretation*, (Oxford: Oxford University Press, 1977), pp. 33-52; Warraq, Why I am not a Muslim, pp. 68-77.

93 Patricia Crone, *Meccan Trade and the Rise of Islam* (Oxford: Oxford University Press, 1987), pp. 231-240.

94 Crone and Cook, *Hagarism: The Making of the Islamic World*, pp. 8-9.

95 Crone and Cook, *Hagarism: The Making of the Islamic World*, pp. 29-32.

96 Some Muslims consider *jihad* to be primarily the preaching of Islam in order to persuade non-Muslims to convert. One such is Dr Mar'uf Al-Dawalibi writing in Kharofa, Ala'Eddin, *Nationalism, Secularism, Apostasy and Usury in Islam* (Kuala Lumpur: A.S. Nordeen, 1994), p. 12.

97 Bernard Lewis, *The Political Language of Islam* (Chicago and London: University of Chicago Press, 1988), p. 71-72.

98 Bassam Tibi, *Conflict and War in the Middle East: From Interstate War to New Security,* 2nd edition, (Basingstoke and London: Macmillan Press, 1998), p. 216.

99 Tibi, *Conflict and War in the Middle East: From Interstate War to New Security*, pp. 61, 109.

100 J. Schacht, "Law and Justice", in P.M. Holt, Ann K.S. Lambton and Bernard Lewis, (eds.), *The Cambridge History of Islam*, Vol. 2B *Islamic Societiy and Civilizaton*, (Cambridge: Cambridge University Press, 1970), pp. 563-564.

101 Thomas Patrick Hughes, *A Dictionary of Islam* (Lahore: Premier Book House, 1885), p. 199.

102 Shi'a Muslims acknowledge the possibility of continuing to practise *ijtihad* (but they constitute only 15%-20% of the world's Muslim population).

103 These are explored by Fred M. Donner in "The Sources of Islamic Conceptions of War" in John Kelsay and James Turner Johnson, (eds.), *Just War and Jihad: Historical and Theoretical Perspectives on War and Peace in Western and Islamic Traditions* (Westport, Connecticut: Greenwood Press, 1991), pp. 31-69. Useful analyses on the sources of Islam in general are found in John C. Blair, *The Sources of Islam: An Inquiry into the Sources of the Faith and the Practice of the Muhammadan Religion* (Madras: The Christian Literature Society for India, 1925) and W. St Clair-Tisdall, *The Sources of Islam: A Persian Treatise* translated and abridged by Sir William Muir, (Edinburgh: T. & T. Clark, 1901). See also S.M. Zwemer's "Analysis of the Borrowed Elements of Islam" in *Arabia: The Cradle of Islam* (Edinburgh and London: Oliphant Anderson and Ferrier, 1900), p. 178.

104 Albrecht Noth, "Heiliger Kampf (Gihad) gegen die 'Franken': Zur Position der Kreuzzüge im Rahmen der Islamgeschichte" in *Saeculum*, Vol. 37 (1986), pp. 240-259.

105 David Cook, *Understanding Jihad* (Berkeley, Los-Angeles, London: University of California Press, 2005), pp. 1-2.

106 Yusuf al-Qaradawi, *Non-Muslims in the Islamic Society*, (Indianapolis: American Trust Publications, 1985), pp. 12, 19.

107 S. Abdullah Schleifer, "Understanding JIHAD: Definition and Methodology - Part One", *The Islamic Quarterly*, London, (Third Quarter, 1983), Sal@m, http://www.salaam.co.uk/knowledge/schleifer1.php, viewed 9 August 2005.

108   This is recorded in the Qur'an "To those against whom war is made, permission is given (to fight), because they are wronged" Q 22:39.

109   Kenneth Cragg discusses the difference between Meccan and Medinan Islam in "A Tale of Two Cities: Helping the Heirs of Mecca to Transform Medina" in *Mission Frontiers* (December 2001).

110   Cook, *Understanding Jihad*, p. 6.

111   S. Abdullah Schleifer, "Understanding Jihad: Definition and Methodology - Part Two", *The Islamic Quarterly*, London, (Third Quarter 1983).

112   Muhammad Hamidullah, *The Battlefields of The Prophet Muhammad*, (New Delhi: Kitab Bhavan, 1983), pp. 2-3.

113   S.K. Malik, *The Quranic Concept of War*, (New Delhi: Himalayan Books, 1986), pp. 145-146.

114   Muhammad Amin Ibn Abidin, *Radd al-Muhtar 'ala al-durr al-Mukhtar*, Vol. 3 (Cairo, 1856 or 1857), pp. 237-238.

115   Mahmoud Mohamed Taha, *The Second Message of Islam*, translated Abdullah Ahmed An-Na'im (Syracuse, New York: Syracuse University Press, 1987), p. 134.

116   The Qur'an often refers to Jews, Christians and Sabeans (followers of John the Baptist) as "the People of the Book", i.e. those who had their own revealed scriptures. They were generally looked on more favourably than were other non-Muslims. Sometimes Zoroastrians were included.

117   By confining himself to Qur'anic verses which actually contain the word "*jihad*" and its variants, Fatoohi has managed to write a book called *Jihad in the Qur'an* without mentioning the Sword Verse. He has also been able to assert that the purpose of armed *jihad* is neither to force non-Muslims to embrace Islam (p. 46) nor to forcibly extend the Islamic state (p. 72).

118   Jalal al-Din al-Suyuti, *al-Itkan fi Ulum al-Qur'an* [*The Perfection of Qur'anic Theology*] Vol. 2, p. 37. See also *al-Kalbi, al-Hafz al-Tashil fi ulum al-tanzil* [*The Easiest Revelation of Theology*].

119   For example 3:156; 3:167-8; 4:74-6; 4:77; 4:95; 9:38-9; 9:42-52; 9:73; 9:86-9; 9:123; 47:4; 61:11; 66:9.

120   For example 5:54; 5:85.

121   For example 2:193; 8:39.

122   Firestone's analysis of war verses is: nonmilitant, giving restrictions on fighting, expressing conflict between God's command and the reaction of Muhammad's followers, and strongly advocating war on behalf of Islam. Reuven Firestone, *Jihad: The Origin of Holy War in Islam* (New York: Oxford University Press, 1999), pp. 67-91.

123   Significantly, Louay Fatoohi, writing with the aim of conveying that *jihad* is primarily spiritual, has deliberately limited his sources to the Qur'an and omitted the *hadith* altogether. Rather misleadingly he writes (*Jihad in the Qur'an* pp. 1-2) "The Qur'an is the undisputed source of and authority on all aspects of the religion of Islam" and goes on to say of his own work, "With its exclusive emphasis on the Qur'an this book sets itself apart from the other studies of *jihad* ...". In other words, he has had to omit all the other usual sources in order not to ruin his argument.

124   Egdunas Racius, *The Multiple Nature Of The Islamic Da'wa*, Academic Dissertation, The Faculty of Arts, University of Helsinki, (Helsinki: Valopaino Oy, 2004), p. 51.

125   The reference to a *hadith* gives first the name of the person who put together the particular collection, then a reference to where that *hadith* is within the collection, then the name of the "narrator" i.e. the first person chronologically in the chain of people who passed the story on. In the original collections the names of everyone in the chain are listed. The word *sahih* before the collector's name means "true" i.e. a particularly reliable and authentic collection. The word *sunan*, which may also appear before a collector's name, is simply indicative of the fact that *hadiths* describe Muhammad's own actions, on which Muslims must model their lives.

126   An excellent text on this subject is Khaled Abou El Fadl's *Rebellion and Violence in Islamic Law* (Cambridge: Cambridge University Press, 2001).

127 For a fuller treatment of the Shi'a understanding of *jihad* and martyrdom, see Mehdi Abedi and Gary Legenhausen (eds.) *Jihad and Shahadat: Struggle and Martyrdom in Islam* (Houston: Institute for Research and Islamic Studies, 1986).

128 A helpful discussion of what various schools of law teach can be found in Majid Khadduri's *War and Peace in the Law of Islam* (Baltimore: The Johns Hopkins Press, 1955), pp. 83-137.

129 *The Islamic Law of Nations: Shaybani's Siyar* translated with an introduction, notes and appendices by Majid Khadduri (Baltimore: The Johns Hopkins Press, 1966).

130 Shaybani's *Siyar* chapter II, pp. 118-123 translated in Khadduri, *The Islamic Law of Nations*, p. 102.

131 Khadduri reviews the stances of various Islamic jurists on this issue in *War and Peace in the Law of Islam*, pp. 106-107.

132 *Dhimmis* (literally "those with a protected status") comprised Jews, Christians and Sabeans in an Islamic state. They were permitted to live and keep their own faith, in return for payment of a poll tax called the *jizya* and adherence to various demeaning regulations. Zoroastrians were sometimes included also. Polytheists were not entitled to *dhimma* status.

133 Shaybani's *Siyar* chapter VII, pp. 1317-1319, translated in Khadduri, *The Islamic Law of Nations*, p. 224.

134 Shaybani, *Kitab Al-Siyar al-Kabir*, I, pp. 14-15, quoted in Khadduri, *War and Peace in the Law of Islam*, p. 74.

135 Abu'l Hasan al-Mawardi, *The Ordinances of Government: al-Ahkam al-Sultaniyya wal-Wilayat al-Diniyya* translated Wafaa H. Wahba, The Centre for Muslim Contribution to Civilization (Reading: Garnet Publishing Ltd, 1996), p. 40. Elsewhere al-Mawardi defines other kinds of enemies who must be fought, such as apostates, insurgents, brigands and highwaymen, but distinguishes this from holy war (see pp. 60-71).

136 Al-Mawardi, *The Ordinances of Government: al-Ahkam al-Sultaniyya w'al-Wilayat al-Diniyya*, p. 59.

137 Al-Mawardi, *The Ordinances of Government: al-Ahkam al-Sultaniyya w'al-Wilayat al-Diniyya*, p. 47.

138 i.e. the school founded by Abu Hanifa

139 Al-Marghinani, *The Hedaya: Commentary on the Islamic laws*, translated Charles Hamilton, Vol. II, Book IX, chapter IV (New Delhi: Kitab Bhavan, 1985), pp. 174-180.

140 Al-Marghinani, *The Hedaya: Commentary on the Islamic laws*, translated Charles Hamilton, Vol. II, Book IX, Chapter II, p. 147.

141 Walter E. Kaegi, *Byzantium and the Early Islamic Conquests* (Cambridge: Cambridge University Press, 1992), p. 127.

142 Ibn Rushd, *The Distinguished Jurist's Primer* (Bidayat al-Mujtahid), translated by Imran Ahsan Khan Nyazee, Vol. 1 (Reading: Garnet Publishing, 1994), pp. 454-487.

143 The meaning of his title is "The beginning for him who interprets the sources independently and the end for him who wishes to limit himself". An English translation, *The Distinguished Jurist's Primer,* (Reading: Garnet Publishing, 1994) has been published in two volumes. A translation of the passages dealing with *jihad* is available in Peters *Jihad in Classical and Modern Islam*, pp. 27-42.

144 Ibn Rushd, *The Distinguished Jurist's Primer* (Bidayat al-Mujtahid), Vol. 1, pp. 455-457.

145 Ibn Rushd, *The Distinguished Jurist's Primer* (Bidayat al-Mujtahid) Vol. 1, p. 480.

146 Ibn Taymiyya, translated in Peters *Jihad in Classical and Modern Islam*, pp. 43-54.

147 Ibn Taymiyya, translated in Peters *Jihad in Classical and Modern Islam*, p. 49.

148 Ibn Taymiyya, *al-Siyasa*, quoted in Qamaruddin Khan, *The Political Thought of Ibn Taymiyah* (Delhi: Adam Publishers, 1982), p. 37.

149 Khan, *The Political Thought of Ibn Taymiyah*, pp. 37-38.

150 Ibn Taymiyya translated in Peters *Jihad in Classical and Modern Islam*, pp. 47-48.

151 Ibn Taymiyya translated in Peters *Jihad in Classical and Modern Islam*, p. 48.

152 Ahmad Ibn Naqib al-Misri, *Reliance of the Traveller: A Classic Manual of Sacred Islamic Law ('Umdat al-Salik)* edited and translated Nuh Ha Mim Keller, revised edition (Beltsville, Maryland: Amana Publications, 1997), pp. 602-603.

153 Ibn Naqib al-Misri, *Reliance of the Traveller*, pp. 603-604.

154 Ibn Khaldun, *The Muqaddimah: An Introduction To History*, translated Franz Rosenthal, Vol. 1 (London: Routledge & Kegan Paul, 1958): p. 473.

155 Ibn Khaldun *The Muqaddimah: An Introduction To History*, Vol. 1, p. 473.

156 Ibn Khaldun *The Muqaddimah: An Introduction To History*, Vol. 1, p. 473.

157 Etan Kohlberg, "The Development of the Imami Shi'i Doctrine of Jihad" in *Zeitschrift der Deutschen Morgenlaendischen Gesellschaft*, Vol. 126 (1976), pp. 64, 68.

158 Abdulaziz Sachedina, "The Development of Jihad in Islamic Revelation and History" in James Turner Johnson, and John Kelsay (eds.) *Cross, Crescent and Sword: The Justification and Limitation of War in Western and Islamic Tradition* (Westport, Connecticut: Greenwood Press, 1990).

159 Al-Muhaqqiq al-Hilli, *shara'i' al-Islam fi masa'il al halal wal-haram*, translated by Hasan M. Najafi, Vol. 1 (Qum: Ansariyan Publications, 2001): pp. 269-292.

160 This principle became a subject of much debate amongst twentieth century Islamists. Some base it on a Qur'anic command: "Fight the unbelievers who gird you about", Q 9:123.

161 Followers of Abul Hasan 'Ali ibn Isma'il al-Ash'ari (873-935), who repudiated his *mu'tazila* beliefs, became a Hanbali Sunni, and established the Ash'arite theology which became the orthodox Sunni doctrine which has dominated Sunni Islam since the tenth century.

162 Fatema Mernissi, *Islam and Democracy: Fear of the Modern World* (Cambridge, MA: Perseus Publising, 1992), pp. 18-19.

163 Mernissi, *Islam and Democracy: Fear of the Modern World*, pp. 19-21, 34-35.

164 Fatema Mernissi refers to Nietzcshe's idea of the "will to power" as the most basic driving force in the universe and in human society, an idea picked up by Fascist and Nazi ideologues and borrowed from them by contemporary Islamists. According to Nietzche living things are not driven just by the mere need to stay alive, but also by the greater need to wield and use power, to grow, to expend their strength, and, possibly, to subsume other "wills" in the process. He regarded a "will to live" as secondary to the primary "will to power". The will to power is a process of expansion and venting of creative energy that Nietzsche argued was the underlying and most fundamental "inner" force of nature. It is also the fundamental causal power in the world, the driving force of all natural phenomena and the dynamic to which all other causal powers could be reduced. Nietzsche argued for the will to power as providing the most elemental foundations for explanations of everything from whole societies to individual organisms, to lumps of matter.

165 Robert R. Reilly, *The Roots of Islamist Ideology*, (London: Centre for Research into Post-Communist Economies, CRCE, February 2006).

166 Sayyid Athar Abbas Rizvi, *Muslim Revivalist Movements in Northern India in the Sixteenth and Seventeenth Centuries* (New Delhi: Agra University Press, 1965), p. 247.

167 Rizvi, *Muslim Revivalist Movements in Northern India in the Sixteenth and Seventeenth Centuries*, pp. 248-249.

168 Rizvi, *Muslim Revivalist Movements in Northern India in the Sixteenth and Seventeenth Centuries*, p. 247.

169 John Esposito, *Islam: The Straight Path* (New York: Oxford University Press, 1988), pp. 119; 123-125. Sayyid Ahmad Barelwi (1786-1831) took Shah Wali Allah's reform teaching a step further by declaring India part of *Dar al-Harb* thus justifying military *jihad* against the Sikhs and the British. After his victory over the

Sikhs at Balakot (1826) he established a state based on *shari'a* and endeavoured to purify Islam by reforming Sufism, denouncing un-Islamic practices and emphasising monotheism (*tawhid*). Esposito, Islam: *The Straight Path*, pp. 125-127.

170 Sayyid Athar Abbas Rizvi, *Shah Wali-Allah and His Times* (Canberra: Ma'rifat Publishing House, 1980), pp. 294-296, 299, 301, 305, quoted in Andrew G. Bostom, (ed.), *The Legacy of Jihad: Islamic Holy War and the Fate of Non-Muslims* (New York: Prometheus Books, 2005), pp. 202-203.

171 Rizvi, *Shah Wali-Allah and His Times*, pp. 294-296, 299, 301, 305, quoted in Bostom, (ed.), *The Legacy of Jihad: Islamic Holy War and the Fate of Non-Muslims*, pp. 202-203.

172 Khadduri, *War and Peace in the Law of Islam*, pp. 158-159.

173 Khadduri *War and Peace in the Law of Islam*, pp. 158-60; Hughes *A Dictionary of Islam* on "Haramu 'l-Madinah" and "Hijaz"; B. Lewis on "al-Haramayn" and G. Rentz on "al-Hidjaz" in *The Encyclopaedia of Islam* (Leiden: Brill, 1986).

174 Abu'l-Hasan al-Mawardi, *The Ordinances of Government: Al-Ahkam al-Sultaniyya wal-Wilayat al-Diniyya*, pp. 152-154.

175 Khadduri, *War and Peace in the Law of Islam*, pp. 158-160.

176 Ibn Taymiyya, *Majmu'at al-fatawa li-Sheikh al-Islam Taq al-Din Ahmad Bin Taymiyya al-Hurani*, (al-Mansourah: dar al-wafa' wal nashr wal tawzi', 1997), p. 308. English translation from Bat Yeor, *Islam and Dhimitude: Where Civilizations Collide*, (Madison, NJ: Fairleigh Dickinson University Press, 2001): p. 59.

177 Ibn Sallam, *The Book of Revenue (Kitab al-Amwal)*, translated by Imran Ahsan Khan Nyazee, (Reading: Garnet, 2002): pp. 51-58.

178 "Conquered Land", Extract from *The Encyclopaedia of Islam*, CD-ROM Edition v. 1.0, © 1999 Koninklijke Brill NV, Leiden, The Netherlands.

179 Ibn Rushd, *The Distinguished Jurist's Primer: Bidayat al-Mujtahid*, Vol. 1, translated by Imran Ahsan Nyazee, (Reading: Garnet, 1994), pp. 480-481 [10.2.5 Section 5: The hukm of land conquered by the Muslims by the use of force (*'anwatan*)].

180   "The Sacred Duty of Defending Jerusalem", 23 August 2005, http://www.islamonline.net/servlet/Satellite?pagename=IslamOnl ine-English-ask_Scholar/FatwaE/FatwaE&cid=1119503543558, viewed 28 November 2005.

181   Yusuf al-Qaradawi, *Priorities of the Islamic Movement in the Coming Phase* (Swansea: Awakening Publications, 2000), p. 163.

182   "Leading Islamist Sheikh Yousef Al-Qaradhawi: We are Fighting in the Name of Islam...", MEMRI: Latest News, Special Dispatch Series No. 1102, 28 February 2006, http://MEMRI.org/bin/ articles.cgi?Page=subjects&Area=antisemitism&ID=SP110206, viewed 31 May 2006.

183   Bernard Lewis, "License to Kill: Usama bin Ladin's Declaration of Jihad", *Foreign Affairs*, (November/December 1998).

184   Isma'il Raji al-Faruqi, *Islam* (Brentwood, Maryland: International Graphics, 1984), p. 60.

185   Zafar Bangash, (ed.), *In Pursuit of the Power of Islam: Major Writings of Kalim Siddiqui* (London: The Open Press, 1996), pp. 253-255.

186   Ghada Hashem Talhami, "The Modern History of Islamic Jerusalem: Academic Myths and Propaganda", *Middle East Policy*, Vol. VII, No. 2 (February 2000).

187   "Palestine in Islamic History", HAMASONLINE, www.hamasonline. com/indexx.php?page=Palestine/palestine_in_islamic_History, viewed 17 March 2005.

188   "The Charter of Allah: The Platform of the Islamic Resistance movement (Hamas)", translated and annotated by Raphael Israeli, Harry Truman Research Institute, The Hebrew University, Jerusalem, Israel, http://www.ict.org.il/articles/h_cov.htm, viewed 28 November 2005.

189   Pnina Werbner, *Imagined Diasporas Among Manchester Muslims* (Oxford: James Currey, 2002), pp. 116-117.

190   Humayun Ansari, *The Infidel Within: Muslims in Britain Since 1800* (London: Hurst & Company, 2004), p. 226.

191   "They destroy the Houses of Allah", The Media Office of Hizb-

ut-Tahrir in Sudan, 12 May 2005, http://www.hizb-ut-tahrir.info/english/sudan/2005/may1205.htm, viewed 28 November 2005.

192 Khadduri, *War and Peace in the Law of Islam*, p. 51.

193 'Ali ibn Abi Bakr al-Marghinani, *The Hedaya: Commentary on the Islamic laws*, translated Charles Hamilton, Vol. II, Book IX, chapter IV (New Delhi: Kitab Bhavan, 1985), p. 141.

194 ibn Naqib al-Misri, *Reliance of the Traveller: A Classic Manual of Islamic Sacred Law*, pp. 602-603.

195 Firestone, *Jihad: The Origin of Holy War in Islam*, p. 54.

196 Firestone, *Jihad: The Origin of Holy War in Islam*, p. 54.

197 The term *mushrikun* in the Qur'an relates to the idolaters (polytheists) of the Arabian Peninsula, as distinct from the Jews and Christians who believed in one God and were termed "People of the Book". Later commentators tend to blur the distinction. Christians in particular were sometimes accused of being *mushrikun* because of their belief in the Trinity and the deity of Christ. Contemporary Islamists often label Jews and Christians as *mushrikun*.

198 Khadduri, *War and Peace in the Law of Islam*, p. 53.

199 Sayyid Qutb, *Milestones* (Indianapolis: American Trust Publications, 1990), p. 102.

200 Ali Sina, "Can Islam be reformed?", http://www.faithfreedom.org/Articles/sina31119.htm, viewed 7 September 2005.

201 In the words of the respected Islamic scholar F.A. Klein: "It is the duty of the Imam to send an expedition, at least once or twice a year, to the land of warfare to fight the unbelievers. If he neglects to do so, he commits a sin, except when he knows that they are not strong enough to subdue the enemy", *The Religion of Islam* (London: Curzon Press and New York: Humanities Press Inc, 1906, reprinted 1971, 1979), p. 175.

202 Brian A. Catlos, *The Victors and the Vanquished: Christians and Muslims of Catalonia and Aragon, 1050-1300* (Cambridge: Cambridge University Press, 2004), p. 82.

203 Khadduri *War and Peace in the Law of Islam*, pp. 52-53.

204 It is noteworthy that the doctrine of *Dar al-Harb* and *Dar al-Islam* is frequently rejected by modern liberal scholars, indicating its importance in justifying violence and conquest in the name of Islam. E.g. Haleem et al., *The Crescent and the Cross*, p. 71; Dr Abdel Mo'ti Bayoumi interviewed by Cornelis Hulsman "Commenting on Bat Ye'or's article" in *Religious News Service from the Arab World*, 28 August 2002.

205 See for example Abu Mansur 'Abd al-Qahir ibn Tahir Baghdadi, *Kitab Usul al-Din*, Vol. I (Istanbul, 1928), p. 270; Abu al-Fath Muhammad ibn 'Abd al-Karim al-Shawkani, *Nayl al-Awtar* 2nd edition, Vol. VIII (Cairo, 1952), pp. 28-29; Abdur Rahim, *The Principles of Muhammadan Jurisprudence* (London: Luzac, printed Madras 1911), pp. 396-397.

206 Kenneth Cragg, *The House of Islam* 2nd edition (California: Dickenson Publishing Co., 1978).

207 Samuel Huntington, *The Clash of Civilizations*, (New York: Simon and Schuster, 1996).

208 Richard Overy, (ed.) *The Times History of the World*, new edition (London: Times Books, Harper Collins Publishers, 1999), p. 303.

209 Bassam Tibi, "War and Peace in Islam", in Terry Nardin, (ed.), *The Ethics of War and Peace: Religious and Secular Perspectives*, (Princeton, NJ: Princeton University Press, 1996, pp. 128-145), p. 130.

210 Quoted in Charis Waddy, *The Muslim Mind*, 2nd edition (Longmans, 1976), p. 100.

211 Al-Qaradawi, *Priorities of the Islamic Movement in the Coming Phase*, p. 171.

212 Speaking at Holy Trinity, Brompton, London. Quoted in Andrew Carey, "Islam's Confused Identity", *The Church of England Newspaper*, 28 August 2003, p. 8.

213 Zaki Badawi, *Islam in Britain* (London: Taha Publishers, 1981), pp. 26-27.

214 The sermon was broadcast live on Palestinian Authority Television. Extracts in English translation in MEMRI Special Dispatch No. 370, 17 April 2002.

215 Muhammad Sayyid Tantawi, Sheikh of Al-Azhar, Muslim Brotherhood in Egypt Website, http://www.ikhwan-info.net/news.asp?id=539, viewed 10 March 2003.

216 Pakistan Penal Code, Section 295-C. The option of life imprisonment, which had been included in the original 1986 law, was removed by a ruling of the Federal Shariat Court in October 1990 that came into effect in 1991. This left a death sentence as the only option. (Points 67 and 69 of a judgement given by Gul Muhammad Khan in a case against Muhammad Isamail Qureshi [Shariat Petitition No. 6/L of 1987] Federal Shariat Court, 30 October 1990. *All Pakistan Legal Decisions* Vol. XLIII (1991) FSC35).

217 Qutb, *Milestones*, pp. 66-68.

218 Shaykh Muhammad Taher, Friday Khutbah, "The Battle of Badr", 24 December 1999, Leeds Grand Mosque.

219 Khadduri, *War and Peace in the Law of Islam*, p. 68.

220 Muhammad Abd al-Salam Faraj, "*The Neglected Duty*" in Johannes J.G. Jansen, *The Neglected Duty: The Creed of Sadat's Assassins and Islamic Resurgence in the Middle East*, (New York: Macmillan, 1986), pp. 159-230.

221 "Appendix III – The Call to *Jihad in the Qur'an*" in *The Interpretation of the Meanings of The Noble Qur'an in the English language, a summarised version of At-Tabari, Al-Qurtubi and Ibn Kathir with comments from Sahih Al-Bukhari, summarized in one volume*, by Dr Muhammad Taqi-ud-Din Al-Hilali and Dr Muhammad Muhsin Khan of the Islamic University, Medina, (Riyadh: Darussalam, 1996), p. 853.

222 Full text in Yonah Alexander and Michael S. Swetnam, *Usama bin Laden's al-Qaida: Profile of a Terrorist Network* (Ardsley, USA: Transnational Publishers, 2001), Appendix 1B, pp. 1-3.

223 Alexander and Swetnam, *Usama bin Laden's al-Qaida*, Appendix 1B, p. 2.

224 Speech posted in three parts on the following web addresses: www.jahra.org/free/131313/Hamza3.wma,www.jahra.org/free/131313/Hamza5.wma,www.jahra.org/free/131313/Hamza6.wma, English translation in MEMRI Special Dispatch No. 539, 18 July 2003.

225 Abu Muhammad 'Abdullah Ibn Abi Zayd al-Qayrawani, *La Risala (Epitresur les éléments du dogme et de la loi de 'Islam selon le rite malakite)* transl. Leon Bercher, 4th edition (Algiers, 1951), pp. 162-163.

226 Khadduri *War and Peace in the Law of Islam*, p. 60. However, Mawlawi in his *fatwa* of 23 March 2003 stressed that "in individual obligation, a Muslim does not need to seek the permission of the imam or the Muslim ruler".

227 Khadduri *War and Peace in the Law of Islam*, p. 141

228 Shaykh Ibn Baz and Shaykh Uthaymeen, *Muslim Minorities: Fatawa Regarding Muslims Living as Minorities* (Hounslow: Message of Islam, 1998), p. 24. Kharofa (*Nationalism, Secularism, Apostasy and Usury in Islam,101*) indicates the same.

229 Faysal Mawlawi, "Seeking Martyrdom by Attacking US Military Bases in the Gulf ", *Islam Online*, http://www.islamonline.net/servlet/Satellite?pagename=IslamOnline-English-Ask_Scholar/FatwaE/FatwaE&cid=1119503546700, viewed 25 June 2006.

230 Khadduri, *War and Peace in the Law of Islam*, pp. 65-66.

231 Ibn Khaldun, *The Muqaddimah* Vol. 1, pp. 257-260, 282-283.

232 From the translation of *Malfuzat-i-Timuri* in Elliot and Dawson, *A History of India As Told by Its Own Historians*, Vol. 3, pp. 394-395.

233 Esposito, *Islam: The Straight Path*, pp. 116-118; Hrair Dekmejian, *Islam in Revolution: Fundamentalism in the Arab World* (Syracuse, NY: Syracuse University Press, 1985), p. 12.

234 Olivier Roy, *The Failure of Political Islam* (London: I.B. Tauris, 1994), pp. 31-32. Roy mentions other movements

representative of this peripheral Sufi-led Islamic renewal and resistance to imperialism, including those of Mullah-i Lang in Afghanistan, the *akhund* of Swat in India, and 'Abd al-Karim in Morocco.

235 Mervyn Hiskett, *The Sword of Truth: The Life and Times of the Shehu Usuman dan Fodio* (Evanston, IL: Northwestern University Press, 1994), pp. 42, 62, 97-100.

236 John Ferguson, *War and Peace in the World's Religions* (London: Sheldon Press, 1977), p. 135.

237 Richard Bonney, *Jihad: From Qur'an to bin Laden*, (Basingstoke: Palgrave Macmillan, 2004), pp. 186-189.

238 Rajmohan Gandhi, *Understanding the Muslim Mind*, (New Delhi: Penguin Books India, 1987), p. 98.

239 Martin Kramer, *Islam Assembled: The Advent of the Muslim Congresses* (New York: Columbia University Press, 1986): p. 55; Andrew Mango, *Atatürk* (London: John Murray, 1999), p. 136. An English translation of the *fatwas* is found in Peters, *Jihad in Classical and Modern Islam*, pp. 56-57. The *beyanname-i cihad* read: "Gather about the lofty throne of the sultanate, as if of one heart, and cleave to the feet of the exalted throne of the caliphate. Know that the state is today at war with governments of Russia, France and England, which are its mortal enemies. Remember that he who summons you to this great holy war is the caliph of your noble Prophet." The *fatwas* and *beyanname*, all in Turkish, Arabic, Persian, Tatar and Urdu, can be found in *Ceride-i ilmiyye* (Istanbul, Muharram 1333 i.e. November/December 1914) 1(7) pp. 437-453 (*fatwas*) and pp. 454-480 (*beyanname*).

240 *Atatürk'ün Tamim, Telgraf ve Beyannameleri* (Circulars, Telegrams and Proclamations by Atatürk published as volume IV (1991) of Atatürk'ün Söylev ve Demeçleri (Ankara, 1989) p. 358. English translation in Andrew Mango *Atatürk* (London: John Murray, 1999), p. 282.

241 Ferguson, *War and Peace in the World's Religions*, p. 135; Gilles Kepel, "The Origins and Devleopment of the Jihadist

Movement: From Anti-Communism to Terrorism" translation Peter Clark in *Asian Affairs*, Vol. 34, No. 2 (July 2003).

242   Bonney, *Jihad: From the Qur'an to bin Laden*, pp. 269-312.

243   Sa'ad Khan, *Reasserting International Islam: A Focus on the organisation of the Islamic Conference and Other Islamic Institutions* (Karachi : Oxford University Press, 2001), pp. 107-108.

244   Hamas Charter, "The Charter Of Allah: The Platform Of The Islamic Resistance Movement (Hamas)", translated and annotated by Raphael Israeli, Harry Truman Research Institute, The Hebrew University, Jerusalem, articles 12, 13, 15; See also: "The Charter of the Islamic Resistance Movement (Hamas)", in Shaul Mishal and Avraham Sela, "*The Palestinian Hamas: Vision Violence and Coexistence*" (New York: Columbia University Press, 2000), pp. 175-200.

245   "Interview With Afghan Islamist Leader On Jihad Against U.S.", *MEMRI, Special Dispatch Series* - No. 455, 6 January 2003.

246   "Afghan Warlord Certain US Troops to Leave Afghanistan soon", *Pravda*, 24 November 2004.

247   "Taliban 'Commander' Out of Hiding; Declares 'Large-Scale' Anti-U.S. Jihad", *The Frontier Post*, 3 August 2006.

248   "Muslims Should Assist Their Afghan Brothers Instead Of Performing Umrah", Jamiatul Ulama (KZN) Islamic Website, http://www.jamiat.org.za/jihadumrah.html, viewed 29 August 2006

249   Muhammad Sayyid Tantawi, quoted in Steven Stalinsky, "Leading Egyptian Islamic Clerics on Jihad Against U.S. Troops in Iraq: March – August 2003", MEMRI, Inquiry and Analysis Series, No. 145, 14 August 2003

250   Muhammad Sayyid Tantawi, quoted in Steven Stalinsky, "Leading Egyptian Islamic Clerics on Jihad Against U.S. Troops in Iraq: March – August 2003", MEMRI, Inquiry and Analysis Series, No. 145, 14 August 2003.

251   "Sheikh Yousuf Al-Qaradhawi: Resistance in Iraq is a Duty of Every Muslim", MEMRI, Special Dispatch Series, No. 828, 14 December 2004.

252 Gilles Kepel in "Political Islam: A Conversation with Gilles Kepel and Jeffrey Goldberg", *Center Conversations*, No. 22, July 2003, www.eppc.org/docLib/20030728_CenterConversation22.pdf, viewed 22 September 2005.

253 "The Prophet Muhammad as a Jihad Model", MEMRI, Special Dispatch Series, No. 246, 24 July 2001.

254 Khadduri, *War and Peace in the Law of Islam*, pp. 74-82.

255 Non-Muslims were either People of the Book or polytheists.

256 "Against them make ready your strength to the utmost of your power including steeds of war to strike terror into (the hearts of) the enemies of Allah and your enemies and others besides whom ye may not know but whom Allah doth know" Q 8: 60.

257 For example " 'Abd-Allah ibn 'Umar stated that the jihad is for combating the unbelievers and the *ribat* for safeguarding the believers."

258 Jonathan Fighel, "Sheikh Abdullah Azzam: Bin Laden's Spiritual Mentor", 27 September 2001, http://www.ict.org.il/articles/articledet.cfm? articleid=388, viewed 28 September 2003.

259 Isma'il Raji al-Faruqi, *Islam*, p. 64.

260 Kalim Siddiqui in Zafar Bengash, (ed.), *In Pursuit of the Power of Islam: Major Writings of Kalim Siddiqui*, pp. 125-126.

261 Hassan Khaled, *"Jihad in the Cause of Allah"*, in D.F. Green, *Arab Theologians on Jews and Israel, Extracts from the Proceedings of the Fourth Conference of the Academy of Islamic Research*, pp. 63-66.

262 Abdullah Ghoshah, "The Jihad is the Way to Gain Victory", in D.F. Green, *Arab Theologians on Jews and Israel, Extracts from the Proceedings of the Fourth Conference of the Academy of Islamic Research*, pp. 67-68.

263 Abdullah 'Azzam, *Defense of the Muslim Lands*, (London: Ahle Sunna Wal Jama'at, no date), pp. 4-6.

264 Khurram Murad, "Prophethood: Root Cause of Islam-West Conflict", *Tarjuman al-Quran* (July 1992) http://www.jamaat.org/Isharat/archive/792.html, viewed 8 September 2005.

265 Yusuf al-Qaradawi, *Priorities of the Islamic Movement in the Coming Phase*, p. 34.

266 Sheikh Muhammad Abu Zahra, "The Jihad (Strivings)", in D.F. Green, *Arab Theologians on Jews and Israel, Extracts from the Proceedings of the Fourth Conference of the Academy of Islamic Research*, pp. 61-63. He also re-stated the accepted view that *jihad* is valid until the end of the world: "*Jihad* would never end, because it will last to the Day of Resurrection."

267 Shaykh Muhammad Taher, Friday Khutbah, "The objectives of the Islamic sacred law", 19 March 2004, Leeds Grand Mosque, http://www.leedsgrandmosque.org.uk/khutbahs/khutba-20040319.asp, viewed 8 September 2005.

268 Fathi Yakan, *Problems Faced by the Da'wah and the Da'iya*, (Singapore: International Islamic Federation of Student Organisations, 1985), p. 231.

269 Ibn Taymiyya, *al-Siyasa*, quoted in Qamaruddin Khan, *The Political Thought of Ibn Taymiyah*, p. 37.

270 Qamaruddin Khan, *The Political Thought of Ibn Taymiyah*, p. 156.

271 Bassam Tibi, "War and Peace in Islam", in Terry Nardin, (ed.), *The Ethics of War and Peace : Religious and Secular Perspectives*, p.130.

272 Tibi, "War and Peace in Islam", p.130.

273 David Cook, *Understanding Jihad* (Berkeley, Los Angeles, London: University of California Press, 2005), pp. 22-25.

274 For further details of what the Qur'an and *hadith* say about the End Times, the reader is referred to David C. Cook, *Studies in Muslim Apocalyptic* (New Jersey: The Darwin Press, 2002).

275 Sultan Firuz Shah of Delhi (d.1388) claimed that he executed those who claimed to be the *mahdi*, but only imprisoned those who claimed to be God. See John Esposito, (ed.), *The Oxford Encyclopedia of the Modern Islamic World*, Vol. 2 (New York: Oxford University Press, 1995), p. 27.

276 See for instance Ibrahim, Abdul-Maajid and Darbaalah, *In Pursuit of Allah's Pleasure*, pp. 30-31.

277 Ibrahim, Abdul-Maajid and Darbaalah, *In Pursuit of Allah's Pleasure*, pp. 30-31. The authors, who are close to the Egyptian al-Jihad movement, include in their declaration of faith (*aqeedah*) the following items: "We have no doubt that the awaited Mahdee (or rightly-guided Imam) will come forth from among the Ummah of the Prophet at the end of time (on earth). We believe in the Signs of the Hour. The appearance of ad-Dajjal (false Messiah, or Antichrist). The descent from heaven of Isa, son of Mary. The sun rising from the West. The emergence of the Beast from the earth. And other signs mentioned in the Quran and the authentic Hadeeth of the Prophet".

278 defined in chapter 12

279 defined in chapter 12

280 Walid M. Abdelnasser, *The Islamic Movement in Egypt* (London: Kegan Paul International, 1994), p. 216; Derek Hopwood, *Egypt: Politics and Society 1945-1990* (London: Harper Collins Academic, 1991), p. 118.

281 Muhammad Abdessalam Faraj. *Al-farida al-ghaiba*, translated in G. H. Jansen, *The Neglected Duty: The Creed of Sadat's Assassins and Islamic Resurgence in the Middle East* (New York Macmillan, 1986), pp. 163-164. Abdelnasser, *The Islamic Movement in Egypt*, pp. 234-235.

282 Juhayman and his followers seized the Grand Mosque and had to be dislodged by the security forces in a violent siege.

283 Ayman Al-Yassini, *Religion and State in the Kingdom of Saudi Arabia* (Boulder, Colorado: Westview Press, 1985), pp. 124-129.

284 Syed Saleem Shahzad, "Armageddon: Bringing it on", *Asia Times Online*, 20 May 2005.

285 David Cook "America, the Second 'Ad: Prophecies About the Downfall of the United States," *Yale Center for International and Area Studies*, Vol. 5, The United States & the Middle East: Cultural

Encounters (2002) pp. 150-93; Timothy Furnish, "Mahdism in the Sunni World Today", *ISIM Newsletter*, (4/99), p. 22.

286   John R. Hall, "Apocalypse 9/11", in Phillip Lucas and Thomas Robbins, (eds.), *NewReligious Movements in the Twenty-First Century: Political and Social Challenges in Global Perspective* (London: Routledge, 2004), pp. 265-282.

287   Matthew Chebatoris, "Islamist Infiltration of the Moroccan Armed Forces", *Terrorism Monitor*, Volume 5, Issue 3, 15 February 2007.

288   For the origins, formulation and development of the concept of *mahdi* in the different Shi'a sects, see Heinz Halm *Shiism* translated by Janet Watson (Edinburgh: Edinburgh University Press, 1991).

289   Cook, *Studies in Muslim Apocalyptic* p. 195.

290   Cook, *Studies in Muslim Apocalyptic*, p. 196.

291   Cook, *Studies in Muslim Apocalyptic*, pp. 198-209.

292   Ayatollah Ibrahim Amini, *Al-Imam al-Mahdi, the Just Leader of Humanity*, translated by Abdulaziz Sachedina, 2nd edition, (Qum: Ansariyan Publications, 1999), pp. 225-227.

293   Al-Hurr al-'Amili, VII, 55-56, quoted by David Cook, *Studies in Muslim Apocalyptic*, p. 233.

294   Amini, *Al-Imam al-Mahdi, the Just Leader of Humanity*, chapters 12-14.

295   Amini, *Al-Imam al-Mahdi, the Just Leader of Humanity*, chapter 14.

296   Daniel Pipes, "The Mystical Menace of Mahmoud Ahmadinejad", *New York Sun*, 10 January 2006.

297   Pipes, "The Mystical Menace of Mahmoud Ahmadinejad", *New York Sun*, 10 January 2006.

298   Kenneth R. Timmerman, "Iran's Nuclear Zealot", *Project Syndicate*, http://www.project-syndicate.org/print_commentary/ timmerman2/English, viewed 13 February 2006.

299 Tom Porteus, "Reading Iran", *Prospect*, Issue 118, 22 January 2006; Patrick Devenny, "True Fanatic", *The American Spectator*, 15 December 2005.

300 Alan Peters, "Mullah's Threat Not Sinking In", *FrontPageMagazine*, 4 November 2006, http://www.frontpagemag.com/Articles/ReadArticle.asp?ID=20065, viewed 14 February 2006.

301 Special Correspondent, "Shi'ite supremacists emerge from Iran's shadows", *Asia Times Online*, 9 September 2005, http://www.atimes.com/atimes/Middle_East/GI09Ak01.html, viewed 17 January 2006.

302 Patrick Devenny, "True Fanatic", *The American Spectator*, 15 December 2005.

303 Raymond Whitaker, "Mahmoud Ahmadinejad: The Nuclear Prophet", *The Independent*, 3 February 2006.

304 Devenny, "True Fanatic", *The American Spectator*, 15 December 2005.

305 Amini, *Al-Imam al-Mahdi, the Just Leader of Humanity*; Tahir-ul-Qadri *The Awaited Imam* (Lahore: Minhaj-ul-Quran Publications, 2003), pp. 15-17.

306 Muhammad ibn 'Izzat and Muhammad 'Arif, *Al-Mahdi and the End of Time*, (London: Dar Al Taqwa, 1997), p. 16.

307 Ibn Katir Ad-Damishqi, *Before & After the Last Hour*, (Karachi: Darul Ishaat, 2004), pp. 47-56; 69-95.

308 Muhammad ibn 'Izzat and Muhammad 'Arif, *Al-Mahdi and the End of Time*, (London: Dar Al Taqwa, 1997), p. 17.

309 Sidheeque M.A. Veliankode, *Doomsday: Portents and Prophecies*, (Toronto: Al-Attique Publishers, 1999), p. 277.

310 Either the Black Stone which is fixed in the south-east corner of the *ka'ba*, or the corner itself which contains the Stone.

311 *Maqam Ibrahim* is a stone situated a little distance from the north-east wall of the *ka'ba*.

312 Cook, *Studies in Muslim Apocalyptic*, p. 232.

313   Cook, *Contemporary Muslim Apocalyptic Literature*, pp. 8-9.

314   Ibrahim, Abdul-Maajid and Darbaalah, *In Pursuit of Allah's Pleasure*, pp. 30-31.

315   David Cook, *Contemporary Muslim Apocalyptic Literature*, (Syracuse, NY: Syracuse University Press, 2005), p. 10.

316   Cook, *Studies in Muslim Apocalyptic*, pp. 165.

317   Cook, *Studies in Muslim Apocalyptic*, pp. 172-182.

318   Cook, *Studies in Muslim Apocalyptic*, p.195.

319   Amini, *Al-Imam al-Mahdi, the Just Leader of Humanity*, translated by Abdulaziz Sachedina, 2nd edition, (Qum: Ansariyan Publications, 1999) chapters 10,12-14.

320   Cook, *Studies in Muslim Apocalyptic*, p. 195.

321   Cook, *Studies in Muslim Apocalyptic*, pp. 209-210.

322   Ancient Israel – see Deuteronomy 20:10-12. Classical antiquity – see Coleman Phillipson, *The International Law and Custom of Ancient Greece and Rome*, Vol. I (London: Macmillan & Co. Ltd, 1911), pp. 96-97.

323   Ibn Abi Zayd al-Qayrawani, *La Risala*, pp. 162-163.

324   In the sense of initiating a campaign against any particular enemy. *Jihad per se* is permanent.

325   Khadduri, *War and Peace in the Law of Islam*, pp. 94-101, 152-154.

326   Abu al-Walid Muhammad Ibn Muhammad Ibn Rushd (Averroes), *Bidyat al-Mujtahid wa-Nihayat al-Muqtasid [The Beginning for him who Interprets the Sources Indepently and the End for him who Wishes to Limit Himself]* English translation in Peters, *Jihad in Classical and Modern Islam*, p. 37.

327   These and other examples are quoted in Yasin Istanbuli, *Diplomacy and Diplomatic Practice in the Early Islamic Era* (Oxford: Oxford University Press, 2001), pp. 46-47.

328   Al-Imam Abu Abdallah Muhammed Al-Bukhari, Sahih Al-Bukhari, (ed.) *Shaikh Qasem al-Rifaie*, Vol. I (Beirut: Dar Al-

Qalam, 1987), p. 65; Muhammad Hamidullah, *Documents sur la Diplomatie Musulmane à l'époque du Prophete et des Khalifes Orthodoxes* (Paris: Librarie Oriental et Americane, Thesis, University of Paris, 1935), p. 33.

329 Hamidullah, *Documents sur la Diplomatie Musulmane*, p. 32. "We who have surrendered" indicates "Muslims", which literally means "those who have submitted" i.e. submitted to God.

330 The letter is displayed in the Topkapi Palace, Istanbul.

331 See also Osama bin Laden's declaration of war against America. It is noteworthy that the first issue of Al-Qaeda's online training magazine *Al-Battar Training Camp* berates the Muslims of today because they "love this world, hate death, and abandon jihad". Mu'aadh Mansour, "The Importance of Military Preparedness in Shari'ah" in *Al-Battar Training Camp*, Issue 1 (December 2003), www.hostinganime.com /battar/b1word.zip. Excerpts in English translation in MEMRI Special Dispatch Series No. 637, 6 January 2004.

332 Khadduri, *War and Peace in the Law of Islam*, p. 67; Professor Sir Norman Anderson, *Islam in the Modern World: A Christian Perspective* (Leicester: Apollos, 1990), p. 31.

333 Government by the Islamic jurists, who are, according to a *hadith*, "the heirs of the prophets". The significance of the term "heirs of the prophets" is that Shi'as believe the imam must be a descendant of 'Ali, the fourth caliph, whose wife was Muhammad's daughter Fatima.

334 Nels Johnson, *Islam and the Politics of Meaning in Palestinian Nationalism* (London: Kegan Paul, 1982), pp. 74-75.

335 Saudi Arabia, where Mecca and Medina are located.

336 The full text can be found in Alexander and Swetnam, *Usama bin Laden's al-Qaida*, Appendix 1A, and also used to be on the website of Azzam Publications www.azzam.com/html/articlesdeclaration. htm (now removed).

337 i.e. William Perry, then US Secretary of Defence.

338 Alexander and Swetnam, *Usama bin Laden's al-Qaida*, Appendix 1A, 15.

339 Ahlus Sunnah wal Jama'ah's Ustadz Ja'far Umar Thalib, commander of the Laskar Jihad, in an address broadcast on Radio SPMM [The voice of struggle of the Maluku Muslims], 1-3 May 2002. This and further excerpts can be found at www.persecution.org/news/report2002-05-15.html, viewed 20 May 2002.

340 Hilmy Bakar Almascaty, *Panduan Jihad Untuk Aktivis Gerakan Islam [A Manual for Jihad for Islamic Movement Activists]* (Jakarta: Gema Insani Press, May 2001), p. 101.

341 "Public Invitation To The British To Embrace The Truth & Justice Of Islam", press release dated 23 June 2000, http://www.hvk.org/articles/0600/47.html, viewed 28 November 2006.

342 Sean O'Neil and Yaacov Lappin, "Britain's online imam declares war as he calls young to jihad", *The Times*, 17 January 2006.

343 Abu Ja'far Muhammad ibn Jarir Al-Tabari, *Ta'rikh al-Rusul wa'l-Muluk (Annales)* (ed.) M.J. De Goeje et al., Vol. 1 (Leiden: Brill, 1879-1901), p. 1850.

344 Including mutilation of the dead. See Khadduri, *War and Peace in the Law of Islam*, p.108.

345 Al-Tabari, *Ta'rikh*, Vol. III, 160; Abu 'Abd-Allah Muhammad ibn 'Umar Waqidi, *Kitab al-Maghazi*, (ed.) Alfred von Kremer (Calcutta, 1856), p. 284.

346 These were the Kharijis who followed Nafi' ibn al-Azraq. See 'Abd al-Qahir al-Baghdadi, *Mukhtasar Kitab al-Farq Bayn al-Firaq*, (ed.) Philip Hitti (Cairo, 1924), pp. 73, 97.

347 Muhammad ibn al-Hasan Shaybani, *Sharh Kitab Al-Siyar al-Kabir*, with commentary by Shams al-Din Muhammad b. Ahmad b. Sahl Sarakhsi, Vol. IV (Hyderabad, 1916-17), p. 79.

348 Shaybani, *Sharh Kitab Al-Siyar al-Kabir*, with commentary by Shams al-Din Muhammad b. Ahmad b. Sahl Sarakhsi, Vol. I, p. 33.

349 He repeats the same guidelines earlier in his *Siyar* as well. See chapter 2:112-113 in Shaybani's *Siyar* transl.ated in Khadduri, *The Islamic Law of Nations*, p. 101.

350   Shaybani, *Sharh Kitab Al-Siyar al-Kabir* with commentary by Sarakhsi, pp. 212-213.

351   Khadduri, *War and Peace in the Law of Islam*, p. 104.

352   Al-Baladhuri, *The Origins of the Islamic State*, a translation of *Kitab Futuh al-Buldan*, translated by Philip Khuri Hitti (Piscataway, NJ: Gorgias Press, 2002), p. 310.

353   From the translation of *Malfuzat-i-Timuri* in Elliot and Dawson, *A History of India As Told by Its Own Historians*, Vol. 3, p. 461.

354   *The History of al-Tabari*, edited by Ehsan Yar-Shater (Albany: New York: State University of New York Press, 1993), Vol. XI, "The Challenge to the Empires", translated by Khalid Yahya Blankinship, p. 26.

355   *The History of al-Tabari*, edited by Ehsan Yar-Shater, Vol. XI, "The Challenge to the Empires", translated by Khalid Yahya Blankinship, pp. 65-66.

356   Muhammad Kasim Hindu Shah, *Ta'rikh-i-Firishta* (Lucknow, 1864), pp. 28-29, quoted in Andre Wink, *Al-Hind: The Making of the Indo-Islamic World*, Vol. II, "The Slave Kings and the Islamic Conquest 11th-13th Centuries", (Leiden: Brill, 1997), p. 124.

357   Wink, *Al-Hind: The Making of the Indo-Islamic World*, Vol. I, "Early Medieval India and the Expansion of Islam 7th-11th Centuries", p. 23.

358   Abu'l Hasan al-Mawardi, *The Ordinances of Government: al-Ahkam al-Sultaniyya w'al-Wilayat al-Diniyya*, pp. 140-157.

359   *The History of al-Tabari*, edited by Ehsan Yar-Shater, Vol. XIX, "The Caliphate of Yazid b. Mu'awiyah", translated by I.K.A. Howard (Albany: New York: State University of New York Press, 1993), p. 213.

360   "Text No. 13: Dionysius Reconstituted", in *The Seventh Century in the West-Syrian Chronicles*, introduced, translated and annotated by Andrew Palmer (Liverpool: Liverpool University Press, 1993), p. 149.

361   Abu Ja'far Muhammad ibn Jarir Al-Tabari, *Kitab al-Jihad wa Kitab al-Jizya wa Ahkam al-Muharibin min Kitab Ikhtilaf al-Fuqaha*, (ed.) J. Schacht (Leiden: Brill, 1933), pp. 103-104; Ya'qub b. Ibrahim al-Ansari Abu Yusuf, *Kitab al-Radd 'ala Siyar al-Awza'i*, (ed.) Abu al-Wafa al-Afghani (Cairo, 1938), pp. 83-87; Joseph Schacht, *The Origins of Muhammadan Jursiprudence* (Oxford: Oxford University Press, 1950), pp. 34-35.

362   Al-Tabari *Kitab al-Jihad*, pp. 106-107.

363   Shaybani's *Siyar* chapter II: pp. 82-89 translated in Khadduri, *The Islamic Law of Nations*, pp. 98-99.

364   *The Holy Qur'an*, Yusuf Ali translation, Note 1234, p. 432.

365   *Interpretation of the Meanings of The Noble Qur'an in the English language, a summarised version of At-Tabari, Al-Qurtubi and Ibn Kathir with comments from Sahih Al-Bukhari, summarised in one volume*, by Dr Muhammad Taqi-ud-Din Al-Hilali and Dr Muhammad Muhsin Khan of the Islamic University, Medina, (Riyadh: Darussalam, 1996).

366   Sayyid Abu'l A'la Mawdudi, *The Meaning of the Qur'an*, Vol. XIII, (Lahore: Islamic Publications, 1986), p. 13.

367   Ibn Naqib al-Misri, *Reliance of the Traveller*, p. 604. Text in brackets comprises the comments of 'Umar Barakat (d.1890) who wrote a commentary on Ibn Naqib's work entitled *Fayd al-Ilah al-Malik fi hall alfaz 'Umdat al-Salik wa 'Uddat al-Nasik [The Outpouring of Sovereign Divinity: an interpretation of the words of "Reliance of the Traveller and Tools of the Worshipper"]*.

368   Abu Yusuf Ya'qub b. Ibrahim al-Ansari, *Kitab al-Kharaj* (Cairo, 1993), pp. 195-196.

369   Shaybani's *Siyar*, chapter II:94-109, translated in Khadduri, *The Islamic Law of Nations*, pp. 100-101.

370   Shaybani's *Siyar*, chapter II:110-111, translated in Khadduri, *The Islamic Law of Nations*, p. 101.

371   Shaybani's *Siyar*, chapter II:80-81, translated in Khadduri, *The Islamic Law of Nations*, p. 98.

372   Abu al-Fath Muhammad ibn 'Abd al-Karim al-Shahrastani, *Kitab al-Milal wa al-Nihal* (ed.) Cureton (London, 1846), pp. 90-93.

373   George E. Nafziger and Mark W. Walton, *Islam at War: A History*, (Westport, CO & London: Praeger, 2003), p. 10.

374   Al-'Utbi, *Tarikh Yamini*, in Elliot and Dawson, *A History of India As Told by Its Own Historians*, Vol. 2, p. 23.

375   Shaybani, *Sharh Kitab Al-Siyar al-Kabir*, with commentary by Sarakhsi, Vol. IV, pp. 223-225.

376   Al-Tabari, *Kitab al–Jihad*, pp. 194-198.

377   Mustafa Abu Sway, "Kidnapping Foreign nationals: An Islamic Perspective", *Christian Science Monitor*, 3 February 2006.

378   Quoted in Quintan Wiktorowicz and John Kaltner, "Killing in the Name of Islam: Al-Qaeda's Justification for September 11", *Middle East Policy*, Volume X, No. 2 (Summer 2003)

379   *Al Qal'ah* website, 14 October 2002, quoted in Christopher M. Blanchard, *Al Qaeda: Statements and Evolving Ideology*, Congressional Research Service (CRS), Report for Congress, 16 November 2004, http://www.fas.org/irp/crs/RS21973.pdf, viewed 8 April 2005.

380   Yassin Musharbash, "The Al-Qaida Guide to Kidnapping", *Spiegel Online*, 1 December 2005, http//www.spiegel.de/international/0,1518,387888,00.html, viewed 27 April 2006.

381   A. Guillaume, *The Life of Muhammad: A Translation of Ibn Ishaq's Sirat Rasul Allah*, (Karachi, Oxford & New York: Oxford University Press, 1955, 13th edition 1998), p. 464.

382   *The History of al-Tabari*, edited by Ehsan Yar-Shater, Vol. XI, "The Challenge to the Empires", translated by Khalid Yahya Blankinship (Albany: New York: State University of New York Press, 1993), p. 24.

383   *The History of al-Tabari*, edited by Ehsan Yar-Shater , Vol. XI, "The Challenge to the Empires", p. 55.

384   *The History of al-Tabari*, edited by Ehsan Yar-Shater, Vol. XI, "The Challenge to the Empires", p. 59.

385 *The History of al-Tabari*, edited by Ehsan Yar-Shater, Vol. XVIII, "Between Civil Wars: The Caliphate of Mu'awiyah", translated by Michael G. Morony, (Albany: New York: State University of New York Press, 1993), p. 127.

386 *The History of al-Tabari*, edited by Ehsan Yar-Shater, Vol. XIX, "The Caliphate of Yazid b. Mu'awiyah", pp. 163-164.

387 G.R. Hawting, *The First Dynasty of Islam: The Umayyad Caliphate AD 661-750*, (London: Routledge, 2000), p. 50.

388 Reinhart Dozy, *Spanish Islam: A History of the Muslims in Spain*, translated by Francis Griffin Stokes (London: Goodward Books, 1913), p. 248.

389 Joseph F. O'Callaghan, *A History of Medieval Spain* (Ithaca, NY: Cornell University Press, 1975), p. 209.

390 George E. Nafziger & Mark W. Walton, *Islam at War: A History*, p. 96.

391 Timothy Furnish, "Beheadings in the Name of Islam", *Middle East Quarterly*, Vol. 12, No. 2 (Spring 2005); "Human Rights in Saudi Arabia: A Deafening Silence", Human Rights Watch (December 2001) hrw.org/backgrounder/mena/saudi/, viewed 27 April 2006.

392 Lord Kinross, *The Ottoman Centuries: The Rise and Fall of the Turkish Empire* (New York: Morrow Quill Paperbacks, 1979), pp. 559-560.

393 Quoted in Hassan Mneimneh and Kanan Makiya, "Manual for a Raid", *The New York Review of Books*, 17 January 2002.

394 Mneimneh and Makiya, "Manual for a Raid".

395 "Where girls are killed for going to school", written by Lara Marlowe for *Marie Claire, Amnesty International Press Awards*, http://www.amnesty.org.uk/news/awards/period.html, viewed 28 April 2006.

396 Timothy Furnish, "Beheadings in the Name of Islam", *Middle East Quarterly*, Vol. 12, No. 2 (Spring 2005); "Van Gogh killer jailed for life", *BBC NEWS*, 26 July 2005.

397 Guillaume, *The Life of Muhammad: A Translation of Ibn Ishaq's Sirat Rasul Allah*, p. 515.

398 See Q 5:36 "The punishment of those who wage war against Allah and His Apostle and strive with might and main for mischief through the land is: execution or crucifixion of the cutting off of hands and feet from opposite sides or exile from the land: that is their disgrace in this world and a heavy punishment is theirs in the Hereafter".

399 Al-Biladuri, in Elliot and Dawson, *A History of India As Told by Its Own Historians*, Vol. 1, p. 124.

400 Wink, *Al-Hind: The Making of the Indo-Islamic World*, Vol. I, "Early Medieval India and the Expansion of Islam 7th-11th Centuries", pp. 13-16, 25, 61.

401 Al-'Utbi, *Tarikh Yamini*, in Elliot and Dawson, *A History of India As Told by Its Own Historians*, Vol. 2, 39.

402 Shams-i Siraj 'Afif, *Tarikh-i Fioz Shahi*, in Elliot and Dawson, *A History of India As Told by Its Own Historians*, Vol. 2, p. 341.

403 For more on the slave soldiers of Islam see: Daniel Pipes, *Slave Soldiers and Islam: The Genesis of a Military System*, (New Haven and London: Yale University Press, 1981).

404 John Eibner, "My Career Redeeming Slaves", *Middle East Quarterly*, Vol. 4. No. 4, (December 1999).

405 Sayyed Wild Abah, "Slavery in Mauritania", *Asharq Alawsat*, 4 June 2006; Pascale Harter, "Slavery: Mauritania's best kept secret", *BBCNEWS*, 13 December 2003.

406 Humphrey J. Fisher, *Slavery in the History of Muslim Black Africa*, (London: Hurst & Company, 2001), pp. 46-54.

407 For example, this verse is quoted in the context of espionage in Almascaty's 2001 *jihad* manual *Panduan Jihad Untuk Aktivis Gerakan Islam*, p. 99.

408 Muhammad Hamidullah, *The Battle Fields of the Prophet* (Lahore: Idra-e-Islamiat, 1993), p. 117.

409 Hamidullah, *The Battle Fields of the Prophet*, pp. 120-131.

410   Hamidullah, *The Battle Fields of the Prophet*, p. 123, citing Ibn Kathir's *History* IV:6. A *hadith* describing the assassination is quoted in chapter 3.

411   Muhammad Zakariyya Kandhalvi, "Stories of Sahabah" in *Tablighi Nisab* (Dewsbury: Anjuman-e-Islahul Muslemeen of UK, no date but probably soon after 1938), pp. 172-173.

412   Hamidullah, *The Battle Fields of the Prophet*, pp. 126-127.

413   Hamidullah states that in peace time there should be no difference in the treatment of male and female adult spies (*The Battle Fields of the Prophet*, p. 131).

414   Shaybani, *Sharh Kitab Al-Siyar al-Kabir*, with commentary by Sarakhsi Vol. IV, pp. 226-227.

415   Shaybani, *Sharh Kitab Al-Siyar al-Kabir*, with commentary by Sarakhsi, Vol. IV, pp. 226; al-Tabari, *Kitab al–Jihad*, pp. 172-173.

416   Omar Saleh Barghuthy, "A Ministry of Propaganda under the Fatimids", *Journal of the Middle East Society* (Spring 1947), pp. 57-59.

417   B. Raman, "Thai dilemma over Muslim anger", *Asia Times*, 3 November 2004.

418   Ibn Asakir, *History of Damascus*, Vol. I (1951 edition), p. 394, cited in Hamidullah, *The Battle Fields of the Prophet*, p. 132.

419   Ibn Sa'd, *Kitab at-Tabaqat al-Kabir*, II/i: 117-118, and Maqriziy *Imta'* I:443, cited in Hamidullah, *The Battle Fields of the Prophet*, p. 133.

420   An expedition authorised with reluctance by Caliph 'Uthman, after Caliph 'Umar I had forbidden it. Caliph 'Umar advised all Muslims not to travel by sea, let alone fight on it. See Khadduri, *War and Peace in the Law of Islam*, p. 112.

421   Abu Muhammad 'Abd-Allah ibn Ahmad ibn Muhammad ibn Qudama, *Kitab al-Mughni*, Vol. VIII, (ed.) M. Rashid Rida (Cairo, 1947 or 1948), pp. 349-350, quoted in Khadduri, *War and Peace in the Law of Islam*, p. 113. See also E. Kohlberg, "Shahid" in *The Encyclopaedia of Islam*. Another interesting

hadith runs "He who becomes sick on a stormy sea will have the reward of a martyr, and he who is drowned will have the reward of two martyrs." *Mishkat al-Masabih 18:2* Narrated by Umm Haram. English translation with explanatory notes by James Robson, Vol. 1 (Lahore: Sh. Muhammad Ashraf, 1990), p. 815.

422 *Sahih Al Bukhari*, Vol. 4, Book 52, Number 175: Narrated by Khalid bin Madan.

423 Shaybani, *Sharh Kitab Al-Siyar al-Kabir*, with commentary by Sarakhsi, Vol. I, pp. 25-26.

424 Hasan Ibn 'Abd-Allah, *Athar al-Uwal fi Tartib al-Duwal* (Cairo, 1878 or 1879), pp. 195-198. The original work dates from 1308 or 1309.

425 Shaybani, *Sharh Kitab Al-Siyar al-Kabir* with commentary by Sarakhsi, Vol. III, p. 265. Al-Awza'i, who opposed attacking an enemy castle with a Muslim human shield, likewise opposed trying to sink or set fire to an enemy ship with a Muslim human shield. See al-Tabari, *Kitab al–Jihad*, pp. 4-5.

426 Al-Tabari, *Kitab al–Jihad*, p. 86.

427 Shaybani, *Sharh Kitab Al-Siyar al-Kabir* Vol. III, p. 269; Ardabili, al-Anwar li-'Amal al-Abrar Vol. II (Cairo, no date), p. 289.

428 Shaybani, *Sharh Kitab Al-Siyar al-Kabir*, Vol. III, pp. 269-270, 272.

429 Shaybani, *Sharh Kitab Al-Siyar al-Kabir*, Vol. III, pp. 270.

430 Stanley Lane-Poole, *The Barbary Corsairs*, (London: Darf Publishers, 1984).

431 Ibn Naqib al-Misri, *Reliance of the Traveller: A Classic Manual of Sacred Islamic Law* ('Umdat al-Salik), p. 602.

432 Ibn Naqib al-Misri, *Reliance of the Traveller: A Classic Manual of Sacred Islamic Law* ('Umdat al-Salik), p. 606.

433 Abdul Jalil Sajid , "Islam and Ethics of War and Peace", 18 May 2002, http://www.preparingforpeace.org/sajid_islam_and_ethics_of_war_and_peace.htm, viewed 7 June 2006.

434 Jonathan Rauch, "The Mullahs and the Postmodernists", *The Atlantic Monthly*, January 2002; Ibn Warraq, "Honest Intellectuals Must

Shed their Spiritual Turbans", *The Guardian*, Saturday, 10 November 2001 http://www.guardian.co.uk/Print/0,3858,4295749,00.html, viewed 8 February 2007; Fred Halliday, "The Left and the Jihad" *openDemocracy*, 8 September 2006.

435 Jonathan Rauch, "The Mullahs and the Postmodernists", *The Atlantic Monthly*, January 2002.

436 Rauch, "The Mullahs and the Postmodernists".

437 Flemming Rose, "Why I published the Muhammad cartoons", *Spiegel Online*, 31 May 2006, http://service.spiegel.de/cache/international/spiegel/0,1518,418930,00.html, viewed 6 June 2006.

438 Kaegi, *Byzantium and the Early Islamic Conquests*, p. 277.

439 Probably from the tribe of Iyad.

440 Al-Tabari *Ta'rikh*, Vol.1, p. 2508. This English translated in *The History of al-Tabari*, edited by Ehsan Yar-Shater, Vol. XIII: *The Conquest of Iraq, Southwestern Persia, and Egypt*, tr. G.H.A. Juynboll (Albany: State University of New York Press, 1989), p. 89.

441 A. Ben Shemesh, *Taxation in Islam*, Vol. 2 (Leiden: Brill, London: Luzac & Co. Ltd, 1965), p. 42; Hugh Kennedy, *The Prophet and the Age of the Caliphates: the Islamic Near East from the Sixth to the Eleventh Century*, (Harlow: Pearson Education Limited [Longman], 1986), p. 63.

442 Hipployte Delehaye, "Passio sanctorum sexaginta martyrum" in *Analecta Bollandiana: A Journal of Critical Hagiography*, Vol. 28 (1904), pp. 289-307; J. Pargoire, "Les LX Soldats Martyrs de Gaza" in *Echos d'Orient: Revue de Théologie, de Droit Canonique, de Liturgie, d'Archaelogie, d'Histoire et de Géographie Orientales*, Vol. 8 (1905), pp. 40-43.

443 Kaegi, *Byzantium and the Early Islamic Conquests*, pp. 95-96.

444 Kaegi, *Byzantium and the Early Islamic Conquests*, p. 89. A similar punishment was given to Muhammad b. Abu Bakr in 658 for his role in the murder of Caliph Uthman. He was not only put in an ass's stomach but then he and the stomach together were burnt – a method of execution intended to bring shame and disgrace because of his terrible crime.

445   Kaegi, *Byzantium and the Early Islamic Conquests*, p. 128.

446   Barnaby Rogerson, *The Prophet Muhammad* (London: Little, Brown, 2003), pp. 164-166.

447   Andrew G. Bostom, "Muhammad, the Qurayza Massacre, and PBS" in *FrontPageMagazine.com*, 20 December 2002.

448   Muhammad took one of the Qurayza women, Rayhanah, as his wife. She converted to Islam but begged to be kept as a concubine rather than become his wife, as she preferred to be a captive of the man who had destroyed her clan rather than enter his house as a free woman.

449   Al-Mawardi, *A'lam al-nubuwwa* (Cairo,1935), pp. 146-147, quoted in M.J. Kister, "The Massacre of the Banu Qurayza: A Re-examination of a Tradition" in *Jerusalem Studies in Arabic and Islam* Vol. 8 (1986), p. 69.

450   Hamidullah, *The Battle Fields of the Prophet*, p. 3, footnote.

451   Sir William Muir, *Mahomet and Islam* (London: The Religious Tract Society, 1895), p. 151.

452   Al-Tabari, *Kitab al –Jihad*, p. 145.

453   Shaybani's *Siyar*, chapter I:44, translated in Khadduri, *The Islamic Law of Nations*, p. 91.

454   Al-Tabari, *Ta'rikh*, Vol. 5, pp. 2557-2559.

455   Khadduri, *War and Peace in the Law of Islam*, p. 128.

456   Ibn Hudayl, *L'ornement des âmes*, French translation by Louis Mercier, (Paris, 1939), p. 195; English translation by Michael J. Miller. Quoted in Andrew G. Bostom, (ed.), *The Legacy of Jihad: Islamic Holy War and the Fate of Non-Muslims* (New York: Prometheus Books, 2005): p. 40.

457   Sophronius, *Sermones*, PG 87.3: 3201-364 in "Weihnachspredigt des Sophronios" (ed.) H. Usener Rheinisches Museum für Philologie n.s. 41 (1886), pp. 506-507.

458   *Doctrina Iacobi Nuper Baptizati*, c.17. See N. Bonwetsch, (ed.) *Abhandlungen der Königlichen. Gesellschaft der Wissenschaften zu Göttingen*, Philologisch-Historische Klasse, Neue Folge Vol.12, No. 3 (Berlin: Weidmannsche Buchh., 1910), p. 88.

459 "Text No. 13: Dionysius Reconstituted", in *The Seventh Century in the West-Syrian Chronicles*, introduced, translated and annotated by Andrew Palmer (Liverpool: Liverpool University Press, 1993), p. 149.

460 "Text No. 13: Dionysius Reconstituted", in *The Seventh Century in the West-Syrian Chronicles*, p. 150.

461 "Text No. 13: Dionysius Reconstituted", in *The Seventh Century in the West-Syrian Chronicles*, p. 150.

462 Peters, *Jihad in Classical and Modern Islam*, pp. 143, 145, 148.

463 Hamid Abdullah Al-Ali, "The Legality of Killing Jewish Women and Children in Palestine" in *Al-Watan*, 31 August 2001, English translation by Shira Gutgold published in the *Jerusalem Post*, 5 September 2001.

464 "Mahathir urges arms as deterrent" in *Straits Times*, 17 September 2003.

465 Haleem et al., *The Crescent and the Cross*, p. 95. Fatoohi, *Jihad in the Qur'an*, p. 44, writes in praise of the sword because it is much more selective than nuclear, chemical and biological weapons or even conventional bombs.

466 'Abd al-Muta'ali Al-Saidi, *Fi Maydan al-Ijtihad* (Helwan: Jam'iyyat althaqafa al-Islamiyya, no date), pp. 133-139.

467 Dr Hashim was speaking at a conference on "Invading Iraq and the Future of the Arab Regime" on 17 April 2003. Reported in Mustafa Suleiman, "The Rector of the Azhar University asks Arabs to Obtain Mass Destruction Weapons" in *Al-Usboa*, 21 April 2003. English translation in *Arab-West Report*, 17-23 April 2003.

468 Abdul Rahman Bilal, *Islamic Military Resurgence* (Lahore: Ferozsons (Pvt.) Ltd, 1991), p. 204.

469 Tashbih Sayyed, "The Islamic Bomb", *Pakistan Today*, 26 December 2003.

470 "We Need Atomic Weapons and Mujahideen, says Daawa" in *Daily Times*, 6 February 2004, www.dailytimes.com.pk/default. asp?page=story_6-2-2004_pg7_15, viewed 6 February 2004.

471 Islamic Republic News Agency, 16 September 2003, reported in MEMRI News Tickers, 17 September 2003.

472 "Iran: Still Failing, Still Defiant", *The Economist*, 9 December 2004.

473 Ephraim Asculai, "Iran After The IAEA Vote: Still In The Driver's Seat", Jaffee Center for Strategic Studies, Tel Aviv Notes, No. 148, 30 September 2005.

474 "Iran Says It Won't Stop Nuclear Program", *Asharq Alawsat*, 21 August 2006.

475 "Security Council Imposes Sanctions On Iran For Failure To Halt Uranium Enrichment, Unanimously Adopting Resolution 1737 (2006)", Security Council SC/8928, 23 December 2006, Department of Public Information, News and Media Division, New York, Security Council 5612th Meeting (AM). http://www.un.org/News/Press/docs/2006/sc8928.doc.htm, viewed 8 February 2007.

476 Ewen MacAskill and Ian Traynor "Saudis Consider Nuclear Bomb" in *The Guardian*, 18 September 2003.

477 Quoted in "Reformist Iranian Internet Daily: A New Fatwa States That Religious Law Does Not Forbid Use of Nuclear Weapons", *MEMRI*, Special Dispatch Series, No. 1096, 17 February 2006.

478 Simon Reeve, *The New Jackals: Ramzi Yousef, Osama bin Laden and the Future of Terrorism* (London: André Deutsch, 1999), p. 261.

479 "Afghanistan invasion halted early stages of al-Qaida WMD programs, security officials say", (*Associated Press*, 27 January 2004, http://www.billingsgazette. com/index.php? display=redn ews/2004/01/27/build/ world/65-alquaidachemicalweapons.inc, viewed 30 January 2004.

480 "Bind a bond firmly (on them): thereafter (is the time for) either generosity or ransom".

481 Wahba Zuhayli, *Athar al-Harb fi al-Fiqh al-Islami: Dirasa Muqarina* (Beirut: Dar al-Fikr, 1965), pp. 403-474; Kamil Salama al-Daqs, *Ayat al-Jihad fi l-Qur'an al-Karim* (Kuwait: Dar al-Bayan, 1972), pp. 550-569.

482 Article 13 states that prisoners of war shall not be exposed to "public curiosity".

483 "Iraq: Muslim law trumps Geneva Convention", *WorldNetDaily. com*, 24 March 2003, quoting a BBC radio interview and Agence France-Presse.

484 S.K. Malik, *The Quranic Concept of War*, (New Delhi: Himalayan Books, 1986) pp. 57-58.

485 Malik, *The Quranic Concept of War*, p.58.

486 Malik, *The Quranic Concept of War*, p. 60.

487 *Hudna* was the term used by Hamas in June 2003 when expressing its willingness for a ceasefire with Israel. While *hudna* is the ordinary Arabic term for a truce or ceasefire, the Islamic religious implications of a merely temporary peace were no doubt clearly understood by Hamas followers.

488 The first *hudna* was made by Muhammad with the Meccans in 628 and was supposed to last ten years (though in fact it was broken after two). See Marshall G.S. Hodgson, *The Venture of Islam*, Vol. 1, *The Classical Age of Islam*, (Chicago: University of Chicago Press, 1974), pp. 193-194. `

489 Ibn Naqib al-Misri, *Reliance of the Traveller* (o9:16), p. 605.

490 Theophanes, *Theophanis Chronographia*, (ed.) C. De Boor (Leipzig, 1883-5): AM 6126.

491 Kaegi, *Byzantium and the Early Islamic Conquests*, pp. 276-277.

492 *The Hedaya* Vol. II, Book IX, chapter III, p. 150.

493 *The Hedaya* Vol. II, Book IX, chapter III, pp. 150-151; Shaybani's *Siyar*, Chapter V, pp. 602-627 translated in Khadduri, *The Islamic Law of Nations*, pp. 154-157.

494 Other Qur'anic commands to keep promises are found in Q 5:1; Q 8:55-6; Q 16:92.

495 Sheikh 'Abdul Rahman 'Abdul Khaliq, *Verdict on the Treaties of Compromise and Peace with the Jews*, reproduced at http://www.islaam.com/articles/treaty.htm, viewed 18 September 2001.

496 Quoted in Dore Gold, *Hatred's Kingdom: How Saudi Arabia Supports the New Global Terrorism* (Washington DC: Regnery Publishing Inc., 2003), pp. 195-196.

497 Shaybani, *Al-Siyar al-Kabir*, with Sarakhsi's Commentary Vol. IV, p. 60; Rahim, *The Principles of Muhammadan Jurisprudence*, p. 282; Sobhi Mahmasani, al-Nazariyya al *'Amma Li'l-Mujibat wa'l-'Uqud*, Vol. II (Beirut, 1948), p. 68 ff.; *Al-Majalla*, Article 103, translated in Charles Hooper, *Civil Law of Palestine and Transjordan*, Vol. I (Jerusalem: Azriel, 1933-6), p. 31.

498 The texts of three of his treaties in English translation may be found in Khadduri, *War and Peace in the Law of Islam*, pp. 205-215.

499 Shaybani's *Siyar*, Chapter VI:628-984a translation in Khadduri, *The Islamic Law of Nations*, pp. 158-194.

500 Mohammad Talaat Al-Ghunaimi, *The Muslim Conception of International Law and the Western Approach* (The Hague: Martinus Nijhoff, 1968), pp. 184-185, 211; Muhammad Abu Zahra, *Al-'Alaqat al-Dawliyya fi l-Islam* (Cairo: al-Dar al-Qawmiyya li-l-Tiba'a wa-l-Nashr, 1964), pp. 74-83; Zuhayli *Athar al-Harb fi al-Fiqh al-Islami*, pp. 362-367.

501 Zuhayli, *Athar al-Harb fi al-Fiqh al-Islami*, pp. 356-357; Sobhi Mahmassani, "International Law in the Light of Islamic Doctrine" in *Academie de Droit International, Recueil des Cours*, Vol. 117 (1966), pp. 53-58.

502 Abu Zahra, *Al-'Alaqat al-Dawliyya fi l-Islam*, pp. 78-79; al Ghunaimi, *The Muslim Conception of International Law and the Western Approach*, pp. 184-185; 'Ali Mansur, *Al-Shari'a al-Islamiyya wa-l-Qanun al-Dawli al-'Amm* (Cairo: al-Majlis al-A'la li-l-Shu'un al-Islamiyya, 1971), pp. 281-286.

503 Al-Tabari, *Ta'rikh*, Vol. I, p. 2349.

504 Ahmad b. Yahya Al-Baladhuri, *Futuh al-Buldan [Conquests of the Countries]* (ed.) M.J. De Goeje (Leiden: Brill, 1866), p. 130.

505 Kaegi, *Byzantium and the Early Islamic Conquests*, p. 165.

506 Eutychius, *Das Annalenwerk des Eutychios von Alexandrien*, p. 282. See Michael Breydy, *Corpus Scriptorum Christianorum Orientalium*, Vol. 471-472, Scriptores Arabici T.44-5 (Louvain: E. Peeters, 1985), pp. 141-142 for text, pp. 120-121 for translation.

507 Theophanes, *Theophanis Chronographia*, AM 6128 (De Boor), p. 340; Michael the Syrian *Chronique* (ed.) and transation J.B. Chabot, (Paris: E. Leroux, 1899-1910) Vol. 2, p. 426.

508 Kaegi, *Byzantium and the Early Islamic Conquests*, pp. 175-176.

509 Kaegi, *Byzantium and the Early Islamic Conquests*, p. 163.

510 Al-Baladhuri, *Futuh al-Buldan*, pp. 150,156-157 whose source is Abu Ubayd al-Qasim Ibn Sallam (770-838), *Kitab al-Amwal*, (ed.) Muhammad Khalil Haras (Cairo, 1968), pp. 248,253.

511 Mehdi Abedi and Gary Legenhausen (eds.) *Jihad and Shahadat: Struggle and Martyrdom in Islam*, p. 15.

512 Abdulaziz Sachedina, "Justification for Violence in Islam" in *Journal of Lutheran Ethics*, 19 February 2003; David C. Rapoport, "Comparing Militant Fundamentalist Movements and Groups" in Martin E. Marty, and R. Scott Appleby (eds.), *Fundamentalisms and the State: Remaking Polities, Economies and Militance*, The Fundamentalism Project Vol. 3 (Chicago and London: University of Chicago Press, 1993), p. 447.

513 A *murid* (literally "one who desires") is a disciple of a Sufi *pir*.

514 Article by J.L. Triaud on "Muridiyya" in *The Encyclopaedia of Islam*.

515 Elizabeth Sirriyeh, *Sufis and Anti-Sufis: The Defence, Rethinking and Rejection of Sufism in the Modern World* (Richmond: Curzon Press, 1999), pp. 38-39.

516 Shaikh Khalid's words are quoted in Butrus Abu-Manneh, "The Naqshabandiyya-Mujaddidiyya in the Ottoman Lands in the Early 19th Century" in *Die Welt des Islams* Vol. 12 (1986), p. 15.

517 Sirriyeh, *Sufis and Anti-Sufis*, p. 39.

518 Bülent Gökay, "Russia and Chechnia: A Long History of Conflict, Resistance and Oppression", *Alternatives: Turkish Journal of International Relations*, Vol. 3, Nos. 2 & 3, (Sumer & Fall 2004); Paul Johnson, *The Birth of the Modern: World Society 1815-1830* (New York: Harper Collins, 1991), p. 275.

519 P.M. Holt, *A Modern History of the Sudan*, 3rd edition (London: Weidenfeld and Nicolson, 1967), pp. 28-32,78-80 & ff.

520 Michael M. Gunter, "The Kurdish Question in Perspective", *World Affairs*, Spring 2004.

521 A radical and now violent Islamic group in South Asia. See chapter 12.

522 Sarah F.D. Ansari, *Sufi Saints and State Power: The Pirs of Sind, 1843-1947* (Lahore: Vanguard Books, 1992), pp. 78-80.

523 Ansari, *Sufi Saints and State Power: The Pirs of Sind, 1843-1947*, pp. 81-83.

524 Later known as Badshah Khan meaning "khan of khans".

525 Olaf Caroe, *The Pathans 550 B.C. – A.D. 1957* (London: Macmillan & Co. Ltd, 1965), pp. 272, 431-435.

526 Ferguson, *War and Peace in the World's Religions*, p. 137.

527 Mukulika Banerjee, *The Pathan Unarmed: Opposition and Memory in the North West Frontier* (Karachi: Oxford University Press, 2000), p. 145.

528 Mirza Ghulam Ahmad, *Tohfah Golrviyah* (1902), p. 82. Republished in vol. 17 of *Ruhani Khaza'in*, the collected works of Ghulam Mirza Ahmad (Rabwa, 1965).

529 Hazrat Mirza Ghulam Ahmad, *Jesus in India: Jesus' Escape from Death on the Cross and Journey to India* (London: The London Mosque, 1978), p. 18.

530 www.real-islam.org (4 October 2001) an Ahmadiyya website. Can now be accessed at http://www.geocities.com/Athens/Delphi/1340/reply/truth/jehad.htm, viewed 4 December 2003.

531 Randall Price, *Unholy War* (Eugene, Oregon: Harvest House Publishers, 2001), p. 191.

532 J.A. Boyle, (ed.), *The Cambridge History of Iran*, Vol. 5, (Cambridge: Cambridge University press, 1986) pp. 424-423.

533 Ayatollah Ja'far Sobhani, *Doctrines of Shi'i Islam: A Compendium of Imami Beliefs and Practices*, translated and edited by Reza Shah-Kazemi (London: I.B. Tauris, 2001), p. 150.

534 Hamid Enayat, *Modern Islamic Political Thought* (Austin: University of Texas Press, 1982), p. 177.

535 Sheikh Mansur Ali Nasif, *Al-Tajj al Jami lil-Usul fi Ahadith al-Rasul*, (Istanbul: Dar Ihya al-Kutub al-'Arabiyyah, 1961). Also published in Cairo by Matba'ah 'Isa al Babl al Halabi (no date). Vol. 5, p. 43.

536 *The Translation of the Meanings of Sahih Al-Bukhari, Arabic –English*, translated by Dr Muhammad Muhsin Khan (Riyadh: Darussalam Publishers and Distributors, 1997), Vol. 9, Book 89.

537 Enayat, *Modern Islamic Political Thought*, p. 176.

538 Ibn Taymiyya, *Iqtida al-sirat al-mustaqim*, Vol. 1, p. 416, quoted in Yohanan Friedmann, *Tolerance and Coercion in Islam: Interfaith Relations in the Muslim Tradition*, (Cambridge: Cambridge University Press, 2003), p. 26.

539 "Iraqi Detainees Forced to Denounce Islam: Disbelievers?", *Islam Online*, http://www.islamonline.net/servlet/Satellite?cid=1 119503548526&pagename=IslamOnline-English-Ask_Scholar/ FatwaE/FatwaEAskTheScholar, viewed 15 August 2005.

540 Enayat, *Modern Islamic Political Thought*, p. 176; Henri Corbin, *En Islam Iranien*, Vol. I (Paris: Gallimard, 1971), pp. 6, 30ff, 117.

541 Enayat, *Modern Islamic Political Thought*, pp. 177-178.

542 Gilbert T. Sewall *Islam and Textbooks*, A Report of the American Textbook Council, (New York, NY: American Textbook Council, 2003), p. 27.

543   See R. Strothmann, "Takiyya" in *The Encyclopedia of Islam*, CD-ROM Edition, Leiden: Koninklijke Brill NV, 2003.

544   Diana Mukalled, "The World is Closely Watching", *al-Sharq al-Awsat*, 30 August 2005. http://aawsat.com/english/news.asp?section=2&id=1465, viewed 6 September 2005.

545   "A question of leadership", transcript, *BBC Panorama*, 21 August 2005. http://news.bbc.co.uk/1/hi/programmes/panorama/4171950.stm, viewed 22 August 2005.

546   "A question of leadership", transcript, *BBC Panorama*, 21 August 2005.

547   "A question of leadership", transcript, *BBC Panorama*, 21 August 2005.

548   "Islamic Perspectives on Peace and Violence", *United States Institute of Peace*, Special Report 82, 24 January 2002 www.usip.or/pubs/specialreports/sr82.html, viewed 5 September 2005.

549   "Egyptian Progressive Criticizes Muslim Intellectual Doublespeak", *MEMRI Special Dispatch Series*, No. 847, 14 January 2005.

550   Mona Anis, "The war of fatwas", *Al-Ahram Weekly*, Issue No. 654, (4-10 September 2003).

551   Roxanne Youssef, "Tantawi still isn't as vitriolic as Gad Al-Haq", *Middle East Times*, issue 20, pp. 1-4. Quoted in Desmond Wiggins, University of South Australia, "Islamic Texts and Circumcision", *Africa Update*, Vol. VIII, Issue 4 (Fall 2001): Conversations on AIDS, viewed 1 June 2006.

552   *Al-Quds* (PA), 17 August 1998, quoted in Yotam Feldner, "Debating the Religious, Political and Moral Legitimacy of Suicide Bombings (I)", *MEMRI, Inquiry and Analysis*, 2 May 2001.

553   "Al-Azhar's Grand Imam Condemns Killing of Civilians", *Islam Online*, News Section, 15 September 2001.

554   "Grand Sheikh condemns suicide bombings", *BBC NEWS*, 4 December 2001; *Al-Akhbar* (Cairo), 16 December 2001, quoted in Haim Malka, "Must Innocents Die? The Islamic Debate over Suicide Attacks", *Middle East Quarterly*, Vol. X, No. 2, (Spring 2003).

555 "Israeli Knesset Protests Comments Made by Azhar Chief", *Islam Online*, News Section, 24 June 2002.

556 "Cleric condemns suicide attacks", *BBC NEWS*, 11 July 2003.

557 "Leading Islamic cleric condemns terror bombing", *Catholic World News (CWN)*, 1 April 2004.

558 "Shaikh of Azhar squares up to rabbis", *Muslimedia*, 1-15 September 1997.

559 Tawfiq Al-Shawi in *Al-Hayat* (London-Beirut), 27 April 2001, quoted in Yotam Feldner, "Debating the Religious, Political and Moral Legitimacy of Suicide Bombings (I)", *MEMRI, Inquiry and Analysis*, 2 May 2001.

560 *Saut Al-Ama* (Egypt), 26 April 2001, quoted in *Al-Hayat* London-Beirut 27 April 2001 and in "Debating the Religious, Political and Moral Legitimacy of Suicide Bombings (I)", *MEMRI, Inquiry and Analysis Series*, No. 53, 2 May 2001.

561 Posted on www.lailatalqadr.com (a website associated with Al-Azhar). Also reported as "Leading Egyptian Government Cleric Calls For: 'Martyrdom Attacks that Strike Horror into the Hearts of the Enemies of Allah' ", *MEMRI Special Dispatch Series*, No. 363, 7 April 2002.

562 "Al Azhar Sheikh: The Door For Jihad Is Open", *Islam Online*, News Section, 13 April 2002.

563 "Female fedaye [self-sacrificing] bombers may take hejab off", *Al-Ahrar*, 19 January 2004, quoted in *Arab-West Report*, Week 3 (2004), 14-20 January 2004.

564 "Sunni Muslim leader calls for jihad", *BBC NEWS*, 13 November 1998.

565 "Whoever Wants to Go to Iraq to Fight , Can Go: Tantawi", *Islam Online*, News Section, *IslamOnline*.net, http://www.islamonline. net/english/news/2003-04/05/article15.shtml, viewed 23 November 2005; Sobhi Mujahid, "Resisting U.S. Aggression Islamic Duty: Al Azhar Grand Imam", *Islam Online*, 22 February 2003, www. islamonline.net/English/News/2003-02/22/article14.shtml, (viewed 13 April 2003); Steven Stalinsky, "Leading Egyptian Islamic Clerics

on Jihad Against U.S. Troops in Iraq: March-August 2003", *MEMRI Inquiry and Analysis Series*, No. 145, 14 August 2003; Yotam Feldner, "Sheikh Tantawi's Positions on Jihad Against Coalition Forces, Saddam's Resignation, and the War in Iraq", *MEMRI Inquiry and Analysis Series*, No. 130, 8 April 2003; Amir Taheri, "Tantawi's Tantrum", in *National Review Online*, 16 May 2003.

566   "Mid-East religions condemn bloodshed", *BBC NEWS*, 21 January 2002; "Leaders intervene in Middle East", *Anglican Journal*, March 2002, http://www.anglicanjournal.com/128/03/world02. htm, viewed 22 August 2005; "Archbishop hosts Holy Land talks", *Anglican Comunion News Service*, 24 October 2002;

567   "Based on Koranic Verses, Interpretations and Traditions, Muslim Clerics State: The Jews Are the Descendants of Apes, Pigs and Other Animals", *MEMRI Special Report*, No. 11, 1 November 2002.

568   Brigadier S.K. Malik, *The Quranic Concept of War*, Indian edition (New Delhi: Himalayan Books, 1986) p. 96.

569   W. Montgomery Watt, *Muhammad Prophet and Statesman* (Oxford: Oxford University Press, 1961) pp. 102-109.

570   Firestone, *Jihad*, p. 134.

571   Watt, *Muhammad Prophet and Statesman*, p. 109.

572   A.A. Vasiliev, *A History of the Byzantine Empire*, Vol. 1 (Madison: University of Wisconsin Press, 1958), p. 207, estimates that not more than a third of the peninsula was actually dominated by Muhammad.

573   Kennedy, *The Prophet and the Age of the Caliphates*, p. 53.

574   Toshihiko Izutsu, *The Structure of the Ethical Terms in the Koran* (Tokyo: Keio Institute of Philological Studies, 1959), p. 49.

575   Dozy, *Spanish Islam: A History of the Muslims in Spain*, p. 7.

576   Julian Obermann, "Early Islam" in Dentan, Robert C. (ed.) *Lectures of the Department of Near Eastern Langages and Literatures at Yale University*, American Oriental Series No. 38 (Yale University Press, 1954), pp. 253-254.

577   Julian Obermann, "Early Islam" in Dentan, Robert C. (ed.) *Lectures of the Department of Near Eastern Langages and Literatures at Yale University*, American Oriental Series No. 38, pp. 254-255.

578   Firestone, *Jihad*, p. 31.

579   Bat Ye'or, *The Decline of Eastern Christianity under Islam: From Islam to Dhimmitude* (Cranbury, New Jersey / London: Farleigh Dickinson University Press and Associated University Presses, 1996), p. 41.

580   Khadduri, *War and Peace in the Law of Islam*, pp. 70-71; Ibn Khaldun, *The Muqaddimah*, Vol. 2, p. 74; Joel Kraemer, "Apostates, Rebels and Brigands" in *Israel Oriental Studies*, Vol. 10 (1980), p. 34. Kraemer suggests that Ibn Khaldun most likely intended to associate the attribute "just" mainly with warfare against seceders and the disobedient.

581   For a discussion of the relative reliability of many of these sources see Walter Kaegi's *Byzantium and the Early Islamic Conquests*, especially pp. 2-18.

582   Al-Tabari, *Ta'rikh*, Vol. 1, p. 3453.

583   John Esposito, (ed.) *The Oxford History of Islam* (Oxford: Oxford University Press, 1999), p. 11.

584   Kennedy, *The Prophet and the Age of the Caliphates*, p. 54.

585   For example Majid Ali Khan, *The Pious Caliphs* (New Delhi: Millat Book Centre, 1976), pp. 35-36.

586   Khadduri, *War and Peace in the Law of Islam*, p. 77. Interestingly, execution of an apostate by burning is specifically forbidden in Islam, and there were those who objected to this method being used.

587   Holt, Lambton and Lewis *The Cambridge History of Islam*, Vol. 1A, (Cambridge: Cambridge University Press, 1970), p. 58.

588   Kennedy, *The Prophet and the Age of the Caliphates*, p. 54; Khan, *The Pious Caliphs*, p. 35.

589   Aisha Bewly, "Introduction", in Muhammad Ibn Sa'd, *The Men of Madina* Vol. 2, a translation of Vol. 5 of Kitab al-Tabaqa), (London: Ta-Ha Publishers, 2000), pp. ix-x.

590 Esposito, *The Oxford History of Islam*, p. 11.

591 Kennedy, *The Prophet and the Age of the Caliphates*, pp. 54-55.

592 Donner, "The Sources of Islamic Conceptions of War", p. 50.

593 Bewly, "Introduction", in Muhammad Ibn Sa'd, *The Men of Madina* Vol. 2, pp. xi-xiii.

594 Bewly, "Introduction", in Muhammad Ibn Sa'd, *The Men of Madina* Vol. 2, pp. xiii-xvi.

595 G.R. Hawting, *The First Dynasty of Islam: The Umayyad Caliphate AD 661-750*, (London: Routledge, 2000), pp. 53-56.

596 Wink, *Al-Hind: The Making of the Indo-Islamic World*, Vol. I, "Early Medieval India and the Expansion of Islam 7th-11th Centuries", p. 210.

597 Kennedy *The Prophet and the Age of the Caliphates*, p. 53.

598 Martin Sicker, *The Islamic World in Ascendancy: From the Arab Conquests to the Siege of Vienna* (Westport, Connecticut: Praeger Publishers, 2000), pp. 10-11; Kamal Salibi, *Syria Under Islam: Empire on Trial 634-1097* (Delmar, New York: Caravan Books, 1977), p. 19.

599 Kaegi, *Byzantium and the Early Islamic Conquests*, pp. 79, 104.

600 Exceptions were Gaza and Ba'labakk where the local inhabitants paid for the repair of their city walls.

601 Kaegi, *Byzantium and the Early Islamic Conquests*, p. 260.

602 Kaegi, *Byzantium and the Early Islamic Conquests*, pp. 112-146.

603 Kaegi, *Byzantium and the Early Islamic Conquests*, p. 144.

604 Kaegi, *Byzantium and the Early Islamic Conquests*, pp. 173-174, 267; John W. Jandora, "Developments in Islamic Warfare: The Early Conquests" in *Studia Islamica*, Vol. 64 (1986), pp. 101-113.

605 Wink, *Al-Hind: The Making of the Indo-Islamic World*, Vol. I, "Early Medieval India and the Expansion of Islam 7th-11th Centuries", pp. 121-122.

606 Al-Baladhuri, *The Origins of the Islamic State*, p. 311.

607   For example, the contemporary or near-contemporary Armenian historian Sebeos in his *History* c.32 (Bedrosian pp.134-6, Macler pp.104-5)

608   Kaegi, *Byzantium and the Early Islamic Conquests*, pp. 189, 198-200, 203.

609   Al-Baladhuri, *The Origins of the Islamic State*, pp. 311, 322, 325, 326, 328, 331, 332.

610   *The History of al-Tabari*, edited by Ehsan Yar-Shater, Vol. XV, "The Crisis of the Early Caliphate", translated by R. Stephen Humphreys (Albany: New York: State University of New York Press, 1990), p. 9.

611   Kaegi, *Byzantium and the Early Islamic Conquests*, pp. 198-200.

612   R. Ernest Dupuy and Trevor N. Dupuy, *The Collins Encyclopedia of Military History From 3500BC to the Present*, (New York: Harper Collins, 1993), p. 233.

613   Dupuy and Dupuy, *The Collins Encyclopedia of Military History From 3500BC to the Present*), pp. 233-234.

614   Dupuy and Dupuy, *The Collins Encyclopedia of Military History From 3500BC to the Present*, pp. 234-235.

615   Fredegarius, *Chronicles* 4:66 (ed.) Bruno Krusch (Hanover: MGH Scriptores Rerum Merovingicarum T.2, 1888, repr. 1984), p. 154; John, Bishop of Nikiu, *Chronicle* 120.33, 121.2, 121,11, 123 translation R. Charles (London, Oxford, 1916); Sebeos, *History* c.32 translation F. Macler, *Histoire d'Héraclius* (Paris: E. Laroux, 1904), pp. 104-105; see also translation by Robert Bedrosian, (New York: Sources of the Armenian Tradition, 1985), p. 135; John Bar Penkaye, *Ris Melle*, in S.P. Brock, "North Mesopotamia in the Late Seventh Century. Book XV of John Bar Penkaye's *Ris Melle*" in *Jerusalem Studies in Arabic and Islam* Vol. 9 (1987), pp. 57-61; Michael the Syrian, *Chronique* 11.5, 11.6 (Chabot Vol. 2), pp. 418, 422-423.

616   Kaegi, *Byzantium and the Early Islamic Conquests*, pp. 26, 87.

617   Kaegi, *Byzantium and the Early Islamic Conquests*, p. 265.

618 Kaegi, *Byzantium and the Early Islamic Conquests*, pp. 274, 269-270, 286.

619 Kaegi, *Byzantium and the Early Islamic Conquests*, pp. 88, 100, 270.

620 Sophronius, *Sermones*, PG 87:3197D.

621 Hodgson, *The Venture of Islam*, Vol. 1, *The Classical Age of Islam*, p. 203.

622 Ferguson, *War and Peace in the World's Religions*, pp. 127-218.

623 Khalid Yahya Blankinship, *The End of the Jihad State: The Reign of Hisham Ibn 'Abd al-Malik and the Collapse of the Umayyads* (Albany: State University of New York Press, 1994), pp. 145-146. Blankinship's book is one of very few works to document and analyse the defeats and disasters suffered by the Muslims at this period.

624 Dupuy and Dupuy, *The Collins Encyclopedia of Military History From 3500BC to the Present*, pp. 247-252.

625 Blankinship, *The End of the Jihad State: The Reign of Hisham Ibn 'Abd al-Malik and the Collapse of the Umayyads*, pp. 199-236.

626 For more details on the disaster of Manzikert, see John Julius Norwich, *Byzantium: The Apogee*, (London: BCA, 1991) pp. 338-361.

627 From the translation of *Malfuzat-i-Timuri* in Elliot and Dawson, *A History of India As Told by Its Own Historians*, Vol. 3, p. 397.

628 For some of the reasons for *The Crusades* see: Jonathan Ridley Smith, "The Events Leading to *The Crusades*", in *The Crusades Revisited: A Consultation*, Cordoba, 31 October-3 November 1996.

629 Nikolas Jaspert, *The Crusades*, translated by Phyllis G. Jestice, (New York and London: Routledge, 2006), pp. 8, 22.

630 Steven Runciman, *A History of The Crusades, Vol. 1*, (Cambridge: Cambridge University Press, 1951), p. 35.

631 Ismail Abaza, "Baybars al-Bunduqdari: The First Great Slave Ruler of Egypt", http://www.touregypt.net/featurestories/baybars.htm, viewed 17 November 2006.

632   Helen Nicholson, *The Crusades*, (Westport, Connecticut: Greenwood Press, 2004), p. xxvi; Bernard Lewis, The *Crisis of Islam: Holy War and Unholy Terror*, (London: Weidenfeld & Nicolson, 2003), pp. 37-40.

633   David Zeidan, "The Islamist view of Life as a Perennial Battle", in Barry Rubin and Judith Colp Rubin, (eds.), *Anti-American Terrorism and the Middle East* (New York: Oxford University Press, 2002) pp. 11-26.

634   Halil Inalcik, *The Ottoman Empire: the Classical Age 1300-1600* (London: Phoenix Press, 2000), p. 3, see also pp. 6-7.

635   Ira M. Lapidus, *A History of Islamic Societies*, (Cambridge, New York & Melbourne: Cambridge University Press, 1988), pp. 306-316.

636   J.A.B. Palmer, "The Origin of the Janissaries" in *Bulletin of the John Rylands Library*, Manchester, Vol. 35, No. 1 (September 1952) passim.

637   Daniel Goffman, *The Ottoman Empire and Early Modern Europe*, (Cambridge: Cambridge University Press, 2002), pp. 157-158.

638   Ann Elizabeth Mayer, "War and Peace in the Islamic Tradition and International Law" in John Kelsay and James Turner Johnson (eds.) *Just War and Jihad: Historical and Theoretical Perspectives on War and Peace in Western and Islamic Traditions* (Westport, Connecticut: Greenwood Press, 1991), p. 196.

639   See Lapidus, *A History of Islamic Societies*, pp. 437-466; Esposito, (ed.), *The Oxford Encyclopedia of the Modern Muslim world*, Vol. 2, pp. 280-284.

640   K.S. Lal, *The Legacy of Muslim Rule in India*, (New Delhi: Aditya Prakashan, 1992), pp. 83-93.

641   Lal, *The Legacy of Muslim Rule in India*, pp. 93-105.

642   In a symbolic gesture, Pakistan has named its latest ballistic missile, capable of delivering nuclear weapons, the *Ghuri* (or *Ghauri*), a not so subtle warning to India to remember the humiliating history of the Muslim invasions.

643 Abdul Hamid Lahori, "Badshah-Nama", in Elliot and Dawson, (eds.), *The History of India: As told by its own Historians*, Vol. 7, p. 36.

644 Muhammad Saki Musta'id Khan, "Ma-asir-i Almagiri", in Elliot and Dawson, (eds.), *The History of India: As told by its own Historians*, Vol. 7, pp. 187-188.

645 Khafi Khan, "Muntakhabu-l Lubab", in Elliot and Dawson, (eds.), *The History of India: As told by its own Historians*, Vol. 7, p. 296.

646 See Lapidus, *A History of Islamic Societies*, pp. 467-488; Esposito, (ed.), *The Oxford Encyclopedia of the Modern Muslim world*, Vol. 2, pp. 284-290.

647 Sharon Siddique, "Conceptualizing Contemporary Islam: Religion or Ideology?" in Ahmad Ibrahim, Sharon Siddique and Yasmin Hussain, (eds.), *Readings on Islam in Southeast Asia*, (Singapore: Institute of Southeast Asian Studies, 1985), p. 345.

648 Peter G. Gowing, "Moros and Khaek: The Position of Muslim Minorities in the Philippines and Thailand", in Ibrahim, Siddique and Hussain, (eds.), *Readings on Islam in Southeast Asia*, pp. 180-192.

649 See Lapidus, *A History of Islamic Societies*, pp. 489-540; Esposito, (ed.), *The Oxford Encyclopedia of the Modern Muslim world*, Vol. 2, pp. 271-290.

650 Jacques Jomier, *How to Understand Islam*, (London: SCM Press, 1989), pp. 30-37.

651 Ann Elizabeth Mayer, "War and Peace in the Islamic Tradition and International Law" in Kelsay and Turner *Just War and Jihad*, pp. 196-197.

652 As well as numerous less well known ones, such as many of the groups to be considered in chapter 12

653 Farhang Rajaee, *Islamic Values and World View: Khomeyni on Man, the State and International Politics* (Lanham, Maryland: University Press of America, 1983), p. 81.

654 Mahmud Shaltut, *Al-Qur'an wa al-Qital*, in Peters, *Jihad in Classical and Modern Islam*, p. 93.

655 Haleem et al., *The Crescent and the Cross*, p. 96.

656 Kaegi, *Byzantium and the Early Islamic Conquests*, p. 142; al-Tabari, *Ta'rikh*, Vol. 1, p. 2089; Irfan Shahid, "Asrar al-nasr al-'arabi fi futuh al-Sham" in *Bilad al-Sham Proceedings* (1985), pp. 137-147.

657 'Abd al-Malik Ibn Hisham, *al-Sira al-Nabawiyya*, (ed.) Heinrich Ferdinand Wüstenfeld, *Sirat Rasul Allah [Das Leben Muhammeds]* (Göttingen: Dieterischen Buchhandlung, 1858-60), p. 958; Muhammad Ibn Sa'd, *Kitab al-Tabaqat al-Kabir*, (ed.) Eduard Sachau et al., Vol. I (Leiden: Brill, 1904-40), pp. 2, 18, 31, 83.

658 Kaegi, *Byzantium and the Early Islamic Conquests*, pp. 68-71.

659 Kaegi, *Byzantium and the Early Islamic Conquests*, p. 142.

660 Al-Baladhuri, *The Origins of the Islamic State*, pp. 284-285.

661 *Sadaka* is the voluntary alms payable by Muslims. Caliph 'Umar simply called the tax he levied from the Banu Taghlib *sadaka* in order to assuage their pride. In fact they payed double the *jizya* rate.

662 Al-Baladhuri, *The Origins of the Islamic State*, p. 286.

663 *The Chronography of Bar Hebraeus*, translated from the Syriac by Ernest A. Wallis Budge, Vol. I, (Piscataway, NJ: Gorgias Press, 2003), p. 106.

664 *The Chronography of Bar Hebraeus*, p. 117.

665 Wink, *Al-Hind: The Making of the Indo-Islamic World*, Vol. II, "The Slave Kings and the Islamic Conquest 11th-13th Centuries", p. 123. The Muslim source mentioned is the *Ta'rikh-i-Firishta* by Muhammad Kasim Hindu Shah, (Lucknow, 1864).

666 Sri Ram Sharma, *The Religious Policy of the Mughal Emperors*, (New Delhi: Munshiram Manoharlal Publishers, 1988), p. 6.

667 Sri Ram Sharma, *The Religious Policy of the Mughal Emperors*, pp. 14-15.

668   Sri Ram Sharma, *The Religious Policy of the Mughal Emperors*, pp. 90-91.

669   Sri Ram Sharma, *The Religious Policy of the Mughal Emperors*, pp. 167-169.

670   Mark R. Cohen, *Under Crescent and Cross: The Jews in the Middle Ages*, (Princeton, New Jersey: Princeton University Press, 1994), p. 166.

671   Karen Barkey, "Ottoman Toleration: The Construction of Mechanisms of Inter-Religious, Inter-Ethnic Peace", Columbia University, Paper prepared for "Religion, Identity, and Empire", 16 & 17April 2005, pp. 23-24, http://www.yale.edu/ycias/europeanstudies/empire/OE_Toleration_revised.pdf, viewed 3 May 2006.

672   Raphael Patai, *Jadid al-Islam: The Jewish "New Muslims" of Meshed*, (Detroit: Wayne State University Press, 1997), pp. 13-16.

673   *The Armenian History attributed to Sebeos*, translated with notes by James Howard-Johnston, Part II. Historical Commentary (Liverpool: Liverpool University Press, 1999), p. 240.

674   Dionysius the Syrian "Text No. 13: Dionysius Reconstituted", in *The Seventh Century in the West-Syrian Chronicles*, introduced, translated and annotated by Andrew Palmer (Liverpool: Liverpool University Press, 1993), p. 163.

675   "Text No. 13: Dionysius Reconstituted", in *The Seventh Century in the West-Syrian Chronicles*, p. 166.

676   "Text No. 13: Dionysius Reconstituted", in *The Seventh Century in the West-Syrian Chronicles*, p. 166.

677   *The Chronography of Bar Hebraeus*, Vol. I, p. 269.

678   *Chronique de Michel Le Syrien*, edited and translated from the Syriac by Jean-Baptiste Chabot, Paris, (1899-1905), Vol. 3, pp. 235-236; quoted in Andrew G. Bostom, (ed.), *The Legacy of Jihad: Islamic Holy War and the Fate of Non-Muslims*, pp. 612-613.

679   Al-Baladhuri, *The Origins of the Islamic State*, pp. 356-357, 360.

680   "Text No. 13: Dionysius Reconstituted", in *The Seventh Century in the West-Syrian Chronicles*, pp. 174-175.

681 Al-Baladhuri, *The Origins of the Islamic State*, p. 236.

682 "Text No. 13: Dionysius Reconstituted", in *The Seventh Century in the West-Syrian Chronicles*, pp. 176-177.

683 S.M. Solihin, *Copts And Muslims In Egypt* (Leicester: The Islamic Foundation, 1991), pp. 7-8; Abdullahi al-Na`im, "Religious Freedom In Egypt: Under The Shadow Of The Dhimma System," in: Leonard Swidler (ed.), *Muslims In Dialogue* (Lewiston, New York: Edwin Mellen Press, 1992), p. 499; B.L. Carter, *The Copts In Egyptian Politics*, 1918-1952 (London: Croom Helm, 1984), pp. 111-114.

684 Y. Masriya, "A Christian Community: The Copts In Egypt," in Veenhoven et al., *On Human Rights And Fundamental Freedoms, A World Survey*, Vol. 4, (The Hague: Martinus Nijhoff, 1976), pp. 60, 84.

685 John of Nikiou, *Chronique de Jean, Eveque de Nikiou*, translated from the Ethiopian with notes by Hermann Zotenberg (Paris, 1879), pp. 228-229; 243-244, 262-263. Quoted in Andrew G. Bostom, (ed.), *The Legacy of Jihad: Islamic Holy War and the Fate of Non-Muslims*, pp. 589-590.

686 Al-Baladhuri, *The Origins of the Islamic State*, pp. 356-357, 360.

687 Ibn Khaldun, *History of the Berbers and the Moslem Dynasties of Northern Africa*, translated from Arabic [into French] by Baron De Slane (Paris, 1925), p. 316.

688 Ibn al-Atir, *al-Kamil fi al-Ta'rikh*, xi, pp. 160-162, quoted in Roger Le Tourneau, *The Almohad Movement in North Africa in the Twelfth and Thirteenth Centurie*, (Princeton, NJ: Princeton University Press, 1969), pp. 57-58.

689 H.Z. Hirschberg, *The Jews of North Africa*, Vol. 1 (Leiden, 1974), pp. 127-128; quoted in Andrew G. Bostom, (ed.), *The Legacy of Jihad: Islamic Holy War and the Fate of Non-Muslims*, p. 612.

690 Wink, *Al-Hind: The Making of the Indo-Islamic World*, Vol. I, "Early Medieval India and the Expansion of Islam 7th-11th Centuries", pp. 14-16.

691 Al-Baladhuri, *The Origins of the Islamic State*, a translation of *kitab futuh al-buldan*, p. 379.

692 Roger Collins, *The Arab Conquest of Spain* 710-797, (Oxford: Blackwell, 1989), pp. 29-30.

693 Dozy, *Spanish Islam: A History of the Muslims in Spain*, pp. 278-288.

694 Dozy, *Spanish Islam: A History of the Muslims in Spain*, pp. 721-722.

695 Wink, *Al-Hind: The Making of the Indo-Islamic World*, Vol. I, "Early Medieval India and the Expansion of Islam 7th-11th Centuries", pp. 121-122.

696 Eliz Sanasarian, *Religious Minorities in Iran* (Cambridge: Cambridge University Press, 2000), p. 50.

697 Darius Jahanian, "Islamic era histroy of Zoroastrians of Iran through political analysis and historical letters", http://www.vohuman.org/Article/Islamic%20era%20histroy%20of%20Zoroastrians%20of%20Iran.htm, viewed 4 May 2006.

698 Jahanian, "Islamic era histroy of Zoroastrians of Iran through political analysis and historical letters".

699 Jahanian, "Islamic era histroy of Zoroastrians of Iran through political analysis and historical letters".

700 Sanasarian, *Religious Minorities in Iran*, p. 30.

701 Sanasarian, *Religious Minorities in Iran*, p. 157.

702 "Text No. 13: Dionysius Reconstituted", in *The Seventh Century in the West-Syrian Chronicles*, p. 213.

703 S. Vryonis, Jr., "A Critical Analysis of Stanford J. Shaw's, *History of the Ottoman Empire and Modern Turkey. Volume 1. Empire of the Gazis: The Rise and Decline of the Ottoman Empire, 1280-1808*, off print from Balkan Studies, Vol. 24, (1983), pp. 57-60, 62, 68.

704 Vryonis, Jr., "A Critical Analysis of Stanford J. Shaw's, *History of the Ottoman Empire and Modern Turkey*, pp. 57-60, 62, 68.

705 Vryonis, Jr., "A Critical Analysis of Stanford J. Shaw's, *History of the Ottoman Empire and Modern Turkey*, pp. 57-60, 62, 68.

706 "Muslim anger grows at Pope speech", *BBCNEWS*, 15 September 2006.

707 *The Armenian History attributed to Sebeos*, Part I. Translation and Notes, pp. 100-101; Part II. Historical Commentary, pp. 246-247.

708 *The Armenian History attributed to Sebeos*, Part I. Translation and Notes, pp. 150-151.

709 *The Armenian History attributed to Sebeos*, Part I. Translation and Notes, pp. 109-111.

710 Vahan M. Kurkjian, *A History of Armenia* (The Armenian General Benevolent Union of America, 1958), pp. 206-209.

711 *The Chronography of Bar Hebraeus*, Vol. I, p. 216.

712 Kurkjian, *A History of Armenia*, pp. 206-209.

713 Count Paul von Wolff-Metternich, German Ambassador to Turkey, quoted in Richard G. Hovannisian, (ed.), *The Armenian Genocide: History, Politics, Ethics*, (Basingstoke & New York: Palgrave, 1992), p. xii.

714 James J. Reid, "Total War, the Annihilation Ethic, and the Armenian Genocide, 1870-1918", in Richard G. Hovannisian, (ed.), *The Armenian Genocide: History, Politics, Ethics*, p. 37.

715 Reid, "Total War, the Annihilation Ethic, and the Armenian Genocide, 1870-1918", in Hovannisian, (ed.), *The Armenian Genocide: History, Politics, Ethics*, pp. 39-47.

716 Ioanis K. Hassiotis, "The Armenian Genocide and the Greeks: Response and Records (1915-23)", in Richard G. Hovannisian, (ed.), *The Armenian Genocide: History, Politics, Ethics*, pp. 146-147.

717 Lal, *The Legacy of Muslim Rule in India*, pp. 83-93.

718 *The Chachnamah, an Ancient History of Sind*, translated by Mirza Kalichbeg Fredunbeg, (Lahore: Vanguard Books, 1985), p. 113.

719 *The Chachnamah, an Ancient History of Sind*, p. 83.

720 Al-Kufi, *The Chachnama*, in Elliot and Dawson (eds.), *A History of India As Told by Its Own Historians*, Vol. 1, p. 181.

721 *The Chachnamah, an Ancient History of Sind*, p. 145.

722 Hasan Nizami, *Taju'l Maasir*, in Elliot and Dawson (eds.), *A History of India As Told by Its Own Historians*, Vol. 2, p. 219.

723 Hasan Nizami, *Taju'l Maasir*, in Elliot and Dawson (eds.), *A History of India As Told by Its Own Historians*, Vol. 2, p. 219.

724 Hasan Nizami, *Taju'l Maasir*, in Elliot and Dawson (eds.), *A History of India As Told by Its Own Historians*, Vol. 2, p. 223.

725 Sri Ram Sharma, *The Religious Policy of the Mughal Emperors*, (New Delhi: Munshiram Manoharlal Publishers, 1988), p. 9.

726 Bostom, (ed.), *The Legacy of Jihad: The Islamic Holy War and the Fate of Non-Muslims*, p. 84.

727 Al-'Utbi, *Tarikh Yamini*, in Elliot and Dawson (eds.), *A History of India As Told by Its Own Historians*, Vol. 2, p. 30.

728 From the translation of *Malfuzat-i-Timuri* in Elliot and Dawson (eds.), *A History of India As Told by Its Own Historians*, Vol. 3, pp. 435-436.

729 Ibn Battuta, *The Travels of Ibn Battutah*, edited by Tim Mackintosh-Smith, (Basingstoke: Macmillan, 2002), p. 250.

730 Muhammad Kasim Hindu Shah, *Ta'rikh-i-Firishta*, in Elliot and Dawson (eds.), *A History of India As Told by Its Own Historians*, Vol. 6, p. 233.

731 *The Baburnama - Memoirs of Babur, Prince and Emperor*, translated and edited by Wheeler M. Thacktson, (Oxford University Press, 1996), p. 188.

732 Nizamu-Din Ahmad, "Tabakat-i Akbari", in Elliot and Dawson, (eds.), *The History of India: As told by its own Historians*, Vol. 5, p. 410.

733 Maulana Ahmad, "Tarikh-i Alfi", in Elliot and Dawson, (eds.), *The History of India: As told by its own Historians*, Vol. 5, p. 171.

734 Maulana Ahmad, "Tarikh-i Alfi", in Elliot and Dawson, (eds.), *The History of India: As told by its own Historians*, Vol. 5, p. 174.

735 Sri Ram Sharma, *The Religious Policy of the Mughal Emperors*, pp.14-15.

736 Khafi Khan, "Muntakhabu-l Lubab", in Elliot and Dawson, (eds.), *The History of India: As told by its own Historians*, Vol. 7, p. 300.

737 Khafi Khan, "Muntakhabu-l Lubab", in Elliot and Dawson, (eds.), *The History of India: As told by its own Historians*, Vol. 7, pp. 457-458.

738 From O. Tafrali, *Thessalonique – Des Origines au XVI Siecle*, 1913, Chapter VI "The Capture and Pillage of Thessalonika by the Saracens (in the year 904)", pp. 151-154.

739 John V.A. Fine, Jr. *The Late Medieval Balkans: A Critical Survey from the Late Twelfth Century to the Ottoman Conquest*, (Ann Arbor, MI: Michigan University Press, 1994), p. 566.

740 Quoted in Colin Imber, *The Ottoman Empire, 1300-1650: The Structure of Power*, (Basingstoke: Palgrave Macmillan, 2002), p. 132.

741 Sima M. Cirkovic, *The Serbs*, (Oxford: Blackwell, 2004), p. 115.

742 Arthur John Evans, *Through Bosnia and the Hrzegovina on Foot during the Insurrection August and September 1875*, (Elibron Classics, originally published by Longmans Green 1876), p. 255.

743 William Montgomery Watt, *The Formative Period of Islamic Thought* (Oxford: Oneworld Publication, 1998), pp. 9-37; Norman Anderson, "Islam" in Norman Anderson, (ed.) *The World's Religions*, 4th edition (Grand Rapids, Michigan: Eerdmans, 1975), pp. 103-104; Kennedy, *The Prophet and the Age of the Caliphates*, pp. 79-80.

744 Anderson, "Islam" in Anderson, *The World's Religions*, pp. 105-106.

745 Bernard Lewis, "The Revolt of Islam" in *The New Yorker*, 19 November 2001. Further details in Bernard Lewis, *The Assassins: A Radical Sect in Islam* (London: Phoenix, 2003).

746   Lapidus, *A History of Islamic Societies*, pp. 374-375.

747   Ayman Al-Yassini, *Religion and State in the Kingdom of Saudi Arabia* (Boulder, Colorado: Westview Press, 1985), pp. 124-129.

748   Rida was building on the ideas of Sir Syed Ahmed Khan (1817-1898) in India, Muhammad Abduh (1849-1905) in Egypt and Jamal al-Din al-Afghani (1838-1897) all of whom sought to reform a decadent and stagnant Islam by looking afresh at the original sources, but without Rida's anti-Western emphasis.

749   Hasan Al-Banna, *Five Tracts of Hasan al-Banna (1906-1949): A Selection from the Majmu'at Rasa'il al-Imam al-Shahid* (Berkeley, California: University of California Press, 1978), pp. 155-156.

750   Sayyid Abu'l A'la Mawdudi, *Jihad fi Sabilillah [Jihad in Islam]*, translation K. Ahmad (Birmingham: Islamic Mission Dawah Centre, 1997), pp. 13-15.

751   Yvonne Y. Haddad, "Sayyid Qutb: Ideologue of Islamic Revival" in John Esposito, (ed.) *Voices of Resurgent Islam* (New York: Oxford University Press, 1983), pp. 85-87; Ronald Nettler, "A Modern Islamic Confession of Faith and Conception of Religion: Sayyid Qutb's Introduction to *tafsir, Fi Zilal al-Quran*" in *British Journal of Middle Eastern Studies* Vol. 21 No. 1 (1994), pp. 102-104.

752   Sayyid Qutb, *The Islamic Concept and its Characteristic* (Indianapolis: American Trust Publication, 1991), p. 12.

753   Yvonne Y. Haddad, "The Quranic Justification for an Islamic Revolution: The View of Sayyid Qutb" in *Middle East Journal*, Vol. 37 No. 1 (Winter 1983), pp. 17-18.

754   Nettler, "A Modern Islamic Confession of Faith", pp. 98-102; S.M. Solihin, *Studies on Sayyid Qutb's Fi Zilal al-Quran* (unpublished thesis, Department of Theology, University of Birmingham, 1993), p. 284.

755   Sayyid Qutb, *Islam and Peace* (Cairo: Dar al-Shuruq, 1988), pp. 80-85; Sayyid Qutb, *Fi Zilal al-Quran* Vol. 3 (Beirut: Dar al-Shuruq, 1987), pp. 1433-1435; Sayyid Qutb, *Milestones* (Lahore: Qazi Publications, no date), pp. 88-89. Also Sayyid

Qutb, *Milestones (Ma'alem Fil Tariq)* (Indianapolis: American Trust Publications, 1990).

756   John Strawson, "Encountering Islamic Law,", essay presented at the Critical Legal Conference, New College, Oxford, September 9 – 12, 1993. The World Wide Web Virtual Library: Islamic and Middle Eastern Law, http://www.uel.ac.uk/faculties/socsci/law/jsrps.html, p. 11.

757   Mamoun Fandy, "Egypt's Islamic Group: regional revenge?" *Middle East Journal* Vol. 48, No. 4 (Autumn, 1994); Michael Collins Dunn. "Fundamentalism in Egypt", *Middle East Policy* Vol. 2, No. 3 (Summer, 1993); Ibrahim, Abdul-Maajid and Darbaalah, *In Pursuit of Allah's Pleasure* (London: Al-Firdous, 1997).

758   Chris Zambelis, "Egyptian Gama'a al-Islamiyya's Public Relations Campaign", *Terrorism Monitor*, Volume 3, Issue 35 (12 September 2006); "Al-Gama'a Al-Islamiyya vs. Al-Qaeda", *MEMRI*, Special Dispatch Series, No. 1301 (27 September 2006).

759   Muhammad 'Abd al-Salam Faraj, *Al-Faridah al-Gha'ibah (The Neglected Duty)*, English translation in Johannes J. G. Jansen, *The Neglected Duty: The Creed of Sadat's Assassins and Islamic Resurgence in the Middle East* (New York: Macmillan, 1986), pp. 163-164; Walid M. Abdelnasser, *The Islamic Movement in Egypt*, pp. 234-235.

760   Nabeel T. Jabbour *The Rumbling Volcano: Islamic Fundamentalism in Egypt*, (Pasadena, CA: William Carey Library, 1993), pp. 143-157; See also Gilles Kepel, *The Prophet and The Pharaoh: Muslim Extremism in Egypt*, (London: al-Saqi, 1985), pp. 95-96, 150.

761   Abdelnasser, *The Islamic Movement in Egypt*, p. 216; Hopwood, *Egypt: Politics and Society* 1945-1990, p. 118.

762   Abdullah 'Azzam, *Defence of the Muslim Lands*, (Ahle Sunnah Wal Jama'at, no date), pp.4-6.

763   Abdullah 'Azzam, *Join the Caravan*, (London: Azzam Publications, 1996), pp. 36-38.

764   'Azzam, *Defence of the Muslim Lands*, p. 7.

765   'Azzam, *Defence of the Muslim Lands*, pp. 7-17.

766 'Azzam, *Join the Caravan*, p. 13.

767 'Azzam, *Defence of the Muslim Lands*, pp. 7-17.

768 'Azzam, *Defence of the Muslim Lands*, pp. 29-33.

769 Esposito, (ed.), *The Oxford Encyclopedia of the Modern Islamic World*, Vol. 2, pp. 125-127; Hizb al-Tahrir Publications: Taqi al-Din Al-Nabhani, *The Islamic State*, (London: Khilafah Publications, no date); Abd al-Qadem Zallum, *How the Khilafah Was Lost*; "Hizb ut-Tahrir"; "Political Thoughts"; "Political Views on Palestine"; Allah's shadow". Zaffar Abbas, "Pakistan bans more Islamic groups", *BBC NEWS*, 20 November 2003.

770 Zahid-Ivan Salam, *Jihad and the Foreign Policy of the Khilafah State*, (London: Khilafah Publications, 2001).

771 For a summary of the development of the jihadist movement in modern times see Gilles Kepel, "The Origins and Development of the Jihadist Movement: From Anti-Communism to Terrorism" translation Peter Clark in *Asian Affairs*, Vol. 34, No. 2 (July 2003).

772 For a study of one network. The Ngruki Network founded in the 1970s in Indonesia, see *International Crisis Group (ICG)*, Asia Report No. 43, "Indonesia Backgrounder: How the Jemaah Islamiyah Terrorist Network Operates", Jakarta/Brussels, 11 December 2002.

773 Cook, *Studies in Muslim Apocalyptic*, pp. 39, 73; Rapoport, "Comparing Militant Fundamentalist Movements and Groups", pp. 447, 450.

774 Khaled Dawoud, "America's Most Wanted" in *Al-Ahram Weekly Online*, Issue No. 552 (20-26 September 2001); Daniel Pipes, "Muslims Love Bin Laden" in *New York Post*, 22 October 2001.

775 Ali Shariati, "Intizar: The Religion of Protest and the Return to Self", in J.J. Donohue, and J.L. Esposito (eds.) *Islam in Transition: Muslim Perspectives* (New York: Oxford University Press, 1982), pp. 298-304; Ali Shariati, *On the Sociology of Islam*, translation Hamid Algar (Berkeley: Mizan Press, 1979), p. 124.

776 Reuven Paz, *The Heritage of the Sunni Militant Groups: An Islamic Internacionale?*, 4 January 2000, http://www.ict.org.il/articles/articledet.cfm ?articleid=415, viewed 5 December 2003.

777 Philip Halden, "Salafi in Virtual and Physical Reality", *ISIM Newsletter* No. 13, Decemebr 2003; "Indonesia Backgrounder: Why Salafism and Terrorism Mostly Don't Mix", ICG Asia Report, No. 83, 13 September 2004.

778 Juan Jose Escobar Stemmann, "Middle East Salafism's Influence and the Radicalization of Muslim Communities in Europe", *Middle East Review of International Affairs*, Vol. 10, No. 3, (September 2006).

779 Maha Azzam, "Al-Qaeda: the misunderstood Wahhabi connection and the ideology of violence", The Royal Institute of International Affairs, Middle East Programme, Briefing No. 1, (February 2003); Richard H. Shultz, Jr. and Ruth Margolies Beitler, "Tactical Deception And Strategic Surprise In Al-Qai'da's Operations", *Middle East Review of International Affairs*, Vol. 8, No. 2, June 2004. Two useful sources are Rohan Gunaratna, *Inside Al Qaeda : Global Network of Terror* (London: Hurst & Company, 2002) and Yonah Alexander and Michael S. Swetnam, *Usama bin Laden's al-Qaida: Profile of a Terrorist Network*, (New Delhi: Aditya, 2002).

780 Alexander and Swetnam, *Usama bin Laden's al-Qaida*, pp. 3, 29, 31; Gunaratna, *Inside Al Qaeda*, pp. 54-69, 95-98.

781 Reuven Paz, "Sawt al-Jihad: New Indoctrination of Qa'idat al-Jihad", Intelliegence and Terrorism Information Centre at the Center for Special Studies (CSS), www.intelligence.org.il/eng/g_j/rp_h_11_03.htm, viewed 24 August 2007.

782 Abdel Bari Atwan, "Total war: Inside the new Al-Qaeda", *The Sunday Times*, 26 February 2006.

783 Michael Scheuer, "Al-Qaeda's Tactical Doctrine: Aiming for a 'Long War' ", *Terrorism Focus*, Vol. 3, Issue 8, 28 February 2006.

784 Stephen Ulph, "Islamist Ideologues Struggle to Raise Morale", *Terrorism Focus*, Vol.3, Issue 6, 14 February 2006.

785 Scheuer, "Al-Qaeda's Insurgency Doctrine: Aiming for a 'Long War' ".

786 Murad al-Shishani, "Salafi-Jihadists in Jordan: From Prison Riots to Suicide Operation Cells", *Terrorism Focus*, Vo. 3, Issue 9, 7 March 2006.

787 Peter Harling and Mathieu Guidère, " 'Withdraw, move on and rampage': Iraq's resistance evolves", *Le Monde Diplomatique* (May 2006).

788 Michael Novak, "What the Islamists have Learned", *The Weekly Standard*, 22 November 2006.

789 See "Serialized Excerpts from Egyptian Al-Jihad Organisation Leader Ayman al-Zawahiri's Book 'Knights Under the Prophet's Banner' ", London: *Al-Sharq al-Awsat* in Arabic, 2 December 2001, http://www.fas.org/irp/world/para/ayman_bk.html, viewed 12 November 2004.

790 Ayman al-Zawahiri in "Serialized Excerpts from Egyptian Al-Jihad Organisation Leader Ayman al-Zawahiri's Book 'Knights Under the Prophet's Banner' ", p. 10.

791 Jonathan Ross-Harrington, "Re-Examining Jemaah Islamiyah in the Wake of the Zawahiri Letter", *Terrorism Monitor*, Volume 3, Issue 21, 3 November 2005; Rita Katz, "It's Real", 21 October 2005, *National Review Online*, http://www.nationalreview.com/comment/katz200510210928.asp, viewed 26 October 2005.

792 Murad al-Shishani, "Al-Zawahiri Addresses Reform in Muslim World", *Terrorism Focus*, Vol. 3, Issue 3, 25 January 2006; Jarret M. Brachman and William F. McCants, "Stealing Al-Qa'ida's Playbook", Combating Terrorism Center at West Point, CTC Report, (February 2006), pp. 11-12.

793 Stephen Ulph, "New Online Book Lays Out Al-Qaeda's Military Strategy", *Terrorism Focus*, Vol. 2, Issue 6, 17 March 2005.

794 Jarret M. Brachman and William F. McCants, "Stealing Al-Qa'ida's Playbook", Combating Terrorism Center at West Point, CTC Report, (February 2006), pp. 6-10.

795 Brachman and McCants, "Stealing Al-Qa'ida's Playbook", Combating Terrorism Center at West Point, CTC Report, (February 2006), pp. 13-14.

796   Daniel McGrory, "Cleric's tape threat to destroy Rome", *The Times*, 3 April 2004.

797   Reuven Paz, "Middle East Islamism In The European Arena", *Middle East Review of International Affairs*, Vol. 6, No. 3 (September 2002).

798   Paz, "Middle East Islamism In The European Arena".

799   Brachman and McCants, "Stealing Al-Qa'ida's Playbook", Combating Terrorism Center at West Point, CTC Report, (February 2006), pp. 15-17.

800   Stephen Ulph, "Setmariam Nasar: Background on al-Qaeda's Arrested Strategist", *Terrorism Focus*, Vol. 3, Issue 12, 28 March 2006.

801   Shane Dennan and Andrew Black, "Fourth generation warfare and the international jihad", Jane's Intelligence Review (October 2006), pp. 18-23. Al-Suri's book is in Arabic *Da'wat al-muqawamah al-islamiyyah al-'alamiyyah*.

802   Shaykh Abu Muhammad al-Maqdisi, "This is Our 'Aqeedah", Reviving Islam.com Research Team, http://www.revivingislam.com/aqeedah/thisisouraqeedah.html, viewed 27 January 2006.

803   Steven Brooke, "The Preacher and the Jihadi", "http://www.futureofmuslimworld.com/research/ctID.7/ctrend.asp" *Current Trends in Islamist Ideology*, Vol. 3, Hudson Institute, 16 February 2006, http://www.futureofmuslimworld.com/research/pubID.41/pub_detail.asp#, viewed 21 June 2006.

804   William McCants, (ed.), *Militant Ideology Atlas: Research Compendium*, (West Point, New York: Combating Terrorism Center, 2006); William McCants, (ed.), *Militant Ideology Atlas: Executive Report*, (West Point, New York: Combating Terrorism Center, 2006).

805   This is more surprising in the case of al-Zawahiri than in the case of bin Laden, as al-Zawahiri has produced more written work than bin Laden. It should be remembered that the methodology of this study is counting citations, which is only a partial measure of influence.

806 *The Oxford Encyclopedia of the Modern Islamic World*, Vol. pp. 2, 121-124; Amaziah Baram, "Two Roads in Revolutionary Shi'i Fundamentalism in Iraq: Hizb al-Da'wa al-Islamiyya and the Supreme Council of the Islamic Revolution of Iraq", in Martin E. Marty and R. Scott Appleby, (eds.), *Accounting for Fundamentalisms: The Dynamic Character of Movements*, (Chicago: University of Chicago Press, 1994), pp. 531-586.

807 *The Oxford Encyclopedia of the Modern Islamic World*, Vol. 2, pp. 129-130; Shahrough Akhavi, "Elite Factionalism in the Islamic Republic of Iran", *Middle East Journal*, 41. 2 (Spring 1987), pp. 181-201; Shaul Bakhash, *The Reign of the Ayatollahs: Iran and the Islamic Revolution* (New York, 1984); John L. Esposito, (ed.), *The Iranian Revolution: Its Global Impact*, (Miami: University of Florida Press, 1990).

808 Gary C. Gambill and Ziad K. Abdelnour, "Hezbollah: Between Tehran and Damascus", *Middle East Intelligence Bulletin*, Vol. 4 , No. 2 (February 2002); *The Oxford Encyclopedia of the Modern Islamic World*, Vol. 2, pp. 130-133; Martin Kramer, *Hezbollah's Vision of the West* (Washington, D.C: The Washington Institute Policy Papers, No. 16, 1989); Martin Kramer, "The Moral Logic of Hizballah", in Walter Reich, (ed.), *Origins of Terrorism: Psychologies, Theologies, States of Mind* (Washington, DC: Woodrow Wilson Center Press, 2001), pp. 131-157; Martin Kramer, "Redeeming Jerusalem: The Pan-Islamic Premise of Hizballah", in David Menashri, (ed.), *The Iranian Revolution and the Muslim World* (Boulder: Westview, 1990), pp. 105-130; Martin Kramer, "Hizbullah: The Calculus of Jihad", in Martin E. Marty and R. Scott Appleby, (eds.), *Fundamentalisms and the State: Remaking Polities, Economies, and Militance*, (Chicago: University of Chicago Press, 1992), pp. 539-556; Chibli Mallat, *Shi'i Thought from the South of Lebanon*, (Oxford: Centre for Lebanese Studies, 1988); J.P. Piscatori, "The Shia of Lebanon and Hizbullah: The Party of God", in Christie Jenet and Randal G. Stewart, (eds.), *Politics of the Future: The Role of Social Movements*, (Melbourne: Macmillan, 1989), pp. 292-231; Shimon Shapira, "The Origin of Hizballah", *Jerusalem*

Quarterly, 46 (Spring 1988), pp. 115-130; Steven Emerson, "The American Connections to Islamic Terror", statement to Senate Judiciary Committee's Subcommittee on Terrorism, Technology, and Government Information, 24 February 1998; *Patterns of Global Terrorism*, 200, United States Department of State, May 2002, http://library.nps.navy.mil/home/tgp/hamas. htm, viewed 28 June 2005.

809 For a recent biography of Fadlallah, see Jamal Sankari, *Fadlallah: The Making of a Radical Shi'ite Leader*, (London: Saqi Books, 2005).

810 Gary C. Gambill and Ziad K. Abdelnour, "Hezbollah: Between Tehran and Damascus", *Middle East Intelligence Bulletin*, Vol. 4 , No. 2 (February 2002).

811 Martin Kramer, "The Oracle of Hizbullah: Sayyid Muhammad Hussein Fadlallah", in R. Scott Appleby, (ed.), *Spokesmen for the Despised: Fundamentalist Leaders of the Middle East*, (Chicago: University of Chicago Press, 1997), pp. 83-181.

812 Martin Walker, "The coming of the Shi'a Empire", *Middle East Times* (3 February 2005).

813 "What can the U.S. do in Iraq?" *International Crisis Group (ICG)*, Middle East Report No. 34, 22 December 2004.

814 Abu Jandal al-Azdi, "Tanzim al-Qaeda wal-harb ghayr al-mutawaziyah", 27 March 2004. See https://www.al-ansar.biz/vb/showthread.php?threadid=7176; the article was circulated by the "News Agency" of al-Qa'eda – Global Islamic Media Front (GIMF).

815 Reuven Paz, "Global Jihad and Wmd: Between Martyrdom and Mass Destruction", in Hillel Fradkin, Husain Haqqani and Eric Brown, (eds.), *Current Trends in Islamist Ideology*, Vol. 2, (Washington, DC: Hudson Institute, Center on Islam, Democracy, and The Future of the Muslim World, 2005), pp. 76-77.

816 Boaz Ganor, "Terror as a Strategy of Psychological Warfare", 15 July 2002, *Institute for Counter-Terrorism*, http://www.ict.org.il/articles/articledet.cfm?articleid=443, viewed 30 October 2006.

817   For example, by a Muslim spy who infiltrated *al-Qa'eda*, interviewed on *Newsnight* BBC2, 16 November 2006

818   B. Raman, "Thai dilemma over Muslim anger", *Asia Times Online*, 3 November 2004.

819   Raman, "Thai dilemma over Muslim anger".

820   Renae Merle, "Pentagon Funds Diplomacy Effort, Contracts Aim to Improve Foreign Opinion of United States", *Washington Post*, 11 June 2005.

821   Simon Tisdall and Ewen MacAskill, "America's Long War", *The Guardian*, 15 February 2006.

822   This phrase is reported to have been used in his confession by Imam Samudra, the Indonesian Islamist accused of masterminding the Bali bombing. Reported in Thomas L. Friedman, "Defusing the Holy Bomb", *The New York Times*, 27 November 2002.

823   "Suicide bombers follow Quran, concludes Pentagon briefing", *WorldNetDaily*, 27 September 2006, http://www.WorldNetDaily.com/news/article.asp?ARTICLE_ID=52184, viewed 30 October 2006.

824   Summarised in MEMRI Special Dispatch Series No. 434, 27 October 2002, taken from www.qoqaz.com. This precisely follows al-Mawardi.

825   Hamid Abdullah Al-Ali, "The Legality of Killing Jewish Women and Children in Palestine" in *Al-Watan*, 31 August 2001, English translation by Shira Gutgold published in the *Jerusalem Post*, 5 September 2001.

826   Tom Roberts (writer and director), *Witness: Inside the Mind of the Suicide Bomber*, Channel 4, 10 November 2003.

827   Suleiman Abu Gheith, "In the Shadow of the Lances", from the Center for Islamic Research and Studies website (originally www.alneda.com then changed to http://66.34.191.223) reported by MEMRI Special Dispatch Series No. 388, 12 June 2002.

828   Lewis, "The Revolt of Islam", *The New Yorker*, 19 November 2001.

829 Shaybani's *Siyar*, chapter II, pp. 142-145, translation in Khadduri, *The Islamic Law of Nations*, p. 105.

830 Carra De Vaux, "Shahada" in *E.J. Brill's First Encyclopaedia of Islam 1913-1936*, Vol. VII (Leiden: E .J. Brill, 1993), p. 259.

831 John Esposito asserts that a new understanding of martyrdom was born out of the "severe dislocations experienced by much of the Muslim world from the eighteenth century to the present". See John L. Esposito, *Unholy War: Terror in the Name of Islam* (Oxford: Oxford University Press, 2002), p. 69.

832 Asra Rasheed, *Death* (Birmingham: Al-Hidaayah Publishing and Distribution, 2001), pp. 24, 28.

833 Rasheed, *Death*, footnote 211, p. 77.

834 Rasheed, *Death*, p. 24.

835 Rasheed, *Death*, footnote 51, p. 188.

836 Sahih Bukhari, Volume 4, Book 52, Number 297.

837 Sahih Bukhari, Volume 5, Book 59, Number 514; Sahih Bukhari, Volume 8, Book 76, Number 500.

838 A *fatwa* carries far more weight with a Muslim than any other kind of statement, command or ban.

839 Quoted at www.lailatalqadr.com (a website associated with Al-Azhar) and also reported in MEMRI Special Dispatch Series No. 363, 7 April 2002.

840 "Islamic Scholars say Suicide Attacks 'Legitimate' ", AFP report dated 10 January 2002, in *Middle East Times* issue 2002-2, 11 January 2002.

841 Richard Lloyd Parry, "Muslim nations defend use of suicide bombers" in *The Independent*, 11 April 2002.

842 *Al-Sharq al-Awsat*, 19 July 2003, extracts in English translation in MEMRI Special Dispatch Series No. 542, 24 July 2003.

843 *Al-Sharq al-Awsat*, 19 July 2003, extracts in English translation in MEMRI Special Dispatch Series No. 542, 24 July 2003.

844 Muslim leaders are often heard making such announcements.

Sometimes some very unexpected kinds of deaths are declared to be martyrdoms. For example a Palestinian student who was killed in a road accident was declared to have died "the martyrdom of learning". See also page 343.

845   A *hadith* states "The Messenger of Allah said: All the sins of a Shahid [martyr] are forgiven except debt." *Sahih Muslim, Book 20, Number 4649: Narrated Amr ibn al-'As.*

846   These detailed promises are derived from various *hadiths*. The Qur'an itself affirms in several places a special reward for those who die in the way of God, but does not go into specifics. See E. Kohlberg, "Shahid" in *The Encyclopaedia of Islam.*

847   Kristen Ashburn, "The Suicide Bombers" in *Telegraph Magazine*, 15 November 2003, pp. 24-27.

848   Hala Jaber and Uzi Mahnaimi, "Suicide Bombing was a Family Affair" in *The Sunday Times*, 18 January 2004.

849   Thauria Hamur, interviewed by Joanna Chen "A Martyr or a Murderer" in *Newsweek*, 23 February 2004, p. 68.

850   There are various other reputed ways of getting straight to paradise, which are believed by some Muslims though probably not with any scriptural basis. For example, some believe that if you memorise the whole Qur'an you and your family will all go to heaven (reported in the *Daily Mail*, 2 May 2003). Others hold that if you kill 40 Christians you will to go to paradise. This was the opinion of a Turkish Muslim during the Armenian massacre in Turkey in the early part of the twentieth century. He first killed 39 Christians, and then found an elderly man whom he also killed to make it up to the figure 40. Reported by Isa Dogdu in Stefan J. Bos, "Christians Near Northern Iraq Persecuted" in *Assist News Service*, 5 April 2003.

851   Esposito, *Unholy War: Terror in the Name of Islam* p. 69.

852   Muhammad said that when God's servant "plunges into the midst of the enemy without mail" it makes God laugh with joy. Ibn Ishaq *Sirat Rasul Allah*, III:445, English translation in Alfred Guillaume, *The Life of Muhammad: A Translation of Ibn Ishaq's Sirat Rasul Allah* p. 300.

853 In his "Declaration of war against the Americans occupying the land of the two holy places", 23 August 1996, quoted in Alexander and Swetnam, *Usama bin Laden's al-Qaida*, appendix 1A, p. 16.

854 Ferguson, *War and Peace in the World's Religions*, p. 132; Khadduri, *War and Peace in the Law of Islam*, p. 62; Jane Idleman Smith and Yvonne Yazbeck Haddad, *The Islamic Understanding of Death and Resurrection* (Albany: State University of New York Press, 1981), pp. 37, 51, 54, 59.

855 Al-Imam Zain-ud-Din Ahmad bin Abdul-Lateef Az-Zubaidi, (compiler) *The Translation of the Meanings of summarized Sahih Al-Bukhari Arabic-English*, translation Dr Muhammad Muhsin Khan (Riyadh: Maktaba Dar-us-Salam Publishers, 1994), p. 335.

856 E. Kohlberg, "Shahid" in *The Encyclopaedia of Islam*.

857 In his "Declaration of war against the Americans occupying the land of the two holy places", 23 August 1996, quoted in Alexander and Swetnam, *Usama bin Laden's al-Qaida*, appendix 1A, pp. 19, 21.

858 Saad Al-Fagih, "The War that Bin Laden is Winning" in *The Guardian*, 13 May 2003.

859 Almascaty, *Panduan Jihad Untuk Aktivis Gerakan Islam*, p. 112.

860 Summary of Tantawi's teachings at http://www.sunnah.org/History/Scholars /mashaykh_azhar.htm, viewed 25 January 2002.

861 Ironically, Europeans consider that the Muslims won the Crusades, despite the initial successes of the Franks.

862 Sheikh Safar bin Abdur-Rahman Al-Hawali, *Open Letter to President Bush*, 15 October 2001, http://www.sunnahonline.com/ilm/contemporary/0025.htm, viewed 24 August 2007.

863 W. Björkman, "Shahid" in *E.J. Brill's First Encyclopaedia of Islam 1913-1936*, Vol. VII, pp. 260-261.

864 Many quotes from the proud relatives are given in Ashburn, "The Suicide Bombers".

865 Itamar Marcus, "UN is Funding Summer Camps Honoring Terrorists" in *Palestinian Media Watch Bulletin*, 25 July 2003.

866 Itamar Marcus, "PA TV Glorifies First Woman Suicide Terrorist – Wafa Idris" in *Palestinian Media Watch Bulletin*, 24 July 2003. The song was broadcast on 24 July 2003, almost eighteen months after her suicide, 27 January 2002, and began:

> "My sister, Wafa, my sister, Wafa,
>
> O, the heartbeat of pride,
>
> O blossom, who was on the earth and is now in heaven..."

867 Ansari, *Sufi Saints and State Power*, pp. 78-79.

868 Qutb, *Milestones*, (Indianapolis: American Trust Publications, 1990) pp. 94-96.

869 Taqiuddin An-Nabhani, *The Islamic State* (London: Al-Khilafah Publications, no date): 188-192.

870 Ayatollah Ruhollah Khomeini, "Islamic Government" in Donohue & Esposito, (eds.) *Islam in Transition: Muslim Perspectives* (New York: Oxford University Press, 1982), pp. 315-316.

871 Eric Ellis, "Mahathir Tirade at 'Jews Ruling World' ", *Times Online*, 17 October 2003, http://www.timesonline.co.uk/printFriendly/0,,1-3-857059,00.html, viewed 5 December 2003.

872 For example, Amr Khaled, who appears on many of the most widely accessed Arab satellite TV channels, calls people to return to traditional Islamic beliefs and lifestyle in order to be able to restore the power associated with Islam's glorious past. One of his arguments is that if women cover their heads and behave modestly, men will not be tempted and fall into sin. The upright behaviour of the men will eventually result in the return of the great conqueror Saladdin. See www.amrkhaled.net.

873 Based on Q 9:123 "Fight the unbelievers who gird you about"

874 Just how un-Islamic the Egyptian government was is open to question. President Gemal Abdul Nasser, famed for his Arab nationalist ideology, was himself a sincere practising Muslim and convinced that Islam was essential to the Arab identity. He emphasised the revolutionary aspect of Islam and established an Islamic Congress. Karen Armstrong, *Holy*

War (London and Basingstoke: Macmillan London Limited, 1988), p. 81.

875 Shaykh Omar Abdul Rahman, *The Present Rulers and Islam. Are they Muslims or Not?* (London: Al-Firdous, 1990), p 23.

876 Osama bin Laden's "Declaration of war against the Americans occupying the land of the two holy places" has already been quoted.

877 Quoted by Martin Woolacott, "The Bali bomb may deal a fatal blow to the Islamists" in *The Guardian*, 18 October 2002.

878 Interestingly he was well aware of the Christian teaching of "turning the other cheek" towards the one who slapped you. But he said that being a Muslim he did not follow this precept.

879 Tom Roberts (writer and director), *Witness: Inside the Mind of the Suicide Bomber*.

880 These are well summarised in E. Kohlberg, "Shahid" in *The Encyclopaedia of Islam*.

881 Hence, presumably, the "martyrdom of learning" referred to a Palestinian student killed in a road accident. See note 844.

882 One apparent example from Britain was Richard Reid who hit the headlines when he allegedly tried to blow up an American plane with explosives in his shoes (22 December 2001). But there are many others, particularly in the Philippines. For further examples see James Hookway, "How a Terrorist Proves his Faith", *Far Eastern Economic Review*, 14 November 2002.

883 The British Muslim, Omar Khan Sharif, who tried to blow himself up in Israel on 30 April 2003, was very unusual in being a married man with two children.

884 "The Role of Palestinian Women in Suicide Terrorism", Israel Ministry of foreign Affairs, 30 January 2003, http://www.mfa.gov.il/MFA/MFAArchive/2000_2009/2003/1/The+Role+of+Palestinian+Women+in+Suicide+Terrorism.htm, viewed 1 September 2006.

885 Jaber and Mahnaimi, "Suicide Bombing was a Family Affair".

886   For example, "Mind of The Suicide Bomber", CBS News, 25 May 2003, http://www.cbsnews.com/stories/2003/05/23/60minutes/printable555344.shtml, viewed 12 February 2007.

887   They believe they cannot enter paradise while in debt.

888   Roberts, *Witness: Inside the Mind of the Suicide Bomber*.

889   Anwar Iqbal, "Islamic schools create Pakistani dilemma", *United Press International*, 17 August 2002.

890   Rick Wood, "Wahhabism: Out of Control?", *Mission Frontiers*, December 2001.

891   Gilles Kepel, *Jihad: The Trail of Political Islam*, translation Anthony F. Roberts (London: I.B. Tauris, 2002), p. 56.

892   "Religious Schools 'breeding ground for future terrorists' ", *Straits Times*, Singapore, 17 January 2003.

893   Duncan Walsh, "Boys Rescued from Kenya's Islamic School of Torture", *The Times*, 19 January 2003.

894   Elizabeth John and K.T. Chelvi, "The Chilling Jemaah Islamiyah Goal", *New Sunday Times*, 19 January 2003.

895   General Hendropriyono, head of Indonesian intelligence (Badan Intelijen Nasional), interviewed shortly after Bali bombing on 12 October 2002.

896   Daniel McGrory and Sam Lister , "Prophets of Hate Prey on Rootless Misfits", *The Times*, 31 January 2003.

897   Bruce Crumley, "Jihad's Hidden Victim", Time, 2 June 2003, p. 48.

898   Almascaty, *Panduan Jihad Untuk Aktivis Gerakan Islam*, p. 92.

899   "The Black Widows' Revenge", *The Economist* (12-18 July 2003), p. 32.

900   Gunaratna, *Inside Al Qaeda*, p. 73.

901   "Holy Warriors Enlisting Online", *WorldNetDaily*, 7 August 2003, http://wnd.com/news/printer-friendly.asp?ARTICLE_ID=33960, viewed 7 August 2003.

902   *Al-Ansar*, No. 16, 24 August 2002, extracts in English in MEMRI Special Dispatch Series No. 418, 4 September 2002.

903   Colonel Karim Sultan, police chief in Karbala, quoted in James Hider, "Iraqis Drugged, Brainwashed and sent to die for Bin Laden", *Times Online*, 22 March 2004.

904   Roberts, *Witness: Inside the Mind of the Suicide Bomber*.

905   Reported in the *Daily Mail*, 2 May 2003.

906   John and Chelvi "The Chilling Jemaah Islamiyah Goal".

907   Almascaty, *Panduan Jihad Untuk Aktivis Gerakan Islam*, pp. 96-112.

908   Almascaty, *Panduan Jihad Untuk Aktivis Gerakan Islam*, p. 95.

909   Gunaratna, *Inside Al Qaeda*, pp. 70-71, 75-76.

910   "Declaration of Jihad Against the Country's Tyrants", Military Series recovered by police in Manchester UK from the home of Nazihal Wadih Raghie, 10 May 2000.

911   Gunaratna, *Inside Al Qaeda*, pp. 71-72.

912   www.hostinganime.com/battar/b1word.zip.

913   English summaries and excerpts in MEMRI Special Dispatch Series No. 637, 6 January 2004.

914   *Declaration of Jihad Against the Country's Tyrants, Military Series*.

915   Gunaratna, *Inside Al Qaeda*, p. 73.

916   "*Jihad* in Cyberspace", *The Economist*, 15 March 2003.

917   "Trouble in the Holy Land" *WorldNetDaily.com*, 3 March 2003, http://www.WorldNetDaily.com/news/article.asp?ARTICLE_ID=31323, viewed 8 February 2007.

918   Hassan Jomass, quoted in Toby Harnden, "Video Games Attract Young to Hizbollah" in *The Daily Telegraph*, 21 February 2004, p. 18.

919   Mayer, "War and Peace in the Islamic Tradition and International Law", pp. 197, 209.

920   Jansen, *The Neglected Duty*, p. 193.

921   Mahmassani, "International Law in the Light of Islamic Doctrine", pp. 307-308.

922   Harifyah Abdel Haleem, Oliver Ramsbotham, Saba Risaluddin and Brian Wicker (eds.) *The Crescent and the Cross: Muslim and Christian Approaches to War and Peace*, (Basingstoke: Macmillan Press 1998; New York: St Martin's Press 1998), pp. 60-103.

923   Haleem et al., *The Crescent and the Cross*, pp. 76-77.

924   The wide range of modern Muslim definitions of the term "self-defence" will be considered later in this chapter.

925   See Abbas Mahmoud al-Aqqad, *Haqa'iq al-Islam wa Abatil Khusumih* (Cairo: Dar al-Hilal, 1957), pp. 187-191, quoting a survey by Ahmad Zaki Pasha of all the battles which took place in Muhammad's lifetime.

926   Mahmud Shaltut, *Al-Qur'an wa al-Qital (The Qur'an and Fighting)* (Matba'at al-Nasr and Maktab Ittihad al-Sharq, 1948). This book was written in 1940 and published in 1948, ten years before Shaltut became the Sheikh of Al-Azhar. English translation in Rudolph Peters, *Jihad in Classical and Modern Islam: a Reader* (Princeton: Markus Wiener Publishers, 1996), pp. 60-101.

927   Ahmed Khan, in *The Pioneer* (23 November 1871) quoted in Peters, *Jihad in Classical and Modern Islam*, p. 123; Judith M. Brown, *Modern India: The Origins of an Asian Democracy*, 2nd edition, in *The Short Oxford History of the Modern World* series (Oxford: Oxford University Press, 1995), p. 153. Sir Syed Ahmed Khan has been vilified by many Muslims for his co-operative attitude towards the British Raj. See for example Maryam Jameelah, *Islam and Modernism* (Sant Nagar, Lahore: Mohammad Yusuf Khan, 1968), pp. 49-55.

928   Dr Abdel-Mo'ti Bayoumi, "Wrong Zionist Perceptions of Jihad in Islam via the Internet", in *Al-Musawwar*, 23 August 2002. English translation in *Religious News Service from the Arab World*, 2 September 2002.

929   Dr Louay Fatoohi, *Jihad in the Qur'an: The Truth from the Source* (Kuala Lumpur: A.S. Noordeen, 2002), pp. 3, 24, 34-35, 50, 52, 60. See also the footnote about Fatoohi's book in chapter 3.

930 Haleem et al., *The Crescent and the Cross*, p. 66.

931 "And fight them on until there is no more tumult or oppression and there prevail justice and faith in Allah; but if they cease let there be no hostility except to those who practise oppression." The very same verse was used by Ibn Taymiyya (1263-1328) to justify Muslims fighting any groups of unbelievers who refuse to convert to Islam. See Taqi al-Din Ahmad Ibn Taymiyya, *al-Siyasa al-Sha'iyya fi Islah al-Ra'i wa-al-Ra'iyya (Governance according to God's Law in Reforming both the Ruler and his Flock)* in Peters, *Jihad in Classical and Modern Islam*, p. 45.

932 Dr Kamal Boraiq'a Abd es-Salam, "Responding to Dr Bat Ye'or", 23 August 2002 in *Religious News Service from the Arab World*, 2 September 2002.

933 "And why should ye not fight in the cause of Allah and of those who being weak are ill-treated (and oppressed)? Men women and children whose cry is: 'Our Lord! rescue us from this town whose people are oppressors; and raise for us from Thee one who will protect; and raise for us from Thee one who will help!' " Q 4:75 appears to encourage Muslims to fight on behalf of anyone who is oppressed, but the traditional Muslim interpretation applies it specifically to oppressed Muslims. See A. Yusuf Ali's footnote 593 to this verse.

934 Ali Asghar Engineer, "Islam and Non-violence" in R. Kumar, (ed.) *Khan Abdul Gaffar Khan: A Centennial Tribute* (New Delhi: Nehru Memorial Museum and Library, Har-Anand Publications, 1995), p. 122.

935 Shaltut, *Al-Qur'an wa al-Qital* in English translation in Peters, *Jihad in Classical and Modern Islam*, pp 76-78.

936 Haleem et al., *The Crescent and the Cross*, p. 77.

937 Shaltut, *Al-Qur'an wa al-Qital*, in English translation in Peters, *Jihad in Classical and Modern Islam*, p. 78.

938 Bayoumi, "Wrong Zionist Perceptions".

939 Haleem et al., *The Crescent and the Cross*, p. 71.

940 Haleem et al., *The Crescent and the Cross*, p. 60.

941 Mahmud Shaltut, *The Muslim Conception of International Law and the Western Approach* (The Hague: Martinus Nijhof, 1968).

942 Fatoohi, *Jihad in the Qur'an*, pp. 27-28, 72, argues that *qital* is one aspect of armed *jihad* which in turn is a specialised kind of *jihad*.

943 Haleem et al., *The Crescent and the Cross*, pp. 75-76.

944 Haleem et al., *The Crescent and the Cross*, p. 79.

945 This is deduced by certain commentators from the words "But do not transgress limits" in Q 2:190 following a command to fight.

946 Haleem et al., *The Crescent and the Cross*, p. 67.

947 Ma'ruf al-Dawalibi, "Islam and Nationalistic and Secularistic Trends", in *Ash-Sharq al-Awsat*, 31 December 1989, reprinted in Kharofa, *Nationalism, Secularism, Apostasy and Usury in Islam*, pp. 11-13.

948 Ahmad Naser Al-Rajihi, "Heavenly Religions Encourage Legitimate War" in *Ash-Sharq al-Awsat*, 28 January 1990, reprinted in Kharofa *Nationalism, Secularism, Apostasy and Usury in Islam*, pp. 25-27.

949 *Al-Ansar*, No. 16, 24 August 2002, extracts in English translation in MEMRI Special Dispatch Series No. 418, 4 September 2002.

950 Ibn 'Uthaymeen, *Riyaadhus-Saaliheen*, Vol.1, pp. 165-66. Available at www.fatwa-online.com/fataawa/worship/jihaad/jih004/0010915_1.htm_, viewed 12 August 2003.

951 'Abd Al-Hamid *Al-Ansari*, "Landmarks in Rational and Constructive Dialogue with the 'Other' ", *Al-Hayat* (London) 31 May 2002. Extracts in English translation in MEMRI Special Dispatch Series No. 386, 5 June 2002.

952 Abdul-Aziz Ibn Baz, Abdul-Aziz Ibn Abdullah Al-Shaykh Abdullah, Salih Ibn Fawzan Al-Fawzan and Bakr Ibn Abdullah Abu Zaid (The Permanent Committee for Academic Research and Ifta) *Unification of Religions*, Fatwa no. 19402 (2 June 1997) available at: www.troid.org/articles/islaamicinfo/Islaamingeneral/whatisislaam/unificationofreligion_, viewed 7 August 2003.

953 *Al-Sharq al-Awsat* (London, 20 April 2002 and 10 May 2002). Extracts in English translation in MEMRI Special Dispatch Series No. 378, 16 May 2002.

954 Khaled Muhammad Batrafi, "Why do we hate the People of the Book?" in *Al-Hayat*, 21 October 2001, extracts in English translation quoted in MEMRI Special Dispatch Series No. 295, 1 November 2001.

955 With regard to law on war, James Turner Johnson identifies five main sources of the Western just war tradition from which international law on war is derived: Hebraic, Roman, Christian, classical and Germanic. See his chapter "Historical Roots and Sources of the Just War Tradition in Western Culture" in John Kelsay and James Turner Johnson (eds.) *Just War and Jihad: Historical and Theoretical Perspectives on War and Peace in Westernand Islamic Traditions* (Westport, Connecticut: Greenwood Press, 1991).

956 Najib Armanazi, *L'Islam et le Droit International* (thesis) (Paris: Librairie Picart, 1929), pp. 50-52; Muhammad Hamidullah, *Muslim Conduct of State*, 3rd edition (Lahore: Sh. Muhammad Ashraf, 1953), pp. 66-68; Mansur, Al-Shari'a al-Islamiyya, pp. 28-30; Al Ghunaimi, *The Muslim Conception of International Law and the Western Approach*, pp. 82-86; Al-Daqs, *Ayat al-Jihad fi l-Qur'an al-Karim*, p. 88.

957 Mayer, "War and Peace in the Islamic Tradition and International Law", p. 199.

958 Mayer, "War and Peace in the Islamic Tradition and International Law", p. 198.

959 Traditionally this involved the payment of tribute in return for a truce or armistice. Historic examples were Muhammad's treaty with the Christians of Nadjran and a treaty in 652 with the Nubians who had to pay a tribute of slaves rather than money. See the article by D. B. Macdonald's on "Dar al-Sulh" in *The Encyclopaedia of Islam*.

960 *Dar al-'Ahd* is acceptable in the Shafi'i school of *shari'a*. The non-Muslims are permitted to continue to have control of their lands on condition that they pay tribute to the Muslims. Examples include Armenia in the early days of Islam, and later various Christian rulers under the Ottoman empire. See the article by Halil Inalcik on "Dar al-Ahd" in *The Encyclopaedia of Islam*.

961   If the non-Muslims must make payments to the Muslims in return for peace or possession of their property there is not much difference between these and the classic *dhimmi* status of non-Muslims living in *Dar al-Islam*, although *dhimmis* were also humiliated in various other ways.

962   Anderson, *Islam in the Modern World*, pp. 30-31; article on "Daru 'l-Harb" in Hughes, *A Dictionary of Islam*, pp. 69-70.

963   Brown, *Modern India*, p. 153.

964   Moulvi Abu Said Mohammed Husain, *A Treatise on Jihad (Iqtisad-fi-Masail-il-Jihad)* translated from Urdu (Lahore: Victoria Press, 1887).

965   Jeremy Reynalds, "Radical Islamic Group Threatens Britain After Police Raid", *Assist News Service*, 30 July 2003; "Insult to the Dead", *Daily Mail*, 9 September 2003.

966   Hasan Moinuddin, *The Charter of the Islamic Conference and Legal Framework of Economic Co-operation among Its Member States* (Oxford: Clarendon Press, 1987), p. 28.

967   Mahmassani, "International Law in the Light of Islamic Doctrine", pp. 320-321.

968   Rosalyn Higgins, "The Attitude of Western States towards Legal Aspects of the Use of Force", in A. Cassese, (ed.) *The Current Legal Regulation of the Use of Force* (Dordrecht: Martinus Nijhoff, 1986), p. 442.

969   Ayatollah Mutahhari in a lecture entitled "Defence – the Essence of Jihad". See Mehdi Abedi and Gary Legenhausen (eds.) *Jihad and Shahadat: Struggle and Martyrdom in Islam* , pp. 109-113.

970   Ala' Eddin Kharofa, "Muhammad the Messenger of God (PBUH) and Westerners", in Kharofa, *Nationalism, Secularism, Apostasy and Usury in Islam*, p. 99.

971   Imam Mohammed Al-Asi, "Qur'anic Teaching on the Justification for *Jihad* and Qital" in *Crescent International* (1-15 June 2003), p. 7.

972   In 1973 the Sheikh of Al-Azhar declared that *jihad* against Israel was incumbent on Egyptians, whether they were Christian or Muslim.

See Rudolph Peters, *Islam and Colonialism: The Doctrine of Jihad in Modern History* (The Hague: Mouton, 1979), p. 134.

973 Mayer, "War and Peace in the Islamic Tradition and International Law", p. 215.

974 Abul A'la Mawdudi, *Jihad fi Sabilillah (Jihad in Islam)*, pp. 3, 8-9.

975 Azzam Tamimi, "Concepts of Life Beyond Death: Martyrdom, Resurrection, Heaven & Hell", Institute of Islamic Political Thought, 26 March 2004, http://www.ii-pt.com/web/papers/concept.htm, viewed 8 September 2005.

976 James Piscatori, *Islam in a World of Nation States* (Cambridge: Cambridge University Press, 1986), pp. 86-87.

977 Moinuddin, *The Charter of the Islamic Conference*, p. 90 and also pp. 186-187 where he reproduces the relevant sections of the Charter.

978 Mayer, "War and Peace in the Islamic Tradition and International Law", p. 206.

979 Rajaee, *Islamic Values and World View*, pp. 82-83.

980 Kharofa, "Muhammad the Messenger of God (PBUH) and Westerners", p. 97 emphasis added.

981 Peters, *Jihad in Classical and Modern Islam*, p. 137.

982 Hamidullah, *Muslim Conduct of State*, pp. 43-44; Muhammad 'Abd Allah Daraz, "Mabadi' al-Qanun al-Dawli al-'Amm li-l-Islam", in *Risalat al-Islam*, 2 (1950), p. 149; Abu Zahra, *Al-'Alaqat al-Dawliyya fi'l-Islam*, pp. 20-25; Mahmassani, "International Law in the Light of Islamic Doctrine", pp. 242-244.

983 Armanazi, *L'Islam et le Droit International*, pp. 73-75; Hamidullah, *Muslim Conduct of State*, pp. 190-194; Abu Zahra, *Al-'Alaqat al-Dawliyya fi'l-Islam*, pp. 94-95; Zuhayli, *Athar al-Harb fi al-Fiqh al-Islami*, pp. 150-61; Mahmassani, "International Law in the Light of Islamic Doctrine", p. 289; Mansur, Al-Shari'a al-Islamiyya, pp. 296-303; al-Daqs, *Ayat al -Jihad fi' l-Qur'an al-Karim*, p. 91.

984 See for example, Mona Abul-Fadl *Where East Meets West: The West on the Agenda of the Islamic Revival*, Islamization of

Knowledge Series (no. 10), (Herndon, Virginia: The International Institute of Islamic Thought, 1992).

985 Yusuf al-Qaradawi, *Priorities of the Islamic Movement in the Coming Phase*, (Swansea: Awakening Publications, 2000), pp. 163-167.

986 *Interpretation of the Meanings of the Noble Qur'an* (1996), p. 47.

987 *Interpretation of the Meanings of the Noble Qur'an* (1996), p. 48.

988 *Interpretation of the Meanings of the Noble Qur'an* (1996), p. 639.

989 *Interpretation of the Meanings of the Noble Qur'an* (1996), pp. 847-848.

990 *Interpretation of the Meanings of the Noble Qur'an* (1996), pp. 863.

991 One of the most significant exceptions is Indonesia, where the progressive reformist organisation Nahdatul Ulama has around 30 million members.

992 "What is Progressive Islam?" *ISIM Newsletter*, No. 13, December 2003; Radwan A. Masmoudi, "The Silenced Majority", *Islam 21*, Issue No. 34, May 2003, http://islam21.net/quarterly/Islam21-May03.pdf, viewed 11 August 2005.

993 Yusuf al-Qaradawi, http://www.islamonline.net/fatwa/english/FatwaDisplay.asp?hFatwaID=61551, viewed 10 August 2005.

994 Ehsan Masood, "A Muslim Journey", *Prospect*, Issue 113, (August 2005), http://www.prospectmagazine.co.uk/article_details.php?id=6989, viewed 5 September 2005.

995 Ulil Abshar-Abdalla, "Freshening Up Our Understanding of Islam", *Kompas*, 18 November 2002. Quotations are an English translation from the Indonesian original.

996 C.W. Troll, *Sayyid Ahmad Khan: A Reinterpretation of Muslim Theology*, (Karachi Oxford University Press, 1979), Roy Jackson, *Fifty Key Figures in Islam* (London and New York: Routledge, 2006), pp. 164-168.

997 Albert Hourani, *Arabic Thought in the Liberal Age 1798-1939* (Cambridge: Cambridge University Press, 1983), pp. 130-160;

Zaki M. A. Badawi, *The Reformers of Egypt* (London: Croom Helm, 1978), pp. 35-95.

998   Gerhard Lichtenthaler, "Muslih, Mystic and Martyr: The Vision of Mahmud Muhammad Taha and the Republican Brothers in the Sudan: Towards an Islamic Reformation?" 1993, MA dissertation, SOAS.

999   Mahmoud Mohamed Taha, "The Second Message of Islam, translation and introduction by Abdullahi Ahmed An-Na'im, (Syracuse, New York: Syracuse University Press, 1987), pp. 132-134.

1000 Fazlur Rahman, *Major Themes of the Qur'an* (Minneapolis: Bibliotheca Islamica, 1980).

1001 Andrew Rippin, *Muslims: Their Religious Beliefs and Practices*, Vol. 2: The contemporary Period, (London & New York: Routledge, 1993), pp. 109-111.

1002 Fazlur Rahman, *Major Themes of the Qur'an* (Minneapolis: Bibliotheca Islamica, 1980) pp. 63-64.

1003 "Islamic Scholar Warns U.S. of 'Two-Faced' Muslims' ", *NewsMax. com Wires, 20 June 2002*, http://www.newsmax.com/archives/articles/2002/6/19/144341.shtml, viewed 11 October 2006.

1004 Basam Tibi, "War and Peace in Islam", in Terry Nardin, (ed.), *The Etrhics of War and Peace: Religious and Secular Perspectives*, (Princeton, New Jersey: Princeton University Press, 1996), pp. 140-143.

1005 Bassam Tibi, *Islam between Culture and Politics*, (Basingstoke: Palgrave Macmillan, 2005), p. 271.

1006 Tibi, *Islam between Culture and Politics*, p. 266.

1007 "Europeans Have Stopped Defending Their Values", Interview With German Islam Expert Bassam Tibi, *Spiegel Online*, 2 October 2006, http://www.spiegel.de/international/spiegel/0,1518,440340,00. html, viewed 11 October 2006.

1008 Ziauddin Sardar, "Rethinking Islam", June 2002, *Islam For Today*,   http://www.islamfortoday.com.sardar01.htm,   viewed

27 May 2005; Thomas Gerholm, "Two Muslim intellectuals in the postmodern West: Akbar Ahmed and Ziauddin Sardar", in Akbar Ahmed & Hastings Donnan, (eds.), *Islam, Globalization and Postmodernity*, (London & New York: Routledge, 1994).

1009   Sardar, "Rethinking Islam".

1010   Sardar, "Rethinking Islam".

1011   Sardar, "Rethinking Islam".

1012   Sardar, "Rethinking Islam".

1013   Sardar, "Rethinking Islam".

1014   Sardar, "Rethinking Islam", June 2002, *Islam For Today*, http://www.islamfortoday.com/sardar01.htm, viewed 5 August 2005.

1015   Ziauddin Sardar, "Viewpoint: The global voices reclaiming Islam", *BBC NEWS*, 6 September 2005.

1016   See articles on FMCAT website, www.freemuslims.org: "Our Positions: What we believe in"; "We are so sorry for 9-11"; "About FMCAT", viewed 22 October 2004.

1017   "Taking our religion back one Muslim at a time", Free Muslims Coalition, http://www.freemuslims.org/, viewed 2 November 2005.

1018   Ehsan Masood, "A Muslim Journey"

1019   "Islam and Secularism", Interview with Soheib Bencheikh, Qantara.de, http://qantara.de/webcom/show_article.php?wc_c=478&wc_id=130&printmode=1, viewed 27 October 2006; Also see Daniel Pipes, book review of Soheib Bencheikh, "Marianne et le Prophète: L'Islam dans la France laïque", *Middle East Quarterly*, (December 2000).

1020   "About SIS", http://www.geocities.com/wellesley/veranda/7502/about/content1.htm, viewed 11 August 2005.

1021   "Islam, Apostasy and PAS", *Resources@Sisters in Islam*, 22 July 1999, http://www.muslimtents.com/sistersinnislam/resources/1apostat.htm, viewed 14 November 2005.

1022   Ioannis Gatsiounis, "Islam Hadhari in Malaysia", Center on Islam, Democracy and the Future of the Muslim World, Current

Trends in Islamist Ideology, Vol. 3, 16 February 2006, www.
futureofmuslimworld.com/ research/pubID.43/pub_detail.asp,
viewed 21 June 2006.

1023 Ziauddin Sardar, "Can Islam Change?", *New Statesman*, 13
September 2004, http://www.newstatesman.com/200409130016,
viewed 20 September 2005.

1024 Abdullah Ahmad Badawi, speech at International Islamic University
Of Islamabad, Pakistan, 17 February 2005, http://www.pmo.gov.my/
WebNotesApp/PMMain.nsf/8b5b580b84fee6b248256db300306a24/
256b2e5f00cd3bb748256fac002a8a71/$FILE/SPEECH%202005%2
002%2017%20I.I.U%20ISLAMABAD%20PRESS%20VERSION.
doc, viewed 3 September 2006.

1025 "Final Declaration", Islam and Reform Workshop Cairo, 5-7
October 2004, Ibn Khaldun Centre for Development Studies (ICDS),
NGO Events/News, Egypt, 7 October 2004, http://www.mengos.net/
events/04newsevents/egypt/october/ibnkhaldun-English.htm, viewed
25 November 2005, also http://www.brookings.edu/fp/research/
projects/islam/cairoclosing.pdf, viewed 25 November 2005.

1026 Y. Yehoshua, "A Cairo Conference Calling for Reform Raises the
Ire of the Egyptian Religious Establishment", MEMRI Inquiry and
Analysis Series - No. 192, 22 October 2006.

1027 Amir Taheri, "Hijacking Islam", *New York Post*, 12 February 2006.

1028 John L. Esposito, "Practice and Theory", in Joshua Cohen and
Deborah Chasman, *Islam and the Challenge of Democracy: A Boston
Review Book*, Princeton & Oxford: Princeton University Press, p. 99.
For more insight into the political thinking of Gus Dur see his website:
http://www.gusdur.net/; See also Abdurrahman Wahid, "Right Islam
vs. Wrong Islam", *The Wall Street Journal*, 30 December 2005.

1029 Sumanto al-Qurtuby, "Seeding Peace on Earth: Abdurrahman
Wahid's Movements on Peace and Nonviolence", http://www.
wahidinstitute.org/pdf-docs/Peace-on-The-Earth.pdf, viewed 3
September 2006.

1030 Niyazi Berkes, *The Development of Secularism in Turkey*, (London:
Hurst and Co., 1998), pp. 431-503.

1031   Derek Hopwood, *Habib Bourguiba of Tunisia*, (Basingstoke and London: The Macmillan Press, 1992); Kenneth J. Perkins, *A History of Modern Tunisia*, (Cambridge: Cambridge University Press, 2004).

1032   Kamel Labidi, "Subversive mourning in Tunisia", *Le Monde Diplomatique* (May 2000).

1033   Salwa Ismail, *Rethinking Islamist Politics: Culture, the State and Islamism*, (London: IB Tauris, 2003), pp. 138-159.

1034   Charles E. Butterworth and I. William Zartman, *Between the State and Islam* (Cambridge: Cambridge University Press, 2001), pp. 179-183.

1035   Gautam Naik, "Tunisia Wins Population Battle, and Others See a Policy Model", *The Wall Street Journal*, 8 August 2003.

1036   The five pinciples of pancasila are: belief in the one and only God, just and civilised humanity, the unity of Indonesia, democracy guided by inner wisdom in the unanimity arising out of deliberations amongst representatives, social justice for the whole of the peoples of Indonesia.

1037   William S. Lind, Keith Nightengale and Joseph W. Sutton, "The Changing Face of War: Into the Fourth Generation", *Marine Corps Gazette* (October 1989), pp. 22-26.

1038   Tony Corn, "World War IV as Fourth-Generation Warfare", *Policy Review*, (January 2006).

1039   William S. Lind, "Understanding Fourth Generation War", AntiWar.com, 15 January 2004. http://antiwar.com/lind/index. php?articleid=1702, viewed 24 October 2006.

1040   Thomas X. Hammes, "Insurgency: Modern Warfare Evolves into a Fourth Generation", *Strategic Forum*, No. 214, January 2005.

1041   Corn, "World War IV as Fourth-Generation Warfare".

1042   Corn, "World War IV as Fourth-Generation Warfare".

1043   Laurent Murawiec, "The Saudi Takeover of Al-Azhar University," *Terrorism Monitor*, Volume 1, Issue 7, 4 December 2003.

1044   It is interesting to note that at Banyas in 1140 it took the combined efforts of the Crusaders and Saracen Muslims to defeat the

Assassins who were attacking both parties. This event gave rise to a new era in Christian-Muslim relations in which Crusader and Saracen nobles gathered together for conversation and sport.

1045 Lewis "The Revolt of Islam".

1046 Ansari, *Sufi Saints and State Power*, p. 96.

1047 Ansari, *Sufi Saints and State Power*, p. 95.

1048 *Daily Gazette*, 4 November 1920, p. 5.

1049 This author has not been able to track down the quoted text within the Qur'an, although two verses state that God will not place a burden on a soul greater than it can bear (Q 2:286 and Q 23:62). One wonders where the Maulvi found his convenient quotation.

1050 Quoted in Banerjee, *The Pathan Unarmed*, p. 49.

1051 Stalinsky's report "Saudi Policy Statements on Support to the Palestinians", is based entirely on official Saudi government sources. Steven Stalinksy, "Saudi Policy Statements on Support to the Palestinians", MEMRI Special Report No. 17, 3 July 2003.

1052 Greg Jaffe, "A General's New Plan to Battle Radical Islam", *Wall Street Journal*, 2 September 2006.

1053 Afzal Bajwa, "Musharraf tells Abizaid where to get off", *The Nation*, 9 March 2006.

1054 John Simpson, "Why Tourists are Now the Ideal Targets", *The Sunday Telegraph*, 1 December 2002, p. 21, emphasis added.

1055 Mark Perry and Alastair Crooke, "How to lose the war on terror", *Asia Times Online*, Part 1: Talking with the 'terrorists' ", 31 March 2006; Part 2: "Handing victory to the extremists", 1 April 2006; Part 3: "An exchange of narratives", 3 June 2006.

1056 Patrick Seale, "Healing the Wounds between Islam and the West", *Al-Hayat*, 10 December 2004.

1057 This is based on two verses in the Qur'an which forbid the eating of pig-meat, Q 2:173, Q 5:4.

1058 Worthington Jukes, *Frontier Heroes: Reminiscences of Missionary Work in Amritsar 1872-1873 and on the Afghan*

Frontier in Peshawar 1873-1890 (manuscript dated Exmouth, 1925, re-typed Peshawar, 2000), p. 47.

1059 Bob Drogin and Greg Miller, "Spy Agencies Facing Questions of Tactics", *Los Angeles Times*, 29 October 2001; Victor Hurley, *Jungle Patrol: The Story of the Philippine Constabulary* (New York: E.P. Dutton, 1938). Also, the threat of being sprinkled with pig's blood was used in the Philippines in 1902 by Pershing to "persuade" some Muslim leaders to sign a treaty to make peace amongst themselves. See Richard O'Connor, *Black Jack Pershing* (New York: Doubleday & Co., inc, 1961), pp. 62-63.

1060 John Murphy, "Psychological warfare and the demise of the new millennium suicide-bomber" LLC White Paper Las Vegas: SusbloodLabs, 2006, http://www.susbloodlabs.com/PsychologicalWarfareandathedemiseofthesuicidebomber.pdf, viewed 28 November 2006.

1061 Philps, "Settlers Use Pigskin to Foil the Martyrs", www.telegraph.co.uk, 26 February 2002, viewed 5 December 2003.

1062 Barbara and David Mikkelson, "Pershing the Thought", in Urban Legends Reference Pages at www.snopes.com/rumors/pershing.htm, 26 February 2002, viewed 11 December 2002.

1063 "Israeli Rabbi urges Pig Fat use to Stop Bombers", Reuters, 12 February 2004, http://news.ft.com/servlet/ContentServer?pagename=FT.com/WireFeed/WireFeed&c=WireFeed&cid=10741 60683676&p=1014232938216, viewed 13 February 2004.

1064 Philps "Settlers Use Pigskin to Foil the Martyrs".

1065 "State Senator Angers Muslims with Flier on Pig Entrails", *Associated Press*, 27 June 2003, available at http://edition.cnn.com/2003/ALLPOLITICS /06/27/senator.pigentrails.ap/, viewed 27 June 2003.

1066 Mark Hosenball and Michael Isikoff, "Al Qaeda Strikes Again", *Newsweek* (26 May – 2 June 2003), p. 24.

1067 "Saudi Clerics Condemn Terrorism", *BBC NEWS* (17 August 2003) http://news.bbc.co.uk/go/pr/fr/-/1/hi/world/middle_east/3157493.stm, viewed 27 June 2003.

1068 "Imam Fired For Praising Suicide Bombers", *The Independent*, 16 June 2003; Estelle Shirbon, "Rome Imam Suspended After Praising Suicide Bombers", Reuters, 13 June 2003 available at http://www.reuters.com/newsArticle .jhtml?type=topNews&stor yID=2928250, viewed 16 June 2003.

1069 W. Björkman, "Shahid", in E.J. Brill's *First Encyclopaedia of Islam 1913-1936*, Vol. VII (Leiden: E.J. Brill, 1993), p. 261.

1070 The Jama'at-i Islami is allied to the Wahhabi movement and to the Muslim Brotherhood. A careful study of Jama'at-i Islami ideology and history can leave no doubt that it is at the forefront of Islamist movements worldwide, committed to attaining political power for the creation of Islamic shari'a states wherever possible, and inherently hostile to Western civilisation.

1071 "Muslim Council of Britain: Much ado about nothing", *Q-News*, March-April 2002, pp. 22-23; "Silencing voices of dissent", *Q-News*, March-April 2002, p. 26.

1072 "In the tent or out?", *The Economist*, 28 October 2004.

1073 Elaine Sciolino, "French Islam Wins Officially Recognized Voice", *The New York Times*, 14 April 2003; "French Muslims back traditional groups", *Aljazeera.Net*, 20 June 2005.

1074 For such misplaced encouragement of Islamists in Britain see Martin Bright, *When Progressives Treat with Reactionaries: The British State's Flirtation with Radical Islamists*, (London: Policy Exchange, 2006).

1075 Fareed Zakaria, "Now, Saudis See the Enemy", *Newsweek* (26 May – 2 June 2003), p. 19.

1076 Angel Rabasa, Cheryl Bernard, Lowell H. Schwartz and Peter Sickle, *Building Moderate Muslim Networks* (Santa Monica, California: Rand Center for Middle East Public Policy, 2007) p. 140.

1077 Michael Y. Park, "Sept. 11 Creates New Lexicon", Fox News, 11 September 2006, http://www.foxnews.com/story/0,2933,213240,00. html, viewed 16 October 2006.

1078 Ahmed Al-Matboli, "German Exhibition Promotes Peaceful Islam", *IslamOnline*, 27 April 2006, http://www.islamonline.net/ English/News/2006-04/27/article02.shtml, viewed 16 October

2006; Daniel J. Nadler, "Muslim Tolerance Post 9/11, Discourse or Dictation?", *The Harvard Salient*, 15 September 2006.

1079   Dr Douglas E. Streusand , LTC Harry D. Tunnell IV, "Choosing Words Carefully: Language to Help Fight Islamic Terrorism", US National Defense University, Center for Strategic Communications, May 23 2006, http://www.ndu.edu/csc/docs/Choosing%20Words%20Carefully--language%20to%20Help%20Fight%20Islamic%20Terrorism%2024%20May%2006.pdf, viewed 3 September 2006.

1080   Robert D. Crane, *Hirabah versus Jihad* Islamic Research Foundation Inc. (2006) http://www.irfi.org/articles/articles_301_350/hirabah_versus_jihad.htm, viewed 22 February 2007; *Haraba* and *hirabah* are alterantive transliterations of the Arabic.

1081   Youssef H. Aboul-Enein and Sherifa Zuhur, "Islamic Rulings on Warfare".

1082   Eric Watkins, "Yemen's Innovative Approach to the War on Terror", *Terrorism Monitor*, Vol. 3, Issue 4, 24 February 2005.

1083   A radical Yemeni Sunni Islamist *jihadi* group linked to al-Qaeda

1084   A Yemeni Zaydi radical group that has fought the regime. The Zaydis are the "fiver" Shi'a (in contrast to the majority "twelver" Shi'a) indigenous to Yemen.

1085   Michael Taarnby, "Yemen's Committee for Dialogue: Can Jihadists Return to Society?", Terrorism Monitor, Vol. 3, Issue 14, 15 July 2005.

1086   Eric Watkins, "Yemen's Innovative Approach to the War on Terror", *Terrorism Monitor*, Vol. 3, Issue 4, 24 February 2005.

1087   Y. Yehoshua, " Reeducation of Extremists in Saudi Arabia ", *MEMRI*, Inquiry and Analysis Series, No. 260, 18 January 2006.

1088   Sun Tzŭ, *The Art of War*, with foreword by James Clavell (London: Hodder and Stoughton, 1981), p. 26.

1089   Kaegi, *Byzantium and the Early Islamic Conquests*, p. 274.

1090   Reported by Judith Mendelsohn Rood, "Why and How Should Christian Students Study World Religions?" in *CCCU Advance* (Spring 2003).

1091 *Remarks by the President to the National Endowment for Democracy*, Ronald Reagan Building and International Trade Center, Washington D.C., 6 October 2005 http://www.ned.org/events/oct0605-Bush.html, viewed 7 March 2007.

1092 For example, Dr Tawfik Hamid's *The Roots of Jihad* (USA: Top Executive Media, 2005).

1093 I am indebted to Daniel Pipes for his analysis pinpointing these four areas (understanding the enemy's motives, defining war goals, defining the enemy, defining the allies) in "Know Thy Terrorists", *New York Post*, 19 November 2002.

1094 William McCants (ed.) and Jarret Brachman, *Militant Ideology Atlas* (New York: Combating Terrorism Center, US Military Academy, 2007).

1095 Speaking at the Royal United Services Institute, UK, 21 November 2002

1096 Sebnem Arsu, "World Leaders Plan for Resolving East-West Rift", *The New York Times*, 14 November 2006.

1097 *NATO: An Alliance for Freedom: How to transform the Atlantic Alliance to effectively defend our freedom and democracies*, a report by Fundación para el Análisis y los Estudios Sociales (president of FAES, José María Aznar), 20 October 2005, p. 15.

1098 *NATO: An Alliance for Freedom: How to transform the Atlantic Alliance to effectively defend our freedom and democracies*, p. 8.

1099 *NATO: An Alliance for Freedom: How to transform the Atlantic Alliance to effectively defend our freedom and democracies*, p. 29 emphasis added.

1100 al-Asi, "Qur'anic Teaching on the Justification for Jihad and Qital", p. 7.

1101 Muhammad Taqi-ud-Din Al-Hilali and Muhammad Muhsin Khan, *Interpretation of the Meanings of the Noble Qur'an in the English Language: A Summarized Version of At-Tabari, Al-Qurtabi, and Ibn Kathir with Comments from Sahih Al-Bukhari*, 15th revised edition (Riyadh: Darussalam Publishers and Distibutors, December 1996).

1102   Bernard Lewis "Roots of Muslim Rage", *The Atlantic Monthly*, Volume 266, No. 3, (September 1990), pp. 47-60.

1103   Hussain Haqqani, "Where's the Muslim Debate?" *The Wall Street Journal*, 22 May 2003.

1104   A selection of extracts from the Saudi press are given in Zakaria, "Now, Saudis See the Enemy".

1105   "The Enemy Within", an editorial in the *Arab News* (an English language Saudi daily) quoted in Zakaria, "Now, Saudis See the Enemy".

1106   Raid Qusti, in the *Arab News*, quoted in Zakaria "Now, Saudis See the Enemy".

1107   Adel Zaid Al-Tarifi, in *Al-Watan*, quoted in Zakaria "Now, Saudis See the Enemy".

1108   This process starts at a young age. The Palestinian Authority Education Ministry set a children's letter-writing competition in which the themes were (1) Lod and Jaffa are Palestinian cities (2) Glorifying violence, hate, death for the sake of Allah – *shahada* (3) Hatred of America. Some of the winning entries were published in the daily newspaper *Al-Quds*, 28 May 2003. English translation in *Palestinian Media Watch Bulletin*, 1 June 2003.

1109   General M. Zia-ul-Haq, Chief of the Army Staff, later President of Pakistan, writing in the foreword to Brigadier S.K. Malik, *The Quranic Concept of War*, Indian edition (New Delhi: Himalayan Books, 1986).

1110   Ferguson, *War and Peace in the World's Religions*, p. 132.

1111   Julian Lindley-French, *British Strategic Leadership: food for thought*, The Shrivenham Papers No. 2 (October 2006), (Shrivenham, UK: The Defence Academy, 2006), p. 17.

1112   Spengler, "Military destiny and madness in Iran", *Asia Times Online*, 6 June 2006.

1113   TV interview for BBC World (screened approximately 23 April 2003).

1114   For example, Eliza Manningham-Buller, the director-general of Britain's MI5, stated in a speech on 17 June 2003 that "Breaking the link between terrorism and religious ideology is difficult", see "MI5 Chief Fears Dirty Bomb is Inevitable", *The Times*, 18 June 2003.

1115   Alongside the other main components of classical *jihad*: the struggle for personal purity, the correcting of wrong and supporting of what is right

1116   Brigadier S.K. Malik, *The Quranic Concept of War*, Indian edition, p. 96.

1117   Excerpts from a speech given by Libyan leader Mu'ammar Al-Qadhafi, aired on Al-Jazeera TV on April 10, 2006, see "Libyan Leader Mu'ammar Al-Qadhafi: Europe and the U.S. Should Agree to Become Islamic or Declare War on the Muslims", MEMRI, TV Monitor Project, Clip No. 1121, 10 April 2006, http://www.MEMRItv.org/Transcript.asp?P1=1121, viewed 22 August 2006.

1118   Frank J. Gaffney and colleagues, *War Footing: 10 Steps America Must Take to Prevail in the War for the Free World*, (Annapolis, Maryland: Naval Institute Press, 2006), pp. 40, 137.

1119   *NATO: An Alliance for Freedom: How to transform the Atlantic Alliance to effectively defend our freedom and democracies*, a report by Fundación para el Análisis y los Estudios Sociales (president of FAES, José María Aznar), 20 October 2005, p. 21.

1120   José María Aznar, "Seven Theses on Today's Terrorism" address at Georgeown University, 21 September 2004, http ://www3. georgetown.edu/president/anzar/inauguraladdress.html, viewed 24 November 2006.

1121   For examples of how psychological warfare has been used see Ron Schleifer *Psychological Warfare in the Intifada: Israeil and Palestinian Media Politics and Military Strategies* (Brighton: Sussex Academic Press, 2006).

1122   Abdeslam M. Maghraoui, *American Foreign Policy and Islamic Renewal*, United States Institute of Peace Special Report 164 (July 2006), p. 9.

1123   Bassam Tibi, *Arab Nationalism: Between Islam and the Nation-State*, 3rd edition (Basingstoke: Macmillan Press Ltd, 1997), pp. 232-233.

1124   For example, as Kennedy records (*The Prophet and the Age of the Caliphates*, p. 35) the Muslim side at the Battle of Badr (624) is known to have consisted of 86 *muhajirun* and 230 *ansar*. The army was not described as a single force of 316 Muslims.

1125   Sicker, *The Islamic World in Ascendency*, p. 9.

1126   Josef Van Ess, *Theologie und Gesellschaft im 2. und 3. Jahrhundert Hidschra. Eine Geschicthe des religiösen Denkens im frühen Islam*, Vol. 1 (Berlin: de Gruyter, 1991-5), p. 17.

1127   The date November 20th 1979 was Muharram 1st 1400 in the Islamic calendar, the first day of a new Islamic century. In Islamic thought the turn of any century is expected to be a time of reformation and religious revival when Islam returns to its original sources. The attack on the mosque in Mecca took place on Muharram 1st itself. This can give rise to eschatological outpouring.

1128   Nathaniel Fick, *One Bullet Away: The Making of a Marine Officer* (Boston: Houghton Mifflin, 2005) quoted in Michael B. Oren Power, *Faith and Fantasy: Amercia in the Middle East 1776 to the present* (New York and London: W.W. Norton & Company, 2007), p. 602.

1129   Answering a question from the audience he was addressing at the Army War College, 27 March 2006 http://www.cbsnews.com/stories/2006/03/27/terror/main1442811.shtml, viewed 4 April 2007.

1130   Quoted in J.M.S. Baljon, *The Reforms and Religious Ideas of Sir Sayyid Ahmad Khan* (Lahore: Shaikh Muhammad Ashraf, 1964), pp. 117-119.

1131   Private gathering attended by the author, London, 29 September 2003.

1132   Rabasa et al., *Building Moderate Muslim Networks*

1133   http://news.bbc.co.uk/1/hi/world/middle_east/3368957.stm, viewed 6 May 2004

Index of *Qu'ran* References

Note: Verse numbers vary slightly between different translations of the Qur'an, so it may be necessary to search in the verses just preceding or just following the verse numbers given here to find the relevant text in any given translation.

Q 2:62	63–64	Q 8:67	152
Q 2:109	63	Q 8:67-9	151
Q 2:114	94	Q 9:4	189
Q 2:177	162	Q 9:5	64, 100, 109,
Q 2:190	99, 119, 357,		167–68, 476
	364, 372	Q 9:7-13	358
Q 2:190-191	64	Q 9:20	65
Q 2:190-193	364	Q 9:23	101–02
Q 2:193 64,	357–58	Q 9:29	65, 100, 358
Q 2:194	182	Q 9:36	364
Q 2:195	199, 325	Q 9:52	360
Q 2:214	359	Q 9:88-89	329
Q 2:216	64, 359	Q 9:123	358
Q 2:251	357	Q 9:193	364, 372
Q 2:256	385	Q 16:91	189
Q 3:28	197	Q 16:106	197
Q 3:64	362	Q 16:125-128	99
Q 3:145	74	Q 16:126	185
Q 3:151	186	Q 17:15	141
Q 3:169	328	Q 21:105	86
Q 4:29	326	Q 22:39	119
Q 4:74	329	Q 24:55	85–86
Q 4:95	65	Q 33:21	47
Q 5:51	175	Q 33:25-26	186
Q 7:128	86	Q 33:50	162
Q 8:12	156, 185–86	Q 40:28	197
Q 8:39	64	Q 47:4	152, 156, 372
Q 8:59-60	65	Q 60:80	362
Q 8:60	122, 182, 186, 426	Q 76:8	185

Index of *Hadith* References

Abu Dawud 14:2478	69
Abu Dawud 14:2526	69–70
Abu Dawud 14:2535	68–69, 329
Abu Dawud 14:2632	67
Abu Dawud 14:2635	1
Ahmad, Musnad 2:50	66
Bukhari 1:24	372
Bukhari 1:121	198–99
Bukhari 1:367	163
Bukhari 2:231:445	326
Bukhari 4:52:73	66
Bukhari 4:52:176	67
Bukhari 4:52:196	67
Bukhari 4:52:261	160–61
Bukhari 4:52:265	67–68
Bukhari 4:52:270	68
Bukhari 4:380	87
Bukhari 6:60:80	69
Bukhari 8:73:72	326
Bukhari 23:37:676	330
Bukhari 54:369	198
Malik, *Muwatta'* 31:1	163–65
Mishkat al-Masabih 18:2	581
Muslim 19:4294	141, 189–90
Muslim 19:4366	68
Muslim 32:6303	198
Muslim 41:6985	205
Al-Tasharraf 1:p.70	193
Tirmidhi 5033	197
Tirmidhi 6284	198

Index

Notes: Names with the prefix 'al-' are listed alphabetically under the next element of the name, e.g. Hasan al-Banna is in the 'B' section of the index, between Bangladesh and Banu an-Nadir:

> Bangladesh 39
> al-Banna, Hasan 89, 280–81
> Banu an-Nadir (Jewish tribe) 480g

Page numbers in **bold** type are for major mentions of people and topics, e.g. in the following example there is most information about Emperor Akbar on pages 264–65:

> Akbar, Emperor 234, 243, **264–65**

Page numbers followed by 'g' are for glossary references, e.g.:

> *ansar* ("helpers") 480g

Abbas I, Shah 252–53

Abbas II, Shah 244

'Abbasid 480g

'Abbasid caliphate 48, 51, 217, 226–27, 228, 271

'Abd al-'Aziz, Shah 114

'Abd al-Mu'min 249

'Abd al-Qader 115

Abd al-Rahman III 251

Abd es-Salam, Kamal Boraiq'a 357–58

Abdel-Rahman, Hamdi 284

'Abduh, Muhammad 377–78, 415

Abdul Hamid II, Sultan 259–60

'Abdul Rahman 'Abdul Khaliq 190

Abdul-Aziz al-Sheikh 410, 473

Abdullah II, King of Jordan 318, 430

Abedi, Mehdi 193

Abizaid, John 405

abrogation (*naskh*) **54**, 63, 413, 486g

Abshar-Abdalla, Ulil 375–76

Abu 'Abd al-Rahman al-Sulami 343

Abu Al-Muntazar 468

Abu Bakr, (first caliph) 145, 149, 177, 179, 215, 219

Abu Gheith, Suleiman 324

Abu Ghreib prison 200

Abu Hanifa 70, 88, 149

Abu Ja'far Muhammad ibn Hasan al-Tusi, *al-Nihaya* 78

Abu Mus'ab al-Suri, *Observations* 306–07

Abu Qatada 468

> *Between Two Methods* 304–05

Abu Yusuf 153

Abu Zahra, Muhammad 125

afa'a (restore) 480g

al-Afghani, Jamal al-Din 377, 388, 442

Afghanistan:

> Al Qa'eda in 293–94
> *jihad* against Soviet Union 116, 279, 338, 434
> Taliban in 278–79
> US support for 434
> US-led Western invasion of 34–35, 117–18

Africa see North Africa; Sub-Saharan Africa; Sudan; West Africa

Africans, black, as slaves 167, 249–50

age, of Muslim populations 29–30

> see also youth

Ahl al-Kitab ("People of the Book") 122, 480g

> see also Christians and Christianity; Jews and Judaism

Ahmad, Khurshid 25–26

Ahmad, Mirza Ghulam 195
Ahmadi 480g
Ahmadinejad, Mahmoud 134–36, 434
Ahmadiyya 195, 438, 480g
Ahmadu Bamba 193
Ahmed, Akbar S. 33
Ahmedinejad, Mahmoud 290
Ahsan, Muhammad 25
'A'isha (wife of Mohammad) 216
Akbar, Emperor 234, 243, **264–65**
Akbar, M.J. 1
Akhtar, Parveen 35
Al-Fayed, Dodi 337
Al-Jama'a al-Islamiyya, in Egypt 283–84
Al-Jihad, Egypt **284–85**, 300–302
Al-Qa'eda 131, 155, 184–85, 231, 274,
   293–99, 319, 339, **352–54**, 400
   deprogramming of members 417
   media support for 468
   recruitment and training 349, 352–54
   and Western response to terrorism 396, 424
Alamut 275, 400–401
Alauddin Shah Bahmani 264
Alexandria Declaration of the Religious Leaders of
   the Holy Land (2002) 208
Alexius I, Comnenus 229
Algeria, civil war in 159–60
Algiers, port of 173–74
Ali, A. Yusuf 151, 325–26
'Ali ibn Abi Talib (fourth caliph) 216, 217, 242,
   272
alienation, and identity loss 32–33
Allah see God (Allah)
Almohads (al-Muwahidun) 244, 251, 276
Almoravids (al-Murabitun) 251, 275–76
Alp Arslan 227, 258
aman (temporary safe-conduct) 480g
America see United States; Western World
American Textbook Council 201–02
al-'Amili, Al-Hurr 132
amir al-mu'minin (prince of the believers)
   480g
'Ammar Ibn Yasir 200
'Amr ibn al-'As 250

analogical reasoning (qiyas) 54, 487g
Anatolia 227, 231
Annan, Kofi 424
al-Ansar (online journal) 298, 350
ansar ("helpers") 480g
Ansar al-Islam (terrorist group), Zarqawi
   Document 458–64
Ansar al-Mahdi ("helpers of the Mahdi") 131
al-Ansari, 'Abd al-Hamid 361
al-Ansari, Seif al-Din 296, 350, 360
Antichrist (Dajjal) 129, 481g
Antioch 229–30
apocalyptic traditions 57–58, 128–31
   see also End-Time; eschatology; Mahdi;
   mahdism
apostasy see ridda; ridda wars; takfir
'aqd ("tie") 480g
Arab Human Development Report 2004 (UN) 31
Arabian Peninsula:
   ethnic cleansing of 68
   Islamic control of 212
   Wahhabi movement in 112
Arabic (language):
   interpretation of 359
   as language of Qur'an 439
   replaced by Turkish 391, 392
Arabs:
   conquest of North Africa 236–37
   and contemporary Islamic reform 439
   and early history of Islam 50, 51, 56, 177,
      214–18, 225
   hostility to non-Shi'as 132
   justification for violence against 72
   reformist anti-terrorism recommendations
      466–78
   violent radical Sunni organisations 311
Arafat, Yasser 117, 143
Armed Islamic Group (GIA) 159–60, 274, 292
Armenia:
   Byzantine 219–20
   impact of jihad in 256–61
armies:
   Byzantine 220–21
   defeat of Islamic 226

Hizbullah militia 318

Ottoman 231, 232

Pakistani 15, 195, 429

state militaries 398–99

see also ghazi; martyrdom; terrorists

"Army of God" 194–95

'asabiyya (tribal loyalties) 213, 218

Asghar Ali Engineer 358

Ash'arites 80, 81

bin al-Ashraf, Ka'b 68, 198

al-Asi, Mohammed 364–65

assassinations **67–68**, 168

Assassins (Isma'ili sect) 275, 324, 329, 400–401, 480g

Assirat al-Moustaqim 348

Association of Muslim Scholars 119

Atatürk, Mustafa Kemal 115–16, 347, **390–91**

bin 'Athamin, Muhammad 473

Atwan, Abdel Beri 36, 468

audiotape transcript, by Bin Laden 450–55

'Auf b. Harith 329

Aurangzeb, Emperor 235, 243, 265

al-Awza'i 72, 149, 169

Ayesha (wife of Muhammad) 75

al-Azdi, Abu Jandal 319

al-Azdi al-Basri, Muhammad 214

al-Azhar University, Cairo 206, 356, 400 480g

Islamic Research Committee 118

al-Aziz, 'Abd al-Qadir bin Abd 309

Aznar, José María 436

'Azzam, Abdullah 122, 124, **286–87**, 295, 307, 309

Baalbek 192

Babur 234, 262, **264**

Badawi, Abdullah Ahmad 386–87

Badawi, Zaki 105–06

Badr, Battle of 151, 154, **168**, 329

Baghdad 226

fall of (2003) 331

Baginda, Abdul Razak 347

al-Baladhuri, Ahmad b. Yahya 214, 247

Balkans 266–68, 268

Bangladesh 39

al-Banna, Hasan 89, 280–81

Banu an-Nadir (Jewish tribe) 480g

Banu Hanifa (Arab tribe) 215, 480g

Banu Qurayza (Jewish tribe) 156, 168–69, 178–79, 480g

Banu Taghlib (Christian Arab tribe) 177, 241–43, 480g

al-Baqir, Abu Ja'far ibn Ali 136

al-Baqir, Muhammad 140

Bar Hebraeus 242–43, 245

Barbarossa, Uruj and Kheir al-Din 173

Barbary corsairs 172–74

Barelwi, Sayyid Ahmad **113–14**, 194

batini (inner or esoteric) 274, 480g

Batrafi, Khaled Muhammad 362

Al-Battar Training Camp (online journal) 353

bay'a (act of swearing allegiance) 334–35, 481g

Baybars, Sultan 401

Bayezid, Sultan 158

Bayoumi, Abdel-Mo'ti 357, 358

beheading 156–58

beliefs:

faith and *taqiyya* 199, 200–201, 205–06

FMC's statement of 384

idha'ah 482g

kufr (unbelief) 484g

Shi'a pacifist beliefs 193

see also political ideology; religious ideology; values

Ben Ali, Zine El-Abidine 27, 394, 395

Bencheikh, Soheib 385

Benedict XVII, Pope 256

Beno, Shamil 349

beyanname-i cihad (declaration of war) 481g

Bhutto, Benazir 427

Bible, Deuteronomy 179

Bilal, Abdul Rahman 182–83

bin Laden, Osama 290, **293–99**

"Bin Laden" audiotape 450–55

on humiliation 332

on *jihad* against America and the West 34, 109, 143, 155

as *jihadi* intellectual 310

on martyr's rewards 329–30

wealth of 405

see also Al-Qa'eda
biradari (group of male kin) 481g
Blair, Tony **17**, 469–70, 472
bombings, organised by Al-Qa'eda 294–95
   see also September 11 attacks; suicide
   bombings
Bourguiba, Habib 393–94
Bouyeri, Mohammed 160
Bridge, Battle of 224
Britain:
   declaration of war on non-Muslims in
     144–45
   foreign policy as cause of Islamic radicalism
     34–35, 434–35
   in India 235
     Islam under British rule 114, 363,
       376–77, 403
     rebellions against 195–96, 278
     repression of terrorism 402–03,
       408–09
   Islamism in 412
   progressive reform in 381, 384
   terrorist groups in 305, 364, 467–68
   terrorist recruitment in 348
Brocquiere, Bertandon de la 267
al-Bukhari, Sahih 66
Bush, George W. 423, 469–70, 472
Buyids 227
   Byzantium (Byzantine Empire) 56–57,
     219–23, 253–56, 481g
   attacked by Turkic tribes 227
   and Crusades 229
   defeated by Muslim Arabs 422
   see also Constantinople; Heraclius
CAIR (Council on American Islamic Relations)
   205–06
caliph (supreme ruler) 288, 481g
   rightly-guided caliphs 179, 213–25,
     487g
caliphate:
   pan-Islamic 280, 294, 297, 304
   succession dispute 216–18
   see also Muslim states; state (Islamic)
Camel, Battle of 216

Cameniates, John 266
Carey, George 208
Carroll, Lewis 432
Casablanca 348
Centron, Marvin 184
CFCM (Council for Muslim Religion) 412–13
Chalcedonian 481g
Chalkis 192
Chartres, Richard 105
Chechnya 349
children:
   enslavement of 152
   executions of 159–60
   as human shield 71
   as non-combatants 146
Choudhary, Anjem 363–64
Christians and Christianity:
   in American culture 39
   anti-Christian radicalism 371
   and anti-Muslim conspiracy theories 41–42
   Byzantine 219, 220, 222, 422
   compared with Islam 21–22, 78
   as *dhimma* 102
   and early Islamic history 19, 49, 50–51,
     177–78
   enslavement of 173
   forced conversion of 241–42
   jihad against 122, 244–48, 362
   martyrs 251
   minorities in Muslim states 370–71
   Qur'anic permissions to attack 100
   reformation of 22, 413
   Western denigration of 176
   see also Crusades; Europe; Jews and
     Judaism; Western World
CIA 279
civilians:
   as combatants 154–55
   and fourth generation warfare 398
   and psychological warfare 319
   as targets 181, 206–07, 473–74
   see also massacres of civilians ;
     non-combatants
clannism 31

Clarke, Charles 35
climate change 39–41
cold war paradigm 431
colonialism:
    Colonial Era 237
    colonial responses to terrorism 402–03
    legacy of Western 18, 25–27
    post-colonial Islamic movements 281–88
    see also imperialism, Islamic
Combating Terrorism Center 309, 424
computer game 354
"Concept Correction Series" 284
"Conflict Forum" think tank 406–07
"conquest, wars of" 218–20
conspiracy theories 41–43, 335–37
Constans II, Emperor 220
Constantinople (Istanbul):
    Ottoman capture of 231–32, 257
    sieges of 225
conversion:
    and declarations of war 140–45
    forced, in Middle Ages 240–44, 251,
        252–53, 256
    in India 234
    in Medina 211–12, 215
    modern Western 334
    as purpose of jihad 68–69, 123–27
    see also Islam; non-Muslims
Copts (Egyptian Christians) 142, 247–48
corsairs 172–74
Council on American Islamic Relations (CAIR)
    205–06
counter-terrorism 320, 435–36
Cragg, Kenneth 103
Crescent International 364
Crone, Patricia 50–51
Crooke, Alastair 406–08
crucifixion 169
Crusades 58, 175, **228–31**, 245
"cultural accommodation" 380–81
cultural values 441
    see also beliefs; political ideology;
        religious ideology; values
Cyprus, impact of jihad in 246–47

Dajjal (the Antichrist) 129, 137, 139, 481g
Damascus 225, 225
Dan Fodio, Usuman **112–13**, 194
Dankowitz, A. 466–78
Dar al-'Ahd (House of Treaty) 363, 481g
Dar al-Harb (House of War) 70, 84, **101–03**,
    191, 481g
    contemporary views on 363, 406
Dar al-Islam (House of Islam) 70, 84, **101–03**,
    188, 363, 481g
    contemporary views on 363, 406
    and globalisation 439–40
Dar al-Shahada (House of Testimony) 363, 481g
Dar al-Sulh (House of Truce) 363, 481g
Davoudi, Parviz 134
da'wa (Islamic mission) 122–27, 369, 481g
el-Dawalibi, Fouad 284
al-Dawalibi, Muhammad Ma'ruf 360
debts, of suicide bombers 328, 410
deception see taqiyya
defensive jihad 99–100, **120–21**, 122, 209,
    238, 293
    contemporary debate on 357, 359–60,
        364, 378, 426–27
Defile, Battle of the 226
Dekmejian, Hrair 37
Delhi 234
Delhi Sultanate 233
democracy:
    as challenge to Islam 80–81
    condemned by Islam 307
    and innocent civilians 154–55
demographic change 29–30, 370, 430
Deobandi 278–79, 481g
dervish 481g
desertification 39
deterrence 221
Deuteronomy (Bible) 179
devshirme (forced levy) 166, 232, 481g
al-Dhahabi, Hasan 286
Al-Dhaydi, Mashari 467
dhimma (the "protected") 20–21, 102, 481g
    defined as the enemy 79
    and ghazwa 213

Hindus as 234

dhimmi (having *dhimma* status) 20–21, 481g

dialogue:

    and language of terrorism 415–16

    as response to terrorism 407–08, 417–19

Diana, Princess 337

Dionysius of Tel Mahre 149

diya (financial compensation) 481g

doctrine *see* beliefs; Islam; Islamism; political

    ideology; religious ideology; source texts; values

dress codes 293, 391, 392

drugs, and terrorist training 350

dynastic cycles, Ibn Khaldun's principle of 78

Earle, Edward Meade 14

economic aid:

    international programmes for 478

    as response to terrorism 404–05

    see also debts; funding; poverty; social

    welfare; socio-economic status

economic strategy, Western 435

education *see* training and education

Egypt:

    Al-Jama'a al-Islamiyya in 283–84

    Al-Jihad in **284–85**, 300–302

    impact of *jihad* in medieval period 247–48

    Islamic *jihad* groups in 291

    Mameluke Sultantate 227, 229

    media support for terrorism 470–71

    Muslim Brotherhood in 280, 403

    progressive reform in 377–78, 387–88

    takfir groups in 291

    Takfir wal-Hijra in 285–86

emigration *see* hijra; *surgun*

Empires *see* Byzantium; colonialism; imperialism

End-Time 40–41, 57, 129, 137–38, 289–90

    see also eschatology; *Mahdi*; *mahdism*

enemy:

    civilians as combatants 154–55

    declaration of war on 140–45

    definitions of 73, 79

    recognition of 422–25

    terrorising of 185–87, 337–38

equality:

    Khariji doctrine of 273

and progressive reform 379, 393–94

Erbakan, Necmettin 347, 392

Erdogan, Recep Tayyip 392

eschatology 129–31, 289

    see also End-Time; *mahdism*

espionage 167–68, 221, 274

Esposito, John L. 328

Esra, Gideon 409

Eurasian tribes, Islamic 58

Europe:

    defence against terrorism 401–02

    Muslim expansion into 103, 430–31

    Muslim minorities in 44, 385

    see also Christians and Christianity; Cru-

    sades; Western World

Eutychius 214

Evans, Arthur John 268

executions 152–53, 156–60

expansionism *see* imperialism

extremism *see* Islamism; terrorism; terrorist

    groups; terrorist motivation; terrorists

Fadlallah, Sayyid Muhammad Husayn 315, 316,

    317–18

al-Fagih, Saad 331, 468

Fahd, King, of Saudi Arabia 333, 404

family planning 395

Fandy, Mamoun 470–72

Faraj, 'Abd al-Salam 108, 130

Faraj, Muhammad 284

al-Faruqi, Isma'il Raji 90–91, 123

Farwa b. 'Amr al-Judhami 240–41

fasad (corruption, immorality) 481g

Fatima (Muhammad's daughter) 216, 274

Fatimid Empire 169, 227

Fatimids 481g

Fatoohi, Louay 357

fatwas 481g

    against heretics 111

    against terrorists 472

    on American military bases 110

fay' 86, **148**, 169, 482g

fi sabil illah (in the way of God) 482g

fida'iyun ("men of sacrifice") 275, 482g

fighters *see* armies; *ghazi*; martyrdom; terrorists

al-Fihri, Habib ibn Maslamah 146
financial restrictions:
    as response to terrorism 404
    see also debts; economic aid; funding
Firestone, Reuven 65–66, 211
Firoz Shah Tughlaq, Sultan 166
fitna (rebellion) 270, 272, 482g
FMC (Free Muslims Coalition) 383–84
fourth generation warfare 398–99, 441
France:
    Islamism in 412–13
    Muslim defeats in 226, 401
    progressive reform in 385
Fredagarius 222
Free Muslims Coalition (FMC) 383–84
freedom, of thought 80–81
Fukuyama, Francis 423
Fuller, Graham E. 29–30
fundamentalism see Islamism
funding:
    of global jihad 400
    restrictions on 435
    for suicide bombings 333
    of terrorist groups 288, 295–96, 317
        financial restrictions as response to 404
        Hizbullah 317
    for training 346
    of Western systems 369
Furrukhsivar 265
Gabrabad 253
Gaul 222
Gazâ (holy war) 482g
Gaza Strip, response to terrorism 409
Genghis Khan 228, 230
genocide 259–60
    see also massacres of civilians
Germany 380
Ghaffari, Hujjat al-Islam Hadi 314
ghanima 148
al-Ghannouchi, Soumaya 37–38
al-Ghannoushi, Rashid 394
Gharavian, Mohsen 184
Al-Gharbawi, Majed 475
Ghayasuddin (Ghiyath al-Din) 263

al-Ghazali 55
ghazi ("one who takes part in a ghazwa") 482g
    Ottoman fighters as 231, 267
Ghaznavids 233
al-ghazw al-fikri (intellectual raid) 35, 482g
ghazwa (inter-tribal raid) 56, **102–03**, 111,
    211–13, 482g
Ghoshah, Abdullah 1, 124
Ghurids 233
GIA (Armed Islamic Group) 159–60, 274,
    292
global jihad 305, 308–09, 399–400
global terrorist networks 295, 311, 399
    see also Al-Qa'eda; terrorism; terrorist
    groups; terrorists
global warming 39–41
globalisation:
    and Dar al-Islam 439–40
    and Islamic identity 33
God (Allah):
    as authority for land ownership 85–86
    duty to, as terrorist motivation 322–28
    non-rationalist (Sunni) view of 80
    protection of God's honour 106–07
    rationalist (mu'tazila) view of 79–80
    and sanctity of mosques 94–95
Granada 227
Greece 266–68
GSPC (Salafi Group for Call and Combat) 292
Gulf War (1990-91) 13, 293, 316, 338
Gus Dur (Abdurrahman Wahid) 389–90
Habib, Kazem 477–78
al-Hadi, Abd 296
hadith 46, 47–49, 482g
    as authority for jihad 66–69, 324, 351–52
    as authority for shari'a 53–54
    as authority for taqiyya 197–99
    denial of, and taqiyya 205
    Maliks' collection of (Al-Muwatta') 149
    promise of martyrs' rewards 329
    ruling on slavery 163–65
    Shi'a apocalyptic in 139
    on spiritual jihad 193
Hajjaj bin Yusuf 233, 252, 261

al-Hakam I, Caliph 158, 158
al-Hakam II, Caliph 251
al-Hakim, Caliph 229
Haleem 358
Halliday, Fred 28–29
Hamas 92–93, 117
Hamdanids 227
Hamidiyye 259–60
Hamidullah, Muhammad 62, 168–69, 179
Hanafi, Hassan 367
Hanafi (Sunni school of *shari'a*) 98, 482g
Hanbali (Sunni school of *shari'a*) 482g
Haqqani, Hussain 427
Haqqani, Jalaluddin 117–18
Haqqania School, Peshawar 347
Haramayn (Mecca and Medina) 84, 482g
harb (war) 482g
Hargey, Taj 203–04
Hariri, Rafiq 317
al-Harra, Battle of 217
Harun al-Rashid 218
Hashim, Ahmed Omar 182
Hassan, (son of Caliph 'Ali) 217
al-Hawali, Safar bin Abdur-Rahman 332
al-Hayat 207, 361, 362
hedaya (guidance) 98, 482g
Hekmatyar, Gulbuddin 117
Heraclius, Emperor 142, 192, 219, 222
heroes, terrorist identification with 333
Hidden Imam 131–32, 482g
Hijaz 84
hijra (emigration) 482g
    Arab, to conquered areas 226
    from British India to Afghanistan 114
    and Islamic resurgence 431
    migrant Muslims in the West 93–96
    model of land ownership 86–88
    post-colonial reformists on 282, 285
    Shi'a teaching on 79
al-Hilali, Abu Ayman 296
al-Hilali, Taqi-ud Din 151, 152, **371–72**, 424
al-Hilli, Muhaqiq 79
Hilmi, Tariq 38–39
Hindus and Hinduism 82, 234, 235, 243,
    261–66
history of Islam *see* Islamic history
Hizb ut-Tahrir 94, **287–88**, 336, 311
Hizbullah 155
    computer game 354
    in Iran 313–14, 318
    in Lebanon 314–19
Hojjatieh 134
Holy Land, Crusades in 228–31, 245
    see also Palestine; Syria
holy war 52, 399
honour:
    protection of God's 106–07
    shame and humiliation 33–34, 331–32
Hossein, Sultan 253
hostage-taking 154–56
House of Islam *see* Dar al-Islam
House of War *see* Dar al-Harb
hubus (or waqf) 482g
hudna (temporary peace) 188, 482g
human rights:
    denial of terrorists' 404
    and Islamic values 381, 384
    violations of 204–05, 320, 371
human shields 71, 172
humiliation, honour and shame 33–34, 331–32
Humud al-Hittar, Abdulhameed 417, 418
Huntington, Samuel 103, 406, 422–23
hurub al-ridda (wars of apostasy) 215–16, 482g
Husain, Moulvi Abu Said Mohammed 363
Hussein, Saddam 118, 312, **331**, 333, 334
Hussein ibn 'Ali 132, 157, 217, 271
al-Husseini, Haj Amin 116
Huzaifah 168
IAEA (International Atomic Energy Agency) 183
'Ibadis 272, 482g
Ibn Abidin 63
Ibn Battuta 263–64
Ibn Baz, Abdel-Aziz (*also known as* 'Abdul 'Aziz
bin 'Abdullah Ibn Baz) **13**, **110**, **190**, 309, 361,
    371, 473
Ibn Hajar al-'Asqalani 309
Ibn Hudayl 179–80
Ibn Kathir 309

Ibn Khaldun 110, 213, 429
 History of the Berbers 248–49
 The Muqaddima 78
Ibn Naqib al-Misri, 'Umdat al-Salik 77–78, 98,
 153
Ibn al-Qayyim al-Jawziyya 309
Ibn Rushd (Averroes) 55, **75–76**, 88, 141
 Bidayat al-Mujtahid wa Nihayat al-Muqtasid
 75–76
Ibn Sa'd 214
Ibn Taymiyya 76–77, 86, 126, 198–99, 309,
 277
Ibn Tumart 276
Ibn 'Uthaymeen 361, 435
Ibn al-Zubair, 'Abdullah 217, 218
Ibrahim 218
Ibrahim, Sa'ad Al-Din 388
identity:
 Arab, and early development of Islam 50–51
 of Islam as separate religion 51, 437–38
 loss of, and alienation 32–33
 umma as core identity 36–37
ideologies see beliefs; Islam; Islamism;
 political ideology; religious ideology; source
 texts; values
idha'ah (propagation of beliefs) 482g
IIF (International Islamic Front) 170
IIIT (International Institute of Islamic Thought)
 24, 369
Ijma' (consensus) 54, 483g
ijtihad 54–55, 483g
 progressive reform interpretation of 375,
 377, 385, 387–88
 renewal of 83, 413–15
 suppression of 80–81
Ikhwan (brethren) 483g
ikrahiyya (enforced taqiyya) 201, 483g
Ilyas, Mawlana Muhammad 279
'Imad al-Din Zangi 245
imam (Shi'a term for supreme ruler) 483g
"The Impacts of Climate Change on the Islamic
 World" (synopsis of seminar) 40
imperialism, Islamic 12–13, 14, **103–06**, 120,
 165–67, **218–20**

Arab settlement in conquered areas 226
Byzantine Empire overthrown 220–23
and Colonial Era 237
conquests in Indian subcontinent 147–48,
 166, **233–35**, 243, **261–66**
and the Crusades 228–31
early Islamic Empire, growth and decline
 225–27
the Ottoman Empire 228, **231–33**
rebellion and internal dissension 214–15
under "rightly-guided" caliphs 213–15
the Sassanid collapse 224–25
in South East Asia 235–36
in Sub-Saharan Africa 236–37
Turks and Mongols 227–28
twentieth century independence 238
ultimate goal of 17
"wars of conquest" 218–20
see also colonialism
India:
 as Dar al-Islam 363
 Islamic conquests and jihad in 147–48,
 166, **233–35**
 forced conversions 243
 plundering and massacres of
 non-Muslims 261–66
 Sufi reform under Barelwi 113–14
 Sunni revival under Sirhindi 81–82
 Islamic sects in 278, 279
 Muslim defeats in 226
 Parsees (Zoroastrians) in 252
 progressive reform in 376–77
 rebellions against British rule 195–96, 278
 Timurlane's campaigns in 228, 234, 263
 violent radical Sunni organisations in 311
Indonesia:
 Laskar jihad 143–44
 progressive reform in 389–90, 439
 recruitment and training in 348, 350–52
 secular democracy in 236
Institute of Peace 437
insurgency doctrine 297
intellectual hypocrisy 16, 469–70
intellectual invasion (al-ghazw al-fikri) 35, 482g

intelligence *see* espionage

Inter-Services Intelligence (ISI) (Pakistan) 279

International Atomic Energy Agency (IAEA) 183

International Institute of Islamic Thought (IIIT) 24, 369

International Islamic Front (IIF) 170

international law 238, 362–64, 364, 368

international programmes 478

internet:
    Islamic websites 200, 298, 302
    online books and journals 298, 307
    as platform for war 399
    used for recruitment 349, 468–69
    see also names of online journals, e.g.
      Sawtal-Jihad

intifada ("a throwing off") 483g

intizar (waiting for the Hidden Imam) 290, 483g

Iran:
    American embassy siege (1979–81) 402
    Hizbullah in 313–14, 318
      Iranian support for 317
    mahdist policies 134–35, 271
    nuclear programme 183–84
    Zoroastrians in 252, 253

Iran–Iraq War (1980–88) 38, 312, 440

Iraq:
    conflict in, and Salafi-Jihad thinking 299
    Hizb al-da'wa al-Islamiyya in 312–13, 317–18
    US strategies in 407
    US-led Western invasion of 34–35, 118–19, 185, 208, 296, 320
    Zarqawi Document on *jihad* in 458–64

'Isa (Jesus) 483g
    see also Jesus

ISI (Inter-Services Intelligence) (Pakistan) 279

Islam:
    belief, faith and *taqiyya* 199, 200–201, 205–06
    bias in contemporary accounts of 201–02
    contemporary radicalisation of 371–73
    contemporary terrorist ideologies 290–91, 292–93, 294, 297, 299–311
    and conversion by violence 256

deviation from as cause of weakness 19

doctrine of war 53–58, 213, 356–59, 425–28

extremism and moderation in 16–17, 430

Islamic conquests and expansion *see* imperialism; rightly-guided caliphs

Islamisation of North Africa 236–37

meaning of 46–47

missionary work *see da'wa*

modern trends in (table) 447

networks of radical Islam (table) 448

reform of 413–15, 425–28, 431–32, 436–40, 442–44

reformist ideologies 280–88

religious authorities and terrorism 474–76

traditional divisions in (table) 446

values *see umma*

world views of 80–81

see also conversion; *jihad*; Muhammad;
    Muslims; progressive reformers; Qur'an;
    secularism; source texts

Islam Hadhari (progressive Islam) 386–87

Islam Online website 200

Islam and Reform Workshop 387–88

Islamic Foundation, Leicester 203–04

Islamic history:
    early history 19, 46–58
    history of revivals 111–15
    and progressive reform interpretations 380, 381–82
    as terrorist motivation 332–33
    textbooks on 201–02, 205–06
    see also source texts

Islamic Research Committee, al-Azhar University 118

Islamic sects and movements:
    bin Laden and Al-Qa'eda 293–99
    contemporary movements 288–92
    early sects 270–76
    later reform movements 276–81
    post-colonial period 281–88
    Salafi-Jihad groups 292–93
    Salafi-Jihadi thinkers and writings 299–311
    use of psychological warfare 319–20

violent radical Sunni organisations 311
   see also terrorist groups; see also names of
      sects and movements, e.g. Isma'ilis
Islamisation 369
   of North Africa 236–37
   see also conversion; da'wa
Islamism ("Islamic fundamentalism") **15–20**, 46,
   280, 483g
      empowerment of, as response to terrorism
         411–13
      ideological threat of 434–35, 468
      and progressive reform 375, 382, 383–84,
         386, 388
      as threat to Islamic societies 440
Islamiyah, Jemaah 350
Isma'ilis (Shi'a sect) 274–75, 483g
Israel:
      civilians as targets 181, 207, 473
      and End-Time discourse 129
      Hizbullah attacks on 316, 317, 318
      jihad against 90, 116–17, 207–09, 365
      response to terrorism 409
      see also Jews and Judaism; Palestine
Israeli–Palestinian conflict 31–32, 365
   see also Palestine
istishad (martyrdom) 483g
Italy, condemnation of suicide bombing 411
Ja'afari, Ibrahim 313
Jabiya-Yarmuk, Battle of 219
Ja'far as-Sadiq (sixth Imam) 199, 274
Jahan, Shah 243
Jahangir 235
jahiliyya 107–08, **282–83**, 285–86,
   308, 483g
Jalal-ud-Din of Bengal 243
al-Jama'a al-Islamiyya 274, 291
jama'a (group, organisation) 95, 483g
Jama'at-i Islami 281, 412
Jamiat Ulema-e-Islam 279
Jammaat ud-Daawa 183
Jan, Abid Ullah 26, 31–32
Janissaries (Yenicheri) 232, 483g
jati (Hindu subcaste) 483g
Al-Jazeerah 468

Jemaah Islamiyah 348
Jerusalem:
      first qibla facing towards 51
      importance of in Muslim world 31–32
      jihad for liberation of 117
      and mahdi apocalyptic 138–39
Jesus 137, 139, 129, 138, 139
      known as 'Isa 483g
Jews and Judaism:
      anti-Jewish radicalism 371
      and anti-Muslim conspiracy theories 41–42
      Banu Qurayza 156, 168–69, 178–79, 480g
      compared with Islam 78
      as dhimma 102
      and early Islamic history 19, 49, 50–51, 61
      forced conversion of 244, 251
      hadith teachings on 67
      jihad against 122, 205, 249, 251, 362
         in Israel and Palestine 90, 116–17,
            207–09, 365
      Khaibar taken by Muslims 87, 162–63
      as oppressors of Islam 18–19
      peace treaties with 190
      and pre-Islamic eschatology 128
      Qur'anic permissions to attack 100
      see also Christians and Christianity; Israel
Al-Jihad 274, 291
jihad:
      Al-Qa'eda's goals for 297–98
      authority to declare jihad 143
      classical theory of 14–15, 98–101, 181
         contemporary debates on 356–59
      concepts and interpretations of 13, 51–53,
         60–61, 120–27, 356–58
         global terrorist ideologies 299–311
         jihad theology in hadith 66
         jihad theology in Qur'an 65–66
         reformist ideologies 280, 281, 282,
            286–87
      definitions and meaning of 78, 98, 359,
         361, 484g
         global jihad 305, 308–09, 399–400
      as a duty **108–11**, 118–19, 120, **360**
      as End-Time struggle 131

hadithic theology of 66
and Islamic imperialism 103–06
and Islamic revivals 111–15
justifications for 21, 76–77, 83
    "Bin Laden" audiotape 450–55
    contemporary debates on 357–58,
      359–62
Khariji theology of 271, 273, 274
modern adaptations of 180–85, 211,
    230–31, 305, **368–73**
    failure of 306–07
    new trends 362–68
    non-violent forms of 430–31
    progressive reformers views of 378,
      380, 382, 387, 388
motives for and objectives of 20, 106–08,
    121–22, 146–48
    apostates and heretics 111, 112,
      121
    slavery 166–67
as non-violent spiritual struggle 193, 279,
    343, 359
Ottoman conquests as 231–33
Qur'anic theology of 63–66, 104
and retrieval of sacred land 89–90
see also conversion; defensive *jihad*; offensive
    jihad; terrorist motivation; violence; war;
    see also names of countries, e.g. Spain
jihad al-dafa'ah (defensive jihad) 120, 484g
    see also defensive *jihad*
jihad almubadahah (aggressive jihad) 120, 484g
jihad groups 290–91
jihad warriors, rewards of 74
jihad-e-akbar (greater *jihad*) 193, 484g
jihad-e-asghar (lesser *jihad*) 193, 484g
jihadi movements:
    contemporary 310–11
    historical 112–15
    see also Islamic sects and movements;
    Salafi-Jihadi
jizya (poll tax) 100, 102, 177, 247, 484g
John the Baptist 342
John Bar Penkaye 222
John of Nikiou 222, 248

Jordan, *takfir* groups in 291–92
July 2005 London bombings 35, 44
just war, Byzantine concept of 57
ka'ba ("cube") 133, 139, 484g
Kaegi 192, 219, 240, 241, 422, 401
kaffara (atonement) 484g
kafir (infidel) 81–82, 484g
Kalb tribe 217, 218
Kaloyeridis, Konstantinos 260–61
Kandhalvi 168
kapikullari 232
Karbala, Battle of 132, 157, 217
Kemalism 391–92
Kenya 347
Kepel, Gilles 120
Khadduri, Majid 1, 84, 85, 110
Khadija Islamic Institute, Nairobi 347
Khaled, Hassan 124
Khalid Ibn al-Walid 147, 156–57, 215
Khalid al-Shahrazuri 194
Khalil, Sa'ad Allah 474
Khamenei, Ayatollah Ali 38, 183
Khan, Abdul Ghaffar 195, 403
Khan, Muhammad Muhsin 151, 152, **371–72**,
    424
Khan, Muqtedar 204–05
Khan, Sir Sayyid Ahmad 357, 363, **376–77**,
    415, 442
khandaq (trench) 484g
kharaj tax 85, 88
Kharijis ("seceders") 153, 216–17, **271–74**,
    324, 400, 484g
    as terrorist face of Islam 411, 424, **441**
Kharofa, Ala' Eddin 364, 367–68
Khashoggi, Jamal Ahmad 472–73
al-Khattab, Hassan 131
khawfiyya (precautionary *taqiyya*) 201, 484g
Khilafat movement 484g
Khomeini, Ayatollah 26, 133, 143, 238, 253,
    312, 336–37
Khomeini, Ayatollah Ruhollah 41–42, 253, 313,
    315
Khudai Khidmatgaran ("Servants of God") 195,
    484g

Khusrau II 224, 225
Khwaja, Maruf 33
kidnapping 154–56
kitmaniyya (arcane *taqiyya*) 201, 484g
Kompas (newspaper) 376
Koran *see* Qur'an
Kosovo, Battle of 231
Kufa **139**, 157
al-Kufi, Abu Muhammad Amad b. 214
kufr (unbelief) 484g
Kuran, Timur 27–28
Kurkjian, Vahan M. 257–59
Laden, Osama bin *see* bin Laden, Osama
Lakhmid kingdom 225
land:
    contemporary teachings on 89–91
    division of conquered land 76, **85**
    and early Islamic expansion 88–89, 102–03
    the *hijra* model of ownership 86–88
    Muslim ownership of 85–86
    in Palestine 91–93
    sacralising of in the West 93–96
    see also property; sacred space
language:
    and definition of "the enemy" 423
    and Islamic reform 443
    of radicalism 412, 415–17
    translations of Qu'ran 426
    see also Arabic; *taqiyya*
Laskar Jihad 143–44
law schools (Islamic) 53, 287
    see also international law; moral law;
      shari'a
Lebanon:
    Hizbullah in 314–19
    Islamic *jihad* groups 291
left (political), and Muslim radicalism 16–17,
    28–29, 175–76, 400, 408
Legenhausen, Gary 193
legislation *see* international law; law schools;
    moral law; *shari'a*
legitimacy:
    of Muslim regimes 37–38
    of "the forbidden" in acts of war 79

Levant, Islamic *jihad* groups 291
Lewis, Bernard 402
liberal reform *see* progressive reformers; reform
liberation struggle, *jihad* as 365
Libya, Sanusiyya order 114–15, 194
Livingstone, Ken 472
loot 74, **146–49**, 172
"loving death"/ "loving to be killed" 143
madrassa (Islamic religious school) 346–47,
    484g
Madrid train bombings 187
Maghreb 275, 276
mahdaviat 134
Mahdi, Ibrahim 106
mahdi (End Time deliverer) 484g
    Ahmedinejad's belief in 134–35, 290
    bin Laden as 290
    characteristics of 135–36
    Hidden Imam as 131–32
    Muhammad Ahmad ibn Abdallah as 114,
      128, 277
    Shukri Mustafa as 286
    twelfth Imam as 133, 135, 193
mahdism 128, 130–31
    Almohad *mahdism* 276
    Faraj's teaching on 284
    Isma'ili *mahdism* 274–75
    Shi'a *mahdism* **131–36**, 143, 271
    Shi'a and Sunni compared 138–39
    Sunni *mahdism* 137–38
    Wahhabi *mahdism* 277
Mahmassani, Sobhi 356, 364
Mahmud of Ghazni 233, 243, 262
Mahmud Ghuri 233, 262
Mahmud Shaltut, (Sheikh of Al-Azhar) 238
Majalla (Ottoman Civil Code) 484–85g
majlis al-shura (consultative council) 295, 485g
Maktab al-Khidmat (Afghan Service Bureau)
    286–87, 295
Malay people 235–36
Malaysia:
    Organisation of the Islamic Conference,
      10th Summit 18
    progressive reform in 385–87

terrorist recruitment in 347
Malik, *Al-Muwatta'* (*The Way Made Smooth*)
  149, 163–65
Malik, Aftab 34, 42
Malik, Brigadier S.K. 14–15, 62–63, 185–86,
  211
Maliki (Sunni school of *shari'a*) 141, 275, 485g
Mamelukes 227, 229
manakh (inter-tribal conflict) 485g
manic 56
mansabdars (military-type ranking) 234, 485g
mansukh 485g
Mansur, Salim 30
Manuel II, Emperor 256
Manzikert, Battle of 227, 229
maqam (*Maqam Ibrahim*) 485g
al-Maqdisi, Abu Mohammad 307–09, 310
Al-Marghinani, Burhan al-Din 146
  Hedaya 74–75
marginalisation, of Muslim youth 32–33
Marighella, Carlos 339
Marj Rahit, Battle of 218
Martel, Charles 226
martyrdom:
  Christian 251
  Islamic 271, 275, 280, **341–43**, 366
    istishad 483g
    justification for 361
    publication of martyrs' names 456–57
    recruitment for 348–49
    suicide killings as 208, 325–28, 333,
      362
    suicide killings condemned by Islamic
      leaders 410–11
  see also Paradise; suicide; suicide bombings
Martyrs of Cordoba 251
Marwan II 218
Al-Masaa (newspaper), editorial 456–57
masjid (mosque) 95, 485g
bin Maslama, Muhammad 198
Masood, Ehsan 34, 375, **384–85**
massacres of civilians:
  in Armenia 259–61
  of Banu Qurayza 156, 178–79

in Byzantium 253–55
in Egypt 248
in India 263–64, 265–68
in Palestine and Syria 244–46
Matta, Juraij bin (Muqawqas) 142
Maurice, *Strategikon* 221
al-Mawardi, Abu'l-Hasan 85, 141, 179
  Al-Ahkam al-Sultaniyya 73–74
Mawdudi, Abu'l A'la 17, 152, 281, 365–66
Mawlawi, Faysal 110
Mayer, Elizabeth 362–63, 365
MCB (Muslim Council of Great Britain) 412, 442
Mecca 485g
  attack on Holy Mosque 440
  in early history of Islam 50
  and *mahdi* apocalyptic 137
Meccan message 378, 379, 413
media:
  apocalyptic material in 129, 130–31
  "Bin Laden" audiotape 450–55
  condemnation of suicide killings 411
  support for Islamic reform 427–28
  support for terrorism 468, 469–71
  use of 200, 203–06, 293, 298
    for global *jihad* 399, 400, 430
    for psychological warfare 319
    for training 354
Medina 485g
  Banu Qurayza in 156, 168–69, 178–79
  early Muslim community in 211–12, 215
  looting of 148–49
  Mohammad's migration to 61, 91
Medinan teaching 378–79, 413
Mehmet II, Sultan 149, 254
Melitene (Malatya) 191
Mernissi, Fatema 80–81
Mesopotamia, Sassanid 219, 224
Michael VII, Emperor 229
Michael the Syrian 222, 245–46
Middle East:
  colonial plan for 25
  demographics of 29–31
  global *jihad* in 300
  peace process in 208–09

see also Israel; Palestine

migration:

    of Arab tribes 225

    Zoroastrian, to India 252

    see also hijra; surgun

militants see terrorist groups; terrorist motivation;
    terrorists

military history, lessons of 62–63

military strategy:

    Byzantine 221

    Islamic 62–63, 296, 297–98, 303–04

    terrorist 396–400, 433–34, 460–64

    Western 435–36, 440

    see also war

military training manuals 350–53

militia see armies; ghazi

missionary work (da'wa) 122–27, 369, 481g

modernisation:

    and Islamic identity loss 32–33, 293

    modern adaptations of jihad 180–85, 211,
        230–31, 305, **368–73**

    modern trends in Islam (table) 447

    modern warfare types 397–400, 441

    see also progressive reformers; secularism

Mohamad, Mahathir 18–19, 181, 337, 434

Moinuddin, Hasan 364

Mongols 58, 228

    see also Mughal; Mughal Empire

Monophysite 485g

Monothelete heresy 222, 485g

moral law 380

    and banning of suicide bombings 472–74

mosques:

    attack on Meccan Holy Mosque 440

    as centres of terrorist activities 471

    role in Muslim communities 94–95, 96

motivation see martyrdom; Paradise; terrorist
    motivation

movements see Islamic sects and movements

Mu'askar al-Battar (online journal) 155, 298

Mu'awiyya ibn Abi Sufyan:

    founds Umayyad caliphate 132, 216, 217,
        218

    as governor of Syria 146–47, 157, 244–45,

        246, 247

Mubarak, Hosni 283

mudarati (symbiotic taqiyya) 201, 485g

mufassala kamila 285

Mughal Empire **234–35**

Mughal ("Mongol") 485g

Mughniyeh, 'Imad 315

al-Muhajiroun 144–45

muhajirun 485g

Muhammad:

    attitude to violence and jihad **61–63**,
        61–63, 156, 160–61, **210–13**, 323

    and conversion of non-Muslims 141–43

    and da'wa 123, 124

    ethnic cleansing of Arabian Peninsula 68

    and ethnic cleansing of Arabian Peninsula 68

    in history of Islam 46, 49

    land conquests of 86–87

    permits slavery 162–63

    and rules of jihad 177

    on spiritual jihad 193

    and taqiyya 198

    use of espionage and propaganda 168–69

Muhammad, Omar Bakri 145

Muhammad Ahmad ibn 'Abdallah (mahdi in
    Sudan) 114, 128

Muhammad ibn 'Abdallah al-Qahtani
    (Saudi mahdi) 130, 277

Muhammad ibn 'Ali al-Sanusi 115–16

Muhammad ibn Ismail 274

Muhtashimi, 'Ali Akbar 315

Muhyi al-Din, Sidi 115

Muir, William 179

mujahid 486g

muqaddas (holy) 486g

al-Muqrin, Abu Hajir 'Abd al-'Aziz 155, 296, 298

Muqtada al-Sadr 313

Murad I 232

Murad II 232

Murad, Khurram 124

murid ("one who desires") 486g

Muridayya 193, 403

Muridism 486g

Al-Musa'ari, Muhammad 468

Musaylima 215

Musharraf, Pervez 405

al-Mushawwah, Khaled 418–19

mushrikun ("associationists") 121, 486g

  see also polytheists

Muslim, Sahih 66

Muslim Brotherhood 125–26, **280–81**, 311, 403, 412, 434

Muslim clerics:

  attitude to terrorism 410–11, 474–76

  counselling programmes 417–18

Muslim Council of Great Britain (MCB) 412, 442

Muslim states:

  authoritarian nature of 30–31

  da'wa in 123

  establishment of Islamic caliphate in 280, 294

  Islamism in 15

  jihad against 337–38

  non-Muslim minorities in 370–71

  poverty of 27–29

  progressive reform in 375–76, 390–93

  repression of terrorism 403–04

  secularism in 390–95

  illegitimacy of 37–38

  Shi'a influence in Sunni Arab states 318–19

  terrorists' aims for 406

  weaknesses of 24–25

  see also state (Islamic); *see also names of countries, e.g.* Iraq

Muslim World League 411

Muslims:

  denunciation of terrorism and suicide bombings 410–11, 471–74, 476–77

  friction between 95–96

  justification for violence against 71–72, 111, 112, 337–38

  as minorities

  in Europe 44, 385

  in South-East Asia 236, 370

  moderate, and terrorism 401, 408, 416, 419–20

  perceived oppression of 17–19

  resentment of West 440–44

  see also Islam; Khariji; non-Muslims; Shi'a; Sufism; Sunni

Mustafa, Shukri 130–31, 285–86

mu'tazila 79–80, 377

Mu'tazilites ("withdrawers") 486g

Al-Muwatta' (The Way Made Smooth) (Malik) 149, 163–65

Mzabis 272, 486g

al-Nabhani, Taqi al-Din 287, 336, 287

Nadwi, Syed Abul Hasan Ali 36

Nageh, Ibrahim 284

al-Nahda movement 394

Nahrawan, Battle of 217, 272

Naji, Abu Bakr, *The Management of Barbarism* 302–04

Al-Najoun min al-Nar 291

Naqshbandiyya (Sufi order) 81, **194**, 486g

Nasif, Mansur Ali 198

nasikh 486g

naskh (abrogation) **54**, 63, 413, 486g

nationalised Islam 390–92, 393

NATO 424–25, 435–36

naval warfare 171–74

navies, Byzantine 221

networks *see* global terrorist networks; terrorist groups

newspapers:

  American 427, 469–70

  Saudi 427–28

Nicephorus 214

al-Nida (online journal) 298

Nihavand, Battle of 219

non-combatants 145–46

  terrorist actions against 323–24

  see also civilians; massacres of non-combatants

non-Muslims:

  alliances with 13–14, 174–76

  and classical theory of *jihad* 98–99, 100–101, 361

  as the enemy 73

  executions of 156–60

  hadith teachings on 67–68

  hostage-taking and kidnapping of 154–56

and Islamic reform 440–42
justification for violence against 71–72, 83,
   103
knowledge of Islam 422–25
minorities in Muslim states 370–71
occupation of Muslim land, seizure of land
   from 84–85, 86, 87–91
as prisoners of war 75–76, 77, **151–54**
rebellions of 214–16
safe conduct (*aman*) agreements 191
and sources of doctrine of war 56–58
and *taqiyya* 197, 199–200
see also Christians and Christianity;
   conversion; Hindus and Hinduism; Jews
   and Judaism; paganism; Western World
North Africa:
   Arab conquest of 236–37
   Fatimids in 227
   impact of *jihad* in medieval period 248–49
   jihad against French 115
NPT (Nuclear Proliferation Treaty) 183
Nubia 250
Nuclear Proliferation Treaty (NPT) 183
nuclear weapons 135, 434
O'Brien, Mike 424, 441
offensive *jihad* 21, 99–100, **120–21**, 360,
   426–27
OIC (Organisation of the Islamic Conference)
   117, 238, 327, 367, 18, 32
oil, Western dependency on 435
Omar, Rageh 44
Organisation of the Islamic Conference (OIC)
   117, 238, 327, 367, 18, 32
Organisation of the Islamic Jihad 315, 316
Osman 231
Othman, Ali 104
Ottoman Empire 228, 231–33
   devshirme system 166
   jihad of 1914 115–16
   jihad and forced conversions in 244,
      254–56, 259–60, 266–68
   naval power of 171, 172
Ottomans 486g
paganism, eradication of 107–08, 121

Pakistan:
   army
      Ahmadis fight alongside 195
      army motto 429
      and concept of *jihad* 15
   Deobandi and Taliban in 278–79
   intelligence agency (ISI) 279
   jama'a (mosque communities) in 95
   madrassa education in 346–47
   nuclear capacity of 182–83
   progressive reform in 379–80
Palestine 31–32
   impact of *jihad* in medieval period 244–46,
      245
   Islamic claims to 90, 91–93
   jihad against Israel 116–17, 365, 404
   suicide bombings 207–09, 456–57
   terrorist training in 350
   US strategies in 407
   see also Israel
Pancasila 389, 439
Paradise:
   promise of 68–69, 74, 172, **328**
      pig body-parts prevent 408–09
Paris Peace Treaty (1856) 233
Pathans 195
Paz, Reuven 290–91
peace:
   classical doctrine of 15, 188–91, 425
   Middle Eastern peace process 208–09
   non-violent spiritual *jihad* 193, 279, 343,
      359
   pacifism 193–95
   peace processes as response to terrorism
      406–08
   peaceful *jihad* 357
   permanent treaties 191
   Qur'anic teaching on 63–64, 189
   strategies for 433–34
peace treaties 188–91
   historical treaties 191–92, 233
   as response to terrorism 406
Pentagon 320
People of the Book (*Ahl al-Kitab*) 122, 480g

see also Christians and Christianity; Jews and
   Judaism
Pershing, John J. 409
Persia see Safavid Empire; Sassanid Empire;
   Zoroastrianism
Peters, Rudolph 181
Philippines, response to terrorism 409
Philps, Alan 409
pig body-parts, prevent entry to Paradise 408–09
pillar of Islam, jihad as sixth 108–09, 273, 284,
   372
pirates 172–74
global piracy 399
pirs (Sufi "saints") 194, 402, 486g
plunder 74, **146–49**, 172
political ideology:
   as cause of terrorism 424
   of Muslim Brotherhood 403–04
   political left and Muslim radicalism 16–17,
      28–29, 175–76, 400, 408
   see also state (Islamic); state–religion
      separation
politico-economic policies 404–05, 435, 441,
   478
polytheists and polytheism 67, 72, 76, 100,
   121, 308
Pomaks 244
population growth 29–30, 370, 430
post-colonial Islamic movements 281–88
poverty:
   as cause of terrorism and radicalism 27–29,
      345–46
   and climate change 39–41
   international programmes for 478
pre-Islamic traditions 56
press reports:
   by Islamic intellectuals 469–70
   on Islamic reform 427–28
   see also media
prisoners of war 75–76, 77, **151–54**, 172, **185**
   executions of 152–53, 156–60, 178,
      323–24
   Muslims as 200
   Qur'an guidance on 151, 152, 155–56

justification for Muslim prisoners'
   behaviour 402
Probst, Peter 184
progressive reformers 374–76, 420
   'Abduh 377–78
   Arab reformists' recommendations 466–78
   Bencheikh 385
   in Egypt 387–88
   FMC 383–84
   Hadhari 386–87
   Khan 376–77
   liberalism and Islamism 15–17
   Masood 384–85
   Rahman 379–80
   Sardar 381–83
   SIS 385–86
   Taha 378–79
   Taheri 388–89
   Tibi 380–81
   Wahid 389–90
   see also secularism
propaganda 168–71
   terrorist 450–64, 476
property destruction 149–51
   see also land; sacred space
psychological training 353–54
psychological warfare 170–71, 297, **319–20**
psychology, of terrorists 344–45
Puin, Gerd R. 50
Pukhtunwali (Pathan code of honour) 486g
puritanical reform movements see Islamic sects
   and movements
Qadhafi, Colonel Mu'ammar 44, 430–31
Qadisiyya, Battle of 219, 224
al-Qa'eda see Al-Qa'eda (under 'A')
Qahtani tribes 217
al-Qaradhawi, Yusuf 60, 89–90, 104, 119, 120,
   125, 281, 327, 370, 375, 472
bin Qasim, Muhammad 233, **261–62**
al-Qassam, 'Izz al-Din 116
qawm 486g
al-Qayrawani, Ibn Abi Zayd 109, 140–41
Qaysi tribes 217, 218
QDR (Quadrennial Defense Review) 12

qibla 486g
    facing Jerusalem 51
al-Qimni, Sayyid 205–06
qital (fighting) 487g
qiyas (analogical reasoning) 54, 487g
Quadrennial Defense Review (QDR) 12
Quraish (Arab tribe) 487g
Qur'an:
    as authority for *shari'a* 53–54
    authority for terrorism and psywar 185–87,
        322–23, 325–26
    definition of 487g
    and early history of Islam 49–51
    English translation of 371–73, 426
    guidance on prisoners of war 151, 152,
        155–56
    interpretations of
        progressive reformers' 376, 378–79,
            382, 384, 385–86
        rationalist (*mu'tazila*) 79–80
        Sunni 80
    justification for Muslim prisoners' behaviour
        402
    Khariji doctrine based on 273
    and legitimacy of nuclear deterrent 182
    and legitimacy of slavery 161–62
    new religious values based on 476
    promise of martyrs' rewards 328–29
    teaching on alliances with non-Muslims
        174–75
    teachings on *jihad* **14–15**, 52–53, 99,
        351–52
    teachings on land ownership 85–86
    teachings on peace 63–64, 189
    teachings on *taqiyya* 197
    teachings on violence 63–66, 63–66
al-Qureshi, Abu Ubayd 296, 310
Al-Qurtubi 309
Qutb, Sayyid 35–36, 101, 107–08, **281–83**,
    309, 310
radda (return, restore) 487g
radicalism, contemporary 16–20, 371–73
    networks of radical Islam (table) 448
    see also Islamic sects and movements;

Islamism; terrorism
Rafsanjani, Akbar Hashemi 183
Rahman, Fazlur 379–80
al-Rahman, 'Umar Abd 283–84
al-Rajihi, Ahmad Naser 360
Ramadan, Tariq 26–27
Rand Center for Middle East Public Policy 414
Al-Rashed, Abdul Rahman 27, 467, 468
Rasheed, Asra 326
rashidun (rightly guided ones) 487g
rationalism:
    mu'tazila school of theology 79–80
    and progressive reform 376, 377, 425
    and religious reform 437
Rayya, Mahmoud 354
Raze, Mohammad Shahid 204
razzia (ghazwa) 487g
Reagan, Ronald 433, 402
reason see *qiyas*; rationalism
rebellions 213–46
recruitment, terrorist 305, 346–50, 468–69
Red-Shirts (*Khudai Khidmatgaran*) 195, 484g
reform:
    Islamic 413–15, 425–28, 431–32, 436–40
    meanings of 374, 425–26, 437
reform movements see Islamic sects and
    movements; progressive reformers; Tunisia;
    Turkey
Reliance of the Traveller see Ibn Naqib al-Misri
religion see Christians and Christianity; Hindus
    and Hinduism; Islam; Jews and Judaism;
    Muslims; religious act; religious ideology;
    state–religion separation
religion, wars of 429
religious acts:
    executions as sacrifice 159
    implementation of *shari'a* as 95
    jihad as 77, 78, 108, 109
religious ideology:
    Islamic and Christian compared 21–22
    not cause of terrorism 424
    promotion of a new Islamic doctrine 443–44
    and terrorism 405, 408–11, 417–20, 468,
        475–76

Western understanding of 428–31
    see also Islam
revenge 33–34
revisionist theories, of Islam 49–51
ribat (defence of frontiers) 122, 487g
Rida, Rashid 277
ridda (apostasy) 487g
ridda wars 215–16, 271–72
rightly-guided caliphs 179, 213–15, 487g
Robinson, Francis 40
Rukn (corner) 487g
Rumsfeld, Donald 424, 440
Russia:
    jihads against 113, 116, 194
    see also Soviet Union
Sabeans (Sabians) 487g
Sabri, Naji 185
Sacranie, Iqbal 31
sacred space:
    doctrine of 84–85, 287
    land in the West as 93–96
    Palestine as 90
    see also land; property
sadaqa (voluntary alms-giving) 177, 241–42,
    487g
Sadat, Anwar 283, 285, 356
Saddam Hussein 118, 312, **331**, 333, 334
Sadiq, Maulvi Muhammad 402
Sadr, Abol-Hasan Bani 314
al-Sadr, Muhammad Baqir 312, 314–15,
    317–18
Safavid Empire 228, 244, 252–53
Saffar-Harandi, Mohammad-Hossein 134
Safiyya bint Huyayy ibn Akhtab 205–06
sahih (true) 487g
Al-Sakina Campaign 418–19
Saladin, Sultan 229
salaf (pious ancestors) 487g
Salafi Group for Call and Combat (GSPC) 292
Salafi-Jihadi:
    groups 131, 292–93
    thinkers and writings 299–311
Salafiyya (neo-Wahhabism) 277–78, 292–93,
    487g

Al-Salami, Hamad bin Hamad 468
Salman b. Rabi'a al-Bahili 220
Samanids 227
Sanusiyya 114–15, 194, 487g
SAR (Sekolah Agama Rakyat) 347, 487g
Sardar, Ziauddin 381–83
Sarkozy, Nicolas 412
Sassanid Empire 57, 219, **224–25**, 251–52
Sassanid (*or* Sassanian) 487g
Saudi Arabia:
    dialogue as response to terrorism 418–19
    funding of *da'wa* 122, 346, 404
    nuclear programme 184
    report on Islamic reform 427–28
    responses to suicide killings 410, 414
    Salafi-Jihadi scholars 309–10
    Wahhabism in 277, 278, 400
Saut al-Ama (newspaper) 207
Sawtal-Jihad (online journal) 302
Schleifer, S. Abdullah 61, 62
SCIRI 313
Seale, Patrick 407
Sebeos 222, **256–57**
sects *see* Islamic sects and movements; terrorist
    groups; *see also* names of sects and
    movements, e.g. Isma'ilis
secularism:
    of Muslim states 37–38, 58
    and privatisation of religion 14
    and progressive reform 385
    in Tunisia 393–95
    in Turkey 390–93
    Western, as cause of Islamic radicalism
    35–36, 176
Sekolah Agama Rakyat (SAR) 347, 487g
Seljuk Empire 227, 231
September 11 attacks:
    and conspiracy theories 42–43, 337
    justification for 34, 72, 364
    Tantawi's condemnation of 206
    terrorists' economic profiles 28
    see also suicide bombings
Seveners 274, 274
    see also Isma'ilis

al-Shafi'i 88
Shafi'i (Sunni school of *shari'a*) 51, **357**, 487g
Shah, Muhammad Kasim Hindu 264
shahada (testimony) 487g
shahid (martyr, witness) 325, 326, **333**, 488g
Shakir, Ahmad 309
Shaltut, Mahmud 357, 359, 358
Sham'ala (chief of Banu Taghlib) 242–43
shame, humiliation and honour 33–34, 331–32
Shamil, Imam **113**, 194
shari'a 488g
    as authority for *jihad* 70, 140
    authority for slavery 167
    as authority for suicide bombings 207, 208
    compatibility with international law 362–63,
        362–64, 364, 368
    as defining characteristic of Islamic state 20,
        280, 281
    in early Islamic history 47, 51, **53–56**
    justification for *devshirme* 232
    in Muslim territories 93–96
    and progressive reform 378–79, 380, 381,
        382, 384, 393, 394
    reform of as response to terrorism 413–14
    ruling on espionage 169
Shariati, Ali 290
al-Sharif Ahmad 115
Sharif, Nawaz 427
Sharon, Ariel 181
    al-Sharq al-Awsat (newspaper) 203, 362,
        467
Shaybani 146, 150–51, 153, 324–25
    Siyar 70–73, 358
Shi'a:
    anti-Sunnism 82, 131–32
    definition of 488g
    history of 216, 270–71
    influence in Sunni Arab states 318–19
    law schools 53
    law on war and *jihad* 78–79
    mahdism **131–36**, 143, 271
    pacifist beliefs of 193
    Salafi attitudes to 302
    sects and movements 312–19

    and *taqiyya* 196, 199, 200–201
    terrorist activities 460
al-Shinqiti 309
al-Shuaybi, Hammoud al-'Uqla 154–55
shura (consultative assembly) 488g
Al-Siba'i, Hani 468
Siddiqui, Kalim 91, 123
Siffin, Battle of 216
"Signs of the Hour" 137–38
Sikhs 265–66
Simpson, John 405–06
Sina, Ali 101–02
Singapore 348, 350
sira (biography of Muhammad) 488g
Sirhindi, Ghulam Mujaddid 402
Sirhindi, Sheikh Ahmad 81–82
Sisters in Islam (SIS) 385–86
Six Day War (1967) 129
siyar ("motion") 71–72, 488g
slave trade 173, 194, 249–50, 267
slavery 152–53, **161–67**
    slave rebellion 250
social welfare services:
    Hizbullah 316
    in Tunisia 395
socio-economic status, of terrorists 28, 345–46,
348, 405
soldiers *see* armies; *ghazi*; martyrdom; terrorists
Sophronius of Jerusalem 214
source texts:
    early Christian 222
    Islamic 46–51, 214
        progressive reform views of 378,
            381–82, 386, 413–15
    Salafi-Jihadi writings 299–311
    see also hadith; Qur'an; shari'a
South East Asia 235–36
Soviet Union, US support for in Afghanistan 116,
279, 338, 434
    see also Russia
space *see* land; property; sacred space
Spain:
    impact of *jihad* in 250–51
    Islamic 103, 122, 158, 173, 227

Madrid train bombings 187
spiritual *jihad* 193, 279, 343, 359
spoils of war 74, **146–49**, 172
Stalinsky, Steven 404
the state (Islamic):
  apocalyptic ideal of 135
  "closing of the gates of *ijtihad*" 80–81
  draft constitution for 287–88
  as *jahili* 282
  jihad and expansionism 104–06, 285–86
  and the nation-state 367
  sacred land principle 90–91
  shari'a as defining characteristic of 20, 280,
    281
  see also caliphate; *da'wa*; Muslim states;
    secularism; *shari'a*; state–religion
    separation
state–religion separation 374, 376, 381, 383,
  388–89, **391**
  of Western Church 22
Streusand, Douglas E. 415
Sub-Saharan Africa 236–37, 249–50
Subuktigin of Ghazni, Sultan 153, 166
Sudan 114, 167, 194, 378
Sufaat, Yazid 184–85
Sufism 55, 488g
  Naqshbandiyya order 81, **194**,
    486g
  rebellions against Western
    colonialism 193–94
  and spiritual *jihad* 193, 343
Abu-Sufyan 132
Sufyani 132, 138
suicide:
  of Assassins 275, 324, 329
  motivation for 324–28
  in Tamil tradition 330
  training for 350
suicide bombings:
  legitimacy of and martyrdom 325–28, 361,
    362
  Madrid train bombings 187
  motivation for 340
  Muslim denunciation of 472–74, 476–77

  organised by Al-Qa'eda 294–95
  the suicide bomber 340–41
  Tantawi's condemnation of 206, 207
  Tantawi's supports legality of 207–09
  see also September 11 attacks; terrorism;
    terrorist motivation; terrorists
Abu Sulayman 24, 25
Sun Tzŭ 7, 422
sunna ("a trodden path") 46, 488g
Sunni:
  definition of 488g
  history of 216
  and Hizbullah 318–19
  law schools 53, 287
  revival movement in India 81–82
  and *shari'a* 55
  Shi'a anti-Sunnism 82, 131–32
  Sunni *mahdism* 137–38
  terrorist activities 460
  view on martyrdom 411
  violent radical organisations 311
sura 488g
surgun (enforced relocation) 232
Surkhposhan (Red-Shirts) 195, 488g
"Sword Verse" 64, 109, 476
Syria:
  conquest of 219, 244–46
  Islamic *jihad* groups 291
  support for Hisbullah 316, 317
al-Tabari 147, 177, 214
Tablighi Jama'at 279
Taha, Mahmud Muhammad (*also spelt*
  Mahmoud Mohamed) 63, **378–79**
Taha, Rifa'i Ahmed 284
Al-Tahawi, Muna 469
Taher, Muhammad 21, 108, 125–26
Taheri, Amir 37, **388–89**, 476–77
takfir 271, 273–74, 276, 277, 488g
takfir groups 291–92
Takfir wal-Hijra 129–30, **285–86**
al-Tali'a al-Islamiyya 291
Taliban 117–18, 278–79, 296, 347, 488g
tamakkun 285
Tamerlane *see* Timurlane

Tamil Tigers 330

Tamimi, As'ad Bayoud 291

Tamimi, Azzam 204, 366

Tannukh tribe 243

Tantawi, Muhammad Sayyid 118–19, **206–09**, 327, 332

Tanzim Al-Jihad 284

taqiyya ("shield", "guard") 196–201, 488g

    contemporary usage of 201–09, 367–68, 408, 426

    Isma'ili practice of 274

taqlid 55

Tarik ibn Ziyad 250

Ta'rikh-i-Firishta 148

Tariqa-i Muhammadiyya movement 114

al-Tawhid 291

tawhid 276, 308

al-Tawhid wal-Jihad 295

tax *see jizya*; *kharaj*

Tayeh, Raeed 409–10

Al-Tayyeb, Ahmad 327

Teheran, American embassy siege (1979–81) 402

television:

    cheap programming and promotion of terrorism 470–71

    taqiyya and presentation of Islam 203–04, 205, 469–70

    see also media

territory *see* land; property; state

terrorism:

    Barbary corsairs as terrorists 174

    and causes of radicalism

        climate change 39–41

        conspiracy theories 41–43, 335–37

        demographic pressures 29–30

        honour and shame 33–34

        identity loss and alienation 32–33

        Islamic world view 81

        legitimacy of secular Muslim states 37–38

        local political conflicts 30–31

        loyalty to *umma* 36–37

        Palestine 31–32

        poverty 27–29

        US global policy 38–39

        and war on terror 477–78

        weaknesses of Muslim world 24–25

        Western colonial legacy 25–27

        Western military action 34–35

        Western secularism 35–36, 176

    Muslim denunciation of 471–74, 476–77

    psychological methods of 155, 319–20

    Qur'anic justification of 186–87

    religious motivation of 184

    responses to 396–400, 419–20, 433–34

        brutal repression 403–04

        change language of radicalism 415–17

        colonialism 402–03

        denial of human rights 404

        dialogue and deprogramming 417–19

        economic uplift 404–05

        elimination 400–401

        empowerment of Islamism 411–13

        financial restrictions 404

        military defeat 401–02

        peace processes 406–08

        peace treaties 406

        reform of Islam 413–15

        theological undermining 408–11

        yielding to terrorists' demands 405–06

    Tantawi's condemnation of 206–07

    Tantawi's supports legality of 207–09

terrorist groups 288–90, 396–97

    bin Laden and Al-Qa'eda 293–99

    Islamic *jihad* 290–91

    Salafi-Jihadi 292–93

    Shi'a 312–19

    Sunni 311

    Takfir 291–92

terrorist motivation:

    bay'a (allegiance) 334–35

    duty to God 322–28

    Heavenly reward 328–30

    identification with heroes 333

    martyrdom 341–43

    networks of radical Islam (table) 448

    sense of history 332–33

shame and humiliation 331–32
specific grievances 335–39
training 333–34
Western understanding of 423–24
terrorists:
and justification for jihad 21, 52–53
psychology of 344–45
socio-economic profiles of 28, 345–46,
348, 405
textbooks, on history of Islam 201–02, 205–06
texts see *hadith*; *Qur'an*; *shari'a*; source texts
al-Thawri 149
theology see beliefs; Islam; religious ideology
Theophanes 214
theories see conspiracy theories;
revisionist theories
Thessaloniki 266–67
Thirty Years War 429
throat-slitting 158–60
Tibi, Bassam 53, 126–27, **380–81**
Timur Lang see Timurlane
Timurid Empire 228
Timurlane 111, 147, **228**, **234–35**, 263
tolerance, Islamic 247
torture 160–61
trade routes, and Islamisation of North Africa
236–37
see also slave trade
training and education:
in secular Muslim states 392, 393
of terrorists 333–34, 346, 350–54, 477–78
tribal loyalties (*'asabiyya*) 213, 218
tribal raiding (*ghazwa*) 56, **102–03**, 111,
211–13, 482g
tribes, migration of Arab 225
see also names of tribes, e.g. Banu Qurayza
Tunisia 393–95
Tunnell, Harry D., IV 415
Turkey 115–16, 259–60, 347, **390–93**
see also Ottoman Empire
Turkic tribes 58, 227
Turkish (language) 391
twelfth Imam 133, 135, 193
see also *mahdis*; *mahdism*

Twelver Shi'a see Shi'a
'Ubaidullah bin Abi Bakra 252
'Ubaydullah 274–75
Uhud, Battle of 330
'ulama (scholars) 488g
'Umair ibn-Sa'd 241–42
'Umar ibn al-Khattab (second caliph) 87, 93,
177, 179
Umayyad 488g
Umayyad caliphate 48, 51, 217–18, 225–26,
250–51
umma 488g
as core identity 36–37
and Islamic expansion 91
and Islamic state 287–88
and liberal Islamic reform 438–39
UN see United Nations
United Kingdom see Britain
United Nations 424
Alliance of Civilisations Initiative 424
Arab Human Development Report 31
charter 238, 364
UN Security Council 183–84
United States:
citizens as Crusaders 231
civilians as combatants 154–55
counter-terrorist strategy 12
economic development in Muslim states 405
embassy siege (Teheran, 1979–81) 402
global strategy against 303–04
jihad against its invasions of Afghanistan
and Iraq 117–19, 144, 208, 296
knowledge of Islam as "the enemy" 423–24,
437
Middle-Eastern strategies 407
Muslim duty to kill Americans 109, 324
Muslim resentment of and opposition to
38–39, 294, 335, **338–39**
progressive reform in 383
and psychological warfare 319, 320,
416–17
supports Afghanistan against Soviet Union
116, 279, 434
textbooks on history of Islam 201–02

tribute payments to Barbary states 174
Urban II, Pope 229
'ushr land 85
Ushurma, Mansur 194
Usmani, Taqi 118, 118
al-'Utaybi, Juhayman 130, 277, 440
al-'Utbi 153–54
'Uthman ibn 'Affan (third caliph) 72, 146, 216, 219
al-'Uyayri, Yusuf 309, 310
Vall, Ely Ould Mohammad 167
values:
    Byzantine 56–57
    new religious culture proposal 475–76
    of progressive reform 384, 387, 389–90, 391
    Western, as cause of Islamic radicalism 35–36, 335–37
    see also beliefs; political ideology; religious ideology
Van Gogh, Theo 160
velayat-e faqih 134, 143, 488g
violence:
    Christian rejection of 22
    hadith authority for 66–69
    justification for 44, 71–72, 79, 103
    legitimation of 270
    and liberal Islamic reform 438
    and medieval *jihad* 240, 242–50, 253–68
    and Muhammad **61–63**, 156, 160–61, **210–13**
    Muslim attitudes to 1, 61–63
    Muslim reputation for 179–80
    in Muslim world 30–31
    non-violence and pacifism 193–95, 390
    non-violent Islam and terrorism 401, 419
    Qur'anic teachings on 63–66
    repression as response to terrorism 403–04
    see also jihad; massacres of civilians; military strategy; suicide bombings; terrorism; terrorist groups; terrorists; war
al-Wahhab, 'Abd 276–77
al-Wahhab, Muhammad ibn **112**, 277
Wahhabism 112, **276–77**, 400, 489g

    see also Salafiyya
Wahid, Abdurrahman (Gus Dur) 389–90
Wali Allah of Delhi 82–83
al-Walid I 242–43
Walid II 218
al-Walid b. 'Uqba 220
Wall Street Journal 427
Wansborough, John 50
waqf (endowment trust) 85, 489g
    Palestine as 92–93
war:
    battlefield martyrs 341–42, 343
    classical doctrine of 14, 53–58, 213, 425–28, 429
    justification for 356–59
    cold war paradigm 431
    declarations of 140–45
    early Islamic defeats 226
    mahdism and the end of time 133–34, 135, 137–38
    military defeat of terrorism 401–02
    modern warfare types 397–400, 441
    Muhammad's justification of 60–63, 210–13
    naval warfare 171–74
    psychological warfare 170–71, **319–20**, 416–17
    rules and conduct of 62–63, 70, 74–77, **145–72**, **177–80**
    weapons of mass destruction 182–85
    see also imperialism; *jihad*; military strategy; peace; peace treaties; *ridda* wars; violence
War Office Training Regulations (British) 62
war on terror 398, 477–78
    goals of 424
    as religious war 429
    US strategy for 12
    see also terrorism, responses to
    wars of apostasy *see ridda* wars
Al-Watan (newspaper) 181, 323
weapons of mass destruction (WMD) 182–85, 434
websites *see* internet
welfare *see* social welfare services

West Africa, Fulani *jihad* 113
Western World:
    attacks on and Islamisation of 368–71
    attitude to "moderate Islamists" 407,
        471–72
    extremist hatred of 16, 477–78
    extremist and terrorist groups in 288, 289
    global dominance of 38–39
    as *jahili* 282–83
    knowledge of Islam as "the enemy" 422–25,
        432–33, 440
    and future action 440–44
    military action of 34–35, 401–02
    modern converts to Islam 334
    Muslim minorities in Europe 44, 385
    political left and Muslim radicalism 16–17,
        28–29, 175–76, 400, 408
    response to terrorism *see* terrorism,
        responses to
    sacralising of land in 93–96
    secularism in 35–36, 176
    Sufism-led rebellions against 193–94
    support for Islamic reform 414
    support for Islamist groups 434–35
    as target for terrorist activity 315–16,
        335–37
    Western theories of Islamic history 49–51
    see also Britain; Christians and Christianity;
        colonialism; Crusades; Europe; France;
        Spain; United States
WMD (weapons of mass destruction) 182–85,
    434
women:
    enslavement of 152, 162–63
    as non-combatants 146
    non-Muslim 77
    rights of 393, 394
    role of, in warfare 75
    and SIS 385–86
    as suicide bombers and martyrs 208, 328,
        333, 349
World War IV 397–400
worship *see* religious act
Yahya, Harun 40–41

Yakan, Fathi 20, 21
Yamama, battle of 215
Yassin, Ahmed 344
Yazdegerd 224
Yazid, Caliph (son of Muawiyya) 132, 157, 158,
    217, 218
Yazid II 218
Yazid III 218
Yediot Aharonot (newspaper) 409
Yemen and Yemenis 217, 218, 417–18
Yenicheri (Janissaries) 232, 489g
YouGov poll (July 2005) 36
youth, Muslim:
    and conspiracy theories 42
    and demographic pressures 29–30
    marginalisation of 32–33
Yusuf ibn Tashufin 275
zamindars (landholders) 234, 489g
Zanj slave rebellion 250
al-Zarqawi, Abu-Mus'ab 295, 300, 301–02,
    307
Zarqawi Document 458–64
al-Zawahiri, Ayman 291, 294, 296, **299–302**,
    310
Zaydi (Fiver Shi'a sect) 489g
Zia-ul-Haq, General 15, 428–29
Ziyad b. 'Amr Nuqil 241
al-Zomor, Aboud 284
Zoroastrianism 251–53, 489g
Zsitivatorok, Treaty of 233
Zuhdi, Karam 284